WORLD PHILOSOPHY

WORLD PHILOSOPHY

Essay-Reviews
of
225 Major Works

3

1726 - 1896

Edited by
FRANK N. MAGILL

Associate Editor
IAN P. McGREAL
Professor of Philosophy
California State University
Sacramento

SALEM PRESS
Englewood Cliffs, N.J.

LIBRARY OF CONGRESS CATALOG CARD NUMBER: 82-060268

Complete Set: ISBN 0-89356-325-0
Volume III: ISBN 0-89356-328-5

First Printing

Some of the material in this work also appears in *Masterpieces of World Philosophy in
Summary Form* (1961)

PRINTED IN THE UNITED STATES OF AMERICA

CHRONOLOGICAL LIST OF TITLES
IN VOLUME THREE

WORLD PHILOSOPHY

FIFTEEN SERMONS PREACHED AT THE ROLLS CHAPEL

Author: Joseph Butler (1692-1752)
Type of work: Metaphysics, philosophy of mind
First published: 1726

PRINCIPAL IDEAS ADVANCED

An examination of human nature reveals not only how man behaves, but also how he ought to behave.

Human nature, according to God's plan, is expressed properly when the passions are controlled by self-love and benevolence, and when the latter are controlled by conscience.

Desires have external objects—such as building a house; the theory that all men act to secure their own happiness is mistaken, for men often desire particular external objects without considering the satisfaction to come from securing such objects.

The fact that pleasure is often the consequence of achieving what we desire does not imply that pleasure is the object of desire.

The claim that even though men desire objects other than pleasure, they are all basically selfish, is in error; it depends on identifying compassion with fear, but experience shows no necessary correlation.

If self-love is enlightened, the course of action it prescribes will coincide with that of benevolence.

Joseph Butler, an Anglican clergyman who was a contemporary of George Berkeley and David Hume, a protégé of Samuel Butler, a favorite of Queen Caroline, Dean of St. Paul's, Clerk of the Closet to George II, Bishop of Bristol at the time John Wesley defected, and Bishop of Durham, and who was not Archbishop of Canterbury because he rejected the office, was the most influential Anglican theologian of the eighteenth century. During his own time and for some time thereafter, his fame as a religious philosopher rested primarily on his very influential book, *The Analogy of Religion*, in which he argued for an enlightened theology designed to woo the deists back into the fold of the church. But his enduring philosophical reputation rests upon his *Fifteen Sermons Preached at the Rolls Chapel* and *A Dissertation upon the Nature of Virtue*, in which he expounds his views about human nature and morality. Indeed, his refutation of psychological egoism, the doctrine that man is always motivated by his own self-interest, is a classic of its kind. This summary will concentrate on this refutation and the analysis of human nature on which it is based. Butler's views on these topics are contained in the Preface to the *Sermons*, in Sermons 1, 2, 3, 11, and 12, and in the *Dissertation*.

Butler's analysis rests upon the thesis that an examination of human nature will reveal not only how man does behave, but also how he ought to behave. This thesis, in turn, rests upon the assumptions that God wants man to act in certain ways, that he has given man such a nature that he will naturally act in these ways if that nature is not corrupted, and therefore, that these ways can be discovered by examining his handiwork. This examination will reveal that human nature has a hierarchical structure, with our many impulses, passions, and desires providing the base, the more general and reflective concerns for ourselves and others providing the intermediate level, and the supreme faculty of conscience providing the apex. Consequently, our nature is expressed fully and properly, not in a life dominated by our impulses, but in one in which these are exercised under the guidance of self-love and benevolence, and in which the latter are controlled in turn by conscience.

This summary will examine each of these levels, starting with the one that provides the basis for the other two. Prior to the exercise of rational control man is a creature of impulse, appetite, passion, and desire, acting in a multitude of ways. Without direction, he seems to be impelled by a host of specific desires to a host of specific and unrelated ends. These desires, or affections, as we shall call them, seem to have several important characteristics that distinguish them from the higher principles. On their first appearance, and usually thereafter, they occur spontaneously, without premeditation or deliberation. As far as the structure of human nature is concerned, they exist prior to any control or regulation the mature personality may later exercise over them. Again, they tend to move spontaneously toward particular goals. It is true that, given the affection, the goal could be sought deliberately but it is not true that it is chosen deliberately. Finally, Butler says, affections have external objects such as eating food, kicking someone, or building a house—objects external in the sense that they are not states of the agent. That is, for instance, the object of hunger is the consumption of food, and not the relief of a feeling of discomfort, or the production of a pleasant sensation. It is to be noted that when Butler speaks of hunger he is not speaking of a state of metabolism or of a feeling in the stomach, but of a desire for something, the desire for food.

Butler overstates his case when he insists that the object of every affection is external, but his major point is sound. The point is this: the crudest form of psychological egoism is false, for in many, if not most, cases, when a man desires something he does not have in mind his own welfare. If a man who is angered springs up and attacks his persecutor, he would not ordinarily be thinking that this is the thing to do in order to maximize happiness. If asked what he wanted, he might reply that he wished to get even, or to save face, or to kick the other person; these are the things he intends to accomplish; these are the objects of his anger.

Of course, Butler agrees, many of our impulsive or passionate acts do bring pleasure to ourselves or to others, whether we had this result in mind or not.

Indeed, affections can be classified according to whether they promote the private or the public good. Thus, the desire for food does tend to keep one alive, even though this is not usually what one has in mind; and the desire for esteem does lead one to treat others considerately, even though the object of one's desire is not their welfare. We might expect that the intelligent agent will recognize these tendencies of the affections to augment either his own or another's general welfare, come to value these two wider possibilities as ends in themselves (if he does not already), and hence be led to satisfy his affections as a means to the achievement of these ends. This, says Butler, we find to be a fact. Emerging from this heterogeneous group of affections are two more general and comprehensive desires: the desire to maximize our own happiness and the desire to maximize that of others. These two desires are present in every normal man.

We do desire our own welfare, but this desire is not to be classified with the affections we have spoken of so far; it is not a passion or an appetite that arises spontaneously and drives impulsively toward a specific goal only to die away when it has been satisfied. Rather, it is a deliberately cultivated, long-enduring desire whose object is such that it cannot be satisfied once and for all at any given time or through the occurrence of any particular event. Furthermore, it functions not merely as a psychological drive, but as a principle according to which we deliberately plan which particular ends we shall pursue in order to enhance our overall welfare. Finally, as experience shows, it is a very powerful motive that exerts a natural authority over the affections; the affections ought to be subordinated to it.

Nevertheless, while it is superior to affections, self-love cannot achieve its object unless they achieve theirs, for pleasures occur only as a by-product of the pursuit and satisfaction of affections. While Butler is not specific, he has in mind such things as the pleasure we experience in pursuing our objective, the satisfaction we experience because we have attained it, and any other pleasures that may follow upon its attainment. Thus, while one goes to the fields because of a desire to obtain food, one may enjoy the walk, enjoy digging in the earth, enjoy the satisfaction of gathering the number of potatoes intended for the meal, and enjoy the physical satisfaction that follows the meal. Though an affection and self-love may seek the same thing, the one seeks it for itself, whereas the other seeks it insofar as its pursuit and attainment bring pleasure to the pursuer. Self-love can attain its own end only by letting selected affections pass into action.

Butler suggests that the intimate relationship between self-love and the satisfaction of affections has led some noted egoists, such as Hobbes, into the error of identifying the particular affections with the principle of self-love, or of regarding them as just so many particular expressions of it. But the fact that our actions do lead to enjoyment and the fact that this fact is exploited by self-love do not indicate at all that the only thing we seek is such enjoyment, or that because such enjoyments do occur we must have been seeking them. Indeed, if we did not seek something other than pleasure we would experience no pleasure. The conclusion that we must be egoists does not follow from the act that all affections belong to the self, from the fact that we never act unless we have such affections, or from the fact that all satisfied affections bring pleasure to the self.

However, for all that has been said so far, there is still room for a subtler egoism, for the egoist might admit that the object of an affection is not the welfare of the agent but insist that insofar as the affections are under the direction of self-love the overriding consideration is always our own welfare. Insofar as man acts reasonably he acts prudently. This type of egoism can be refuted only if there are actions that are not subsumed under the principle of self-love, or subsumed under it alone.

But there are such actions, Butler says, for most men do act part of the time in a genuinely benevolent fashion. He realizes that he will have to defend this position against the most sophisticated egoist. Hobbes had argued, and many were prepared to believe, that what appears to be benevolence is really subtly disguised selfishness. Thus Hobbes claimed that when a man feels pity for another he is really feeling thankful that he has escaped the calamity and fearful lest such a thing should happen to him in the future. A man feels more "sympathetic" toward his unfortunate friend than he does toward strangers because his friend's life is much more like his own and therefore the probability of a similar calamity befalling him is higher. Butler admits that such selfish reflections might occur, but he insists that they must be distinguished from genuine compassion. Hobbes' view requires that we equate compassion with fear, an equation that any man can see to be mistaken. If it were correct, then the more compassionate a man is, the more fearful he would be, but this is simply not the case. In the second place, the more compassionate a man is, the more we admire him; but the more fearful he is, the less we admire him. In the third place, while it is true that the sight of friends in distress evokes greater compassion than the sight of others in distress, it is quite questionable whether the sight of friends in distress raises in us greater fear for ourselves than does the sight of others in distress. This is the classic refutation of Hobbes' doctrine, a refutation that was accepted and polished by men such as David Hume and Adam Smith.

Butler supports his position, not simply by criticizing his opponents, but by drawing our attention to the way people do behave. Human behavior will show, he says, that we do have a propensity to help each other, a propensity that cannot be confused with self-love. He offers examples to support this view. Granted that in some cases an apparently benevolent action may be performed solely for the satisfaction it gives the agent, or for the sense of power he experiences. Yet, has the reader never known of a man who was not in a position to help another but who nevertheless rejoiced when a third party assisted the second? And has the reader never known a man to assist one person rather than another where the choice between the two could not be accounted for in terms of the sense of power? Are there not cases where the choice is made in terms of need? And if you examine your own behavior, will you not find it ridiculous to try to explain your benevolent behavior entirely in terms of your love of power, of being dominant, or of hoped-for reciprocation? Nor will it do to reply that acting benevolently gives you pleasure. Of course it does, but first, this does not mean you sought that pleasure; and second, the action would not have given you pleasure unless you had a concern for the other person. In this way Butler answers the more sophisticated egoist.

Although Butler clearly maintains that there is genuinely benevolent action that cannot be explained away, he is not as clear as he might be about the status of benevolence. There are some passages in which benevolence is spoken of as an affection, but there are many others in which it is spoken of as a rational principle. It is true that benevolence is not as strong a motive as self-love and it is also true that the scope of its application is more restricted, for whereas every affection has consequences that affect the agent, not every affection has consequences that affect others. Most of the passages in which Butler speaks of benevolence as an affection occur when he is making these contrasts, and consequently they seem designed to emphasize the contrasts rather than to express his full view about benevolence. In view of the numerous passages in which benevolence is spoken of as a principle, it seems reasonable to conclude that Butler was not being inconsistent, that he meant that insofar as benevolence transcends spontaneous compassion it becomes a principle functioning as a guide and having a relationship, like that of self-love, to a multitude of affections. Because it is psychologically weaker it needs to be fostered and cultivated in a manner in which self-love does not, but it has a similar function and enjoys the same sort of authority over the affections.

Since these principles are coequal in authority, one might expect conflicts in interest between them, but Butler believes that if self-love is really enlightened; the course of action it prescribes will coincide with that of benevolence. No one who is callous to his fellows will be really happy, not only because this involves thwarting natural affections of sympathy and the like, but also because such behavior invites a similar reaction on the part of those so treated. Furthermore, even though it should appear that the selfish will prosper more on this earth than the benevolent, one should not overlook the fact that there is an afterlife in which God will at least compensate for the earthly imbalance. Once again, because two different motives suggest the same actions we must be wary of falling into the error of identifying them or repudiating one of them. Butler sometimes leaves himself open to misunderstanding on this point when he writes that we are never required to act against our own self-interest. However, when he said this he was pointing out to his worldly and sophisticated congregation that benevolent action does not have consequences that are incompatible with those pursued by self-love. He was not suggesting that benevolence should be placed under the dominance of self-love, but, rather, that if there is a conflict, we had better check to see if we really have discovered what is to our self-interest, for the conflict provides *prima facie* evidence that we have not.

So far we have discovered two principles in addition to the basic affections, but neither of these has to do with duty as such. Consequently, as an examination of our nature will show, there is a faculty whose function it is to point out what is right and wrong, the faculty of conscience. It should be noted that we must distinguish between action motivated by compassion or benevolence on the one hand and that motivated by a sense of duty on the other. Of course, benevolence and conscience may, and frequently do, suggest the same course of action, but the motivation is different. As the supreme faculty, conscience should stand above and coordinate the activities of the other principles. Its supremacy does not rest upon its power, for impulse and self-love often override it, but it carries upon itself the mark of authority, as is evidenced by the feeling of wrongdoing or guilt we experience when we do not heed it. "Had it strength as it has right, had it power as it has manifest authority, it would absolutely govern the world." Of course, it need hardly be mentioned that the existence of conscience indicates in yet another way the inadequacy of the egoist's position.

Conscience is not a criterion used in reaching decisions or planning courses of action, as are the rational principles of benevolence and self-love, but a faculty that makes pronouncements about what is right or wrong. It tells us *what* to do and *what* to approve of, but not *why*. Butler suggests that God might be a utilitarian, but he insists that we cannot be, for certain things are simply seen to be praiseworthy or unpraiseworthy quite apart from any tendency they might have to further or hinder the public welfare. Thus, for instance, conscience reveals the baseness of treachery and the meanness of a small mind as well as the praiseworthiness of fidelity, honor, and justice. Conscience does not proceed by reasoning, nor does it seek to justify its deliverances in terms of some underlying principle; it simply pronounces on specific matters and does so with authority. It functions in all "plain honest men" as the vice-regent of God, cutting in a direct and simple manner through the moral perplexities of their daily lives.

Butler believed not only that there is no conflict between conscience and benevolence, but also that there is none between conscience and self-love. There cannot be if we are clear about what is to our self-interest. After all, God intends that we should be happy, and conscience is the faculty he has given us to ensure that we do as he intends. Consequently, as Butler saw it, human nature exhibits a complexly structured system of motives, resting upon the affections which are controlled by the principles of self-love and benevolence and capped by the faculty of conscience which has authority over all. When developed as God intended it should be, it is a nature in which these various factors supplement and complement one another to produce an integrated and harmoniously organized life.

Butler did not develop his views as fully as we could wish, but he traced out in bold outline a view that embodies the classic refutation of psychological egoism, ancient or modern; a view that had a profound effect upon Hume and Smith insofar as it stresses compassion and benevolence; and a view that has influenced such recent philosophers as H. A. Prichard, W. D. Ross, and C. D. Broad insofar as it brings conscience and duty to the fore. Butler is one of the most important moral philosophers of the eighteenth century. —*L.M.*

PERTINENT LITERATURE

Duncan-Jones, Austin. *Butler's Moral Philosophy*. Harmondsworth, England: Penguin Books, 1952.

Austin Duncan-Jones's book is, as its title makes clear, devoted to the moral philosophy of Joseph Butler. In his Preface the author states his purpose: "to expound and criticize Joseph Butler's ethical doctrines, and to pursue further some of the questions Butler raised." In carrying out this purpose Duncan-Jones conducts an analytic investigation into the central concepts that appear in Butler's ethical writings, such as "passion," "cool self-love," "egoism," "benevolence," "conscience," "desert," and so on, and into the main lines of argument that Butler offers in support of his views regarding the moral life. Going beyond Butler, particularly in the final chapter, he raises several problems of a very general nature concerning the status of ethics as a discipline and its proper methodology—problems which have been of particular concern to writers in our own century.

Following an introductory chapter devoted to Butler's life and general philosophy, Duncan-Jones begins his study of the Butlerian ethics by an inquiry into his conception of human nature. He analyzes the three ways in which Butler uses the terms "nature" and "natural" and proceeds to explain why only the third provides a satisfactory standard in terms of which we can properly conclude that virtue consists in following human nature, and vice in violating it. On the controversial issue of the relationship of the passions to the principles of human nature that Butler is usually understood to believe rational, he takes a somewhat unorthodox position. Although he concedes the rationality of the principle of cool self-love—hence its moral superiority to the various passions—he argues that Butler did not accord the same status to the principle of benevolence. Although Butler's views on the nature of benevolence and its role in human nature are a little uncertain, Duncan-Jones concludes that on the whole he leans toward "representing benevolence as one of the passions. . . ." Turning to the highest principle of moral action, conscience, Duncan-Jones argues that Butler's account rests on three assumptions: (1) the authority of conscience, (2) the uniformity of conscience, and (3) the uniformity of duty. The first of these needs little comment; Duncan-Jones amplifies it by saying that the dictates of conscience offer not only decisive but also "prepotent" reasons for action, meaning that they offer reasons so overwhelming as to outweigh all contrary reasons, not only in the situation at hand but also on all occasions. The third is an expression of what is often called ethical objectivism, the view that the basic moral relationships in which persons stand to one another are not conditioned by time and place but apply to everyone everywhere. The second is closely related to the third, being the view that all human beings are capable of recognizing the uniform rules of duty and, if conscience governs their conduct, of abiding by them. Since conscience is, for Butler, our sufficient (and, indeed, only) guide to moral conduct, if anyone follows his conscience, he will, of necessity, be acting rightly. Here, however, Duncan-Jones raises a serious objection to the Butlerian position. In his opinion assumption (2) is questionable; we cannot assume the uniformity of conscience. As a result, we cannot share Butler's optimistic conclusion that conscientiousness always leads people to act in a way that is morally right. Duncan-Jones explains Butler's views on this issue as an expression of a general optimism about human nature characteristic of the eighteenth century, of which the wider knowledge and darker experiences of our times have disabused us.

Other phases of Butler's moral philosophy to which Duncan-Jones devotes attention include his views on egoism, utilitarianism, and the relationship of religion to ethics. On the issue of egoism, he considers Butler to have pursued a dual aim—on the theoretical side, to refute Hobbesian psychological egoism and, on the practical side, to convince ordinary people that life does not present them with an antithesis, between acting self-interestedly and acting morally. Turning to the question of utilitarianism, Duncan-Jones points out that Butler's writings contain several passages that appear to offer a utilitarian justification for moral action. On the other side, however, are passages that appear to reject utilitarianism, primarily because his appeal to conscience as the final moral arbiter eliminates the necessity for the agent to calculate consequences, in the way that a utilitarian must, in order to reach a decision about how he ought to act. Finally, Duncan-Jones points out that, although Butler accepted the view that in a universe governed by a just and providential God everyone would receive rewards or punishments according to his deserts, the question of what is right and what is wrong in human conduct can be answered by an understanding of the nature of man, and so no appeal to the will or dictates of God is required.

Broad, C. D. "Butler," in *Five Types of Ethical Theory*. London: Routledge

& Kegan Paul, 1930.

Joseph Butler is one of five moral philosophers to whom C. D. Broad devotes chapters in his *Five Types of Ethical Theory*, now generally regarded as a minor classic in the field. Broad's discussion of Butler is both expository and critical. He begins by pointing out that Butler's chief merit was as a moral psychologist, and much of his chapter is devoted to analyzing psychological points made by Butler in his moral writings.

Broad begins his account by arguing that Butler viewed the moral life from the perspective of a conception of an ideal human nature. In Butler's view virtue consists in acting in accordance with this ideal nature, and vice in acting against it. Because the human mind is an organized system, composed of various principles and propensities related to each in a hierarchical order of moral authority, virtuous action results when each of these propensities functions according to its proper place in the hierarchy; but vice is the result when one of the propensities usurps the function and authority of another. Then the constitutional hierarchy is thrown out of balance.

Following Butler into the details of his conception of the human moral constitution, Broad next distinguishes the four main propensities that move us to act: (1) Particular passions or affections, (2) the general principle of cool self-law, (3) the general principle of benevolence, and (4) conscience. In ideal human nature these springs of action are organized in an order of ascending moral authority with (1) lowest, (2) and (3) on a par, and (4) at the top. Vice occurs when a lower propensity disregards the dictates of a higher. For example, cool self-love leads us to disregard our obligations to others and we act selfishly, or our recognition of our duties to others leads us to overlook our well-being and we act in a way that is too benevolent. In both cases conscience would have directed us to act differently. Again, at a lower level, acts of passionate revenge or even thoughtless sympathy can lead us to act in ways inconsistent with our own best interest (cool self-love) or that of others (benevolence).

Broad turns next to a discussion of one of the most influential of Butler's arguments: his critique of Thomas Hobbes's psychological egoism, taking special note of the way in which he refutes Hobbes's attempt to give an egoistic interpretation of actions motivated by sympathy. Although he agrees that Butler's arguments destroy Hobbesian egoism, he believes that certain refinements need to be made in Butler's psychological analysis on this point. To understand the relationships between our various particular impulses (as originators of action) and the principles of cool self-love and benevolence, Broad argues, we must draw certain distinctions that Butler does not. (1) Some of our impulses result from causes originating in the agent (for example, hunger), some in causes originating in others (pity), and some in causes originating in inanimate objects (covetousness). (2) Some impulses aim at producing results in the agent (the aim of hunger is to eat); some at producing results in others (the aim of pity is to help someone in need); and some at producing results in inanimate objects (the aim of blind rage may be to smash crockery). (3) The satisfaction of our impulses produces collateral effects either in the agent or in others, or in both. The collateral effects of satisfying one's hunger are confined almost exclusively to the agent; those of satisfying one's sympathetic impulses are primarily felt by others; and those of satisfying one's ambition are felt by oneself and by others. (4) Finally, when an impulse to act is satisfied through action, whatever the impulse may be, the agent experiences the pleasures of satisfied impulse. Such an expanded analysis of our motivations and actions, Broad believes, buttresses Butler's conclusion that Hobbesian egoism offers a grossly inadequate view of human nature.

After drawing some distinctions between the principle of self-love and that of benevolence and noting the relationships between the two, Broad concentrates on Butler's supreme principle of morality—namely, conscience. He agrees with Butler that it has both a cognitive and an authoritative aspect. As cognitive, it reflects on our actions from the point of view of their rightness and wrongness, and makes moral judgments about them. As authoritative, it offers us reasons for performing actions or refraining from them which, whether or not we actually abide by them, we nevertheless recognize to be conclusive reasons either for doing or not doing the actions in question. We recognize, that is to say, the moral right of conscience to have supreme authority over what we do. To this account Broad adds a third characteristic of conscience, pointing out its efficacy as an active principal. We do, at least sometimes, act in a certain way because our conscience so directs us.

Broad concludes his chapter by discussing two problems that have long divided commentators on Butler's moral views. The first concerns a famous remark Butler makes to the effect that, if we reflect coolly, we can never justify an action that will be detrimental to our own happiness. Although apparently a defense of ethical egoism, this remark, according to Broad's interpretation, is not meant to be a statement of Butler's own position but rather a hypothetical view put forward to make the quite different point that conscience should remain one's practical guide in life. The second issue concerns Butler's "utilitarianism." Once again, he makes several remarks that seem to imply his belief that the only good in life is happiness. Broad thinks these remarks can be explained away in terms of their context and that Butler's considered opinion involves a rejection of utilitarianism.—*O.A.J.*

ADDITIONAL RECOMMENDED READING
Carlsson, P. A. *Butler's Ethics*. The Hague, The Netherlands: Mouton and Company, 1964. A study relating Butler's ethics to his theology and to eighteenth century moral philosophy.

Collins, W. L. *Butler*. Edinburgh: W. Blackwood, 1881. A survey of Butler's ethics in the context of his theology.

Hudson, W. D. *Ethical Intuitionism*. London: Macmillan and Company, 1967. A short critical account of English intuitionism in the classical period.

Mossner, E. C. *Bishop Butler and the Age of Reason*. New York: Macmillan Publishing Company, 1936. Butler's thought viewed in its relationship to the history of ideas during the age of reason.

Norton, W. J. *Bishop Butler: Moralist and Divine*. New Brunswick, New Jersey: Rutgers University Press, 1940. A study of Butler's ethics in its relationship to psychology, social theory, and theology.

A TREATISE OF HUMAN NATURE (BOOK I)

Author: David Hume (1711-1776)
Type of work: Epistemology
First published: 1739

PRINCIPAL IDEAS ADVANCED

All of our knowledge comes from impressions and ideas; the impressions are more forceful and lively than the ideas.

By the use of memory and imagination we preserve and arrange our ideas.

We have no abstract, general ideas but only ideas of particular things which can be considered collectively by the use of general terms.

Certainty comes from the intuitive recognition of the similarity or differences in ideas, or from the demonstrative process of connecting a series of intuitions— as in arithmetic and algebra.

Our knowledge of causal relationships is simply the habit of expecting events of one kind to follow events of another kind with which they have been observed to be conjoined; there are no necessary relationships between events.

We have good reason to be skeptical about all conclusions reached by the use of reason or on the basis of sense experience.

Hume's *A Treatise of Human Nature* is his earliest philosophical work and the one that contains the most complete exposition of his views. Apparently it was planned when he was in his early twenties, when he claimed to have discovered a "new scene of thought." The work was composed during a sojourn in France from 1734 to 1737 and was revised shortly thereafter in an unsuccessful attempt to gain the approbation of Bishop Joseph Butler. The first book of the *Treatise* was published in 1739, and the other two the next year. Hume had hoped that his views would attract a great deal of attention; instead, the work "fell dead-born from the presses." His novel theories did not attract attention until after he had published a more popular version in *An Enquiry Concerning Human Understanding* in 1748. The *Treatise* was subjected to a full-scale attack by Thomas Reid in 1764. By this time, Hume was so successful as an author, especially on the basis of his essays and his *History of England* (1754-1762), that he refused to defend his first book, and called it a juvenile work. Over the years it has become more and more important as the fullest and deepest statement of Hume's philosophical views; in fact, Book I of the *Treatise* has come to be regarded as one of the finest achievements of English philosophy.

On the title page of Book I, Hume announces that the *Treatise* is "an attempt to introduce the experimental Method of Reasoning into Moral Subjects." In the Preface, he explains that he intends to develop a "science of man" by applying Sir Isaac Newton's experimental method to human mental behavior. Following in the footsteps of various English and Scottish moral philosophers, and of the French skeptic Pierre Bayle, he hoped to discover the limits of human knowledge in such areas as mathematics, physics, and the social sciences (the moral subjects). By scrupulously observing human life, Hume thought he could discover certain general laws about human thinking and behavior. He admitted at the outset that it was probably not possible to uncover "the ultimate qualities of human nature," but he thought it should be possible to learn something about the origin and nature of what we think we know.

All of our information, Hume writes, is composed of impressions and ideas. The only difference between these is that the former strike us more forcefully and with greater vivacity than do the latter. Ideas and impressions can be simple or complex, the simple ones being those which cannot be divided into parts or aspects, while the complex ones are composed of simples. There is a great deal of resemblance between the impressions and the ideas. The simple ideas, in fact, exactly resemble simple impressions in all respects except with regard to their force and vivacity. Further, in terms of their appearance in the mind, the simple impressions always precede the simple ideas (except for one unusual case that Hume brings up). The complex ideas are composed of simple parts which are exactly like the simple ingredients of impressions that we have already experienced, though the complex idea itself may not actually be a copy of any complex impression. These discoveries about impressions and ideas indicate, Hume says, that all of our ideas are derived from experience (the world of impressions), and that we have no innate ideas in our minds; that is, ideas that are not based on what we perceive.

In the first part of the *Treatise*, Hume proceeds to explore the bases of our knowledge. We possess two faculties, memory and imagination, for dealing with the ideas that we receive. The memory preserves the ideas in the exact order in which they entered the mind. The imagination, on the other hand, is free to arrange the ideas in any manner that is desired. But, contrary to what might be expected, our imaginations do not function at random. Instead, we imagine ideas in ordered sequences, so that whenever a particular idea comes to mind, other related ideas automatically follow it, according to certain principles of the association of ideas that Hume calls "a kind of ATTRACTION, which in the mental world will be found to have as extraordinary effects as in the natural." Ideas tend naturally to be associated when they are similar, or contiguous in time or space, or when they stand in the relation of cause and effect. The importance of association is brought out when Hume comes to discuss causality in Part III.

Before applying these "discoveries" about the way we think, Hume takes up a few other questions. He argues first for a point Bishop Berkeley had previously made, that we possess no abstract general ideas, but only ideas of particular things. General terms, such as "man" or "triangle," designate the collections of similar particular ideas that we have acquired from experience.

Hume then tries to explain mathematics as being about particular experiences. He knew relatively little about mathematics and based many of his views on comments in Pierre Bayle's *Dictionary* (1695-1697). Hume's empirical mathematical theory has generally been regarded as, perhaps, the weakest part of his book, though he was always proud of having shown that mathematics is "big with absurdity and contradiction." Hume conceived of arithmetic as being a demonstrable science dealing with relations of quantity, whereas geometry was thought of as an empirical science dealing with observable points. Because of the limitation of our ability to see and count the points, the theorems in geometry are always to some degree uncertain.

The most famous part of the *Treatise* is the third part of Book I, which treats "Of Knowledge and Probability." Genuine knowledge is gained by an intuitive inspection of two or more ideas to see if they stand in a particular relationship to each other. We can be completely certain by intuition that two ideas do or do not resemble each other, or that they differ from each other, or that one has more or less of a given quality than another, as, for instance, that one is darker than another. Such knowledge is certain in that it depends solely on what one "sees" when two or more ideas are brought together by the imagination, but it gives us relatively little information. By connecting a series of intuitions, we gain the sort of demonstrative knowledge that occurs in arithmetic and algebra. Intuition and demonstration are the sole sources of complete certainty and knowledge.

Our information about the causal relation of ideas does not arise from an intuitive examination of our ideas, and almost all of our information about what is happening beyond our immediate experience is based upon causal reasoning. How do we decide which ideas are causally related? When we examine two ideas, or two impressions that we think are so related, we find that we do not perceive any necessary or causal connection between them. We perceive only that the ideas are contiguous and successive. We do not, however, perceive that they are necessarily connected in any way, although we do feel that there must be more to the sequence than merely one idea following after another. We believe that one of the ideas must make the other occur. But, Hume asks, what evidence do we have for such a belief, and where do we acquire the belief? If we admit that we do not perceive any necessary connection between events, then Hume suggests that we ought to ask ourselves why we believe that every event must have a cause and why we believe that particular causes necessarily must have certain effects.

When the first problem is examined, we discover something that is surprising. Even though we all believe that every event must have a cause, this proposition is not intuitively obvious, nor can it be demonstrated. When we conceive of events, we neither see them as caused nor necessarily think of them in terms of their causes. Because of the freedom of our imagination, each event can be thought of separately and independently. If events can be thought of as uncaused, it is also possible that they occur uncaused. If that is a genuine possibility, then there can be no valid demonstration proving the impossibility of uncaused events. The demonstrations that had been offered by previous philosophers, Hume believed, are all unsatisfactory. They beg the question in that they assume what they are attempting to prove; namely, that every event has a cause. Apparently, the causal principle, which is not self-evident nor demonstrable, is so basic that we all accept it for reasons that seem to be unknown.

To explore the matter further, Hume turns to the other problem: What is the basis for our belief that particular causes have particular effects, and how do we infer one from the other? The actual constituents of our causal reasoning, he asserts, are a present impression of sense or memory, an imagined idea of a related event, and an unknown connection between them. When we hear a certain sound, we think of somebody ringing the doorbell. Why and how do we infer from the impression to its supposed cause? Many other ideas might have come to mind. When we hear the sound, we do not, at the same time, experience its cause, yet we implicitly believe that said cause must also be occurring to produce the perceived effect. This reasoning process is not a logical one, Hume maintains, since there is no *reason* for us to think of one idea rather than another when a particular experience takes place.

If reason cannot be what makes us connect events causally, perhaps experience is responsible. We find that when a sequence of events is constantly repeated in our experience, and when the events are conjoined, we tend to associate ideas about them in our minds. Then, when we experience just one of the events, we also think of the other. One of them we call the cause and the other, the effect. What is there in the fact that certain events have been constantly conjoined in the past that leads us to think of them as being causally related? Hume points out that if the process involved were a rational one, we would have to presuppose that the principle of the uniformity of nature was true. This principle asserts *"that instances, of which we have had no experience, must resemble those, of which we have had experience, and that the course of nature continues always uniformly the same."*

Hume next questions whether we possess any evidence that this principle is true, or that it has to be true. Since we can readily imagine that the world might change in many respects in the future, it is not possible to demonstrate that nature must be uniform. Our experience up to the present moment does not constitute evidence as to what the future course of nature will be, or must be. Just because the sun has risen every day up to now does not prove that it has to rise tomorrow. We can only judge the future if we know that nature is uniform. But our information up to this point is only that, so far, nature has always been uniform. Experience can provide us with no clue about what has to be the case in the future. Hence, we can neither demonstrate nor prove from experience that the all-important principle of the uniformity of nature is true, even though much of our reasoning about the world depends upon it.

The acceptance of this principle, Hume contends, is a fundamental characteristic of human nature. We have a habit or custom that operates upon us for unknown and unknowable reasons. After we have experienced the same sequence of conjoined events several times, then, when we perceive one of the conjuncts, habit or custom leads us to think of the other, and to think of it in a lively and forceful way. Although we are able to think of any idea we wish, we are led psychologically to think only of a particular conjoined idea and to conceive of it with some of the force and vivacity of its conjoined impression. Such force and vivacity constitute our belief in the actual occurrence of the conjoined item. In terms of this explanation, the principle of the uniformity of nature is more a principle about how we think and feel than it is one about the order of events in the world.

Hume uses his discovery of the psychological origins of our belief in the uniformity of nature to explain the basis for our conviction that there is a necessary connection between events. The necessary connection is never perceived, no matter how often the same sequence is observed. But, after a constant conjunction of events has been perceived many times, we then feel that one of the conjuncts causes or produces the other. It is not any discoverable fact about the events that makes us believe this, but rather our psychological attitude toward the events. We possess a fundamental propensity or determination of the mind to think of a conjoined idea after experiencing the conjunct or thinking of it, once we have perceived the constant conjunction of the two in our experience. This determination, which is a strong feeling, is the necessary connection that we think exists between events. Although it is felt in us, we have a tendency to conceive of it as existing in the events themselves. This idea is actually a feature of the way we think about events, rather than a feature of them. Thus, the term "cause" can be defined as *"An object precedent and contiguous to another, and so united with it in the imagination, that the idea of the one determines the mind to form the idea of the other, and the impression of the one to form a more lively idea of the other."*

In Hume's explanation of causality, he joins Father Nicolas Malebranche's contention that there is no necessary connection between events with his own psychological account of how we react to the uniformities in experience. Because of our habits, we expect the future to resemble the past, and we feel that when we observe certain events, their constant conjuncts must also be taking place, even if we cannot observe them. We have no actual knowledge of what is taking place, but only beliefs. Since we can never be completely sure that our beliefs correspond to the actual state of affairs, our causal information is always, at best, only probable.

Hume sees the task of the sciences as that of carefully establishing bases for "reasonable belief" by collecting data about the constant conjunctions that occur in human experience, and organizing such data in terms of scientific laws. These laws provide a form of rational expectation, in that they allow us to predict the future course of events on the basis of detailed information about what has happened up to now. The scientist, like anyone else, expects, because of his habits and propensities, that the future will resemble the past. Science, for Hume, is not the search for the "real" cause of events, but for the best available probable predictions about the course of nature, founded on correlations of constant conjunctions of events and the psychological habits of human beings.

After presenting his explanation of the source of our information, the nature of our beliefs about the world, and the character of scientific "knowledge," Hume turns in Part IV of the *Treatise* to the full statement of his skeptical views. He first presents a series of reasons to show why we should be doubtful of the conclusions that we come to because of our reasoning and those that we come to because of our sense experience and our attitudes towards it. Then Hume contends that though there are basic difficulties with regard to both our reason and our senses, we still have to believe many things because of our psychological structure. Unfortunately, what we believe is often either indefensible or contradictory.

The argument offered to engender a "scepticism with regard to reason" purports to show that even the most certain conclusions of reasoning are actually only probable and that their degree of probability diminishes the more that we examine them. Since we all make mistakes, every time we reason there is a possibility that we may err. When we check our reasoning, it is still possible that we have erred in our checking, and that we will err in checking our checking, and so on. Each judgment that we make about the merits of our reasoning is merely probable, and the combined probability, Hume says, will get smaller and smaller the more we judge our judgments of our judgments of our judgments. Hence, if this checking process were carried on indefinitely, we should begin to lose confidence even in our most certain reasonings in arithmetic or algebra.

With regard to our sense information, Hume insists that we are naturally convinced that the objects we observe exist continuously and independently of us. But as soon as we begin to examine this belief we find that it is completely unjustified and that it conflicts with what we know about our impressions. Neither sense information nor valid reasoning can supply any basis for concluding that there are independent and continuous objects. If our imaginations, through some propensities, supply us with this belief, it is still "contrary to the plainest experience." All that we ever perceive are impressions which, as far as we can tell, are definitely dependent on us. An alteration in our sense organs, or in the state of our health, changes what we perceive. In view of this, we should not think that our perceptions are things that exist independently from us, continuing to exist even when not perceived. But,

Hume observes, no amount of argument on this subject makes us give up our natural belief in the existence of the external world.

The discussions of the bases for skepticism indicate that for Hume even complete skepticism is impossible because of the force of natural belief. "Nature, by an absolute and uncontrollable necessity has determined us to judge as well as to breathe and feel." Nature forces us to accept certain views, in spite of the evidence for or against them. Philosophy, Hume said elsewhere, would make us into complete skeptics, were not nature so strong. Philosophy would make us completely skeptical about the status of the objects that we perceive with our senses, but nature prevents us from taking the philosophical arguments seriously.

In his discussion of our knowledge of ourselves, Hume brings out a similar point. We all believe that we possess a personal identity that continues throughout our lives. But when we try to discover the entity we call "ourselves," we discover that all that we are acquainted with is the succession of impressions and ideas. By certain psychological habits and propensities, we have created a fiction which makes us believe that we are also aware of an identical self that perseveres through all our various experiences.

Hence, there is a type of complete skepticism that results from a careful and profound study of human nature. In theory, we realize that there is inadequate evidence to support the bulk of what we believe about the world. Our reasoning and our senses are too unreliable to support these beliefs, which are due to our psychological character and not to any legitimate conclusions of rational processes. Some of these natural beliefs conflict with one another. Hume contends that the factors which make us connect events causally in our experience should make us disbelieve in the continuous and independent existence of sense objects. The more we examine human nature, the more we should realize how dubious and unreliable human opinions are. In the conclusion to Book I of the *Treatise*, Hume points out that his skepticism even undermines his faith in his psychological findings.

But nature prevents us from carrying out this skeptical attitude to its final destructive conclusion. Regardless of the difficulties, in practice we find that we have to believe all sorts of things, even incompatible things. When we go out in the world, the skeptical doubts lose their force; we are overwhelmed by our natural feelings and beliefs, and we act and live in the same way as anyone else. Hume's final advice is that one should be skeptical when one has to be, and be a natural believer when one must, while realizing that neither of these attitudes has any final justification. In periods when doubts are not being taken seriously, one can go on and examine other aspects of the human world, as Hume does in Books II and III of the *Treatise*, and seek for laws about human passions. (One of his findings in this regard is that reason is, and ought only to be, the slave of the passions.)

The *Treatise* has been a rich source of many contemporary views. The more

empirical side of it has greatly influenced the logical positivists and the language analysts. Some of the psychological analysis of human belief and behavior has influenced the pragmatists and instrumentalists. The extreme skepticism and irrationalism have had some impact on neoorthodox theologians. It is for these reasons that *A Treatise of Human Nature* is regarded by many as perhaps the best philosophical work in the English language.
—R.H.P.

PERTINENT LITERATURE

Chappel, V. C., ed. *Hume*. Garden City, New York: Anchor Books, 1966.

This collection of twenty-one essays on David Hume by scholars from different parts of the English-speaking world contains several essays which are important for studying the fundamental issues that appear in Hume's *A Treatise of Human Nature*, Book I. T. E. Jessop, the bibliographer of Hume, seeks in his essay "Some Misunderstandings of Hume" to show that although modern critics constantly attack the *Treatise* for its inconsistencies, it is nevertheless Hume's basic work, setting forth his philosophical goals. Further, Jessop argues for the value of the basic theme of the *Treatise*, Hume's naturalistic analysis of human nature.

R. H. Popkin's essay on Hume's Pyrrhonism and critique of Pyrrhonism tries to delineate exactly what kind of skepticism Hume advocated and to show how such advocacy could be reconciled with Hume's constant jibes at the Pyrrhonian skeptics in all of his works. Popkin argues that Hume developed a "consistent" Pyrrhonism, consistent in that his arguments and analyses indicated the inability of human beings to find truth and certainty in any area whatsoever. Sextus Empiricus, after pointing this out in case after case, declared that therefore we should suspend judgment. Hume saw that this consequence did not follow and that we could only actually do what nature allowed us to do. Our natural propensities could be analyzed but not justified. Popkin then tries to show that Hume's "consistent" Pyrrhonism was compatible with his naturalism.

The article by R. P. Wolff on Hume's theory of mental activity attempts to show that what Hume held to was more than associationism or the copy theory of ideas, even though he began his inquiry in the *Treatise* with these views.

Four of the essays are directly on Hume's analysis of causality. Three concern the two definitions of cause that Hume presented at the end of Book I, Part III, Section XIV of the *Treatise*, and one of the essays is on Hume's defense of causal inference. J. A. Robinson begins his discussion of Hume's two definitions of cause by pointing out that many of the peculiarities of the text in the *Treatise* are due to the fact that Hume was seeking to propound empirical laws of psychology at the same time that he was trying to give a philosophical analysis of the concept of "cause." Robinson claims that this confusion of tasks misled Norman Kemp Smith in his commentary on Hume. An answer to Robinson by T. H. Richards is presented, together with a further answer by Robinson. The discussion is very helpful in clarifying what Hume may have intended to accomplish. The essay by J. W. Lenz on Hume's defense of causal inference broadens the discussion and clarifies some of the possible interpretations of the theory. Hume's analysis of causality leads to his theory of probability and induction, at least as it is presented in Part III of Book I in the *Treatise*. D. Stove's essay on this point argues that by now Hume is credited with having proven much more on this subject than he actually did in his discussion of inductive arguments. Hume is usually portrayed as having developed a skepticism about all inductive arguments. Stove instead contends that there are probable inductive arguments that are not canceled out by Hume's analysis.

The essay by T. Penelhum treats Hume's discussion on personal identity in the *Treatise*, Book I, Part IV, Section VI. Penelhum is concerned to evaluate Hume's arguments on the subject. He very carefully examines what Hume's case rested on and finds that it was on a confusing notion of identity, which led to Hume's denying that we can discover any personal identity within us. (Hume appeared to have second thoughts about this point.) Penelhum offers a way of avoiding Hume's skeptical results.

The remaining essays by A. C. MacIntyre, R. F. Atkinson, Anthony Flew, Geoffrey Hunter, W. D. Hudson, Bernard Wand, and F. A. Hayek deal with crucial issues that appear in Books II and III of the *Treatise* and in Hume's later essays. The last three items in the volume—James Noxon, "Hume's Agnosticism"; William Capitan, "Part X of Hume's *Dialogues*"; and G. J. Nathan, "Hume's Immanent God" are important and stimulating discussions of Hume's religious or irreligious views, especially as they appear in the *Dialogues*.

Stroud, Barry. *Hume*. London: Routledge & Kegan Paul, 1977.

Barry Stroud's work presents a general interpretation of David Hume's theory of knowledge and his theory of morals and passions. The study deals with Hume's two main philosophical statements, the *Treatise of Human Nature* and the two *Enquiries*. Issues in these texts are related to current philosophical discussions of similar questions. Six of the ten chapters deal primarily with the theory Hume set forth in the bulk of the *Treatise*, Book I.

Stroud, from the outset, sets out to show that Hume was not simply an arch skeptic offering negative views about everything. He was also, and more important, a philosopher of human nature attempting to establish a Newtonian science of man which would account for all of human behavior. Hume sought to build on the work of John Locke, Lord Shaftesbury, Bernard Mandeville,

Francis Hutcheson, and Joseph Butler. Stroud follows out Hume's attempt to develop his new science at the beginning of the *Treatise*, carefully examining Hume's contentions about the origin and nature of our ideas. Stroud points out that Hume never really questioned his own theory or gave much evidence for it and that there are serious problems in the theory that Hume never grappled with. Hume's theory of the association of ideas also is full of difficulties, according to Stroud, which Hume often acknowledged but did not resolve.

When Hume came to deal with the central issue of how we think about causal relationships, he was, of course, first of all very negative in the sense that he showed that such thinking is not a rational process that can be justified as deductive or inductive. Stroud turns from this to the positive side of Hume's theory of causal belief; namely, Hume's presentation of the psychological process by which we "connect" causes and effects. Many difficult or baffling parts of Hume's analysis are clarified in Stroud's account. For example, his interpretation of the kind of necessity that Hume believed existed between cause and effect makes more sense of the matter than Hume's text appears to do. One may doubt this interpretation and some of the others that Stroud offers, but usually they are illuminating and helpful in getting Hume's often confusing and sometimes seemingly contradictory explanations into a coherent pattern. Stroud traces several of these difficulties back to confused starting points of Hume. By showing how Hume could have overcome the difficulties, Stroud sets forth a more consistent analysis that Hume could have presented. In the case of causality, Stroud attempts to suggest a way for Hume to avoid psychologism while retaining his ideas about necessity.

Similarly, with the difficult discussions in Hume's *Treatise* of our knowledge of the existence and nature of external and internal objects (bodies and minds), Stroud patiently examines Hume's steps. He blames skeptical conclusions on Hume's facile acceptance of the Cartesian model of how we know about the external world. Stroud asserts that one should follow the spirit of Hume's work, examine how we do function in ordinary life, and then use what we find as a source of naturalistic explanation.

The discussion of the problem of personal identity is even murkier in Hume. Stroud ably shows how Hume was unable to find a satisfactory answer in his own terms and finally, in the Appendix to Book I of the *Treatise*, was ready to give up. Stroud contends that at this point Hume should have recognized "a fatal deficiency" in his theory of ideas.

Having presented a lucid and careful examination of the many strands of the *Treatise*, Book I, Stroud devotes the rest of his study to Hume's second and third books on man's moral and emotive behavior and to the application of Hume's naturalistic analysis of how human beings act to their actions in society. Stroud stresses the importance of Hume's naturalistic science of man for providing a program for examining the human situation rather than for offering specific answers to specific problems. Hume's own skepticism, even about this positive achievement, Stroud believes, could not really be taken seriously, even by a Humean.

Smith, Norman Kemp. *The Philosophy of David Hume: A Critical Study of Its Origins and Central Doctrines*. New York: Macmillan Publishing Company, 1941.

Norman Kemp Smith's study of the most important of David Hume's ideas, especially as they are expressed in *A Treatise of Human Nature*, Book I, deals both with interpreting Hume's overall views and with revealing their likely sources. Kemp Smith had been arguing since the beginning of this century that Hume was not really a skeptical thinker trying to destroy all positive views. Instead, Kemp Smith insisted, Hume was a naturalist who believed that reason is and ought only to be the slave of the passions. (Thus by analyzing how the passions function, we ought to be able to understand how the whole intellectual world functions.)

In developing such a reading of Hume, Kemp Smith also argued that Hume's sources, principally the writings of the Scottish moralists and of Pierre Bayle, formed the basis for a naturalistic point of view. One of the main lines by which Kemp Smith approached his subject was to argue that Hume developed his philosophy from concerns about ethical questions rather than from epistemological ones. From Francis Hutcheson, Hume learned that moral judgments were not rational but were based on feelings. Hume then went on to evaluate rational judgments as also based on feelings, and he took over the experimental method of John Locke and Sir Isaac Newton. Also, Hume used some of the most paradoxical portions of Pierre Bayle's *Dictionary*, especially the articles on Benedictus de Spinoza and Zeno of Elea, to show that even our most basic notions, such as those of space and time, are unintelligible.

From these different ingredients, Kemp Smith sought to construct a theory of the order in which Hume actually developed his ideas. It is central to Kemp Smith's interpretation to contend that Hume's theory of the role of the passions was his basic discovery. Through his theory of the actions of the passions Hume could explain all of human nature, including so-called rational behavior. Such an explanation was a positive naturalistic view and not the skeptical position with which Hume is usually credited. Hume later worked out the epistemological views of Book I of the *Treatise*. Carefully analyzing the discussions in this book, Kemp Smith brings out how they differ from what was said in Books II and III. He also stresses how these discussions led to unsatisfactory and skeptical results, or to Hume's emphasis on natural belief. The latter, his positive view, is what Kemp Smith sees as connecting the two parts of the *Treatise*. Natural belief is the result of strong feelings, and it is this kind of belief which Hume said "peoples our world." Hume's theory of belief became its author's explanatory device for the major problems of knowledge and metaphysics. It is, Kemp Smith stresses, essentially the same kind of naturalistic explanation that Hume offered in ethics. At the same time, Kemp Smith admits that there were so many conflicting tendencies in Hume from his empirical, his naturalistic, and his skeptical sides that he failed to work out one overall consistent document.

Kemp Smith's emphasis on Hume's naturalism flies in the face of the skeptical interpretation of Hume that has been popular for more than two hundred years. Kemp Smith has given a strong provocative statement of his case. Those who disagree have been forced to examine the texts most carefully to see if they can be given other interpretations. In spite of the disagreement of many scholars with Kemp Smith's interpretation, it remains perhaps the major commentary on Hume in this century.—*R.H.P.*

ADDITIONAL RECOMMENDED READING

Capaldi, Nicholas. *David Hume: The Newtonian Philosopher*. Boston: Twayne Publishers, 1975. Interesting recent interpretation of Hume in terms of the science of his time.

Hall, Roland. *Fifty Years of Hume Scholarship*. Edinburgh: Edinburgh University Press, 1978. Best available bibliography of recent writings on Hume.

Hendel, Charles W. *Studies in the Philosophy of David Hume*. Indianapolis: Bobbs-Merrill, 1963. An important interpretation of Hume.

Leroy, André. *David Hume*. Paris: Presses Universitaires de' France, 1953. The most complete interpretation of Hume by a French scholar.

Noxon, James. *Hume's Philosophical Development*. Oxford: Clarendon Press, 1973. A controversial work on how Hume's views developed.

Passmore, John A. *Hume's Intentions*. Cambridge: Cambridge University Press, 1952. A highly critical evaluation of Hume.

Penelhum, Terrence. *Hume*. New York: St. Martin's Press, 1975. A general presentation of Hume by a major contemporary philosopher.

THE NEW SCIENCE

Author: Giovanni Battista Vico (1668-1744)
Type of work: Philosophy of history
First published: 1744 (Definitive edition; earlier edition, 1725)

PRINCIPAL IDEAS ADVANCED

The only way to know man is in terms of his own creations—language, history, law, and religion.

The new science consists of reasoning (philosophy) and investigation (philology, considered as the empirical study of language, history, and literature).

After the Deluge the world was dominated by giants; the giants lived like wild animals until storms turned their eyes toward heaven and led them to invent gods; this is the origin of religion.

Because of his fear of the gods man became ashamed of himself; in acting accordingly he created morality.

The practice of burying the dead, undertaken for sanitary reasons, led to the belief in the immortality of the soul.

All cultures must pass through three stages: the age of gods, the age of heroes, and the age of men; corresponding to these stages are three kinds of customs, three kinds of laws, commonwealths, and religions.

Like many an eighteenth century scholar, Giovanni Battista Vico was in agreement with Alexander Pope's slogan, "The proper study of mankind is man." But whereas the typical representative of The Enlightenment thought that the way to study man was to apply to him the principles of Newtonian mechanics (for example, David Hartley, *Observations on Man*, 1749; Julien La Mettrie, *L'Homme Machine*, 1748), Vico maintained that the only way to know man is in terms of his own creations—language, history, law, religion—in short, through the study of civilization.

Vico professed to be carrying on the work of Descartes, and he took sharp issue with both the Cartesians and the Newtonians for supposing that nature is properly understandable by man. Is it not true, he asked, that we can know only what we make? Then only God can understand nature, because it is his creation. Man, on the other hand, can understand civilizaton, because he has made it. This was Vico's Archimedean point, a truth beyond all question: "that the world of civil society has certainly been made by men, and that its principles are therefore to be found within the modification of our own human mind."

Vico professed, at the same time, to be an adherent of the method of Francis Bacon; he claimed that he was merely carrying over into the study of civil affairs the method Bacon had applied to the study of nature. What he seems to have borrowed from Bacon, however, is not the inductive principle which most people associate with the English thinker, but the practice of turning to sensible evidence to verify one's theories. Vico explained that his science consisted of two parts, reasoning and investigation. The former, which he called "philosophy," had to do with the development of theories on the basis of axioms, definitions, and postulates. The latter, which he called "philology," was the empirical study of language, history, and literature. He maintained that because these latter are founded on memory and imagination and are mixed with emotion, they do not give us the truth; but when they are consulted by an intelligent investigator, who has a theory to test, they are of paramount importance and make possible a science of man.

Vico's central thesis was that modern civilized man has come into existence through a process which is intelligible in terms of certain tendencies inherent in the human constitution. He conceived that initially men roamed the forest like wild beasts, giving no evidence of reason or compassion or any of the traits which have come to distinguish them. Only gradually did man modify his passions and discipline his powers, learning reverence and devising the institutions and inventions with which he has subjugated the earth. Vico did not regard the process as accidental in any sense: it was all part of God's design. But the elements which Divine Providence made use of were, in his opinion, simple and understandable, and finding them was the aim of the "new science." He emphasized the role of providence in history, in order to guard against the belief in fate and chance of the Stoics and Epicureans. In his view, however, providence was a rational principle immanent in the world, rather than a mysterious will transcendent over it.

His work opens with a long list of axioms and corollaries, which should be studied carefully before one reads the rest of the book. They purport to give the fundamental traits of human nature that provide the dynamism for cultural evolution, together with the traits which determine the habits of poets and chroniclers whose creations must serve the scientist as sources. For example: "Because of the indefinite nature of the human mind, wherever it is lost in ignorance, man makes himself the measure of all things." "It is another property of the human mind that whenever men can form no idea of distant and unknown things, they judge them by what is familiar and at hand." "When men are ignorant of the natural causes producing things, they attribute their own nature to them."

When, on the basis of such axioms, Vico turned to study the myths and legends of the past and with their help to reconstruct the prehistory of the race, the results were hardly in agreement with the assumptions of the eighteenth century drawing room. It was the fashion to think of primitive man as a tender, rational creature, who spontaneously worshiped the God of Nature and knew none of the prejudices or vices of artificial civilizations. Moreover, men took it for granted that Homer was a cultivated philosopher and gentleman, well suited to be a tutor of their youth—except they could not understand why he attributed such scandalous behavior to his heroes and his gods. In Vico's opinion, however, Homer was sublime as a poet in virtue of the fact that he was no philosopher, but a poet with a childlike mind, the product of a childlike age. We must read Homer with this in view and make allowances when we use his material in any attempt to understand his times. Similarly, his gods and heroes must not be judged by our moral standards. They echo the memories of an age when reason and morality had scarcely begun to tame the savage spirit or soften the features of the gods men feared.

Ransacking the myths of pagan peoples, and fitting what he found into the biblical tradition, Vico constructed the following account. First, there seemed among all peoples to be a recollection of the Deluge; second, all traditions mentioned a time when the world was dominated by giants. Vico argued that God took the children of Shem to be the people of the Promise and conducted their development along supernatural lines which science was not designed to explain. But the descendants of Ham and Japheth were permitted to wander abroad, unattended by divine grace, and to develop the civilization which was Vico's concern. They became a gigantic folk, said Vico, from the fact that after their mothers had weaned them they left them to draw their nourishment from the earth. They became fierce and wild, cohabiting like beasts, and fighting for their food. So it continued until climatic changes, which followed the drying out of the earth, brought thunderstorms into being. The lightning and roar of thunder astonished these savages, causing them to lift their eyes to heaven; and the fear which was in their hearts caused them to invent the first gods. Thus, according to Vico, religion came into being—the first step toward civilization.

The fear of the gods made man take a look at himself and made him ashamed of some of the things he did, particularly concerning matters of sex. When he took his woman into a cave, however, he initiated a series of consequences which he could never have anticipated. In a word, he created morality, the second great principle of civilization, and by bringing his passions one by one under control he liberated his higher capacities, notably reason.

The third principle of civilization recognized by Vico is witnessed by the universal practice among early men of burying their dead. Occasioned at first by the offensiveness of decaying corpses, it came to be the basis of his belief in the immortality of the soul.

In opposition to the orthodox views of his day, Vico held that civilization originated independently in many different lands—a principle which had importance for the study of etymology, to which he gave so much attention. Since each language had a separate origin, it was useless to try to find common roots. On the other hand, different languages could be expected to show parallel developments. For example, because law originally came from God, the Greeks, who called God "*Dios*," called divine things "*diaïon*" and law "*dikaion.*" Correspondingly, the Romans called God "*Jove*," and law "*jus*," which is a contraction of "*jous.*"

It was a general principle with Vico that, on account of the unity of human nature, all cultures must pass through identical stages, namely, the age of gods; the age of heroes; and the age of men. He found their existence attested not merely in mythology and epic poetry, but also in the history of religion, in compilations of laws, and, above all, in etymologies. For, following these three ages, there are three kinds of natures characteristic of men, three kinds of customs, three kinds of laws, commonwealths, religions, and so forth. Thus, in the first age man's nature was fierce and cruel, in the second noble and proud, in the third benign and reasonable. Again, customs of the first age were tinged with religion, those of the second with punctilio (for example, Achilles), those of the third with civic responsibility.

It was Vico's ambition to develop his science along seven different branches. First, he proposed to make it a "rational civil theology of divine providence." He was not alone, in the eighteenth century, in marveling at the "divine legislative mind" which fashions private vices into public virtues. "Out of ferocity, avarice and ambition, the three vices which run through the human race, it creates the military, merchant, and governing classes and thus the strength, riches and wisdom of commonwealths. Out of these three great vices, which could certainly destroy all mankind on the face of the earth, it makes civil happiness."

Second, his science was to be a "philosophy of authority." In place of the usual speculation about social origins, contracts, the beginnings of property, and so forth, it offered a framework within which to trace the development of sovereignty and right—from the time when authority first sprang from the will of the gods, through the age when it was lodged with princes whose might obligated those who came to them for asylum, to the time when free men concluded by means of reason that authority resides in laws of nature.

In the third place, it was to be a "history of human ideas." Poetry, for Vico, was the wisdom of the heroic age, when men thought in images and confused fancies with memories. It was, however, the beginning of "the knowledge of good and evil," and all the ideas which speculative science was later to bring to refinement were present there in the rough.

The remaining four branches of the new science led to a speculative reconstruction of world history, including such matters as the span of time required for each period, the courses the nations run, the common elements of law and custom among the peoples, and, finally, the principles of universal history.

Because Vico came to his investigations through the study of jurisprudence, he developed the implications of the new science more completely in that direction and in the field of political thought than in most others. He maintained that civil societies evolve through three stages. All begin as aristocracies, which come into being because of the tendency of the weak to seek asylum at the altars of the strong. The peace and prosperity which result from this arrangement gradually strengthen the productive classes, who demand guarantees from their superiors. In time, a republic of free men, governed by law, replaces the aristocracy. But wealth and leisure breed effeminacy and greed. Citizens grow careless, and lawlessness prevails. Deliverance comes when a strong prince establishes order and takes authority into his hands. In Vico's words, "Since in the free commonwealths all look out for their own private interests, into the service of which they press their public arms at the risk of ruin to their nations, to preserve the latter from destruction a single man must arise, as Augustus did at Rome, and take all public concerns into his own hands, leaving his subjects free to look after their private affairs. . . . Thus are the peoples saved when they would otherwise rush to their own destruction." Vico regarded aristocracies and republics as unstable, and maintained that states normally "come to rest under monarchies."

In the century of Frederick the Great, it was nothing unusual for an enlightened thinker to argue in favor of an absolute monarchy. Voltaire did also. But the development which we have so far described was, in Vico's view, only half a cycle. A nation might flourish for some time under a prince, as did Imperial Rome; but the fate of Rome serves notice that the irresponsibility of civilized men in an "age of reason" may pass all bounds and bring about the destruction of everything that had been built up through the centuries. And such was, in Vico's opinion, the eternal law of history. He saw civilization as a fragile achievement which Divine Providence frames out of violence, greed, and pride; but when the zenith has been passed it is destroyed by these same forces. No need, with Gibbon, to place the blame on alien influences and external barbarians! A new "barbarism of reflection" turns civilized men into worse than beasts. Reason disintegrates into skepticism: "learned fools fall to calumniating the truth." Civic loyalties forgotten, the restraints of morality are turned into jests. Men throng together in cities and jostle each other at public festivals, but they live in deep solitude of spirit: under soft words and polite embraces they plot against one another's lives. Their factions grow into civil wars, which decimate the land and let their cities return to forests. Those who survive are reduced again to "the barbarism of sense," until they learn once more the things necessary for life. "Thus providence brings back among them the piety, faith, and truth which are the natural foundation of justice as well as the graces and beauties of the eternal order of God."

Vico gained only a limited fame in his own time. The curious manner in which many twentieth century points of view are anticipated in his work has, however, brought him belated recognition. Pragmatists can see their doctrine of knowledge in his contention that we know only what our minds contrive. Humanists find much wisdom in his account of civilization. Persons concerned with history as a science admire the way in which he combined hypothesis and investigation, and those whose interest is in plotting the cycles of cultures find fruitful suggestions in his work. James Joyce did much to popularize his name among students of literature. And, inevitably, his account of the early giants creating their gods and fleeing in shame to caves has caught the attention of some existentialists.—*J.F.*

Pertinent Literature

Pompa, Leon. *Vico: A Study of the New Science.* Cambridge: Cambridge University Press, 1975.

Leon Pompa's book is a study of Giovanni Battista Vico's theory of history, a complex and subtle philosophical work unfortunately written in a style which is baroque and obscure. All the more valuable then, is the fact that Pompa's study of Vico's theory is presented in a clear and exact form with careful exegesis backed up by sustained argument.

The principle which runs through all of Vico's thought and not just his theory of history is that what is true depends on ideas that are created. We can have complete knowledge only of that which we ourselves have made. Although this principle applied only to geometrical and mathematical propositions in Vico's early thought, it is used in *The New Science* as the method of historical interpretation, governing all causal connections and relationships in history. According to Vico, the propositions of mathematics were, as René Descartes had maintained, irrefutable and clear only because they were the creations of our own mind—not, as Descartes had also maintained, because such propositions were simple and unanalyzable, the atomic entities of thought conceived as being connected with one another by necessary logical links. From this underlying epistemological claim Vico arrives at his central anti-rationalist (anti-Cartesian) position that philosophy and history must be worked into a systematic form of synthetic *a priori* knowledge wherein the philosopher of history uses both metaphysical deduction and the true historical method. All of Vico's ideas on the nature of human history are informed by this central position. If we are to understand the principles of historical knowledge, we must pay close attention to specific historical factors and conditions, such as the human institutions of marriage and religion in different historical periods and in different nations. But historical specifics such as these are unable to yield the principles of historical science, which can be discovered only by close examination of the beliefs and ideas belonging to a definite period in the history of all nations. The implication here, as Pompa emphasizes, is clear. Since man created history informed by a particular web of beliefs and ideas in a particular time, man the historian can know history, just as God knows the world of nature which is his creation. Thus, it is to the human mind that we must look for the principles of a science of history.

Having explained and analyzed Vico's theory of history, Pompa turns to address the problems with which this theory is beset. The central issue here involves the interpretation of the underlying epistemology of Vico's theory of history as man-made. If the characteristics of man's mind determine social institutions, then how exactly is the relationship between developing human traits and modifications of man's mind, and the evolving social institutions (customs, practices, religion) through the different stages, supposed to work? Vico believes that the fundamental characteristics of human nature are themselves the source of this activity of cultural and historical evolution. This position, however, must be explained, for it presupposes the intelligibility of the relation between the principles of historical knowledge (the study of which is the business proper of "philosophy") and the history of the particular (which Vico called "philology" and by which he meant the empirical study of language, history, and literature).

Pompa rejects a number of attempted solutions to this problem. Benedetto Croce's Hegelian suggestion that the mind of the historical agent and the mind of the reconstructing historian are together equivalent to "objective reason" is rejected because such an explanation demands that one accept rather heavy doses of metaphysical necessity and the *a priori*. Some have put forth the theory that the kind of knowledge Vico has in mind as being necessary for the possibility of a science of history is knowledge by introspection, and Pompa dismisses such an interpretation of Vico's intent on the grounds that the principles of causal relationships and change in history can hardly be thought to be discovered by self-awareness of whatever form. Still others have suggested that for Vico knowledge of the fundamental facts of human existence, such as war, religion, poverty, and familial loyalty, can help reveal the truth about the facts of history. Here again, however, one would have to accept the completely uncritical presupposition that personal experience could somehow reveal the nature and structure of historical causation and change, and Pompa is left unconvinced by such an argument.

Pompa's own proposal is that Vico has a twofold conception of knowledge: knowledge of the formal conditions of history and knowledge of the factual conditions of history. The formal conditions of history are said to consist of facts, such as that institutions affect human nature. These are structural truths expressing the relationships holding between human institutions, decision-making at various levels, capacities for social development, and other such general facts pertaining to historical change in societies. Knowledge of the factual conditions of history can be concrete, practical knowledge, the source of which can range from an emotionally directed perspective on certain stages in history and the individual historian's own appreciation of such a perspective, through his own experience (and the modifications of his own mind), and through the possession of universal beliefs throughout history about institutions such as marriage and religion. Also cited as an example of the sort of factual condition for history are specific facts about man's nature—his lack of foresight, his tendency toward prudential rather than altruistic behavior, and other familiar characteristics making for difficult social relations and development. Pompa is careful to emphasize that Vico is not here merely appealing to matters of fact; or, at least, the importance of the conception of a factual condition of history is not that these "facts" are searched for and trotted out but that the recovery of such factual knowledge consists in man as historian making use of his imaginative and critical faculties. For Vico, only critical reflection on the past from the standpoint of the present can produce "true knowledge" of the historical world.

Pompa does not pretend that this suggestion is a definitive answer to the problems in Vico's theory; indeed, Pompa is quick to discuss the philosophical difficulties which Vico's theory of the "New Science" must overcome. How, for example, does Vico's science of history choose between different and often conflicting historical interpretations? How, ultimately, can Vico's emphasis on the metaphysical principles of the development of human history be reconciled with his insistence that history is a science?

Berlin, Isaiah. *Vico and Herder: Two Studies in the History of Ideas*. New York: The Viking Press, 1976.

The "two studies" contained in Isaiah Berlin's urbane and invigorating work in the history of ideas can be read as related pieces or as independent examinations of their subject, Giovanni Battista Vico and J. G. Herder. The essay on Vico, however, is considerably longer than the Herder effort and shows signs of having received a greater share of Berlin's philosophical acumen. While Berlin deals with Vico's work other than with *The New Science*, the latter is the center of the discussion; commentary on Vico's other books only serves to illuminate our appreciation and understanding of the central themes of *The New Science*.

Berlin casts Vico as an eighteenth century thinker who opposed the doctrines which lay at the heart of the Enlightenment, in particular, the doctrine that human nature was uniformly capable of rationality and that ideas, beliefs, and practices which were not founded on a rational basis were unworthy of serious consideration by any thinker interested in genuine human progress. Vico, both in *The New Science* and elsewhere, swam against the current in arguing that human rationality did *not* imply universal values, that the social groupings of men and women in past societies were more than just so many inferior stages in the inevitable movement toward a better world. In coming down firmly on the side of historicism, Vico claimed that each stage of man's social development was unique and indispensable; indeed, that each passing phase of man's past and future development retains a validity relative to its own stage of progress. The implication here is that the Enlightenment thinkers were seriously mistaken in describing the earlier stages of human evolution and social progression as almost inhuman and certainly barbaric. According to Berlin, Vico's fundamental conception of what it is to be human—that man has a soul with its own immanent laws of growth, subject only to non-mechanical change, that man understands himself in a different way from that in which he understands the material world, and that history is first a humane study, a science of man unlike all other sciences—shapes the Italian philosopher's work.

Vico's central tenets are presented in a theory of history based on a metaphysical conception of the nature of man. According to this conception, there is no unalterable state of human nature, a truth which a study of history—man's history—reveals. For Vico, human history is a field of enquiry in which the historian is involved in a continuous process of self-analysis, an idea which Vico regards as unproblematic because for him man is not something other than the actual process of his development—individual (physical, moral, intellectual) and social (political, artistic). Thus, says Berlin, the very idea of man's nature is for Vico intelligible only in terms of men's relations with the external world and other men. In a word, this interaction is the history of mankind. Growth and change in the mental life of men is one with the growth and development of the institutional life of the society, and this explains why, according to Berlin, the historian's activity seemed to Vico to be a genetic one. The value of the study of history, as one might expect from such a conception, is indisputable and essential: historical enquiry points out the existence of many, various, and autonomous cultures, each possessing a distinct way of life, set of values, and world view.

One appreciates why Vico has been called "the father of sociology"; his humanist theory of history—according to which the past is necessary to any understanding of the present—contains the seeds of a vitalist sociology. It was possible to know more about history than the physical sciences, for only in the former were men actual participants, seeking out the past in legends, myths, language, and other expressions of societies' forms of life. For Vico, such an examination formed a part of man's ancestral creation, and the study of history, so conceived, gave men the opportunity to exploit their unique capacity for imaginative understanding and reconstitution. The result was a sort of introspective knowledge (without mystical associations) which imparts an understanding of the causal and social conditions of history.

Berlin defends Vico's peculiar conception here that the basic facts of human existence (war, terror, religion) can convey the significance of historical facts. It remains to be shown, however, how such personal experience and imagination can of themselves produce knowledge of causation in history or a solid understanding of the conditions for the development of social life. It should be pointed out that Vico did think that empirical data and deductive reasoning were important contributions to historical investigation; he simply maintained that without imaginative reconstruction historians could not but produce a distorted picture of human history. It was essential for Vico that man enter into the imagination of past cultures, into their mental life, a process begun by a study of a culture's means of expression, and then onward to a grasp of the culture's world view or "vision of reality." This, according to Berlin, is what Vico tried to describe in *The New Science* and along the way provided the essential perceptions of what was to become the social sciences.—*J.P.D.*

ADDITIONAL RECOMMENDED READING

Fisch, Mat H. and T. G. Bergin, eds. *The Autobiography of Giambattista Vico*. Ithaca, New York: Cornell University Press, 1962. As well as the interesting autobiography, the book contains a most helpful introduction by Fisch to possible influences on Vico, Vico's influence on other important thinkers, and the overall importance of Vico's contribution to the philosophy of history.

Kelley, Donald R. *The Foundations of Modern Historical Scholarship*. New York: Columbia University Press, 1970. This book, by a historian, concerns the origins of cultural history and is valuable in relation to Vico because it places the latter's contribution to the idea of a historical science in the context of his predecessors and successors. Pertinent discussions of Vico throughout the book.

Pompa, Leon. "Vico's Science," in *History and Theory*. X, no. 1 (1971), pp. 49-84. An excellent argument that Vico's "science" really is scientific. The entire article is invaluable as a clear, analytic, and well-balanced exposition of Vico's theory of history.

Tagliacozzi, G. and H. White, eds. *Giambattista Vico, an International Symposium*. Baltimore: Johns Hopkins University Press, 1969. A collection of expository and critical articles on Vico's thought from a variety of thinkers. Very useful.

MAN A MACHINE

Author: Julien Offray de La Mettrie (1709-1751)
Type of work: Metaphysics and natural philosophy
First published: 1748

PRINCIPAL IDEAS ADVANCED

Both animals and men are machines that feel.

The soul is a material part of the brain, as is shown by the fact that when the body is diseased, so is the soul.

Man is distinguished from other animals by his larger brain and by his ability to use language.

Although it is highly probable that a supreme being exists, this information has little practical value.

Descartes had declared that all animals except men are "machines": very complicated automata, responding to external stimuli in a mechanical way. Thus, man alone, because he possesses an immaterial soul, is conscious and endowed with free will, hence capable of being virtuous or sinful. La Mettrie's leading idea was the denial of any sharp distinction in kind between man and other animals. In his *Natural History of the Soul* (1745) he put this in the form of a strong objection to Descartes' calling brutes "machines," thereby denying that they think and feel. But three years later he changed his terminology (not his doctrine) and argued that animals are machines that feel, and so is man. "The human body is a machine which winds its own springs; . . . the soul is but a principle of motion or a material and sensible part of the brain."

(It is unfortunate that *Man a Machine* has become traditional as the translation of *L'Homme machine*, for in English, unlike French, it is absurd on grounds of usage to call a man or a dog a *machine*, though it makes sense to speak of them as *mechanisms*—which is what La Mettrie meant.)

Man a Machine is for the most part a treatise on physiological psychology, containing also certain ethical and antitheological reflections. It is in the form of an oration, without subdivisions.

La Mettrie begins with a defense of experience and observation as foundations of knowledge even about the soul, as against the claims put forward for revelation as a source superior to reason. "If there is a God, He is the Author of nature as well as of revelation; . . . if there is a revelation, it can not contradict nature." To be sure, nature stands in need of interpretation; but so does the Bible. Concerning the soul, the requisite "experience and observation . . . are to be found throughout the records of the physicians who were philosophers, and not in the works of the philosophers who were not physicians. . . . Only the physicians have a right to speak on this subject." Theologians have the *least* right.

What experience and observation show the philosopher-physican about the soul is that its character is patently dependent on bodily conditions. When the body is diseased, so is the soul: a genius may be reduced to idiocy by a fever; it sometimes happens, conversely, that "the convalescence of an idiot produces a wise man." Extreme bodily fatigue produces a sleep amounting to the temporary extinction of the soul. The effects of opium, wine, and coffee are cited. Diet influences character: the English are savage because they eat their meat red and bloody. In La Mettrie's opinion the English diet accounts for their vices of "pride, hatred, scorn of other nations, indocility and other sentiments which degrade the character"—but education can counteract this. Extreme hunger, and prolonged sexual abstinence, can produce raving maniacs. When the body degenerates in old age, so does the soul. Female delicacy and male vigor correspond to the different bodily constitutions of the sexes. When you look through a gallery of portraits "you can always distinguish the man of talent from the man of genius, and often even an honest man from a scoundrel." Differences in national characters correspond to differences in climate. In sum, "the diverse states of the soul are always correlative with those of the body."

Comparative mammalian anatomy, especially brain anatomy, bears out and explains this conclusion. Man is the most intelligent animal because he has the largest and most convoluted brain; the descending order of intelligence— monkey-beaver-elephant-dog-fox-cat—is also the descending order of brain size and complexity. La Mettrie makes three generalizations about animals: "1st, that the fiercer animals are, the less brain they have; 2nd, that this organ seems to increase in size in proportion to the gentleness of the animal; 3rd, that . . . the more one gains in intelligence the more one loses in instinct." But among men, brain defects are not *always* gross: "A mere nothing, a tiny fibre, something that could never be found by the most delicate anatomy, would have made of Erasmus and Fontenelle two idiots."

The higher animals can do surprising things when properly trained. It would be interesting to attempt to teach an ape to speak by application of the method that Amman has used so brilliantly with deaf-mutes. If one chose a fairly young ape, "one with the most intelligent face, and the one which, in a thousand little ways, best lived up to its look of intelligence," the experiment might well succeed. Then the ape "would no longer be a wild man, nor a defective man, but he would be a perfect man, a little gentleman, with as much matter or muscle as we have, for thinking and profiting by his education." For man is not distinguished qualitatively from the other animals except in possessing language. And language itself is not an inherent possession of the human species as such, but must have been invented by certain geniuses who taught it to the others.

Knowledge consists in the comparison of the sensory ideas (images) produced in the brain, and this comparison can hardly proceed without language, a system of symbols for classifying. This comparison La Mettrie calls "imagination," and he asserts: "All the faculties of the soul can be reduced to pure imagination. . . . Thus, judgment, reason, and memory are not absolute parts of the soul, but merely modifications of [the] medullary screen upon which images of the objects painted in the eye are projected as by a magic lantern." Hence, all talent and genius, whether of Newton or of Corneille, is fundamentally the same thing: lively imagination.

"Man's preeminent advantage is his organism. . . . An exaggerated modesty (a rare fault, to be sure) is a kind of ingratitude towards nature." There is nothing wrong with taking pride not only in skill, learning, and virtue, but even in mind, beauty, wealth, nobility; these, "although the children of chance, all have their own value."

It is wrong to try to distinguish man from other animals by the former's alleged exclusive acquaintance with natural (moral) law. Natural law is "a feeling that teaches us what we should not do, because we would not wish it to be done to us." It manifests itself to *me* when, for example, I feel remorse after bad conduct; my belief that *you* have a similar experience can only be based on my inferences from your behavior. But we see the same signs in animals, such as the "crouching and downcast air" of a dog who has offended his master. La Mettrie cites the story of Androcles and the lion to prove that animals feel gratitude. If, however, it is maintained that despite appearances animals do not really have any awareness of natural law, then it follows that men do not either, for "man is not moulded from a costlier clay; nature has used but one dough, and has merely varied the leaven." But in fact, remorse and gratitude are universal, even among the most hardened criminals. These persons commit their atrocities from morbid impulses and they are punished adequately by their consciences. It would be better to hand them over to doctors than to burn them or bury them alive, as is the custom.

It is clear that for these reasons virtue is its own reward, and that "Nature has created us all solely to be happy—yes, all of us from the crawling worm to the eagle lost in the clouds." (La Mettrie developed the ethical implications of this doctrine in his *Discourse on Happiness*, 1748.)

La Mettrie next turns his attention to religion. It is highly probable, he says, that a supreme being exists; but this is "a theoretic truth with very little practical value." It does not follow that a highest being ought to be worshiped just because he exists; nor does religion (as everyone knows) insure morality, any more than atheism excludes it.

The "zealous writers" who pile up evidences of design in nature to prove the existence of an intelligent Creator are misguided. "Either the mere structure of a finger, of an ear, of an eye, a single observation of Malpighi proves all, . . . or all the other evidences prove nothing." For even if it be admitted that these facts rule out the possibility of a merely "chance" universe, the existence of a supreme being is not thereby proved, "since there may be some other thing which is neither chance nor God—I mean, nature." All we know is that there is an infinite variety of ingenious mechanisms in nature; we know nothing of their ultimate causes; in this situation recourse to God is a mere disguise of ignorance. "The weight of the universe therefore far from crushing a real atheist does not even shake him."

At this point La Mettrie writes (more astonishingly than convincingly): "Such is the *pro* and the *contra*, and the summary of those fine arguments that will eternally divide the philosophers. I do not take either side." A friend of his, however, "an abominable man," maintained to him that "the universe will never be happy, unless it is atheistic." The extirpation of religion would put an end to religious wars; "Nature, infected with a sacred poison, would regain its rights and its purity. Deaf to all other voices, tranquil mortals would follow only the spontaneous dictates of their own being, the only commands which can never be despised with impunity and which alone can lead us to happiness through the pleasant paths of virtue."

Returning to the subject of the soul, La Mettrie next shows that it is not necessary to postulate the soul as a principle or cause of motion of the body, since muscular fibre is inherently motile. He offers ten observations and experiments in proof. One is that portions dissected from polyps regenerate into whole polyps; the other nine are concerned either with spontaneous motions of parts of organisms severed from bodies or with the motion of parts of the body after death. "The soul is therefore but an empty word, of which no one has any idea, and which an enlightened man should use only to signify the part in us that thinks."

La Mettrie describes at considerable length the physiology of reflex and involuntary movements to illustrate the mechanical nature of the body. (He cites, among other things, the phenomenon of erection. This and all other references to sex, as well as whole pages on prenatal influence, embryology, and heredity, are omitted in the Open Court translation, which was made in 1912 by a committee of learned ladies. Oddly, or perhaps not, the one really indecent *double entendre* in La Mettrie's text escaped their vigilance. See pp. 95ff.) The bodily effects of emotional states show moreover that there is no sharp division between what is under control of the will and what is not. Though La Mettrie does not deny (or even discuss) the "freedom of the will," he remarks that the will "can not act save by permission of the bodily conditions." But having shown (to his satisfaction) that the body is self-moved, and that consciousness is a property of its organized matter, not an independent substance, La Mettrie confesses that he can go no further in explanation. "The nature (origin) of motion is as unknown to us as that of matter."

Descartes is praised for having proved that animals are machines. His insistence on the distinctness of mental from material substance was, says La Mettrie, a ruse to throw the theologians off the scent; for the analogy of men with animals is so striking that it could only be overlooked by "animals and

machines which, though upright, go on all fours." There is no contradiction
in the notion of a thinking, feeling, moral animal-machine. "Thought is so
little incompatible with organized matter, that it seems to be one of its properties on a par with electricity, the faculty of motion, impenetrability, extension, etc."

Only pride and prejudice lead men to resist these conclusions. But "matter
contains nothing base, except to the vulgar eyes which do not recognize her
in her most splendid works."

We are told (again to our surprise) that immortality is not impossible. To
suppose it out of the question would be to reason like caterpillars who can
have no conception of their coming metamorphosis. We should admit that
we are invincibly ignorant in this domain, and will remain so.

La Mettrie concludes by picturing the wisdom, justice, tranquillity, reverence (for nature), gratitude, affection, tenderness, kindliness, pity, and forgiveness—in a word, the happiness—of the materialist. "Convinced, in spite
of the protests of his vanity, that he is but a machine or an animal, the
materialist will not maltreat his kind, for he will know too well the nature of
those actions, whose humanity is always in proportion to the degree of the
analogy proved between human beings and animals; and following the natural
law given to all animals, he will not wish to do to others what he would not
wish them to do to him.

"Let us then conclude boldly that man is a machine, and that in the whole
universe there is but a single substance differently modified. . . . Such is my
system, or rather the truth, unless I am much deceived. It is short and simple.
Dispute it now who will."

Two centuries after La Mettrie one is likely to smile wryly at the pretty
picture of grateful lions regulating their conduct by the Golden Rule, and at
the conviction that once religion is got rid of, all will be well—as if religion
were something imposed on men from outside, contrary to "the spontaneous
dictates of their own being"! But these are amiable eighteenth centuryisms
which should not deceive us into supposing that La Mettrie was a naïve
thinker. He deserves the credit (or blame) for many insights usually attributed
to such men as Rousseau, Condillac, Helvétius, and Holbach. His brief remarks on the relation of evidence to conclusion in the design argument for
the existence of God penetrate to the essential logical point in a manner not
inferior to the more celebrated critiques of Hume and Kant.

Materialists, at least since Lucretius, argued that no chasm separates man
from the rest of nature and that the soul must be material, or a property of
matter, because mental states obviously vary with the condition of the body.
La Mettrie did not have a new argument; he only added to the old one such
evidence as was available to him from recent investigations of brain anatomy.
But just as La Mettrie questioned the relevance of piling up evidence for
design in nature for the purpose of proving a Great Designer, so here also

one can ask whether more and more detail about the *dependence* of soul on body strengthens the conclusion that soul *is* body. Except for theological considerations (which La Mettrie justifiably ignored), philosophers who were well aware of all the facts concerning the effects of bodily constitution on the soul still upheld the separateness of body and soul for three reasons: (1) Our thoughts and feelings, of which we are directly aware, are obviously not bodies, nor properties of bodies, since it makes no sense to raise such questions about them as where they are, or how big they are. (2) We know (again immediately) that the self has an identity that no material thing, or property, could have: for anything spatial can be divided, whereas we have no notion of what it would be like to split one self into two selves. (3) Matter is essentially inert; if it moves, there must be a cause of its motion; and our experience reveals that volition, which is mental, is capable of moving the body. (Note that all these purport to be deductions from "experience and observation.")

It is incumbent upon materialists at least to cope with these objections. Now La Mettrie paid attention to the third, and he gave good reasons for denying the inertness of matter, especially organic matter. An answer to the second is implicit in his writing: the unity of the self is only a unity of functions, and when the organism is malformed (as in congenital idiocy or deafness) the corresponding functions ("faculties") are absent.

There is discernible in La Mettrie the bare beginning of a materialist reply to the first objection. He says, in the passage already quoted above, that "judgment, reason, and memory are not absolute parts of the soul, but merely *modifications* of [the] medullary screen upon which images of the objects painted in the eye are projected as by a magic lantern." (Emphasis supplied.) That is, when an image is formed on the retina, it is transmitted by the optic nerve to the visual cortex, and the visual sensation *is* the resulting "modification" or "brain-event." This doctrine requires considerable argumentation and explication before it becomes plausible, and La Mettrie provides none. However, he has at any rate progressed beyond the childish view of Descartes, according to whom the immaterial soul somehow "inspects" (directly, infallibly, and unintelligibly) the "medullary screen." In any case, it would be unreasonable to complain of La Mettrie that he did not, once and for all, explain how one is to conceive the identity of thought and brain process—that is, solve the mind-body problem, still the most vexed question on the philosophical agenda despite well-meant attempts to dismiss it as nonsensical.

La Mettrie was the first, the most consistent, and the most extreme of the eighteenth century French materialists. He was a thinker of great originality who insisted on saying what he thought, in print, well knowing that to do so would expose him to the rage of fanatical obscurantists. In fact, he was forced to flee from France to Holland, thence to Prussia, where Frederick the Great granted him asylum. In Potsdam he resumed the practice of medicine. He enjoyed but two years of security and prosperity; he died at the age of forty-one. (The pious claimed that Epicurean gluttony was the cause of death.) Frederick himself composed his eulogy, saying of him (with justice that the much-maligned philosopher has yet to receive from the historians, with the honorable exception of Lange): "La Mettrie was born with a fund of natural and inexhaustible gaiety; he had a quick mind, and such a fertile imagination that it made flowers grow in the field of medicine. Nature had made him an orator and a philosopher; but a yet more precious gift which he received from her, was a pure soul and an obliging heart. All those who are not imposed upon by the pious insults of the theologians mourn in La Mettrie a good man and a wise physician."—*W.I.M.*

PERTINENT LITERATURE

Callot, Émile. "La Mettrie," in *La Philosophie de la vie au XVIIIe siècle.* Paris: Marcel Rivière, 1965, pp. 195-244.

In this volume Émile Callot examines seven theoreticians of biology, from Bernard Le Bovier de Fontenelle to Karl Linnaeus. Regarding Julien Offray de La Mettrie, he tells us that he was the most denounced thinker of his time, and the most unknown in the following century. Only in the last fifty years has he been rediscovered in spite of the fact that he was the bravest thinker of the Enlightenment, advancing a thoroughgoing materialism. His materialistic view preceded that of Denis Diderot and Baron Paul Holbach and opened the way for a new evaluation of man biologically and psychologically.

After a brief biography of La Mettrie, pointing out that he wrote all his important works in seven years, 1744-1751, when he was thirty-five to forty-two (when he died), Callot begins by analyzing La Mettrie's medical and biological theories. The basic mechanistic view about animal and human bodies came from René Descartes and from La Mettrie's teacher, Herman Boerhaave. His classmate, Albrecht von Haller, provided specific detail about the mechanism of animals and humans in terms of the irritability of muscles and the sensibility of nerves. Haller still believed in a spiritual part of living beings. It was La Mettrie's critical contribution to claim that, using mechanistic explanations, including those of physiology, one could describe the man-machine. Callot examined La Mettrie's early medical writings to show how he was moving towards materialism. Next the philosophical influences, Epicurus and Lucretius, Francis Bacon, Thomas Hobbes and John Locke, René Descartes, Nicolas de Malebranche and Pierre Gassendi, as well as Benedictus de Spinoza, are considered. Influenced by all these men, La Mettrie became both a firm empiricist and a staunch materialist.

From such a background, La Mettrie worked out a special kind of materialistic theory of man which differs somewhat in his *Natural History of the Soul* (1745) and *Man a Machine.* Man is a living material being with a unity. Callot insists that as La Mettrie developed his conception he was led to adopt two positions, one a kind of vitalism, the other pure materialism. Citing passages in which La Mettrie spoke of an animated body which is capable of self-motion and feeling, Callot shows the vitalistic element that goes along with La Mettrie's inert materialism. The matter of which La Mettrie spoke (and of which Diderot and Holbach spoke after him) was not merely the collection of atoms of Democritus, but was something much richer—a kind of matter capable of engendering from itself all its forms of existence. As La Mettrie developed his conception with regard to men, it became obvious that there is no real separation between men and animals; there is only a difference of degree. This view set the stage for a theory of evolution.

Callot also describes how La Mettrie used his theory to develop an atheistic position. If everything can be explained materialistically, God is then just a useless metaphysical hypothesis. Nature contains what it requires and is all-powerful, self-ordering, and determined. Hence God is an idea which has no theoretical or practical interest and no philosophical base.

After surveying much of La Mettrie's view, Callot concludes that his materialism has special properties. It is on the one hand a pure mechanism, which can explain brute bodies, and it is on the other hand a dynamism, involving the sensibility of matter under the biological aspect of the irritability of tissues, including the cerebral ones in man. In terms of these two aspects one can explain man as a machine. La Mettrie's dynamic materialism, offered by him as a hypothesis, was the richest form of the doctrine put forth in the eighteenth century. Through it Descartes' animal-mechanism could be really advanced and his explanation expanded to explain man. Self-moving matter could account for the soul, without requiring any spiritual categories. On this basis Callot concludes that La Mettrie was the most thorough and advanced materialist of the Enlightenment.

Rosenfield, Leonora Davidson. *From Beast-Machine to Man-Machine*. New York: Octagon Books, 1968.

This work is the major study of the intellectual developments from René Descartes' conception of the animal machine up to Julien Offray de La Mettrie's proposal that man is a machine. Leonora Davidson Rosenfield starts by examining how Descartes worked out his theory of the nature of beasts in opposition to the scholastic as well as the humanistic views of the time asserting that animals had souls. Descartes' theory about the nature of animals is shown to be a basic part of his philosophy. Rosenfield traces how this Cartesian doctrine spread in the seventeenth century intellectual world. The later Cartesians such as Louis de La Forge, Johann Clauberg, Jacques Rohault, Pierre-Sylvain Régis, Géraud de Cordemoy, and others argued for the beast-machine theory, both as a scientific view and as a metaphysical one. Nicolas de Malebranche, who deviated from many of the Cartesian positions, nevertheless strongly maintained the distinction between animals and people on Cartesian grounds. Malebranche did this largely in terms of metaphysical considerations. It was his formulation that shaped the views of the later Cartesians, who found the beast-machine theory a basis for arguing for the immortality of the human soul and the Providence of God. Descartes' thesis became more and more a religious view by the end of the seventeenth century. The Cartesians saw that making animal psychology purely mechanistic buttressed a spiritual view of man.

The Cartesian animal-machine theory was opposed from its inception by a wide range of thinkers holding various traditionalist and scholastic views. The French Jesuits fought against Descartes' view as well as the counterclaim that animals think. They were trying to undermine his whole metaphysical system. A stronger challenge to Cartesianism came from empiricism, especially that fostered by John Locke at the beginning of the eighteenth century. With their strong emphasis on facts discovered in experience, empiricists from Pierre Gassendi onward saw some experiential signs of animal intelligence. Locke contended that animals had a lower form of intelligence than human beings. Pierre Bayle saw animals as having less complex souls than humans. Bernard Le Bovier de Fontenelle used empirical science to attack the theory of animal automation and to convince people that beasts are capable of simple ideas. Voltaire then contended that beasts are not mere machines but are animated by a degree of thought. Locke had said that it is possible that matter can think. For Voltaire the case of the animal proved this.

Various eighteenth century thinkers discussed whether animals can have forms of intelligence, such as speech. As they worked out explanations of animal behavior, these became more and more mechanical in accounting for intellectual activity of animals. It was while this discussion was going on that La Mettrie proposed his shocking and revolutionary theory that man is a machine.

Rosenfield devotes only a few pages to La Mettrie, although the whole book has been pointing to him. La Mettrie was a complete materialist. He accepted Descartes' theory of the beast-machine and simply extended it. All animal and human activity are natural phenomena. All intellectual activity of either is conditioned by the organization of the body. The functioning of the bodies of humans and beasts is mechanical. Back in Descartes' day, the traditionalists had said that the Cartesian mechanistic theory of animals implied the same kind of a theory about humans. And a century later La Mettrie was propounding the latter theory. Once he had adopted a thoroughgoing materialism, La Mettrie had eliminated the possibility of Descartes' spiritual human soul. At that point, as Rosenfield says, "La Mettrie's mechanism became the logical outcome of Descartes' mechanistic physiology." La Mettrie's mechanism thus became a serious challenge to religion since it denied the existence of any independent soul. By implication La Mettrie also denied that there was any need to bring theological considerations into what he now claimed were purely scientific matters. Animal intelligence would have to be examined empirically as part of animal psychology, whose domain include the human animal, the man-machine.

Rosenfield's book closes with an examination of some of the other eighteenth century discussions of the matter, as well as the literary uses of the various theories. The notes and bibliography are invaluable for anyone studying the background of La Mettrie's theory.

Vartanian, Aram, ed. *La Mettrie's L'Homme Machine: A Study in the Origins of an Idea*. Princeton: Princeton University Press, 1960.

Aram Vartanian, a specialist on science during the Enlightenment, presents a detailed analysis and evaluation of Julien Offray de La Mettrie's *Man a Machine*, while placing the work in its historical setting. Vartanian's monograph begins with a biographical sketch of the author based on the small amount of information that we possess. La Mettrie's medical writings prior to *Man a Machine* are discussed to show how the author was moving toward a materialistic view. His *Natural History of the Soul* was his first venture into philosophy and was immediately condemned by those who were religiously oriented. *Man a Machine* caused a sensation and made its author a major figure in both the philosophical world (as a materialist and atheist) and in the scientific world as a psychologist.

The character of La Mettrie's psychology is carefully analyzed by Vartanian. La Mettrie, he points out, clearly breaks with the entire theological and metaphysical tradition by proposing to consider the problem of understanding the mind as a problem in physics, with the machine as the model. Man as the machine would be a mechanical entity in which psychic events occur as the result of organic causes. This theory is, Vartanian insists, a hypothesis which purports to give a better explanation of human phenomena than any prior psychological theory, when the evidence is judged empirically. La Mettrie's principle of explanation is not just mechanical, but is also based on the principle of irritability in human tissues. La Mettrie also saw that the same principles operated in subhuman species and that there was a gradual difference in how it operated. This view led him to an early version of the theory of evolution. La Mettrie offered a new and different way of conceiving the relationship of mind and body. According to Vartanian, he offered it not as a metaphysical or antireligious dogma, but as a "heuristic hypothesis" which has proved valuable in psychophysiological investigations up to the present time.

In tracing the background of La Mettrie's thought, Vartanian shows that he came to the man-machine theory only in 1747, when he wrote the book. His previous work was dualistic, and La Mettrie rejected much of his earlier work. In the *Natural History of the Soul*, he opposed René Descartes and supported Aristotle and John Locke. Two years later he was using Benedictus de Spinoza as well as new scientific data. In the four years after *Man a Machine*, before La Mettrie died, he defended and expanded his theory. In so doing he gradually fell out with the *philosophes* in opposing their conception of nature.

Vartanian next traces the historical background of the man-machine theory from Descartes' conception of the animal machine. Nicolas de Malebranche and Locke are each seen as crucial in leading away from Descartes' limited concept. Spinoza, whom La Mettrie thanks for his idea, is only really a source in terms of how he was interpreted during the Enlightenment. Gottfried Wilhelm von Leibniz is also a source. Thomas Hobbes, whose views are closer to La Mettrie's, was probably unknown to him. Then, examining eighteenth century literature, expecially the medical work of La Mettrie's teacher, Herman Boerhaave, one sees thinkers getting closer and closer to La Mettrie's idea, even in its medical detail about irritability as a basic factor. Albrecht von Haller had discussed this in his notes to Boerhaave's lectures. Vartanian also shows the developments in psychiatry that led to La Mettrie's view. Altogether, it is maintained that La Mettrie's theory is the outgrowth of Descartes, stripped of its metaphysics, and the outgrowth of certain clandestine ideas about materialism and atheism. La Mettrie fused the antireligious views involved with medical findings and developed a view that has been significant in medicine and psychology ever since he stated it.

Vartanian concludes his monograph with a chapter on the critical reaction of La Mettrie's contemporaries, covering the critiques up to 1762. He then closes with a survey of the man-machine from 1748 onward, showing that after the Enlightenment rejection of La Mettrie's views, his views were revived by Pierre Cabanis (who never mentioned their source). He was then rediscovered by the nineteenth century materialistic biologists and psychologists and since then has been a major figure in intellectual history. His theory is still being debated in modern form concerning whether machines (computers) can think.—*R.H.P.*

ADDITIONAL RECOMMENDED READING

Lange, F. A. *The History of Materialism*. London: Kegan Paul, Trench, Trubner & Company, 1925. An overall history of materialistic thought; places La Mettrie's work in its historical setting.

Needham, Joseph. *Man a Machine*. London: Kegan Paul, 1927. An attempt to present La Mettrie's theory in twentieth century scientific terms.

Perkins, Jean A. "Diderot and La Mettrie" and "Voltaire and La Mettrie," in *Studies on Voltaire and the Eighteenth Century*. X, pp. 49-111. Two important studies of La Mettrie's relationship with two important Enlightenment thinkers.

Poritzky, J. E. *Julien Offray de La Mettrie, sein Leben und seine Werke.* Berlin: F. Dümmler, 1900. A full-scale biography of La Mettrie and a summary of his works.

AN ENQUIRY CONCERNING THE PRINCIPLES OF MORALS

Author: David Hume (1711-1776)
Type of work: Ethics
First published: 1751

PRINCIPAL IDEAS ADVANCED

The purpose of ethical inquiry is to discover those universal principles on which moral praise and blame are based.

Benevolence is approved partly because of human sympathy and partly because of its social utility, but justice is approved for its utility alone.

Utility accounts for the worth of such virtues as humanity, friendship, integrity, veracity—and it is by its utility that government is justified.

Theories which attempt to explain all human conduct as springing from self-love are mistaken.

Whatever is worthwhile is so in virtue of its utility or its agreeableness.

Moral judgment is essentially a matter of sentiment, not reason.

Hume's *An Enquiry Concerning the Principles of Morals* is a philosophical classic which grows older without aging, which remains lively with a wisdom that speaks to the present. It is not the most profound of Hume's works or the most original, being to some extent a revision of Book III of Hume's masterpiece, *A Treatise of Human Nature*. But its author considered it the best of his works, and many critics have agreed with this judgment.

Dealing decisively with major ethical issues the *Enquiry* presents in clear, carefully organized form an analysis of morals. It continues the attack begun by Bishop Butler against the self-love theory (psychological egoism) of Hobbes, and in so doing achieves a measure of objectivism frequently either overlooked or denied by Hume's critics. On the other hand, after preliminary recognition of the significant but auxiliary role of reason in moral judgment, Hume sides with the eighteenth century school of sentiment against the ethical rationalists, on grounds shared today by those who regard ethical judgments as emotive utterances. But while Hume is frequently cited as a predecessor of the latter philosophers, he avoids the utter relativism and moral nihilism frequently, but erroneously for the most part, attributed to them. Hence, although it would be worthwhile to read the *Enquiry* for its historical importance alone, it also has a unique relevance to some fundamental problems of mid-twentieth century ethical philosophy, particularly to those concerning the nature of moral judgment.

While the *Enquiry* can be clearly understood without previous reading of Hume's other works, it is an application to ethics of the theory of knowledge and methodology presented in *A Treatise of Human Nature* and *An Enquiry*

Concerning Human Understanding, and its interest is enhanced by familiarity with these books. Like them, the present *Enquiry* contains a measure of skepticism which, while fundamental, has been greatly exaggerated and widely misunderstood. Indeed one of the chief merits of Hume's philosophy lies in the "mitigated" skepticism which recognizes the limits of human reason without succumbing to what he calls "Pyrrhonism" or excessive skepticism, which in practice would make belief and action impossible. But those who accuse Hume of the latter skepticism must ignore one of his chief aims: to apply the Newtonian method of "philosophizing" to a study of human nature.

The object of the study is to trace the derivation of morals back to their ultimate source. Hume's proposed method was to analyze the virtues and vices of men in order "to reach the foundation of ethics, and find those universal principles, from which all censure or approbation is ultimately derived." Since this was a factual matter it could be investigated successfully only by the experimental method, which had proved itself so well in "natural philosophy," or physical science.

This "scientific" approach will appeal to many modern readers, but herein lies an ambiguity which, in spite of the clarity of Hume's style, has misled some critics. One must realize that Hume was at this point writing of ethics as a descriptive study *about* morals—about acts, characters, and moral judgments. In this sense ethics is a behavioral science and its statements are either true or false. This may suggest what today would be called an objectivist position, but Hume was not describing the way in which moral attitudes are affected; moral judgments, strictly speaking, are matters of sentiment, although before they can properly occur reason must furnish all the available relevant information. To avoid misinterpretation, it is hardly possible to overemphasize this distinction between inductive conclusions *about* moral acts and judgments, on the one hand, and moral approvals and disapprovals themselves, on the other.

Hume's analysis begins with an examination of the social virtues, benevolence and justice, since their explanation will have relevance to other virtues as well. Such benevolent sentiments and characters as are described by words like "sociable" or "good-natured" are approved universally. But it is not the mere fact of approval but the principle underlying it which is the object of investigation. We approve benevolence in part because of the psychological principle of what Hume calls *sympathy*, an involuntary tendency in an observer to experience the same emotions he observes in a fellow man, but the more immediate reason for such approval is that we perceive the utility (usefulness, conduciveness to happiness) of this virtue. When we praise a benevolent man, Hume says, we always make reference to the happiness and satisfaction he affords to society. Since benevolence is regarded as one of the highest virtues, it reflects in turn the fundamental importance of utility. Even in our nonmoral judgment of value, usefulness is a paramount consideration.

In cases of uncertainty about moral questions, Hume adds, there is no more certain way of deciding them than by discovering whether the acts or attitudes involved are really conducive to the interests of society. Hume describes several reversals in the estimation of practices, such as generosity to beggars, when it was seen that their tendencies were harmful rather than helpful, as had been supposed at first.

Whereas benevolence is approved partly but not exclusively for its beneficial consequences, justice has merit for no other reason. (One must realize that Hume conceives justice as concerning only property relations, thus omitting "fair play" and equality, ordinarily considered essential to the concept; actually he accounts for impartiality by his account of truly moral judgment, as is shown below.) To prove this apparently controversial claim, Hume cites a number of cases in which the connection of justice and utility is demonstrated by their joint occurrence or nonoccurrence, increase or diminution. Too many and too lengthy to admit adequate recapitulation here, Hume's arguments may be suggested briefly by a few illustrations: In situations of superfluity or of dearth of material goods, the observation of property distinctions becomes useless and is suspended; a virtuous man captured by outlaws flouting justice would be under no restraint from justice if the opportunity to seize and use their weapons arose, since regard for ownership would be harmful; societies suspend international justice in times of war because of its obvious disadvantages.

Examination of particular laws confirms this explanation of justice; they have no other end than the good of mankind, to which even the natural law theorists are forced to appeal ultimately. Particular laws would in many cases be utterly arbitrary and even ridiculous, were it not that the general interest is better served by having specified rules rather than chaos. In individual cases the fulfillment of justice may even be detrimental, as when an evil man legally inherits a fortune, and abuses it, but consistent observance of the law is ultimately more useful than is deviation.

Were individuals completely self-sufficient, again justice would not arise, but actually men mate and then rear children; and subsistence of the family requires observance within it of certain rules. When families unite into small societies, and societies engage in commerce, the domain of utilitarian rules of property enlarges accordingly. Thus the evolution of social groups shows a direct proportion between utility and the merit of justice.

In finding the essence of justice and its moral obligation in utility alone, thus making it of derivative rather than intrinsic value, is Hume degrading this virtue? Not so, he insists: "For what stronger foundation can be desired or conceived for any duty, than to observe, the human society, or even human nature, could not subsist without the establishment of it; and will still arrive at greater degrees of happiness and perfection, the more inviolable the regard is, which is paid to that duty?"

At the end of his section on justice he repeats his conclusion that utility accounts for much of the merit of such virtues as humanity, friendship, and public spirit, and for all that of justice, fidelity, integrity, veracity, and some others. A principle so widely operative in these cases can reasonably be expected to exert comparable force in similar instances, according to the Newtonian method of philosophizing. Hume then finds utility to be the basic justification for political society or government, and he notes that "the public conveniency, which regulates morals, is inviolably established in the nature of man, and of the world, in which he lives."

But is utility itself a fundamental principle? We may still ask *why* utility is approved, to what end it leads. The alternatives are two: it serves either the general interest or private interests and welfare. Hume recognizes the plausibility of the self-love or self-interest theory holding that all approvals are ultimately grounded in the needs and passions of the self, but he claims to prove decisively the impossibility of thus accounting for moral judgments.

The skeptical view that moral distinctions are inculcated through indoctrination by politicians in order to make men docile is very superficial, Hume says. While moral sentiments may be partially controlled by education, unless they were rooted in human nature the terminology of ethics would awaken no response.

But granted this response, must it still be traced to self-interest, perhaps an enlightened self-interest that perceives a necessary connection between society's welfare and its own? Hume thinks not. We often praise acts of virtue in situations distant in time and space, when there is no possibility of benefit to ourselves. We approve some virtues in our enemies, such as courage, even though we know that they may work to our harm. When acts praised conduce to both general and private welfare, our approbation is increased, but we still distinguish the feelings appropriate to each. Now if the first two considerations are rejected by arguing that we approve what is not really to our own interest by imagining our personal benefit had we been in the situation judged, Hume replies that it is absurd that a real sentiment could originate from an interest known to be imaginary and sometimes even opposed to our practical interest.

Even the lower animals appear to have affection for both other animals and us; surely this is not artifice, but rather disinterested benevolence. Why then deny this virtue to man? Sexual love produces generous feelings beyond the merely appetitive, and common instances of utterly unselfish benevolence occur in parent-child relationships. It is impossible, Hume holds, to deny the authenticity of such affections as gratitude or desire for friends' good fortune when separation prevents personal participation.

But if the evidence is so clear, why have self-love theorists been so persistent? Hume blames a love of theoretical simplicity. The self-love theory, as Butler forcibly argues, mistakenly attempts to reduce all motivation to this one principle, and so is psychologically false. Man has physical appetites each having its own object; that of hunger is food, that of thirst is drink; gratification of these needs yields pleasure, which may then become the object of a secondary, interested desire—self-love. Unless the primary appetites had occurred, there could have been no pleasures or happiness to constitute the object of self-love. But the disinterested primary passions also include benevolence or desire for others' good, satisfaction of which then similarly yields pleasure to the self. Hence self-love actually presupposes specific and independent needs and affections, which complexity is again shown by occasional indulgence of some particular passion, such as the passion for revenge, even to the detriment of self-interest.

Since self-love cannot account for our moral approval of utility, then the appeal of the latter must be direct. In any theoretical explanation some point must be taken as ultimate, else an infinite regression occurs; hence we need not ask why we experience benevolence—it is enough that we do. Actually, however, Hume further explains it by reference to sympathy, the almost inevitable emotional reaction to the feelings of others. Yet Hume is careful not to claim that "fellow-feeling" is necessarily predominant over self-love; both sentiments vary in degree. But in normal men there is close correlation between strong concern for one's fellows and sensitivity to moral distinctions. Benevolence may not be strong enough to motivate some men to *act* for the good of another, but even they will feel approval of such acts and prefer them to the injurious.

Having admitted not only interpersonal differences in sympathy, but acknowledging also intrapersonal variations of feelings for others, how can Hume account for any uniformity and objectivity in our moral judgments? Here he offers one of his most significant contributions to ethics. Even while our sentiments vary we may judge merit with practical universality, analogously to judgmental correction of variations in sensory perception. Though we do not all, or always, perceive the same physical object as having the same color, shape, or size, as when we approach an object from a distance, we do not attribute the variations to the object; instead we imagine it to have certain stable, standard qualities. Such adjustment or correction is indispensable to mutual understanding and conversation among men.

Likewise, men's interests and feelings vary. Thus, moral discourse would be impossible unless men took a general rather than a private point of view: "The intercourse of sentiments . . . in society and conversation, makes us form some general unalterable standard, by which we may approve or disapprove of characters and manners." Although our emotions will not conform entirely to such a standard, they are regulated sufficiently for all practical purposes, and hence ethical language becomes meaningful: "General language . . . being formed for general use, must be moulded on some more general views, and must affix the epithets of praise or blame, in conformity to sentiments, which arise from the general interests of the community." In order for this standard to be effective there must of course be a sentiment or emotion to implement it, and here again Hume produces a telling argument against the self-interest theory. Self-love is inadequate to the prerequisites of the concept of morals, not from lack of force, but because it is inappropriate. Such a concept as this implies (1) that there be in existence a universal sentiment producing common agreement in approving or disapproving a given object, and (2) that this sentiment comprehend as its objects actions or persons in all times and places. None but the sentiment of humanity will meet these criteria. Hume's account of a "general unalterable standard" based principally on social utility and hence on benevolence is strongly objectivistic and balances subjectivistic strains in his ethics; it also provides the impartiality apparently neglected by his definition of justice.

Having thus accounted for our approval of qualities conducive to the good of others, Hume continues his analysis of virtues and finds three other classifications. "Qualities useful to ourselves" ("ourselves" here meaning persons exhibiting the qualities) may be approved also for general utility, but primarily for benefit to the agent; examples are discretion, frugality, and temperance. Now a second major division and two other categories of virtues are added: the "agreeable" (pleasant or enjoyable) to their possessors or to others. "Qualities immediately agreeable to ourselves," approved primarily for the satisfying feelings aroused, are such as greatness of mind and noble pride, though some like courage and benevolence may also be generally useful. Good manners, mutual deference, modesty, wit, and even cleanliness illustrate "qualities immediately agreeable to others."

Only when the analysis is almost completed does Hume offer the first formal definition of "virtue" as "*a quality of the mind agreeable to or approved by every one who considers or contemplates it.*" A second definition, better summarizing the *Enquiry*'s results, is that "Personal Merit consists altogether in the possession of mental qualities, *useful* or *agreeable* to the *person himself* or to others." A definition of value in general follows: "Whatever is valuable in any kind, so naturally classes itelf under the division of *useful* or *agreeable*, the *utile* or the *dulce*. . . ."

Readers familiar with the history of ethics will thus see hedonistic and utilitarian themes which received subsequent expression in Bentham and Mill. The only goal of Virtue, Hume says, is cheerfulness and happiness; the only demand she makes of us are those of careful calculation of the best means to these ends and constancy in preferring the greater to the lesser happiness. Such an obligation is *interested*, but the pleasure it seeks, such as those of peace of mind, or awareness of integrity, do not conflict with the social good, and their supreme worth is almost self-evident.

Having discovered what he calls the true origin of morals through the experimental method, Hume is now ready to return to the Reason vs. Sentiment issue he mentions at the beginning of the *Enquiry* but defers for settlement until the end. Throughout the book statements occur which indicate his final position, but unfortunately there are also a number which appear to make moral judgment a matter of reason. This ambiguity is dispelled by Hume's final treatment showing that moral judgment proper is noncognitive and affective in nature. It is true that reason is indispensable to approval or disapproval, for it must provide the facts which pertain to their objects. Very detailed and precise reasoning is frequently required to determine what actually is useful in a given case; nothing other than reason can perform this function. In view of the importance of the question, of whether moral judgment is rational or sentimental (affective), to both the eighteenth century and ours, Hume's full recognition of the auxiliary role of reason must be kept in mind. But he cannot agree with those rationalists who hold that moral judgments can be made with the same mental faculties, methods, and precision as can judgments of truth and falsity, and who frequently make comparisons between our knowledge of moral "truths" and those of mathematics and geometry.

Besides the evidence of the origin of moral sentiment from benevolence, there are perhaps even more cogent arguments based on comparison of the two types of judgment. The judgments of reason provide information, but not motivation, whereas blame or approbation are "a tendency, however faint, to the objects of the one, and a proportionable aversion to those of the other." That is, moral "judgment" is essentially affective and conative, while rational judgments are neither. Although reason can discover utility, unless utility's *end* appealed to some sentiment the knowledge would be utterly ineffective.

Rational knowledge is either factual or relational (logical or mathematical) in nature; its conclusions are either inductive or deductive. But the sentiment of blame or approbation is neither such a conclusion nor an observation of fact; one can examine at length all the facts of a criminal event, but he will never find the vice itself, the viciousness, as another objective fact in addition to those of time, place, and action. Neither is the vice constituted by some kind of relation such as that of contrariety, for example, between a good deed and an ungrateful response, since an evil deed rewarded with good will would involve contrariety but the response then would be virtuous. The "crime" is rather constituted such by the sentiment of blame in the spectator's mind.

In the process of rational inference, we take certain known facts or relations and from these deduce or infer a conclusion not previously known; but in moral decisions, says Hume, ". . . after every circumstance, every relation is known, the understanding has no further room to operate, nor any object on which it could employ itself. The approbation or blame which then ensues, cannot be the work of the judgement, but of the heart; and is not a speculative proposition or affirmation, but an active feeling or sentiment." This is one of the clearest and most definitive statements of Hume's position on moral judgment.

Finally, reason could never account for ultimate ends, as can be shown very shortly by asking a series of questions about the justification of an act. For example, if one says he exercises for his health, and is asked why he desires health, he may cite as successive reasons its necessity to his work, the necessity of work to securing money, the use of money as a means to pleasure. But it would be absurd to ask *why* one wished pleasure or the avoidance of pain. Similarly we have seen that virtue appeals to sentiments which neither have nor require any further explanation. Whereas the function of reason is to discover its objects, that of moral (and aesthetic) sentiment (or taste) is to confer value.

Hence, in a radical sense, moral distinctions are subjective, but the subject from which they derive is the whole human race, and individual subjectivity is corrected by the general unalterable standard. The *Enquiry* thus affords both a naturalistic, empirical description of the origin of moral values and a persuasive account of an ethical norm by which consistent judgments may be made, without appealing to a doubtful metaphysics. It is in this eminently sane recognition of the functions and limits of both reason and emotion that modern readers can learn much from David Hume.—*M.E.*

PERTINENT LITERATURE

Glossop, Ronald J. "Hume, Stevenson, and Hare on Moral Language," in *Hume: A Re-evaluation*. Edited by D. W. Livingston and J. T. King. New York: Fordham University Press, 1976.

Ronald J. Glossop observes that although a focus on ideas was as philosophically popular in David Hume's time as a focus on language is in ours, Hume paid a considerable amount of attention to language, especially in his work on ethics. In this article, Glossop compares what Hume said about moral language with what more recently has been said in C. L. Stevenson's *Ethics and Language* and R. M. Hare's *The Language of Morals*. In the course of making such comparisons, Glossop attributes to Hume a form of ethical naturalism. (Ethical naturalists claim that any moral prescription is equivalent to or reducible to some kind of descriptive statement.)

Both Stevenson and Hare, Glossop says, claim that Hume not only was concerned with the issues in which they are interested but also held views about them which are in general similar to their own. Glossop denies that Hume's moral theory is importantly similar to that of either Stevenson or Hare. With regard to Hume, Glossop makes the following claims.

In the *Enquiry* (and in *A Treatise of Human Nature* as well), Hume recognizes that his concerns are what we should call metaethical rather than normative, and his sensitivity to issues of linguistic usage is evident in the most central aspects of his ethical theory. Although Hume describes in three different ways the procedure he intends to follow to discover the general principle of morals—namely, compiling a list of virtues on the basis of (1) the evaluative meanings of terms, (2) the sentiments of a single disinterested spectator, and (3) the moral judgments of all persons—it seems clear that he would have believed the results would be the same regardless of what procedure he used, since he believed that terms used to describe virtues simply reflect approbation which everyone feels toward certain qualities because nature has made such feelings universal among human beings. Even those who reject "qualified spectators" and "unanimous approbations" would be unlikely to disagree that terms such as "generous" and "industrious" have favorable (positive) evaluative meanings, while terms such as "selfish" and "lazy" have unfavorable (negative) evaluative meanings. Hume examines the list he compiles to try to discover what the favorable evaluative meanings have in common.

Hume then offers three arguments all of which conclude that everyone, when not constrained by particular biases, in fact approves of whatever promotes the welfare of humankind. His first argument involves the claim that sympathizing with other people is an essential aspect of being human. The second is a summary of the overall argument of the *Enquiry*: What is common to all the virtues is that directly or indirectly they promote the happiness of their possessor himself or of others. The third is concerned with moral language. Hume argues that a logical requirement for both stable thought for the individual himself and communication with others is that our moral language reflect a general point of view which includes a concern for the good of the human species. (A similar argument, Glossop points out, can be found in *A Treatise of Human Nature*.) That is, Hume argues that even if we cannot "correct" our sentiments (cannot overcome the effects of our biases on our feelings), stable thought and interpersonal communication require that the linguistic formulation of our moral judgments reflect a concern for human happiness.

The third argument does not depend on the first two. Even if people in fact did not sympathize with others or approve of what promotes the general welfare, the private and interpersonal use of moral language presupposes a common viewpoint.

Glossop then considers Stevenson. Stevenson takes "X is good" to be roughly synonymous with "I approve of X; do so as well." He appears not to recognize that "approve" suggests a disinterested rather than a personal point of view; he claims that the term may be used to indicate what he calls a peculiarly moral attitude, but that such an attitude differs from others in being more intense, or an attitude about other attitudes. Hume, however, explicitly states in *A Treatise of Human Nature* that moral sentiment differs from other kinds of sentiment in that moral sentiment can arise only from a disinterested point of view. As mentioned above, he later argues in the *En-*

quiry that even where one cannot "correct" his sentiments, his moral *judgments* must reflect a disinterested or general viewpoint.

According to Glossop, Stevenson's failure to recognize that moral language reflects a disinterested point of view leads him to a misinterpretation of Hume's theory. He "correctly sees that for Hume only the sentiments of *informed* spectators are trustworthy indicators of virtue and vice, but he fails to note that for Hume a distinct point of view is indicated by the notion of approbation." Not only does Stevenson's misinterpretation lead him incorrectly to identify Hume as a fellow emotivist but (Glossop claims to show) his criticisms of Hume's theory can also be seen to be inapplicable on the correct interpretation.

Turning to Hare, Glossop argues that although Hare would not agree with such an assessment, Hare and Hume differ with regard to the relation between statements of fact and moral judgments. Hare holds that all naturalistic ethical theories are mistaken, that moral language is irreducibly prescriptive, and that there is an unbridgeable gap between prescriptive and descriptive language. On the other hand, Hume, when correctly interpreted, does not claim that one can never get an "ought" statement from an "is" statement, but rather claims that such an important move has not been given sufficient attention by moral theorists. Hume claims, further, that such a move cannot be made on the basis of reason alone: we move from "is" to "ought" on a bridge of sentiment rather than reason.

Glossop describes what he takes to be Hume's ethical theory as a theory which involves an analytical part in which the term "virtue" is defined and a synthetic part in which a generalization is drawn with regard to all human qualities called virtues. Glossop says that once Hume's list of virtues has been drawn up on the basis of his definitions (the list includes such terms as benevolence or generosity, justice, discretion, industry, frugality, honesty, prudence, dignity, courage, and wit), Hume concludes that what is common to all virtues is that they are useful or agreeable to oneself or others. Then Glossop attempts to imagine how Hume would attack Hare's claim that a naturalistic approach to ethics fails because in making moral judgments descriptive, it leaves out their commending function.

Glossop argues that if one adopts Hume's definitions of "virtue," in attributing a virtue to a particular person one is making a *descriptive* statement which is itself *commendatory*. Hare is simply assuming that language cannot be both descriptive and prescriptive, and Glossop offers arguments which conclude that there is good reason for the naturalist or anyone else to reject such an assumption.

Either Stevenson or Hare, Glossop admits, might now raise the issue of resolving disagreement about moral issues. That is, they might ask Hume: "How are we to determine that any particular person has become a completely informed, completely disinterested, perfectly normal spectator?" Glossop proposes that Hume could answer as follows. Although we cannot determine *exactly* when one is completely informed, completely disinterested and perfectly normal, we can understand when one person is *better* informed, *more* disinterested, and *less* abnormal than another. So we can determine when some persons' value judgments are *more likely* to be correct than others', and we can know what we must do to *improve* our own value judgments. Furthermore, there would be something wrong with any view which said that when some person who is "completely qualified" says "P is true," he *cannot* be mistaken. So the fact that the Humean definition cannot make such a claim is an asset rather than a liability.

One thing which Hume did not do, and should have done, according to Glossop, was to distinguish between what *are* virtues and what are *thought* to be virtues. What one *thinks* is a virtue, he says, depends on what arouses one's approbation; what arouses one's approbation depends on what one *thinks* is useful and agreeable, and that in turn depends on one's metaphysical views about the nature of reality. So modified, Glossop contends, Hume's views might receive wider acceptance because "one would no longer feel bound to accept Hume's own metaphysical views as a basis for what is useful."

Norton, David Fate. "Hume's Common Sense Morality," in *Canadian Journal of Philosophy*. V, no. 4 (December, 1975), pp. 523-543.

David Fate Norton contends that David Hume's moral theory, taking into consideration both *A Treatise of Human Nature* and the second *Enquiry*, is explicitly and fundamentally a commonsense theory. Norton claims to show how three features of that theory come together to form an outlook which is appropriately so designated. Two of those features—Hume's claim that moral distinctions rest on sentiments, and that it is by means of the principle of sympathy that the sentiments of a person come to be experienced by others—are, he says, widely accepted; whereas the third—Hume's concern to refute moral skepticism and his explicit use, for this purpose, of appeals to "common sense"—has to a great extent been overlooked.

In support of his claim, Norton argues that Hume is not, as is usually supposed, a moral "subjectivist"; that, quite to the contrary, his intention is to establish morality's "objectivity." In addition, Norton gives detailed consideration to Hume's concern with moral skepticism and his appeals to common sense. Finally, he argues for the fundamental role, at least in the original formulation of Hume's theory, of the principle of sympathy. The reader is warned against taking Norton's arguments as supporting the claim that, in Hume's philosophy as a whole, reason is thoroughly subordinated to feeling and instinct. That concept, he argues, is incorrect.

Skeptics doubt that there is something which is known or is real. Commonsense philosophers counter by showing or insisting that something is known or is real. Therefore, if it is correct to describe Hume as a commonsense moralist, then it must be shown that he is a moral realist; that is, that he holds the distinction between virtue and vice to be not merely subjective or entirely dependent on private psychological factors.

Such a task may appear to be an impossible one, Norton writes, because of Hume's comparison of vice and virtue to perceptions of sounds, colors, heat, and other sense properties in *A Treatise of Human Nature*. An examination of his immediately following statements, however, calls for a careful consideration of which of obviously inconsistent claims better represents his position; for there Hume holds that vice, far from being a sentiment, is the (independent) *cause* of the sentiment. The choice must go against the subjectivistic claim, for Hume suggests in more than one way that virtue and vice are themselves independent of the sentiments which nature has provided for their recognition. In addition, Hume argued in *A Treatise of Human Nature* that virtue and vice are quite independent of the mind of an observer who states that the acts or character of another are virtuous or vicious; "virtuous" and "vicious" are terms, Hume claims, which refer to actions reflecting or proceeding from the enduring *qualities* or *character* of moral agents. A character, he says, is not virtuous because it pleases; rather, it pleases because it is virtuous.

Norton goes on to show that Hume's account in *A Treatise of Human Nature* of the indirect passions—pride, humility, esteem, hatred—as well as his discussion there of the unusual nature of our moral sentiments, supports the claim that epistemologically as well as metaphysically Hume is a moral realist. Hume believes, Norton contends, that when oneself and others manage to assume a disinterested stance, an interchange of sentiments enables the formation of a "general unalterable standard" of morality. Hume holds, he continues, that although we may not always feel or act as the standard suggests, its effectiveness as a standard is not thereby impaired.

Hume's theory is formulated not only in opposition to rationalist moral theory, an opposition generally recognized, but also against egoistic moral theories. His "anatomical" approach to morality in *A Treatise of Human Nature*, Hume himself believed, made that work appear to lack "Warmth in the cause of Virtue," an appearance he attempted to explain away and made sure did not infect the *Enquiry*. The latter begins by finding the viewpoint of those who deny the reality of moral distinctions so absurd that Hume recommends leaving them alone, in the belief that it is highly likely that they will in time "come over to the side of common sense and reason" on their own. However, the position of the ethical egoist, whom Hume also considers a moral skeptic, is subjected to a sustained attack in the *Enquiry*.

In *A Treatise of Human Nature*, common sense is employed as a primary weapon against moral skepticism both indirectly (Norton cites numerous passages) and directly: Hume holds that there are general principles which are "authorized by common sense, and the practice of all ages," giving as an example the right of people to resist a tyrannical ruler. Those who deny such a right, he says, "have renounc'd all pretensions to common sense and do not merit a serious answer." Serious arguments involving appeals to common sense, however, are given by Hume, not only in *A Treatise of Human Nature* but also in other works.

The systematic importance in Hume's moral theory of reliance on common sense is shown by his claim that our commonsense views rest on an absolutely fundamental and natural principle: sympathy. Sympathy makes possible intercommunication of sentiments and understanding between human beings. Sympathy enables the creation of a common point of view, the pursuance of common interests, and the creation of a common moral standard by which to determine the rightness or wrongness of acts. From our observation of another's passions and our perceptions of the usual causes of such passions, we are led to the perception of the usual effects and feel the passion itself. It is through sympathy that we know and care about the good of mankind; consequently, sympathy causes us to approve of that which has a tendency toward the good of mankind. It is through sympathy that we know and care about the good of someone who may even be a stranger to us; and sympathy causes us to approve of that which has a tendency toward the good of only the stranger himself. The principle of sympathy, then, according to Hume, enables us to escape the perspective of our own narrow interests, to know and share the judgments, opinions, and feelings of others, and to establish a general and intersubjective standard of right and wrong.

Norton concludes that if we grant that Hume's principle of sympathy exists and that it functions as he claims, "then we can see that his appeals to common sense are not merely casual appeals, nor appeals to mere vulgar prejudice. They are, rather, appeals to the collective judgment and feeling of a mankind equipped to produce disinteresterd and intersubjective judgments of an objective moral reality."—*B.C.S.*

ADDITIONAL RECOMMENDED READING

Capaldi, Nicholas. *David Hume: The Newtonian Philosopher*. Boston: Twayne, 1975. Capaldi argues that in the *Enquiry* the passions are no longer an essential feature of Hume's moral theory.

Frankena, William K. *Ethics*. Englewood Cliffs, New Jersey: Prentice-Hall, 1973. Frankena's view is similar to that of Glossop in the paper summarized above, although Frankena does not consider Hume an ethical naturalist.

Glossop, Ronald J. "The Nature of Hume's Ethics," in *Philosophy and Phenomenological Research*. XXVII, no. 4 (June, 1967), pp. 527-536. Glossop doubts that Hume can be considered an ethical naturalist in the strictest sense.

King, James T. "The Place of the Language of Morals in Hume's Second

Enquiry," in *Hume: A Re-evaluation*. Edited by D. W. Livingston and J. T. King. New York: Fordham University Press, 1976, pp. 343-361. King holds that although in some respects *A Treatise of Human Nature* and *Enquiry* views are similar, their logical and epistemic ordering is not. As one consequence, he argues, the problem in *A Treatise of Human Nature* of correction of the sentiments does not arise in the *Enquiry*. King denies that Hume is in the strictest sense an ethical naturalist.

Noxon, James. *Hume's Philosophical Development*. Oxford: Clarendon Press, 1973. Noxon observes that in the *Enquiry*, as opposed to *A Treatise of Human Nature*, Hume's method involves the observation of moral, not psychological, phenomena.

THOUGHTS ON THE INTERPRETATION OF NATURE

Author: Denis Diderot (1713-1784)
Type of work: Philosophy of science, epistemology
First published: 1754

PRINCIPAL IDEAS ADVANCED

The rationalistic approach to nature is useless; to study nature one must proceed from facts by the use of methods of inference.

Inferences should be checked by experiments; reflection and observation should supplement each other in empirical inquiry.

By acts of interpretation one succeeds in becoming more than a mere observer of nature; by drawing general conclusions from the order of things one arrives at an understanding of the world's order.

There is one causal principle operative in the world, but there are numerous elements, divisible into molecules themselves indivisible.

Experimental physics is the basis of all true knowledge.

A small book consisting of fifty-eight numbered paragraphs, Diderot's *Thoughts on the Interpretation of Nature* was composed with a view to arousing young men's interest in scientific experimentation. It did not propose to instruct them, but to exercise them. "A more capable one than I will acquaint you with the forces of nature: it is sufficient if I have made you employ your own," he wrote in his dedicatory epistle, "To Young Men who are Disposed to Study Natural Philosophy."

That an essay of this sort was called for in France as late as the middle of the eighteenth century was not entirely due to religious censorship. Quite as much as scholastic metaphysics, the rationalistic temper of Cartesian science had prejudiced French thinkers against the experimental methods which had been in vogue for a century in England. Voltaire's *Letters Concerning the English Nation* (1732), written after two years spent in exile in that country, had endeavored to acquaint the French people with such thinkers as John Locke and Isaac Newton. Diderot's *Thoughts on the Interpretation of Nature*, although not expressly mentioning the British authors, had a similar intention.

At a time when ability to read English was as rare among Frenchmen as ability to read Russian is among Americans today, Diderot mastered the language and employed himself in translating English works for publication. The present work is clearly an echo of Francis Bacon, whose *Novum Organum* (1620) bore the subtitle, "True Directions Concerning the Interpretation of Nature."

Diderot was convinced that the rationalistic approach to nature, which supposed that there is an exact correspondence between the processes of logic and the laws of the universe, held little promise. The followers of Descartes were accustomed to regard geometry as the only true science because of the certitude of its results. They left to experimenters only the task of deciding which mathematical expressions happened in fact to fit the order of nature. In Diderot's opinion this plan reversed the true procedure. Insofar as it merely elaborates the connection between ideas, mathematics is, he said, merely a branch of metaphysics. It is a kind of game which does nothing to increase our understanding of the world. He acknowledged that mathematics had been put to good use by astronomers, but he believed that there was little more to be hoped for in that direction. He predicted that mathematics had reached its zenith and that a hundred years hence there would not be three great geometers in the whole of Europe.

On the other hand, Diderot found no promise in the methods employed by "naturalists" such as Carolus Linnaeus, whose system of classification he ridiculed because it placed man in the class of quadrupeds and (admittedly) lacked means of distinguishing him from apes. He called such investigators "methodists," on the ground that they revised the world to fit their method, instead of revising their method to fit the world.

The proper method for studying nature, according to Diderot, was to proceed from facts by way of inference to further facts. Thoughts, he said, are significant only insofar as they are connected with external existence, either by an unbroken chain of experiments, or by an unbroken chain of inferences which starts from observation, or by a series of inferences interspersed with experiments "like weights along a thread hung by its two ends." He favored the latter. "Without these weights, the thread will be the plaything of the least breath of air."

Diderot distinguished three stages of experimental reasoning. First is the observation of nature, by which one becomes acquainted with the facts; second is reflection, by which the facts are combined in the mind; third is experiment, by which the combination is tested with reference to further facts. In a simile reminiscent of Bacon, he said that the scientist is like a bee: he must constantly pass back and forth from reflection to the senses. The bee would wear out its wings to no purpose if it failed to return to the hive with its burden; but it would accumulate only useless piles of wax if it were not instructed how to fashion its harvest into honeycomb.

In contrast to the facile optimism with which many enthusiasts for science have written about method, Diderot recognized that the path of the experimenter is straight and narrow and that there are few who find it. The mysterious combination of gifts which makes up "creative genius" intrigued him. Men who combine the insight necessary for fruitful observation with powers of reflection and with the skill and patience required for fruitful experiment are exceedingly rare, he said; and he saw nothing that could be done about it. Like a maladroit politician who finds it impossible to take hold of a situation, the average person can spend his whole life observing, say, insects, whereas another takes a passing glance and discovers a whole new order of life.

It was the hope of Diderot that experimenters could learn a lesson from skilled craftsmen, who, without any formal teaching but purely as a result of long experience in handling materials, are able to "smell out" the course of nature and adapt their methods to its ways. As the son of a master cutler, Diderot retained throughout his life a high regard for technical skills, as numerous articles and engravings in the famous *Encyclopédie* (1751-1766), which he edited, attest. The workers themselves, he said, believe that they divine the ways of nature through a kind of "familiar spirit." But he explained their gift as being no more than the faculty of perceiving analogies between the qualities of objects which have certain things in common and a massive knowledge of the ways things affect one another when brought into combination. With this insight into the workings of the craftsman's mind, the experimenter should be able not merely to equal but to surpass him in ability.

Diderot would have some sympathy with the man who said that genius is ninety-nine percent perspiration and only one percent inspiration, and he recognized that discoveries are often happy accidents, in which error and folly have a share. To make his point, he adapted the story of the man who on his deathbed told his lazy sons that there was treasure buried in the orchard. They spent the summer digging it over. Though they failed to find the object of their greed, they did receive an unusually good crop of fruit. So, said Diderot, experimentation commonly fails to unlock the secrets of the universe in the way men expect, although it yields a reward in pragmatic truth.

But Diderot continued the parable. The next year one of the boys told his brothers that in the course of digging over the orchard he had noticed a peculiar depression in one corner. With his mind still on treasure, he convinced them that since the prize did not lie near the surface it must have been hidden in the bowels of the earth. In this way he persuaded them to join him in the strenuous task of sinking a deep shaft. After many days, they were at the point of abandoning the project when they came upon, not the treasure which they had hoped for, but an ancient mine, which they began to work with profit. "Such," concluded Diderot, "is sometimes the outcome of experiments suggested by a combination of observation with rationalist theories. In this way chemists and geometers, while trying to solve problems which are probably unsolvable, arrive at discoveries more important than the solutions which they sought."

The strength and originality of Diderot's book has sometimes been said to lie in his own peculiar ability to "smell out" directions which were far beyond the intellectual horizon of the typical eighteenth century *philosophe*. This gift appears not only in his insights into experimental method, but also in his own "interpretation of nature." For Diderot was not a positivist and had no intention of limiting human knowledge to the results of observation and experimentation. "One of the main differences," he said, "between the observer of nature and the interpreter of nature is that the latter takes as his point of departure the place where the former leaves off. He conjectures from that which is known that which is yet to be known. He draws from the order of things conclusions abstract and general which have for him all the evidence of sensible and particular truths. And he arrives at the very essence of the world's order."

Thoughts on the Interpretation of Nature includes several paragraphs devoted to Diderot's own "conjectures" as to the direction that science should take—suggestions such as "that magnetism and electricity depend upon the same causes." It also includes an ironical analysis of the philosophy of Pierre de Maupertuis, whose *System of Nature* had recently appeared (Latin, 1751; French, 1753). Diderot agreed, on the whole, with Maupertuis' position, and he assumed a critical air in order to develop further implications of the theory while professing to be scandalized at the outcome. Diderot had already spent three months in prison for advanced thinking and had learned to envelop his speculations in studied ambiguity.

Perhaps the "thought" which governs all the rest of Diderot's "interpretations of nature" is that when man has discovered that every event must have a cause, he has reached the frontier of metaphysical knowledge. There is no point in speculating about any higher cause, nor in asking "why" things are constituted the way they are. At an earlier stage of his development, Diderot had embraced the deistic account of origins which he found in Shaftesbury's *Characteristics* (1711). In the present work, he took his stand on the side of what today would be called naturalism, which at that time was called Spinozism.

It seemed to Diderot that the possibility of experimental science rested upon the assumption that there is only one causal principle operative in the world. But he was so much impressed by the variety which nature exhibits at every level that he shied away from the view that the world is made of a uniform substance. Instead, he favored the materialistic version of Leibniz's philosophy suggested in Maupertuis' book. In this view, every "element" that goes to make up nature is essentially different from every other. Each element is divisible into molecules, themselves incapable of further division. Moreover, the molecules must be thought of as "organic," endowed with the rudiments of desire and aversion, of feeling and thought. Only thus could the whole range of nature be accounted for.

In his oblique fashion, Diderot gave thanks for the biblical account of creation. For, he said, if we had been left to our own speculations, the best we could do would be to infer that the elements of living beings had been mingled with other elements from all eternity in the total mass, and that they have joined together to form beasts and men "merely because it was possible for it to happen!" He allowed himself to speculate that a species of animals might come into being, reach maturity, and perish—just as we observe happens in the case of individual members of a species. And, giving full rein to his imagination, he suggested that living beings must have passed through infinite stages of development, acquiring in turn "movement, sensation, imagination, thought, reflection, consciousness, sentiments, passions, signs, gestures, sounds, articulate sounds, speech, laws, sciences, and arts," with millions of years between each of these acquisitions—that perhaps still other developments are yet to come, of which we are ignorant; that the process may come to a standstill, and that eventually the product of these transformations may disappear from nature forever. "Religion," he said, "spares us all these wanderings and the mental labor which it would require to follow them out."

Diderot's interest in biological evolution was not merely of this speculative sort. Familiar with comparative anatomy, he observed that every one of the quadrupeds is patterned on the same "prototype," that nature merely lengthens, shortens, modifies, or multiplies the same organs. "Imagine the fingers of a hand bound together and the material of the nails increased to envelop the whole: in place of a man's hand you would have a horse's hoof." Such considerations led him to conclude that there is no real division between the animal kingdoms. Nature, he said, is like a woman who loves to vary her costume. She does not require many different outfits because she knows how, by varying a sleeve or a collar, adding a pleat or letting down a hem, to achieve an infinite number of effects while using the same pattern.

Diderot's greatest boldness, however, lay in the view which he took of man's role in nature, and of the role of science in human affairs. The Copernican revolution had convinced enlightened thinkers that the earth is not the center of the universe, but the majority of them continued to think of man as occupying a favored position. In rejecting Deism and turning back to the more expansive tradition of Bruno and Spinoza, Diderot sharply challenged the optimism of his day, particularly as it pertained to the advancement of learning.

In principle, Diderot admitted that, just as mathematicians, in examining the properties of a curve, find the same properties present under different aspects, so experimental physicists may eventually find a single hypothesis which covers such different properties as weight, elasticity, electricity, and magneticism. But how many intermediary hypotheses, he exclaimed, had to be found before the gaps could be filled in. Nor could there be any shortcut, such as exists in mathematics, where intermediary propositions can be arrived at by deduction. On the contrary, he saw a deplorable tendency for various branches of science to build mutually exclusive systems of explanation. Classic mechanics was such a system. Diderot said it was a labyrinth in which men must wander without hopes of ever reaching understanding with other sciences.

Diderot expressed most vividly the disparity between our fragmentary knowledge and the vastness and variety of nature. "When one begins to compare the infinite multitude of the phenomena of nature with the limits of our understanding and the weakness of our faculties, can one be surprised that our work lags and frequently drags to a halt, and that all which we possess is a few broken and isolated links of the great chain of being?" Suppose that experimental philosophy should continue for several centuries. Where is the mind that could take it all in? How many volumes would be required to record it? And how far would any one person be able to read? Are we not, he asked, "as foolish as the men of Babel? We know the infinite distance that separates earth from heaven, yet we do not cease to build the tower." A confusion of tongues is bound to result which will lead to men's abandoning the effort.

This pessimism was directed against barren intellectualism, the attempt to understand the world in abstract terms, and finds its counterpart in Voltaire's *Candide* (1759), where wisdom is said to consist in cultivating one's garden instead of speculating about matters too high for us. Diderot complained that men are content to live in hovels while raising uninhabitable palaces which reach to the clouds. It was his hope that experimental science would alter that condition and would bring into being vast stores of knowledge which would alleviate man's condition. But he predicted that when this change had come about men would lose interest in science just as they had (in his opinion) already lost interest in geometry. "Utility circumscribes everything. It is utility which, in a few centuries, will set the limits to experimental physics as it is on the point of doing to geometry. I accord several centuries to this study because the sphere of its utility is infinitely more extensive than that of any abstract science, and because it is undeniably the basis of all true knowledge."—*J.F.*

PERTINENT LITERATURE

Wilson, Arthur M. "Thoughts on the Interpretation of Nature," in *Diderot*. New York: Oxford University Press, 1972.

Arthur M. Wilson describes Denis Diderot's *Thoughts on the Interpretation of Nature* as a milestone in the history of scientific method. Not so much a scientist as a philosopher of science, Diderot was endowed with an extraordinary imagination which enabled him to suggest what could be done by persons with more specialized interests. *Thoughts on the Interpretation of Nature*, says Wilson, was a tentative work which took account of current problems in the sciences and sent out patrols along the frontiers of knowledge. Perhaps on account of its aphoristic style, students of the Enlightenment have failed to give it a place alongside the more pretentious writings of Julien Offray de La Mettrie and Paul Henry Thiry, Baron d'Holbach, and have neglected it in favor of Diderot's own *Letter on the Blind* (1749) and

D'Alembert's Dream (1769), in which many of the same themes are developed in a novelistic setting. Nevertheless, Wilson finds the work unrivaled in the understanding which it reveals of fundamental shifts that were taking place in eighteenth century thought. "We are verging on a great revolution in the sciences," Diderot wrote. And better than any of his contemporaries he understood what was taking place.

Time had come for students of nature to take a new fix on their course. The geometrically inspired methods which had guided workers in astronomy and physics were not suited to the new sciences of biology and chemistry. In the writings of Francis Bacon, Diderot found insights that had been neglected by the followers of René Descartes and Sir Isaac Newton. Calling attention to the fact that the conceptual reasoning which comprises mathematics has no direct bearing on what we experience, he proclaimed science the purlieu of skilled experimenters who, acquainted with one another's findings, possess the genius necessary to recognize the new questions to which these discoveries give rise and to invent appropriate experimental procedures. Says Wilson, Diderot closely forecast the actual working methods of such scientists as Robert Koch and Louis Pasteur.

Along with this emphasis on observation and experimentation, Wilson calls attention to Diderot's epistemological presuppositions. Inveighing against the arguments of rationalists and empiricists, as Bacon had done against scholasticism, Diderot declared that knowledge had too long been bound up with words and ought now to be concerned with things. Our thoughts, he said, "take on consistency only by being linked to externally existing things. This linking takes place either by means of an uninterrupted chain of experiments, or by an uninterrupted chain of reasoning that is fastened at one end to observation and at the other to experiment, or by a chain of experiments, dispersed at intervals between reasoning." Emphasizing the disproportion between man's capacity for knowledge and the complex world presented to our senses, he stressed the need for rigorous rules of inquiry, and promised no more than a gradual approximation of our thoughts to things, with new problems constantly calling for solution.

Probably the most revolutionary change that was taking place in mid-eighteenth century science was the abandonment of the static conception of nature that had been presupposed alike in the physics of Newton and in the biology of Karl Linnaeus. Wilson quotes Ernst Cassirer as crediting Diderot with being one of the first to replace this static conception with one which took full account of time and change. Wilson mentions the boldness of passages in *Thoughts on the Interpretation of Nature* which clearly anticipate the theory of evolution: for example, the conjecture "that the animal world has had its separate elements confusedly scattered through the mass of matter; that it finally came about that these elements united—simply because it was possible for them to unite; that the embryo thus formed has passed through an infinite number of successive organizations; that it has acquired in turn movement, sensation, ideas . . . that millions of years have elapsed between each of these developments."

Wilson also notes that Diderot's evolutionism "moved him very close to a materialist view of the universe," mentioning the favor which he has found with left-wing Hegelians as a transitional figure, well ahead of his contemporaries in surmounting the traditional mechanical form of materialism and recognizing the dialectical character of natural phenomena.

Diderot's place in the history of materialism is the subject of controversy. F. A. Lange, in his *History of Materialism* (1865), protested against the Hegelian passion for construction which made Diderot the leader in French materialism when "the facts are that he was no materialist before the appearance of La Mettrie's *Man a Machine*, and that his materialism developed through his intercourse with the group that gathered around Holbach, and that Pierre Maupertuis, Jean Robinet, and La Mettrie exercised more influence on him than he on any of them." Wilson agrees that what led to Diderot's conversion from deism to atheism was the possibility, put forward by Maupertuis but not recognized in the older materialism associated with Lucretius, that even nonorganic atoms may be thought of as endowed with sensitivity— a possibility, says Wilson, that was "destined to bulk ever greater in his thought." Thus, in his chapter on *D'Alembert's Dream*, Wilson discusses three ways in which Diderot's materialism differed from that of the Epicureans: first, following John Toland, whose *Letters to Serena* had recently been translated by the Holbach group, he accepted the idea that motion is an inherent property of matter; second, influenced by Georges Louis Leclerc, Comte de Buffon, he replaced the mechanistic concept of the atom with a vitalistic one; third, following the physician Bordeau (who is one of the interlocutors in *D'Alembert's Dream*), he introduced the notion of a leap from mechanical interaction of individual particles to the formation of organic wholes. Notwithstanding this dependence on others, it is Wilson's opinion that only Diderot succeeded in making materialism credible. Pointing to his rare combination of literary skill, knowledge of current research, and speculative power, he remarks that not many "could bend such a bow."

Crocker, Lester G. *Diderot's Chaotic Order: Approach to Synthesis*. Princeton, New Jersey: Princeton University Press, 1974.

Although Denis Diderot wrote on a wide range of subjects, he nowhere undertook to bring his thoughts together in a systematic fashion. Lester G. Crocker's book, consisting of chapters on cosmic order, aesthetics, morals, and politics, is a contribution in this direction. *Thoughts on the Interpretation of Nature*, viewed more as a metaphysical than as a scientific work, is considered in Chapter One.

The theme that Crocker has chosen for his synthesis is order and chaos. In his opinion, the deeper significance of the Enlightenment lay in the gradual dissolution of the "stable, benign cosmic order" which was taken for granted through the time of Sir Isaac Newton and Gottfried Wilhelm Leibniz (witness Voltaire's Pangloss in *Candide*) and the consequent need to replace the conception of a finite universe with that of one which is infinite. Pierre Bayle, Baron de Montesquieu, Voltaire, and Jean Jacques Rousseau were, at one level or another, all dealing with the problem of order and disorder. But Crocker holds that Diderot had a clearer grasp on the problem as a problem than any of these, and that a sense of the interplay between chaos and order determined the way he thought about moral and aesthetic no less than about scientific questions.

Crocker puts the problem in perspective by observing that *Thoughts on the Interpretation of Nature* appeared in the same month as the volume of the *Encyclopédie* which contained Diderot's article "Chaos," where it is explained that, as opposed to Moses, the early Greeks were of the opinion that in the beginning nothing existed but a chaos of particles of all kinds, each moving in its own fashion, and that they represented cosmic history as a succession of combinations of matter, culminating in the stable order which makes up our world. In Diderot's words, "the moving mass, by internal fermentation, collapses, and attractions, gradually brought forth a sun, an earth."

Thoughts on the Interpretation of Nature filled in this outline. Strictly speaking, Diderot explained, chaos is an impossibility. Matter can never be completely disorganized because it is of the nature of each molecule to move around until it finds other molecules with which to unite. The formation of the solar system, the distribution of elements on our planet, and the emergence of living forms are all part of the ceaseless struggle of material particles to form ever more stable combinations in the midst of perpetual change. Such systems, says Diderot, "will resist a force that tends to disturb their coordination, and will always tend either to return to their original ordering, if the perturbing force happens to cease, or to restructure their arrangement according to the laws of their attraction, their shape, etc., and according to the action of the perturbing force, if it continues to act." Crocker tries to capture Diderot's meaning in terms of energy-systems resisting entropy.

Scholars have argued about how far Diderot escaped from mechanism. In Crocker's opinion the question can never be answered because of the imprecision of Diderot's vocabulary. The statement in *Thoughts on the Interpretation of Nature*, according to which molecules move about until they find a place where they are "comfortable," is interesting as combining mechanical and vital causes. These same two principles are acknowledged in *Elements of Physiology*, Diderot's last work on the subject, where the ordering and conserving principle in the universe is said to be rigorously subject to geometrical laws. But Diderot certainly abandoned the simple mechanism of Lucretian materialism for a complex mechanism which took account of what we know as emergent qualities, and maintained that there are lower and higher kinds of machines, each requiring to be understood in its own fashion. Crocker suggests that Diderot's conception of animals as machines accords very well with what modern thinkers have in mind when they speak of animals as cybernetic machines.

Crocker has written elsewhere about Diderot's contribution to the theory of evolution, and his treatment of this subject is here marked by restraint. Diderot believed that species evolve, but it is not clear whether he thought of new species as emerging from a line of variations occurring in a previously existing species or as variations of a common type. He certainly included man in the process. In a letter written about 1769, he spoke of the sun as conceivably dying and being rekindled and of plants, insects, and animals being reborn. "And man? you will ask me. Yes: man, but not as he is. First, a certain something; then another certain something; and then, after several hundreds of millions of years and so many more certain somethings, the bipedal animal who has the name of man." Yet, Crocker reminds us, although this is evolutionary, "it was certainly not the present-day theory of organic evolution, with its tight interrelationship of mutations, adaptation to environment, and survival of the fit."

A point of interest to Crocker is that, in spite of the many characteristics shared by man and other animals, man's self-awareness and the kind of freedom which it implies does not exist at lower levels. In other creatures the individual's behavior is determined by the law of the species, but at the human level each individual organizes the chaos of its private sensations into a unique self. Morality, which is a creation of the human species, is a novel element in the universe, and, by what Crocker calls "cosmic irony," it is an element of disorder.

Diderot saw the limitations of materialism as a philosophy, and this is the point of the title *Chaotic Order*. The categories of human thought compel man to look for rational explanations, but the facts which require explaining, particularly those dealing with life and with the inner world of human thought, lead to the conclusion of "an order of disorder."—*J.F.*

ADDITIONAL RECOMMENDED READING
Cassirer, Ernst. *The Philosophy of Enlightenment*. Princeton, New Jersey: Princeton University Press, 1951. Essential background for *Thoughts on the Interpretation of Nature*, especially pages 73 to 77.

Crocker, Lester G. "Diderot and Eighteenth Century French Transformism," in *Forerunners of Darwin: 1745-1859*. Edited by Hiram Bentley Glass. Baltimore: The Johns Hopkins University Press, 1959, pp. 114-143. A study of the genesis and development of Diderot's evolutionary thinking.

Grava, Arnolds. "Diderot and Recent Philosophical Trends," in *Diderot Stud-*

ies. Edited by Otis Fellows. Vol. IV. Geneva: Librairie Droz, 1963, pp. 73-104. Diderot is viewed as a forerunner of the organic philosophy of Whitehead.

Torrey, Norman L. "Diderot," in *Encyclopedia of Philosophy*. Edited by Paul Edwards. Vol. II. New York: Macmillan Publishing Company, 1967, pp. 397-403. An authoritative introduction to Diderot's philosophy.

Wartowsky, Marx W. "Diderot and the Development of Materialist Monism," in *Diderot Studies*. Edited by Otis Fellows and Norman L. Torrey. Syracuse, New York: Syracuse University Press, 1952, pp. 275-309. Diderot is viewed as a forerunner of Marx and Engels.

FREEDOM OF THE WILL

Author: Jonathan Edwards (1703-1758)
Type of work: Metaphysics, theology
First published: 1754

PRINCIPAL IDEAS ADVANCED

The will is the ability men have of choosing one course of action rather than another.

The will is determined when, as a result of certain actions or influences, a decision is made.

The will is always determined by the greatest apparent good.

To be free is to be able to do as one wills.

Freedom is compatible with determination of the will; if the will were not determined, there would be no possibility of moral motivation and no sense in praise or blame.

The Arminians claim that the will is self-determining and that it wills indifferently and without cause; but this idea is inaccurate and self-contradictory; furthermore, it makes virtuous action impossible and moral injunctions senseless.

The problem of the freedom of the will, like many of the traditional philosophical problems, remains a problem for many philosophers because of the manner of its formulation. Even to consider the title of the problem is to be led astray. "The Freedom of the Will"—*what* is the problem? Is it *whether* the will is free? Or is it *how* the will is free? Or is it a question as to *what* the will is? Or freedom? Does it even make sense to talk about the will as free? A man can be free, but what is the sense of saying that the *will*—whatever that is—can be free? Or is the question the familiar question as to whether the will is free or determined?

Jonathan Edwards, the great Puritan philosopher of the eighteenth century, the first significant creative mind in American philosophy, taking his cue from John Locke, whose *An Essay Concerning Human Understanding* (1690) he much admired, recognized the difficulties involved in the formulation of the problem. Consequently, his careful study of the problem begins with explanations of the terms involved in discourse concerning freedom of the will; he begins with "will," proceeds to "determination," "necessity," "liberty," and to other terms whose ambiguity and vagueness have made the problem a particularly troublesome one for philosophers. And unlike many philosophers, Edwards did not use the occasion of definition as an opportunity for framing the problem to suit his own purposes; with an analytic acumen which would do credit to twentieth century semanticists, he hit upon the meanings relative to common use; and he clarified those meanings without neglecting consideration of the function of terms in conventional discourse. Thus, in considering "liberty," he noted that, in common speech, "in the ordinary use of language," the words "freedom" and "liberty" mean the "power, opportunity, or advantage, that anyone has, to do as he pleases." "To *do* as he pleases"—in recognizing that to be free is to be able to do as one pleases, Edwards prepared the way for his next point: that it is nonsense to talk about the will as free. It is nonsense because the will is not an agent, not a person who is somehow able to do as he pleases! Thus, Edwards wrote, "it will follow, that in propriety of speech, neither liberty, nor its contrary can properly be ascribed to any being or thing, but that which has such a faculty, power or property, as is called 'will.'" It makes sense to talk about a free *person*, for a person can be in a condition of being able to do as he pleases; but it violates "propriety of speech" to talk about a free *will*, as if a will could do as it pleased, could act as *it* wills.

If, then, to have a free will is to be able to do as one wills, and if the will, the power of choice, is determined by the apparent values of the alternatives brought to the attention of the person, it follows that a free will is determined: a man, who is able to choose, is *free* if, when his choice is *determined* by various considerations, he *can do as he pleases*. If this is the resolution of the problem—and, except for introducing the careful definitions, the arguments, and the qualifications, this is the essential resolution as Edwards presents it— then it is apparent that the formulation of the problem is misleading. It is misleading to consider the "freedom of the will," as if the will were an agent, capable of doing as it willed; and it is misleading to take the problem as the one put by the question, "Is the will free *or* is it determined?"—as if the alternatives were incompatible. Jonathan Edwards deserves credit not only for resolving the problem in a manner that continues to win the admiration of professional philosophers, but also for making his method cleat: the method of destroying a problem by clarifying its formulation.

Jonathan Edwards was a vigorous defender of Calvinism, a minister who was an effective combination of intellectual and emotional power. As minister at Northampton, Massachusetts, he argued for predestination, the depravity of man, and the doctrine of irresistible grace. He held with Puritan fervor to the conviction that God is unlimited in his use of grace; he can save whomever he chooses. In support of these hard doctrines he employed a remarkable talent for developing, defending, and propounding ideas. But he did not expect to win anything by the use of intellect alone; although he disdained religious emotionalism, he declared the necessity of conversion and faith. His extraordinary personality brought about an enthusiastic movement in support of the faith he defended; the church at Northampton became the origin and center of religious revival which came to be known as "The Great Awakening." His strict Calvinism eventually had its effect; as a result of an argument concerning the qualifications for communion, probably only the focal point of a number of doctrinal quarrels, he was dismissed in 1750 from the ministry of Northampton. He moved to the Indian mission at Stockbridge and continued work on the problem of the freedom of the will, an enterprise undertaken sometime in 1747. Written in support of the Calvinistic doctrine of predestination and of the necessity which it entails, the resultant work is nevertheless philosophically relevant to the general problem of the freedom of the will. The full title of the study, which is Edwards' masterpiece, is *A Careful and Strict Enquiry into the Modern Prevailing Notions of that Freedom of Will which is Supposed to be Essential to Moral Agency, Virtue and Vice, Reward and Punishment, Praise and Blame.*

The *Freedom of the Will*, which Edwards referred to as the *Inquiry*, was Edwards' answer to Arminianism, a doctrine based upon the ideas of Jacobus Arminius, a sixteenth century Dutch Reformed theologian. To Edwards the most objectionable feature of Arminianism, which was a view calling for a moderation of Calvinist doctrine, was the claim that divine grace is resistible. Arminianism, in advocating a less strict conception of election and redemption, prepared the way for an increasing emphasis on the moral and the human, with decreasing emphasis on the divine and on the absolute dependence of man on God. The "modern prevailing notions" to which the title refers are the Arminian notions, in particular the Arminian idea of the liberty of the will. According to Edwards, the Arminians regarded the will as acting contingently, not necessarily, and without cause—a conception often referred to as indeterminism of the will.

The work has four major parts and a concluding section. The first part defines the terms of the inquiry and explains the problem. Part II considers the Arminian conception of the freedom of will, inquiring whether there is any possibility that the will is indifferent; that is, free from any influence by causal or determining factors. Part III deals with the question whether liberty of the will in the Arminian sense is necessary to moral agency. Part IV continues the criticism of the Arminian conception of the freedom of will by examining the reasons offered in support of that conception. The conclusion reaffirms the basic Calvinistic doctrines: universal providence, the total depravity and corruption of man, efficacious grace, God's universal and absolute decree, and absolute, eternal, personal election.

Edwards begins his treatise with an analysis of the meaning of the term "will." He quite sensibly reminds the reader that definition would probably not be necessary had not philosophers confused the issue. The will, then, is "that by which the mind chooses anything"; it is the power to choose. There is no suggestion that the will is a substantial entity of some sort, an internal mechanism that hands out decisions; the will is what common discourse makes it to be: simply the faculty that a man has of choosing to do one thing rather than another. Where there is no inclination one way rather than another, there is no act of will, no volition.

Next, he considers what is meant in talking about the "determination" of the will. The answer is that the will is "said to be determined, when, in consequence of some action, or influence, its choice is directed to, and fixed upon a particular object." To say that the will is determined, then, means simply that choices are caused.

The "good" is defined as the agreeable, whatever wins acceptance or "tends to draw the inclination. . . ." Thus, Edwards points out, "the will always is as the greatest apparent good is." In other words, if the will is the power to choose, and if choices are inclinations toward some alternatives at the expense of others, and if the greatest apparent good is what most of all provokes the interest, the inclination, of the person, then what is chosen, in every case, is whatever is the greatest apparent good. The factors affecting choice are several: they include the apparent characteristics of the object considered (allowing for the possibility that the object is not precisely what it appears to be), the apparent degree of difficulty involved in attaining the object, and the apparent time it would be before the object was attained. The apparent good, according to Edwards, is a function not only of the apparent character of the object considered, but also of the manner in which the object is viewed or considered, and the circumstances of the mind that views. There is no objection to saying that the greatest apparent good *determines* the will— indeed, that is a proper way of speaking—but to say that the will "is" as the greatest apparent good "is" serves to emphasize the point that an object's appearing most agreeable and its being chosen are not two distinct acts.

The term "necessity" is critical in the problem of the freedom of the will. Edwards states his intention of showing that necessity is not inconsistent with liberty. He rejects several customary definitions of necessity, showing that either they say very little or else they ignore the relativity of necessity: anything which is necessary is so *to us* "with relation to any supposable opposition or endeavor *of ours*." The necessity relevant to a consideration of free will is philosophical necessity, defined as "the full and fixed connection between the things signified by the subject and predicate of a proposition which affirms something to be true."

A distinction is then drawn between natural necessity and moral necessity. Natural necessity is the result of natural causes other than such moral matters as habits, dispositions, motives, or inducements. Thus, by a natural necessity falling bodies move downward. We are naturally unable whenever we cannot do something, even if we will it; we are morally unable when we are not sufficiently motivated to do a particular act.

"Freedom" or "liberty," as we have noted, signifies the power to act as one wills.

Having completed the definition of crucial terms, Edwards turns to an explication and criticism of the Arminian conception of the free will. According to the Arminians, the will is self-determining. Edwards points out the impropriety of saying that the *will* determines its own choices; after all, the will is not an agent. But even if it be contended that not the will, but the soul, determines the will, and does so without causal influence of its action, the further difficulty remains that every act of choice would be determined by a preceding act of choice. If a first act of choice, in a series of acts, is self-determined, it must be the consequence of a previous choice and, thus, be not first: a contradiction. If, on the other hand, it is not self-determined, then it is not free in the Arminian sense. In either case, the Arminian notion is self-defeating.

The next important consideration is whether it would be possible for an event to occur (say, an act of volition) without a cause of its occurrence. Defining a cause as any antecedent on which the existence or nature of something depends, Edwards claims that no event could occur without cause. He affirms the principle of universal causation as one on which all reasoning about matters of fact depends, and he adds that no proof of the being of God would be possible without that principle. If no event could occur without a cause, then no act of volition could occur without a cause.

The argument that the will has the freedom of indifference; that is, that the will can choose any course indifferently, on its own, without being influenced—or that the soul's power of choice is in that way indifferent—is rejected by Edwards because of the contradiction involved in the implicit claim that the soul, while indifferent (in a state of *not* being inclined one way rather than another), chooses (is in a state of being inclined one way rather than another).

Referring to the Arminian contention that the will is contingent in the sense that acts of will are free from all necessity, Edwards argues that there could not be any act free from both cause and consequence. He adds that, even if an act could in this way be free from necessity, it could not be an act of volition, for acts of volition are *necessarily* connected with motives. To will is to be moved to action by the greatest apparent good; volition, then, necessarily involves being moved, or motivation; consequently, an act entirely unnecessary could not be an act of will.

In order to strengthen further his point that volitions are not contingent, in the sense of being without necessity, Edwards maintains that God's foreknowledge of events is possible only because of the necessity of those events, a necessity he recognizes.

In Part III, Edwards argues that the Arminian notion of an indifferent will, a will free from all causal necessity, is not only not necessary to moral virtue; it is inconsistent with it. To establish his point, he first of all advances a number of considerations to show that necessity is not incompatible with virtue or vice. God's moral excellence, the holiness of Jesus' acts, the sin of man—these are all necessary, but surely God's nature is virtuous and praiseworthy, as are Jesus' acts; and the acts of the sinner, although morally necessary, are nevertheless instances of vice and blameworthy.

Having argued that necessity is not incompatible with virtue, Edwards then maintains that freedom of indifference is not compatible with virtue, for virtue cannot reside in a soul which is indifferent; what common judgment requires is that a person commit himself, that he be inclined toward commendable action.

The conclusion is that virtue depends upon necessity; if the person could not be moved by exhortations, considerations, and inducements, neither virtue nor vice would be possible, and neither praise nor blame would be sensible. Even the commands of God would have to be acknowledged as senseless, if a virtuous soul could not be moved by those commands without losing its moral freedom.

In Part IV, Edwards considers, among other objections to the doctrine he proposes, the claims that if choices are determined, men are machines; if choices are necessary, fate rules men; the doctrine makes God the author of sin and (ironically) encourages atheism; and, finally, the doctrine is metaphysical and abstruse.

Answering the charges, Edwards argues that men are entirely different from machines in that men are able to reason, to will, to do as they will, to be capable of moral acts, and to be worthy of praise, love, and reward. On the Arminian conception, however, men would be worse than machines, the victims of "absolute blind contingence." If fate, as conceived by the Stoics, involves any limitations of human liberty, as Edwards has described it, then he rejects that notion of fate. It is misleading, Edwards continues, to argue that God is the author of sin, for even if God permits sin and so orders events that sin occurs, he does so for holy purposes and must be distinguished from the human agents who are the actual sinners. If atheists have embraced the doctrine of the determined will and have used it to defend their ways, Edwards argues, that in no way implies that the view is to blame. To the charge that his philosophy is metaphysical and abstruse, Edwards replies that it seems to be the other way about: the Arminian philosophy depends upon vague and undefined ideas and self-contradictory suppositions.

Edwards concludes by claiming that the chief objections to Calvinism have been met by his discourse. The principal objections against the notions of God's universal and absolute decree and the doctrine of personal election are that they imply a necessity of human volitions and of the acts of men; but the argument has shown that unless choices and acts are necessary, in the causal sense described, no volition is possible, and no judgment of moral action is justifiable.—*I.P.M.*

PERTINENT LITERATURE

Foster, Frank Hugh. *A Genetic History of the New England Theology.* Chicago: University of Chicago Press, 1907.

Although Frank Hugh Foster's book *A Genetic History of the New England Theology* was published in 1907, it ought not be overlooked by anyone interested in an analysis of Jonathan Edwards' *Freedom of the Will*. Foster's critique of Edwards' thought is rigorous and wide-ranging. His primary conclusion is that Edwards' position in *Freedom of the Will* is seriously flawed. Foster contends that Edwards is guilty of two major errors: he used the term "cause" ambiguously, and he confused emotion and volition. These two errors vitiate Edwards' positive thesis—that freedom of the will is compatible with complete determinism—as well as his negative thesis—that the Arminian doctrine which holds that the will determines itself is absurd.

According to Foster, Edwards sometimes used the term "cause" to mean any antecedent event, either natural or moral, which partially or wholly determines a subsequent event, and at other times to mean the occasion at which change occurs. It is thus impossible to understand in what sense motives act as causes in relation to the will. Are motives antecedent realities which partially or wholly determine the will, or are they simply aspects of occasions on which the will acts? Edwards was free to adopt either of these very different positions since he used the word "cause" ambiguously.

The second major error in Edwards' thought, according to Foster, is that he confused emotion with volition. Foster argues that because Edwards accepted the threefold division of mind into faculties, understanding, and will, he confused emotion, which is compelled, with will, which is free, and attributed to the latter the necessity belonging to the former. Foster points to Edwards' use of the word "inclination" as proof that this is the case. At times Edwards used the word "inclination" to denote emotion; and at other times, often in the same sentence, he used it to denote volition. (Foster cites specific passages so that one can decide for oneself the validity of such an assessment.)

Foster recognizes the theological success of *Freedom of the Will*, despite what he judges to be its philosophical failure; theologically Edwards did succeed in reinstituting Calvinist doctrines in New England theology. Arminianism had placed too much emphasis on the human side of the divine/human relationship, just as Calvinism in the early colonial period had placed too much emphasis on the divine side. With the publication of *Freedom of the Will* the emphasis shifted back in God's favor.

Foster also comments on the influence of *Freedom of the Will* on the development of theology after Edwards. He maintains that Edwards' distinction between *natural* and *moral* ability, while not correct as presented, becomes the basis for a correct distinction between actual incapability and personal unwillingness. Moreover, Edwards' remarks on the origin of evil stimulated others to address themselves to this important issue.

Foster's critique of Edwards' work, although predominantly negative, is persuasive and should be given careful attention.

Miller, Perry. *Jonathan Edwards*. New York: Meridian Books, 1959.

In his book *Jonathan Edwards*, Perry Miller, the leading modern scholar on Jonathan Edwards and American Puritanism, presents a perceptive and interesting interpretation of Edwards' *Freedom of the Will*. In Miller's estimation *Freedom of the Will* operates on two levels: it is a rejection of Arminianism and a defense of Calvinism, while at the same time it is an analysis of modern culture and the role America has played in shaping it.

Miller is not concerned with simply summarizing Edwards' arguments against the Arminian doctrine that the will is self-determining. What interests Miller are three features of Edwards' work: Edwards' definitions of certain key words (words he had used as "oracular symbols" ever since his Boston lecture of 1731), the solidification of motifs in Edwards' thought, and the "hidden meaning" of the text. The crucial words to which Miller refers are: *will, desire, determine, motive, good, necessity, impossibility, inability, contingency, liberty, freedom*, and *moral agency*. The motifs that Miller notes are (1) the unity of the self in perception and will, (2) the location of the self in nature, and (3) the dignity of God and of the human individual.

The idea of the unity of the self in perception and will, according to Miller, reflects Edwards' idealism—the view that what is perceived depends entirely on the perceiver for both its being and character—as well as his agreement with John Locke that it is the total self which acts and not simply some faculty of the self. (Miller disagrees with Frank Hugh Foster's judgment that Edwards adopted John Calvin's threefold analysis of mind.) In Miller's opinion, Edwards' rejection of the prevailing view that mind consists of faculties, understanding, and will is important because he thereby dismisses the possibility that the will is dependent upon understanding and that an increase in knowledge will lead to the perfection of will.

The second motif is the placement of the human self in the natural world. For Edwards the self is wholly within nature and is thus subject to natural laws. Miller terms this view "radical naturalism."

The third motif discussed by Miller is Edwards' defense of the dignity of God and of the human individual. Edwards assails Arminianism for requiring God to react to the free actions of human beings. Such a view of God, in Edwards' estimation, impugns God's dignity—it places God in the role of adapter and mender. Arminianism also impugns human dignity. By contending that acts of will are not determined, Edwards' argued, Arminianism undercuts the basis of moral responsibility, since undetermined acts are not morally accountable.

The "hidden message" of *Freedom of the Will* is that, in rejecting complete determinism, the modern era, and specifically the modern era in the United States of America, labors under the delusion that history is meaningless, that events are random, and that one future is as likely as another. In the name of progress and free enterprise, Americans have given up the belief that history has a purpose—that is, that it has a predetermined goal.

Miller's interpretation of Edwards' *Freedom of the Will* is perceptive and important. Whether or not he is finally correct about its "hidden meaning," he is surely correct in holding that the book is a complex text which operates on various levels and sheds light on the whole of Edwards' writings.

Cherry, C. Conrad. *The Theology of Jonathan Edwards: A Reappraisal.* Garden City, New York: Doubleday & Company, 1966.

C. Conrad Cherry maintains that in an effort to render Jonathan Edwards' thought relevant, or perhaps to make it more palatable to the contemporary person, Perry Miller and other Edwardian scholars tended to emphasize those elements of Edwards' thought which presumably "transcend" Calvinism. In Cherry's estimation, to do this is to distort Edwards' thought, for nothing in Edwards' work transcends Calvinism. All of his mature works, Cherry contends, must be interpreted in light of his primary interest and, although he read Sir Isaac Newton, John Locke, Francis Hutcheson, and the Cambridge Platonists, Edwards' primary interest was theology.

According to Cherry, Edwards' thought developed between two sets of religious extremes which were prevalent in eighteenth century New England: (1) Rationalism (the belief that reason alone is sufficient for understanding reality) and Enthusiasm (the belief that divine inspiration is required if one is to know all that there is to know); and (2) Neonomianism (a revival of Nomianism, which is the belief that salvation is contingent upon a person's following certain divinely ordained rules) and Antinomianism (the belief that salvation is *not* contingent upon following rules or laws). In *Freedom of the Will* Edwards is concerned with rejecting Neonomianism, which he considered to be heretical because it makes salvation the result of human activity rather than divine activity; it denies that it is only through the atonement of Christ that one is saved.

Arminianism, the position that the human will is capable of self-determination is the essence of Neonomianism, according to Edwards. Edwards argued that the doctrine of a self-determining will tended to prevent the exercise of faith in God because it denied any dependence upon the divine. Edwards believed that if he could refute Arminianism, if he could show it to be self-contradictory to suppose that the will can determine itself, he could undermine Neonomianism; for without the presumed ability of self-determination it would make no sense to contend that one's salvation is entirely in one's own hands.

Cherry's analysis of Edwards' thought is helpful in two ways. First, he provides an excellent discussion of the religious issues that were paramount in Edwards' time. Second, he indicates how Edwards' various writings are related to one another; for example, according to Cherry, *Freedom of the Will* and *Original Sin* are both conceived as responses to Neonomianism. Cherry may be guilty of overemphasizing the importance of Calvinism on Edwards' thought, but he is surely correct in contending that it is a major determining factor in all of Edwards' writing. Cherry's "reappraisal" of Edwards' theology is an excellent corrective to those studies of Edwards' thought which, for whatever reasons, shy away from his Calvinistic concerns.—*M.F.*

ADDITIONAL RECOMMENDED READING

Allen, Alexander V. G. *Jonathan Edwards*. Boston: Houghton Mifflin Company, 1889. Once the standard biography of Edwards, this book still merits reading. Allen is particularly helpful in facilitating an understanding of Edwards' theology.

Elwood, Douglas J. *The Philosophical Theology of Jonathan Edwards*. New York: Columbia University Press, 1960. Elwood emphasizes Edwards' concern to integrate scientific, philosophical, and theological knowledge. He notes the contemporary relevance of Edwards' thought.

Faust, Clarence H. and Thomas H. Johnson. *Jonathan Edwards*. New York: Hill and Wang, 1935 and 1962. This is an excellent collection of Edwards' most important writings. The introductory remarks are very helpful, as is the annotated bibliography.

Miller, Perry. *Errand into the Wilderness*. Cambridge, Massachusetts: Harvard University Press, 1956. A collection of Miller's articles, including "The Marrow of Puritan Divinity," "From Edwards to Emerson," "Edwards-Locke—and the Rhetoric of Sensation," and "Edwards and the Great Awakening." Some of these articles are controversial; all are important and ought to be considered.

THE THEORY OF MORAL SENTIMENTS

Author: Adam Smith (1723-1790)
Type of work: Ethics
First published: 1759

PRINCIPAL IDEAS ADVANCED

The origin of moral sentiments is sympathy, placing oneself imaginatively in the situation of another in order to realize the passions which affected him.

We approve the passions of another and regard them as suitable if, imagining ourselves in like circumstances, we find that we would have similar feelings.

The amiable *virtues of condescension and indulgence stem from sympathy; and the* respectable *virtues of self-denial and self-command arise in those who are the objects of sympathy.*

The unsocial *passions, hatred and resentment, are disagreeable; the* social *passions such as generosity, kindness, compassion, are agreeable; and the* selfish *passions are mixed, neither as disagreeable as the unsocial passions nor as agreeable as the social.*

The propriety of an action is the fitness of its motivating feeling to the cause of that feeling; the merit or demerit of an action rests upon the character of the consequences of the action.

Conscience is the faculty of judgment of the man within the breast, the inward man who knows the actual motivations of his actions.

Adam Smith was a professor of moral philosophy in the University of Glasgow. He is perhaps better known for his work in economic theory, *An Enquiry Concerning the Nature and Causes of the Wealth of Nations* (1776), than for this, his other major publication. Smith was a contemporary and friend of David Hume. Accepting Hume's moral doctrines on the whole, he offered the theory of moral sentiments as a treatment of an area Hume left only vaguely outlined. Smith considered the science of ethics to have as its business the description of the moral rules with a justness and nicety which would both ascertain and correct our ideas of proper conduct.

Smith was close on the heels of the "moral sense" philosophers, Shaftesbury and Francis Hutcheson. Unlike them, however, he did not ascribe moral perception to an inner sense like the exterior senses, a sense capable of recognizing moral quality in a manner analogous to the way the eye perceives color and shape. Smith asserted that philosophers should give greater attention to the causes of the passions, along with the due heed paid to their consequences.

Smith regarded the origin of the moral feelings to be in the process of sympathy with the passions. This consists of placing ourselves in imagination in the place of another, of conceiving ourselves as undergoing the same events and, consequently, having the same feeling as the other person. We do not have *his* feelings, which is simply impossible; but imagination copies our own feelings upon earlier occasions and supplies them anew to our minds. Thus, a sympathetic feeling could be one of compassion for the misery of an unfortunate person, or also the joy of one delivered from danger. And since we are not actually, but only imaginatively, in the situation of the other, we can never have feelings in such great strength as he. Furthermore, some passions do not arouse fellow feeling but rather act as stimuli to some opposing feeling. Sometimes when we perceive a person's anger, we are aroused against him rather than against those toward whom his anger is aimed; or we may experience fear of him rather than anger. A sympathetic response is aroused more by the knowledge of the situation in which the other's feeling first arises than it is by the perception of the other's feeling. This is shown when we occasionally sympathize with the dead, who can actually have no feeling at all.

The exercise of sympathy brings a pleasure both to him who gives and to him who receives it. The pleasure of receiving sympathy in the disagreeable passions is more intense than in the agreeable, and may serve as a measure of relief.

The basis of our approval of the feelings of another man is whether there is perfect concord between our own sympathies and his, when we are aware of his situation. We determine in this way that his passions are suitable and proper to their objects. Just as to have the same opinion as another is to approve of his having it, so with the feelings; we approve the other's feeling if we, in like circumstances, would have the same feeling. Even in cases in which we do not actually have sympathetic feeling with another, experience leads us to learn the nature and the amount of feeling appropriate to his circumstances, and thus to approve of his feelings.

Our natures are so constituted that we can be at variance with our fellows in our feelings, yet tolerate or even enjoy one another's company, as long as the matters which arouse them are items of indifference to our particular lives. But when an event touches us directly, we hope for the greatest possible concord of the spectator's feeling with ours, and we are likely to select our company only from those who display it. Yet recognizing that no other can feel precisely what we feel, since he cannot imagine to himself all the conditions which stir the feeling in us, we restrain and moderate our own feeling to a degree which those around us can attain when it arises in them upon our behalf. Thus, our desire for their approval and the satisfaction we expect from it act as a curb on the extremes of our feelings, and the society of those who have fellow feeling with us aids in restoring and preserving the tranquillity of our minds.

Two classes of virtues follow from these tendencies. The *amiable* virtues of "candid condescension and indulgent humanity" stem from the sympathy of the spectator, and the *respectable* virtues of self-denial and self-command come from the moderation of passion in the person involved. "To feel much for others and little for ourselves . . . to restrain our selfish, and to indulge our benevolent affections, constitutes the perfection of human nature; and can alone produce among mankind that harmony of sentiments and passions in which consists their whole grace and propriety." The *propriety* or the impropriety of an affection consists in the "suitableness or unsuitableness, in the proportion or disproportion which the affection seems to bear to the cause or object which excites it." Certain qualities are favorable but not necessarily admired; those which excite not only approbation but also wonder and surprise are the admirable qualities. This is true of our actions. Many, perhaps most, actions exhibiting propriety do not require virtue; but those which arouse our admiration at their uncommon delicacy of feeling or strength of self-command are signs of the admirable degree of the amiable or respectable virtue.

Passions originating with the body, such as hunger or pain, are objects more of disgust than of sympathy, since the onlooker can enter into them only to a very low degree. But those which take their origin from the imagination can readily take on the configuration of the imagination of the person affected. Such would be the loss of one's fortune or the frustration of an ambition. A tragic drama may fitly turn on such an event, but not even on so great a physical loss as the loss of a leg.

The passions fall into a set of classifications. The *unsocial* passions are hatred and resentment, with their variations. They arouse in the spectator rival feelings, which must work against each other, for he has as much tendency to sympathize with the person hated as with the person showing hatred. These passions are disagreeable alike to the spectator and the person feeling them. They tend to drive men apart and destroy society. The *social* passions, such as generosity, humanity, kindness, compassion, friendship, and all the benevolent affections, are felt with enjoyment; they bring men together and cement society. We enter into the feeling of satisfaction both of him who shows them and of him who is their object. Finally, the *selfish* passions take a middle place between the others. They are grief and joy when arising over the particular good or bad fortune of the person by whom they are felt. These become neither as disagreeable as the unsocial passions, for there is no rival to arouse a contrary sympathy, nor as agreeable as the social passions, for there is no additional beneficiary in whose satisfaction also we would share.

The qualities of merit and demerit are the qualities of deserving reward or punishment, distinct species of approbation and disapprobation. Whereas the propriety of an action is the fitness of its motivating feeling to the cause of that feeling, the merit or demerit of the action rests upon the beneficial or hurtful effects which the action tends to produce. An action appears to deserve reward which is the proper object of gratitude. Similarly, an action appears to deserve punishment which is the proper object of a fitting resentment.

These passions of gratitude and resentment, like every other, "seem proper and are approved of, when the heart of every impartial spectator entirely sympathizes with them, when every indifferent bystander entirely enters into, and goes along with them."

In one passage, Smith refers to the impartial spectator as "every human heart," but again he modifies this to "every body who knows of it." While he thus apparently sets up a standard of popular approbation, he seems to regard its basis—"the impartial spectator"—as an abstraction from instances of the human heart, rather than as a census by count. Thus it is possible to have moral judgments in a case in which no feelings, or the "wrong" feelings, have been stirred; it is possible to judge of the demerit of an injury to a person who is unaware he has been injured; and it is possible to alleviate the apparent demerit of an act which is accidental rather than springing from an improper resentment. Judgments of merit are based on direct sympathy with the agent, through which we approve or disapprove the affection giving rise to the action, and upon a sympathy, indirect but no less strong, with the recipient affected. Smith's view makes retaliation a natural impulse and incorporates it, in due degree, into the body of proper actions.

But the standard of the impartial spectator undergoes a further transformation. "I divide myself, as it were, into two persons; . . . I, the examiner and judge, represent a different character from that other I, the person whose conduct is examined into and judged of. The first is the spectator . . . The second is the agent, the person whom I properly call myself. . . ." The first of these persons Smith refers to again and again as "the man within the breast." Thus imagination and sympathy become the account of conscience or the voice within.

Man naturally desires not only to be approved of by society but also to be what ought to be approved of, to be worthy of approbation. Therefore, the "man within the breast" has a powerful voice in determining one's actions, so much so that in many cases inward approval may completely replace that of actual fellow men. The inward man knows one's inmost secrets of motivation and is not contented to approve merely external appearances of rightly motivated actions.

The general rules of morality are formed inductively upon instances of what our moral faculties approve or disapprove. These rules, together with good habits of action, serve as guides to our conduct when our involvement is great and our passions violent, conditions in which the "ideal man" within is deceived or haste prevents his being consulted. Our sense of duty is our regard for these general rules. Some actions, such as marks of gratitude, are of course better when they are prompted by an immediate feeling than when done solely from a sense of duty. The commandments of justice are the most exact duties; they admit of only such exceptions as may also be derived from the same just principles and with the same precision. Justice is an ordinary virtue, largely negative because on most occasions it only avoids harm rather than doing positive good. Nevertheless, it is the foundation of society, for where men are ready to do each other harm without restraint there can be no society. On the other hand, benevolence, which is free and never required, is the ornament of society and often an admirable virtue.

Nature has made every individual concerned first of all for the preservation and health of his body. Men soon learn to transfer their diligence in these regards toward obtaining social desires, such as the respect of our equals and credit and rank in society. The care of such objects as these, upon which one's happiness depends, is the virtue called prudence. It is perfectly respectable, yet neither endearing nor ennobling. Insofar as our actions may injure or benefit others, the character of the individual may affect the happiness of others. The concern for others prompts the virtues of justice and benevolence. The only motive which can justify our hurting or interfering with the happiness of our neighbor is proper resentment for injustice attempted or actually committed; and the punishment should be more aimed at making him aware of the hurt he has done, and at drawing his disapproval toward the motive of it, than at inflicting harm upon him. While prudence, justice, and benevolence may often summon the approval of a man, his passions may yet mislead him. Therefore, still another virtue is needed, that of self-command. Its best form shows greatness and steadiness of the exertions over self-love, with the strong sense of propriety needed to make and maintain that exertion. The degree of self-estimation, neither too high nor too low, which the impartial spectator would approve, is the same as that which will secure for the individual himself the most happiness.

Smith sharpens the outlines of his doctrine by adding, as the final part of his book, an examination of various systems of moral philosophy. He divides his subject according to two questions: (1) Wherein does virtue consist? (2) By what power or faculty of the mind is this character of virtue recommended to us? These represent the traditional questions, respectively metaphysical and epistemological, around which the philosophy of morals has centered in Western thought. Smith recognizes three possible answers to the first question: (1) Virtue consists either in propriety, the "proper government and direction of all our affections," which considered singly may tend either toward good or toward evil; or (2) virtue consists in prudence, the pursuit of one's own happiness; or (3) it consists in benevolence, the promotion of the happiness of others.

Smith places the ethical systems of Plato, Aristotle, and the Stoics within the group making the first answer. He claims the consistency of Plato's system with his own description of propriety. Aristotle differs in having virtue consist in habits of action rather than sentiments and judgments. The Stoics, he insists at some length, mistake entirely the kind of a system Nature made for man, for they reduce to nothing the importance of what we have the most power over, our immediate circumstances; and they would deaden the sentiments which are the very basis of moral judgments. Smith adds to the group the systems of Samuel Clarke, William Wollaston, and Shaftesbury, remarking that they fail to supply what he has provided, the element of sympathy on which morality is based.

Smith finds Epicurus giving the second answer, that virtue is in prudence. Epicurus, however, was too eager to rest everything on a single principle, bodily pleasure and pain; he failed to notice the powerful satisfactions which we take in the approval of our fellow man.

Philosophers proposing the third answer, regarding the principle of benevolence as the primary virtue, included Ralph Cudworth, Thomas More, and John Smith of Cambridge, but most especially Francis Hutcheson, "the soberest and most judicious." Smith commends these philosophies of benevolence as nurturing the most agreeable and noblest affections, but he objects that Hutcheson and the others fail to provide an adequate account of the real worth of the lesser virtues, such as prudence. Their works in that respect are not true to human nature. Bernard Mandeville, who urges that all society and all virtue are founded on self-love, also did men an injustice, for he presents any passion which is ever vicious as always vicious, and to the utmost degree.

For Smith, the problem of the knowledge of moral worth is the problem of approbation. The three possibilities to him seem to be self-love, reason, and sentiment. Against Hobbes, Puffendorf, and Mandeville, he argues that society cannot have been founded simply as a means of furthering private interest because sympathy is not a selfish principle; rather, a sympathetic feeling arises entirely on account of the other individual. Cudworth and other opponents of Hobbes advanced reason as the source of moral knowledge. Smith agrees that reason gathers the moral rules inductively, but argues that we must have some source, some "first perceptions," from which the reason gathers its instances. Smith commends Hutcheson for first seeing to what extent moral distinctions arise in reason, and to what extent they are founded on immediate sense and feeling. But, on grounds of the nature of experience, he opposes Hutcheson's claim to have discovered an inner moral sense. The inner sense, said to have as its sole purpose the judging of the rightness of actions, could not function as claimed because right actions do not always have the same appearance or form. Further, sentiments, whether proper or improper, feel inwardly the same. And if the inner sense is devoted to identifying proper approbations, a species of moral feeling, it is superfluous, for we do not require particular inner senses to account for other species of feelings which are unrelated to the moral. Still further, the inner moral sense is never detected operating apart from allied feelings such as sympathy or antipathy, and there is therefore no evidence of its existence such as its single operation would afford.

Finally, Smith affirms that the ancient sort of moralists, who delineated characters in general, in accordance with recognizable virtues, were much superior to later writers, such as the casuists, who attempted to lay down particular rules covering human conduct in advance of the fact. For conduct will always be various, and systems of human law will never be equal to natural justice, made known to man by his sympathies.

The moral system of Adam Smith stands at an interesting place in the development of ethics. It was not a brilliant constructive performance in itself, being here and there imprecise, and advancing very few grounds for the claims made. It did, however, serve to ameliorate some of the more extreme views of its time by helping to emphasize the complexity and subtlety of human experience and conduct. While it was among the last of the works to found morality upon a plan of virtues, it was among the early efforts to provide a sound psychological basis for choices of conduct. While we can see in it clear glimpses of the narrowing influence of the author's own temperament and of the culture and times in which he lived, we can also discover acute and instructive interpretations of human motives. Despite its copious didactic passages, the work shows a hearty desire not to let our wishes for the moral elevation of man get in the way of our seeing the facts of man's actual moral life.—*J. T. G.*

PERTINENT LITERATURE

Campbell, T. D. *Adam Smith's Science of Morals*. The University of Glasgow Social and Economic Studies, 21. Totowa, New Jersey: Rowman and Littlefield, 1971.

T. D. Campbell's *Adam Smith's Science of Morals* is certainly the most substantial modern treatment of Adam Smith's moral philosophy. It is in addition extremely enlightening, not only in its analysis of *The Theory of Moral Sentiments*, but also especially in its explanation of the place of Smith's moral philosophy within the larger context of his thought, of which, according to Campbell, *The Wealth of Nations* was one relatively specialized part.

Basic to Campbell's general thesis is his view that Smith's *The Theory of Moral Sentiments* is best regarded not as a work on moral philosophy in the modern sense (that is, as a work concerned with the logical analysis and the logical foundations of morality) but as an early psychological and sociological theory of morals. Campbell maintains that although there is a normative framework to *The Theory of Moral Sentiments*—he is concerned to give advice to "statesmen"—Smith is primarily concerned with causal rather than logical analysis of morality and its role in human life. In other words, he is concerned with "the origins and function of moral judgments rather than with the clarification or criticism of moral language."

Smith's objective, according to Campbell, was ultimately a complete science of society, of which *The Theory of Moral Sentiments* was to have formed a basic part. That project is one which was to have continued with a study of jurisprudence, which Smith regarded as the study not only of justice but also of what concerns "police, revenue, and arms, and whatever else is the object of law." It is under these later headings that Smith placed economics. Therefore, the progression from his moral theory to his economic theory which was to take place by way of his unfinished work on jurisprudence is one of increasing specialization. According to Campbell, and contrary to those who allege an incompatibility between *The Theory of Moral Sentiments* and *The Wealth of Nations*, there is a definite connection between those two important works such that a proper understanding of his economics is greatly enhanced by a study of his theory of morality.

The foregoing is a summary of the general picture Campbell has of Smith's thought. However, Campbell also deals with great clarity and persuasiveness with specific aspects of Smith's moral philosophy. In his chapter on "The Impartial Spectator," he criticizes the view that Smith's conception of the impartial spectator is equivalent to the conception of the ideal observer as found in contemporary ethical theory. Among the differences he cites are that the impartial spectator in Smith is not perfectly knowledgeable, nor the possessor of an imagination vivid enough to imagine simultaneously all relevant facts. Nor is he without ordinary emotions.

In his chapter on "Smith's Social Theory," Campbell persuasively explains why there is, as mentioned above, no incompatibility between Smith's views of human motivation in *The Theory of Moral Sentiments* and his views in *The Wealth of Nations*. Those who maintain that there is such an incompatibility—that there is "The Adam Smith Problem"—often argue that in *The Theory of Moral Sentiments* Smith gives the social passions the central role, whereas in *The Wealth of Nations* self-interest is always the dominant motive. Campbell explains that on the one hand Smith does not deny, even in *The Theory of Moral Sentiments*, that self-interest constitutes the most efficacious motive of human action. On the other hand, neither does he ever hold that all human actions are selfish in the ordinary sense that they are incompatible with a concern for others. Instead, what Smith calls "selfish passions" need not aim at one's own welfare at the expense of others. Indeed, in Smith's view, as with many others of that period, a desire for the good of others could become a part of one's own happiness such that the pursuit of the latter need not be narrowly self-interested.

In the chapter "Approval and Sympathy," Campbell illuminates Smith's conception of sympathy by distinguishing it from pity or compassion. Smith's notion of sympathy was not, Campbell points out, the normal meaning of the term, even in his own day. Indeed, taking it in its more usual sense leads to serious misreadings of Smith. In contrast with philosophers such as Lord Shaftesbury, David Hume, and Francis Hutcheson, Smith did not take sympathy to be a particular sentiment or as any process by which the feelings of one person are transferred to another. For Smith, sympathy in general means our awareness of the agreement, coincidence, or harmony of sentiments between ourselves and others. It is "our fellow-feeling with any passion whatsoever." More narrowly, Smith, who is particularly concerned with that type of sympathy in which the coincidence of sentiments is brought about by imaginatively taking on the position of another, uses "sympathy" to refer to the capacity to achieve such a coincidence through imaginative means.

Other perceptive portions of this book deal with the relation of Smith's science of society and morals to his religious views, his analysis of virtues in terms of the impartial spectator, and an assessment of his work as a sociological and psychological resource.

Raphael, D. D. "The Impartial Spectator," in *Dawes Hicks Lecture on Philosophy*. Vol. LVIII. London: Oxford University Press, 1972.

According to D. D. Raphael, what is original in Adam Smith's moral philosophy is the development of the idea of an impartial spectator (which originated in Francis Hutcheson and was adopted by David Hume) to explain the judgments of conscience made by an agent about his own actions. Thus Smith dealt with two difficulties inherent in spectator theories of moral judgments: namely, that they most easily account for second- and third-person judgments, but not so easily with judgments made in the first person; and they are more comfortable with judgments of things done in the past than in deciding what should be done in the future. In addition, by explaining the origins of conscience and hence judgments of duty he helped to correct an inadequate treatment of duty and obligation in both Hume and Hutcheson.

According to Smith, conscience, by which he means approbation or disapprobation of oneself, is an effect of judgments made by spectators. Thus he is establishing the psychological origins of conscience. He is not saying that conscience is merely what others think of us. What happens in the development of conscience is that we first judge and are judged by others from the point of view of a spectator. Since we naturally care how others regard us, we then come to judge our own conduct by imagining how others would judge us. Since we soon discover, however, that we cannot win everyone's approval, we imagine whether an impartial spectator would approve or disapprove of it.

The impartial spectator is not, then, any actual bystander, but the product of one's own imagination. In fact he is oneself in the position of a spectator. That impartial spectator might judge differently from any actual spectator because he has a more intimate knowledge of the situation, especially of his own motives, and because he judges without bias. By means of this impartial spectator Smith can explain why it is that even though conscience is a social product, it can nevertheless sometimes oppose public sentiment, and indeed often be superior to it even without our conceiving of it as the voice of God.

Raphael points out that Smith's conception of the impartial spectator differs in important ways from Roderick Firth's conception of an ideal observer who is omniscient, omnipercipient, disinterested, and dispassionate, and from John Rawls's conception of the impartial spectator who is perfectly rational, identifies perfectly with the desires of others, and hence is capable of organizing the interests of all persons in society into a single ordered system. Raphael also compares Smith's conception of conscience with Sigmund Freud's notion of the superego, commending Smith on not underestimating the role society in general plays in the formation of conscience and on not stressing, as Freud did, the force of disapproval and fear.

According to Raphael, Smith's theory was meant to provide a satisfactory alternative to purely *a priori* accounts of conscience and morality generally. As such, he attempts to give a thoroughgoing empiricist account of conscience. As with Hume and Hutcheson, he attempted an explanation of ethics in terms of human nature—what we would today call empirical psychology. Smith appreciated that the theories of Hutcheson and Hume were inadequate to account for the peculiarities of conscience, and he attempts to show how conscience can be accounted for by a moral sense theory.

Raphael concludes with three questions concerning Smith's views on conscience and morality. He dismisses all but the third. The first is whether Smith remained true to his empiricism. Certain remarks that Smith makes concerning God's laws and conscience as an authority superior to social approval and disapproval notwithstanding, Raphael maintains that Smith does not depart from his empiricism. The second question is whether it is reasonable to attribute greater complexity to moral judgments made about ourselves than to those made about others. Smith is not guilty of this charge, according to Raphael, because he does not claim that moral judgments about oneself have more complex meanings than judgments about others. It is simply that the former have a more complicated history. Finally, Raphael suggests that Smith's concept of the impartial spectator is too complicated to be acceptable when one works it out fully in terms of his general theory of approval. An agent who consults his conscience has to imagine himself in the position of an uninvolved spectator who, in turn, because it is the nature of moral judgments, imagines himself in the position of involved agent and compares those feelings with those he actually has. Raphael thinks that although this is not impossible it seems too complicated to be a common occurrence.—*C.K.I.*

ADDITIONAL RECOMMENDED READING

Bitterman, H. J. "Adam Smith's Empiricism and the Law of Nature," in *The Journal of Political Economy*. XLVIII (1940), pp. 487-520 and 703-737. Discusses Smith's methodology in the light of *Essays on Philosophical Studies*.

Bonar, James. *Moral Sense*. New York: George Allen & Unwin, 1930. Important study of Smith's moral philosophy as part of the moral sense tradition.

Oncken, A. "The Consistency of Adam Smith," in *The Economic Journal*. VII (1897), pp. 443-450. The beginning of the controversy about the alleged incompatibility between *The Theory of Moral Sentiments* and *The Wealth of Nations*.

Sprague, Elmer. "Adam Smith," in *The Encyclopedia of Philosophy*. Vol. VII. New York: Macmillan Publishing Company, 1967, pp. 461-463. A concise presentation of Smith's moral philosophy.

THE SOCIAL CONTRACT

Author: Jean Jacques Rousseau (1712-1778)
Type of work: Social philosophy
First published: 1762

PRINCIPAL IDEAS ADVANCED

Whatever rights and responsibilities the rulers and citizens have in a state are derived from some agreement; no social right is derived from nature.

In a state of nature men live to preserve themselves; to make cooperation possible and to assure common security, states are instituted by social contracts.

According to the contract, when a man places himself under the control of a sovereign, he is placing himself under the control of himself and his fellow citizens, for a sovereign exists in order to safeguard the citizens.

The sovereign is limited to the making of general laws; he cannot pass judgment upon individuals.

As a result of the joining of wills by the social contract, a general will, distinguishable from a collection of individual wills, comes into being.

The ideal government is a small, elected group; and the ideal state is small enough to allow the citizens to know one another.

Jean Jacques Rousseau is the most interesting and the most important political thinker of the eighteenth century. He is known for his famous *Confessions* (1784) and for his discussion of education in *The New Héloïse* (1760) and *Émile* (1762), but he is best known today, in philosophical circles at any rate, for *The Social Contract*, which is one of the great classics in the field of political philosophy. Rousseau was very much concerned with the relationship between the state on the one hand and the individual on the other. He recognized that the state has tremendous power over the individual, that it can command him, coerce him, and determine the sort of life he is to live, and also that the individual makes many demands on society, even if he does not have the power to back them up. But surely, he insisted, the relations between the state and the individual cannot be simply those of naked power, threats, coercion, arbitrary decrees and fearful or cunning submission, for we do speak of justified authority, the legitimate exercise of force, the rights of citizens, and the duties of rulers. The big question, then, is this: What is the source of the rights and responsibilities of both the citizen and the ruler?

In *The Social Contract*, Rousseau repudiates those who argue that the stronger have the right to rule the weaker, insisting that strength as such amounts to coercion and not justified coercion. If a highwayman brandishing a pistol leaps at me from a thicket and demands my purse, I am forced to hand it over, but his strength does not justify his act and my weakness does not make my reluctance blameworthy. Nor does this right of society over the individual flow from nature. True, the simplest social group, the family, does rest upon the natural requirement that the parents care for the child—survival is the first law of nature—but since the family usually holds together much longer than is needed to satisfy this requirement, it is evident that the rights and obligations that continue to exist within the family organization are not supported or required by nature. Rather, these obligations and rights depend upon tacit agreements between parents and children that certain relationships shall be maintained and respected within the group, agreements tacitly admitted when the son chooses to stay within the family and the father welcomes his continued presence. Agreements of this sort mark the transition from the amoral state of power and submission to power to the moral state of acknowledged rights and responsibilities. What is true of the family is also true of that larger society, the state, for whatever rights and responsibilities the rulers and citizens possess could only have evolved as the result of some agreement among men. Rousseau insists, like Thomas Hobbes, John Locke, and many others, that society is based upon some implicit contract.

This contract delivers us from a prior state of nature. Before men lived in societies they were motivated primarily by the basic urge to preserve themselves, an urge that manifested itself in physical appetites and desires and released itself instinctively through actions designed to satisfy these. Man was not governed by reason or by moral considerations, for there were no rights or moral relationships to be respected. Rousseau does not claim that presocietal man was vicious or the natural enemy of every other man, or that he had no gregarious instincts at all, but he does claim that the life of the individual was dominated by the amoral, unreflective pursuit of his own welfare. As a result of this marked individualism and the rude circumstances of nature, life was uncertain and precarious, cooperation impossible, and aggression common. Such a state could be transcended only by instituting, by common consent, some sort of body politic within which cooperation would be possible and security guaranteed.

According to Rousseau, the society instituted by the contract brings about a marked transformation in man, for rational behavior replaces instinct, a sense of responsibility replaces physical motivation, and law replaces appetite. Latent capacities and faculties finally flower, and out of "a stupid and dull-witted animal" there emerges "an intelligent being and a man." In these respects Rousseau differs from Locke and Thomas Jefferson, who maintained that prior to the contract man is already rational and moral and already possesses rights. The contract does not change man or affect his rights; it only safeguards what he already has. But for Rousseau man's debt to society is far greater, for rights, morality, and his very status as a man are consequences of his being a member of a body politic. Rousseau also differs from Hobbes, not about the nonexistence of morality in a state of nature, but about human nature. The Hobbesian man is so egoistic that he can only be restrained, not transformed. For Hobbes, Locke, and Jefferson, man is essentially individualistic, whereas for Rousseau he is essentially a social creature. This view leads to two different conceptions of the function of political society. In the former, social institutions have only the negative function of securing what man already has by controlling excessive individualism, whereas in the latter, social institutions have the positive function of enabling man to fulfill his nature. In the former, political institutions are a necessary evil, but for Rousseau they are a blessing.

In the contract that establishes the state, men agree with one another to place both themselves and their possessions under the complete control of the resultant body politic, and to give to it the power and responsibility of safeguarding them and of providing the framework within which they can jointly pursue their common welfare.

It may sound as if Rousseau were advocating a rather extreme despotism, but this is not so. In the first place, according to the terms of the contract, civil power and responsibility are not turned over to a king or to some small group of persons, but are kept in the hands of the contractors themselves, who thus become jointly sovereign. Consequently, when a man contracts to place himself under the control of the sovereign, his action means only that he, like every other person, places himself under the control of himself and his fellow citizens.

Secondly, while the state shall have control over the individual, the scope of its control is limited to matters pertaining to the preservation and welfare of all. If it transgresses these limits, the contract is void and the citizen is released. Thus, for instance, while the new citizen hands all his possessions over to the state, the state immediately hands them back and, by giving him title to them, institutes property rights as distinguished from mere possession. According to the contract, the state retains control only in the sense that it has the right to appropriate the individual's property if the public interest should require that it do so. Similarly, the state can command the individual only to the extent that control is needed for the public welfare. At all other times and in all other respects it guarantees his freedom from the encroachment of the government and of other individuals. In this way the contract brings human rights into being and specifies their scope.

Again, the individual is safeguarded insofar as the function of the sovereign group is restricted to the making of laws and insofar as the object of the law is always general. The sovereign power can pass laws attaching rewards or punishments to types of action and privileges to certain offices, but it cannot pass judgment upon individuals. The latter is the function of the executive or administrative branch, not that of the legislative. Rousseau maintains emphatically that the legislative and administrative functions shall not be discharged by the same group.

The transformation wrought in the individual and the nature of the sovereign act are both expressed in what is perhaps the most nearly basic of Rousseau's concepts, that of the "general will." Even though man is initially motivated by self-interest, the awareness that a contract is desirable forces him to think about others and their interests. Once the contract is made and the mechanism of democratic assemblies put into practice the individual will be forced to consider those other interests more seriously than ever before. This consideration may result from prudence alone in the first place, but the deliberate joining of lots, the debating, the compromises to accommodate others, and the conscious recognition that they have common ideals cannot fail to encourage a genuine concern for the welfare of all. Man becomes a social creature with a social conscience, and what would otherwise have been a mere collection of individuals with individual goals and individual wills becomes a collective person with a single general will and a single goal. There comes into being a *res publica*, a republic, a body politic with many members.

Rousseau stressed the point that man is not really a citizen so long as he accepts society from prudence alone, that he becomes a real citizen only when he develops a genuine concern for the welfare of all. There is an emphasis here that is not found in the English and American social contract writers. Of course, Rousseau does not write that man's interest in himself will disappear; he claims, rather, that a new dimension has been added. Insofar as he is still self-centered, man must be a subject, but insofar as he is a socially conscious person he can assume his responsibilities as a sovereign.

Rousseau insists that the general will must be distinguished from the many individual wills. If the citizens jointly form a body politic, the general will is the will of that body, a will that comes into being when they jointly concentrate their attention on the needs of that body. This will exercises itself through democratic assemblies of all the citizens and lets its intentions be known through the decisions of such assemblies. An assembly expresses the will of the whole people and not that of a part, but it requires only the voice of the majority *if* the views of the minority have been fairly heard and fairly considered. The general will cannot be ill-intentioned; it is concerned with the good of all, and it cannot be mistaken unless it is ill-informed. Simple, unsophisticated men are quite capable of exercising sovereign power provided that they are socially conscious, and well informed, and provided further that they act after full discussion, and are not subject to pressure groups. Since sovereignty is the expression of the general will, and the general will is the expression of the will of all, sovereignty cannot be alienated by anyone or delegated to anyone—king or elected representative.

While he sometimes spoke in a rather idealistic manner, Rousseau could also be rather hardheaded. He was quite aware that the conditions just mentioned are not always fulfilled. Pressure groups do occur; citizens become so indifferent or so preoccupied with their own concerns that they fail to discharge their civic responsibilities, and administrators seek to control those they are supposed to serve. In these and other ways sovereignty can be destroyed. No human institution, he writes, will last forever. In addition, it is not likely that simple men can themselves establish the proper kind of state. Some well-intentioned and exceedingly gifted lawgiver is needed to provide a constitution, help establish traditions, and guide the fledgling state with a hidden but firm hand until the people have developed the ability, stability, and desire to carry on for themselves.

Through the expression of their general will, then, the people exercise the sovereignty which they have and must retain in their own hands, but as we have already noted, they do not administer the resultant laws. To do so they establish an executive branch that functions as their agent. The form and structure of the administration will depend upon the size of the state, and, other things being equal, the number of rulers tolerable for efficiency will vary inversely with the number of citizens. This is so since a larger state will require the tighter administrative control that can be achieved only if the executive power is restricted to a small number of administrators. On the other hand, a very small state might get along by allowing all the citizens to take part in the administration. Having in mind a moderately sized city-state, such as his native Geneva, Rousseau suggests that the ideal government would be a small elected group. He says that the function of the executive is restricted to the support and administration of the law and to the preservation of civil and political liberty, and that the sovereign assembly is restricted to legislating, but he does not specify these functions in detail nor does he discuss the relationship between them. Furthermore, he does not discuss a judiciary, but this is presumably included in the administrative complex.

He is clear, though, in his insistence that the administrator be the servant of the assembly. To ensure that this be so, the people enter into no contract with their administrator and, unlike the Hobbesian contractors, transfer no rights to him. They extend to him nothing more than a revocable commission, thereby retaining control over him without being bound by him. When the sovereign assembly meets, as it does very frequently, all commissions granted by it at previous meetings become void until they are renewed.

Rousseau favors a moderately sized state something like the communes of Switzerland wherein every citizen can come to know all the others, for in the large state relations between citizens become impersonal, and their interests, problems, and fortunes become diversified. If there are many provinces, mores will not be uniform and one body of law will not be sufficient. The number and levels of subordinate government will multiply, and as the cost increases liberty will decrease. Chains of command become attenuated to such an extent that administration at the bottom levels becomes indifferent, weak, or corrupt, and supervision from the top becomes difficult. The control of the government by the people becomes impossible, as does the democratic legislative process. Indeed, a very large state cannot avoid being a dictatorship both legislatively and administratively, and that is the best form of government for it. If a state is to be a democratic state it must be small, as small as it can be without inviting encroachment by its neighbors.

It is interesting to speculate about what Rousseau would say of modern democracies which have millions of citizens and embrace hundreds of thousands of square miles. He would perhaps admit that contemporary means of communication obviate some of the difficulties he had in mind, and that security usually requires a considerably larger state than was necessary then. Quite possibly he would admire many of the ingenious ways by which we have delegated both legislative and administrative powers and controlled these powers, but he might argue sadly that we are bedeviled by many of the difficulties inherent in size. Gone forever is the small autonomous political group with its intimacies, its personal concern, its shared interests and problems, and its joint endeavors.

Rousseau's views have influenced many thinkers and political movements, partly because of the central problem with which he was concerned and partly because of the vigor and clarity with which he wrote. But his influence is due also to the fact that unresolved tensions in his thought have permitted partisan readers to place rather different interpretations upon him. On the one hand, his emphasis on equality, liberty, and the supremacy of the citizen made him a favorite author among the leaders of the French Revolution, and these emphases plus those on democracy and the control of the administrators have always made him attractive to those who have supported a republican form of government. On the other hand, his claim that man realizes his full nature only by participating in the life of a society has impressed those who believe that the state should play more than a negative regulatory role. This claim, along with his assertion that the individual is under the complete control of the sovereign power, and his sometimes near reification of the general will have seemed to others to foreshadow the engulfing national spirit of Hegel and his followers and to be congenial to the recent German and Italian cult of the Fatherland. The truth, of course, is that each of the above views requires that the interpreter select his passages and, in some cases, stretch them considerably, whereas in fact, Rousseau presents us with a rich array of ideas that are not worked out completely or consistently. These fresh ideas are what make *The Social Contract* one of the great classics of political philosophy.—*L.M.*

Pertinent Literature

Plamenatz, John. "On le forcera d'être libre," in Maurice Cranston and Richard S. Peters' *Hobbes and Rousseau: A Collection of Critical Essays.* Garden City, New York: Anchor Books, 1972, pp. 318-332.

John Plamenatz dedicates this essay to dissipating the shocking effect of

Jean Jacques Rousseau's famous contention that people may be forced to be free. Rousseau's critics have been divided about their true meaning. Some have accused him of being a traitor to liberty, allowing its suppression in its own name. Plamenatz feels that this accusation is misguided, since Rousseau insisted that genuine liberty exists only when every man (or perhaps one should say every citizen) is a member of the legislative assembly. Everyone who was not excluded from the assembly and was free to vote his conscience without unreasonable pressure or coercion was obliged to abide by the laws enacted by it.

Nevertheless, Plamenatz concedes that the expression "forced to be free" is obscure, and that if one takes it literally, it is impossible to make any sense of it. In order to understand it, he suggests that it not be taken literally, and argues that if his meaning is properly understood, it will lead to new insights into Rousseau's theories on the connections between law, duty, and freedom, and more especially to a greater appreciation of the novel contributions Rousseau made to the concept of liberty.

Rousseau distinguishes three kinds of liberty: natural, civil, and moral. Natural liberty, a state in which men are totally independent of one another, can exist only in a state of nature, where there are no laws. In such a state, where rules, rights, and obligations are unknown, man is not yet a moral being. Civil liberty consists of the right to do that which the rules permit. Moral liberty is obedience to rules imposed by the individual upon himself. The essential difference between civil liberty and moral liberty, then, is that civil liberty is conditioned by the laws or social rules imposed by the state or other citizens through some form of collective action and the threat of sanctions, while moral liberty concerns only the individual's relation to himself. According to Plamenatz, Rousseau's paradoxical slogan about forcing a man to be free has to do only with moral liberty.

In the state of nature, man enjoys natural liberty or independence because he can satisfy his relatively simple wants without the assistance of others. In such a state he is not a slave to his passions, not because he totally lacks passions, but because the passions he has are moderate to begin with, like those that brute animals have. Only in society, where men become vain and grasping, can they become true slaves to their passions. Of course, man in the state of nature has no conception either of freedom or of slavery; but men who live in civil society can look back upon the state of nature and, realizing their own acquired needs and desires and the extent to which they have become dependent upon others for their satisfaction, can reflect upon the state of nature and recognize the fact that in that state men enjoyed a kind of freedom which is denied to them.

To be free in the complete sense of that word, man must want only what he can get. He must not have insatiable appetites or desires that are incompatible with one another. Such appetites and desires are acquired only in civil society, where men develop the "unnatural" passion to be preferred over all others—a passion which is unnatural since it does not exist in the state of nature. This passion is also unnatural in that it prevents man from achieving the very goal for which he presumably organized himself into civil society—happiness.

If a society could produce two conditions, it could be said to be truly free: if it could prevent the development in its members of needs that they could not satisfy, and if it could meet those demands that its members did have, then in the sense discussed above, its members would be free, for they would not be dependent upon one another for the satisfaction of unmet needs.

In actual societies, however, there is a tendency for people to develop passions and wants which cannot be satisfied, and for inequalities to develop which result in jealousies and the consequent desire on the part of those who do not have all that their neighbors enjoy to acquire a greater share of the wealth (however that term may be defined). Inequalities give rise to prejudices, passions, and laws which serve to perpetuate the very inequalities which create the problems they are designed to treat. This leads inevitably to even greater unhappiness.

It is therefore reasonable for men in civil society to be equalitarian—to be recognized by others as equals, and to treat them equally—in short, to require of others no more than they would be willing to concede to them. No matter how rich or powerful one may be, someone always has greater power or wealth (in some sense); so, according to Rousseau, it is to everyone's interest to invoke the principle of equality.

How, then, can a man in civil society be free? He can be free in obeying the law if the law itself expresses his will. But since the laws govern all, and since equality is a reasonable goal for men to pursue (in their own self interest), it follows that it is best if *all* men are free—which means that the law must express the will of all alike. Thus, all the citizens must take part in making the law. This, of course, is the sense of Rousseau's conception of the general will.

But suppose a man has voted against a law which was enacted by the majority. Or suppose he changes his mind and no longer approves of a law which he approved of when it was first enacted. The law then—it would seem—no longer expresses his will, and his obedience to it is no longer an expression of his freedom, but is rather an instance of coercion and enslavement. Plamenatz argues that, according to Rousseau, one who participates in the deliberations that lead to a decision (for example, a piece of legislation) binds himself to accept that decision even if he votes against it. In a sense, then, he has freely accepted the conclusions arrived at by the legislature.

As for the lawbreaker, or the one who no longer wishes to be bound by the dictates of a particular law, Plamenatz interprets Rousseau to be saying that even he respects the law. He may want to abide by the law, and at the same time want what he cannot have unless he breaks the law. Consider, for example, the citizen who is making out his tax return—wanting, on the one hand, to be honest and to fulfill the mandates of the law, and on the other hand wishing that he could keep some of the money that an honest tax return obliges him to pay to his government. If he is honest, he regrets the loss of the funds he would otherwise have and the goods and services he might have purchased with them; and if he cheats on his return, he feels guilty or tries to find some excuse for his behavior.

It is precisely this sort of situation which Plamenatz feels Rousseau draws to our attention more than any other writer before him. We feel both thwarted and liberated by our sense of duty. A person who has a sense of duty does not submit to anyone else's will, but nevertheless feels bound to abide by the rule, even when he fears no sanctions. At the same time, he wants everyone else to abide by the rule as well. Thus, men not only adopt and live by rules because of their self interest; but also they wish to keep the rules because they are moral beings—despite the fact that their appetites are such that they feel thwarted by the very rules which they want so strongly to adopt and to obey. Even when their appetites overwhelm their moral sense of duty, they wish that they were law-abiding. It is this feeling that Rousseau calls the *constant will*—a will to abide by the law even when one disobeys it.

In *The Social Contract*, Plamenatz says, Rousseau describes the social and political conditions most likely to lead men to feel this way about the laws they must obey. Those conditions, he says, are also unfavorable for the development of those passions which induce men to disobey the law. Where all men are equal, they are most likely to want only what they are capable of achieving and to do what they wish to do. To get what he wants, the citizen of such a state is not dependent upon the favors of others, and is therefore independent in Rousseau's sense of the word—although he is dependent upon laws which they and he desire be obeyed.

The phrase "to be forced to be free" cannot be taken literally, then. It can, however, be understood to express Rousseau's explanation of those conditions which are necessary for men to find a moral support in the laws established in a just society for the discipline they need to be free of the passions that would otherwise enslave them.—*B.M.L.*

Cassirer, Ernst. *The Question of Jean-Jacques Rousseau*. Translated and edited by Peter Gay. New York: Columbia University Press, 1954.

The question referred to in the title is whether it is possible to reconcile discordant elements in Jean Jacques Rousseau's thought. Rousseau insisted on the unity of his work, but well-known scholars have argued that the political system sketched in *The Social Contract* is a foreign element, out of harmony with Rousseau's passion for individual freedom. Ernst Cassirer holds that

Rousseau's assessment was correct, that although his thought was always in motion and cannot be reduced to a system, the movement is nevertheless continuous and gives organic unity to his writings. Rousseau wrote by impulse and, at the beginning, had no notion of his goal; but gradually he perceived the direction he must take and was able to give objective and universal expression to the problems which caused him such personal anguish.

According to Cassirer, what mainly disturbed Rousseau was the shallowness and falsity of the Enlightenment view of man, first as he met it in Parisian society and later as he listened to his friends the Encyclopedists. The success which he had enjoyed in the salons did not blind him to the fact that this highly touted existence was a kind of slavery, and when by chance he saw the notice of an essay contest on the question "Has the restoration of the sciences and the arts helped to purify morals?" he was ready with his answer. This essay, known as the *First Discourse*, was a popular success mainly because of its eloquence and passion. Cassirer says, however, that there was nothing novel in the thesis that man, naturally good, is corrupted by society; that was what many advanced thinkers were saying. The assumption of the Enlightenment was that, like other creatures, man has a fixed nature, and that in order to discover it we need only think what he was like in his natural condition. The real shock came when, in the *Second Discourse*, "The Origins of Inequality," Rousseau denied the fixity and intelligibility of human nature and argued that what sets man apart from other creatures is that his nature is unfinished. Rousseau was the first, says Cassirer, to oppose the static eighteenth century view of the world, setting against it his own dynamic view according to which man's form and essence are plastic. In other words, he had come to consider that it is not possible to consider what man *is* apart from the question of what man *ought* to be.

For the most part, Rousseau's readers missed the main point. When he exalted the natural man over the artificial man, railed against the learned, set feeling over intellect, and called upon individual persons to free themselves from the bondage of custom and dare to live their own lives, he was understood as advocating capricious subjectivism at best and amoral self-seeking at worst. According to Cassirer, however, Rousseau was speaking a new language. The natural man which he held up in opposition to the product of civilization was not a creature of instinct and passion but one who had freed himself from his animal condition by establishing for himself a moral law; the feeling to which he appealed was not sympathy or sentiment, but conscience; and the freedom which he cherished was not arbitrary self-will, but a canopy of voluntary submission to law which the person erects over himself.

From the beginning, says Cassirer, Rousseau maintained the primacy of the ethical will over both passion and empirical knowledge. "Virtue! Sublime science of simple souls!" he cried in the *First Discourse*; "To learn your laws, is it not enough to return to ourselves and to listen to the voice of conscience in the silence of passions?" The truth must be apprehended by each person for himself, but it is denied to no one because it belongs to man's essence. All that we need in order to discover what is right is to remove hindrances that stand in our way. That was the thesis of *Émile*, his work on education; it was also the foundation of his political thought. In the *Confessions* he says that he was not long in discovering that human existence is a political achievement. Past states have grown up as battlegrounds for men's ambition and self-love, with the result that states have been oppressive; but man can control his destiny and transform a curse into a blessing. "The great question seemed to reduce itself to this: which is the form of government fitted to shape the most virtuous, the most enlightened, the wisest, and, in short, the 'best' people?" The Encyclopedists, Cassirer points out, were also interested in political reform, but where they were looking for ways to increase men's happiness, Rousseau was looking for ways to make men good. In the state that he envisaged, legislation, giving voice to the General Will, would not merely focus the wills of people but would form them, enabling men to raise themselves above the life of appetite and desire.

According to Rousseau, law, when it is the expression of moral reason, does not diminish spiritual freedom. Rousseau hated servility as much as the next person. He could endure natural evils; indeed, he saw it as part of man's greatness that he can learn to absorb the shocks of nature. What he could not endure was having to submit to the arbitrary wills of other men. Law, as the expression of ethical will, is not arbitrary, however; one need not even think of himself as having to *obey* the law if the law is one that has been arrived at in a way that expresses the ethical will.

Cassirer mentions the high compliment which Immanuel Kant paid to Rousseau when he said that just as Sir Isaac Newton was the first to see order in the seemingly irregular motions of the heavenly bodies, so "Rousseau was the first to discover in the variety and shapes that men assume the deeply concealed nature of man and to observe the hidden law that justifies Providence." It is well known that Kant learned from Rousseau to respect the moral judgment of the common man. Cassirer brings out other parallels between the writings of the two men.—*J.F.*

ADDITIONAL RECOMMENDED READING

Chapman, John W. *Rousseau: Totalitarian or Liberal.* New York: Columbia University Press, 1956. Contrasts Rousseau's liberalism with the classical British variety.

Cobban, Alfred. *Rousseau and the Modern State.* London: George Allen & Unwin, 1934. Considers the relevance of Rousseau's principles to the problems of modern democracies.

Grimsley, Ronald. *The Philosophy of Rousseau.* Oxford: Oxford University Press, 1973. A professor of French literature surveys Rousseau's ideas, with emphasis on his social thought.

Hendel, Charles W. *Jean-Jacques Rousseau: Moralist*. Indianapolis: Bobbs-Merrill, 1962. Detailed account of the development of Rousseau's philosophy. Useful for the advanced student.

Masters, Roger D. *The Political Philosophy of Rousseau*. Princeton, New Jersey: Princeton University Press, 1968. A commentary on pertinent writings of Rousseau by a political scientist.

NEW ESSAYS ON THE HUMAN UNDERSTANDING

Author: Gottfried Wilhelm von Leibniz (1646-1716)
Type of work: Epistemology, ontology
First published: 1765

PRINCIPAL IDEAS ADVANCED

Locke was mistaken in thinking that at birth the mind is like a blank tablet; certain ideas are innate, but they rise to consciousness only when the mind is provoked by experience.

Sense perception is active, not passive.

Locke's conception of simple ideas ignores such physical phenomena as the color spectrum and light waves; and his distinction between primary and secondary qualities is not necessary since it is possible to qualify perceptual generalizations carefully enough to allow for individual differences.

Locke's suggestion that substance might be nothing but a collection of properties cannot be tolerated, for reason has difficulty in accepting the idea of properties which are not the properties of anything.

External spatial and temporal relations cannot guarantee identity; it is by the internal modifications of substance that an individual acquires its identity.

An exact analysis of the signification of words would show us the workings of the understanding.

In 1707 Leibniz wrote to a friend concerning his *New Essays on the Human Understanding*: "My purpose has been to throw light upon things rather than to refute the opinions of another." He had undertaken this work in response to the criticisms of Cartesian rationalism appearing in John Locke's *An Essay Concerning Human Understanding* in 1690. It was completed about 1707, but Leibniz hesitated to publish it because of Locke's death in 1704; consequently, it did not appear in print until Leibniz himself had been dead for almost half a century. A study of the *New Essays* not only bears out the author's contention that his aim was constructive rather than merely critical, but also makes clear to the reader that Leibniz was one of the ablest and most universal thinkers of all time. Certainly European rationalism at that time had no better exponent than this thinker who combined a deep appreciation of past accomplishments in philosophy with a penetrating originality of his own.

The argument of the *New Essays* follows faithfully Locke's *Essay* and so is itself divided into four books dealing first with the question over innate ideas and truths, second with perception and ideas in general, third with the cognitive use of language, and fourth with the different kinds of cognitive statements and reasoning in which they appear.

The question of the existence of innate ideas and truths arose when Locke compared the human mind at its inception to a blank sheet of paper upon which experience alone wrote. In order to support the Platonic and Cartesian view that certain ideas and truths are innate and not inscribed by experience, Leibniz changed similes and compared the mind to a block of marble whose veins require the accommodation of experience—a view which was to become the foundation of Kant's theory of knowledge. Locke's objections to the contrary, ideas and truths did not have to be consciously entertained by all men, let alone enjoy universal assent, to be regarded as innate. They arose in consciousness and became known only when the mind was provoked by experience to reflect upon the necessary principles underlying the sensible world. Such reflection was not always easy and not all men were capable of it, for it required great powers of analysis and inventiveness in addition to the presentation of sense-experience. To illustrate his point Leibniz fondly recalled Socrates' midwifery in extracting from an ignorant slave boy knowledge of certain necessary and rather complicated geometrical relations (in Plato's *Meno*).

Though experience was often helpful to rational activity in bringing to light innate ideas and truths, Leibniz went on, the validity of such ideas and truths was certified by reason alone. The Pythagorean Theorem, he pointed out, established a necessary relationship of equality between the sum of the squares of the sides of a right-angled triangle and the square of its hypotenuse, but it was a proposition whose truth did not depend upon the empirical findings of surveyors. Ancient Egyptians discovered empirically that a corner of land whose sides measured three and four units would measure five units along its hypotenuse, but they never perceived the general and necessary truth behind this discovery. Their observation yielded to them what Leibniz called a truth of fact, but it was Greek geometers who perceived the truth of reason implicit in the factual discovery.

Leibniz, then, in defending the theory of innate ideas and truths was making an important epistemological distinction between those truths whose validity rested upon sense-experience and those truths whose validity did not; contingency earmarked the former and necessity the latter. Leibniz stole a march on Hume in claiming that the fact that things have been observed to happen in a certain way in the past is no guarantee that they will always happen that way. But he associated with this epistemological view the psychological proposition that innate ideas and truths existed in the mind prior to reflection or analysis as dispositions or preformations of their postanalytic emergence in consciousness. This theory was a modification of Plato's doctrine of reminiscence, though it is still unacceptable to some who however accept Leibniz's epistemological distinction. Perhaps still less generally acceptable is the metaphysical thesis Leibniz associated with the foregoing to the effect that truths of reason are identical with the timeless truths of nature which state what is always the case because they are ultimately the principles by which Supreme Reason or God has ordered the world for the best.

This intrusion of psychology and metaphysics into his theory of knowledge was regarded as quite natural by Leibniz, who did not believe it possible to separate epistemology altogether from psychological and metaphysical considerations. He was concerned throughout his philosophizing to exhibit the systematic interdependence of such various considerations and to find illumination in their interplay.

In the second book of the *New Essays* Leibniz turned his attention to Locke's theories of perception, of ideas in general, of substance, and of qualities and relations. He not only disputed Locke's contention that all ideas originate in either sense-experience or introspection—for Leibniz believed that such ideas as God, Being, Unity, and Substance, for example, cannot be traced either to sense-experience or to introspection and so are innate— but also the thesis that sense-perception is a purely passive affair. According to Locke and his successors, our senses are presented with clearly defined phenomena; different colors, shapes, sizes, feelings salute our senses and reveal their identity as they parade by. But Leibniz was convinced that this concept was a myth (now called by Kantians the myth of the given) and held it to be a gross oversimplification of what goes on in sense-perception. He said we must distinguish between what we now call subliminal perception— which is relatively passive but at the same time indistinct—and apperception, which is the attention paid to things within our range of perception in order to determine what kinds of things they are. One can see, for example, that something is actually a whirring hummingbird by attending apperceptively to it. But the terms "attending to" and "noticing" connote activity and not lazy passivity, and it is just such intellectual activity, according to Leibniz, which gives us clear and distinct ideas of what we perceive.

Together with this criticism Leibniz expressed doubt concerning the reality of Locke's simple ideas of such primary qualities as motion and rest and such secondary qualities as colors and tastes. Is the idea of motion really simple and unanalyzable, asked Leibniz? Do we not have to understand the motion of an object in terms of time spent and space covered by the moving object as well as by its relation to other objects? And is not any color to be understood as part of a color spectrum in which it is sometimes difficult to tell where one color leaves off and another begins, and are not all colors, moreover, reducible to different wave lengths of light? Such questions concerning these and other so-called simple ideas led Leibniz to reject their existence.

He was also unable to accept Locke's distinction between primary and secondary qualities, which was based upon the dependence of the latter upon conditions of perception. Honey might taste sweet, for example, to someone in good health but quite bitter to someone who was not. But what this and other examples of the vagaries of perception show, said Leibniz, is that although sensible qualities are indeed relative to the senses, there is nothing to prevent us from making an objective classification of such qualities on the basis of what normal percipients experience under normal conditions of perception. On this basis, he concluded, there is little point in distinguishing between primary and secondary qualities.

Here Leibniz anticipated Berkeley's rejection of this distinction, though, unlike Berkeley, he continued to believe in the real existence of an external physical world and did not erase the distinction between qualities and our ideas of them. Rather, he held with Descartes and Locke that the evidence of our senses faithfully represents the actual qualities of the physical world—though both Descartes and Locke made this claim only of primary qualities and not of their alleged secondary qualities.

To understand the doctrine of representation in the history of the theory of perception we should perhaps bear in mind that the thinkers we have been discussing were attempting to assimilate the physical hypotheses of their age concerning the role of light waves or corpuscles in making objects visible and concerning the reducibility of matter to colorless, tasteless atoms. Such hypotheses did not agree with common sense-experience, and the necessary but difficult task of drawing careful distinctions between the presuppositions of ordinary discourse on the one hand and scientific discourse on the other was only begun by such thinkers as Locke and Leibniz. Neither was entirely free of the confusions which result from failing to make such distinctions; but neither are many present-day philosophers and scientists.

Talk of qualities naturally leads to talk of substances, and indeed Leibniz's concern was with Locke's analysis of the presumably complex idea of substance. Gold, said Locke, is said to be a physical substance. Analyze it, however, and what does one find? Only, Locke argued, an assemblage of qualities such as yellowness, solidity, heaviness, fusibility, malleability, and dissolvability in *aqua regia*, but apart from such qualities one can discover nothing answering to substance as such. Deprive gold of these and its other properties and nothing remains. Thus, for Locke, the idea of substance either signified collections of qualities only or stood for something unperceivable— "a something, I know not what."

Leibniz agreed with Locke that to deprive a material object of all properties would be to leave nothing, the reason being that such properties are determinations of the object and one can more readily imagine an object losing some of its properties than one can imagine properties that are not properties of something. Had Leibniz been a contemporary of Lewis Carroll he might have pointed out that the Cheshire cat is not ridiculous when it ceases to grin, but that something is awry when it departs leaving its grin behind—something that could happen only in Wonderland. Leibniz was therefore more at home with the idea of concrete substances than with the idea of qualities abstracted from such substances, and unlike Locke he regarded the idea of substance as perfectly clear and distinct. He acknowledged that it was not an empirical notion, but held it to be a product of reason instead, and thus he laid the groundwork for Kant's analysis of substance as a category of knowledge.

It is, moreover, just this idea of substance, said Leibniz, which provides the key to the vexing problem of individuality. In Locke's view, no two entities could ever be confused with each other because they could never occupy the same point in space at the same time. All objects are externally related in time and space; since no two of them can have exactly the same temporal and spatial relationships to any other, they are each assured of separate numerical identity. But Leibniz argued that external relations could not of themselves guarantee separate identity, not only because it is far from clear that no two objects can occupy the same position in time and space (he challenged Locke's theory of the impenetrability of things and cited the possibility of two rays of light coinciding in time and space), but also because location in time and space is determined by reference to concrete physical objects in the first place; and so one cannot use time and space determinations to establish the identity of things without begging the question.

Leibniz therefore countered with a doctrine of internal relations to satisfy the requirements of physical and personal identity according to which individual substances affect and are affected uniquely by their environment. A person, for example, as a substantial being in interaction with the universe through ceaseless activity of body and mind (subliminally as well as consciously) has been undergoing internal modification from the moment of his inception. It cannot suffice to say, Leibniz declared in opposition to Locke, that personal identity is assured by the qualitative patterning of his life, since on the level of qualities and external relations only, in abstraction from the substances they qualify and relate, personality development is in principle duplicable over and over again. It is only when personality development is seen as involving the evolution of mind and body substances that genuine individuality is assured.

In this subtle line of argument the application of Leibniz's principles of natural continuity and the identity of indiscernibles is apparent, as was the application of his famous (and contentious) principle of preestablished harmony in his espousal of the representational theory of perception. The application of such principles is worth noticing because it illustrates once more Leibniz's eagerness to apply metaphysical principles to the solution of philosophic puzzles.

Human beings use language to express their ideas, and though language has more than one use its cognitive employment is extremely important. Thus, it became the subject of the third book of the *New Essays* where we find Leibniz contending against Locke's nominalistic tendencies. Such tendencies manifested themselves in the belief that only particular objects enjoy actual existence and that the essences, species, and genera debated by medieval philosophers are only abstract ideas existing in the human understanding. Nothing in the real world corresponds to such ideas, and Locke therefore wanted to treat them as somewhat arbitrary inventions. Leibniz sided with the realists and argued that talk of different species and genera as well as of the essential properties of things answered very definitely to reality. Was not discourse about species and genera founded upon undeniable and actual resemblances between, let us say, individual tigers on the one hand and tigers and other members of the cat family on the other? And do not all tigers have certain properties in common which make them what they are rather than something else, and do not all felines have certain properties which distinguish them? How can such talk be avoided, asked Leibniz, in giving a factual account of nature? And if it cannot be avoided, there is nothing arbitrary about it.

It is furthermore a *non sequitur*, he went on, to argue as Locke did from the difficulty we sometimes encounter in defining the essential characteristics of natural kinds to the conclusion that there are no such characteristics. All definitions are provisional or hypothetical and subject always to revision, but it does not follow that they are therefore vulnerable to subjective caprice; what it does mean, however, is that the search for the distinguishing characteristics of natural kinds is continuous, as is all scientific inquiry.

But we do not define only for purposes of natural classification, Leibniz pointed out. For other purposes we may give different connotations to general referring terms, but when we do so we should call such definitions logical in order to distinguish them from physical definitions grounded upon natural resemblances between objects. We might, for example, define "mate" for legal purposes more strictly than we do for biological purposes, but it would not follow that the legal term would then designate individuals not designated by the biological term and would thus unnaturally increase the world's membership. If we understand our varied aims in constructing definitions—biological, legal, and otherwise—we shall not be tempted to overpopulate the universe. There is fetching irony in the fact that Leibniz's realism permitted him to match Locke's concern for the possible abuses of words, and yet to warn against ungrounded mistrust of language and to conclude with what could well serve as the clarion call of modern linguistic analysis in philosophy: "I truly think that languages are the best mirrors of the human mind, and that an exact analysis of the signification of words would show us better than anything else the workings of the understanding."

In the remaining book of the *New Essays* Leibniz undertook to correct such Lockian impressions as that the laws of logic are trivial and unessential, that the family of cognitive statements includes only those that are either self-evident or follow from self-evident truths, and that deduction is the only accredited form of reasoning. He strongly defended the importance and utility of such intuitive general logical principles as those of identity, contradiction, and excluded-middle as well as other self-evident principles involved in formal reasoning such as the rules of syllogistic deduction. Appeal to such principles was useful in establishing the validity of deductive arguments even if it were true, as Locke maintained, that in common argumentation such principles were not explicitly mentioned. They did not have to be mentioned, said Leibniz, or even clearly recognized by men to count as the principles of correct reasoning and be relevant to logical appraisal. It was, moreover, in accordance with such principles that important theorems of mathematics and formal logic were derived. Leibniz therefore agreed with Locke that self-evident propositions and demonstrated theorems as found in mathematics and logic must be regarded as cognitive statements, but he rejected Locke's characterization of the general principles of logic as rather unnecessary to rational discourse. In so doing he anticipated well in advance the emphasis of our own day upon formal logic as an indispensable tool of inquiry.

Leibniz also went beyond Locke in stating that deductive reasoning is by no means the only acceptable mode of reasoning and that self-evident and demonstrated truths are not the only cognitive statements. He proposed that inductive reasoning and the statements found in the empirical sciences receive accreditation from the logician and epistemologist; he not only expressed the hope that a logic of probability and induction would receive speedy recognition and attention, but went further in suggesting that other modes of logic, such as judicial process, be investigated. It is interesting to note that Leibniz's farsighted advice in these respects went largely unheeded by logicians until quite recently.

We may also discover in Leibniz's views on logic and scientific method the outline of what has come to be called the hypothetico-deductive or explanatory-inductive method of modern science, according to which hypotheses are suggested by reason to account for an accumulation of empirical data; further consequences are then deduced from such hypotheses in order that they may be tested by sense-experience. Leibniz appreciated the importance of this method of scientific inquiry, and also saw clearly that modern scientific theory is a function of both empirical discovery and deductive theory. That is why he wanted to make room for "mixed" truths alongside straightforward truths of reason and truths of fact. Mixed truths would be those propositions derived from empirical hypotheses in accordance with the rules of deduction, enjoying no greater probability than their contingent empirical premises but yet entitled to cognitive status as probable truths. Leibniz even allowed for the possibility of certainty in the empirical sciences where there was sufficient confirmation for empirical propositions, but he carefully distinguished such practical or physical certainty from rational or metaphysical certainty.

What all this strongly suggests to the reader of the *New Essays* is that its author had a profound insight into the principles of human knowledge (including those of modern science), perhaps exceeding that of the author of the first *Essay*. Certainly the acceptance of many of Leibniz's insights into the theory of logic and knowledge by empiricists and rationalists alike is good evidence of the basic soundness of his ideas, or at least of their precious ability to stimulate further inquiry in these important areas of philosophic concern. No better tribute is possible to Leibniz's amazing stretch of mind and originality.—*F.S.*

PERTINENT LITERATURE

Broad, C. D. *Leibniz: An Introduction*. Edited by C. Lewy. Cambridge: Cambridge University Press, 1975.

C. D. Broad, author of *The Mind and Its Place in Nature* (1925) and Knight-bridge Professor of Moral Philosophy at Cambridge from 1933 to 1953, taught Gottfried Wilhelm von Leibniz to undergraduates at Cambridge, and after Broad's death in 1971, Dr. C. Lewy, Fellow of Trinity College and Reader in Philosophy, University of Cambridge, edited Broad's lectures, sought out the references, and prepared the book as an introduction to Leibniz.

The book begins with a five-page account of Leibniz's life, works, and influence. Broad then develops in considerable detail an account of general principles employed in Leibniz's work, with an emphasis on the "Predicate-in-Notion Principle," the Principle of Sufficient Reason, and the principle of the identity of indiscernibles. The author then deals with Leibniz's theory of corporeal substances, his theory of monads, and his psychology and theory of knowledge. The final two chapters are concerned with the ethics and theology. Broad's lectures are useful in that they are organized, comprehensible to students, analytical and critical, and informal (illuminated by relevant examples and parallels).

By the "Predicate-in-Notion" principle, Broad explains, is meant the principle that every substance has a complete "notion"; that is, for every individual there is an idea that exhausts everything that is true about or of the individual, including past, present, and future. Hence, the notion of an individual is complete, exhaustive, and exclusive. The notion of the predicate in a true judgment is contained in the notion of the subject. According to the "Principle of Sufficient Reason," there is a reason for every contingent fact. Broad explains that for Leibniz this principle is equivalent to the principle that there is an *a priori* proof that would show the connection of subject and predicate (in a factual judgment) to be based on the "natures" of the two terms. Leibniz believed the Predicate-in-Notion principle to be compatible with contingency because, as Broad explains it, he distinguished between absolutely and hypothetically necessary connections, and he regarded the connection between subject and predicate in a contingent proposition to be hypothetically necessary in that the connection was made freely by God.

Leibniz argued for the principle of the identity of indiscernibles—the principle that no two individuals can be exactly alike in all their properties—by attempting to relate it to the Predicate-in-Notion principle, Broad states. But, in Broad's opinion, Leibniz could not have proved the principle of the Identity of Indiscernibles by deducing it from the principle of Predicate-in-Notion. (Broad does point out, however, that Leibniz did not attempt such a proof.) Broad himself attempts to cast doubt on the connection by arguing that if the idea of two minds exactly alike is meaningful, there is nothing in the principle of Predicate-in-Notion that entails the impossibility of such a state of affairs.

In Chapter 5, "Psychology and the Theory of Knowledge," Broad deals specifically with the *New Essays*. According to Broad, Leibniz's views of mind and its activities were developed, or at least expressed, primarily in the criticism of René Descartes and John Locke. Broad emphasizes Leibniz's claim that there are unconscious perceptions, as well as Leibniz's distinction between perception and apperception. By "perception," Broad explains, Leibniz meant any kind of experience—feelings (of toothaches, of hunger), dreams, seeing a ghost, and so forth.

Broad considers whether unconscious experiences are possible, and in doing so he abandons Leibniz for the time being and considers the question directly by asking, in effect, whether under some circumstances (such as when a person is not paying attention or has a disposition that is not made manifest) we might be willing to describe his state of mind as that of having an "unconscious experience." For various reasons, which he gives by way of examples, Broad thinks that, in at least some senses of the expression, there are "unconscious experiences," but he points out that Leibniz assumes this proposition to be true without showing that it is.

Why did Leibniz need the belief that there are unconscious experiences? According to Broad, the belief was needed because if monads (simple substances: bare monads, animal souls, and rational souls) are to perceive other monads by the action of God, then, since one is not consciously aware of perceiving everything else in the universe, one must be unconsciously aware of doing so. (There are also a number of other claims that are supported by the presupposition that unconscious experiences are possible.)

The doctrine of unconscious experiences is also useful in accounting for the fact that we are often not aware of the innate ideas that Leibniz says we all have. As Broad explains it, Leibniz believed that whatever difficulty we may have in bringing innate ideas to the surface is occasioned not by our being ignorant but by our being unable to attend to and recognize those ideas.

Leibniz can still make the distinction between empirical and *a priori* ideas, Broad claims. The empirical ideas are derived by abstraction from sense experience; the *a priori* ideas involve necessities which are independent of sense experience.

Leibniz held a theory of representative perception, as most critics claim, but Broad suggests that the famous proposition "The monads have no windows" may have been used to mean not that the world cannot be viewed, but that the causal influence of the world cannot affect the monad. Broad then argues for the possibility of direct acquaintance of one monad with another, but he does not suggest that Leibniz held any such view.

Russell, Bertrand. *A Critical Exposition of the Philosophy of Leibniz*. London: George Allen & Unwin, 1900.

In the Preface to the first edition of his study of Gottfried Wilhelm von Leibniz, Bertrand Russell first of all makes clear his intention to provide a philosophical, not a historical, examination of Leibniz's work. He then explains how he came to believe that a new book on Leibniz was called for: previous studies had not shown how the various ideas central to Leibniz's thought—the noninteraction of the monads, the identity of indiscernibles, the principle of sufficient reason—could have arisen—as well as the grounds on which Leibniz presumed that they rested. Upon reading Leibniz's *Discours de métaphisique* and the letters to Arnauld, Russell realized that what appeared to be the "fantastic fairy tale" of the *Monadology* was deducible from "a few simple premises," premises that most philosophers would be willing to admit. Accordingly, the book begins with passages that provide the premises from which the essential doctrines of Leibniz's thought were deduced, and an Appendix provides a set of extracts supporting the various key points.

In the Preface to the second edition (1937), Russell announced that shortly after publication of the first edition, his central thesis—that Leibniz's philosophy was based on his logic—was confirmed by Louis Couturat's *La Logique de Leibniz*, published in 1901. Couturat had unearthed a considerable number of writings that supported the view Russell had abstracted from the *Discours* and the letters to Arnauld. The paper "Primae veritates," for example (published in the *Opuscules et fragments inedits de Leibniz*, 1903, contains the following passage (as translated by Russell) from which, Russell claims, "all the main doctrines of the 'Monadology' are deduced . . .": "Always therefore the predicate or consequent inheres in the subject or antecedent, and in this fact consists the nature of truth in general. . . . But this is true in every affirmative truth, universal or singular, necessary or contingent." Russell reports that Couturat showed that, according to Leibniz, the Principle of Sufficient Reason asserts that every true proposition is analytic (to be distinguished from the more familiar claim that every analytic proposition is true) and that from the analytic character of true propositions could be deduced the principle of the Identity of Indiscernibles (which requires that there be some difference other than numerical difference if there is to be individual difference).

Russell notes that the papers unearthed by Couturat show that Leibniz's logic was simpler (more direct) than Russell had supposed it to be. Russell mentions two important respects in which his views had changed between 1900 and 1937: in the first edition he declared that the propositions of pure mathematics are synthetic, but by 1937 (having come to know a great deal more of mathematical logic and of Georg Cantor's theory of infinite numbers) he realized that the propositions of mathematics are deducible from logic and hence are in that sense "analytic"; he also came to realize that his conclusion that not every monad could have a body composed of subordinate monads was based on the erroneous supposition that the number of monads must be finite (while the *Opuscules* contains Leibniz's remark that "In every particle of the universe, a world of infinite creatures is contained").

Russell sets forth five basic premises from which, he claims, the rest of Leibniz's philosophy follows: (1) "Every proposition has a subject and a predicate," (2) "A subject may have predicates which are qualities existing at various times (*Such a subject being called a substance*)," (3) "True propositions not asserting existence at particular times are necessary and analytic, but such as assert existence at particular times are contingent and synthetic [the latter depending upon final causes]," (4) "The Ego is a substance," and (5) "Perception yields knowledge of an external world, *i.e.* of existents other than myself and my states." Russell claims that the first premise is inconsistent with the fourth and fifth premises and that the inconsistency provides the ground for a general objection to Leibniz's philosophical view.

In Chapters II through V Russell discusses the first four premises and argues that most of the necessary propositions of Leibniz's system can be deduced from them; Chapters VI through XI present Russell's account of Leibniz's system (except for references to final causes and the good), while Chapters XII through XVI are concerned with Leibniz's accounts of the soul and the body, of perception, of knowledge, or proofs for the existence of God, and of ethics. (Russell comments that in dealing with the latter problems Leibniz followed Benedictus de Spinoza without acknowledgement and accordingly shows little originality in his work. Also, Russell says repeatedly, Leibniz avoided the expression of certain logical consequences of his views because of his wish to avoid unpleasant political consequences.)

Russell's discussion of Leibniz's claim that all propositions are reducible to subject-predicate form is interesting and acute; it foreshadows some of his later logical preoccupations in analysis. He proposes as the best examples of propositions that cannot be reduced to subject-predicate form such statements as "There are three men," which "assert plurality of subjects." Also, propositions asserting relations betwen subjects—such as relations of greater or less, whole and part—are irreducible to subject-predicate form, Russell contends, and he cites a passage in which Leibniz recognizes the problem but finally dismisses it by declaring that a relation is "a mere ideal thing, the consideration of which is nevertheless useful." (Russell suggests not only that Leibniz failed to recognize the difficulties residing in propositions about numbers and relations but also that a careful analysis of propositions would show that relations are more fundamental than subject-predicate form and that, in fact, the latter can be understood only by reference to the former.)

As to the *New Essays*, Russell argues (in Chapter XIV, "Leibniz's Theory of Knowledge") that the views expressed in this work are inconsistent with Leibniz's metaphysics. In any case, Russell claims, Leibniz's theory of knowledge is more a matter of psychology than it is of epistemology. Leibniz regarded knowable truths as innate; but innate truths come to be known only insofar as they become objects of apperception. Leibniz's effort in the *New Essays* is limited to a consideration of *necessary* truths, Russell points out, although his metaphysics would require that all truths be innate. The doctrine of innate necessary truths is "more like Kant's doctrine than it has any right to be," Russell declares: space, time, and the categories are innate, but the "qualities" are not.

The argument for the innateness of necessary ideas depends upon the presupposition (described by Russell as "radically vicious") that either knowledge is caused by what is known—as by physical objects in perception—or it is uncaused; hence, since Leibniz rejected the causal theory of perception, he argued that necessary ideas that can be known are innate. Russell calls the argument "scandalous."

At the close of the chapter Russell takes Leibniz to task for supposing that philosophy can be a kind of "universal mathematics," reducing all problems to symbolic expression and resolving them by means of logic. The business of philosophy, Russell declares, is the discovery of simple, indefinable, indemonstrable ideas which can serve as primitive axioms and upon which logical reasoning or scientific thinking can be based. The problems of philosophy, Russell concludes, are "anterior to deduction," and he points to Leibniz's belief in the analytic character of necessary truths as the root of Leibniz's error. (However, by the time of the second edition, as already noted, Russell was prepared to admit that the propositions of mathematics are analytic, not synthetic.—*I.P.M.*

ADDITIONAL RECOMMENDED READING

Rescher, Nicholas. *Leibniz: An Introduction to His Philosophy*. Totowa, New Jersey: Rowman and Littlefield, 1979. Rescher, a professor at the University of Pittsburgh, provides a clear and unifying account of Leibniz's views; he is critical of Russell's contention that Leibniz should have adopted the idea that all known truths are innate.

Schilpp, Paul A., ed. *The Philosophy of Bertrand Russell*. Evanston, Illinois: The Library of Living Philosophers, 1946. This collection of critical essays about Russell's work (including Russell's replies) contains many references to his study of Leibniz. See the *Index*.

Wiener, Philip P. "Method in Russell's Work on Leibniz," in *The Philosophy of Bertrand Russell*. Edited by Paul A. Schilpp. Evanston, Illinois: The Library of Living Philosophers, 1946. Wiener's analysis of Russell's method of criticism and its relation to Russell's developing philosophical views is penetrating and useful.

DIALOGUES CONCERNING NATURAL RELIGION

Author: David Hume (1711-1776)
Type of work: Philosophy of religion
First published: 1779

PRINCIPAL IDEAS ADVANCED

The argument from design is an argument which attempts to prove God's existence on the basis of signs of adaptability in nature, but it is an unsatisfactory argument because, although plausible, it does not demonstrate with logical certainty the truth of the claim that the universe was designed.

Furthermore, if we try to deduce the nature of God from the characteristics of nature regarded as his handiwork, God must be finite, imperfect, incompetent, and dependent.

It is possible that order in nature is the result of a natural generative process.

A priori *arguments designed to prove God's existence are inconclusive and establish only that something, not necessarily God, may have been a first cause.*

Although the cause of order in the universe probably bears some resemblance to human intelligence, nothing can be concluded concerning the moral character of such a cause.

Hume's *Dialogues Concerning Natural Religion* is one of the most famous works criticizing some of the arguments offered by philosophers and theologians to establish the existence and nature of God. Hume, who was known as the "Great Infidel" in his own time, began writing the *Dialogues* around 1751. He showed the manuscript to several of his friends, who dissuaded him from publishing it because of its irreligious content. Over the years, he revised the manuscript many times and finally, just before his death in 1776, he made his final revisions. He was very much concerned to make sure that the work would be published shortly after his death. In his will, he first requested his friend, the economist Adam Smith, to arrange for the publication of the *Dialogues*. When Smith refused, Hume next tried to get his publisher to do so, and when he also refused, Hume altered his will, instructing his nephew to take charge of the matter if the publisher had not done so within two years of his death. Finally, in 1779, the work appeared, gaining both immediate success and notoriety. It has remained one of the classic texts in discussions about the nature of the evidence presented to prove the existence of God and the character of his attributes.

The *Dialogues* are patterned after Cicero's work on the same subject, *The Nature of the Gods*, in which a Stoic, an Epicurean, and a Skeptic discuss the arguments about the nature and existence of the gods. Both Cicero and Hume found that the dialogue form enabled them to discuss these "dangerous" subjects without having to commit themselves personally to any particular view. They could allow their characters to attack various accepted arguments and positions, without themselves having to endorse or reject any specific religious view.

Hume begins the *Dialogues* with a letter from Pamphillus, a young man who was a spectator at the discussion, to his friend Hermippus. Pamphillus explains that the dialogue form is most suitable for discussing theology, because the subject, on the one hand, deals with a doctrine, the being of God, that is so obvious that it hardly admits of any dispute, while on the other hand, it leads to philosophical questions that are extremely obscure and uncertain regarding the nature, attributes, and decrees and plans of God. The dialogue form, presumably, can both inculcate the "obvious" truth, and explore the difficulties.

After having Philo and Cleanthes debate the merits of skepticism in Part I, Hume presents Philo and the orthodox Demea as agreeing that human reason is inadequate to comprehend divine truths. They concur in the view that there is no doubt concerning the existence of a deity, but that our natural and rational information is insufficient to justify any beliefs concerning the nature of the deity. Philo sums up the case by asserting that our ideas are all based upon experience and that we have no experience at all of divine attributes and operations. Thus, the nature of the Supreme Being is incomprehensible and mysterious.

Cleanthes immediately objects and states the theory that Hume analyzes in great detail throughout the *Dialogues*. The information and evidence that we have about the natural world, Cleanthes insists, enable us to infer both the existence and nature of a deity. He then presents what is called "the argument from design," an argument that had been current in both ancient and modern theological discussions, but which had become extremely popular in the form in which it was stated by Sir Isaac Newton. Look at the world, Cleanthes declares, and you will see that it is nothing but one vast machine, subdivided into smaller machines. All of the parts are adjusted to one another, so that the whole vast complex functions harmoniously. The adaptation of means to ends through all of nature exactly resembles the adaptation which results from human design and intelligence. Since natural objects and human artifacts resemble one another, we infer by analogy that the causes of them must also resemble one another. Hence the author of nature must be similar to the mind of man, though he must have greater faculties, since his production is greater.

Philo proceeds to criticize the argument from design by pointing out first that the analogy is not a good one. The universe is unlike a man-made object, such as a machine or a house. Also, we discover causes only from our experience; for example, from seeing houses being built or machines being constructed. We have never seen a universe being produced, so we cannot judge if it is made analogously to human productions. We have perceived many causal processes other than human design, processes like growth, attraction, and so on. For all that we can tell from our experience, any of these may be the cause of the natural world.

Cleanthes insists, in Part III, that the similarity of the works of nature to the works of human art is self-evident and undeniable. When we examine various aspects of nature in terms of the latest scientific information, the most obvious conclusion that we come to is that these aspects must be the result of design. By citing several examples, Cleanthes tries to show the immense plausibility of the argument from design. (In other works such as the *Natural History of Religion*, 1755, Hume always stressed the fact that a reasonable man could not help being impressed by the order and design in nature, and could not avoid coming to the conclusion that there must be some sort of intelligent orderer or designer of nature. However, Hume also insisted, as he did over and over again in the *Dialogues*, that no matter how convincing the argument may be, it is not logical, and can be challenged in many ways.)

To counterattack, Hume has Demea point out another failing of the argument from design. If we gained knowledge about God by analogy with the human mind, then we would have to conclude that the divine mind is as confused, as changeable, as subject to influence by the passions, as is man's. Such a picture of God is incompatible with that presented by traditional religions and by the famous theologians. In fact, as Philo and Demea point out in Parts IV and V, if the argument from design is accepted, then strange theology will ensue. Since man's mind is finite, by analogy so is God's mind. If God's mind is finite, he can err and be imperfect. If we have to judge God's attributes from the effects that we are aware of, what can we actually ascertain about God's nature? We cannot determine, from looking at the world, whether it represents a good achievement, as we have no standards of universe-construction by which we can judge. We cannot tell if the world that we perceive was made by one God or by many deities. If one takes the analogy involved in the argument from design seriously, all sorts of irrelevant conclusions are possible and any conclusion about the type of designer or designers is pure guesswork. "This world, for aught he [man] knows, is very faulty and imperfect, compared to a superior standard; and was only the first rude essay of some infant Deity, who afterwards abandoned it, ashamed of his lame performance; it is the work only of some dependent, inferior Deity; and is the object of derision to his superiors: it is the production of old age and dotage in some superannuated deity; and ever since his death, has run on at adventures, from the first impulse and active force, which it received from him. . . ." These and all sorts of other hypotheses are all possible explanations, by means of the argument from design, of the order in the universe.

Philo, in Parts VI-VIII, maintains that other explanations can be offered to account for the order in the world besides the explanation of a designer, and that these alternatives can be shown to be at least as probable. Two theories are considered, one that order results from a generative or growth process, and the other, that order is just the chance result of the way material particles come together. Over and over again we see order develop in nature as the result of biological growth. Seeds grow into organized plants. We do not see any outside designer introduce the order. Hence, if we judge solely by our experiences, one genuine possibility is that order is an unconscious result of the process of generation. The world, for all that we can tell, generates its own order just by developing. Since every day we see reason and order arise from growth development, as it does in children maturing, and never see organization proceeding from reason, it is a probable as well as a possible hypothesis to suppose that the order in the world comes from some inner biological process in the world, rather than from some designing cause outside it.

Even the ancient hypothesis of Epicurus, that the order in the world is due to "the fortuitous concourse of atoms" and that there is no external or internal designing or organizing force, suffices to account for the world as we know it. From our experience, it is just as probable that matter is the cause of its own motions as that mind or growth is. Also, nothing that we perceive proves that the present order of things did not simply come about by chance. Philo concludes the discussion on this point by asserting that an empirical theology, based solely on information gained from experience, would be inadequate to justify acceptance of any particular hypothesis about the source or cause of order in the world, or any particular religious system about the nature of the force or forces that govern the universe.

Demea, the orthodox believer, who has agreed with Philo's attack up to this point, now contends, in Part IX, that there are rational *a priori* arguments, not based on any empirical information whatsoever, that show that there must be a divine being. Demea states the classical theological argument that there must be a first cause, or God, that accounts for the sequence of causes occurring in the world. Hume has Cleanthes challenge this argument by introducing some of the skeptical contentions about causality and the inconclusiveness of *a priori* arguments that Hume had presented in his *A Treatise of Human Nature* (1739) and his *An Enquiry Concerning Human Understanding* (1748). Further, Hume points out that even if the *a priori* were legitimate, and even if it actually proved that there must be a first cause, or a necessarily existent being, it still would not show that this being had to be God. Perhaps the material world is itself the first cause, the cause of itself.

With this criticism, Hume concludes his considerations of arguments purporting to establish the existence of God, and turns to what can be known about God's nature or attributes. At the beginning of Part X, Philo and Demea rhapsodize about the misery and weakness of man, which Demea presents as the reason why man must seek God's protection. Philo uses the same information about man's plight to indicate that we cannot infer moral qualities of a deity from what is going on in the human world. If we knew what the deity is like, we might be able to explain, in terms of his perfect plan, why the evils of this world occur, and why there is so much human misery. But, since we do not know God's nature, we are not able to infer that he is perfect, wise, and good, from our limited knowledge of man's dismal and painful existence. Demea offers a religious explanation of the evils; namely, that our present existence is just a moment in the course of our existence. The present evil events will be recompensed and rectified in another realm, in an afterlife. But, Cleanthes insists, if man is to judge of divine matters from his experience, he has no information to support this religious supposition. The only way in which man can accept a belief in a benevolent deity is to deny Philo and Demea's thesis that human life is absolutely miserable. To this, Philo replies that the occurrence of any evil, any misery, any pain, no matter how small a part of human life it might be raises difficulties in ascertaining if God has the moral attributes accepted by traditional religions. If God possesses infinite power, wisdom, and goodness, how does anything unpleasant happen?

Cleanthes argues, in Part XI, that if one goes back to his analogy between man and the deity, an explanation can be offered. If the author of nature is only finitely perfect, then imperfections in the universe can be accounted for as being due to his limitations. Philo, in turn, argues that present experience provides no basis whatsoever for any inference about the moral attributes of the deity, and that the more we recognize man's weaknesses, the less we are capable of asserting in support of the religious hypothesis that the world is governed by a good and benevolent deity. If we knew that a good and wise God existed, then we might be able to account for the evils in this world by either the theories of Demea or Cleanthes. But if we have to build up our knowledge and our hypotheses from what we experience, then we will have to admit that there are four possibilities concerning the first causes of the universe: that they are completely good, that they are completely bad, that they are both good and bad, and that they are neither good nor bad. The good and the evil events in human experience make it difficult to conclude from our experience alone that one of the first two possibilities is the case.

As Philo explores the four possibilities and seems to be leaning toward the last, Demea realizes with dismay that he and Philo are not really in accord. Demea stresses the incomprehensible nature of God, the weakness of man's intellectual capacities, and the misery of his life as the basis for accepting orthodox theology. Philo employs the same points to lead to an agnostic conclusion, that we cannot know, because of our nature and God's, what he is actually like, and whether there is any explanation or justification for the character of the experienced world. Demea apparently accepted revealed information as the basis for answering the questions that man, by his own faculties, could not, while Philo turned only to man's experience for the answers and found that no definite ones could be given. As soon as Demea sees how wide the gap is between them, he leaves the discussion, and Philo and Cleanthes are left on the scene to evaluate the fruits of their arguments.

In the last part, XII, Philo offers what has been taken as a summary of Hume's own views about religion. Everywhere in nature there is evidence of design. As our scientific information increases, we become more, rather than less, impressed by the order that exists in the universe. The basic difficulty is that of determining the cause or source of the design. The difference between the atheist and the theist, and between the skeptic and the dogmatist, on this matter, is really only a verbal one. The theist admits that the designer, if he is intelligent, is very different from a human being. The atheist admits that the original principle of order in the world bears some remote analogy to human intelligence, though the degree of resemblance is indeterminable. Even a skeptic like Philo has to concede that we are compelled by nature to believe many things that we cannot prove, and one of them is that there is in the universe order which seems to require an intelligent orderer. And the dogmatist has to admit that there are insoluble difficulties in establishing any truths in this area as well as in any other. The skeptic keeps pointing out the difficulties, while the dogmatist keeps stressing what has to be believed.

When these arguments are taken into account, Philo points out, we are still in no position to assess the moral character of the designer. The evidence from the observable world is that works of nature have a greater resemblance to our artifacts than to our benevolent or good acts. Hence, we have more basis for maintaining that the natural attributes of the deity are like our own than for maintaining that his moral attributes are like human virtues. As a result, Philo advocates an amoral, philosophical, and rational religion. In 1776 Hume added a final summation: "the whole of natural theology . . . resolves itself into one simple, though somewhat ambiguous, at least undefined proposition, *that the cause or causes of order in the universe probably bear some remote analogy to human intelligence.*" Nothing more can be said, especially concerning the moral character of the cause or causes.

The dialogue concludes with two perplexing remarks. Philo announces as his parting observation that "To be a philosophical sceptic is, in a man of letters, the first and most essential step towards being a sound, believing Christian." This contention, which was made by all of the Christian skeptics from Michel de Montaigne to Pierre Bayle and Bishop Pierre-Daniel Huet, may have been a sincere conviction on their part. In Hume's case, there is no evidence that his skepticism led him to Christianity, but rather that it led him away from it.

At the very end, Hume has Pamphillus, the spectator, evaluate the entire discussion by saying that "PHILO'S principles are more probable than DEMEA'S; but . . . those of CLEANTHES approach still nearer the truth."

Critics have variously interpreted this ending, pointing out that Pamphillus and Hume may not agree, and that this conclusion may have been intended to quiet possible critics. Others have held that Hume himself may have felt, in spite of his devastating criticisms of Cleanthes' position, that it contained more truth than Philo's almost complete skepticism.

The *Dialogues Concerning Natural Religion* has been a central work in discussions about religious knowledge ever since its publication. It is generally recognized as presenting the most severe criticisms of the argument from design, in showing its limitations as an analogy and as a basis for reaching any fruitful conclusions about the nature of the designer of the world. Since Hume in the *Dialogues* discusses only the natural evidence for religion, some later theologians, especially Søren Kierkegaard, have insisted that Hume's arguments only make more clear the need for faith and revelation as the sole basis of religious knowledge.—*R.H.P.*

PERTINENT LITERATURE

Smith, Norman Kemp, ed. "Introduction," in David Hume's *Dialogues Concerning Natural Religion*. Indianapolis: Bobbs-Merrill, 1977.

This essay, first published in 1935, is probably the most important study on the *Dialogues Concerning Natural Religion*. First, Norman Kemp Smith corrects the published text of the work by comparing it with the manuscript in David Hume's own hand. (This is one of the very few works of Hume for which the manuscript has survived.) Thus Kemp Smith is able to show that some of the most skeptical portions of the *Dialogues* were added during the last years of Hume's life, when he knew he was dying.

Second, Kemp Smith makes a significant attempt to place Hume's critical views about religion in the context of the Scottish Calvinist background in which he was reared, and in the general Enlightenment background in which he flourished. Third, he compares the discussion in the *Dialogues* with the other major discussions of religion in Hume's writings, such as *The Natural History of Religion* and *An Enquiry Concerning Human Understanding*, which contain some apparently divergent views on the subject. Fourth, Kemp Smith carefully traces out some of Hume's sources for his *Dialogues*, especially Hume's use of the format in Cicero's *Nature of the Gods* and his use of fundamental arguments taken over from Pierre Bayle's *The Historical and Critical Dictionary*.

In analyzing the content of the *Dialogues*, Kemp Smith insists, in contrast to most of the interpreters of his time, that the skeptic, Philo, represents Hume's views from the beginning of the *Dialogues* to the perplexing end of the work. On the other hand, Kemp Smith claims that the Newtonian empiricist, Cleanthes, is Hume's mouthpiece only when he explicitly agrees with Philo. The drama of the *Dialogues* is the result of using both Cleanthes and

Demea as foils, so that the reader will see that the arguments in favor of religion, especially the argument from design, are not adequate to support any serious religious conclusions. Nature produces some conviction about the source of the order in the universe, but this conviction cannot support any definite, unambiguous claim about *an* or *the* Author of Nature. According to Kemp Smith, Hume stated his skeptical view about religious knowledge, both in the *Dialogues* and in *The Natural History of Religion*, with the least possible emphasis. This was done presumably so that the reader would have the least difficulty in first accepting Hume's devastating critique of arguments for religion, and then following on to Hume's quite negative view of religion. The conclusions of both the *Dialogues* and *The Natural History of Religion* indicate the inability of human reason to penetrate the enigma of religious knowledge. Hume placed the problem in the context of the rest of his philosophy and showed the basic limits of human reason. In the *Dialogues* as a whole, Kemp Smith points out, Hume indicated that the traditional arguments for religion are logically defective. At this point, it is up to the reader to decide whether to go along with Hume into a thoroughgoing skepticism about religious and other matters, or whether to consider the *Dialogues* as simply instructive of the defects of certain kinds of theological arguments. This second alternative could lead, as it does in the case of Demea, to a negative way to faith. In any case, Kemp Smith insists, Hume's analysis of religious argumentation and its influence on Immanuel Kant has greatly affected discussions of Divine Existence from the late eighteenth century on.

Pike, Nelson. "Hume on the Argument from Design," in David Hume's *Dialogues Concerning Natural Religion*. Edited by Nelson Pike. Indianapolis: Bobbs-Merrill, 1970.

Nelson Pike's essay deals primarily with the argument from design, which was David Hume's primary consideration in the *Dialogues*, and with Hume's reflections on that argument. Pike very carefully examines both Hume's formulation of the argument, in contrast to other significant versions of the time, and Hume's criticisms of the version of the argument he had stated. He begins by showing that one of the key weapons that Hume employed, that of separating the way terms are used to describe the Deity from the way they were normally used, had been analyzed by theologians such as St. Thomas Aquinas and Bishop Berkeley, who had patiently explained how the terms could be used significantly without the need for a separate and distinct meaning when referring to God.

Further, Pike insists that Hume unfairly criticized the empirical and scientific character of the analogy involved in the argument from design. Working carefully through the debate between Cleanthes and Philo (Demea's contribution is rarely considered), Pike attempts to show that a version of the argument from design could and did survive all of the challenges. Pike notes several dubious steps taken by Philo, or acceded to by Cleanthes, which, if rejected, would give the argument more force.

Similarly with the discussion in Dialogues X and XI, Pike carefully considers whether Philo had eliminated all possibilities for holding that God is moral in the face of human suffering, and contends that there is still a defensible religious position. The view of Philo in Dialogue XII becomes, for Pike, Hume's own attentuated theism, which is taken over from positions Cleanthes had held earlier in the work.

Contrary to Norman Kemp Smith, Pike argues that Hume was not giving a sop to the religions in the last dialogue. He stresses that the *Dialogues* was the one work Hume knew would be published only after his death; therefore, he had no reason at all to dissimulate. Further, in *The Natural History of Religion* and in his letter to his friend Gilbert Eliot in 1751, when he began working on the *Dialogues*, Hume clearly seemed to accept the argument from design as convincing to any rational person. The letter to Eliot can be read— and Pike has done so—as saying that Cleanthes, the believer in the argument, is supposed to represent Hume. From this evidence and from his very careful examination of the way the argument proceeds in the *Dialogues*, Pike concludes that Hume and Philo rejected the "scientific" version of the argument that contended that the same kind of empirical reasoning as used in science could be used in theology to prove that an intelligent designer exists. In contrast, from the time of his letter to Eliot onward, Hume was talking of an "irregular" argument that would lead from design to designer. Philo's espousal of the argument at the end, Pike argues, was on this basis. And he also stresses, as Philo also did, that this "irregular" argument from design provides very little, if any, support for a Christian theory.

The position that Pike sees Hume working out through the central discussion of the *Dialogues* was rather close to that set forth in portions of George Berkeley's dialogue on religion, *Alciphron*. Although Hume did not refer to that work in any of his writings on religion, Pike nevertheless offers the amusing suggestion that the best answer to the query "Who speaks for Hume in the Dialogues?" is not Philo or Cleanthes but rather Bishop Berkeley.

This essay provides both a very careful analysis of the mainstream of the argument in the *Dialogues*, and a most thought-provoking interpretation.

Yandell, Keith E. "Hume on Religious Belief," in *Hume: A Re-evaluation*. Edited by D. W. Livingston and J. T. King. New York: Fordham University Press, 1976.

Writing on the occasion of the two hundredth anniversary of David Hume's death, Keith E. Yandell declares that "There is no universal consent as to what view of religion Hume embraced." He then shows that apparently conflicting claims stated in Hume's *Dialogues* and *The Natural History of Religion* have been employed to support widely differing interpretations. Yandell insists that in spite of what appears in the texts, Hume had one clear view, often stated with studied ambiguity because of the emotional factors involved. This clear view can be found in a careful examination of Hume's way of expressing himself.

One thing that has led other commentators astray, Yandell asserts, is that they have first asked which of the characters in the *Dialogues* speaks for Hume. A variety of answers have been given, pointing to all of the characters except Demea. However, Yandell insists that no single character is always Hume's spokesman. Cleanthes, who states some of Hume's views, does hold to a very un-Humean thesis—that morality is dependent on religion, no matter how corrupted religion may be. Hume had attacked this view in his major works. Philo, in the early part of the *Dialogues*, had contended that one could suspend judgment about religious belief. Later, he joined Cleanthes in denying that position.

In the light of the conflicting data, Yandell holds that each of the characters, Cleanthes, Demea, and Philo, is at various times Hume's spokesman. To understand Hume's message, one should look into the significance of the *Dialogues* in the context of Hume's other writings on religion. His *The Natural History of Religion* asserts explicitly what the *Dialogues* say only implicitly. For Hume, the basic question here is, How is religious belief related to human nature? Hume contended in *The Natural History of Religion* that there is a propensity of all mankind to believe in some kind of invisible, intelligent power—which might be said to constitute a minimal theism. Beyond that, there are contrary propensities, built upon ignorance, hope, and fear, which lead people to develop more elaborate religious beliefs and to anthropomorphize their conception of the deity.

In terms of the sources of our beliefs, what does Hume (through Philo in the last dialogue) seem to believe? Has Philo (or Hume) suddenly changed his mind on the value of the argument from design? Yandell attempts to show that Hume is thoroughly consistent in having Philo at the end be a severe critic of natural theology and at the same time be a spokesman for natural religion. The latter arises naturally; but the attempt to interpret it as a set of theistic beliefs always remains open to a devastating Humean attack. Natural religion is not based on arguments; it rests only on passions and propensities. Philo (or Hume) in defending a minimal theism in the last dialogue is not thereby defending any kind of natural theology—only a natural belief. Even this natural belief, like belief in causality, the existence of the external world, and personal identity, is in conflict with other beliefs. Hume's thrust in all of his works was to show that we can never obtain adequate reasons for believing; yet we have to believe. Natural religion, as analyzed in both *The Natural History of Religion* and the *Dialogues*, rests on natural propensities; but beyond the most minimal theism is "a riddle, an enigma, and inexplicable mystery." Yandell contends that Hume in the *Dialogues* was advocating his general theory that although basic beliefs cannot be justified, neither can they be avoided. What can be examined is what these beliefs represent in terms of human nature. To appreciate what Hume accomplished in the area of religion, Yandell insists, the *Dialogues* should be examined not simply by reference to the views of the characters, but also by the consideration of Hume's other works on religion and philosophy. —*R.H.P.*

ADDITIONAL RECOMMENDED READING

Hurlbutt, Robert H. *Hume, Newton, and the Design Argument*. Lincoln: University of Nebraska Press, 1965. A study of the discussions of the design argument among the Newtonians and Hume.

Mossner, Ernest C. *The Life of David Hume*. Oxford: Clarendon Press, 1980. The definitive biography; extensive quotations from letters and other materials.

_____ . "The Religion of David Hume," in *Journal of the History of Ideas*. XXXIX, no. 4 (October-December, 1978), pp. 653-663. An attempt to characterize what Hume actually believed.

Penelhum, Terence. "Hume's Skepticism and the *Dialogues*," in *McGill Hume Studies*. Edited by David Norton, *et al*. San Diego: Austin Hill Press, 1979. An examination of whether Hume's discussion in the *Dialogues* is compatible with his skepticism.

Taylor, A. E., *et al*. "Symposium: The Present-Day Relevance of Hume's *Dialogues Concerning Natural Religion*," in *Aristotelian Society Proceedings*. XVIII (1939), pp. 179-205. A collection of discussions by some leading scholars of Hume's views about religion.

Wollheim, Richard, ed. "Introduction," in *Hume on Religion*. New York: World Publishing Company, 1963. A helpful explanatory introduction to a collection of Hume's writings on religion.

CRITIQUE OF PURE REASON

Author: Immanuel Kant (1724-1804)
Type of work: Metaphysics
First published: 1781

PRINCIPAL IDEAS ADVANCED

To establish the possibility of metaphysics as a science, it must be shown that synthetic a priori *truths are possible.*

Synthetic a priori *truths are universally and necessarily true (hence,* a priori*), but their necessity cannot be derived by analysis of the meanings of such truths (hence, they are synthetic).*

The two sources of knowledge are sensibility and understanding.

Space and time are the a priori *forms of sensibility (intuition); we are so constituted that we cannot perceive anything at all except by casting it into the forms of space and time.*

The a priori *conditions of our understanding are called the categories of our understanding; the categories of* quantity *are unity, plurality, and totality; of* quality*: reality, negation, and limitation; of* relation*: substance and accident, cause and effect, and reciprocity between agent and patient; of* modality*: possibility-impossibility, existence-nonexistence, and necessity-contingency.*

The principles of science which serve as presuppositions are synthetic a priori*; the possibility of such principles is based upon the use of* a priori *forms of intuition together with the categories of the understanding.*

Immanuel Kant's *Critique of Pure Reason* is an established classic in the history of epistemology. First published in 1781 and then revised in 1787, it is the fruit of Kant's later years and as such clearly reflects the insight and wisdom of a mature mind. It is a work in which the author attempted to conciliate two conflicting theories of knowledge current at his time—British empiricism as represented by Locke, Berkeley, and Hume; and Continental rationalism as represented by Descartes, Leibniz, and Wolff. The latter theory maintained that important truths about the natural and the supernatural world are knowable by pure reason alone, independently of perceptual experience, whereas the former held that perceptual experience is the source of all our legitimate concepts and truths of the world. Kant believed that both these doctrines were wrong, and he tried in the *Critique of Pure Reason* to correct the pretensions of each while saving what was sound in each. We can best see to what extent Kant succeeded in this undertaking by reviewing the main arguments of this great work.

Kant began his inquiry by asking why metaphysics had not kept pace with mathematics and natural science in the discovery of facts about our world. Celestial mechanics had been developed by Kepler at the beginning of the seventeenth century and terrestrial mechanics by Galileo later in the same century, and the two theories were soon united into one by Newton. These developments represented astonishing progress in natural science, but Kant could detect no parallel progress in metaphysics. Indeed, in metaphysics he saw only interminable squabbling with no apparent method for settling differences. So he asked whether it is at all possible for metaphysics to be a science.

Metaphysics can be a science, Kant reasoned, only if there exists a class of truths different in kind either from the straightforward synthetic truths of nature discoverable through sense-experience or from the straightforward analytic truths which owe their validity to the fact that the predicate term is contained in the subject term of such judgments—in other words, to the fact that they are true by virtue of the meanings of their terms, true by definition. This distinction is illustrated by the statements "Peaceful resistance is effective" (synthetic) and "Peaceful resisters shun violence" (analytic). This distinction had been recognized by Hume, who regarded it as exhausting the kinds of statements that can be true or false. But Kant believed that there are statements neither empirical nor analytic in character—synthetic *a priori* statements. These are statements which are true neither by definition nor because of facts discoverable through sense-experience. Rather, they can be seen to be true independently of sense-experience; in this sense they are *a priori* and necessarily true since no sense-experience can possibly confute them. Kant believed that all mathematical statements are of this sort—for example, "Seven plus five equals twelve." He also believed that synthetic *a priori* truths constitute the framework of Newtonian science, as we shall see shortly. But if such truths exist, Kant next asked himself, how are they possible?

They are possible, he said, if it can be shown that human knowledge is dependent upon certain concepts which are not empirical in origin but have their origin in human understanding. But even before he revealed the existence of such concepts he attempted to show in the first major division of the *Critique of Pure Reason*, entitled the "Transcendental Esthetic," that *a priori* considerations form the basis even of human perception or sensibility. This view was important to Kant, for in his proposed Copernican revolution in epistemology the two sources of knowledge are sensibility and understanding working in inseparable harness together. He had already written in the introduction to the *Critique* that all knowledge begins with experience, but it does not necessarily arise out of experience.

What are these *a priori* foundations of sensibility? According to Kant they are space and time. He reasoned that all objects of perception are necessarily located in space and time. Such objects may vary over a period of time in color, shape, size, and so on and still be perceptible objects, but they cannot be deprived of space and time and still remain perceptible. Even to establish ourselves as perceivers, and objects in our environment as objects of perception, requires the use of spatial and temporal terms; hence, the concepts of space and time. As percipients we regard perceived objects as separate from or distant from us; and we realize that our perceptions themselves, whether of external objects or of our own thoughts and feelings, succeed one another in time. We cannot represent them otherwise and still sensibly preserve the meaning of the terms "perceiver" and "object of perception." In this sense space and time deserve recognition as presuppositions of sense-experience. All our empirical, descriptive characterizations of perceptible objects take for granted their fundamental nature as objects in space and time. This is why Kant calls space and time *forms of intuition* in order to distinguish them from the *contents* of sense-experience. To be sure, portions of space and moments of time can be perceived, but such parts must always be understood as forming parts of an underlying continuum of space and time. (British phenomenalists like Berkeley and Hume were not in agreement with this interpretation of space and time, but whether we can agree with Kant in the details of his argument, we probably can agree with him that the perception of anything presupposes the existence of space and time.)

Believing that he had already exhibited the dependency of human knowledge upon conditions prior to immediate sense-experience, Kant next proceeded to a consideration of the *a priori* conditions of human understanding. We saw above that, in Kant's view, all knowledge is the product of human understanding applied to sense-experience. Does the understanding organize the contents of sense-experience according to its own rules—rules which must originate elsewhere than in sense-experience if their function is to categorize it? Such rules exist indeed, declared Kant, and he called them the *categories of the understanding*. He argued that there are twelve such categories and that they can be discovered and classified by careful scrutiny of the logical forms of the judgments we characteristically make about the world. For example, if we look at our categorical judgments we see that they contain a referring expression which we call the grammatical *subject* and a characterizing expression which we call the *predicate*. In "Beethoven was a great composer" the referring or subject term is of course "Beethoven," and our characterizing or predicate term is "great composer." Now a tremendous number of the factual claims we normally make are of this same basic form—*substance* and predicated *property*—and for Kant, therefore, the concept of substance deserves the status of a category of knowledge. Under it are subsumed all the substance-words in our conceptual scheme of things, such as "table," "tree," "moon," "nail," and so on, which denote material objects in our environment. It is thus a familylike concept denoting all those objects which have *substantiality* in common, something which none of the individual terms in this category does.

Much the same point can be made about the concept of *causality*, to take another of Kant's categories, which he derived from the form of hypothetical or conditional judgments—our "if . . . then" judgments. "If water is heated under normal atmospheric conditions to 212°F, it will boil" and "If one suppresses his guilt-feelings he will become neurotic" are examples of hypothetical judgments which assert a causal connection between the states of affairs mentioned by the antecedent and consequent of such judgments. Such judgments also appear frequently in our factual reports on the world and suggest that the concept of causality is an important and fundamental concept in our way of recording experience. It is a concept embracing numerous words in our language, such as "create," "produce," "bring about," "make," and so forth, all of which are causal terms. By virtue of designing such a large family of terms the concept of causality must be regarded as one of the relatively few root concepts or categories at the basis of our conceptual scheme which give this scheme its flavor by influencing it throughout. The importance of causality is something which Kant clearly saw, even though it had been missed by the British phenomenalists.

Many philosophers have disagreed with Kant over his number and selection of categories as well as his method of arriving at them, but they have not taken issue with him as to the existence of categories in our conceptual framework and their importance in any account of human knowledge. But many others have rejected Kant's major contention that human knowledge is dependent upon such categories as substance and causality and so have sided with Hume, who, not finding anything answering to such categories in immediate sense-experience, proceeded to dismiss them as fictitious. Kant, of course, agreed with Hume that substance and causality are not to be found *in* sense-experience, but he insisted nevertheless that they are necessary ingredients in a world about which we can hope to have knowledge. The Kantian point is sometimes made by saying that unless one assumes that the general features referred by one's judgments persist in time and are public entities independent of any particular percipient, there can be no confirmation judgments and consequently no knowledge at all. Kant saw this simple but essential point when he stated that the categories are necessary conditions for our having any knowledge whatsoever.

He also saw that categories such as substance and causality are by no means arbitrary impositions upon sense-experience, as is sometimes implied by Hume and his followers, but are useful concepts since sense-experience testifies to a great amount of orderliness in the world rather than to a befuddling chaos. It is the presence of order observable by all which vindicates the use of such ordering principles as substance and causality—they would have no utility whatever in a chaotic world.

It is chiefly as ordering principles that Kant viewed the categories. What they order or synthesize in his partly phenomenalistic theory of knowledge are the items of experience—colors, shapes, sizes, sounds, tactile impressions, odors, and so on. But Kant believed that there is a problem in showing how such *a priori* principles can be applied to empirical data, and he thought that the answer to this problem is to be found in the mediatory power of time which, as seen above, is an *a priori* ordering form which is a necessary condition of sense-experience. Kant proceeded to relate the categories to the concept of time, and it was this merger of the concepts of substance, causality, and time which paved the way to his discussion of the presuppositions of Newtonian science. Kant believed that there are three such presuppositions; namely, the principles of the conservation of matter, of universal causality, and of the universal interrelation of all things making up the natural world. (We recalled that in the Newtonian view of the universe all objects were considered to be made up of material particles governed in their behavior by the universal laws of motion and attraction.)

Such principles are not analytic truths, according to Kant, since their denials are not self-contradictory, nor are they empirical generalizations since we know them to be necessarily true, and no empirical generalization is ever necessarily true. They must therefore be genuine synthetic *a priori* truths, and their possibility arises from the fact that they utilize *a priori* concepts whose use is indispensable to human knowledge and yet whose only sanctioned cognitive use is in relation to the objects of sense-experience in the manner dictated by the principles in question themselves.

Kant's argument in this respect is somewhat circular, though it has been defended as illuminating by thinkers who believe that any examination of basic principles must inevitably be circular in that they must be elucidated in terms of one another. But his argument has not been convincing to many others who, although granting that Kant isolated the main presuppositions of the scientific thinking of his day, do not concede that the presuppositions are synthetic *a priori*. Such critics argue that is it one thing to show that certain concepts are not empirical in origin and another to show that the judgments in which they figure are *a priori*. Concepts such as substance and causality may indeed underlie our factual discourse about the world and so be necessary and ineradicable concepts to intelligible and informative discourse, but it is not at all evident that the principles in which they occur—such as that the quantity of substance remains invariant throughout all physical transformations—are necessarily true. Such principles may be fruitful guideposts in scientific inquiry, yet not be true or false judgments at all, merely heuristic rules in the way that Kant himself was to regard certain metaphysical concepts as we shall see shortly.

Up to this point Kant's concern was to explore the foundations of scientific knowledge and to disclose the dependency of such knowledge upon a handful of forms, concepts, and principles. In this exploration he clashed sometimes head-on, sometimes obliquely, as we have seen, with accounts of human knowledge provided by British empiricists. But his conclusions thus far were also brewing trouble and embarrassment for Continental rationalism as well. For what follows from showing that concepts such as causality and substance are presuppositions of empirical knowledge? It follows, Kant said, that their use independent of sense-experience is illegitimate and can only result in conceptual difficulties and empty noise. We recall that Kant's initial concern was to determine whether men can fruitfully engage in metaphysical speculation. In his time such speculation chiefly revolved around such matters as the immortality of the soul, the origin and extent of the universe, and the existence and nature of God. Was a science of such matters really possible? In the third and concluding portion of his inquiry, called the "Transcendental Dialectic" (that dealing with the categories and principles he had termed the "Transcendental Analytic"), Kant's answer to this burning question was an unequivocal "No!"

Kant identified the main concepts of the above-mentioned metaphysical issues as the psychological idea, or *soul*; the cosmological idea, or *world*; and the theological idea, or *God*; and he considered the author of such ideas to be human reason rather than human understanding or sensibility. But why is human reason unable to develop these ideas cogently and scientifically? Kant's chief explanation for this debility was that nothing in sense-experience corresponds to the ideas of pure reason and thus there can be no control over their speculative use.

Cartesians and Leibnizians, for example, argued that the soul was an immaterial, simple, therefore indestructible substance. But where is the empirical support for such claims? It does not exist, said Kant, and furthermore the reasoning leading up to such conclusions is wholly fallacious. These Cartesians and Leibnizians have treated the "I think" or *cogito*—that is presupposed by all acts of knowing—as the logical subject of our judgments analogous to the way in which "Beethoven" is the subject of the judgment "Beethoven became deaf in his later years"; further, Cartesians and Leibnizians have argued that just as "Beethoven" designates a real person, so does the knowing subject of the *cogito*. Kant's rebuttal to this argument consisted of saying that it is an analytic truth that acts of knowing presuppose a knower, but the existence of the knower is an empirical question which cannot be inferred from an analytic truth whose validity is founded upon the meaning of terms. The existence of the soul as well as its properties must remain an empirical question, and the concept of substance is properly applied only to the self that is the object of empirical psychology.

Kant next turned to metaphysical speculation about the universe at large. Men have always asked themselves with respect to the universe whether it had a beginning in time or has always existed, whether it is finitely or infinitely extended in space, and whether it was created. Kant showed that no definitive answers are possible to such questions. Indeed, he argued that reasoning can establish with equal cogency alternative answers to such questions. His explanation for such a disconcerting and paradoxical state of affairs in meta-physics was that one cannot regard the universe as a substance or given entity in the way a desk, for example, can be so regarded. It is of course meaningful to ask when a certain desk was made, how it was made, and what its spatial boundaries are. Such questions can be settled empirically, for we can trace the history of the desk and have it before us to measure. But this investigation of the properties of the desk and the countless ones like it which we undertake in our daily lives occur within the framework of the universe, so that the questions that can significantly be raised about things within the universe cannot significantly or profitably be asked of the universe itself. If the cate-gories of substance and causality have as their proper epistemic function the characterization of given and possible objects of perception, it is an improper use of such categories to apply them to what is neither a given nor even a possible object of perception such as the universe. Because it is not such an object, the universe cannot serve as a check or control upon our speculations about it; and it is this basic consideration again which explains reason's in-competence in this area.

Can human reason do any better, then, in the area of theological specu-lation? Can it, in the absence of empirical evidence, produce convincing arguments for God's existence, his benevolence, omniscience, and so forth? Kant surveyed the standard arguments or alleged proofs for the existence of God and concluded that none of them have any real force. He found that arguments which use the facts of existence, design, and causality in nature to support claims on behalf of divine existence not only make an unwarranted leap from the known to the unknown, but also fall back on the ontological argument for the existence of God as propounded successively by Saint An-selm, Descartes, and Leibniz. This famous and captivating argument begins with the premise that God is the being greater than which nothing is con-ceivable, and with the help of a subordinate premise to the effect that existence in the real world is better than existence merely in idea proceeds to the conclusion that God must exist, for if he did not he would not then be the greatest conceivable entity.

Kant's rebuttal of the ontological argument consists of saying that all ex-istential statements of the form "X exists" are synthetic a posteriori and must be established on empirical grounds. If the major premise of the ontological argument is analytic, then existence is included in the definition of "God" and one has in effect defined God into existence. But, Kant asked, can we by definition define anything into existence, or must we not look beyond our concept of something in order to determine whether it genuinely exists? Kant added that it is in any case a mistake to view existence as a predicate like any other, since in all statements in which referring expressions such as "God" occur as subject terms the existence of the denoted object(s) is not asserted by such statements but rather taken for granted in order to see what is attributed truly or falsely to the denoted object(s). But if existence is taken for granted in this way, then as far as the ontological argument is concerned one has assumed the very point in question and the argument is question-begging.

The results of Kant's inquiry into classical metaphysics prompted him to reject the view that the leading concepts of such speculation have any constitutive place in human knowledge at all. Such concepts do not enter into the weblike structure of our knowledge of the world, as do the categories in his view. But Kant did not progress further to the Humian conclusion that metaphysical works containing these concepts should therefore be consigned to the flames. On the contrary he argued that although such concepts do not have a constitutive role in human knowledge, they nevertheless have a vital regulative function in the scientific quest, for they posit a systematic unity to the world and so stimulate scientists to look for connections in nature, even between such diverse elements, say, as falling apples and orbiting planets. It is pure reason with its concept of an ordering, purposeful, and wholly rational God, for example, which proposes for investigation the idea that the world created by God must be rationally constructed throughout and so reward experimental inquiry by men similarly endowed with reason. No other faculty of the mind was for Kant capable of such a stirring vision.

In this remarkable conclusion to his inquiry into the contributing factors of human knowledge, Kant plainly conceded enormous importance to pure reason, although not that exactly which rationalists defended. He therefore no more appeased the rationalists than he did the British empiricists.

Many philosophers since Kant have appreciated his middle road between rationalism and empiricism, even if they have not been able to accept the details of this reasoning, and they have credited Kant with the rare ability to raise problems worthy of philosophical investigation.

But other philosophers have not been impressed by Kant's strictures against rationalism and empiricism, and they have borrowed from his meticulous genius (happily wedded to broad vision) what suits their purposes while ignoring what does not. Thus Hegel, for example, was stimulated by Kant to seize upon pure reason's dialectical tendencies—so futile in Kant's view—and erect upon such tendencies a complete picture of history and the world—quite often at the expense of empirical facts. And latter-day phenomenalists such as John Stuart Mill and Bertrand Russell have persisted in the search for the foundations of human knowledge among sense-data (more lately in conjunction with formal logic), which in all their fleeting transiency are so much unlike Kant's enduring and causally ordered substances.

But most philosophical critics assent to the rich stimulation of Kant's ever surprising fertile mind and rank him among the great philosophers of all time.—*E.S.*

PERTINENT LITERATURE
Ewing, A. C. *A Short Commentary on Kant's Critique of Pure Reason*.
London: Methuen, 1938.

In his Preface, A. C. Ewing acknowledges his indebtedness to Norman
Kemp Smith for his *Commentary to Kant's Critique of Pure Reason* (1918)
and to H. J. Paton for his *Kant's Metaphysic of Experience* (1936), but he
notes that their influence "often operates in reverse directions." Paton's commentary changed many of Ewing's ideas that were influenced by Kemp Smith's
commentary, but Ewing admits that he was strongly influenced by both.

Ewing's Introduction points out that Immanuel Kant wrote the *Critique of
Pure Reason* as a preliminary investigation of the human faculties of knowledge to prepare the way for the intellect's most important task—that of
constructing a satisfactory metaphysics; but Kant realized, when his work was
completed, that there was no room for any further metaphysics: the *Critique
of Pure Reason* had done it all.

Although originally profoundly influenced by Gottfried Wilhelm von Leibniz's views, Kant was led by accounts of David Hume's *Treatise of Human
Nature* to deny the possibility of *a priori* knowledge of the real world. He
designed the *Critique of Pure Reason* to answer two fundamental questions
(according to Ewing): (1) How can the *a priori* categories be applied to
appearances in advance of experience, and (2) Is there any justification for
applying the *a priori* categories to reality?

Ewing argues that despite verbal inconsistencies in Kant's work (composed
over an eleven-year period), it is possible to put together a consistent doctrine,
and it is reasonable to assume that had the work been purged of its contradictions, it would have been so unified.

According to Ewing, the *Critique of Pure Reason* has two main aims: (1)
to provide science with a philosophical basis in the *a priori*, and (2) to provide
faith with adequate grounds even though such grounds fell short of knowledge.
The latter aim, if achieved, was to prepare the way for the ethical arguments
of the *Critique of Practical Reason*, and Kant hoped that in solving the problem
of freedom, by showing freedom to be compatible with causality, he would
make sense of ethics.

Kant realized that although it can be shown that the categories apply to
objects of experience and that the *a priori* rests on that possibility, the categories could not be referred to in the attempt to prove propositions having
to do with God, freedom, and immortality, for the categories did not apply
to matters falling outside the realm of experience.

Ewing compares Kant's effort in "critical" philosophy to that which would
be made by investigators who compared objects they saw clearly with objects
they saw dimly and then made generalizations about the two kinds of objects
so seen, and explained by reference to a theory of vision why the one kind

was seen clearly and the other dimly.

The author warns the reader that his work is intended to be a commentary to be read in conjunction with Kant's work and not as a self-contained essay on the *Critique of Pure Reason*. It falls between the more detailed and extensive commentaries of Edward Caird, Kemp Smith, and Paton on the one hand, and the brief accounts given by Robert Adamson and A. D. Lindsay on the other. He also comments that his work is one of exegesis, not criticism, although occasionally, for the sake of clarity, some criticism is advanced.

Ewing describes Kant's claim to completeness and certainty (in the Preface to the first edition) "audacious," and he points out that even a great philosopher may commit errors (and hence can hardly lay claim to certainty) and that there is always something more to be said about any important subject.

Among the most useful comments made in Ewing's Introduction is that having to do with the term *Anschauung*, usually translated "intuition." Ewing indicates that the sense of the term in Kant is different from the sense of the term "intuition" in English (an *a priori* insight not based on conscious reasoning). In Kant the term *Anschauung* means, Ewing suggests, "awareness of individual entities" (as by looking at something). But Ewing rejects the use of the word "perception" in translation since it is at least possible that there are beings other than human beings that are aware of individual entities without having to perceive them.

Ewing's discussion of the question as to whether there are synthetic *a priori* judgments (propositions) is also interesting and useful. Many philosophers confuse two possible meanings of the term "analytic proposition," according to Ewing: some think that an analytic proposition is that which yields no new knowledge, while others suppose it is a proposition that becomes self-contradictory when denied. Ewing claims that the proposition that a judgment which is analytic in the second sense must be analytic in the first sense is itself a synthetic judgment—hence, the effort to deny synthetic *a priori* propositions yields a synthetic *a priori* proposition.

The distinction between "transcendent" and "transcendental" is also important, Ewing points out. The term "transcendent" refers to what is not a possible object of knowledge, while the term "transcendental" refers to the necessary conditions of experience. Hence, transcendental knowledge is possible, according to Kant, in that by reference to the conditions of knowledge one understands how synthetic *a priori* propositions are possible as applying to the "appearances" or objects of experience.

Ewing's commentary is careful and thorough, and he is particularly careful to point out differences between what terms in translation ordinarily mean and what they mean in the context of Kant's thought. He is also determined to show the development of Kant's thought even in cases—and perhaps especially in cases—in which the development or transition is not at all clear in the *Critique of Pure Reason* itself.

In his commentary Ewing discusses "The Transcendental Aesthetic" (which has to do with perception, not beauty), "The Transcendental Deduction of the Categories," "The Individual Categories and Their Proofs," "Kant's Attitude to Material Idealism. The Thing-in-Itself," "The Paralogisms and the Antinomies," and "Theology and the Ideas of Reason."

Weldon, T. D. *Introduction to Kant's* Critique of Pure Reason. Oxford: Clarendon Press, 1945.

In the Preface to the first edition of his study of Immanuel Kant's *Critique of Pure Reason*, T. D. Weldon disclaims any intention of writing another commentary; he cites H. J. Paton and Herman Jean de Vleeschauwer as having provided substantial and authoritative commentaries. Weldon's intention is to discuss the *Critique of Pure Reason* as an account of Critical Philosophy, and he maintains that such an account must make clear the context in which Kant's book was written (as influenced by René Descartes, Gottfried Wilhelm von Leibniz, and Sir Isaac Newton—not Albert Einstein, Werner Heisenberg, and Erwin Schrödinger).

Weldon's book begins with a discussion of the European influences (Descartes, Leibniz, John Locke, and David Hume) and the "local" influences (Christian von Wolff, A. G. Baumgarten, and G. F. Meier) on Kant. The problem for the Europeans, Weldon suggests, was that of reconciling the new experimental methods of science (including the use of mathematics) with metaphysics and theology. Many of the problems were of the sort we now call linguistic, Weldon claims, but he warns that it is an oversimplification to presume that the linguistic approach does justice to the issues. (One notes, however, that in his conclusion to the book Weldon claims that Kant's distinction between things-in-themselves and phenomena was "not a distinction between two types of entity but a distinction between two alternative ways of talking about the world.")

Weldon then comments on Kant's early works—from the *Correct Method of Calculating the Active Force of Bodies* (1747) through *Dreams of a Spirit-Seer* (1766, an examination of issues raised by the doctrines of Emanuel Swedenborg) to the Dissertation of 1770 (*De mundi sensibilis atque intelligibilis forma et principiis*). Weldon points out that although in the *Dissertation* Kant argued that things *qua* sensuous are apprehended through sensibility, he was inclined to think that through pure reason one could know independently existing real objects *qua* intelligible. The transition to the viewpoint of the Critical Philosophy was perhaps incited by Hume's work, Weldon suggests.

In Part II Weldon summarizes and discusses in detail the argument of the *Critique of Pure Reason*, including the Prefaces, the *Aesthetic*, the *Analytic*, and the *Dialectic*.

Weldon describes Kant as a "logician rather than an epistemologist" in the formulation and answering of the fundamental question about the limits of knowledge and the consequences of limitation to beliefs in God, freedom, and immortality. Although Kant argued that only phenomena can be known—and that they are known *a priori*: "objects must conform to our knowledge"—the distinction between things as they appear and as they are "in-themselves" made it possible to argue that belief in God and immortality, and hence the belief in freedom, was compatible with the limitation of knowledge to the phenomena.

The aim of the *Aesthetic* is described by Weldon as that of demonstrating that the axioms of arithmetic and geometry are applicable to phenomena; the aim of the *Analytic* is to do the same for physics. (The solution, of course, was to refer to the forms of space and time as imposed on what is given in experience, and to the concepts of the understanding as making possible the derivation of the axioms of physics.)

The purpose of the *Dialectic*, Weldon writes, was to account for the transcendent ideas of God, freedom, and immortality, and to explain how metaphysics can yield knowledge. Just as the *Aesthetic* developed the "transcendental implications of sensibility," and the *Analytic* the transcendental implications of the understanding's use of concepts, so the *Dialectic* develops the transcendental implications of reason's capacity for inference.

In Part III, "Inner Sense and Transcendental Synthesis," Weldon examines Kant's assumption of an "inner sense" and his unanalyzed assumptions about modes of perception. Weldon contends that if Kant had concentrated on the *function* of "models," such as the Newtonian model of physical reality, instead of on the *origin* of such models (in the "transcendental imagination") he would have come closer to what modern scientific theory concentrates on and would thus have avoided many of the problems occasioned by adopting a deficient or unclear empirical psychology.

Weldon contends that Kant's achievement was that of making clear what happens in the course of scientific thinking and in emphasizing (although, Weldon says, he did not realize that he was doing so) ways of talking about the world. His work provides a foundation for the philosophical analysis of scientific method. Insofar as Kant falls short, Weldon states, he did so because he was handicapped by the limitations of Newtonian physics, Aristotolian logic, and the empirical psychology of Locke, Hume, and J. N. Tetens. —*I.P.M.*

ADDITIONAL RECOMMENDED READING

Cassirer, H. W. *Kant's First Critique*. New York: Humanities Press, 1954. A commentary on the *Critique of Pure Reason* that emphasizes both Kant's contributions and his errors and weaknesses.

Paton, H. J. *Kant's Metaphysic of Experience*. New York: Humanities Press,

1936. A widely used commentary on the first half of the *Critique of Pure Reason*. Paton argues, in opposition to Kemp Smith, that the *Critique of Pure Reason* is a coherent work and that its critical method provides the philosophy of science with a useful tool.

Smith, Norman Kemp. *A Commentary to Kant's "Critique of Pure Reason"*. London: Macmillan and Company, 1918. One of the standard commentaries despite Kemp Smith's adoption, at least in part, of what Paton calls the "mosaic or patchwork" theory defended by Erich Adickes and Hans Vaihinger—the theory that the *Critique of Pure Reason*, especially the "Transcendental Deduction" of the first edition, was put together by combining passages written at different times and sometimes conflicting.

FOUNDATIONS OF THE METAPHYSICS OF MORALS

Author: Immanuel Kant (1724-1804)
Type of work: Ethics
First published: 1785

PRINCIPAL IDEAS ADVANCED

Nothing is unconditionally good except the good will.

The good will, which is the rational will, acts not merely in accordance *with* duty but from *duty.*

The good will wills as obedient to the moral law.

Duty consists in observing the categorical imperative: Act only according to that maxim by which you can at the same time will that it should become a universal law.

A second form of the categorical imperative is: Act so that you treat humanity, whether in your own person or that of another, always as an end and never as a means only.

A third form of the categorical imperative is: Act always as if you were legislating for a universal realm of ends.

Ethics, like physics, so Immanuel Kant holds in the *Foundations of the Metaphysics of Morals* (*Grundlegung zur Metaphysik der Sitten*), is partly empirical and partly *a priori*. This work deals only with the *a priori* part in that it is based entirely on the use of reason without recourse to experience. Everyone must recognize, Kant writes, that since moral laws imply absolute necessity, they cannot be merely empirical. For example, "Thou shalt not lie" applies not merely to all human beings but to all rational beings. Its ground, therefore, must be found in pure reason. Moreover, what is done morally must be not only in accordance with law but also done for the sake of law; if this were not its motivation, different circumstances of the agent would call forth different responses.

This book, issued as a preliminary to an intended metaphysic of morals, the *Critique of Practical Reason* (1788), comprises a critical examination of purely practical reason and establishes the supreme principle of morality. The order of inquiry is from common moral knowledge to the supreme principle (analysis), then back to application in practice (synthesis).

Kant begins by claiming that "Nothing in the world—indeed nothing even beyond the world—can possibly be conceived which could be called good without qualification except a *good will*." Not intelligence, wit, judgment, courage, or the gifts of fortune; possession of them is a positive evil if not combined with good will, which indeed is the indispensable condition even of worthiness to be happy. And although moderation, self-control, and calm deliberation are all conducive to good will, they can also characterize the cool villain and make him even more abominable. The goodness of the good will does not depend on its accomplishments; it "would sparkle like a jewel in its own right, as something that had its full worth in itself," even if external circumstances entirely frustrated its actions.

The good will is the rational will. Why has nature appointed reason to rule the will? Not for the sake of adaptation, which would be more efficiently accomplished by instinct. Moreover, when a cultivated reason makes enjoyment its end, true contentment rarely ensues. Reason, then, is intended for something more worthy than production of happiness. Being a practical faculty, yet not suitable for producing a will good merely as a means (instinct would do better), reason must be given us to produce a will good in itself. Everyone knows, at least implicitly, according to Kant, the concept of a will good in itself. We need only bring to light that to which we give first place in our moral estimate of action.

Kant considers the concept of duty, distinguishing between what is done *in accordance with* duty (but motivated perhaps by a natural inclination or a selfish purpose) and what is done *from* duty. Moral import is clearly seen only in those cases where on account of absence of inclination, duty is exhibited as the motive. It is our duty to be kind, and amiable people are naturally inclined to kindness. But do they act from duty or inclination? Ordinarily we cannot be sure which; however, suppose that someone in such deep sorrow as to be insensible to the feelings of others yet tears himself out of this condition to perform a kind action. We see then that his action has genuine moral worth. Or we know a man who by nature is unsympathetic yet behaves beneficently: he must be acting from duty, not inclination.

Moral worth attaches to action from duty even with respect to the pursuit of happiness, according to Kant. Everyone has an inclination to be happy, and particular inclinations toward what are regarded as the particular constituents of happiness. Still, all these subtracted, the duty to pursue one's happiness would remain, and only the dutiful pursuit would have true moral worth. (Pursuit of happiness is a duty because unhappiness could tempt to the neglect of other duties.) The commandments to love our neighbors and our enemies should be read as requiring us to exercise beneficence from duty; love cannot be commanded.

A central idea in Kant's work is that the moral worth of action performed from duty lies not in its purpose but in the maxim (rule, principle) by which it is determined. Otherwise, moral worth would depend on inclinations and incentives, which, as we have seen, cannot be the case. "Duty is the necessity of an action executed from respect for law," writes Kant, I cannot have respect for a mere consequence or inclination, but only for what can overpower all inclination: this can be no other than law itself. To be an object of respect is the same as to be valid as a source of command. The law determines the will objectively; subjectively I am determined by respect for the law; this subjective element is the maxim of my action, that I ought to follow the law whatever my inclination may be. Respect, the conception of a worth that overrides self-love, can be present only in a rational being.

The only kind of law the conception of which is capable of determining the will without reference to consequences must be the notion of conformity to law as such. That is to say: Never act in such a way that you could not also will that your maxim should be a universal law requiring everybody in these circumstances to do this action. This is what the common reason of mankind has constantly in view in moral matters, Kant claims.

For example: May I extricate myself from a difficulty by making a false promise? A prudential calculation of consequences might or might not recommend this course. But to determine whether it is consistent with duty I need only ask whether I could wish that everyone in difficulty might extricate himself similarly. I see that the maxim would destroy itself, for if it were a universal law, no one could derive any help from lying, since no promise made in a difficult situation would be believed. So there is no difficulty in deciding whether a proposed course of action would be morally good; I need only ask myself whether my maxim could become a universal law. If not, it must be rejected and the action forgone. Reason compels respect for universal legislation. Every other motive must defer to duty.

Common reason habitually employs this test: "What if everybody did that?" It is the advantage of practical over theoretical reason to be everybody's possession. Ordinary people are as likely to hit the mark as philosophers— indeed, more so, being less liable to be led astray by subtle fallacies. Nevertheless, philosophy is called upon to buttress reason against the assaults of inclination and against specious arguments on their behalf. That is why a metaphysic of morals is required.

Although only what is done from duty has moral worth, it is not possible to be certain in even one instance that an action was in fact done from duty. Some philosophers have indeed attributed all motivation to self-interest. They may be right as a matter of psychology; for how can we be sure that what we most sincerely and carefully conclude to be action from duty was not in reality prompted by some hidden impulse of inclination?

Duty, therefore, is not an empirical concept, according to Kant. Moreover, its universality and necessity also show its nonempirical nature. Nor could it be derived from examples: How would we know in the first place that the cases were fit to serve as examples, if we did not presuppose knowledge of the concept? Even if we consider the actions of God himself, we must antecedently possess the concept of duty in order to judge them as moral. Duty, therefore, is a concept *a priori*. While this fact is obvious, it nevertheless needs to be explicitly argued for on account of the popularity of empirical rules recommended as bases of morality. It is a mistake to try to popularize morality by holding out the inducement of happiness. On the contrary, the picture of disinterested duty has the strongest appeal even to children, because here reason recognizes that it can be practical.

Kant argues that if reason, which tells us what principles of action are objectively required, infallibly determined the will, we would always choose the good. But in fact the will is affected also by subjective incentives that clash with the dictates of reason. Thus the will when not completely good (as it never is in human beings) experiences the pull of reason as constraint. This command of reason, the objective principle constraining the will, is also called an imperative. A perfectly good or "holy" will, being always determined to action only by objective laws, would not experience constraint.

According to Kant, imperatives are either *hypothetical*, commanding something to be done in order to achieve a desired end: if you want X, do A; or *categorical*, commanding an action as objectively necessary: Do A (never mind what you desire). Hypothetical imperatives are further subdivided into rules of skill, which tell what to do in order to achieve some end which one may or may not wish to achieve: heal a person, or poison him; and counsels of prudence, telling what to do to achieve happiness, the one end that all rational beings in fact do have. But the counsels of prudence are still hypothetical, depending on what the agent counts as part of his happiness. Only the categorical imperative is the imperative of morality.

How are imperatives possible—how can reason constrain the will? There is no problem with respect to rules of skill, since it is an analytic proposition that whoever wills the end wills the indispensable means. Because the notion of happiness is indefinite and infallible, means for attaining it cannot be prescribed; counsels of prudence do not strictly command, but only advise. Still, there is no difficulty here as to how reason can influence the will. The puzzle arises only with respect to the categorical imperative.

We cannot show by any example that a categorical imperative does influence the will. When someone in trouble tells the truth it is always possible that not the categorical "Thou shalt not make a false promise" influenced his will but the hypothetical "If thou dost not want to risk ruining thy credit, make no false promise." Hence the question of the possibility of the categorical imperative must be investigated *a priori*. Moreover, the categorical imperative is synthetic *a priori*—*a priori* in that the action prescribed is necessary, synthetic in that the content of this action is not derived analytically from a presupposed volition.

The categorical imperative is simply the demand that the subjective principle of my action, my maxim, should conform to the objective law valid for all rational beings. Therefore, Kant contends, there is only one categorical imperative: "Act only according to that maxim by which you can at the same time will that it should become a universal law." Here are some of Kant's examples:

1. Suicide. Maxim: Out of self-love I shorten my life. But a system of nature

in which this maxim was a law would be contradictory: the feeling impelling to improvement of life would destroy life. Therefore the maxim could not be a law of nature, and the action is contrary to duty.

2. False promises. A universal law of nature that people in trouble escape by making false promises is incoherent, as they would never be believed.

3. Is it all right to amuse myself at the expense of failing to develop my talents? While it could be a law of nature that all people do this, a rational being could not *will* it to be a law of nature, for rationality entails willing that faculties be developed.

4. Should we help other people, or is "Every man for himself" morally permissible? A world could exist without altruism; but again, a rational person could not will it, for his will would conflict with itself: there must often be occasions when he needs the love and sympathy of others, from which he would be cutting himself off.

Examples 1 and 2, in which the idea of the maxim as law of nature is self-contradictory, show strict duties. Examples 3 and 4, where the maxim could be law of nature but not willed to be, illustrate meritorious duties. If we were perfectly rational, then every time we thought of transgressing duty we would notice a contradiction in our will. But in fact we experience no such contradiction but only antagonism between inclination and what reason prescribes. This does show us, however, that we acknowledge the validity of the categorical imperative.

Kant contends that the form of the categorical imperative can also be deduced from the consideration that "rational nature exists as an end it itself." Rational beings (persons) do not exist as mere means to some other end but as themselves bearers of absolute worth. Everyone thinks of his own existence in this way, and the rational ground for his so doing is the same for all others. It is therefore not a merely subjective principle of action, but objective. The categorical imperative can thus be phrased as "Act so that you treat humanity, whether in your own person or in that of another, always as an end and never as a means only." This principle also condemns suicide (which is using oneself merely as a means to maintaining a tolerable life up to its conclusion) and false promising, and shows the merit of self-development and altruism.

The notion of rational beings as ends leads in Kant's ethics to a third formulation of the categorical imperative. We can form the conception of a universal realm of ends, an ideal society of completely rational beings. Such beings would act toward each other not from interest but from pure practical reason; that is, they would always do their duty. This action would be in conformity to the laws of reason, which they had imposed upon themselves. Therefore: "Act always as if you were legislating for a universal realm of ends."

The categorical imperative, in all its forms, is the principle whereby a rational being gives a law to himself: it is thus the principle of autonomy (self-legislation). All other principles, based on interest, are heteronomous (other-legislation), the "other" being the object determining the will: riches, say, or happiness, or any external object of interest. All heteronomous principles are spurious. The worst is that based on happiness, which is neither empirically nor conceptually connected with morality and virtue. It undermines morality by making the difference between virtue and vice to be a mere matter of calculation instead of a difference in kind. The appeal to a moral sense can furnish neither an objective standard of good and bad nor a basis for valid judgment; nevertheless it does have the merit of ascribing intrinsic worth and dignity to virtue. Morality based on an ideal of perfection is empty and involves circular reasoning, as it does not explain our moral ideals but pre-supposes them. Theological morality, based on the notion of the divine will, either presupposes an independent standard or tries to base morality on the notions of glory, dominion, might, and vengeance—a system directly opposed to morality. All these heteronomous moralities look not to the action itself but to the result of the action as incentive—"I ought to do something because I will something else" is a hypothetical imperative, and hence not a moral imperative.

Kant attempts to show not that the autonomous will is actual but that it is possible. To show even this much is difficult, Kant admits, inasmuch as if nature is a system of effects following by natural laws from their causes, and if human beings are part of nature, it seems that every human action is necessitated by natural causes, and thus could not be otherwise than it is. The will could not then be autonomous, "a law to itself," unless it is free.

Kant's strategy in establishing the possibility of freedom depends on the distinctions, elaborated in the *Critique of Pure Reason*, between things as they are in themselves and things as they appear to us. With regard to con-ceptions that come to us without our choice, such as those of the senses, we can know only how they appear, not how they are in themselves. This applies even to the individual's concept of himself: he knows himself only as he appears to himself and is ignorant of the reality underlying the appearance. However, man finds in himself the faculty of reason, which transcends the conceptions given through the senses. Man must therefore conclude that his ego as it is in itself belongs to the intelligible world (world of things in themselves). The upshot is that man has a dual citizenship: in the world of the senses his actions are explainable in terms of natural causation, thus heteronomously; but as a denizen of the intelligible world, the causality of his will is and must be thought of under the idea of freedom, as autonomous.

If we belonged only to the intelligible world, all our actions would conform to the law of freedom and would be moral. If we belonged only to the sensible world (as nonrational animals do), all our actions would be effects of natural causation—that is, determined by incentives. Belonging as we do to both worlds, we experience the dictates of practical reason as *ought*: even in following material incentives we are conscious of what reason requires. We must assume, although we cannot prove, that there is no ultimate contradiction between natural necessity and freedom in human action. And the assumption is justified, for there is no contradiction in a thing-in-itself's being independent of laws to which the thing-as-appearance must conform. In this way we can "comprehend the incomprehensibility" of the unconditional necessity of the moral imperative.—*W.I.M.*

PERTINENT LITERATURE

Ebbinghaus, Julius. "Interpretation and Misinterpretation of the Categorical Imperative," in *The Philosophical Quarterly*. IV, no. 15 (April, 1954), pp. 97-108.

There is no question about what Immanuel Kant's concept of a categorical imperative is: a law unconditionally valid for the will of every rational being. Julius Ebbinghaus contends, however, that there is controversy about its contents and the inferences to be drawn from it. The opinion has been heard that Kant's philosophy is typical of—or even responsible for—the notorious German fondness for obedience to superiors, and hence for National Socialism.

But the categorical imperative, Ebbinghaus points out, is an expression of the notion of what it is to be under a moral obligation. It does not say what in particular our moral obligations are. If Kant was wrong, the consequence is not that some principles of obligation other than those which Kant acknowledged are the right ones; rather, it is that there is no such thing as being under a moral obligation of any kind.

Every moral philosophy must begin with a characterization of duty. The first misinterpretation of Kant's moral philosophy, according to Ebbinghaus, is that it is empty formalism—it does not go beyond this characterization. But the special feature of Kantianism is that it abstracts not only from the matter of duty, but also from the matter of will: from all purposes or ends.

In a moral theory based on a necessary end, such as Aristotle's or John Stuart Mill's, duty is whatever promotes the final end. But can other ends conflict with the final end? If they can, there must be a superfinal end to resolve the conflict, and the allegedly final end is not final after all. If they cannot, then there is no such thing as duty: the will is necessarily (in fact) in all its decisions subordinated to the highest end. This is why, according to Ebbinghaus, Kant determined the form of ethical obligation not by ends but by fitness to be universal law. This does not mean that obligation has no content: it has precisely *this* content.

Ebbinghaus reports Mill's criticism that when Kant attempts to deduce actual duties of morality, he fails to show that there would be any contradiction in the adoption by all rational beings of obviously immoral rules of conduct.

Georg Wilhelm Friedrich Hegel makes a similar objection. And John Dewey, also believing that the categorical imperative is empty of content, supposes that it naturally lends itself to being filled up by whatever authority, specifically the national leader, may prescribe; these dictates then become unconditionally binding. This reasoning, however, as Ebbinghaus points out, is exactly contrary to Kant, whose doctrine forbids a man to subject his own will to the will of any other person. That would be for the will to will its own annulment, which Kant held to be self-contradictory. The obedience required by the categorical imperative is thus the exact opposite of subjection to arbitrary power.

But, then, must not the autonomous will be able to legislate for itself anything it likes? Mill supposes that it can—and that Kant admitted as much in bringing in consideration of the agent's advantage in his examples. In showing the wrongness of hard-heartedness Kant allegedly appealed to the agent's self-interest, a piece of "commonplace egoism." Ebbinghaus replies: (1) It is at any rate not "commonplace egoism," for there is no contention that the agent wills his own happiness exclusively. (2) But Kant's argument is that insofar as happiness is an end for the agent, he cannot possibly will to be abandoned in need. (3) What Kant says is that the will to hard-heartedness would be "in conflict with itself." (4) The universalized maxim of hard-heartedness would be: Everyone who feels himself immune from need may be deaf to the need of others. This cannot be willed, as it would be a will to let oneself be abandoned, in a case that for all one knows might actually arise. One could indeed assent to this formulation: I will never help anyone who is immune from need—but that offers no difficulty to Kant.

Ebbinghaus claims that Kant's critics overlook the word *through* in the categorical imperative: Act only on that maxim *through* which you can at the same time will that it should become a universal law. This means that the reason for the possibility of willing the maxim as law must be found in the maxim itself, not in external circumstances of the agent. This condition is not met in hard-heartedness; anyone able to will it must feel himself immune from need, and this is an external circumstance.

All, then, that is left of the egoism charge is that Kant holds that a man cannot will to be abandoned. To be sure, Kant does insist that we be prepared to sacrifice our happiness—but never as a possible end altogether. And that would be required were hard-heartedness universalizable.

The categorical imperative indeed abstracts from all ends, Ebbinghaus insists; but this is not to be confused with saying that the categorical imperative demands that my will have no ends at all, which would be not to be a will at all.

Utilitarians say, in effect, according to Ebbinghaus, "You must help others because it will promote your own happiness." Kant says, in effect, "You must help others whether it promotes your own happiness or not, because to will the maxim of hard-heartedness as a universal law contradicts your inevitable (and permissible) end." The difference is this: while for Kant there can be no taking into account the consequences for my happiness of willing the maxim as a law, nevertheless I must consider whether the maxim as law would make it impossible to take my own happiness as an end.

Ebbinghaus argues as follows: I will my own happiness. I *can* will the happiness of others. But in willing my own happiness I will on the principle that others should also will my happiness. Suppose now I do not will the happiness of others: I cannot then will that others should act on my maxim, for then they would not will my happiness. Thus to will my happiness and not will the happiness of others is (if the categorical imperative is valid) a contradiction. Therefore it is a definite command of duty that I must include the happiness of others in my own end of personal happiness. This shows how it is, after all, possible to deduce particular precepts from the categorical imperative.

Harrison, Jonathan. "Kant's Examples of the First Formulation of the Categorical Imperative," in *The Philosophical Quarterly*. VII, no. 26 (January, 1957), pp. 50-62.

According to Immanuel Kant, Jonathan Harrison reminds us, there are duties to oneself and to others, and perfect and imperfect duties. There are therefore four kinds of duty: perfect duty to oneself, perfect to others, imperfect duty to oneself, imperfect to others. Kant gives one example of each. Kant holds it to be impossible that everybody adopt the maxim of an act that infringes on a *perfect* duty; but although it is possible for everybody to adopt the maxim of an act that infringes on an *imperfect* duty, it is not possible to *will* that everybody should adopt such a maxim.

The first form of the categorical imperative is supposed to be the supreme principle of morality. It is not just the demand that moral principles be general, which Kant takes for granted. This formula, moreover, is used by Kant not to test alleged moral principles, but to test maxims. He takes for granted that moral principles must be universal, and endeavors only to show what maxims are universalizable. Maxims are rules that I make for myself. They are not true or false. They are not moral principles: maxims can be made, but moral principles cannot. Maxims, however, can conform to moral principles. Maxims apply only to the person making them.

According to Harrison, Kant held that a maxim is morally unacceptable if it cannot be universalized and that it is acceptable (that is, *may*—not must or ought to be—adopted) if it can be universalized. He may also have thought that it must be adopted if its "contradictory" is not universalizable. Presumably Kant meant this by "impossible to will": Were I able to bring about a certain state of affairs, I could not bring myself to do so. There are maxims that it is logically impossible for everyone to act on: for example, Be first through every door. There are others which I would be unlikely to act on if as a result everybody else did: for example, Consume without producing.

In Kant's example of suicide, Harrison writes, we must expunge the words "From self-love I make it my principle," as this phrase has nothing to do with the maxim but only with motives for adopting it. The maxim is: "To shorten my life if its continuance threatens more evil than it promises pleasure." Now, what contradiction would result from universal adoption of this rule? None at all, Harrison claims; nor does Kant attempt to show it. All he does try to show is that it contradicts the statement that the purpose of self-love is to stimulate the furtherance of life, which amounts to saying that the purpose of self-love is to prevent people from committing suicide. But even here there is no contradiction. Things can have purposes that they do not, or do not always, fulfill. Besides, the maxim is not simply to commit suicide, but to do so if I would be happier dead—and people in this situation are presumably a minority. The universal adoption of the maxim, then, would not lead to universal suicide, or even have the consequence that self-love usually or frequently caused people to commit suicide.

Harrison comments on Kant's other examples follow.

On false promises: Contradiction arises only if certain contingent statements are true; for example, people frequently find themselves in circumstances where they can obtain services in no other way than by making false promises. Furthermore, people are egotistical; they remember what promises have been made. These contingent statements are no doubt true. But that aside, there is still trouble for Kant, since the rule as he put it was "when you find yourself in certain circumstances. . . ," which is an antecedent that could be vacuously satisfied even if nobody believed promises.

Never to help others in distress: Kant is not here appealing to self-interest; he says rather that the will would be at variance with itself, for it would also necessarily will to receive aid in distress. However, one often does things in spite of motives not to do them. All "variance with itself" means is that one could not will this maxim wholeheartedly, not that one could not will it.

Neglecting to develop my natural gifts: Kant says one cannot will the universal neglect of talents, because talents are useful. This is odd; the usefulness of talents to oneself is a better reason for not neglecting one's own than for not willing that others should neglect theirs. Further, Kant says that "as a rational being" one cannot will to neglect one's talent, evidently because it is obvious that as a partially nonrational being one can. But the "as a rational being" qualification begs the question.

According to Harrison Kant does not appeal to consequences. Although in the third example Kant points out that failure to develop one's talents would have harmful consequences for the agent, this is not a utilitarian argument: it does not say anything about harmful consequences for society.

Moreover, the harmful consequences do not provide the reason why the maxim is *wrong*—they show why one cannot will it. Nor does Kant appeal to the bad consequences of everybody's adopting a maxim, according to Harrison.

Furthermore, although Kant mentions purposes he never argues that something is wrong because it is contrary to what something was intended for. Kant seems to think that if maxims are wrong, then the question of the morality of actions falling under them is settled. But it cannot be, Harrison contends. One can do the right thing for the wrong reason. Moreover, for every wrong action, a universalizable maxim enjoining it can be found.
—*W.I.M.*

ADDITIONAL RECOMMENDED READING

Broad, C. D. *Five Types of Ethical Theory*. London: Routledge & Kegan Paul, 1930. Chapter 5 is a penetrating discussion of the Kantian ethics.

Duncan, A. R. C. *Practical Reason and Morality*. London: Nelson, 1957. A brief but authoritative exposition and criticism of the *Foundations*.

Levin, Michael E. "Kant's Derivation of the Formula of Universal Law as an Ontological Argument," in *Kant-Studien*. LXV, Heft 1 (1974), pp. 50-66. Argues that Kant illicitly derived the existence of a categorical imperative from the mere concept of a rational action.

Paton, H. J. *The Categorical Imperative: A Study in Kant's Moral Philosophy*. London: Hutchinson, 1946. The definitive commentary.

ESSAYS ON THE INTELLECTUAL POWERS OF MAN
ESSAYS ON THE ACTIVE POWERS
OF THE HUMAN MIND

Author: Thomas Reid (1710-1796)
Type of work: Epistemology, ethics, philosophy of mind
First published: Intellectual Powers, 1785; *Active Powers*, 1788

PRINCIPAL IDEAS ADVANCED

There is no intermediate between the mental act and the object of knowledge; perception is the direct experience of things present to the senses.

All the intellectual powers involve apprehension of some content and judgment.

We have immediate experience of spatial extension and of temporal duration, and this intuitive knowledge supplies first principles.

Through perception and memory we acquire probable knowledge; through conception and abstraction, knowledge of necessary truths.

God has supplied men with consciences which provide intuitive knowledge of the right and the wrong; in following his moral sense no man need fear a conflict of interest and duty.

At the age of seventy-one, Thomas Reid resigned from his University of Glasgow professorship to prepare for publication his celebrated classroom lectures on mental and moral philosophy. The intellectual world already knew the general thrust of the new Scottish Realism through his *Inquiry into the Human Mind* (1764). But the full articulation and defense of the system awaited the appearance of his two books of *Essays*, works so lucid and so plausible that they became almost at once the basis of the orthodox philosophy of the English-speaking world. Reid's philosophy is everything that a "public philosophy" should be. While it lacks the graceful style of certain eighteenth century philosophers, it has a masculine strength and a directness which still arouses admiration.

The *Essays on the Intellectual Powers of Man* contains eight essays of rather unequal length, each (except the Introduction) given over to one of man's intellectual powers or faculties. It is characteristic of Reid's philosophy that, like those of Joseph Butler and Francis Hutcheson, it makes no effort to reduce the different activities to a common denominator. Sense-perception, memory, conception (imagination), abstraction, judgment, reason, and taste are so many distinct and irreducible activities, although they may also occur in combination. Reid begins each essay by identifying the power in question and explaining its typical features. There follows a historical account telling how other philosophers have dealt with the subject. Often, in addition, one of the British empiricists is selected for quotation and detailed refutation—not the least profitable part of the work.

Reid was a conscientious empiricist, pledged to carry out the program of Francis Bacon for the mental and moral sciences. By observation and investigation he hoped to arrive at fundamental laws comparable to those which Newton had found in natural philosophy. His method is basically introspective: one can learn to attend to one's own mental activities, describe them, and relate them to one another. In this manner we can map out the "human constitution." But description is all that we can attain to, since to man it is not given to know the causes of things. In fact, with Reid, as with most of his contemporaries, the underlying assumption (as basic to them as evolution was to the late nineteenth century) was that by a perfect wisdom all the parts of the world are adjusted to each other.

Besides introspection, Reid makes frequent appeal to common speech to support what he takes to be the witness of man's constitution. An example: Is beauty properly said to be an emotion in the mind of the perceiver, or a property of the object viewed? Language witnesses the latter. Again, are heat, hardness, and the like perceived as ideas in the mind or as qualities in bodies? Our speech testifies that they are perceived as qualities.

Reid's attitude toward the history of philosophy (which he regarded as the history of error) is central to his own commonense point of view. He shared the optimism of the eighteenth century which held that the truth is always near at hand and that the first step toward enlightening mankind is to clear away ignorance, prejudice, and artificiality. In Reid's view, all the complications in mental philosophy stem from the very old error of thinking of the mind after the analogy of body. Men observe that, in the physical world, there is no action at a distance, and they suppose that similarly the mind can act and be acted upon only by what is immediately present to it. The ancient philosophers taught that bodies give off films which, passing through the sense organs, leave impressions on the mind. The moderns, following Descartes, have refined their doctrine, but have retained the old "phantasms" under the new name of "ideas." These ideas are "hypothetical" in the bad sense of the word which Newton implied when, setting aside the entities of the schoolmen, he said, "*non fingo hypotheses.*" According to Reid, the progress of philosophy is assured if the "ideal hypothesis" (which remains to plague the writings of Cartesians and Lockians alike) is relegated to the rubbish heap along with other scholastic notions.

In Reid's theory of knowledge there is no intermediate between the mental act and the object of knowledge. Perception is the direct experience of things present to the senses; memory, of things past; consciousness, of the mind's own activity; and sensation and emotion are pure states of consciousness. It is characteristic of all these powers that they include (1) a notion or apprehension of some content and (2) a judgment or belief about existence. Reid is full of scorn for Hume's suggestion that belief is simply a degree of the vivacity of an object.

He makes use of the distinction between primary and secondary qualities of things, even though he does not hold to the existence of ideas. Perception is a complex act which includes sensation but is not reducible to it. Thus, says Reid, when I touch the table I have a sensation which, however, I do not ordinarily attend to, the mind passing over it to attend to the quality of the thing—that is to say, hardness, smoothness. There is, according to Reid, a natural symbolism here which we cannot understand: the Creator has attached the perception of the quality to the particular sensation, and this is a mystery— just as it is a mystery that certain vibrations in the brain are regularly attached to certain sensations. The case is otherwise with secondary qualities. When we smell an odor, Reid says, the sensation is likely to be mistaken for the physical object, although introspection reveals that when we smell, say, a rose, all that is really attested is the existence of some external cause of the characteristic sensation: we learn to connect the odor with the object of our other senses. Partly this is true also of vision, where, however, the purely mental experiences of color are inseparably blended with spatial properties.

Perception and memory, besides the notion of and belief in the object toward which they are directed, carry with them other truth. As Reid says, I know that I exist as knower, and that some external cause exists adequate to give rise to my perceptions and memories. Through perception I come to know the reality of space, and through memory I know the reality of time— these are presupposed by extension and by duration of which we have immediate experience. Here are examples of what Reid calls intuitive truths. They serve as first principles for our knowledge of the world and man. Other truths follow from them by reasoning or demonstration; but the first principles (requisite to every science) must be known immediately.

The principles so far mentioned all have to do with existence. By means of conception and abstraction it is possible for the mind to invent objects of a different order. These could be called "ideas" without offense—Platonic, rather than Cartesian ideas. They are objects of the mind, and do not represent anything beyond themselves. They do not, as Plato supposed, exist apart from the mind, but are pure essences completely discerned by the mind. Among these theoretical objects, axioms of a different sort are discovered. We call them intuitive also; but they differ from those axioms which deal with contingent truths in that they are seen to be necesssary.

The two kinds of principles just mentioned yield two kinds of knowledge— necessary truths (for example, mathematics) yield demonstrative knowledge; contingent truths (astronomy) yield probable knowledge. Reid is dissatisfied with Hume's suggestion that probable knowledge is less certain than demonstrative, and accuses that philosopher of using the word "probability" in a strange fashion. One's knowledge, for instance, that the capital of France is Paris is no less certain than a demonstration in geometry.

Discussing demonstrative knowledge, Reid takes issue with Locke's contention that moral judgments are of this sort since the terms of moral judgments are not real essences but nominal ones. According to Reid, moral judgments are judgments about contingent matters, and flow not from definitions but from intuitions. They depend on moral axioms, more or less clearly discerned by all civilized peoples. And they are properly discussed under the actual rather than the intellectual powers of the mind.

Problems of taste, however, which very much interested the eighteenth century, are dealt with under intellectual powers. Reid is interested in the power of the mind to combine images in meaningful patterns—he is dissatisfied with the purely mechanistic account of thinking expounded under the name of associationism. Here, in the broadest sense, is the basis for art: purposiveness. We not only invent meaningful combinations; but we recognize them and rejoice in them in the handiwork of other men and in nature.

Reid follows the usual division of aesthetic objects into those of curiosity, grandeur, and beauty. The perception of any of these is a complex act involving on the one hand an emotion and, on the other, a notion and judgment respecting the object. There is an analogy between this and his analysis of sense-perception: as sensation is to physical quality, so emotion is to aesthetic quality. Curiosity (like smell, for example) is almost entirely subjective. Not so with grandeur and beauty where we are aware of a property in the thing. It may be that the property is "occult"—in which case our judgment of beauty is like our perception of color, and we do not understand what it is in the object that gives rise to our pleasant emotion. But sometimes the property is perfectly intelligible—in which case our judgment of beauty is analogous to our perception of primary qualities.

Reid's philosophy radiates confidence and good will. He is not nervous about his position, and although he indulges in ridicule (he justifies it as one of the ways in which common sense asserts itself) it is never cruel or malicious as is so much eighteenth century wit. Nevertheless, Reid has a genuine enemy: it is skepticism. He thanks Hume for carrying the "spirit of modern philosophy" (Reid's own expression) out to its logical conclusion: if one hypothesizes "ideas" skepticism is inevitable. But skepticism, in Reid's eyes, is merely defeatism of the sort that prevailed in natural philosophy until the miasmas of peripateticism were cleared away by such men as Galileo and Newton. Happily, a return to common sense makes possible new experimental gains in mental and moral philosophy also.

The *Essays on the Active Powers of the Human Mind* carries the investigation from mental philosophy into the field of moral philosophy. This work is only half as long as the former, and hence we rightly infer that it was not Reid's major field of interest, but not that he considered the active life less important than the speculative one. On the contrary, he glows with enthusiasm for those remarkable endowments which set man above the other animals and give him the means of remaking the world in the interests of human happiness. The intellectual powers are only instruments in the service of man's active powers.

Moral philosophy, until almost our own time, included the psychology of motives as well as the principles of normative action. In Reid's philosophy these can scarcely be disjoined. The clue to his system may be found in Pope's *Essay on Man* (1734) as well as in Joseph Butler's *Sermons* (1726). It lies in the belief that man's constitution has been fashioned by a wise and benevolent Creator who always orders the part with a view to the perfection of the whole. There are many motives in man and, though often they seem to be at odds, careful examination reveals a hierarchy among them. Every motive is good at the right time and place: and there are superior principles which determine when and where the inferior are intended to function. Thus, a purely descriptive account of human nature contains by implication a moral code. But in practice man has a readier guide. One of the higher principles with which he is endowed is conscience, which gives him an intuitive sense of right and wrong. Since it bestowed upon him by the Architect of his being, it can be trusted to lead him toward his proper end.

By the same token, interest and duty are seen to be complementaries. It is part of the office of reason to judge between desires and to steer the course which promises to be good for man on the whole. The man who follows reason is said to be prudent, and insofar as he is successful he achieves a happy life. But such intelligence never extends very far; and for mankind as a whole it is not an adequate guide. In addition to calculating his interest, man should study duty, disclosed to him through the moral sense. Here he is not merely provided with moral truth, from which he may infer his obligation; but the deliverances of conscience are also attended with strong feelings of approval and disapproval, which add greatly to its effectiveness as a guide. While there can be no opposition between these two principles, the rule should be to follow duty rather than interest, on the reasonable presumption that under a wise and benevolent Administration it is impossible that the issue of doing what is right should ever be anything but happy.

In somewhat the same way, egoistic and altruistic motives are proved not to be in conflict. Our animal impulses, whether appetites or desires, by themselves are neither selfish nor unselfish, neither bad nor good. It is only with reference to larger considerations that they become one or the other. Rightly ordered, they both promote our own happiness and serve our fellow men. Reason would, if it were perfect, so regulate them. But because of the limits of man's reasoning power, God has taken the precaution of undergirding his intention and, to secure our social well-being, has implanted in us certain affections which are above the particular desires but beneath reason and conscience. Benevolence, the first of these, is the source of such affections as filial love, gratitude, compassion, friendship, and public spirit. But there is also malevolent affection, which manifests itself in emulation and resentment. (Reid is not sure that they should be called "malevolent.") In themselves they are not evil, being the basis for such honest attitudes as the desire to excel and the disposition to resist and retaliate injury. If they are not brought under the government of reason or conscience they become evil; but this is also true of our benevolent affections.

The question of moral liberty inevitably finds a place in Reid's discussion. The problem, as he sees it, is not whether a man has power to act, but only whether he has power to will. Hobbes, who defined the question in the former manner, equated liberty with freedom from external impediment; at the same time he held that all man's actions are causally determined. For Reid, it is this last contention which needs to be examined. The matter is complex. Reid holds it to be a self-evident truth that every event in the material world, including the motion of a man's body, must have an efficient cause, but that the nature of the causal nexus is mysterious. Presumably the divine Spirit is the source of the motions in nature at large. The question in hand is whether the human spirit has received a somewhat analogous power. Reid holds that it has, else all our notions of duty and responsibility, praise and blame would be without foundation. As he looks for the source of this freedom in the human constitution, it seems to him to lie on the side of reason as opposed to passions. The latter are impressions upon the mind which have their origin in matter; but the former seems to be independent of these motives and free to direct its attention from one object to another, to weigh their respective merits, to select a goal, and to plan a course of action. Insofar as it is externally motivated, the things that influence reason are final (not efficient) causes, together with such considerations as truth and duty.

Although Reid regards the active powers as a natural endowment, he does not suppose that they occur full-blown in any person. Conscience is a good example. It does not make itself felt at all in infants or in imbeciles. And even in the adult it is extremely subject to education, both for weal and for woe. In this respect, moral competence is like other natural endowments— like the ability to dance or sing, or to reason logically. The unpleasant fact is that the great part of mankind in every age is sunk in gross ignorance and fettered to stupid and unprofitable customs. But even as the intellectual powers have a natural affinity for truth, so the active incline man toward virtue and well-being. This is manifest in the institutions of all civilized people and in the Law of Nature and of Nations widely recognized as the foundation of political rights and duties.

Reid distinguishes between the moral judgment and the theory of morals. Just as a person may have a good ear which has been improved by practice in the art of music, and still be ignorant of the anatomy of hearing and the theory of sound, so one may have exact and comprehensive knowledge of what is right and wrong in human conduct and yet be ignorant of the structure of our moral powers. Moral theory is important as a part of the philosophy of the human mind, but not as a part of morals.

It is usual to think of Thomas Reid as the apostle of "common sense." The term occurs frequently in his writings, not always with the same meaning. In some places it means "good sense"—that degree of reason which makes a man capable of managing his own affairs and answerable in his conduct toward others. In other places it refers to the opinions of the man in the street. But in the technical sense which came to characterize the system of Reid and of the Scottish school, it stands for that part of man's mental constitution by which he knows the truth of the principles or axioms which, underlying all experience and all inference are the indispensable foundations of science and morality.

"We ascribe to reason two offices, or two degrees. The first is to judge of things self-evident; the second to draw conclusions that are not self-evident from those that are. The first of these is the province, and the sole province, of common sense; and, therefore, it coincides with reason in its whole extent, and is only another name for one branch or one degree of reason."

The most obvious difference between the two kinds of reason mentioned here is that, whereas the second is "learned by practice and rules," the first is "purely natural, and therefore common to the learned and the unlearned, to the trained and the untrained." Whatever the difficulties of formulating its deliverances, there is, native to man's mind, a capacity to grasp the essential truths concerning human existence.

Common sense, so understood, underlies the realism of Scottish philosophy. In his analysis of experience, Reid avoided sensationism and nominalism only because, at each critical juncture, he refused to wear the blinders of technical reason. He professed to repudiate metaphysics, and agreed with his age that man ought to content himself with observed laws and phenomena. But he was little disposed to measure heaven with a span.

"A man who is possessed of the genuine spirit of philosophy will think it impiety to contaminate the divine workmanship, by mixing it with those fictions of human fancy, called theories and hypotheses, which will always bear the signature of human folly, no less than the other does of divine wisdom."—*J.F.*

PERTINENT LITERATURE

McCosh, James. *The Scottish Philosophy, Biographical, Expository, Critical, from Hutcheson to Hamilton.* London: Macmillan and Company, 1875.

As used in the title of this book, "the Scottish philosophy" means what we nowadays mean by the expression "The Scottish enlightenment."

The expression also is used by James McCosh in the narrower sense, however, as synonymous with the school of commonsense realism which rose in opposition to the skepticism of David Hume. McCosh, who came to America in 1868 to be president of Princeton, was a noteworthy representative of this school. His account of Thomas Reid is entirely sympathetic, although, like Dugald Stewart, Thomas Brown, and other members of the school, he was aware of points at which Reid needed to be corrected.

"It has been the aim of the Scottish school, as modified and developed by Reid, to throw back the scepticism of Hume," writes McCosh in his chapter on Hume, remarking that Hume's skepticism was assailable at two junctures: first, where he claimed that all ideas are copies of sensations; second, where he maintained that all truth is derived from experience. Reid, says McCosh, met Hume at both these points, the former by inquiring more accurately into the role of the senses in perception, the latter by proving that the mind has independent rational capacities for apprehending and judging the truth.

Reid's claim that the senses give us direct knowledge of material objects McCosh holds to be basically sound, especially commending Reid's efforts to disprove the scheme found in both René Descartes and John Locke, according to which we perceive by means of ideas coming between the mind and the object perceived, so that we can reach knowledge of external objects only by means of inference. Even supposing that no philosopher held the doctrine in quite the crude form in which Reid represented it, Reid performed a great service in compelling philosophers who persist in using the word "idea" to make plain what they mean by the term. Unfortunately, Reid failed to develop an acceptable alternative. In describing what he took to be a law of our mental constitution, Reid said that sensations in the mind give rise to intelligible notions and beliefs, thereby enabling us to know physical objects, our own minds, and past events. George Berkeley had used the term "suggestion" to designate habitual associations by which visible figure calls to mind tangible figure. Reid maintained that there are also natural suggestions by which, for example, the sensations of touch present to the mind the notions of extension, solidity, and motion; but this, says McCosh, is hardly more satisfactory than the hypothesis of ideas which Reid rejected. There is no evidence that sensation precedes perception, the two being, in his view, one concrete act which we separate only by abstraction. When our senses are affected, says McCosh, we *know* the colored surface or the tangible figure.

It was this account of perception by Reid, McCosh states, which led Reid's most distinguished disciple, Sir William Hamilton, to doubt whether, strictly speaking, Reid subscribed to the doctrine of direct realism. McCosh argues, however, that even Hamilton would have to admit that there are natural processes intervening between the object and our perception of it; and Reid, although he included sensations among these intermediaries, was steadfast in holding that extended objects and not sensations are the objects of the mind in perception.

Hume's broad claim that all knowledge comes through the senses Reid met by listing truths which he claimed are self-evident to every man who is in a sound state of mind, calling these truths "principles of common sense." This expression McCosh regards as unfortunate, pointing out that although it contributed to the popularity of Reid's philosophy, it damaged his reputation with those who, like Immanuel Kant, were seriously engaged in meeting Hume's skeptical assault. Even Joseph Priestley, who took the trouble to understand what Reid meant by common sense and agreed with him that there are genuine mental principles, rightly complained that Reid admitted first principles too readily and failed to define their nature and the laws governing their use.

Furthermore, McCosh points out, Reid did not make clear how common sense is supposed to resolve philosophical doubt. Does it do so because it is a sense, or because it is common to all men, or because we are compelled to believe it? Reid sometimes calls the truths of common sense "principles of our constitution," and says that we can have no better reason for trusting them than the fact that our minds are determined to give them implicit belief. If, however, someone were to say that our constitutions may deceive us, Reid seems to have no answer.

We are in debt to McCosh for reprinting in his Appendix selections from an unpublished manuscript by Reid dealing with this question. Quite possibly it was written as a reply to Priestley. The question, Why do I believe first principles?, admits of two answers, says Reid. It can be taken as meaning, To what cause is my belief to be ascribed?, or as meaning, What reason have I for my belief? The former is answered by an appeal to man's constitution; the latter by an appeal to the self-evidence of what is believed. Reid then goes on to distinguish two kinds of self-evidence, much as he does in the *Essays* where he speaks of necessary truths and of contingent truths. In this way, McCosh suggests, Reid arrived at Kant's distinction between analytic and synthetic *a priori* judgments, although he failed to see its importance or to elaborate it in a meaningful way.

Grave, S. A. *The Scottish Philosophy of Common Sense*. Oxford: Clarendon Press, 1960.

As S. A. Grave points out, the career of Scottish philosophy terminated in 1865 with the publication of John Stuart Mill's *Examination of Sir William Hamilton's Philosophy*, both for those who agreed with David Hume and Mill and for those who did not, the latter turning away from Thomas Reid to Immanuel Kant and Georg Wilhelm Friedrich Hegel. Still, in our day, according to Grave, there is much to be said for the philosophy of common sense. Its claim that there are genuinely philosophical questions which can be answered by common sense and not otherwise compels us to ask both what we understand by common sense and what we understand by philosophical questions, and its claim is not easily settled, if indeed it can be settled at all.

Grave would not have been misleading had he titled his book "The Philosophy of Thomas Reid," because the book is in fact an exposition of the *Essays*, amplified here and there by opinions of other representatives of the school. Chapters are devoted to Reid's criticism of the doctrine of ideas, to his examination of perception, to his account of personal identity and free will, and to his theory of aesthetic and moral judgment. Of special interest to contemporary philosophers are his two chapters titled "Common Sense," the first of which deals with what is ordinarily meant by the term, the second with the special meaning given it by the Scottish school.

Contemporary philosophy might seem to have cut the ground from under anyone who attempts to resolve philosophical problems by appealing to common sense. Taking their cue from George Berkeley, modern analytical philosophers sometimes appear to think with the learned and speak with the vulgar. Hume ordinarily disdained to conceal the radical nature of his conclusions in this way; but his modern interpreters, by exciding a few passages from his writings and by distinguishing between two levels of language, make it seem that Hume was not questioning the existence of material objects, self-identity, causation, or anything that common sense is convinced of, but merely analyzing these terms so as to show what they mean.

Grave suggests, however, that a real dispute remains: namely, whether it is possible to entertain metaphysical opinions. For example, the commonsense belief that there is a trunk in the attic when everyone is downstairs does not reduce without remainder to a trunk's being able to be seen by anyone going into the attic. In other words, the empiricist interpretation of common sense, framed to agree with boundaries of significant speech drawn up by phenomenalist philosophers, does not do justice to the metaphysically loaded opinions of the plain man. If the latter seems to be at a disadvantage in explaining to the philosopher what he means by unperceived objects, the analyst must find himself attempting to say what cannot be said if he undertakes to explain where the plain man has gone wrong.

Grave has more difficulty defending Reid's attempt to reduce common sense to a set of axioms intended to serve as the foundation for all human knowledge. Joseph Priestley had put his finger on the problem when he charged the Scottish school with making truth depend on "the arbitrary constitution of our nature," hence, "relative to ourselves only." Grave admits the totally unphilosophical manner in which, on occasion, Reid appealed to man's constitution as a reason for assenting to first principles. Still, says Grave, it is clear that Reid did not mean to be putting forward the view that the principles of common sense are merely ways in which human beings have to think because made so by God, regardless of whether their thoughts correspond to the nature of things. That every event must have cause, that objects of perception exist independently of our perception of them, and that memory can give knowledge of past events, are truths which, although not seen to be evident in the same way as are analytic truths, must be taken as self-evident at least in the Aristotelian sense of being truths without which other truths could not be reached. As Grave puts it, however, the language of self-evidence is half-logical and half-psychological, and this appeal leaves Reid with many questions to answer. To begin with, Reid must show how, if these truths are self-evident, many philosophers dissent from them; but he also has to show that, in spite of dissent, the principles are evident in themselves. To appeal to the opinion of the masses, or even to show that philosophers have to act according to them while denying them in theory, Grave says, is too easy, playing as it does on the ambiguity already noted as to whether the content of commonsense beliefs is metaphysical or empirical only.

Turning from the *Essays on the Intellectual Powers of Man* to the *Essays on the Active Powers of the Human Mind*, Grave shows that Reid's place in the history of moral philosophy is that of a critic of the emotive theory of value. Against the view that moral approbation and disapprobation are merely feelings, Reid maintained that, although attended by feelings, they are real judgments which, like other judgments, must be either true or false.

Grave considers, first, Reid's attempts to show that moral approbation includes a judgment of fact by drawing an analogy between aesthetic and moral judgments. Common sense dictates the belief that some things possess real excellence and that they have this excellence from their own constitutions and not from that of the observer. Thus, moral judgments state facts about facts, calling attention to facts of the unique kind indicated by such words as "good" and "right." Second, Grave takes up Reid's contention that moral judgments operate as motives. In the early part of our lives, we are motivated by appetites and desires; but, as reason develops, we weigh these against conceptions, such as good on the whole, which everyone recognizes as taking precedence over particular desires. In conclusion, Grave reminds us that Hume himself said that moral skeptics are disingenuous disputants who, if no one argued with them, would come over to the side of common sense. Pointing to impressions, Hume could claim to have verified what common sense holds with respect to moral distinctions. Still, for Reid, the moral skeptic would not be fully restored to common sense until he acknowledged what he presumably once knew: namely, that moral distinctions are immutable and independent of anyone's impression. Here again, for Reid, common sense has a metaphysical character.—*J.F.*

ADDITIONAL RECOMMENDED READING

Barker, Stephen F. and Tom L. Beauchamp, eds. *Thomas Reid: Critical Interpretations*. Philosophical Monographs 3. Philadelphia: Temple University Press, 1976. Papers representative of the recent revival of interest in Reid's philosophy.

Beck, Lewis White, ed. "The Philosophy of Thomas Reid," in *The Monist*. LXI, no. 2 (April, 1978). The entire issue consists of articles dealing with aspects of Reid's philosophy.

Grave, S. A. "Reid, Thomas," in *The Encyclopedia of Philosophy*. Edited by Paul Edwards. New York: Macmillan Publishing Company, 1967. An authoritative summation of Reid's doctrine.

Reid, Thomas. *Essays on the Intellectual Powers of Man*. London: Macmillan and Company, 1941. A. D. Woozley's "Introduction" to this edition is a classic.

_____ . *Essays on the Intellectual Powers of Man* and *Essays on the Active Powers of the Human Mind*. Cambridge, Massachusetts: M.I.T. Press, 1969. See particularly the Introductions to the respective volumes by Baruch A. Brody, who brings out Reid's relevance to our times.

CRITIQUE OF PRACTICAL REASON

Author: Immanuel Kant (1724-1804)
Type of work: Ethics
First published: 1788

PRINCIPAL IDEAS ADVANCED

Morality can claim objectivity and universality only by being founded on pure reason itself.

Moral laws are universal and categorical because of their form, not their empirical content.

The fundamental law of the pure practical reason is so to act that the maxim of the will could always function as a principle establishing universal law.

Were it not for the moral law, man could never know himself to be free; for man, "thou ought" implies "thou canst."

The rational postulates of the practical reason are that man is free, that the soul is immortal, and that God exists.

None of Kant's writings can be understood without a clear recognition of the "Copernican revolution" in philosophy effected by his first critique, the *Critique of Pure Reason* (1781). Previously, the predominant rational tradition in Western philosophy was founded on the assumption of reason's capacity for discovering the forms or essential structures characterizing all things. Whether the form of "treeness" was an innate aspect of every existent tree (as Aristotle believed) or a transcendent form in which each existent tree participated (as Plato held), the capacity of reason for perceiving such forms was not doubted. The medieval controversy over "universals" centered not in reason's ability for such perception, but in the nature of this rational activity.

From the first questioning of the nominalists, however, through the break between self and "exterior world" in Descartes, doubt as to the precise authority of rational apprehension increased. Human error and empirical deception began to be seen as intervening between perceiver and perceived, thus raising powerfully the question of the criteria for truth. The Aristotelians, especially from the time of St. Thomas Aquinas on, affirmed that knowledge begins with sense perception; however, because of reason's capacity for extracting forms, human knowledge possessed not only the qualities of necessity and universality, but made possible an inductive knowledge of trans-empirical realities. It was the empiricists, especially David Hume, who provided the most serious challenge to this rationalist claim. Centering his attack on the problem of universal causality (cause and effect as universally operative), Hume raised the question of necessity. On what grounds, he asked, can one insist that, *of necessity*, all "effects" have causes and, similarly, that such causes *necessarily* produce identical effects? Hume's conclusion was that the category of causality, like all human ideas, is derived from sense impressions, having the status simply of a habitual assumption and expectation; human ideas are forever bereft of necessity.

It was Kant who saw the seriousness of this empiricist challenge. Reason was bankrupt as an agent of knowledge if it could no longer claim necessity and thus universality for its findings. Man and the world had been severed, and skepticism seemed the inevitable result.

The answer provided by Kant's first critique was a revolution, a complete reversal of the previous conception of the knowing process. If human knowledge cannot claim a necessity which is resident within the empirical world itself, it is possible, nevertheless, to claim universality for it if the locus of necessity is within the universal operations of human reason. With this new conception of rational necessity and universality, Kant proceeded to exhibit what he conceived to be the necessary operations of rational apprehension, the manner in which the understanding, by its very structure, has and of necessity will always perceive and organize whatever realities encounter it.

As Kant interpreted it, Hume's error was in seeing subjective necessity as grounded only in habit instead of being a result of the *a priori* structure of reason. If the latter is the case, rational necessity and universality are guaranteed, although on a far different basis from before. For Kant, the forms perceived through sense experience are the product of the categories of the human mind, but now the externality so encountered is never known as it is in itself (as "noumenon"), but only in its relation to man (as "phenomenon").

While reason attempts to complete this knowledge by bringing it into a comprehensive unity, it is barred from success in this speculative operation by certain antinomies, both sides of which are in harmony with man's phenomenal knowledge. In the area of speculative psychology, these antinomies make it impossible to affirm a soul existing apart from the physical. In the area of speculative cosmology, the consequence of the antinomies centers in the impossibility of establishing man as free of the determined processes of cause and effect. And in the area of speculative theology, the antinomies negate the possibility of proving the existence of God. In all cases, the antinomies defy resolution of these questions *either* positively or negatively.

As a result, reason, in its theoretical function, is barred from any cognitive penetration into the noumenal. This does not mean that the noumenal realm is necessarily unlike man's phenomenal knowledge of it and that human categories do not apply there; rather, the problem is that pure reason can provide no guarantee of any correspondence.

What is most significant about the first critique is that while Kant revives the old Platonic distinction between noumenon and phenomenon, in exploring reason along the narrowly Aristotelian lines of his day (as a strictly cognitive activity), the Platonic distinction became a severe human limitation. Plato had stressed the noetic aspects of reason, which was deeply imbued with an intuitive or mystical quality. But in the Preface to the second edition of the first critique Kant gave indication that he was moving toward a broader, or more Platonic, conception of reason: "I have found it necessary to deny *knowledge* [of super-sensible reality] in order to make room for *faith*." Although "faith," for Kant, was to be understood largely in moral terms (stemming from his pietistic background), we have here a beginning indication of his recognition of modes of human apprehension far broader than simply discursive or cognitive reason. Much of the impetus for exploring this possibility came from Kant's tremendous interest in ethics, made urgent by the seemingly undermining affect of his first critique upon this realm. His understanding of the experience of the form of duty, like Plato's experience of the form of the good, has about it a near mystical quality.

The *Critique of Practical Reason* is of major importance not only as the attempt to create a purely rational ethic, but also as a defense of a nondiscursive mode of apprehension, as an insistence that the "rational" is not restricted in meaning to the "cognitive." It is this point which Kant develops further in the third critique, the *Critique of Judgment* (1790), in terms of beauty and the purposiveness of nature. In order to understand these points, one must beware of the misleading title of the second critique. In distinguishing between *pure* reason and *practical* reason, Kant is not speaking of two human agents or loci of activity; in both critiques he is speaking of pure reason as such, but in the first he is concerned with its theoretical or speculative function, in the second with its practical or ethical function. For Kant, this second function is the activity known as will. It is his purpose to show that will is not divorced from reason, controlled internally by drives or impulses, or externally by pleasure stimuli. In its fulfilled operation it is a purely rational enterprise; it is pure reason in its practical operation which must *control* drives and *determine* external ends.

Likewise, in this realm it was Hume who haunted Kant, for Hume understood reason as being the pawn of passions, and morality as being rooted in subjective feeling. Just as Kant's answer in the cognitive realm depended on exhibitng the *a priori* or categorical laws of man's cognitive activity, so his answer in the second critique depended on discovering the *a priori* or categorical laws of the rational will. Morality could claim objectivity and universality only by being founded not on experience, but on pure reason itself. The task of the second critique, then, is to discover the *a priori* or necessary principles of the practical reason.

At the heart of the problem of ethics is the problem of freedom; without freedom, morality is an impossiblity. But according to the first critique, since all things are seen, of necessity, under the category of causality, all things are seen as determined. Yet, Kant insists, the same noumenon-phenomenon distinction applying to the object of such knowledge also applies to the subject as well. It is man as phenomenon who is seen under the category of necessity, but the nature of the noumenal man remains unknown. Although the speculative function of reason strives for an understanding of the human "soul," the antinomies, as we have seen, left the matter of freedom for the noumenal self as "problematic but not impossible." If Kant can exhibit the will as free, he believes, he can also show the capacity of pure reason to determine the will's total activity.

If there is to be an objective ethic, an ethic based on freedom, the only possibility for it can be reason presupposing nothing else but itself, for a rule can be objective and universal only if it is not subject to any contingent, subjective conditions. Thus, moral *laws* cannot be based on the pleasure principle, for the objects of pleasure and pain can only be identified empirically, thus having no objective necessity. Further, hedonism can make no legitimate distinction between higher and lower pleasures; only if reason is able to determine the will can there be a higher faculty of desire than base feeling. Likewise, there is no objective, universal basis for an ethic of happiness, for happiness is simply the general name for satisfaction of desire.

Consequently, maxims (subjective, personal principles) of man's commonplace activity can claim the ethical status of law not according to their content, which is always empirically gained, but only according to their form. Every maxim can be tested for such universality of form by inquiring whether that maxim, if made a universal law, would negate itself. For example, all men seeking only their own happiness would soon render happiness impossible; thus, the goal of individual happiness is judged to be lacking the universality required of a moral law.

Now, since it is only the form of the maxim which makes objective claim upon the will, the will must be seen as independent of the natural law of cause and effect; that is, we have here a case in which the will operates in isolation from the phenomenal realm. The act is rooted totally in reason itself. This is the heart of Kant's ethic—"freedom and unconditional practical law imply each other." Since freedom cannot be known through the theoretical function of reason, its objective reality is discovered by experiencing the moral law as duty, as a rational necessity. This means that the pure practical laws are discovered in the same manner as the pure theoretical laws, by observing what reason directs in indifference to empirical conditions. Without the moral law, Kant insists, man would never know himself to be free—"thou ought" implies "thou canst."

For Kant, the fundamental law of the pure practical reason is this—"So act that the maxim of your will could always hold at the same time as a principle establishing universal law." Such rational control of the will is objective, for the legislation is made in indifference to any contingencies. Yet a distinction must be drawn between a *pure* will and a *holy* will; although the moral law is a universal law for all beings with reason and will, because the free man has wants and sensuous motives, he is capable of maxims which conflict with the moral law. Thus, this law comes to man as a "categorical imperative." It is categorical because it is unconditioned; it is an imperative because it is experienced as "duty," as an inner compulsion provided by reason. Holiness is above duty, but in this life it remains the ideal to be striven for, but never reached. Each maxim must strive for unending progress toward this ideal; it is such progress that deserves the name "virtue."

Kant's formulation of the moral law is, in effect, a philosophical statement of the "Golden Rule." As Kant says, the moral law of universality alone, without the need of any external incentive, arises as duty "to extend the maxim of self-love also to the happiness of others." Or, put on a commonsense level, Kant's moral formula is rooted in the integrity required by reason. It is self-evident that reason, to be rational, must operate in complete self-consistency; since the rational is the universal, reason qua reason must consent to will only that which can consistently be willed universally.

For Kant, the demand of duty is unmistakable and can, without difficulty, be perceived by the simplest person. Where the difficulty arises is in following the imperative. Kant's estimate of man is such that he goes so far as to maintain that the good act is done only when duty and inclination are in conflict. What he really means here is that aversion is a sign that the individual has gone beyond self-interest to real duty. It is necessary to insist, Kant maintains, that satisfaction follows but does not precede awareness of the moral law; there is certainly a "moral feeling" that should be cultivated, but duty cannot be derived from it.

Kant's rejection of all ethical theory but his own formal principle provides a helpful summary of alternative ethical systems. He sees six types. Of the subjective type, there are two kinds—external and internal. In the former, men like Montaigne root ethics in education, while others, such as Bernard Mandeville, see its basis in a civil constitution. Of the internal variety, Epicurus sees physical feeling as central, while Francis Hutcheson grounds ethics in "moral feeling." There are likewise internal and external types within the objective ethical systems. The former is the ethic of perfection, held by Christian von Wolff and the Stoics; the latter is the "will of God" ethic of theological morality. The subjective group Kant quickly discards as empirically based, thus, by definition, failing to meet the requirements of universal morality. Also, the objective types, though rational, depend on a content which, within the confines of Kant's first critique, can be gained by empirical means only; consequently, these too must be disqualified as being neither universal nor necessary.

Man's capacity for obeying the moral law in independence of empirical conditions establishes, for Kant, the objective fact of man's free, supersensible (noumenal) nature. As Kant puts it, the necessity of the practical reason makes freedom a rational postulate. Freedom is not known, in the theoretical sense, but it must be subjectively affirmed as necessary. This does not mean that freedom is simply subjective, but that its objectiveness is perceived through reason's practical rather than theoretical operation. Moral need has the status of law, while the antinomies render the completions of speculative reason hypothetical or arbitrary. Thus, the former provides the certitude which the latter lacks, establishing the factuality of freedom as valid for both the practical and pure reason. Here we see the breadth of Kant's conception of reason—such a moral postulate is both objective and rational, even though it is not cognitive.

Since it is Kant's concern to show that it is pure (speculative) reason itself which is practical, the postulates of reason in its practical function become objective for reason as such. In actuality, the practical function is prior and the speculative function must submit to it, for "every interest is ultimately practical, even that of speculative reason being only conditional and reaching perfection only in practical use." The result of this insight is that the agnosticism of the first critique is transcended by the second, for while still insisting upon his former severe limitations on speculative reason, Kant here provides an alternative mode for metaphysical affirmation. This is most apparent in the two additional moral postulates that Kant draws from the postulate regarding freedom. What is required by the moral law is complete "fitness of intentions," which would be holiness. But since this is impossible for finite man, the practical reason requires that one affirm an "endless progress" in which such fitness can be completed. And since such progress requires the immortality of the soul, this affirmation becomes an objective postulate of the practical reason. Such a proposition is not demonstrable, but is "an inseparable corollary of an a priori unconditionally valid practical law." Thus the second antinomy of speculative reason is practically resolved.

Likewise, a third postulate is involved. The postulate of immortality can be made only on the supposition of a cause adequate to produce such an effect; thus, one must affirm as an objective postulate the existence of God, an affirmation sharing the same necessary status as the other two moral postulates. A further basis for this postulate rests in the fact that although finite existence supports no necessary connection between morality and proportionate happiness, such a connection is morally necessary.

The affirmation of such postulates Kant calls the activity of "pure rational faith," for although they are objective (necessary), freedom, the soul, and God are not known as they are in themselves. This, he affirms, is in truth the essence of "the Christian principle of morality." It is from morality that religion springs, for religion is nothing more than "the recognition of all duties as divine commands."

Since morality has to do with the moral law, with the form of an action, it follows that no "thing" is good or evil; such designations properly apply only to an acting will. Good and evil are defined only after and by means of the moral law; to reverse this procedure is to develop an empirical, subjective ethic. It is the practical judgment which determines the applicability of a universal maxim to a concrete act. To make an application such as this is very difficult, for it is here that the laws of freedom (the noumenal realm) are applied to the laws of nature (the phenomenal realm). Such a meeting is possible because the moral law is purely formal in relation to natural law. That is, it raises this question: if this proposed act should take place by a law of nature of which you were a part, would your will regard it as possible? The center of the moral act thus rests in one's intentions, not in consequences. If the right act occurs but not for the sake of the moral law, it is not a moral act. The only incentive which is valid is the moral law itself.

For man as he is, his natural feelings of self-love are ever at war with the moral law. The very fact that morality resides in law reveals the severe "limitation" of man. The moral law is victorious only if all inclinations and feelings are set aside out of respect for the moral law, in and of itself. An act not performed out of such a sense of duty is inevitably tainted with the self-pride of believing goodness to be a spontaneous reflection of one's nature.

Perhaps the major difficulty in Kant's ethic is the problem of application. There are few acts which a performer would not defend as universally valid if the hypothetical performer and situation were in every way identical with those of the actual performer. Every evil has been defended by the exigencies of person and circumstance. Kant's moral formula is designed to eliminate all such individualized decisions. Yet to the degree that the formula is interpreted, not in such a particularized fashion but in an absolutely universal sense, its inadequacy becomes evident. Total truth-telling, total promise-keeping, and the like, all have obvious moral exceptions. Likewise, how is one to resolve conflicts between these objective duties? And further, law for its own sake tends to be elevated above the individual men between whom moral relations arise.

Kant's moral position has stimulated generations of heated conflict. For certain theologians, Kant's ethic seems to be only an ethic of the fall and not a redemptive ethic; for others, it is a classic Protestant ethic, judging human pretension and incapacity. For philosophers, the difficulty, as with Anselm's ontological argument, rests in its deceptive simplicity (despite the difficulty of its expression). Such a position is uncomfortable in its rather wholesale rejection of consequences, moral incentives, absolute good, and the like. But there is no denying Kant's realistic appraisal of human capacity, the absolute quality of moral activity and yet the relativity of concrete ethical situations. It may be that Kant's ethic is too simple, discards too much, and is too uncompromising, but consequent ethicists have found it impossible to bypass this second critique.

In regard to their larger ramifications, Kant's critiques have been a powerful damper on speculative metaphysics. Philosophically, they have stimulated an exploration of noncognitive modes of human apprehension; theologically, they have encouraged exploration of the moral dimensions of religion and of theological method.—*W. P. J.*

PERTINENT LITERATURE

Beck, Lewis White. *A Commentary on Kant's* Critique of Practical Reason. Chicago: University of Chicago Press, 1960.

Lewis White Beck's excellent commentary on the *Critique of Practical Reason*, the most comprehensive published in English, is chiefly devoted to a section-by-section analysis of Immanuel Kant's work. In addition, the text is supplemented by a wealth of footnotes of interest primarily to the Kant scholar, while accessibility of the work to students is not sacrificed.

Two additional goals are set by Beck for the commentary: to place the *Critique of Practical Reason* within the framework of Kant's philosophy as a whole and within the context of eighteenth century philosophy, and to assess the *Critique of Practical Reason* on the basis of its philosophical merit. The former aim is accomplished in part through a tracing of the incubation period of the *Critique of Practical Reason*. Beck shows that the work moved from its initial conception to publication in the remarkably short period of less than one year. The motivating force behind its writing was the objection by the critics that the *Foundation of the Metaphysics of Morals* had failed to address the connection between theoretical and practical reason. It is this independence, according to Beck, which in fact has made the *Foundation* the more popular introduction to Kantian ethics. The *Critique of Practical Reason*, on the other hand, born as a result of the incompleteness of the *Foundation*, by necessity had to deal with topics addressed in his first critique, the *Critique of Pure Reason*. Understanding of it, therefore, requires knowledge of Kant's entire critical philosophy and the relation of his thought to that of his contemporaries. Beck's work is thus to a large extent a contextual one and demonstrates a thorough acquaintance with the thought of David Hume, Jean Jacques Rousseau, and Christian Wolff, among many others.

The critical aspect of the commentary is based on the same insight into Kant's reason for producing his second critique, the *Critique of Practical Reason*, that is, the question of the unity of theoretical and practical reason. This, along with the claim that the moral law must apply specifically to man rather than solely to rational beings in general, Beck takes as being Kant's governing hypothesis for the critique. While the criticisms occur in a scattered fashion throughout the commentary, their overall thrust is clear: Kant failed in his attempt to unite the theoretical and practical aspects of the moral law and, more generally, failed to unite theoretical and practical reason.

The moral law, Beck claims, can indeed assert its necessity; but it can do so only on the practical level. The Copernican insight of the second critique is that freedom is the source of the law itself, rather than the law being a restriction on freedom. It is man's will which is at the same time both the creator and the executor of obligation. By relating the law to the will in this manner, however, it is established for Beck that the law has practical validity only; it cannot breach the "doors" of pure theoretical reason. The ultimate question of whether practical reason and theoretical reason have the same foundation is thus left unanswered. Furthermore, on the specifically human or psychological level Kant is unable to show that the desires man has are those desires which will lead to universally identical formulations of moral rules subsumed under the moral law. Kant's analysis is thus flawed on two levels: it fails to make the vital connection to pure reason and it fails in its attempt at reconciliation with human nature.

Williams, T. C. *The Concept of the Categorical Imperative*. London: Oxford University Press, 1968.

Throughout Immanuel Kant's writings on ethics the categorical imperative occupies a prominent position and has therefore become the well-deserved object of concern for many Kant scholars as well as beginning students of ethics. Yet no concensus of interpretation of the categorical imperative has emerged. T. C. Williams' book provides a readable introduction to the reasons for this lack of concensus, an analysis of the major strains of interpretation, and an interpretation of his own (which to a large extent is rooted in previous interpretations).

Williams deals with three previous types of interpretation: the traditional formalist reading of the categorical imperative, the position of H. J. Paton that the categorical imperative is important primarily as a motivating force, and A. R. C. Duncan's view of the discussion as a continuation of the critical task developed in the *Critique of Pure Reason*.

For several centuries the standard conception of the categorical imperative was that it should serve as a precise and unequivocal test of the morality of proposed actions. This absolutist interpretation, however, meant that Kant's foundation for ethics was weak at best, for it implied that either some of his moral claims were only arbitrarily derived from the categorical imperative or that all kinds of nonmoral actions were derivable from it as morally obligatory. Paton recognized that such a consequence would surely have been recognized by a philosopher of Kant's stature. He therefore shifted the emphasis from immediate application of the principle to its being a motivating guide which would move one to a recognition that one ought to act on the basis of a rational attitude. The practical usefulness of the principle, according to Paton, is simply that it subverts selfish interests through imaginative projection of how agents ought to act in general. Duncan, then, denied even this ethical component and argued that the principle itself is not intended as a guide to moral conduct at all. He asserted rather that it is strictly a descriptive principle which describes the working of pure practical reason. Duncan consequently considered Kant's own claim to prescriptivity to be an illegitimate extension of the principle.

The Concept of the Categorical Imperative attempts to harmonize the above three previous strains of interpretation. Williams argues that both Paton and Duncan had the same fundamental insight: the categorical imperative cannot be applied in a narrow prescriptive sense. Yet Kant seems to be committed to the claim that specific universal moral laws can be derived from the categorical imperative. Williams shows that both of these aims can be accomplished if the various Kantian formulations of the categorical imperative are categorized on two different logical planes: as an instance of a formal principle on the one hand and as particular categorical imperatives on the other. The supreme principle of morality for Kant is that one should "act only on that maxim which you can at the same time will that it should become a moral law." This imperative, in conjunction with the principle of autonomy, describes the presupposition on which morality is founded. It is therefore, in terms of the second critique, not subject to a philosophical proof. The other formulations of the categorical imperative, which all make reference to ends, are to be regarded as subsidiary practical principles. They serve as concrete guides to action and arise out of the spontaneous activity of pure practical reason. It is the supreme principle of morality which manifests to the conscience the need to act on a rational basis, but it is the particular categorical imperatives which give the principle a concrete moral content, for without some reference to ends no morality is possible.

Williams' interpretation thus unites two strains of thought in Kant's position: the analytical and the ethical. It does so, however, at the price of denying Kant's claim to objectivity on the practical level. The supreme principle of morality as a precondition for morality is indeed objective since it makes no reference to ends, but the particular categorical imperatives are founded on the moral intuitions of the agent. No formal unity between these two logical planes can, according to Williams, be established.

Benton, Robert J. *Kant's Second Critique and the Problem of Transcendental Arguments*. The Hague, The Netherlands: Martinus Nijhoff, 1977.

Robert J. Benton's book is not a commentary on Immanuel Kant's second critique. It is rather a sustained and complex argument demonstrating the unity of the section called "The Analytic" within that work. In order to accomplish that end Benton focuses on the structure of the "Analytic" and argues that it is an instance of the transcendental argumentation with which readers of the *Critique of Pure Reason* are well acquainted.

A transcendental argument is one which establishes the conditions of the possibility of a type of experience. In the first critique Kant had shown that the intellect and sensible intuition are essential to theoretical knowledge. This result, however, seemingly eliminated the possibility of freedom and therefore the possibility of moral obligation as well. Benton seeks to demonstrate that moral obligation can still be rescued by Kant because the conditions of the possibility of practical knowledge involve a different set of elements from those required for theoretical knowledge: the intellect and the faculty of desire. Practical knowledge is therefore not required to be interpreted in terms of a model where all experiences have a strictly causal sequence. Yet the two forms of knowledge have a common ground—the finitude of the human mind. It is from that unifying element which guides all experience that Benton derives his major insight for analyzing the "Analytic" and transcendental arguments in general: the "must/can" structure of transcendental arguments.

Such arguments, Benton claims, are designed to show initially that something *must* be the case in general and then to show that it *can* be the case in particular instances. Seen within the overall structure of the "Analytic" this means that Chapter One shows that there must be a practical viewpoint, which is that the moral law is the sole law of practical reason; and Chapters Two and Three show that the objective realm and the realm of subjectivity are reconcilable within that viewpoint. Thus actual instances of application of the moral law are granted status only as making possible a general principle of experience rather than as involving the assertion of actual duties.

The support given for the interpretation involves asking the questions: What is the overriding purpose of the "Analytic" as a whole? and What can be the reason for the order in which the chapters are presented? According to Benton, it is these critical questions which are overlooked in a chapter-by-chapter commentary such as Lewis White Beck's. Briefly stated, the entire argument is concerned with setting up a point of view on the basis of which morality is possible, rather than establishing the moral law. Chapters Two and Three thus provide the necessary "can" or justification for adoption of a practical viewpoint, rather than an explanation of how the moral law is to be applied in concrete contexts. The interpretation thus avoids the difficulties associated both with the supposed deduction of the moral law and with the application of a strictly formal principle in specific situations.

Benton recognizes that his interpretation of the *Critique of Practical Reason* conflicts with Kant's own stated aims and the views of the majority of commentators. What makes the interpretation significant is that it provides a framework for interpreting Kant's seemingly muddled procedures in parts of the second critique. It also means, however, that Benton is committed to denying that the intention of the *Critique of Practical Reason* is to aid man in determining how he should act in particular situations.—*H.C.L.*

ADDITIONAL RECOMMENDED READING

Aune, Bruce. *Kant's Theory of Morals*. Princeton, New Jersey: Princeton University Press, 1979. A good analytical introduction to Kant's entire moral philosophy, intended for the student rather than for the Kant scholar.

Duncan, Alistair R. C. *Practical Reason and Morality*. Edinburgh: Thomas Nelson and Sons, 1957. An influential work on Kant's *Foundation of the Metaphysics of Morals* which argues against the traditional interpretation that it and the *Critique of Practical Reason* express the same fundamental ideas.

Gregor, Mary J. *Laws of Freedom*. Oxford: Basil Blackwell, 1963. An important contribution to the study of Kant's moral philosophy in that Gregor emphasizes his theory of virtue above his theory of obligation.

Murphy, Jeffrie G. *Kant: The Philosophy of Right*. London: Macmillan and Company, 1970. This book, which is part of a series on *Philosophers in Perspective*, is an excellent introduction for the beginning Kant student. While focusing specifically on the moral dimension, it considers the entire context of Kant's life and thought.

Nell, Onora. *Acting on Principle: An Essay on Kantian Ethics*. New York: Columbia University Press, 1975. Nell makes a concerted effort to examine how Kant's categorical imperative can be applied concretely to the guidance of action, while at the same time pointing out some serious flaws in his theory of right.

Paton, Herbert J. *The Categorical Imperative*. London: Hutchinson and Company, 1965. A sympathetic interpretation by one of the foremost Kant commentators. While it places the categorical imperative within the framework of Kant's entire moral philosophy, its primary text is the *Foundation of the Metaphysics of Morals*.

AN INTRODUCTION TO THE PRINCIPLES
OF MORALS AND LEGISLATION

Author: Jeremy Bentham (1748-1832)
Type of work: Ethics
First published: 1789

PRINCIPAL IDEAS ADVANCED

The first principle of moral philosophy is the principle of utility which states that every man is morally obligated to promote the greatest happiness of the greatest number of persons.

The principle of utility takes account of the fact that all men are governed by an interest in securing pleasure and in avoiding pain.

Only the consequences of acts are good or bad; intentions are good or evil only insofar as they lead to pleasure or pain.

Since suffering is always bad, all punishment is bad; but punishment must sometimes be administered in order to avoid the greater suffering that an offender against society might bring to others.

Bentham's aim in writing *An Introduction to the Principles of Morals and Legislation* was to discover the foundations for a scientific approach to penal legislation. Because he found these in human nature, rather than in statutes and precedents, his work is also a book on morals.

Two distinct elements appear in Bentham's theory. The first is a psychology of motivation according to which all the actions of men are directed toward pleasures or away from pains. The second is a principle of social ethics according to which each man's actions ought to promote the greatest happiness of the greatest number of persons. That the two principles are independent in their origin and application is not altered by the fact that happiness, according to Bentham, consists in nothing other than pleasure and the avoidance of pain.

The obligation to promote the happiness of the greatest number Bentham called *the principle of utility*. In the manner of the eighteenth century, he frankly admitted that this first principle of his philosophy cannot be proved, because a chain of proof must begin somewhere, and there can be no principle higher than a first principle. The principle, he said, is part of "the natural constitution of the human frame," and men embrace it spontaneously in judging others if not in directing their own actions. Bentham believed that, in addition to this principle, there are in man social motives, including "goodwill" or "benevolence," which work in harmony with the principle of utility; but the inclination to kindness is one thing, and the principle of utility something else. The latter is an intelligible rule which lies at the foundation of all morals; hence, also of legislation.

What chiefly distinguished Bentham from other eighteenth century moral philosophers was, first, that he recognized only one ultimate principle of morals and, second, that the principle which he maintained was one which admitted of empirical application. The "Age of Reason" commonly appealed to a whole array of self-evident principles, intuitive convictions, and laws of nature. But Bentham complained that none of them provided an external standard which men could agree on. In many instances, the alleged truths of nature were an expression of the principle of utility: but at other times they were nothing but expressions of private feelings, prejudices, and interests. The principle of utility, on the other hand, made it possible to define good and evil, right and wrong, in terms which everyone understood and accepted. "Nature has placed mankind under the governance of two sovereign masters, *pain* and *pleasure*. . . . The *principle of utility* recognizes this subjection, and assumes it for the foundation of that system, the object of which is to rear the fabric of felicity by the hands of reason and of law."

These fundamentals having been laid down, Bentham devoted the remainder of his work to detailed analyses of the psychology of human behavior, chiefly as it bears upon problems of social control. His aim was to find the natural divisions of his subject and to arrange the matter in tables which would be of help in drawing inductions.

First, he treated of pleasures and pains. The legislator, he said, has a twofold interest in these. Inasmuch as the general happiness consists in pleasure and the avoidance of pain, the legislator must consider these as ends or final causes; but since, as legislator, he has to employ motives, he must also consider them as instruments or efficient causes. It is the latter consideration especially that makes it necessary to consider the *sources* of pain and pleasure. The legislator is advised that, in addition to such internal motives as men have toward benevolence, there are several external forces or "sanctions" which reinforce virtue and right. The physical sanction is the pain and loss which nature attaches to certain imprudent acts; the religious sanction is fear of divine displeasure or hope of divine favor; the popular sanction is the favor or disfavor of our fellow men. Political sanction is a fourth source of pain and pleasure, being the rewards and punishments which the ruling power of the state dispenses in cases where the other sanctions are not effective.

The *value* of particular pains and pleasures is obviously relevant in connection with the ends of legislation, but not less so in connection with the means, since the deterrent must be made to outweigh the temptation to crime if it is to serve its purpose. Bentham believed that it is possible to estimate the amount of a pain or pleasure, and he suggested seven calculable factors: intensity, duration, certainty, propinquity, fecundity, purity, and extent. Besides the quantitative side of pain and pleasure, Bentham recognized that there are different kinds of pains and pleasures, and he devoted a chapter to tabulating them. Perceptions, he held, are usually composite, made up of more than one pain or pleasure or both. He undertook to analyze them into their simple parts, and to enumerate these. Besides pleasures of the senses he noted pleasures of acquisition and possession, of skill, of friendship, of a good name, of power, and even of malevolence. Besides pains of the senses, he recognized the pains of privation (desire, disappointment, regret), and the kinds of pains that are opposite to the pleasures listed above. The lawmaker, according to Bentham, must have all these in view. When he considers an offense, he must ask what pleasures it tends to destroy and what pains to produce in order, on the one hand, to estimate its mischief to the public, and, on the other, its temptation to the wrongdoer. Furthermore, when he considers the punishment, he must take into account the several pains which it is in the power of the state to inflict.

Besides these accounts of the general value of pains and pleasures, a special chapter is devoted to individual differences. Bentham listed thirty-two factors which influence men's sensibilities to pain and pleasure, reminding lawmakers that there is no direct proportion between the cause of pain or pleasure and its effect, since differences of health, sex, education, religion, and many other conditions must be taken into account.

Bentham then considered human *action*. The legislator is interested in acts in proportion to their tendency to disturb the general happiness; hence, his judgment has regard only to consequences, not to motives. Bentham distinguished carefully between the intention of an act and its motive. The intention of an act, he maintained, may have two things in view, the act and its consequences, but not equally: one must intend at least the beginning of the act, as, for example, when a person begins to run; but he may have none of the consequences in view, and rarely does he have more than a few. To make his point, Bentham took the story of the death of William II of a wound received from Sir Walter Tyrrel when they were stag-hunting, diversifying it with different suppositions. Had Tyrrel any thought of the king's death? If not, the killing was altogether unintentional. Did he think, when he shot the stag, that there was some danger of the king's riding in the way? If so, the act was intentional but obliquely so. Did he kill him on account of hatred and for the pleasure of destroying him? If such was true, the deed was ultimately intentional. Such examples show that intention involves, besides the motive or will to act, an understanding of the circumstances in which the action takes place. It is the latter which, according to Bentham, must chiefly be taken into account when an intention is praised or blamed, for it is the consequences which are properly good or evil; the intention is good or evil only in so far as the consequences were in view from the start.

Bentham maintained that the will or motive of an intentional act is neither good nor evil. One desire is as legitimate as another, and the pleasure which a man receives from injuring an enemy is, considered by itself, a good, however we may judge the act in terms of its consequences. Bentham was alert to the role which fictitious entities play in human discourse, and noted the difficulties which they place in the way of exact analysis. For example, "avarice" and "indolence" are supposed to act as motives, although they correspond to nothing in the heart of man. Similarly, real motives, such as the pleasure of eating or of sexual satisfaction or of possession are obscured by calling them "gluttony," "lust," and "covetousness." To help clear up the confusion, Bentham went over the whole catalog of kinds of pleasures and pains, and noted how many of them have several names. Thus, pleasures of wealth are called "pecuniary interest" (a neutral term), "avarice," "covetousness," "rapacity," "lucre" (terms of reproach), and "economy," "thrift," "frugality," "industry" (terms of approval), according to the circumstances and our estimate of their consequences. But the motive, in each case, is the same, and may neither be praised nor blamed.

Nevertheless, some motives are more harmonious with the principle of utility than others. Bentham classified the motives as *social* (good will, love of reputation, desire for friendship, and religion), *dissocial* (displeasure), and *self-regarding* (physical desire, pecuniary interest, love of power, and self-preservation). But not even the purest social motive, good will, always coincides with the principle of utility, particularly when it confines itself to the interests of a limited set of persons.

Bentham recognized that when a man is contemplating an act, he is frequently acted on by many motives which draw him in different directions. Some of them are more likely to prompt mischievous acts, others to oppose them. The sum of the motives by which a man is likely to be influenced make up his disposition. "Disposition" was, in Bentham's view, another fictitious notion which represents no more than one man's estimation of how another man is likely to behave. Nevertheless, so far as it can be estimated, the disposition of an offender is important to know. And Bentham admitted that judgments of good and bad do apply to dispositions, as they do not to single motives. He suggested that the degree of depravity of a criminal's disposition is inversely proportional to the strength of the temptation needed to prompt him to a mischievous act.

True to the principle of utility, however, Bentham maintained that, strictly speaking, only the *consequences* of an act are good or bad. Pleasures and pains are real, as dispositions are not. And acts and intentions, which are internal to the doer, are good or evil only as they attach to consequences. Bentham devoted approximately the last half of his book to distinguishing and classifying mischievous acts. The main division is between primary mischief, which is suffered by one or more individuals whose happiness is directly affected by the offense, and secondary mischief, which is the alarm or danger apprehended by the citizenry from the presence of the offender at large in their midst. Penal legislation must take account of both, since the latter diminishes the general happiness (by disturbing men's sense of security) no less than the former.

Bentham's principles for penal legislation are frankly calculative. The law-maker must estimate the strength of temptation to do mischief, and make the punishment sufficiently severe to act as a deterrent. Bentham argues that there is no kindness in making the punishment light because if it is strong enough persons disposed to crime will not have to endure it, whereas if it is too light, they will. Severity, of course, is not the only thing to be considered. Applying his method of calculating the amount of pleasure and pain, Bentham argued that the certainty and proximity of the punishment must also be taken into account, as well as its appropriateness.

There is no detailed account in the *Introduction* of the purposes of punishment. But in a footnote, referring to a separate work called *The Theory of Punishment*, the author explains that the principal end of punishment is to control action, whether that of the offender or of others who might be tempted to similar misdeeds. It may work through reformation of the man's disposition, through prohibiting action, or through making him an example. Bentham recognized that vindictive pleasure is also a good, but he could not tolerate making it a basis for punishment.

Like his liberal disciple John Stuart Mill (as in *Essay on Liberty*, 1859), Bentham held that all punishment is mischief and to be admitted only for the exclusion of greater evil. In many cases, to use his words, "punishment is not worth while." This is the case when the act was freely entered into by the party injured, or when the penalty cannot be efficacious (for example, when it comes too late), or when the evils of detecting and prosecuting the crime are more costly than the evils they are intended to prevent. In some cases the mischief is better countered in other ways—for example, the disseminating of pernicious principles should be overcome by educating people in wholesome ones.

The limitations of effective penal legislation were a matter of primary concern to Bentham. He emphasized private ethics and education as more important than legislation. His view of ethics is usually designated "enlightened self-interest" because he maintained that in most instances a man's motives for consulting the happiness of others are dictated by his own interest. But he conceded that there are occasions when social motives act independently of self-regarding motives. Private ethics he called the art of self-government; education, the art of governing the young. Admittedly these do not always achieve their full intention; but it is dangerous and unprofitable to try to make up for their defects by criminal procedures.

Bentham was especially critical of the jurisprudence that existed at the time, and he distinguished his approach to the subject by coining a new name. A book of jurisprudence, he said, could have one of two objects: to ascertain what the law is, or to ascertain what it ought to be. Most books are devoted to the former—he called them "expository"; his was devoted to the latter—

he called it "censorial" jurisprudence, or the *art of legislation.—J.F.*

PERTINENT LITERATURE

Plamenatz, John. *The English Utilitarians*. Oxford: Basil Blackwell, 1958.

Jeremy Bentham has always been considered important as a reformer and as the head of the philosophical movement known as utilitarianism; but many, including John Stuart Mill, have not regarded him as, properly speaking, a philosopher. John Plamenatz agrees with this estimate in *The English Utilitarians*, where he represents Bentham as a practical man who embraced whatever doctrines of the Enlightenment suited his purpose without subjecting them to serious criticism. The famous hedonistic calculus is an example: Bentham's rough indication as to how it would work seems to imply that putting it into practice is a mere detail, whereas, says Plamenatz, "the truth is that even an omniscient God could not make such calculations, for the very notion of them is impossible."

Bentham's greatest confusion lay in trying to employ an egoistic psychology and an altruistic theory of morals at the same time. According to Plamenatz, Bentham did not notice that there was any difficulty here, because he was too busy showing the world how to form a society in which selfish interests can be so harmonized that as a matter of fact everyone will desire what as a matter of right he ought to desire. Plamenatz says, however, that even if it could be brought about that men's selfish interests were perfectly harmonized, it would still be impossible to reconcile egoism and utilitarianism in principle.

The English Utilitarians remains an important statement of the philosophical issues to which Bentham's *Introduction* gives rise, even though the conclusion seems to be "that it is not possible to make sense of what Bentham is saying." In *Man and Society* Plamenatz tries, as he says, to be more sympathetic and more adequate, which he does by distinguishing two lines of argument, one of which he finds relatively free of philosophical difficulties.

Insofar as Bentham believed that it is possible to deduce moral propositions from psychological observations, he was surely mistaken. His initial enterprise was to define value terms in such a way as to eliminate emotive and intuitive connotations and to give to each an objective, empirical content by way of reference to the tendency of an act or a thing to increase pleasure or diminish pain. This would have been legitimate had he been content, as David Hume was, merely to give a descriptive account of moral phenomena. Bentham, however, was primarily a reformer; and, having stipulated new meanings for the words "good" and "right," he proceeded to use them in the old way, according to which what is good ought to be desired and what is right ought to be done. In this manner he convinced himself that his utilitarian rule followed logically from his empirical definitions.

Plamenatz, however, allows that there is another strain of thought in Bentham's *Introduction*. In some passages Bentham takes his stand boldly on naturalistic assumptions about the world and man. When arguing in this vein he assumes that everyone, willy-nilly, seeks pleasure, and that ethical terms need to be redefined so that men can pursue pleasure more efficiently and without bad conscience. Taken in this second way, the utilitarian scheme is no longer an attempt to derive moral rules from psychological truths, for in this view morality in the traditional sense is an illusion which must disappear when men throw off their superstitious beliefs about God and about natural law.

Taken in a naturalistic sense, the utilitarian principle is merely a prudential rule and, as such, is compatible with psychological egoism. If "I ought to do this" means no more than that there is a social rule of which I generally approve, it is possible for me to will my own pleasure in every case while affirming that I ought to will other people's pleasure also. The possibility turns on keeping in mind the difference between what I will as a means and what I will as an end. The function of a rule is to achieve social control; and it is in my interest to support such a rule even when it deprives me of some pleasures. Stated in these terms, Bentham's system is self-consistent.

Nevertheless, in Plamenatz's opinion, utilitarianism, in both its psychological and moral claims, rests on rather simple mistakes. Against egoism, he argues that, while it is a truism that when a person gets what he wants he is satisfied, it does not follow from this that what he wants is his own satisfaction, and that therefore he is selfishly motivated. Similarly, against hedonism, he argues that although it may be the case that one always experiences a pleasant feeling when one gets what one wants, it does not follow that what a person wants is a pleasant feeling. On account of confusions such as these, together with the absurdity of the attempt to measure and sum up pleasure, Plamenatz finds himself obliged to reject the greatest happiness principle. He proposes an emendation, however, which he thinks might have received Bentham's approval. Instead of trying to calculate what would make everyone happy and acting accordingly, why not follow the rule of trying to help others "get what they want according to their own preferences"? To a modern liberal such as Plamenatz, there is something sinister about one person trying to help another get what the former thinks is good for him.

Plamenatz believes that the spirit of Benthamism is against any system which would result in sacrificing the happiness of people to an abstract scheme or program. For this reason, he regards utilitarianism as more promising than John Locke's appeal to natural law. He even suggests the possibility of reframing the doctrine of natural law in the light of his improved reading of Bentham: Act so as to help other people get what they want and not what you think is good for them.

Lyons, David. *In the Interest of the Governed: A Study in Bentham's Philosophy of Utility and Law.* Oxford: Clarendon Press, 1973.

This closely reasoned study attempts to differentiate between Jeremy Bentham's utilitarianism and that of the school which goes by his name. David Lyons' "new interpretation" finds no place in Bentham's own thought for either egoism or the greatest happiness of the greatest number. He arrives at this view by focusing attention on two main passages from the *Introduction*—the initial sections of the first and last chapters respectively. In the former passage, Bentham defined "utility" as the principle which judges actions by reference to "the happiness of the party whose interest is in question," mentioning two parties, the community in general and the particular person. In the latter, Bentham defined "ethics" in terms that, although similar, are significantly different: that is, as "the art of directing men's actions to the production of the greatest possible quantity of happiness on the part of those whose interest is in view." Then he proceeded to divide ethics into two parts, the art of directing one's own actions (private ethics), and the art of directing the actions of other human beings (the art of government). Both of these passages speak of those whose interest is concerned; but the latter, by emphasizing the notion of directing actions, defines the utility principle in a way that would otherwise remain obscure.

The traditional interpretation, according to Lyons, assumes that when Bentham spoke of the happiness of those whose interests are in view, he meant persons who are affected by a given act. Interpreted in this way, Bentham has been understood in a universalistic sense. Lyons shows, however, that, even in the first chapter, Bentham's intention was parochial—that is, limited to one's own community. When, in addition, the passages from the final chapter are taken into account, it appears that he was guided neither by universal nor by parochial interest but by what Lyons calls a dual standard. This means that Bentham envisaged the principle of utility as applying, in the first instance, to acts of government proper, and in the second to what may be called self-government. Lyons admits that, in this interpretation, Bentham was silent respecting other areas of activity where a person is responsible for directing the interests of others—for example, the family or the school—but he sees no difficulty in extending the application. What is excluded is the universalistic interpretation, according to which the rightness or wrongness of a particular act is said to be measured by the total lot of happiness it is thought of as producing.

Much of the book is given over to showing, by an examination of texts, how the dual standard of ethics can be derived from the general principle of utility. Lyons finds a useful clue in the division by Bentham of acts of government into two classes—those of the government considered as an individual, and those of individual government officials. Here, at least, is a precedent for the twofold division of ethics. The argument assumes that, in his earlier writings, which dealt with law and government, Bentham had not seriously thought of making utility the basis for private morality and that the novel feature of the *Introduction* was his attempt to generalize the principle.

Incidental to his argument for the dual standard, Lyons maintains that Bentham was not committed to egoistic hedonism. Admittedly, he was a determinist; but when he said that every act is determined by the desire for pleasure or for the avoidance of pain, he was using the term "pleasure" loosely, as equivalent in meaning to "happiness" or "welfare." Moreover, Lyons finds clear evidence in the *Introduction* that Bentham acknowledged, with David Hume and against Thomas Hobbes, that men are often motivated by sympathy with other people's pleasure and pain. Lyons also points out that in later writings Bentham admitted to finding men more self-centered than he had originally supposed, thereby showing that he regarded it as an empirical question whether and how far man is an egoist.

With the "loosened, non-egoistic hedonistic theory of goals" which he attributes to Bentham, Lyons is in a position to reject the charge that Bentham's psychology and his ethics are necessarily in conflict. A similar question, however, arises on the ethical plane: namely, whether it is possible for one person to follow two independent rules, one of which directs him to seek his own happiness, and the other which directs him to seek the happiness of the community as a whole. Here Lyons takes up the problems of modal logic involved in determining the sense in which two or more "ought" statements can be said to conflict. For the rest, he reduces the problem to a question of fact: Is the world so constituted that private interests can be harmonized with those of the community at large? According to Lyons, Bentham, when he wrote the *Introduction*, believed that it is. Another question, related to this one, has to do with the adequacy of legislation, and how far, in specific circumstances, a person is obliged to obey the law.

Lyons believes that, with the current renewal of interest in ethical theories which provide a "standard for judging what is right and wrong," as opposed to the philosophical analysis of value-terms, the time is ripe for a reexamination of Bentham's writings. Nevertheless, he argues, until there is understanding, the time has not come for a comprehensive exposition of Bentham's doctrines.

(As the subtitle indicates, Lyons' book includes a study on law, based on a separate work by Bentham, entitled *Of Laws in General*. The two parts of the book are independent, and the present review deals only with the study of utility.)—*J.F.*

ADDITIONAL RECOMMENDED READING

Baumgardt, David. *Bentham and the Ethics of Today*. Princeton, New Jersey: Princeton University Press, 1952. Stresses the scientific pretensions of Bentham's work. See the review by Everett W. Hall, in *Ethics*. LXIII, no. 4 (July, 1953), pp. 308-311.

Long, Douglas G. *Bentham on Liberty*. Toronto: Toronto University Press, 1977. Views Bentham as a social theorist and designer of culture.

Mack, Mary P. *Jeremy Bentham: An Odyssey of Ideas*. New York: Columbia University Press, 1963. Full-scale intellectual biography.

Parekh, Bhikhu, ed. *Jeremy Bentham: Ten Critical Essays*. London: Frank Cass, 1974. Includes papers by J. S. Mill, H. L. A. Hart, and others.

CRITIQUE OF JUDGMENT

Author: Immanuel Kant (1724-1804)
Type of work: Aesthetics, metaphysics
First published: 1790

PRINCIPAL IDEAS ADVANCED

Judgment in general is the faculty of thinking the particular as contained under the universal; if a judgment brings the particular under a given universal, it is determinant, and if it discovers a universal by which to judge a given particular, it is reflective.

Taste is the faculty of judging an object by a satisfaction (or dissatisfaction) which is not dependent on any quality of the object itself; the satisfaction is a subjective response to the mere representation of the object; hence, it is disinterested.

Even though beauty is subjective, it is universal; the beautiful is that which pleases universally because it satisfies the will as if it served a purpose.

The sublime is found when a formless object is represented as boundless, even though its totality is present in thought.

Since its publication the *Critique of Judgment* has been of highest importance to the philosophy of art and of religion. It met opposition as radically skeptical and destructive of theology; indeed, Kant intended to set limits on religious thinking. It opened promising new pathways in aesthetics, still found highly worthy of exploration.

The work is based wholly on the psychology of faculties and the logic Kant adopted in the *Critique of Pure Reason* (1781) and the *Critique of Practical Reason* (1788). The former treats the faculty of *understanding*, which, presupposing natural law, brings us our knowledge of nature. The latter treats *reason* ("practical" reason, will, or desire), which presupposes freedom and legislates for us in accordance with moral law. While writing the first two critiques, Kant believed that the faculty of pleasure and pain could have no critique, being passive only. But he came to regard this faculty to be the same as the judgment, which subsumes representations under concepts, always accompanied by a feeling-response. He declared finally that judgment could have a *regulative* critique of its own, showing its functions and limitations, even though the faculty brings us no objective knowledge. Indeed, the *Critique of Judgment* would show the ground of union between understanding and reason, although their presuppositions had seemingly forced them irrevocably apart.

The desire or will when realized is actually a natural cause, specifically that cause which acts in accordance with concepts. Concepts are of two kinds, natural concepts and concepts of freedom. The understanding carries on a theoretical legislation through natural concepts resulting in knowledge; the practical reason carries on a moral legislation through precepts resulting in choices of actions. Understanding and reason legislate over the very same territory of experience, yet without conflicting. However, the practical reason presupposes a *supersensible substratum*, which cannot be experienced but which is necessary as a condition of freedom of choice. The understanding can give knowledge only through intuition, which can never reach the *thing-in-itself*; the concept of freedom, on the other hand, represents its object as a *thing-in-itself* but cannot give it in intuition. The region of the thing-in-itself is supersensible; but while we cannot *know* it, we can *impute* reality to it. This must be a *practical* reality founded on our necessity of acting, not on any source of substantive knowledge concerning it. To postulate such a substratum enables us to transfer our thought between the realm of nature and the realm of freedom and think according to the principles of each in turn.

The deduction of the principle of judgment is crucial to the book. "Judgment in general," says Kant, "is the faculty of thinking the particular as contained under the universal." Either the universal or the particular might be given. If the universal, then the judgment which brings the particular under it is *determinant*; the judgment brings knowledge according to *a priori* law and with finality. But if the particular is given, then the judgment must find for itself a law to judge by, in the absence of a concept. Hence it is *reflective*; and if the judgments delivered are to be regarded as laws this must be on the assumption of some underlying unifying principle. The principle must be this: as universal laws of nature have their ground in our understanding (as shown in the *Critique of Pure Reason*), particular empirical laws must be considered in accordance with such a unity as they would have if an understanding had furnished them to our cognitive faculties, so as to make possible a system of experience according to particular laws of nature. The concept of an actual object contains its purpose; the principle of judgment which we take, then, on these suppositions, is *purposiveness* in nature. (For nature to realize a purpose would be to carry out a "particular law of nature.") *If* nature were guided by an understanding, then purposiveness would underlie its variety as the unifying factor. This concept of purposiveness is *a priori*—it provides a principle for reflecting upon nature without needing specific experience of nature. Yet we can never prove real purpose in nature; we only justify our way of thinking about it.

The faculty of judgment functions also as the faculty of pleasure and pain. When the understanding shows us an order of nature and the judgment apprehends it under the aspect of purposiveness, we feel a pleasure, since the attainment of any aim is bound up with the feeling of pleasure. Because the ground of this feeling is a principle *a priori*, the judgment is valid for every man. The *imagination* is the faculty of *a priori* intuitions; our pleasure arises when the judgment of purposiveness places the imagination in agreement with the understanding—shows a form such as an understanding would furnish.

The judgment of taste represents purposiveness without mediation of a concept. But purposiveness may also be represented objectively as the harmony of the form of an object with the possibility of the thing itself according to some prior concept which contains the basis of this form. In two ways a concept of an object may be realized: a person may make an object which fulfills his preconceived concept; or nature may present an object realizing a concept which we supply. Thus we can regard *natural beauty* as the presentation of the concept of subjective purposiveness, and *natural purposes* as the presentation of the concept of an objective purposiveness. Hence, the *Critique of Judgment* is divided into the "Critique of the Aesthetical Judgment" (considering the former) involving the feeling of pleasure, and the "Critique of the Teleological Judgment" (treating the latter) involving the understanding and reason, according to concepts. While the aesthetical judgment is the special faculty of taste, the teleological judgment is not a special faculty but only the reflective judgment in general, judging of certain objects of nature according to reflective principles.

True to his critical logic, Kant considers in turn the quality, quantity, relation, and modality of the judgment of taste, in a subdivision called the "Analytic of the Aesthetical Judgment." Then in its "Dialectic," he resolves an antinomy or contradiction which arises in aesthetics.

By the *aesthetical* Kant means that element whose determining ground can be no other than subjective. Consequently, the aesthetic apprehension does not depend on existential relations of the judged object with other things (its usefulness, for example) but only on the relation of the *representation* of the object to the observing subject. In contrast, the pleasant and the good always involve a representation not only of the object but of some connection of the judging subject with that object; hence, they bring an interested rather than a free satisfaction. Taste is the faculty of judging of an object, or of the method of representing one, by a satisfaction (or dissatisfaction) which as to quality is entirely disinterested. The object of such satisfaction is called beautiful.

Since the satisfaction does not depend on a particular relationship with a particular subject, it may be thought of as resting on something present in everyone and hence binding universally. Since this element inheres in the subject, not in the objects judged, the quantity is a "subjective universality." What we postulate is that all rational minds are constituted alike in the relation of their cognitive faculties. For a representation to be capable of becoming a cognition at all requires *imagination* for bringing together in ordered fashion the manifold of phenomena, and *understanding* for providing a concept under which the representations may be united. But this requires as its condition a free play in the action of imagination and understanding. Aesthetic pleasure must be communicable among all minds so constituted. What the judgment of taste asserts as universally valid is not some attribute of the object (as in the claim that something is pleasant or good), but rather the claim of our presupposition of the communicability of aesthetic pleasure among subjects. As to quantity, then, the beautiful is that which pleases universally without requiring or providing a concept.

A purpose is a concept of an object insofar as the concept is regarded as the cause of the object. When we can think of an object only as though caused by a concept, *for us* that object has purposiveness, even though we cannot know whether it has purpose. That is, it has *purposiveness without purpose.* The mere form of purposiveness is given, and it is that in which we take pleasure. As to relation, beauty is the form of the *purposiveness* of an object, so far as this is perceived in it *without any representation of a purpose.*

The modality of the judgment of taste is necessity. It is, however, neither objective necessity nor practical necessity, like those respectively of understanding and reason, but *exemplary* necessity. It requires the assent of all "to a judgment which is regarded as the example of a universal rule that we cannot state." This assent may be expected only on the assumption introduced above, the communicability of our cognitions. Under this presupposition, an individual has a right to state his judgment of taste as a rule for everyone and thus assert of all subjects the particular judgment arising from his own experience. The beautiful, then, is that which without any concept is cognized as the object of a *necessary* satisfaction

The judgment of the sublime has the same quality, quantity, relation, and modality as that of the beautiful, but there are important differences. The beautiful pleases through its form and its bounds; but the sublime is found when a formless object is represented as boundless, even though its totality is present in thought. Hence while beauty is a satisfaction in quality, the sublime is a satisfaction in respect to quantity. Furthermore, in the sublime the form may seem to violate purposiveness and be quite unsuited to our presentative faculty. It rather should be said that the object is fit for the presentation of a sublimity found in the mind, producing in us a feeling of purposiveness of our powers, independent of nature.

The sublime has two kinds: the mathematical, and the dynamic. Whereas that of the beautiful is restful, the judgment of the sublime stirs a movement of the mind which is judged as subjectively purposive and is referred either to the cognition, generating (A) the mathematically sublime, or to the will, generating (B) the dynamically sublime.

(A) We can always think something still greater than whatever the senses give us. While we cannot have an intuition of the infinite, which is absolutely great, we can comprehend it logically. To do this without contradiction presupposes a supersensible faculty. Thus we refer to the ideas of reason (God, freedom, immortality). Comparing the objects of nature, however grand, with these ideas, we gain a feeling of respect for our own destination according to the law of reason. (B) On observing in nature mighty objects from which we are in no danger, if we can think of a case in which we would fear them, we feel the emotion of the sublime. It calls up a comparison with our own power, which is small physically but which in our *rational* faculty has a superiority to nature even in its immensity, in the sublimity of the mind's destination. The judgment of either kind of sublime is thus not so much upon the object but on our state of mind in the estimation of it. Like the judgment of the beautiful, the judgment of the sublime postulates a common faculty among men, in this case the feeling for the legislation of reason, that is, for what is moral.

Kant considers it requisite to provide a *deduction* or proof of its grounds for any judgment claiming necessity. But since the judgment of taste is neither cognitive nor practical, it can draw its necessity from no concepts. Rather, it has a twofold peculiarity: (1) it claims the universality of a singular, not a universal, proposition; and (2) it claims the necessary assent of everyone *a priori*, but cannot depend on *a priori* grounds of proof for doing so. And because of what they are, Kant asserts, the explanation of these peculiarities suffices as a deduction. As to the necessity, although the judgment of each individual improves with exercise, at each stage it claims the necessary assent of others. It claims autonomy. If it submitted to external principles, it would be something other than taste. As to quantity, since it judges without a concept, this must always be singular: "This tulip is beautiful," never "All tulips are beautiful," since the universal subject term of the latter is a concept and brings the understanding into the process. Obviously, then, no objective principle of taste is possible, and no rule can be given to art. Rather, the principle of taste is the subjective principle of judgment in general, operating on the condition solely of the faculty of judgment itself.

Unlike mere labor, or science, or commercial handicraft, beautiful art is free. Yet we must be conscious of it as art and not nature, to keep it within the framework that will allow it to please in the mere act of judging. Beautiful art is the work of genius, which is the "innate mental disposition (*ingenium*) *through which* nature gives the rule to art." Genius is an original productive talent, not a capacity for following rules. Its products serve as examples setting standards for others. Natural beauty is a beautiful thing, but artificial beauty is a beautiful representation of a thing. In some beauties, such as the latter, inevitably a concept enters, and enjoyment through reason as well as aesthetic judging enters with it. Taste, but not genius, is a requisite for judging works of beautiful art. Genius is a faculty of presenting *aesthetical ideas*, representations of the imagination which occasion much thought where no one thought is adequate. This is a particular kind of the play which harmonizes the imagination and the understanding. It goes beyond the limits of experience to find presentations of such completeness that they have no example in nature, presentations which will communicate the aesthetic pleasure to others.

The chief aesthetic problem of Kant's times was how to controvert seriously matters of taste as though taste had an objective standard, when we also assert that there is no disputing tastes. Kant cast the problem as an antinomy in the "Dialectic of the Aesthetical Judgment." The thesis is "The judgment of taste is not based upon concepts, for otherwise it would admit of controversy (would be determinable by proofs)." The antithesis is "The judgment of taste is based on concepts, for otherwise, despite its diversity, we could not quarrel about it (we could not claim for our judgment the necessary assent of others)." The apparent contradiction is resolved when we recognize that "concept" has a different reference in each proposition. A concept may be either determinable or not. The thesis refers to determinable concepts; the antithesis refers to the one indeterminable concept, the supersensible, on which the faculty of judgment rests. So understood, both are true, and the contradiction disappears.

The beautiful is the symbol of the morally good, in that it gives pleasure with a claim for the agreement of everyone else. It makes the mind feel an elevation of itself above mere pleasantness of sensation, and enables it to estimate the worth of others in this regard also. For just as the reason does in respect to the practical, the judgment gives the law to itself with respect to objects of pure aesthetic satisfaction. The propaedeutic to the beautiful arts lies in humane studies, not in precepts, and it reaches art through the social spirit and the communication of men which is distinctive of humanity. Taste "is at bottom a faculty for judging of the sensible illustration of moral ideas. . . ."

The sequel of the study of purposiveness in nature without purpose is the study of the basis of judging nature as having purpose—the "Critique of the Teleological Judgment." We have absolutely no grounds to ascribe purpose objectively to nature, but must regard purpose as a principle supplied by ourselves for bringing this phenomena of nature under rules wherever the laws of mechanical causality do not suffice to do so.

A purpose is a concept which functions as a cause of that of which it is the concept. In order to see the possibility of a thing as a purpose, it is a requisite that its form is not possible according to natural laws and that the empirical knowledge of its cause and effect presupposes concepts of reason. The things regarded as natural purposes are organized, living beings. The understanding takes causes to be immediate preceding conditions (efficient causes) of their effects, but the reason can think a final cause. For a thing to be a natural purpose, its parts must be possible only through their reference to the whole, and they should so combine in the unity of the whole that they are reciprocally cause and effect of each other. Thus nothing is in vain in it. The being so constituted may be regarded as the product of both efficient causes and final causes, an organized and self-organizing being—in a word, a *natural purpose.*

Organized beings give the basis for teleology, as they first afford objective reality to the concept of a natural purpose. From regarding them, we are carried farther, reflectively to regard the mechanism of all of nature as subordinated according to principles of reason.

The reflective judgment must subsume presentations under a law not yet given; hence, it must serve as principle for itself. Therefore it needs maxims for its reflection, so as to attain to concepts and cognize nature even according to empirical laws. Among its maxims the following antinomy arises. Thesis: All production of material things and their forms must be judged possible according to merely mechanical laws. Antithesis: Some products of material nature cannot be judged to be possible according to merely mechanical laws. But these are maxims, not substantive propositions. The concepts involved in maxims of the judgment (including "mechanical laws") are not accorded objective reality but are merely guides to reason. Now the thesis may be acceptable as a maxim of the determinant, and the antithesis of the reflective judgment. Hence, no contradiction in fact exists between them.

To unite the mechanism of nature and the principle of purposes, teleology places the supersensible tentatively at the basis of phenomenal nature, but of it we can have no theoretical knowledge whatever. We should explain everything in nature by mechanism as far as this is in our power. But we should acknowledge that some things, which we cannot even state for investigation without a concept of a purpose of reason, must finally be accounted for by purposes.

For anything in nature, if we ask why it exists, the answer is either that it rose solely out of nature's mechanism without design, or else that it has somewhere a designed ground as a contingent being. And if the latter, we can say either that its purpose lies in itself—a final purpose—or that the ground of its existence is external to it in another natural being. Apparently, man is the only being we can regard as the ultimate purpose of creation here on earth, for he is the only creature "who can form a concept of his purposes and who can, by his reason, make out of an aggregate of purposively formed things a system of purposes." That within him which is to be furthered as a purpose must be either what nature could perhaps satisfy, his happiness, or else his aptitude and skill with which he can turn nature to all kinds of purposes, his culture. But if man makes happiness his whole purpose, a purpose dependent upon nature, this renders him incapable of positing his existence as a final purpose and of being in harmony with it. The culture of skill, and particularly of the will, of discipline, makes us receptive of higher purposes than nature itself can supply. Through culture of the beautiful arts and the sciences we are prepared for a reign in which reason alone shall have authority.

The moral law, as the rational condition of the use of our freedom, obliges us *a priori* (as shown in the *Critique of Practical Reason*) to strive for the highest good in the world possible through freedom. The highest physical good is happiness. But the reason supposes virtue to be the worthiness to be happy; and it is impossible to represent virtue and happiness as connected by natural causes or as harmonized in life. Thus, in order to represent to ourselves a final purpose consistent with the moral law, we must assume a moral world cause. While the final purpose cannot be regarded as having objective reality, it has subjective practical reality by being embodied in our actions toward the highest good. Through it we gain the possibility of thinking the world as a purposive order, although we gain no proof of the existence of its original Being. "For the existence of the original Being as a Godhead, or of the soul as an immortal spirit, absolutely no proof in a theoretical point of view is possible. . . ." Faith (as *habitus* or disposition, not act) is the moral attitude of reason toward belief in something unattainable by theoretical cognition. The mind assumes that, since it is so commanded, the duty to attain the highest good is possible to fulfill. It has grounds for such a faith in the faculty of the reason freely to legislate in accordance with the moral law. Only freedom, among the three pure rational ideas—God, freedom, and immortality—proves its objective reality by its effects in nature; and thus it renders possible the reconciliation in thought and nature of God, immortality, and freedom.—*J. T. G.*

PERTINENT LITERATURE

Crawford, Donald W. *Kant's Aesthetic Theory*. Madison: University of Wisconsin Press, 1974.

Recent work on Immanuel Kant's *Critique of Judgment* tends to eschew line-by-line commentary. In part this is because it is now commonly acknowledged that Kant's way of organizing his argument does not always bring out its real thread. Kant tended to cast all his work into the Procrustean forms that he had worked out for the *Critique of Pure Reason*. The relevance of this model for the *Critique of Judgment* is debatable, and its perspicuity even for the first has not gone unchallenged. Given these assumptions, what can replace commentary is a kind of reconstruction designed to exhibit the underlying pattern of the argument in such a way that its sound points can be made more attractively than Kant himself makes them and its weak points can be pinpointed and criticized.

Donald W. Crawford's exercise in the direction of reconstruction starts by focusing on the first "moment" of Kant's analytic of the beautiful, disinterestedness. The role of this concept has been frequently misunderstood, most often by exaggerating it as stating necessary and sufficient conditions for the judgment of beauty. (This sometimes occurs under the tacit influence of aesthetic theories focusing on the quite different concept of aesthetic distance.) To determine the true role played by disinterestedness in Kant's argument, Crawford invokes the distinction appearing elsewhere in Kant between "empirical" and "transcendental" deductions. "Disinterestedness," he believes, plays the first role: it explains by way of a regressive psychological causal analysis, after the fashion of John Locke and David Hume, why we *think* we are entitled to expect agreement from others in our judgments of beauty. The reason is that by inner inspection we claim to exclude by our lights any egocentric motive which could keep our judgment from being disinterested and hence universalizable. This "empirical deduction," however, cannot really justify such judgments. This can be done only by a "transcendental" deduction which sets forth the presuppositions under which we are really entitled to make such demands. Nevertheless, for Crawford "disinterestedness" does more than pass into this further demand. It enables us to mark off, descriptively, judgments of beauty from others, notably from judgments of fact and goodness on one side and judgments of the pleasant and the charming on the other. Judgments of beauty are both disinterested *and* aesthetic, in the sense that they report our feeling-states and in particular our liking-states (pleasure). They thus claim a disinterested *pleasure* that excludes the former types of judgments, which, while disinterested, involve subsumption of their objects under definite concepts that undermine the feeling dimension of the judgment; while the latter are also excluded as involving feeling-reports, but not disinterest. It is under their description as *disinterested pleasure reports* that the transcendental justification of aesthetic judgments is to be worked out.

This deduction, according to Crawford, occupies the rest of the *Critique of Judgment*. It may be summarized in five steps. Since what we want is justification for ascribing universally sharable pleasure states, the first step will be to get past the objection that pleasure is so inherently subjective that it can never be sharable in this way. To obviate this objection, one must hold, as Kant does, that the pleasure in question is consequent upon a *judgment*, while at the same time avoiding the absurdity of holding that some object causes the pleasure of beauty just because we say it does. The way out is to distinguish between the judgment that some object has a certain quality that causes pleasure (this will turn out to be formal purposiveness) and the judgment that *therefore* it is beautiful. The former sort of judgment precedes the latter and is the source of the pleasure that is reflected upon by it.

The second step proves that the required communicability rests on a state of the *cognitive* faculties, since only such faculties involve what is universally communicable. At the same time this state must be sufficiently nonconceptual to keep the reference to feeling-states. Kant concludes that the state which meets these demands is that of a harmony between the imagination and the understanding. In such a state sensory material is held in the imagination in a preconceptual but still structured way. In step three the character of an object describable as a correlate of this state is shown to be that of formal purposiveness. We thus go on in Crawford's step four to generate what Kant more narrowly calls the transcendental deduction of taste by proving that this characteristic, and the pleasure which intrinsically accompanies it as the exercise of these capacities, is a prerequisite for any objective experience and cognition, and hence can be presupposed as sharable by all beings who are capable of the kind of cognition we have. This is the ground of our expectation that others can and will concur in our judgments of beauty.

For Crawford, however, the judgment of beauty involves more than this expectation. It involves a *demand* that has the ring of duty. In explicating this further dimension Crawford hopes in one swoop to complete the deduction and to clarify Kant's contention that aesthetic judgments connect with moral judgments. His argument is that the concept of formal purposiveness becomes available for reflective consideration as the assumption that nature is ordered for our cognition. This is for Kant a "supersensible" idea in the technical sense that it cannot be fully justified by facts but is continually used in our orientation to the totality of facts. Beauty is a symbol of this comforting presupposition. But the same assumption undergirds our sense that human *purposes* are generally coherent with the natural order, and in particular that nature is amenable to our highest purpose, the realization of the rational will. Since this is also a basic postulate of morality for Kant, beauty thus also serves as a symbol of morality. The "duty" that attaches sensibility to beauty is so explained and justified.

Although Crawford's book is limited to an account of the *Critique of Judgment*, it suggests something of the relation Kant intends between that part of the book and the part on teleology in nature. Both focus on objects made accessible under the concept of formal purposiveness. Aesthetic judgment focuses this concept toward the subject, teleology toward the object, although the latter also falls short of objective constitution, despite its relevance to knowledge claims and their acquisition.

Guyer, Paul. *Kant and the Claims of Taste*. Cambridge, Massachusetts: Harvard University Press, 1979.

Like Donald W. Crawford's study (see above), Paul Guyer's book is a critical reconstruction of Immanuel Kant's argument in the *Critique of Judgment*, undertaken on the assumption that Kant's ordering of his argument is not always perspicuous. Guyer is especially sensitive to places in which Kant makes bigger claims than he can support.

A striking feature of his reconstruction is the claim that Kant's theory of aesthetic judgment is not an explanation of judgments that are independently describable in terms of disinterestedness. The identification of aesthetic judgments with their explanation (that they are reflections on pleasures caused by the awakening of a harmony between imagination and understanding occasioned by objects "estimated" to be formally final or purposive) lies in Kant's (hypothesized) attempt, recorded in both the published and unpublished introductions to the *Critique of Judgment*, to revise the views of the *Critique of Pure Reason* about the relation between an assumed "systematicity" of nature as a whole and empirical knowledge. In the *Critique of Judgment* the postulation of a nature whose laws form a perfectly coherent hierarchy that cannot be grasped except in relation to the Idea of design is made a condition of empirical knowledge itself, and not simply an ideal helpful in acquiring it. While still regulative in nature, this assumption is now seen to be as much *about* objects as about us. The presumption that natural objects are related in such a coherent way with one another suggests to Kant that *singular* objects in nature are themselves purposively coherent with the tendencies of our cognitive faculties apart from, and prior to, full conceptual knowledge. It is this notion that provides the key to an *a priori* principle of taste which Kant had hitherto thought impossible, and generates his explanatory hypothesis of a harmony between the faculties occasioned by formally final objects. This interpretation is helpful in showing how the heterogeneous materials of the *Critique of Judgment* are tied together. Guyer himself, however, is interested in determining how this setting of Kant's theory of taste predisposes him toward a concrete aesthetic which places more stress on beauties of nature and the property of "designedness" than is actually warranted by the theory of faculty-harmony itself.

It is a burden of Guyer's reading that it must explain the moments of the analytic as flowing from, rather than leading to, the explanatory hypothesis. This burden is met by claiming that the four moments provide conditions for bringing the explanation to bear on the assessment of given judgments. Employing reconstructive methods not unlike Crawford's, Guyer rearranges the second and fourth moments, universality and necessity, to state logical constraints that will apply to any judgment which is a candidate for this explanation. The first and third moments, disinterestedness and formal finality, then offer guidance as to how to link these conditions with particular acts of judging (disinterestedness) and particular objects (finality). These last notions operate analogously to schematization of concepts in the *Critique of Pure Reason*. This is Guyer's contribution to the art of using pieces of Kantian machinery deployed elsewhere to illuminate stretches of work where Kant's own machinery is alleged to be creaky. An interesting consequence of treating "disinterestedness" this way is that we no longer need to torture out of that concept a phenomenological description of "lack of interest." "Disinterest" is simply a consequence of the lack of definite concepts already built into the explanatory hypothesis: without a concept of *what* one is interested in, one *cannot* have an interest. With respect to finality, Guyer concludes that it does yield an informative aspect of objects judged to be beautiful, but nothing like the primacy of natural over artistic beauty or the love of purely "architectural" formal designedness that, as noted above, Kant wants. Perhaps it is because he obscurely sensed that his theory of taste was beginning to cut loose from its origins in a general theory of reflective judgments that Kant reintroduced the notion of a "supersensible Ideal" of the fittingness between nature and human faculties when he got to the "dialectic" of aesthetic judgment. Guyer, however, thinks this does little work in undermining aesthetic skepticism that is not already done in the deduction of such judgments.

The deduction grounds these judgments on the strictly cognitive presuppositions of the harmony theory: their sharability rests on capacities possessed by knowers. Moreover, the harmony of the faculties stands to the cases it explains as a strictly *causal* hypothesis. Together these considerations suggest that the claim on others by the judgment of beauty is best taken as a *predictive* claim. It is, however, for Guyer, an "ideal prediction" that is never verifiable in practice, since in the absence of definite concepts one can never know for sure whether he has *correctly* subsumed a judgment under this explanatory ground. Such a view preserves the corrigibility of aesthetic judgments: they can be right or wrong. This requirement, Guyer believes, is undermined by treating the claim as a weakened expectation, a quasiperformative imputation, or something closer to a moral demand. For this reason Guyer is skeptical of arguments which see in a moral demand for aesthetic sensitivity a "completion" of the deduction. Although Kant may well wish for a stronger link between beauty and the good, what he can at most expect to have shown is that there are interesting analogies between independently justified aesthetic and moral judgments.—*D.J.D.*

ADDITIONAL RECOMMENDED READING

Elliot, R. K. "The Unity of Kant's 'Critique of Aesthetic Judgement,'" in *The British Journal of Aesthetics.* VIII, no. 3 (July, 1968), pp. 244-259. Stresses the importance of reference to morality in Kant's justification of aesthetic judgments.

Genova, A. C. "Kant's Complex Problems of Reflective Judgment," in *The Review of Metaphysics.* XXIII, no. 3 (March, 1970), pp. 452-480.

_____ . "Kant's Transcendental Deduction of Aesthetical Judgments," in *Journal of Aesthetics and Art Criticism.* XXX, no. 4 (Summer, 1972), pp. 459-475. Genova stresses reflective judgment as linking together the realms of freedom and nature.

McFarland, J. D. *Kant's Concept of Teleology.* Edinburgh: Edinburgh University Press, 1970. A sound explication of the second part of Kant's third critique.

Neville, M. "Kant's Characterization of Aesthetic Experience," in *Journal of Aesthetics and Art Criticism.* XXXIII, no. 2 (Winter, 1974), pp. 193-202. Criticizes the alleged centrality of "disinterestedness" in Kant's aesthetics.

Podro, M. *The Manifold in Perception: Theories of Art from Kant to Hilde-*

brand. Oxford: Clarendon Press, 1972. Theories of perception are linked to theories of art, starting with Kant.

Warnock, M. *Imagination*. Berkeley: University of California Press, 1976. Sees Kant's aesthetics as standing behind the Romantic theory of creativity.

Zimmerman, R. "Kant: The Aesthetic Judgment," in *Kant: A Collection of Critical Essays*. Edited by R. P. Wolff. Garden City, New York: Doubleday & Company, 1967. Views Kant's aesthetics as resting on intuitions of the noumenal world.

A VIEW OF THE EVIDENCES OF CHRISTIANITY

Author: William Paley (1743-1805)
Type of work: Theology
First published: 1794

PRINCIPAL IDEAS ADVANCED

Either no religion is true, or Christianity is true because it is superior.

Once believe there is a God, and miracles are credible; revelation is a miracle, and through revelation God's will is made known to man.

From historical evidence contained in pagan and Christian writings the truth of Christianity is borne out.

The auxiliary evidences of the truth of Christianity are the prophecies of the Old and New Testaments, the morality of the Gospels, the consistency of the various accounts concerning the life and character of Christ, and the rapid growth of Christianity.

Although there are inconsistencies in the Gospels, they are attributable to historical errors or to the effect of different perspectives.

William Paley is the last of the important English theologians to write on the philosophy of religion without taking seriously the views of David Hume and Immanuel Kant. When he published his *Evidences* in 1794, all three of Kant's great *Critiques* and Hume's *Dialogues Concerning Natural Religion* had appeared within the previous fifteen years. Paley's writings sum up an era in theology. His literary style is clear but uninspired; his doctrine is unoriginal.

His principal works, he argued, form a system which establishes Christianity on a firm and reasonable basis. He has written on the evidences of natural religion, the evidences of revealed religion, and on the duties that result from both. Paley argues that by the argument from design one can prove that there is a God. That this God is the Christian God can be inferred from the excellence of his teachings which are true because they are confirmed by evidence within the Bible and by external accounts of historians. Having accepted in general outline the Christian documents as true, one must then accept the details which, supplemented by the natural light of reason, delineate one's Christian duties. In cases where the moral precepts of the Bible seem not to fit a particular problem, one may use as a basis for moral decision God's general purpose in the universe, which is that he wishes men to be happy. To provide the greatest happiness for the greatest number is an essential property of any moral act, is consistent with the explicit morality of the Bible, and is an infallible test of any moral precept.

A View of the Evidences of Christianity, by dealing with the evidences for revealed religion, holds a central place in his scheme. A typical eighteenth century work in theology, it is divided into three books which reveal in their titles Paley's plan of organization. Part I he calls "Of the Direct Historical Evidence of Christianity, and Wherein It Is Distinguished from the Evidence Alleged for Other Miracles." Part II has the title, "Of the Auxiliary Evidences of Christianity," and is concerned with Christ's moral character. Part III, "A Brief Consideration of Some Popular Objections," deals with the discrepancies in the Gospels and with the effects that the spread of Christianity has had in history.

Part I opens with a statement of the position from which Paley will argue. Either no religion is true, he believes, or Christianity is true because from every point of view it is far superior to any other. To prove that Christianity is true is to prove in this sense the very possibility of religious belief. Christianity is in part a revealed religion, and one can be convinced by an examination of the nature of man that revelation is necessary. God intends in his plan of creation that through moral obedience to him man will gain happiness in this world and in the world to come. But man must know a precept in order to obey it, and it is incredible that God should demand obedience without supplying the rules for man to obey. These rules could be supplied to all men only through revelation because reason is too weak to be a sufficient guide. But a revelation requires a miracle; and consequently, miracles are as credible as is the fact of revelation. But if miracles are credible, then some proof of their actuality is at least possible.

The only human evidence that a miracle has occurred is the testimony of witnesses. An objection to this argument, Paley points out, had been made by David Hume. He had maintained that miracles would be contrary to experience and that therefore testimony of witnesses could not be credible. "Contrary to experience," Paley thinks, must mean either contrary to the experience of a particular witness, or contrary to the general or usual experience of witnesses. Miracles have never been thought to fall into either category. Thus, to say that they are "contrary to experience" is not to state an objection to their credibility but to state a fact about them. Hume, Paley argues, has confused miracles with occurrences due to natural law. An event in accord with natural law can recur time after time in the presence of a diversity of witnesses, but miracles by their very nature are unique or nearly so. Hume's criticism is not to the point. The laws of nature are laid down by an intelligent being. However, we are justified in expecting that these laws would be suspended on occasions of particular importance, but infrequently, and only in the presence of a few people. "In a word, once believe that there is a God, and miracles are not incredible." Here lies Hume's error, Paley writes, that he did not first assert the existence and power of God for, in consequence, he maintained that miracles would be incredible to the believer and the unbeliever alike.

Paley shows to his own satisfaction that Hume is wrong and that miracles can be substantiated by the testimony of reliable witnesses. His first argument in support of the truth of Christianity and of the genuineness of miracles is that those who attest genuine miracles would not have acted in the way that they acted, according to the Bible, unless the miracles were genuine. The very fact that Christianity became an established religion is testimony to the effectiveness of miracles and the authenticity of Christ. The exponents of Christianity at its beginnings fought the state and its established religion; they were punished by torture and death; but still Christianity prevailed. It demanded a morality which was contrary to that of the dissolute, pagan age; and yet it was accepted by the people. These paradoxical facts can be explained only by admitting the truth of Christianity and the genuineness of miracles.

Many pagan writers such as Tacitus, Suetonius, Juvenal, and Pliny the Younger testify to the spread of Christianity and to the tenacity with which its adherents believed. In addition to pagan sources, we have four histories of Jesus Christ, the Gospels of Matthew, Mark, Luke, and John. We have also the Acts of the Apostles and a collection of letters written by adherents to the faith.

From this material we learn that the faith had certain characteristics which distinguish it from all other religions. It is an exclusive religion in that it denied every article of heathen mythology, says Paley. It went to the common people and preached renunciation of the world around them and pursuance of the world to come. Containing a system of values that was alien to the pagan world, it exposed its adherents to ridicule and violence. Christianity separated church and state in a way that no pagan religion had. The Gospels foretell the harassment and persecution that the propagators of the new religion had to suffer. That its adherents persisted in the face of all their difficulties is ample evidence of the strength of their belief in the truth of their preaching that Christ is the Son of God. Paley avers that one must either think of their belief as true or think of their account of it as a vast conspiracy entered into by pagans and Christians alike.

Paley now turns to the question of whether the New Testament gives an accurate account of the activities of Christ and the early Christians. Here again he finds corroborative evidence. There is no trace of an alternative story, although in ancient history we often find conflicting accounts of a single incident. Josephus in his *Antiquities* mentions John the Baptist; James, the brother of Jesus; and, though the authenticity of this passage has been questioned, the facts of Christ's own life. Tacitus, Suetonius, and Pliny, all anti-Christian writers, give us details of the story consistent with the New Testament.

If the Gospels are regarded as separate accounts by different historians, they substantiate one another; and thus the probability of their truth is higher than if there were only one account. We have the same reasons for believing that the Gospels were written by their reputed authors as we have that Caesar wrote his *Commentaries* or that Vergil wrote his *Aeneid*. The Gospels are quoted by Christian writers, beginning with those who were contemporary with the apostles. Paley cites Polycarp, the first bishop of Smyrna, who in a short letter includes forty clear allusions to the New Testament. This is evidence that he had the same books that we have and that he accepted them as the word of God. About the year 170, Hegesippus traveled from Palestine to Rome, visiting churches on the way. He remarks that "in every succession, in every city, the same doctrine is taught . . . which the Lord teacheth." The earliest Christian writers refer to the Scriptures as we have them, and later writers prove that they never lost their authority as canonical books.

Justin Martyr, writing in the year 140, tells us that the Scriptures were read in the churches. In this early period when some living Christians must have spoken with the apostles, the Scriptures were accepted as the authentic word of Christ. Indeed, the high regard in which they were held explains their survival to the present day.

Paley selects, as the three most important controversies among the early Christians, the relation of the Old Testament to the New, the origin of evil, and the nature of Christ. Many opinions were advanced and many opinions were defended, but all the disputants agreed on the same Scriptural canon. Paley quotes Saint Augustine on the Donatists that they ". . . produce some proof from the Scriptures, whose authority is common to us both." The same can be said of quotations in anti-Christian writers such as Celsus, Porphyry, and the Emperor Julian.

In the first centuries of Christianity, as Paley admits, there was some controversy about certain parts of the canon of the New Testament. But, in general, questions of authenticity were raised only about minor Epistles.

To sum up this part of the *Evidences*, Paley writes that he has shown that the account of the life of Christ and the apostles which we have is true, and that the lives of the early exponents of Christianity prove it to be true as do the writings of the early Church Fathers. He believes that if we bring the same tests of authenticity to the Christian texts that we bring to ancient secular texts, then the proof that the Christian texts are genuine is stronger than that for any secular work.

Paley's next general point concerns the credibility of biblical miracles. He throws doubt on a number accepted by the Roman Catholic Church and discusses the three miracles mentioned by David Hume in Chapter 10 of his *An Enquiry Concerning Human Understanding* (1748). In all of the cases that Paley cites, the alleged miracles will not stand under the tests that prove the biblical miracles. These tests are that the miracle is unequivocal, that it overthrows established persuasions, that it is contrary to secular authority, that it is believed by many, and that this belief leads men "to a life of mortification, danger and sufferings."

In Part II of the *Evidences*, Paley begins his discussion of prophecy, of

Christ's character, and of his resurrection. A prophecy is a statement describing an act before it takes place, before it can be foreseen by natural means. The coming of Christ was foretold in the Old Testament, for example, in Isaiah LII:13-LIII:12. These intentionally prophetic words are fulfilled by the life of Christ. Jesus himself made prophecies. He predicted the destruction of Jerusalem, an event which occurred thirty-six years after his death and under the circumstances he described.

The morality of the Gospels is an argument for their truth. Paley says that morality is not the main object of Christ's mission, which is the redemption of the world, but that it is a secondary object and that Christ put morality on a sound and effective basis. Christianity shifts the emphasis in ethics from acts to intent; and "a moral system which prohibits actions but leaves thoughts at liberty will be ineffectual and is therefore unwise." Christianity gave men a reason for doing their duty, assurance of the reality of the future existence of the soul. The Gospel omits as moral injunctions some of the qualities which other moral systems accept; for example, patriotism, friendship, and active courage. The Gospels stress certain virtues which had been overlooked but which possess high intrinsic value. These are passive courage, patience, humility, and the like. "No two things can be more different than the heroic and the Christian character," Paley points out. However, Christian virtues are those that contribute most to the happiness of society. This stress on happiness is in keeping with Paley's ethical theory as expressed in his *Principles of Moral and Political Philosophy* (1785). This moral doctrine, the Sermon on the Mount, and the Lord's Prayer are without equal or rival and could only have their source in an inspired religion, promulgated by someone with the character of Christ.

Although the four Gospels were written by different people, there is a consistency in the character of Christ which could only have come from acquaintance with the same real person. There is a similarity of phrases in all the Gospels. To give one example, Christ applies the name "Son of Man" to himself seventeen times in Matthew, twelve times in Mark, twenty-one times in Luke, and eleven times in John. The Jewish concept of the Messiah had been primarily political. A fabricated story of the Messiah would have made Jesus a political figure. But his message was in fact original and unique, almost the opposite of political.

Continuing his argument for the truth of the New Testament, Paley now turns to the references to historical facts that can be confirmed by independent accounts. These show that the biblical narrative was composed by people living at the time and who were familiar with what was happening around them. To select one example from many, in Acts XVII:23 Paul, preaching in Athens, says, "For as I passed by, and beheld your devotions, I found an altar with this inscription, 'TO THE UNKNOWN GOD.' Whom therefore ye ignorantly worship, him declare I unto you." This inscription is referred to by Diogenes Laertius, Pausanius, Philostratus, and Lucian.

The New Testament canon contains thirteen letters ascribed to Saint Paul and an account of his ministry in the Acts of the Apostles. Careful examination had convinced Paley that these two accounts of Saint Paul were independent and in consequence guaranteed each other's authenticity. His elaborate proof of this point had appeared in the book, *Horae Paulinae, or the Truth of the Scripture History of Saint Paul*, published in 1790.

Every part of the New Testament affirms the fact of the Resurrection, and all of the early teachers of Christianity agreed upon it. Saint Matthew relates that the Jews accused the followers of Christ of stealing his body. Paley replies, "It is impossible our Lord's followers could believe that he was risen from the dead, if his corpse was lying before them." But the fact is that they did believe.

Paley argues that the wide and immediate spread of Christianity is evidence of the authenticity of the Scripture. A short time after Christ's ascension, there were about three thousand Christians (Acts II:41). A little time later this number had increased to five thousand (Acts IV:4). The next chapter of Acts records that multitudes of both men and women had joined the new religion. In Chapter VI the number has increased still more—all this within a year of the ascension and in one city, Jerusalem. Four years later there were churches throughout Judea, Galilee, and Samaria. About seven years after the ascension a great number of Gentiles were converted. Eighteen years later the faith had spread through Greece, the coast of Africa, Rome, and into rural Italy. Non-Christian authors attest this spread. Only thirteen years after the ascension, Nero accused the Christians in Rome of burning the city. Tacitus refers to them as a vast multitude. Clement of Alexander, writing one hundred and fifty years after Christ's ascension, said that Christianity had spread throughout the whole world, and he was seconded by Origen about thirty years later. In eighty more years the Roman Empire had become Christian under Constantine.

This spread of Christianity is remarkable, Paley asserts. We are not watching the spread of an idea or an opinion but of a new religion, a new way of life, of thinking, and of acting. If we compare the spread of Mohammedanism with that of Christianity, it is possible for us to better appreciate the marvelous success of early Christianity. Since the later history of Christianity is not marked by such rapidity of conversion, the early Church must have had some means of conviction that we lack. This means could only have been the constant occurrence of miracles.

In Part III of *Evidences of Christianity*, Paley considers some of the objections that might be made to his historical argument for the truth of Christianity. The first of these is the contention that the Gospels disagree among themselves. Paley's answer is that the disagreements can be accounted for by the fact that the same story is being told from different points of view. For example, Saint Matthew's account of Christ's appearance in Galilee differs from that in the other Gospels, but none of the other accounts contradicts his.

It is sometimes argued that the apostles held erroneous opinions, that they misquoted the Old Testament or used material out of context to make dubious points, that they believed in the imminence of the Day of Judgment. These objections can be met by distinguishing Christ's revelation from extraneous matter in the New Testament. In no case will inconsistencies be found in his religious doctrine, and the errors in extraneous matter can be accounted for as historical errors.

Christianity cannot be held responsible for every error in the Old Testament. It recognizes as divine the origin of the Jewish religion, but not of every institution that it gave rise to. Attacks on the New Testament through the Old, such as those of Voltaire and his followers, depend on the mistaken belief that every point in the Old Testament is binding on Christians—an absurd contention.

Paley next tries to account for the fact that Christianity has not been universally convincing. Some people have heard the Christian message and yet have rejected it. For people living in a Christian nation, the acceptance or rejection of Christianity depends on one question, "whether the miracles were actually wrought." Paley argues that "from acknowledging the miracles, we pass instantly to the acknowledgement of the whole." However, we find from reading the New Testament that some Jews could accept that fact of the miracles and yet not accept Christ as the Messiah. Many Jews fancied that the Messiah would have a political mission that Jesus did not fulfill and rejected him for this reason. To heathens Christianity comes with its demand that they change their whole way of life. Many men of arrogant character would rather ignore the Christian evidence than yield to its reform. God could have formed men so that the evidence of Christianity would have been immediately apparent to them; but he did not, and thus it is consistent with his plan that some for a variety of reasons might continue to reject the truth.

Although the evidence for Christianity may not convince every mind, there is sufficient to convince the reasonable mind. God has created a world whose order is beneficent, a nature marked by goodness both of design and effect. It is a nature which bears strong marks of its origin in God. Here is evidence, convincing to the fair mind. Suppose that the evidence were unavoidable; suppose that rain fell whenever it was needed or on the just alone. Men, then, would have no freedom of choice. But free will is an essential part of God's benevolent plan. Too much evidence would be as harmful as too little; the fact is that God has supplied enough.

This argument of Paley's is an interesting use of the argument from design which he developed at length in his book, *Natural Theology, or Evidences of the Existence and Attributes of the Deity, Collected from the Appearances of*

Nature. This book, its title explaining its content, was published in 1802, eight years after the *Evidences*. In it Paley argues that just as one could reason from examining a watch that it is a human contrivance, so by examining the nature of the world one can infer that it was created by God.

Paley next takes up the problem of the effects of Christianity. It has been argued that although Christianity advocates high moral standards, its actual practice has been detrimental to morality. Paley answers that Christianity could not be expected to eliminate every act of immorality. He believes that in the course of history one cannot help being conscious of a gradual improvement. Not everyone who cries, "Lord, Lord," is acting in his name. So not everyone who persecutes in the name of Christ is acting in the spirit of Christian morality.

In conclusion, Paley repeats that there is evidence to support the leading facts of Christianity. However, he warns us not to forget that Christianity is also a revelation and an act of belief.—*J.Co.*

PERTINENT LITERATURE

Clarke, M. L. *Paley: Evidences for the Man*. Toronto: University of Toronto Press, 1974.

Natural theology, M. L. Clarke remarks, is theology as it can be deduced from the world of nature. Within the Christian tradition, its opposite is "revealed theology," as given in the contents of the Bible; the major arguments of natural theology, Clarke continues, were developed prior to the dawn of Christianity. The argument from design is a central part of natural theology.

Clarke says that the essentials of the argument from design are found in Xenophon's *Memorabilia*, I, 4, 5-7, developed by the Stoics, and classically stated in Book Two of Cicero's *De Natura Deorum*. The universe is compared to various artifacts, with the result that such features as natural beauty and utility for human purposes are taken as evidence that the universe has an architect. The Stoic version of the argument, Clarke notes, stresses the degree to which the universe is suitable to human ends, and tends to regard the universe itself as divine. As Clarke points out, when the argument from design was stated by Christian theologians, God as creator was clearly distinguished from the creation (nor did William Paley stress suitability to human ends).

During the Middle Ages, Clarke continues, *a priori* arguments were preferred, and only with the rise of modern science in the seventeenth century did the argument from design come again into the forefront of philosophical reflection. Sir Isaac Newton's discoveries, popularized by Richard Bentley and rehearsed in Joseph Addison's hymn concerning the "spangled heavens" which "their great Original proclaim," presented the universe as the product of a cosmic mathematician. Clarke records that such authors as John Ray, William Derham, and Colin Maclaurin argued from (in Maclaurin's phrase) "the evident contrivance and fitness of things" to a Mind which planned and executed this fitness.

David Hume, in his *Dialogues Concerning Natural Religion*, presented the character Philo, who, Clarke reminds us, pressed hard on the disanalogies between the universe, and any product of human contrivance; the *Dialogues* at most sanction the suggestion that the cause of order in the universe bears some remote analogy to human intelligence. Nevertheless, this skepticism regarding the design argument did not take popular root.

Clarke begins his explicit exposition of Paley's *Natural Theology* by quoting the famous watch passage in which a person crosses a heath. If the person's foot strikes a stone, it may be reasonably supposed to have been there forever; but if it is a watch rather than a stone, this supposition will not do. The difference lies in the fact that the watch, but not the stone, has parts which work together in a way that must have been contrived to yield a result.

Paley's version, Clarke points out, has comparatively little material on astronomy, the data for which was obtained for him by the astronomy professor at Dublin, John Law. His focus, rather, was on natural history, especially the parts and processes of the body. He also deals with fish, birds, insects, and plants, offering, Clarke adds, instance after instance of what he takes to be the contrivance of the Creator.

Further, Clarke mentions, a reviewer of *Natural Theology* observed that Paley's work was different from others in that he dealt with answers to objections. Important in this regard is his reply to the contention that the universe is not well constructed; to this, Paley replies that this is so only if we mistakenly suppose the universe to have been created for human benefit, a view Paley rejects. Clarke quotes Paley to the effect that the hinges in the wings of an earwig and the joints of its antennae are as carefully wrought as if God had nothing else to make. Yet this seems hardly essential to human weal.

Clarke adds that there is an element of hedonism in Paley's view. He contends that the world is essentially a happy place, as species after species lives a life of pleasure. Thus Clarke finds Paley, in his *Moral and Political Philosophy*, holding that God intends persons to be happy. Evil, Paley contends, is not the object of contrivance; people do not design it for its own sake. Evils serve their practical purposes—pain as a means to self-preservation, for example.

Clarke tells us that Erasmus Darwin, in 1794, suggested that the parts of an animal or plant, by slow improvement, have become fitted for the ends they serve, without design having played any role in the process. His grandson, Charles, was to refine these remarks in *On the Origin of Species*. Paley's *Natural Theology* was reprinted often, and its gist was defended in the *Bridgewater Treatises*, commissioned by the will of the Earl of Bridgewater, who died in 1829. These works, Clarke records, were written by eight authors between 1833 and 1836, many of them eminent scientists.

Clarke sees Paley's *Natural Theology* as essentially an eighteenth century product, bound by its perspective to its time. Still, he notes, Darwin himself thought there must be a first cause with a mind somewhat analogous to the human, and Paley's allowance for the existence of "trains of mechanical dispositions" between present order and the action of a Designer—"trains" fixed long ago and kept in power until now—suggests a way in which a defender of Paley might deal with the Darwinian objections.

Ferré, Frederick, ed. "Introduction," in William Paley's *Natural Theology: Selections*. Indianapolis: Bobbs-Merrill, 1963.

William Paley, Frederick Ferré tells us, was born in 1743, four years after the publication of David Hume's *Treatise of Human Nature*, while John Wesley's first lay preachers held forth in the fields near Bristol, England. Paley's *Natural Theology*, Ferré suggests, is perhaps best seen as an attempt to show that Hume's skeptical views on the one hand, and the enthusiasm of Wesley's preachers on the other, do not exhaust the alternatives with regard to religious belief.

Although Hume's arguments are generally conceded to be among the most forceful against Paley's type of argument, Ferré notes that James Beattie's *Essay on Truth* was thought to have refuted Hume, and Immanuel Kant was not yet well known in England. Still, *Natural Theology* gives superlative statement to the teleological argument after the powerful Humean and Kantian critiques were offered against it.

Ferré records that Paley, having graduated from Giggleswick School, where his father was headmaster, graduated from Cambridge in 1763, and became a fellow there in 1766 and a tutor in 1768. He married in 1776 and took the first of a variety of ecclesiastical appointments. Ferré notes that Paley was, with Jeremy Bentham, one of the founders of utilitarianism, and authored *The Principles of Moral and Political Philosophy* (1785), *Horae Paulinae* (1790), *View of the Evidences of Christianity* (1794), and *Natural Theology* (1805). In *Natural Theology*, Paley was a lucid expositor, not an originator. Others, Ferré indicates, had earlier said what Paley was to say so well. For a half-century or so after its publication, the book was very influential; after that, it was mainly ignored.

Ferré indicates that the argument of the *Natural Theology* falls into two parts. The first concerns an argument for the existence of God, conceived as a cosmic designer. The second deals with the attributes, or properties, of the designer. Relying on data of sensory observation, Paley's goal, Ferré notes, was to establish the strong probability that a cosmic designer exists. One observed items in which parts work together to produce a common end, whether the end was of use to humankind or not. Then one recognized these phenomena as evidence of intelligence. Ferré suggests that Paley spends the bulk of his effort in establishing that the first-stage observations are made and then does little by way of discussing the crucial second stage. Although aware that the argument requires this second stage, Paley does not explain how the "previous knowledge" of the characteristics of design, knowledge requisite to the second stage, is acquired, nor how reliable it is, nor what its status is within an empiricist theory of knowledge. Yet, as Ferré insists, these questions are basic when we come to ask whether proper inference from natural objects to a cosmic designer is possible, particularly in the light of Hume's argument.

In any case, Ferré adds, Paley contends that, by a combination of sensing and recognition, we are able to recognize the cooperation of parts in production of a common end and may then infer an intelligent designer as their cause. Further, he notes, Paley replies to objections by clarifying what exactly his argument amounts to. For one thing, Paley contends, the argument does not require that the objects in which cooperating parts are observed be seen in the process of being produced by a designer; and, of course, the design need not be one that human beings can produce. Nor must we be able to identify what purpose, if any, is served by the end that is produced. Nor, Paley continues, need the object (or its parts) be without defects. Still further, the argument need not claim that it is impossible, but only that it is improbable, that design and order be produced randomly. Again, Ferré's exposition continues, Paley maintains that appeal to "a principle of order in things" is either unintelligible or else simply is another way of referring to a designer: a natural law is but a *description*, not a *cause*, of order. Yet again, were designed and orderly objects to descend from other such objects, this, Paley holds, would but put off, not escape, the appeal to an intelligent cause of design and order.

The second stage of the argument, as noted, concerns the attributes of the being whose existence was allegedly established by the argument's first stage. Paley emphasizes that a designer must be personal (conscious, purposeful), and that, although the intelligence and power of such a being is beyond comparison, the designer need not be omniscient and omnipotent. Ferré states that Paley offers an "empirical interpretation" of the divine attributes; religious terminology uses superlatives such as "omniscience" and "omnipotence," while great wisdom and power are all that the design argument shows and all that religion requires. Analogously, the unity proved to be possessed by God is, for Paley, not greater than that possessed by a jury agreed on its verdict.

While written a half-century prior to *On the Origin of Species*, and before a mature concept of natural selection had been presented, *Natural Theology* is still a relevant work, Ferré believes, appealing to the complexity and subtlety of natural laws exhibited in the evolutionary process. Knowledge of contemporary science, Ferré believes, would not alter Paley's basic convictions, although it would require him to drop contentions to the effect that species are fixed and that species never become extinct.

Ferré also asserts that Paley's official methodology is one thing and his actual procedure of argument another. Paley declares that he will inductively derive what he says about God from observations of natural objects and processes. In fact, Ferré maintains, Paley's argument concerning the problem of evil defends the position that not only is the belief that God is good *compatible* with scientific evidence (even though it may seem otherwise), but the evidence also actually provides support for the view that there is a God, a Designer, and that he is good. In this case, then, and in others he discusses, Ferré believes we can interpret Paley in such a manner as to strengthen his sort of position against the critiques of Hume and Kant and thereby learn much from a careful study of *Natural Theology.—K.E.Y.*

Additional Recommended Reading

Bertocci, Peter. *Introduction to the Philosophy of Religion.* Englewood Cliffs, New Jersey: Prentice-Hall, 1951. An extended defense of the teleological argument.

Butler, Joseph. *The Analogy of Religion,* in *The Works of Joseph Butler.* Edited by W. E. Gladstone. Oxford: Oxford University Press, 1897. A classic attempt to show that the belief in God is reasonable. In some ways, a companion piece to Paley's.

Gaskin, J. C. A. *Hume's Philosophy of Religion.* New York: Barnes and Noble, 1978. A careful contemporary treatment of Hume's views, including his critique of the design argument.

Swinburne, Richard. *The Existence of God.* Oxford: Clarendon Press, 1979. A contemporary defense of the rationality of the belief in God.

Tennant, F. R. *Philosophical Theology.* Cambridge: Cambridge University Press, 1928-1930. Contains post-Paley statements of the argument from design.

Webb, C. C. J. *Studies in the History of Natural Theology.* Oxford: Clarendon Press, 1915. A discussion of various figures and arguments from the history of natural theology.

THE VOCATION OF MAN

Author: Johann Gottlieb Fichte (1762-1814)
Type of work: Epistemology, ethics
First published: 1800

PRINCIPAL IDEAS ADVANCED

Each self appears to be a self-conscious, intelligent, willing element in a rigidly determined system which results from a fundamental forming power in nature.

But the world of experience (together with the causal laws which appear to govern it) is a construction by the self.

The self, therefore, is free and morally responsible.

By faith the self is assured of the existence of other selves; and by action man fulfills his moral obligation: to act, to do—this is man's vocation.

Johann Gottlieb Fichte is a transitional figure in the history of German philosophy. His philosophical impetus came from Kant, and his work began the modifications of Kant which ultimately resulted in the Absolute Idealism of Hegel. He had some trying experiences as a young man, finding himself in financial want during the latter days of his formal education and during the five years that passed between his engagement to his future wife and their marriage. He was forced to scrape along as a tutor during his early career, work that was not always satisfying and rewarding. But during these early years as a private tutor he came across the writings of Kant, and these provided him with background and inspiration for his career as a philosopher. In fact, his emergence from obscurity to national recognition almost overnight resulted from his being mistaken for Kant. A book of Fichte's on philosophy of religion was published without his name appearing as author. The literary world assumed the book had been written by Kant himself. Kant then made it known that the book was from Fichte's pen, not his own, and he also praised the work, thereby immediately making Fichte a national figure.

Fichte was attracted most strongly to the ethical views of Kant. He saw himself in his youth as a Spinozist, but he was not happy with Spinoza's rigid determinism. He had considerable passion and enthusiasm, and he apparently also had a need to feel that his acts were subject to ethical appraisal in that he himself was a free and responsible ethical agent. In the Spinozistic world, of course, all acts followed from their causal antecedents in a necessary way. This view comforted Spinoza, but it was too somber for Fichte. Kant's conviction, expressed in the *Critique of Practical Reason* (1788), that men are free ethical agents, opened a new philosophical possibility for Fichte. But even Kant was not strong enough for Fichte, since Kant did not begin his philosophy with a free ethical agent but with an account of the world of experience which the scientist investigates. Kant's metaphysics and episte-mology only made it *possible* that there are free, ethically responsible selves; proof that such is indeed the case was not given. Since Fichte wanted a firmer base than this for his own philosophy, he introduced modifications which, although they seemed innocent enough at first, ultimately resulted in a no-ticeably different kind of idealism from that of Kant. Kant was moved by both the heavens above and the moral law within; Fichte was too much involved with the moral law within to pay much attention to the heavens.

On the epistemological side, Fichte dropped out the Kantian *ding an sich*. For Kant, the world of experience is a world constructed out of the sensuous material given in the manifold of intuition as ordered by the forms of space and time, a construction which is ordered by the categories. But the manifold of sense is caused by the unknown and unknowable *ding an sich*, things in themselves. We can know only the world of our experience; we cannot know anything of the things *in themselves*. (Except, perhaps, that they cause the sensuous manifold out of which we produce the world of our experience.) Things in themselves, then, initiate a process which ultimately yields the world of our experience, but the world of experience, as we are able to know it, includes no things in themselves, and it is, furthermore, something which we ourselves unconsciously construct. We do not experience things in themselves; we cannot know them. It is a short step from this idea of things-in-themselves to saying that we do not need them and that they are therefore not real. This is the step Fichte made. The world of experience was for Fichte, as it was for Kant, a construction made unconsciously by the self. But while Kant saw this construction as a kind of response to the stimulus of an unknown and un-knowable thing in itself, Fichte did away with the thing in itself and merely said that the world of experience is an unconscious construction by the self.

Fichte, however, did offer a causal account to explain how the world of experience comes to be constructed, an account which results from his fun-damentally ethical orientation. At the base of Fichte's system is the self as an ethical agent. The self, in becoming aware of itself, sees itself as a free ethical agent, and therefore posits the Ego. The self, or Ego, posits its own existence. It is as if Fichte were offering a variation of Descartes' "I think, therefore I am" argument; we might paraphrase Fichte's starting point as "I am obligated, therefore I am." It is not the knowledge problem with which Fichte begins, but the ethical problem. But after the Ego posits itself, it finds that there is need for an additional posit. One cannot be ethical in a vacuum; there must be an arena of action—one must be obligated to other persons. It is this circumstance that produces the world of experience. The Ego, having posited itself as ethical agent, also posits the Non-Ego as a world of experience (which includes other selves) in order that the Ego may have an arena in which to perform its tasks and discharge its obligations. The world of expe-rience is not fundamental in its own right in Fichte's philosophy as it is in

Kant's. Rather, the world of experience exists in order that a man can be ethical.

It is against this background that *The Vocation of Man* must be viewed. It is less technical than most of Fichte's writings, and it is addressed to the ordinary reader rather than to the professional philosopher. Fichte says in the Preface that the book "ought to be intelligible to all readers who are able to understand a book at all." He therefore avoids the words "Ego" and "Non-Ego," as well as other technical terms which appear elsewhere in his writings. Nevertheless, the position is the same. This avoidance of technicality is one of the considerable merits of this book as contrasted with Fichte's *The Science of Knowledge*. The latter is liberally sprinkled with technical terminology and arguments which Fichte himself thought important and sound, but which recent philosophers have judged to be almost the opposite. *The Vocation of Man* is thus the most understandable and the most popular statement of Fichte's position.

The book has three divisions which are entitled "Doubt," "Knowledge," and "Faith." Roughly, they may be said to represent the Spinozistic, the Kantian, and the Fichtean positions, at least as Fichte understood them.

Book I, "Doubt," has the tone of Descartes' *Discourse on Method* (1637) or his *Meditations* (1641). Fichte writes in the first person and addresses himself to the problem of discovering what he can know about himself and the world in which he lives. He considers the information he gets from sense-experience and draws conclusions about what the world is like. He accepts the view that there are independently real objects, each occupying a place in a system which is connected throughout by necessary causal relations. Each object or each event in nature is what it is and is what it must be. Nothing could possibly be other than it is. Removing even a single grain of sand, Fichte says, would change the entire structure of nature; all past and future history would be different.

Each man, including Fichte himself, is, of course, "a link in this chain of the rigid necessity of Nature." There is a "forming power" in nature, or perhaps better, behind or lying under the nature we observe, which gives rise to all the objects and events that make up the system of nature. Fichte himself was produced by the forming power. And as he becomes aware of this power, he says, he feels himself sometimes free, sometimes restrained, and sometimes compelled. Yet this is merely Fichte's awareness of how the underlying power operates in his own existence and consciousness. It explains his own consciousness, his awareness of himself as a discrete item in the system of nature. But this self-consciousness of the forming power as manifested in himself provides the ground from which he infers that the forming power also manifests itself in other objects in nature. There are varieties of individual selves, each resembling Fichte. Finally, the summation of the self-consciousnesses of these selves make up the "complete consciousness of the universe." Fichte, as a self, then, is one element—a self-conscious, intelligent, willing element—in a rigidly determined system which is the result of a fundamental forming power in nature.

Yet this Spinozistic system of nature fails to satisfy Fichte. There is no freedom in it. If Fichte, together with all his acts, is merely a set of necessary consequences in a rigidly determined system, then he is not an ethical agent. Whatever he does, he necessarily has to do, and his conduct is therefore not subject to ethical evaluation or to praise and blame. This is the outcome of his reflection. But what he desires, on the other hand, is to know that he is free and ethically responsible. He wants to be, in some sense, himself the cause of his behavior, instead of feeling that his behavior is merely the effect of external causes.

The conclusion reached in Book I of *The Vocation of Man*, then, is this: Fichte has stated two possibilities: either he is merely one element in a rigidly determined system, or else he is a free moral agent. One view, he says, satisfies his heart, while the other destroys his own sense of worth. Which view should he adopt? This is the issue he must resolve, but he is left, at the end of Book I, in doubt.

Book II, "Knowledge," is a dialogue, not unlike Berkeley's *Three Dialogues Between Hylas and Philonous* (1713). Fichte writes that he is tormented by the doubt which issued from the first attack on the problem, and he awakens in the night, his sleep interrupted by the unresolved problem. A Spirit then comes to him to lead him out of doubt and into knowledge. The knowledge offered is subjective idealism, and Book II is as fine a statement of the position as is generally available.

The Spirit begins by questioning Fichte about how he knows objects in the external world, to which Fichte replies that he knows them by sensation. But the sensations are merely modifications of Fichte himself, the Spirit points out, and so Fichte has knowledge only of his own condition—not knowledge of the independently real, external world. "In all perception," the Spirit points out, "thou perceivest only thine own condition."

Fichte is not yet convinced, however. The argument moves on to consider the ordinary belief that sensations are caused by independently real, external objects. But such independent objects cannot be known by sense, for if Fichte has sensations, they are merely modifications of Fichte himself, not characteristics of independent objects. If there are external, independent objects, they cannot be known by sense, at any rate. They can only be known in virtue of applications of the principle of causality. But how can the principle of causality itself be justified? Certainly not by appealing to the fact that sense objects are causally connected, for that would be to argue in a circle. The argument would then go: I know there are independent objects because of the principle of causality, and I know the principle of causality because independent objects are examples of it. Such an argument fails to do the required job. The principle of causality must, therefore, be justified in another way. The alternative taken is that the causal principle is a statement of how men really do interpret experience; that is to say, the principle is contributed by the knower, not by the objects known. The principle is thus another modification of Fichte himself, not a feature of the world he believes is external to himself. If this is the case, however, the justification previously given for believing that there are independent objects which cause sensations collapses, and Fichte's world of experience loses all of its independent status. Kant's things in themselves are removed from the philosophical terrain since they are erroneously inferred from an inadequately formulated version of the causal principle. The world of experience is not a response to a set of stimuli from independently real things in themselves; instead, it is from beginning to end a projection of, or a construction out of, the self's own modifications. The "object" of knowledge is only a modification of the knower, and, as such, is (in Fichte's terminology) a "subject-objectivity." Subject and object merge into the subjectivity of the knower.

Such is the subjective idealism developed in the second book of *The Vocation of Man*. His subjective idealism was developed by Fichte in order to settle the doubt which marked the outcome of Book I. Fichte wanted to reject rigid determinism but needed a ground which would justify the rejection. He saw subjective idealism as providing such a ground. If the world of experience is constructed freely by the self, then the self need no longer labor under the onus of rigid determinism. The Spirit tells Fichte that he need "no longer tremble at a necessity which exists only in thine own thought; no longer fear to be crushed by things which are the product of thine own mind."

But other selves, the necessary additional elements which make the ethical situation plausible, do not have fundamental reality in the subjective idealism which is presented in Book II. The doubt of Book I is replaced by knowledge, yet this knowledge does not assure a fundamental reality for other selves. To get full reality for other selves Fichte must go still further; he must go beyond knowledge. If knowledge must be transcended, it is inadequate. The opinion is what lies behind the strikingly strange statement Fichte makes near the end of Book II, that "knowledge is not reality, just because it is knowledge." Knowledge does not disclose reality, according to Fichte. Its function differs from this commonly held view. Really, knowledge is less powerful. Fichte writes that "it destroys and annihilates error," but it "cannot give us truth, for in itself it is absolutely empty." Knowledge is not the avenue to reality. It must make way for a higher power; it must make way for faith, the subject of Book III. Faith assures the self that there are really other selves.

Book III opens with Fichte's dissatisfaction at the outcome of Book II. If all there is to the world is the construction Fichte himself unconsciously makes out of the modifications of his own self, then the world is empty. Yet this is all one can get from knowledge. But knowing does not exhaust human life;

there is more to it than just that. "Not merely TO KNOW, but according to thy knowledge TO DO, is thy vocation," Fichte declares. And the "doing" here is clearly an *ethical* doing; it is striving, achieving, fulfilling obligations. Fichte regards himself as under an immediate and underived sense of obligation to act; this is his, it is all men's vocation. Yet if one is to *act*, there must be an arena in which to act; there must be an externally real world to act in and to act on. To justify such a world on the basis of knowledge is not possible. One must transcend knowledge and place his reliance in faith. Early in Book III Fichte resolves to do just this. He turns from knowledge to faith, from intellect to will, and thus he arrives at a real, external world which is populated with other selves related to Fichte and to one another by mutual ties of ethical obligation.

This discussion brings to a conclusion the strictly philosophical segment of *The Vocation of Man*. Fichte goes on for quite a time, however, into what is really more religion than philosophy. Once he has established his own existence and the existence of a world in which he can strive, he sermonizes about fulfilling his obligations. If Book I is similar to Descartes, and Book II is similar to Berkeley, it can be said with equal justice that Book III resembles a sermon enjoining strenuous ethical striving. Fichte tries to sound a clear call to plain living and high thinking, and his fervor, if not the details of his message, cannot fail to strike the reader.

Essentially the position he took is a mystical one. Somehow or other, according to his account, Fichte's own ethical will merged with the Universal Will, a kind of metaphysical ultimate that functioned as Fichte's God. He seemed to feel affinities with St. John's Gospel, but he insisted on de-anthropomorphizing God, and he thus lost what has always been at the center of the devotional life of the saints. Fichte had much of the emotion of the Christian mystic, but little sympathy for the object of Christian devotion. He replaced St. John's incarnate Word (Jesus Christ) with a pantheistic extension of his own ethical sensitivity. The result is quite a frightening projection of Fichte's own passions set up as God. The control exercised over the saint by his worship of a truly transcendent God is missing in Fichte; he remained an egocentric German romantic.

The Vocation of Man is a kind of guided tour beginning with Spinoza, leading through Kant, and ending in a subjective ethical idealism with deep romantic footings. It is an excellent introduction to the philosophy of nineteenth century Germany, and it shares with that general movement its characteristic strengths and weaknesses. The logic is often unsound, feeling often overrules reason, selfish concerns are sometimes read out as the Will of God. Yet the Romantics generally, and Fichte among them, certainly were ethically concerned; they were trying to spell out the moral ideal and to set men moving toward a better world.

However, while *The Vocation of Man* is a fine example of romantic idealism, it is at the same time, paradoxically, a work which foreshadows significant developments in philosophy of a sort opposed in spirit and method to much of what Fichte endorsed. In rejecting the *ding an sich* of Kant, in emphasizing the role of the self in the effort to know reality, in basing his philosophy on the self's declaration of its own existence, and particularly in urging the definitive importance of action, Fichte suggested the basic ideas of later pragmatic and existentialistic philosophies. Of course, Fichte remains a subjective idealist, and he never developed the pragmatic and existentialistic features of his thought; philosophically speaking, he remains a nineteenth century German idealist. But the resolution of the paradox of moral action—the paradox in which man as a free moral agent finds himself involved because of his presence in a causally determined universe—is similar to the resolution achieved by the existentialists, Christian and atheistic alike. To begin with the striving self, to regard man as what he can become as a result of his moral efforts, to take his moral "vocation" as prior to his essence—all of this is strikingly similar to the ideas later to be defended by such radically different philosophic personalities as Søren Kierkegaard and Jean-Paul Sartre.

It is the emphasis on will which makes a philosopher such as Fichte a transitional figure, borrowing from the old idealistic philosophy and suggesting the lines of development of the new pragmatic-existentialistic philosophy. A thinker who extends the principle of the will to the entire universe, deifying will and rejection all else on its behalf, exhibits a metaphysical radicalism that is today's philosophical conservatism. But one who regards will, the striving of the stubbornly independent self, as definitive of self, of man, but not of all reality—such a one may very well oppose himself to the idealist while, at the same time, refusing to commit himself to realism; he remains pragmatic, testing not only his own nature, but the nature of everything else, in terms of action and consequences.

In arguing that the moral will involves the assumption of a moral law that admits no exceptions, and in regarding the Infinite Will as that law—"a Will that in itself is law"—Fichte shows that he is in the great tradition of idealistic philosophy; but in arguing that it is "the vocation of our species to unite itself into one single body" through the moral striving of the free self, and in suggesting that "All my thoughts must have a bearing on my action," Fichte passes from the metaphysical to the moral, and from the moral to the pragmatic and existential. In his philosophy, then, the old and the new combine, neither one in a pure state but each aspect enlivened by the presence of the other.—*R.E.L.*

PERTINENT LITERATURE

Chisholm, Roderick, ed. "Introduction," in Johann Gottlieb Fichte's *The Vocation of Man*. New York: Liberal Arts Press, 1956.

In this introductory essay which accompanies his edition of Johann Gottlieb Fichte's *The Vocation of Man*, Roderick Chisholm provides a concise and thorough analysis of a philosophical work which has earned the reputation of being one of the clearest statements of the beginnings of nineteenth century German idealism. After the publication of *The Science of Knowledge*, his major philosophical work, Fichte was widely accused of being an atheist. The charge was probably evoked by his doctrine, propounded in *The Science of Knowledge*, that God is an unrealized and unrealizable ideal. In addition, Fichte does not personify God in his major treatise but presents the Absolute or Divine as a state of being. *The Vocation of Man* was written largely to clarify his position to the public and to those who opposed his work on the ground that it was really a disguised atheism.

Chisholm maintains that Fichte's central argument in *The Vocation of Man*, or the conclusion arrived at, is a paradox. The argument, according to Chisholm, proceeds as follows. If we consider man's position in the system of nature (the determinist view) and derive our conception of the nature of man therefrom, we would succeed only in completely misunderstanding man's true nature. But this is an easy error to fall into; indeed, Fichte had been a determinist of the Spinozist variety in his early philosophical years. If we regard man as a product of natural forces, then it follows that all of human action is, like other physical events, merely a link in the causal chain of events. For every human action there is a natural cause such that every human action becomes the inevitable result of the conditions under which it occurs. Chisholm elaborates nicely on this picture by explaining that the main thesis of the determinist position is that every natural event takes place under conditions such that, should those conditions be absent, the event in question would not occur, and with these conditions, the event in question "must" occur. Furthermore, these conditions are themselves only so many events which are part of an unending causal sequence.

According to Chisholm, the problem for Fichte is that there is no room for moral responsibility in a system which is governed solely by causal principles. Man's actions thus being determined by the conditions which necessitate them, there would be no justification for the attribution of responsibility to anyone. For example, a man stealing would be both physiologically and psychologically conditioned so that, at the precise moment, he could do nothing else but steal. He would steal, as it were, necessarily, which is to say that he would not freely choose to steal. For Fichte, following Immanuel Kant, such a conclusion is unacceptable, for human action is essentially independent of external causes in that the source of human action is ourselves.

The way out of this dilemma is to consider the way in which we come to *know* the physical world around us. This will reveal the truth about the world and ourselves—that the world is a product of our mental activity. It is at this point in the argument that Chisholm is reluctant to accept the line of reasoning advanced by Fichte. The latter begins by contesting the commonsense belief that it is by means of our senses that we perceive things to be external to us. In perceiving things to be outside ourselves we are really perceiving something about ourselves. If I claim to see a car in the center of the road, my claim is based on what *I think* I see when I believe that I am standing near the road looking into its center. This knowledge of what I seem to see, or what I believe myself to see, is knowledge about myself. Thus, all perception is really perception of myself and my condition.

The important move in the argument, according to Chisholm, is when Fichte asks what is the private condition of all perception of external things. Fichte's own response is that when you perceive an external object, you perceive sensible qualities (color, sound, taste) which you *assume* signify the object. All perception is thus regarded as being a condition of the perceiver's own state; in other words, in perception, the perceiver perceives his own condition.

This line of reasoning Chisholm takes to be paradoxical without really explaining in detail why. However, it is fairly plain that the alleged paradox consists in the fact that if all perception is really of myself, then it is hardly perception at all, for I am not involved with something other than myself, which would seem to be a minimal condition for calling something a perception. Chisholm points out that Thomas Reid attacked George Berkeley for holding a similar position about perception and that Reid's argument was being used again in the twentieth century against the sense-data philosophers. The position, however, is central to an idealist position similar to Fichte's, and Arthur Schopenhauer was to argue in similar fashion that "the World is my idea."

The next question Fichte poses, now that he has his paradoxical conclusion, is why we should regard these sensible qualities as reliable signs of external objects at all. Our justification is that we assume our sensations have a cause and that the cause is something outside us—namely, objects. But this is just another use of the general causal principle that every event must have a cause (the importance of which Fichte had learned from Kant).

Fichte's next step in the argument, states Chisholm, is characteristic of his way of thinking. Since we have immediate knowledge only of sensible qualities, how do we know the truth of the causal principle? We cannot say, as most people in their unphilosophical moments would say, that objects in the world behave according to the causal principle, and that this is proof enough. Such a defense is circular in the context that Fichte has constructed. For if I use the principle of causality to defend my belief in the external world of nature (that my sensations are caused by external objects), then I cannot justify use of the principle by appealing to my beliefs about external objects in the world of nature.

The necessary conclusion, as Chisholm reads Fichte's argument, is that the principle is an "inward law of thought." The impossibility of an uncaused event in the external world is really an impossibility with respect to our way of thinking. The argument here is Kant's, according to which the causal order of the world is intimately connected to the way in which the subject must think about the world. Fichte, however, goes beyond Kant in concluding from the above argument that what we take to be knowledge of external things is really knowledge of our own mental activity. Chisholm, not giving Fichte's idealist language any second-guessing, says that objects one supposes to exist are really a product of one's own thought. Chisholm does point out that Fichte describes in detail just what this mental activity consists in. In *The Science of Knowledge*, with its doctrine of the Absolute Ego who necessarily posits something other than itself, Fichte makes clear how sensation is possible. Experience, according to Fichte, consists of a subject's having an experience which is only of sensations. Sensations are accompanied with the thought that they are the objects of immediate knowledge and the thought of a subject as experiencing them. The Absolute Ego thus posits both itself and the non-Ego. Consciousness of the external world is really a representation of myself to myself.

Chisholm now turns to how Fichte uses this Absolute Idealist conclusion to solve the problem about moral responsibility. Not surprisingly, Fichte says that since the rigid necessity of the natural world is really a product of my own consciousness, and not an order independent of me, the necessity is just a human necessity which makes it possible for us to organize the world of appearances.

Now, however, the further problem arises which Chisholm regards as inevitable, given Fichte's reasoning. The world we are left with is a world of appearances, a product of our own mental states—a "system of pictures," Fichte states. What about reality and its apprehension? Here Fichte turns to our moral consciousness, again appealing to Kant. As a moral, practical being, I have to act *as if* other persons really existed; we all have obligations to act in a certain way toward one another, and in doing this we will believe that such actions pertain to a "real world." We will have *faith* in such a world, a spiritual or supersensual world whose reality is revealed to us by our moral consciousness. The awareness of these two orders, the one ruled by my will, the other by my deed, comes to use through my moral consciousness. Chisholm makes no bones about the fact that the arguments Fichte employs to reach this conclusion are unacceptable to someone who has not already accepted the premises and assumptions. Nor is the final conclusion any easier to accept—that God is the foundation for the moral order in the world and that each of us exists in and through the Divine. In fairness to Fichte, this conclusion is presented as a truth of our moral consciousness, not of the understanding.

Royce, Josiah. *The Spirit of Modern Philosophy*. Boston: Houghton Mifflin Company, 1931, pp. 135-169.

Josiah Royce was in the forefront of the Modern Idealism movement in America in the early part of the twentieth century. He possessed an uncommon ability for presenting the works of the great philosophers, especially the Moderns and the nineteenth century idealists, in a fashion which was at once exhilirating and perspicacious. The lecture in the present volume given to a discussion of Johann Gottlieb Fichte's brand of German idealism exemplifies both Royce's philosophical style and his peculiar approach to philosophical problems.

Royce introduces and then expands on the central doctrines in Fichte's idealism, including those contained in *The Vocation of Man*, which, in any case, is a condensed version of Fichte's main ideas. Like almost all other philosophers acquainted with Fichte's work, Royce places the starting point of the latter's work in a denial of Immanuel Kant's thesis that there exist things-in-themselves which are the causes or origins of reality as we know it. Having rejected Kantian things-in-themselves, Fichte was faced with the problem of explaining how it is that we come to know reality and what the origin of reality *as we know it* is.

Fichte found the solution which was palatable to one of his philosophical disposition in another problem which he had inherited from Kant and with which he had been concerned throughout his career: namely, the problem of freedom and determinism. As a part of nature, man would seem to fit into the rigid system of causal necessity within which all of his actions are the inevitable results of the conditions under which they happen to occur. If so, then there is no room for freedom in the world, for we can hardly be said to choose freely our course of action—and in so choosing, cause it—when our action merely follows necessarily upon the event or condition which preceded it. Furthermore, if man is not a free agent, then he is not a morally responsible one either; it is nonsense to attribute responsibility to someone who is not free to choose in the first place. According to Royce, Fichte's "way out" of this dilemma is to make man himself, through the agency of the self, the cause of the world; more precisely, the world is the world that the self makes. Thus, Fichte answers his question concerning the causal basis of the world without having to appeal to things-in-themselves and at the same time resolves the freedom-determinism difficulty—at least to his satisfaction—by making man the "maker" of the world as he knows it.

According to Royce, Fichte sees man as free both in the sense that he is self-determined even within a rigidly determined system, and in the sense that man freely causes the experienced world to which the causal network of events gives a formal structure. A fundamental truth of philosophy, then, is that living and voluntary selves freely choose to assert themselves and organize their world in so doing. It follows from this that the moral consciousness, or knowledge of the moral law, is prior to theoretical knowledge; for, if knowing a world is making a world, then we must consciously recognize the truth by acting in this way or that. In this way, says Royce, Fichte's law of action becomes the basis for all theoretical knowledge. The external world becomes, for Fichte, the stuff or material, indeed, the opportunity, for the self's duty to make itself manifest. The point of this last remark of Royce is that the everyday world is essential if our moral activities are to have significance. Both the external world, even if it is ultimately the creation of my mind, and other selves *must be assumed to exist* if I am to think, and most important, to act and live.

It is clear, according to Royce, that the recognition of the necessity of there being other selves and a phenomenal world is a matter of *faith* for Fichte, as the latter presents it in Book III of *The Vocation of Man*. This faith is, as it were, imposed on us by our moral natures, which strive toward the improvement of the world and the eradication of misery and evil. All men share the common task of carrying out their moral duties, and the material world is but the condition for this task. Furthermore, Royce interprets Fichte's concluding doctrine in *The Vocation of Man*—that God is the foundation of the moral order of the world—to mean that the universe of self-creating and world-making selves constitutes the life and embodiment of the one true and infinite Reason—God's will. Fichte himself regarded this conclusion as difficult to grasp intellectually, but that fact did not bother him unduly as the alleged truth expressed therein he considered to be a subject matter proper to the moral consciousness, not the understanding.

Fichte's philosophy has been called "subjective idealism" because the self is considered to be the source of both consciousness and the external world. Royce, however, thinks that "ethical idealism" is a more accurate description of the heart of Fichte's system, as it is in keeping with what Fichte regarded as the true significance of his work, that it is only through the moral consciousness that we can apprehend "reality"—infinite Reason, elsewhere described by Fichte as "Being." It is Reason or Being in this sense that Fichte equates with God and it is why he was charged with atheism. Because each individual self is a partial embodiment of Reason or Being, or God's will, we all have a "vocation" to work together toward a better life; in so doing, something of this divine will is realized—but only partially, for the task is endless.

For all of his admiration of the spirit of Fichte's system of thought, Royce rejects it as a candidate for an acceptable form of idealism. Fichte's work lacks a genuine respect for the natural order and for experience, a requirement Royce considers necessary for any form of idealism. Ultimately, then, Fichte's dismissal of the external world must be judged to be totally unwarranted.—J.P.D.

ADDITIONAL RECOMMENDED READING

Copleston, Frederick. *A History of Western Philosophy*. Vol. VII. London: Burns and Oates, 1963. An excellent account of the development of Fichte's thought, especially of its movement in an increasingly religious direction, signs of which are already present in *The Vocation of Man*.

Green, Garrett, ed. and tr. "Introduction," in Johann Gottlieb Fichte's *Attempt at a Critique of All Revelation*. Cambridge: Cambridge University Press, 1978, pp. 1-30. This introductory essay to Fichte's first philosophical work provides a concisely informative discussion of the context of the development of Fichte's thought—especially of its relationship to the philosophy of Kant.

Scott, Charles E. "Fichte Today?," in *Idealistic Studies*. VIII, no. 2 (May, 1978), pp. 169-178. A summary and discussion of themes pursued at a 1977 Fichte conference in Austria; provides some idea of how Fichte is being read by contemporary philosophers.

Verweyen, Hans J. "New Perspectives on J. G. Fichte," in *Idealistic Studies*. VI, no. 2 (May, 1976), pp 118-159. Besides containing an invaluable bibliography of Fichte's works and commentaries on him, the May, 1976, issue of *Idealistic Studies* is devoted completely to papers on Fichtean themes. Although some of them are fairly technical, the issue as a whole is essential for an appreciation of what philosophers consider valuable in Fichte's work today.

PHENOMENOLOGY OF SPIRIT

Author: Georg Wilhelm Friedrich Hegel (1770-1831)
Type of work: Metaphysics, philosophy of history
First published: 1807

PRINCIPAL IDEAS ADVANCED

As the science of appearances, phenomenology is distinct from metaphysics, which is the science of being.

Phenomenology of spirit observes and describes the forms of unreal consciousness and the necessity which causes consciousness to advance from one form to another.

Knowledge of the dialectical structure of reality makes possible the scientific study of the forms in which consciousness appears.

In its evolution, mind has passed through three moments: consciousness of the sensible world; consciousness of itself and of other selves; and consciousness of the identity of the self and the sensible world.

While Napoleon was defeating the Prussians outside the walls of Jena, G. W. F. Hegel inside the walls was completing his *Phenomenology of Spirit.* Napoleon's victory signified for Hegel the triumph throughout Europe of enlightened self-rule and marked the beginning of a new social era; and in the Preface to the *Phenomenology of Spirit* he drew a parallel between Napoleon's achievement and his own. "It is not difficult to see that our epoch is a birth-time and a period of transition," he wrote. "The spirit of man has broken with the old order of things and with the old ways of thinking." Changes leading up to the present had, he said, been quantitative, like the growth of a child in the womb, but recent events had marked a qualitative change such as happens when the child draws its first breath.

When Hegel made this optimistic assessment of his own achievement, he was thinking not merely of the book in hand but of the system of knowledge for which he was later to become famous and which, even then, he was expounding in university lectures. The *Phenomenology of Spirit* was to introduce the system to the public. Originally he had planned to include it in the first volume of his *Logic*, but the project outgrew the limits of an introduction and was published as a separate work. Today it lives not as an introduction to the system but as a classic in its own right. Indeed, many who appreciate the *Phenomenology of Spirit* find nothing to their taste in the system. Jacob Loewenberg, for example, speaks of the need "to save Hegel from the Hegelians—nay, from Hegel himself," adding that the insights that abound in the *Phenomenology of Spirit* make the task well worth attempting. This is somewhat like eating the filling of a pie and leaving the crust, for the Hegelians are undoubtedly correct in insisting that, read as it was intended to be read, the *Phenomenology of Spirit* is very much a part of the system.

Like Immanuel Hermann von Fichte and F. W. J. von Schelling before him, Hegel was a metaphysician in the tradition that stemmed from Parmenides. The problem of philosophy in the broadest sense had to do with the identity of being and knowing. Admitting that the way of mortals is mere seeming, each of the three in his own way was trying to expound the way of truth. For Fichte, the Absolute (ultimate reality, the Kantian thing-in-itself) is the self which produces the phenomenal world and then overcomes it. For Schelling, the Absolute is the common source of the self and the world. Both men held that the task of philosophy is to lead the finite mind to the level of immediacy at which the difference between knowledge and being disappears in vision. Hegel thought that both men went too far in their attempts to abolish diversity. In his opinion, an intuition which leaves all difference behind is ignorance rather than knowledge. He said, rather unkindly, that Schelling's Absolute is "the night in which all cows are black." He agreed that knowledge demands immediacy but he denied that the distinctions present in human consciousness are incompatible with the unity demanded of knowledge, it being sufficient that the logic of thought and the logic of being are the same. In short, when one thinks dialectically he thinks truly. This, as is often pointed out, was also Aristotle's solution to the Parmenidean problem. According to Aristotle, divine mind—mind fully actualized—"thinks itself, and its thinking is a thinking of thinking" (*Metaphysics* XII.9).

An obvious difference between Aristotle and Hegel is that for the latter the divine mind is immanent in the world process. Hegel expresses this by saying that Substance and Subject are one. Spirit, which is Hegel's Absolute, is said to be "the inner being of the world." It exists in itself (*an sich*) as Substance, but it also exists for itself (*für sich*) as Subject. "This means, it must be presented to itself as an object, but at the same time straightway annul and transcend this objective form; it must be its own object in which it finds itself reflected." The process Hegel describes as a circle which has its end for its beginning. What he means is that when the movement begins Spirit is one, and when it ends it is again one, while in between it is divided and tormented by the need to end the division. From Hegel's point of view, the circular movement was not in vain. In the beginning Spirit was potentially everything but actually nothing. Only by means of the processes which we know as nature and history does Spirit attain to actuality.

All of this is metaphysics. Like Parmenides, Hegel, when he speaks of Absolute Spirit, views the world not as it *appears* to mortals but as it is *known* by the gods. Metaphysics, which is the science of reality, is not phenomenology, which is the science of appearances. In the *Phenomenology of Spirit* Hegel, without abandoning the standpoint of one who knows, observes and describes the opinions of finite spirits in their multiplicity and contrariety. It is like history, says Hegel, in that it includes the sum of human experience, both individual and communal; but, whereas history views these experiences "in the form of contingency," phenomenology views them "from the side of their intellectually comprehended organization." Most of the book is a far cry from metaphysics; and if one finds some parts indigestible, the explanation is usually that Hegel is alluding to things we have never encountered in our reading. Incidentally, it is an advantage of the German word *Geist* that, unlike our words "mind" and "spirit," which translators have to use in its place, it covers the whole range of human concerns. Psychology, history, philology, sociology, theology, ethics, and aesthetics, each of which Hegel manages to illuminate, are all referred to in German as *Geisteswissenschaften*—"sciences" of *Geist*.

The *Phenomenology of Spirit*, therefore, is the story of mankind. It is concerned directly with finite spirits and only indirectly with the Absolute, which must be thought of as hidden behind these appearances. Nevertheless, in order to understand the layout of the book, one needs to keep in mind what he is told in the Preface about the movement of the Absolute realizing itself in a threefold process: first, a process of positing itself as a living and moving being, in constant change from one state to its opposite; second, a process of negating the object and becoming subject, thereby splitting up what was single and turning the factors against each other; third, a process of negating this diversity and reinstating self-identity. This final movement, Hegel reminds us, is a new immediacy, not the immediacy with which the process began. "It is the process of its own becoming, the circle which presupposes its end as its purpose and has its end for the beginning; it becomes concrete and actual only by being carried out, and by the end it involves."

In the *Phenomenology of Spirit* the three movements are designated not from the standpoint of Absolute Spirit but from the standpoint of man. Part A, "Consciousness," is concerned with man's attempts to achieve certainty through knowledge of the sensible world. Part B, "Self-consciousness," has to do with man as doer rather than as knower, but it is mainly concerned with the self-image to which man's action leads. Part C, not titled in Hegel's outline, exhibits the stage in which man sees himself reflected in the external world. Hegel explains that these three moments are abstractions arrived at by analysis; he does not mean for us to think that the dialectic which he traces in the development of consciousness was anterior to that which he traces in the development of selfhood. On the other hand, because what is meaningful in history comes from man's efforts to attain self-knowledge, the great moments in history may be seen as illustrative of this triadic movement. Thus, the extroverted mind of pre-Socratic Greece serves to illustrate the first stage; the introverted mind of late antiquity and the Middle Ages, the second; and the boisterous, self-assertive mind of modern man, the third. The plan was simple, but the execution is complicated by Hegel's tendency to loop back into the past in order to give a fuller exhibition of the dialectic.

Part A, "Consciousness," is an essay in epistemology. Specifically it is a critical history of man's attempt to base knowledge on sensation. Although it seems probable that Hegel first envisaged the problem as it appeared to Plato in the *Theaetetus*, his exposition makes full use of the light shed on it by modern empiricism. In three chapters Hegel traces man's attempt to find certainty through knowledge, first on the level of sensation, then on the level of perception, then on the level of scientific understanding. Sensations are indeed immediate; but they cease to be such the moment we make them objects of knowledge. The object of perception, of which common sense is so sure, turns out to be a congeries of properties. And the chemical or physical force in terms of which man tries to explain these properties turns out to be unknowable and has to be abandoned in favor of descriptive laws, which, although satisfactory from a practical standpoint, are unsatisfactory to consciousness bent on knowledge. In the end, consciousness learns that the sensible world is like a curtain behind which an unknown inner world "affirms itself as a divided and distinguished inner reality," namely, self-consciousness. But, says Hegel, to understand this "requires us to fetch a wider compass."

In Part B, "Self-consciousness," Hegel makes a new start. The wider compass means taking account of man's animal condition. Life, says Hegel, is an overcoming. The animal does not contemplate the sensible world but consumes it. Self-consciousness dawns when man's appetites turn into desires. Unlike appetites, desire is universal. What man desires is the idea of overcoming. He is not content to consume what he needs: he destroys for the sake of proving that he is an overcomer; but not satisfied with proving it to himself, he needs to prove it to others. Thus, says Hegel, self-consciousness is a double movement. In order to be certain that he is a self, man needs to be recognized as such by other selves.

Hegel works through the dialectic of self-consciousness in a famous section titled "Lordship and Bondage." It is by killing a rival in life-and-death combat that primitive man attains to selfhood. If the rival lacks mettle and cries out to be spared, the double movement is still accomplished: the rival survives not as a self but as a slave who exists only to serve the lord's desires. The slave, however, although he has no independent existence at first, learns to value himself as a worker and through the skills that he acquires gradually wins the recognition of his master. In the end, the master, who wanted nothing more than to be independent, finds himself dependent upon his slave.

Much has been made, by Friedrich Wilhelm Nietzsche and others, of the two types of consciousness, that of the master and that of the slave. For Hegel, however, this section is scarcely more than an introduction to the one which follows, entitled "The Freedom of Self-consciousness." Failure of consciousness to find independence in the mutual relation between the two selves leads to the negation of the double movement. "In *thinking* I am free, because I am not in another but remain simply and solely in touch with myself." This bold attempt to recover immediacy Hegel illustrates by reference to the sub-jective philosophies of late antiquity, when culture was universal and life was burdensome to master and slave alike. In Stoicism, thought affirmed itself indifferent to all the conditions of individual existence, declaring its univer-sality. In skepticism, individuality reasserted itself in the giddy whole of its disorder. In Christianity, the attempt was made to combine the universality of the former with the facticity of the latter, giving rise to the consciously divided self which Hegel calls "the unhappy consciousness." For example, the Apostle cries out (*Romans* VII), "O wretched man that I am! Who shall deliver me from the body of this death? For I delight in the law of God after the inward man; but I see another law in my members warring against the law of my mind." Devotion, ceremony, asceticism, mysticism, and obedience are viewed by Hegel as means of overcoming this rift; but the healing remains a mere "beyond." Meanwhile "there has arisen the idea of Reason, of the certainty that consciousness is, in its particularity, inherently and essentially absolute." And so man enters the last stage of his pilgrimage.

Part C, left untitled by Hegel, is the synthesis of consciousness and self-consciousness; but the synthesis, insofar as it falls within the compass of the *Phenomenology of Spirit*, is incomplete. This incompleteness must be kept in mind when we consider the titles which Hegel gave to the three subdivisions of Part C. They are: AA. Reason; BB. Spirit; CC. Religion. The titles are part of the passing show, banners around which modern men are accustomed to rally.

Reason, as understood in this major division, is the reason of newly awak-ened modern man. In contrast to the ascetic soul of the Middle Ages, modern man is blessed with sublime self-confidence, certain of his vocation to pull down the rickety structures of the past and to build new ones on the foundation of reason. Hegel discusses the rise of science, modern man's pursuit of plea-sure, and the doctrine of natural law. This section is memorable mainly for the comical situations into which man's zeal and good intentions get him. Disregarding his objective nature, he plunges like Faust into life, only to find himself mastered by fates beyond his control. Retreating somewhat, he takes refuge in "the law of the heart" which the cruel world refuses to understand. Or, as the "knight of virtue," he engages in sham fights with the world. All of this appeal to immediacy, Hegel says, is "consciousness gone crazy, . . . its reality being immediately unreality." A delusory objectivity is achieved in the third section of this division when the individual undertakes to find mean-ing in life by devoting himself to some worthy cause. Hegel's title for this section, "The Spiritual Zoo, or Humbug!" indicates that high-mindedness has its low side. Loewenberg catches the flavor in his heading, "Animal Behavior in the Realm of Reason."

The excessive claims made for reason provoked reactions, known histori-cally as pietism, illuminism, and romanticism. These are all dealt with in the section "Spirit," which represents man looking for the truth within himself. The fact that Hegel loops back in time in order to draw a contrast between the conscientiousness of the Greek heroine Antigone and that of the "beautiful soul" cherished and cultivated by German romantics somewhat obscures the dialectical movement. We may take up the story with court life in France under the ancien régime, which, for Hegel, is a brilliantly orchestrated variation on the old theme of self-alienation. To be recognized as a self one had to sacrifice himself to society, either by fighting or by working or by talking. Almost everybody who was anybody chose the third way. The prerevolutionary salon, as J. N. Findlay comments, made Paris "the most agreeable city in the world" to outsiders such as David Hume; but to insiders such as Rameau's nephew in Denis Diderot's classic, it was a snake pit. Hegel points out that the revolt against the meanness and duplicity of the existing order was two-pronged—religious and philosophical. Wilhelm Bossuet exemplifies one party, François Marie Arouet de Voltaire the other. But the difference, Hegel tries to show, was superficial. Both parties were otherworldly, taking flight to the Absolute, whether it was called the Trinity or the Supreme Being. The philosophical party was to triumph as the party of Enlightenment. It lacked cohesion, however, and splintered into political sects which stoked the fires of revolution and, in their pursuit of absolute freedom, were consumed in the Terror.

Absolute freedom is undoubtedly what every self demands. But the lesson Hegel draws from the Enlightenment is that the individual cannot claim to be absolute: the truth that is in him must be in everyone else as well. And this was the new morality from Königsberg just then enjoying great success in romantic circles. Morality has the task of harmonizing thought and inclination. It recovers the wholeness known to the ancient Greeks but it does not do so by means of custom but by means of the voice of conscience, moral reason present in every man.

This section of the *Phenomenology of Spirit* is important chiefly for its criticism of deontological ethics. Universal law raised above all the contingency and duty divorced from all advantage made obvious targets for Hegel's satire. Far from harmonizing the soul, morality gives rise to dissemblance. The beautiful soul is divine in conception—the "self transparent to itself" is similar to Hegel's definition of the Absolute. Unfortunately, reality did not match the concept, as everyone must recognize when he judges his fellows, but also occasionally when he judges himself. On such occasions the conscientious person wants to confess his fault and ask forgiveness; and this can be rewarding, except when one has to do with one who is hard-hearted, and who "refuses to let his inner nature go forth." Here, as Hegel points out, morality anticipates religion.

Hitherto, consciousness has conceived of itself alternately as object and subject, as individual and social. At each level spirit has taken into itself more of the content of human experience, although it continues to mistake each new experience for the whole toward which it aspires. This wholeness Hegel finds in "Revealed Religion," by which he means Christianity. But once again he loops back in time and, in the final section, presents an entire phenomenology of religion.

Religion had been of major concern to Hegel from the time when, as a theological student, he had found difficulty reconciling biblical revelation with Greek *paideia*. His survey traces religion through three stages: the cosmological stage represented by Persia and Egypt; the anthropological stage represented by classical Greece; and the revelational stage represented by Christianity. We merely note that the first stage removed the divine too far from man and that the second brought it too close (for example in classic comedy), leaving it for the gospel of the incarnation of God's Son to find the proper distance. For Hegel, the doctrine of the Trinity—one God revealed to man simultaneously as being, as being-for-itself, and as the self knowing itself in the other—comes as close as religion can possibly come to Absolute Knowledge. However, in religion self-consciousness is not fully conceptualized. The self does not yet know itself directly but only as appearance.

"The last embodiment of spirit," Hegel explains in a brief concluding chapter, "is Absolute Knowledge. It is spirit knowing itself in the shape of spirit." Consciousness, which in religion is not perfectly one with its content, is here "at home with itself." Although the particular self is "immediately sublated" to the universal self, however, it is not absorbed into it, for the latter also is consciousness; that is to say, "It is the process of superseding itself." But here we have left phenomenology and are on the threshold of the System.—*J.F.*

PERTINENT LITERATURE

Royce, Josiah. *Lectures on Modern Idealism*. New Haven, Connecticut: Yale University Press, 1919.

The three lectures in this series which Josiah Royce devoted to G. W. F. Hegel's *Phenomenology of Spirit* have served successive student generations as an introduction to this work, the entire series providing much-needed background in post-Kantian idealism. Like Immanuel Hermann von Fichte and F. W. J. von Schelling, Hegel started with the assumption that "the world of reality is to be defined in terms of whatever constitutes the true nature and foundation of the self." Immanuel Kant had spoken of a single consciousness the laws of which determine the conditions of all experience, and the boldest of his successors went on to formulate the conception of an impersonal Absolute as the ground and source of human personality.

Royce protests against the common impression that these idealists were arbitrarily imaginative and calls attention to the philosophically important use to which they put the dialectical or antithetical method. One finds the method, says Royce, in Plato's dialogues, which often develop and compare antithetical doctrines not merely in order to expose ignorance but also for the sake of winning a view of truth in its complexity. But while Plato restricted the dialectical process to human thinking, the idealists took it to be inherent in the nature of truth itself. According to Royce, this was partly owing to Kant's declaration, in connection with the antinomies of pure reason, that reason always expresses itself in antitheses; but it was also partly due to the storm and stress of the Napoleonic era, which brought to the light a host of contradictions deeply rooted in human nature.

Royce's chapters on Schelling are helpful to the student of the *Phenomenology of Spirit* in view of Hegel's famous description of Schelling's Absolute as "the night in which all cows are black." Royce, it should be said, does not prejudice his readers by approaching Schelling through Hegel, but takes two lectures to show how, applying the dialectic to the problem of the unity between the self and the universe, Schelling, after affirming that the world is simply the objectification of the "I" whose true nature is to know and not to be known, went on to distinguish between the "I" as conscious and the "I" as unconscious. As the artist loses himself in his work, so the intelligent activity of the self forgets itself in its product. Philosophy transcends these distinctions. The Absolute, Schelling concluded, is neither subject nor object but Indifference.

Hegel, however, held out for difference. By means of the dialectic he showed that the Absolute becomes aware of itself only by passing through a process of inner differentiation into many centers of selfhood, each of which affirms itself in a manner that when taken in isolation is false and self-contradictory but when taken as a stage in the series is true and justified.

Royce's extended tour through the *Phenomenology of Spirit* is picturesque. Taking his cue from the way in which Hegel speaks of consciousness as "passing over" from one stage to another, Royce uses the metaphor of transmigration and imagines the World-Spirit as undergoing repeated incarnations. Hegel's use of the term "world-spirit" was, according to Royce, purely allegorical, portraying consciousness as subject to historical change—a kind of Everyman, appearing successively as master and slave, as monk and pleasure-seeker, as rationalist and romantic. In Hegel's Absolute all the diversity of life is preserved—every struggle, every sacrifice, of the vanquished as well as of the victor.

In his own philosophy, Royce tries to bring knowledge and action together; hence, it is not surprising that he finds the same tendency in Hegel's dialectic. For example, the lower stages of consciousness are divided by Royce into two types according to whether the finite spirit is too practical or too theoretical in its attitude toward life. In those stages in which it is excessively practical man appears as enthusiastic, hopeful, and even heroic, but also blind, failing to understand what he is doing. On the other hand, in those stages in which spirit is excessively intellectual, man's life is empty of content and he finds himself estranged from the world. The Absolute, says Royce, is "the world of human life . . . characterized by a complete unity or harmony of what one might call a theoretical and practical consciousness."

A further point Royce liked to make and which he finds emphasized in the *Phenomenology of Spirit* is that man attains to full consciousness of self only in a social context. Even the headhunter, says Royce, referring to Hegel's early chapter on self-consciousness, depends on his neighbor to furnish him another head. But it is in the later chapters, dealing with society and the state, that this social consciousness attains full realization. All previous stages, says Royce, were "a sleep and a forgetting of the unity upon which all individual life is based. An organized social order is the self for each one of its loyal subjects. The truth of the individual is the consciousness of the people to which he loyally belongs." And what appears on the social plane appears once again on the level which we call culture, notably in religion, which in its higher forms Hegel regarded as "an interpretation of the world by the social self and by the individual only as he identifies himself with the social self."

In his own philosophy of religion, Royce maintains that the Absolute is a superhuman consciousness which, although including the consciousness of individuals, is more than the sum total of individual consciousnesses. He admits that this teaching is not explicit in the *Phenomenology of Spirit*, where Hegel seems to think that the Absolute finds its highest expression in the consciousness of individuals who have attained to awareness of the rational nature of the world. Still, he regards it as implicit in Hegel's thought and argues that it is explicit in his later writings. Royce is careful to point out that this is not traditional theism: the Absolute is not thought of as being first perfect by itself and then as creating an imperfect world; rather it becomes perfect in the process of bringing man to a realization of his place in the Divine life.

Kojève, Alexandre. *Introduction to the Reading of Hegel: Lectures on the* Phenomenology of Spirit. Edited by Allan Bloom. Translated by James H. Nichols, Jr. New York: Basic Books, 1969.

Alexandre Kojève's lectures at the *École Pratique des Hautes Études* helped to bring G. W. F. Hegel to the attention of the intelligentsia in France during the late 1930's. His lectures contrast nicely with those of Josiah Royce, because Kojève denies that Hegel was an idealist.

According to Kojève, Hegel anticipated Karl Marx's dictum that life is not determined by consciousness but consciousness by life, because he fully understood that the spirit or mind is from first to last a false consciousness, and that the motivating principle of history is not thought but action. History ends not in a higher state of consciousness but in man's return to the unconsciousness proper to his animal nature. Kojève suggests that the *Phenomenology of Spirit* might as well have been entitled "Phenomenology of Man" or "Anthropogenetics" because it is an account of the experience of the animal called man which set out to master nature and succeeded at last but had to overcome innumerable difficulties along the way. Marx erred, says Kojève, in viewing man's victory as yet future, Hegel having correctly perceived that the struggle had come to a virtual end with Napoleon.

Kojève is also at some pains to show that Hegel anticipated Martin Heidegger in his comments on being and time. In the *Phenomenology of Spirit*, although not in his later writings, Hegel identified nature with space and history with time. By discourse and by action man reveals being in thought, and time is generated by these means. Although René Descartes had already identified space with static being, it was Hegel who first opposed self (thought and time) to being (space), concluded that man is nonbeing or nothingness, and exhibited history as man's attempt to preserve his nothingness by overcoming being—namely, by transforming it into something new in a nonexistent, nonspatial past.

Kojève finds in the *Phenomenology of Spirit* four irreducible premises which, taken together, explain history: first, the revelation of being by speech, which results from man's attempt to seize the world given through the senses; second, nonbiological desire, which arises as man attempts to become a self; third, the existence of many individuals aspiring after selfhood, each seeking the destruction of every other; and fourth, the difference in quality of desire between those individuals whose aspiration after selfhood is stronger than their natural desire after life, and those in whom the opposite is the case— that is, between future masters and future slaves. History, and therefore humanity, came into existence with the first fight which resulted in one self consenting to be the slave of another. History is the dialectical relation between mastery and slavery. And history will be completed as soon as the synthesis of these two is realized in the "whole man, the citizen of the universal and homogeneous states created by Napoleon."

The specifically human, nonbiological desire which is the moving force of history is desire for recognition. The master gets recognition from the slave and by means of the slave's work his biological desires are also satisfied. But, as Hegel showed, there is more future in being a slave than in being a master. The human ideal, which arose in the master, of being recognized and also of having one's animal desires satisfied, is completely realized only by the specifically human activity of work, which is the province of the slave, who in the course of serving his master not merely rises above nature but transforms nature and mankind in the process. That the slave acts means that he obeys an idea, and in the course of his action he creates a nonnatural, technical, humanized world. His acceptance of the idea of slavery created a social order;

his techniques gave birth to reason; even the glimpse of his own nothingness which led him to choose slavery rather than death anticipated the wisdom of posthistorical man.

The editor gives special prominence to Kojève's lectures on mastery and slavery and to those lectures which trace the history of the state from pagan to modern times. Here the dialectic of master and slave appears as the dialectic of universality and particularity, mastery corresponding to the former and slavery to the latter. It is noteworthy that the two concepts are dialectically present in the desire for recognition: each self wants his particular value to be recognized universally. Thus, in order for mankind to find satisfaction and bring history to an end, a society must be formed in which the individual worth of each is respected by all. Kojève notes that it was not actual slaves but self-employed bourgeoisie with highly individualistic ideologies who completed the historical evolution of mankind by realizing the ideal of a self-satisfied citizenry.

In footnotes written later, Kojève spells out for the uninitiated what he means when he speaks of the end of time and the cessation of history. To be sure, the results of the French Revolution had to be extended geographically: two world wars and numerous large and small revolutions were needed to bring its benefits to backward civilizations. But in all this time nothing new has taken place. Historical action has come to a halt and with it the conflict of ideologies, including philosophy. With light irony Kojève points to "the American way of life" as prefiguring the "eternal present" which eventually all humanity will come to enjoy, the final Marxist communism in which everyone appropriates what seems good to him without working any more than he pleases.—*J.F.*

ADDITIONAL RECOMMENDED READING

Findlay, J. N. *Hegel: A Re-examination.* New York: Macmillan Publishing Company, 1958. Chapters V and VI on *The Phenomenology of Spirit* are the best brief guide in English. The author is a philosopher in the analytic tradition.

Hyppolite, Jean. *Genesis and Structure of Hegel's* Phenomenology of Spirit. Translated by S. Cherniak and John Heckman. Evanston, Illinois: Northwestern University Press, 1974. Full-length commentary, essential for a close study of the text.

Kaufman, Walter. *Hegel: Reinterpretation, Texts, and Commentary.* Garden City, New York: Doubleday & Company, 1965. A detailed treatment of the Preface of the *Phenomenology of Spirit*, with much information concerning the circumstances under which the book was written.

Loewenberg, Jacob. *Hegel's Phenomenology: Dialogues on the Life of the Mind.* La Salle, Illinois: Open Court, 1965. The dialogue form permits the author to raise objections which might occur to a nonphilosophical reader and to answer them in a nontechnical manner. Rewarding for the careful student.

LOGIC

Author: Georg Wilhelm Friedrich Hegel (1770-1831)
Type of work: Logic, metaphysics
First published: 1812-1816

PRINCIPAL IDEAS ADVANCED

What is real is rational, and what is rational is real.

Logic, which is a systematic creative process, has three stages: the abstract stage, the dialectical stage, and the speculative stage.

In the abstract stage terms of thought are considered separately; in the dialectical stage one realizes that for something to exist it must be, not separate, but in relation to others; and in the speculative stage one understands the unity of opposites in their opposition.

There are three subdivisions of logic: the Doctrine of Being, the Doctrine of Essence, and the Doctrine of Idea—by which being is known not only for itself and for another, but in-and-for itself.

Hegel is in the idealist tradition that evolved in Germany in the late eighteenth and the nineteenth centuries. Kant and the post-Kantians felt that the empirical philosophy of Hume, with its skeptical consequences, was inadequate; that mind through intuition, understanding, and reason could discover the grounds of experience either in an *a priori* categorical structure or in experience itself, if that experience were looked upon as primarily rational. Kant took the first alternative and argued that although events in themselves are unknowable (thus, keeping an element of Humean skepticism), as phenomena which we perceive they are constructed according to the categories of the understanding and the forms of intuition. As such they have their intelligible basis in mind, although there is an empirical content given from the external world. Hegel believed that the categories and forms are as much a part of reality as anything else, that the dichotomy between mind and its objects is a false one, and, hence, that reality is as rational as thought itself. He expressed this view in his famous statement, "What is real (actual) is rational; what is rational is real (actual)."

How is thought to express the nature of reality? Philosophy from Hume through Kant (and earlier) held that the agreement of thought with reality is the criterion of truth. But Hegel claimed that thought alone brings to light the nature of things; this is the true sense of thought and reality being in agreement.

Like all idealists, Hegel maintained that since reality is known by means of ideas, and since the only thing that can agree with an idea is something like an idea, reality must be mindlike. In seeking to know the nature of things via reflection the individual concentrates upon the universal character of things. But thought so directed loses its individual character, for in proceeding in this way a person reflects as any other individual would who was in pursuit of the truth. Reflective thought thus loses its subjective aspect and becomes objective; thought and reality become one.

As is well known, Hegel held that thought expresses itself in triads, each of which usually has its own triadic structure, a structure which often has a triadic structure of its own. Thus, logic has three stages; its subdivisions are three, and each of these has a triadic structure. It is interesting that Hegel apparently did not use the expression, "thesis-antithesis-synthesis," which has been correctly used to characterize his position. At any rate the emphasis upon the development of thought in terms of a point of view, its negation, and the reconciliation of the two is reminiscent of the dialectical procedure of Socrates and Plato. Hegel, keenly aware of this resemblance, used the term "dialectical" for his own philosophy.

Hegel uses the word "logic" in somewhat the same sense that St. John spoke of "logos." That is, the word refers to a systematic creative process rather than to an analysis of language and argument. For him there are three stages of logic: (1) the abstract stage, or that of the understanding, (2) the dialectical stage, or that of negative reason, and (3) the speculative stage, or that of positive reason.

In the *abstract* stage every term or product of thought appears separate and distinct from one another. The understanding believes that they exist on their own account. What Hegel is saying is that on reflection the individual initially considers the elements of his thought—that is, whatever he is reflecting upon—as taken from the context of experience (or abstracted) and as having an existence of its own independent of anything else. This stage in thinking occurs throughout the history of thought; so that in each stage of philosophical development, men begin by abstraction. Thus the first stage has its own abstract beginning, but the stage itself, when compared to the next stage, will be seen as abstract.

As an illustration, consider the philosophical view called "empiricism." In the abstract stage of empiricism only the immediately given, that which is presented here and now, has ultimate reality. These data, usually called "impressions," turn out to be bare "givens" devoid of relations and predicates and hidden in a skeptical mist, yet held to be separate and distinct and existing on their own account. But as we read the empiricist, he seems to pass from this "reality" about which he can say nothing, to his ideas about which he says everything that he can say. But his ideas belong to a different level of knowledge; memory and reflection are involved, and thus the empiricist passes from the stage of abstraction to that of dialectic wherein mediate thought is now the subject matter.

The *dialectical* stage is one in which the understanding views the elements in their separate and distinct capacity and as such recognizes that no more can be said of them. (In Hume's work this stage can be seen in his denial of necessary connection in experience and in his skepticism regarding reason and the senses.) There is a "positive" side to dialectic, however, in its indication that whatever is finite, when seen as separate and distinct and as free from all relations to others, ceases to exist. To be one without others is impossible. Existence involves a relationship between at least two entities.

The last stage of logic is the *speculative*, in which reason is wholly positive. For Hegel, the contradictory character of certain metaphysical principles is finally reconciled. In the concept of causation it is argued that for every effect there must be a cause, and that every cause is an effect for which there is yet a cause. This concept is such that the notion of a first cause is untenable, since it too would have to have a cause. But, since causation which has no limits leaves any system of philosophy incomplete, such a concept is repugnant to reason. The same sort of analysis may be made with regard to time as a sequence of events which can have neither a beginning nor an end but still must have both. These paradoxical philosophical problems which Hegel argued had not been solved are reconciled by speculative reason which apprehends the unity of the categories in their very opposition.

As noted earlier, the subdivision of logic has three parts also. These are the Doctrine of Being, the Doctrine of Essence, and the Doctrine of Notion or Idea. Let us first indicate briefly the sense of each doctrine before discussing them in more detail. It should also be pointed out that in these doctrines Hegel intended the sort of development that we mentioned earlier; that is, implicit in the exposition of each is to be found the grounds for the next. Although each may be taken as a doctrine in itself, each would then be an abstraction (another instance of the first stage of logic) and hence untrue as well as incomplete.

In the doctrine of Being we are faced with an analysis of the given in its immediacy. In the history of philosophy there have been innumerable ideas concerning the nature of Being advanced by philosophers claiming to have identified the basic ontological stuff. The One of Parmenides, Aristotle's primary substance, and Hume's impressions are all candidates wearing the label of "Being." Under this doctrine Hegel analyzes the full meaning and consequences of the immediately given and indicates wherein he thinks it false.

The doctrine of Essence takes up where the failure of Being as a satisfactory philosophical doctrine occurs. If the immediate nature of things cannot reveal their essential characteristics to thought, if the search for them forces us to mediate knowledge—that is, to look for intervening features, to wonder how the given came to be as it is—then we can no longer consider the given in itself, but only in its relation to an other. (The other need not be an entity in addition to the immediately given; it may simply be the recognition that the given has limits, a recognition which Hegel believed takes us beyond the immediate.) It is here that the doctrine of Essence enters, for in order for the essential features of a thing to be known by thought, it must be seen in its relations to an other. The doctrine of Essence, however, is concerned in itself with an exclusive analysis of the mediate; hence it, too, is incomplete.

The doctrine of Notion or Idea is that in which the inadequacy of the previous two is reconciled. Being must be known not only for itself and for an other, but in-and-for itself. (We noted that "for an other" need not imply a second given, that it might indicate the limits of the given, its finiteness, and hence refer to itself. In its immediacy nothing can be said about Being.) But when seen in this way, Being is understood as a Notion or Idea, and the truth of the given is grasped by reason.

In discussing the doctrine of Being, Hegel attempted to accomplish two things: to present the totality of Being and to abolish the immediacy of Being. There are three grades to Being which are necessary to our discussion of it: quality, quantity, and measure. Here we are concerned not only with the history of philosophic thought, but also with the evolution of thought itself.

In the bare beginnings of thought we have, as it were, an indeterminate something from which something determinate is to come; Hegel calls this bare beginning "Being." This impression of which there is not yet an idea cannot be talked about. It is taken as a here-now; in order to talk about it, think about it, predicate anything of it, we would have to take it out of the here-now and make of it something determinate, but as something determinate it would have a quality. A bare datum is without distinction, without time, and to say of it that it is here in a specified way is already to take it out of the immediate and determinate it.

The bare beginnings then pass to a stage in which the given is qualified, is made something; it is saved from not being anything. That it is something and not others, that it has a distinct character which differentiates it from others, subjects it to change and alteration. No longer indeterminable (Being itself) or nothing (not-Being), it stands between the two in the world of becoming.

Perhaps Hegel's discussion will be easier to follow if a philosophical illustration is considered. Impressions may be regarded as similar to indeterminable Being. Impressions are sensations below the level of consciousness, about which we can say nothing because of their fragmentary, fleeting nature; they are gone before they can be talked about. Consciousness arises concomitantly with the birth of ideas. From the fleeting impressions, mind selects and holds for observation—determines, as it were—one of these, and thus ideas are born. In the analysis of ideas, mind finds qualities, time, cause, change. So for Hegel, Being is quality—that determining characteristic without which the given would cease to be.

If we consider a determinate entity, we observe that it is what it is independently of any increase or decrease of its quantity, since a qualitative characteristic defines it. Quantity is both discrete and continuous, for it rests upon a unit construction which is exclusive and which is equalized. Numbers, for instance, fulfill this requirement and may be used to determine both discrete and continuous magnitudes. Yet quantity itself cannot be considered as an absolute notion, for as an object is decreased or diminished, eventually a quantitative difference will make a qualitative one.

Generally, Hegel views change of quantity in terms of absolutes; that is he conceives of increase or decrease to the infinitely large or infinitesimally small; the one approaches the entire universe, the absolute; the other approaches nothing, not-Being. A house may be a house no matter how large or small; but "no matter how" must be taken relatively, a house cannot be nothing or everything. Hegel considers this an instance of the dialectical at work in quantity, making it what it is not; that is, quality.

Thus, we arrive at the third grade of Being, a quantified quality, or measure. In measure we attain the knowledge that everything is not immediate, but relative or mediate. For everything has its measure, its proper qualitative and quantitative range, as it were, beyond which it cannot remain the same. To know the proper measure of a thing, of Being, is to know its Essence.

Hegel thus accomplished what he set out to do; that is, he presented the totality of Being by analyzing its three grades, quality, quantity, and measure, and he abolished the immediacy of Being by showing that its Essence, whatever makes it what it is, rests not upon its immediately given appearance, but upon its measure, which is a mediate or relative concept demanding that the given be seen in terms of an other. This analysis depended not upon mere perception of the immediately given, but rather upon reflective thought. Thought and its object are progressing together. Being is the immediate appearance of reality; through reflection the philosopher has proceeded to the mediate aspect of reality, its Essence. Neither Being nor Essence is more real than the other; reflective thought has gone from one to the other to give us a greater insight into reality.

In the doctrine of Essence we also find three grades: identity, diversity, and ground. We have seen that an analysis of a thing is such that it is conditioned by, and conditions, something else. In order to be determinate, not only are the boundaries of the thing needed, so that it can be defined as a finite object, but in its very definition it is distinguised from what it is not. Thus, not only is it related to itself in terms of its identity, but also it is related to others in terms of its difference.

Hegel's argument is reminiscent of Plato's analysis of the One and the Many in the *Parmenides*. Plato showed that the paradox of the One—that it is and yet that it is not—can be resolved if we introduce the concepts of identity, difference, and other than. The One is (identical with itself) and the One is not (others); that is, the One is other than or different from. Hegel's work contains a similar (although in many ways different) analysis. In order to understand the essence of a thing we must grasp the apparently contradictory characteristics of identity and diversity in some sort of unity. Unity is found in the concept of the ground. In order for a thing to be, that is, to exist, there must be more than its self-identity. For self-identity when not contrasted with what the self is now would once more lead to an indeterminate, abstract Being. On the other hand, there must be more than the mediating relations which indicate that there are others than the self. That is, we cannot concentrate only upon what the self is not. In the concept of a ground Hegel finds the proper meaning of Essence, for the thing is seen in its inward relations (its self-identity) *and* in its relations to an other also; but this is the concept of the ground.

The final subdivision in Hegel's logic is that of the doctrine of Notion or Idea. (Hegel's term in the German is "Begriff"—a term which, replete with difficulty, has the conflicting shades of meaning alluded to earlier and, as it were, all present at the same time.) The three grades of this doctrine are universal, particular, and individual.

Having presented two aspects of reality, its immediate and mediate appearance, its Being and its Essence, Hegel was ready to consider reality in its totality. The movement from Being to and through Essence is a dialectical process involving reflection, a process by which the nature of the given is revealed. The doctrine of Idea emphasizes for us that the only way in which we can discover the nature of a thing is to proceed through this kind of process. Hegel points out in the doctrine of Idea that in the process of development the thing is revealed to reflective thought in the aforementioned grades. In its bare beginnings as immediate Being, it is an indeterminate, undefinable thing in itself—the very *ding an sich* that Kant spoke of. It is an undeveloped universal. From the immediately given, one proceeds to a consideration of the thing as a differentiated something. (Hegel refers to this as the particularizing phase of development.) Finally, in reflecting upon the further development of the thing into a Being which is both immediate and mediate, identical and different, universal and particular, the individual is realized. But to see the individual as it is, it must be understood in terms of its process from undifferentiated universal to differentiated particular to individual. If the parts are to be understood, we must understand the process as a whole. Thus, for Hegel, the process of knowledge and that which is known, Being, ultimately are one. Reality and rationality are interchangeable.—*T.W.*

PERTINENT LITERATURE

McTaggart, John McTaggart Ellis. *A Commentary on Hegel's* Logic. Cambridge: Cambridge University Press, 1910.

It is now widely agreed among commentators on Georg Wilhelm Friedrich

Hegel's *Logic* that although John McTaggart's work may well be the most influential—J. N. Findlay, for example, admires it the most—it is the commentary with which they most disagree as well. Its influence is due to several factors. It was the first full-scale commentary on Hegel's logical writings available in English, and therefore generated much of the terminology commonly associated with Hegel (for example, thesis, antithesis, synthesis; triad and triadic) for which there is no direct German counterpart in Hegel. It is also, perhaps primarily, one influential philosopher's critical analysis of the writings of another. Finally, it is the version of Hegel which Bertrand Russell and George Edward Moore learned and against which they rebelled. McTaggart's commentary is the most disagreed with primarily because the vision and version of Hegel which emerges is Hegel as Oxford idealist: Hegel is scarcely to be distinguished from Francis Herbert Bradley or McTaggart himself.

McTaggart's aim is clear and precise: to take the reader, by means of a detailed critical account of the various transitions, from Hegel's category of Being to the category of the Absolute Idea. It is the dialectical process itself which McTaggart regards as the one absolutely essential element in Hegel's system. To reject the dialectical process is to reject the system. Moreover, McTaggart accepts the general validity of the dialectic method; he maintains that Hegel is justified in passing from category to category in cases in which they do stand to one another in the relations in which he asserts that they stand.

McTaggart's disagreements with Hegel are spelled out in the first chapter of the book. There are major differences, disagreements which are then rehearsed in greater detail throughout the remaining nine chapters of this commentary. First, McTaggart believed that Hegel committed serious errors in applying the results of his logical investigations to concrete phenomena. Second, Hegel failed to understand specifically the nature of the dialectic relations which obtained between the ideas he had discovered.

Specifically, Hegel misunderstood the dialectic, according to McTaggart, by exaggerating both its objectivity and its comprehensiveness. By exaggerating the objectivity of the dialectic, McTaggart meant that Hegel would have rejected the notion that there could be possible alternative routes from category to category, from the lower to the higher ones. In short, the argument is that Hegel would have considered it *a priori* impossible that two valid chains could proceed from the same starting point to the Absolute Idea.

By claiming that Hegel exaggerated the dialectic'c comprehensiveness, McTaggart argues that Hegel thought that nothing in philosophy can be logically prior to the dialectic process itself, and this McTaggart considers to be not merely arbitrary but also mistaken. For when one asks the question: To what subject matter does the dialectic apply?, McTaggart believes that Hegel's answer would have been "to all reality." Hegel would not have been justified in this assertion, however, because, according to McTaggart, the dialectic may properly apply only to "what is existent," which rules out "propositions" and "possibilities," for example. Other alleged deficiencies are discussed in McTaggart's opening chapter, and these determine the author's subsequent treatment. It is said, for example, that Hegel errs in particular transitions as a result of his failure to confine himself to what is existent, or as a result of his desire to include important results of science within his logic, or as a result of his own confusion between categories and the concrete states-of-affairs after which they are named.

McTaggart's commentary divides into ten chapters which amount to 296 sections. The thirteen-section introductory chapter is followed by a forty-two-section discussion of Quality; a twenty-five-section discussion of Quantity; a twenty-section discussion of Measure; a thirty-six-section discussion of Essence; a twenty-two-section discussion of Appearance; a twenty-six-section discussion of Actuality; a thirty-nine-section discussion of Subjectivity; a twenty-nine-section discussion of Objectivity; and a thirty-two-section discussion of The Idea. The book's final section makes the point that a commentary of this sort, one which emphasizes points of difference more than agreement, is likely to mislead. To correct this impression McTaggart remarks that Hegel has managed to penetrate more deeply into "the true nature of reality" than any philosopher before or after him has done.

Mure, Geoffrey Reginald Gilchrist. *A Study of Hegel's* Logic. Oxford: Clarendon Press, 1950.

Geoffrey Mure's study is a sympathetic and profound treatment of Georg Wilhelm Friedrich Hegel's logical writings. It differs from its predecessors in that it does not insist that Hegel's dialectic displays the logically necessary transitions of an otherwise monistic timeless absolute. Rather, Mure finds that the *a priori* and empirical sources of the dialectic often travel by the double method of compass and dead reckoning.

Chapters II-XVII constitute a sympathetic reconstruction of Hegel's categories as these are found in the *Encyclopedia of the Philosophical Sciences in Outline*, Part I; the exposition is modified slightly by supplementation from *Wissenschaft der Logik*. In Chapter I, Mure briefly but precisely sets down his own reactions to Hegel's philosophy, concentrating on Hegel's theory of language. This discussion is again taken up in Chapters XIX-XXII, where a definite line of criticism emerges.

According to Mure, Hegel's central task was to show that reality is a necessarily ordered whole in which the elements ordered are the phases of a single timelessly self-constituting activity; this activity is mind or spirit (*Geist*). This self-constituting activity is, in turn, self-manifestation. Moreover, this is a self-manifestation in a double sense in that it is not only a complete and unreserved manifesting *of* itself but also a manifestation *to* itself. Expressed in a formula, self-constitution is self-manifestation, self-manifestation is self-consciousness, and this alone is complete activity, activity in the full sense.

This activity *is* dialectical thinking, according to Mure. Its self-manifestation is a progressive cycle of self-definition by thesis, antithesis, and synthesis; each antithesis is the completely mediating and determinant contrary of its thesis, and each synthesis is, in turn, the coincidence of these opposites in a fuller definition. This dialectic is explicit self-definition in its supreme form when it becomes philosophical thinking. For the forms through which spirit progresses it also sublates; and these are chiefly three: (1) forms which are spirit's explicit self-definitions—namely, the categories; (2) forms of nature which are "real" only as sublated in the activity of spirit, even though required for spirit's self-manifesting; and (3) forms of spirit which are not yet explicitly the philosophic thought in which they culminate but, like Nature, are really only as sublated in thought. The explicit self-definition of spirit in philosophical thinking is the self-explication of philosophy in and through the categories, the forms of nature, and the forms of Concrete Spirit.

Mure takes great pains to remind the reader that Hegel's logic is an onto-logic—that is, an ontology, a theory of being. Indeed, even with reference to formal logic, Mure reminds the reader of three of Hegel's most important assumptions: that pure thought is itself both form *and* content, that no category can signify in isolation—can have meaning apart from a dialectical relation to other categories—and that no principle or category of thought can be held to be absolutely *a priori* and eternally exempt from criticism. This last point, the refusal to argue for an Archimedian standpoint within Hegel's logic, distinguishes Mure's approach sharply from that of John McTaggart.

Mure accepts Hegel's original identification of being and self-conscious thought as a unity, the view that the real is the single self-developing and self-developed activity of spirit. Although the difference between pure thought and perception is perhaps the deepest and most immediately available in human experience, we cannot achieve a world of pure thought untainted by contingency, Mure argues; and he suggests that the empirical material which Hegel struggled to incorporate in the *Logic* reveals this impossibility. This point has a deeper application still, for it suggests that while the unity of thought and being may save us from total skepticism, it also precludes any hope of finality to human thought. Because the single activity of spirit is of its own nature not only self-developed but self-developing, self-manifesting in finitude, an ambiguous duality is omnipresent in human experience, Mure argues.

Mure's sensitive and penetrating work on Hegel was virtually complete when World War II broke out. It was later revised and published after the war in a philosophic climate as hostile as any has been to historical/philosophical research. The alliance of empiricism and logical analysis had so come to dominate that Mure sometimes feared civilization itself had been uprooted, that a terrifying return of the dark ages was afoot. It was to light one candle in the encroaching darkness that Mure wrote his Hegel studies.—*B.M.*

ADDITIONAL RECOMMENDED READING
Findlay, John N. *Hegel: A Re-Examination.* New York: The Macmillan Company, 1958. A brilliant reexamination of Hegel's philosophy, acclaimed by Continental European as well as Anglo-American philosophers.
McTaggart, John McTaggart Ellis. *Studies in the Hegelian Dialectic.* Cambridge: Cambridge University Press, 1896. An investigation of the concept of dialectic in Hegel's philosophy.
Mure, Geoffrey R. G. *An Introduction to Hegel.* Oxford: Clarendon Press, 1940. An examination of Hegel's philosophy which stresses his connection with the tradition, particularly with Aristotle.
Stace, W. T. *The Philosophy of Hegel.* New York: Dover Publications, 1955. First published in 1924, this is a clear and thorough account of Hegel's philosophy which centers on the *Encyclopedia of the Philosophical Sciences in Outline.*
Taylor, Charles. *Hegel.* Cambridge: Cambridge University Press, 1975. A massive volume which examines Hegel's philosophy and relates it to its time and ours. Perhaps the best recent book on Hegel available in English.

THE WORLD AS WILL AND IDEA

Author: Arthur Schopenhauer (1788-1860)
Type of work: Metaphysics
First published: 1818

PRINCIPAL IDEAS ADVANCED

The world is my idea—this is a truth for every man, since the world as it is known depends for its character and existence upon the mind that knows it.

By his understanding man forms the world of phenomena, and by his reason he achieves harmony in a world of suffering.

The entire world of phenomena, including the human body, is objectified will.

The will is a striving, yearning force which takes various forms according to its inclinations.

By losing oneself in objects, by knowing them as they are in themselves, one comes to know the will as Idea, as eternal form.

In his Preface to the first edition of *The World as Will and Idea*, Schopenhauer states that his chief sources are Kant, Plato, and the *Upanishads*. He does indeed blend these three into his own philosophical system, but he gives the whole his own philosophical interpretation.

The opening book is entitled, "The World as Idea," and in it Schopenhauer presents his modified scheme of Kant's "Copernican Revolution" in philosophy. Kant had held that the world of phenomena which we perceive is to be understood as a world which is made known to us through various features of our understanding. Events appear to us as in space and time; for Kant these were ultimately to be understood as forms of intuition or perception which, as it were, gave to events their spatial and temporal characteristics. In his famous analogy, the forms of intuition are the spectacles through which we view the world in its spatial and temporal aspects. In addition, we know the world in terms of traditional categories among which cause is a primary one; for Kant these categories are also of the understanding. Thus, the world of appearances is in the final analysis one in which undifferentiated "stuff" is formed in space and time and categorized by the understanding into the related events that science studies. But, to repeat, at bottom it is a mind-formed world. Schopenhauer accepted the Kantian view of the world, and rather brilliantly reduced the twelve categories to the *Critique of Pure Reason* to one, that of the principle of sufficient reason (causation). This principle, with its fourfold root in science, logic, morality, and metaphysics, formed the basis of Schopenhauer's analysis of the world of phenomena.

"The world is my idea" means, then, that the world of objects that I perceive depends for its existence as a perceived system of things upon the mind of consciousness that perceives it. Schopenhauer follows Kant in that he distinguishes mere sense impressions from perceptions (or ideas). Sense impressions are received by the mind from the external world; through the forms of space and time and the principle of sufficient reason, the understanding gives form to sensations, making them into ideas. Since it is the understanding which makes ideas what they are, perception is essentially intellectual. The subject or conscious mind becomes aware of object or body first through sense knowledge of its own body. Schopenhauer believed that the subject infers from sense effects immediately known to the self's body and to other bodies. It is in this way that the world of ideas is constructed. The world of ideas may be considered in two ways. The understanding itself contains the potentiality to form a world of perceptions. But it would remain dormant, as it were, did not the external world excite it. In this sense, then, there is an objective side to the possibility of knowing the world; the world must be capable of acting upon the subject to make perceptions possible. The subjective expression of the world, however, actually converts this possibility into a world of phenomena, for the law of causality springs from and is valid only for it. This means that the world of events as existing in space and time and causally related to one another is formed by the understanding. Additionally, as we noted, the sensibility of animal bodies makes possible the body as an immediate object for the subject.

Although the understanding makes meaningful the world of objects (there would be but undifferentiated sensations otherwise), there is yet another aspect of mind which has an important role to play, and that is reason. Reason distinguishes man from other animals in that by its use he is able to deal in abstract ideas or concepts, and thus to plan, choose, and build—in general, to act prudently. If he merely perceived the world of objects through his understanding he would never be able to transcend and contemplate it. In the quiet life of contemplation, he rises above the hustle and bustle of everyday activities; he can achieve stoical calm, peace, and inner harmony in a world of pain and suffering.

In the second book, "The World as Will," Schopenhauer considers the reality behind the world of appearances, what had been for Kant unknowable, the thing-in-itself. It is traditional for philosophers to speculate upon the why of things, to try to understand what makes things what they are. For Schopenhauer, this question cannot be answered by searching within the world of phenomena, but only beyond that world. The key is to be found in the subject himself who, as an individual, has knowledge of the external world rooted in the experience of his body—object to his self. Body is given to the individual in two ways. As we have seen, it is given (1) as an idea; an object among objects subject to the law of objects, that is, to the law of cause and effect. It is also given (2) as an act of will; when the subject wills, the apparent result is a movement of the body. This aspect of Schopenhauer's philosophy can also be found in Kant. Kant had held that for morality to be possible, the will must be autonomous and not subject to the same laws as phenomena. Otherwise our actions would be causally explainable, and hence no more morally responsible than a rolling stone's action. As autonomous, the will is part of the noumenal world of things in themselves and is thus free. The result of willing, for Kant, was a physical movement subject to scientific laws, part of the world of phenomena. The cause of the movement was not itself part of the world of phenomena; hence, not a cause in the scientific sense, it was thus morally free.

We must understand that the term "cause" has a curious history in philosophical works. There is a sense of cause which we might term the creative sense, that which brings an event into being and keeps it existing. In this sense the word is often used to refer to something outside the world of events (usually a being such as God) regarded as responsible for the creation and continuity of that world. But there is another sense of "cause" which while not original with David Hume has since his time been in more popular use among many philosophers. That is cause as a constant conjunction of events within the world of phenomena; what there might be outside that world as a cause of it is held to be subject not to knowledge, but perhaps to faith. It is a religious sense of cause. When Kant refers to the autonomous action of the will, he refers to an action that is not part of the world of events, yet one which has a consequence there—a bodily movement. The sequence of bodily movements is a sequence of events (or ideas) that is subject to causal analysis in the second sense mentioned above; but since the will is not part of the world of phenomena its activities are free from scientific analysis, and thus responsible. It is this sense of the Kantian notion of will that Schopenhauer accepts.

Since an act of will is known as a movement of body which is itself an idea, Schopenhauer regards the body as objectified will. He states also that the entire world of ideas, the realm of phenomena, is but a world of objectified will. For Schopenhauer, the world of noumena is nothing but a world of will, that which is "beyond" the world of events, yet its very ground. We also have knowledge of the noumenal world; there is a unique relationship between the subject and his body in which he is aware of his "noumenal" willing and the resulting physical movements. It is possible to look upon the entire world of events, including other subjects known only as ideas, as one's own world. But Schopenhauer would not be satisfied with solipsism.

In holding that body is but objectified will, Schopenhauer argues that the various parts of the body—for example, teeth, throat, and bowels—are but expressions of will, in this case of hunger. For Schopenhauer, there is a force in all things which makes them what they are: the will. Recall, however, that phenomenally this force is not perceived; since all we know are events subject to the principle of sufficient reason, the will here is groundless. But in self-consciousness the will is not hidden but is known directly, and in this consciousness we are also aware of our freedom. We are aware of an activity that cannot itself be part of the world of events that follows from that activity.

Although it has been customary in the history of philosophy for philosophers to raise questions concerning the purpose or end of existence, of creation, Schopenhauer claims that such questions are groundless. In effect they refer to the activity of the will; but the will has no purpose. It moves without cause, has no goal; it is desire itself, striving, yearning, wanting without rhyme or reason.

The third book of Schopenhauer's work is also entitled, "The World as Idea," but "idea" is now seen as a product of reason rather than as a perceptual event. It is here that Plato's concept of the idea or form is used by Schopenhauer, and his prime purpose is to develop his theory of art by means of it. He begins by pointing out that the will is objectified not only in the many particulars that we come to know as events in space and time, subject to change and, hence, explainable under the principle of sufficient reason; but it also manifests itself in universals, which are immutable and thus not susceptible to causal analysis. Schopenhauer holds that the will as universal presents us with a direct objectification, a Platonic form, whereas as a particular it is indirect.

How is the individual to know these direct objectifications? He may gain knowledge of them by transcending the world of events, of space and time and causality, and looking at things as they are in themselves. He does so by losing himself in the object, by giving up his own subjectivity and becoming one with that which he perceives. In such a state. Schopenhauer holds, the individual becomes the pure will-less, painless, timeless subject of knowledge. He becomes a knower of ideas or forms, and not of mere particulars; the object to him is now the *Idea*, the form, of the species. This seems to be something like the sort of knowledge that has been attributed to the mystic, and, no doubt, the influence of the Far East upon Schopenhauer can be seen here also; but he likens the apprehension of forms to art. The artist repeats or reproduces Ideas grasped through pure contemplation; knowledge of the Ideas is the one source of art and its aim is the communication of this knowledge. With this in mind we can see that Schopenhauer's definition of "art" fits closely with his views. It is the way of knowing things independently of the principle of sufficient reason. The man of genius is he who by intuition and imagination most completely frees himself from the world of events to grasp the eternal present within it.

Schopenhauer writes that the aesthetic mode of contemplation involves two features: (1) the object known as a Platonic idea or form and (2) the knowing person considered not as an individual in the ordinary sense, but as a pure, will-less subject of knowledge. When the knower gives up the fourfold principle of sufficient reason as a way of knowing things and assumes the aesthetic mode of contemplation, he derives a peculiar pleasure from that mode in varying degrees depending upon the aesthetic object.

Ordinarily it is difficult and, for most persons, impossible, to escape from the world of desires and wants, the world which gives rise to our willing and which can never be satisfied. Our wants are without satiation; thus, suffering, frustration, and a sense of deficiency are ever-present to us. But if by some external cause or inner disposition we are raised above the cares of the daily world, our knowledge is freed from the directives of will and the temporal aspects of events, and we can achieve that transcendent state of peace, the painless state that separates the world of forms from that of suffering. This is the state of pure contemplation that the great Greek philosophers spoke of.

The artist who has attained this state and then represents it to us in his works allows us to escape the vicissitudes of life and to contemplate the world of forms free from the machinations of the will. His work of art is a means by which we can attain his heights. Nature, too, in certain circumstances, can present us with her objects in such a way that we transcend the world about us and enter into the realm of forms. But the slightest wavering of attention on our part once more returns us to the world of phenomena; we leave contemplation for desire. Aesthetic enjoyment can also be obtained in the remembrance of things past. Schopenhauer points out that the individual in contemplating his memories finds them freed from the immediate tinges of suffering and pain that events often have. Generally speaking, aesthetic pleasure arises whenever we are able to rise above the wants of the moment and to contemplate things in themselves as no longer subject to the principle of sufficient reason; pleasure arises from the opposition to will; it is the delight that comes from perceptive knowledge. When a contemplated object takes on the Idea of its species, we hold it to be a beauty. The nineteenth century aestheticians were concerned with the sublime also; Schopenhauer sees it in the exaltation which arises when one forcibly and consciously breaks away from the world of events and enters the world of forms. The object transfigured in this contemplative act yet carries an aura of its existence as an event created by will. As such it is hostile to the perceiver, yet in being "made" into a form it is the object of pleasure and beauty. If the hostility crowds out the beauty, then the sublime leaves. When the sublime is present we recognize our own insignificance alongside that which we perceive, yet, Schopenhauer feels, we also recognize the dependence of the object upon us as one of our ideas. We are both humble and monumental in its presence.

Tragedy is the summit of poetical art; it presents the terrible side of life, the pain and evil, the want and suffering. We see in nature the all-consuming war of will with itself. When we learn of this inner struggle through tragedy, we are no longer deceived by the phenomena about us. The ego which is so involved in the world of events perishes with that world as we see it for what it is. The motives which keep the will striving are gone; they are replaced by knowledge of the world. This knowledge produces a quieting effect upon the will so that resignation takes place, not a surrender merely of the things of life, but of the very will to live. (This is not to be confused with a "desire" to commit suicide, which is a definite, if ill-advised, act of will tormented by the world of events; rather, it is a renunciation of all desire as one becomes one with the eternal.)

The last book is also entitled, like the second, "The World as Will," but in the second aspect of will Schopenhauer further examines the renunciation of the will to live. In this particular book, Schopenhauer emphasizes the Eastern religious and philosophical view of denial and renunciation. He also concentrates on the idea of life as tragic. It is interesting that Schopenhauer develops a theory of the act of generation as an assertion of the will to live. His discussion is reminiscent of Freud's account of the libido as a general drive manifesting itself throughout mankind and accounting for much, if not all, of human behavior. Freud is supposed to have been shown the passages in Schopenhauer which were similar to his. He claimed not to have read Schopenhauer, but he did acknowledge the similarity of the views.

Schopenhauer believed that in each phenomenal object the will itself is present fully, in the sense that the object is the reification of the will. But the will in its noumenal nature is most real; in inner consciousness the individual, as we noted, is directly aware of the will. The individual within the world of events, aware of pure will in himself, desires everything for himself. Schopenhauer believed that in this way selfishness arises. Recall that each has within himself, for himself, the entire world of phenomena as ideas as well as the world as will. Recall, too, that all other selves are known by the individual as his own ideas—thus he hopes to have all, to control all. His death ends all for him, although while he lives he seeks the world for himself. In this eternal war with one another men deserve the fate which the world as will has for them: a life of tragedy, of want, of pain and suffering. Ultimately, also, the will, in trying to express itself at the expense of others, punishes itself.

As we saw, only those who can rise above their principle of individuation, above the world of cause and effect, who can see the world as one of woe and suffering, can triumph over it. Once one has seen the world for what it is, there is no need to go on willing and striving. One renounces the world of ideas and of will; knowledge quiets the will. This freedom found outside the world of necessity is akin to grace, therein, believed Schopenhauer, lies one's salvation.—*T.W.*

Pertinent Literature

Copleston, Frederick C. *Arthur Schopenhauer: Philosopher of Pessimism.* London: Burnes, Oates & Washbourne, 1946.

Frederick C. Copleston, S. J., Professor of the History of Philosophy at Heythrop College at the time of publication, presents a careful and authoritative analysis of Arthur Schopenhauer from a Roman Catholic perspective. Copleston's interest is in presenting an objective exposition of "that system of philosophy which Schopenhauer propounded in *The World as Will and Idea*" and in criticizing it; the result is as Copleston intended: the criticism does not intrude on the exposition. The book is valuable, then, both as a discerning report on Schopenhauer's ideas and as a source of penetrating criticisms well worth serious attention.

Copleston concludes that for Schopenhauer, since life is the manifestation of "the Will to live," and since such a manifestation entails suffering and evil, the ideal would be "nothingness." Accordingly, the view is in radical contrast to that of Georg Wilhelm Friedrich Hegel: "Instead of optimism, pessimism and the worst possible world; instead of Reason, irrational Will; instead of the manifestation of the Idea, the goal of nothingness."

It is impossible so to interpret Schopenhauer's philosophy as to arrive at a positive view of deep import, Copleston claims. The author himself made the effort after having composed his exposition of Schopenhauer's philosophy: he attempted to interpret Schopenhauer as meaning by "Will" force or energy, or the *élan vital*, life itself—or as propounding a psychological doctrine, or an ethic or theory of value—and in every case the doctrine developed by Schopenhauer frustrated Copleston's effort.

Some persons have attempted to see Schopenhauer as an "esoteric" Christian, but Copleston rejects that view as absurd; Christianity, he contends, is the opposite of Schopenhauer's pessimistic denial of the value of life.

Copleston considers the effect of Schopenhauer's philosophy on the views of Eduard von Hartmann (1842-1906, author of *The Philosophy of the Unconscious*) and Friedrich Nietzsche. Neither thinker salvages anything of worth from the philosophy of Schopenhauer, Copleston concludes. In fact, he writes, Hartmann, although making Idea correlative to Will (the Will must have an end by way of Idea), posited an unconscious Absolute and then, while accepting Schopenhauer's pessimism, agreed also with Gottfried Wilhelm von Leibniz in regarding this world as the best of all possible worlds. Such a view is a "fantastic dream, that passes under the name of philosophy."

As for Nietzsche, according to Copleston, the effort to achieve an optimistic position by venerating the Superman as the ultimate expression of the will to power amounts to nothing more than a futile effort to give priority to the body's biological function of consciousness and, from an atheistic viewpoint, to endorse as the moral ideal the emancipation of moral "prejudices."

Copleston's study of Schopenhauer begins with a survey of the philosophic situation prior to Schopenhauer: Continental Rationalism, on the one hand (despite radical differences in thought among the rationalists), and British Empiricism, on the other. Copleston traces the development from Immanuel

Kant (who emphasized the creativity of the individual human mind and in-sisted on the "thing-in-itself") through J. G. Fichte, F. W. J. Schelling, and Hegel, to Schopenhauer. Although Schopenhauer began with Kant's *Critique of Practical Reason* (in contrast to Fichte and Hegel, who developed ideas from the *Critique of Pure Reason*, thereby ending up with a rationalistic metaphysics) and developed a metaphysics of Will, Copleston warns the reader that Schopenhauer's conception of will is quite different from Kant's.

In a brief biography, Copleston recounts Schopenhauer's efforts to correct the philosophical tendencies of his contemporaries and calls attention to his misanthropy (he had no real friends). Copleston attributes the misanthropy in part to Schopenhauer's strong will and egoism, and he finds the remainder of the explanation (and, in fact, the persistence of the egoistic will) in the conflicts between Schopenhauer and his mother (which also may have stim-ulated Schopenhauer's relentless diatribes against women).

Copleston's account of Schopenhauer's proposition that "the world is my idea" is fair and detailed, and the author makes an effort to find what is acceptable in the idea that the world is phenomenon, including the objectified will; but Copleston argues that although the world is known by a subject and thus by way of phenomena, matter-in-itself—that is, an independent world existing apart from any subject, even the infinite Subject, God—is a "dream world."

The relation of the pessimistic attitude which pervades Schopenhauer's work to the ideas developed in his work and especially to the affirmation of will as fundamental is spelled out by Copleston under the title "The Tragedy of Life." Copleston then writes of art as providing Schopenhauer a "partial escape" through his idea that the arts express different grades of the Will's objectification (except for music, which expresses the Will itself, and hence is the highest of the arts).

The book concludes with discussions of Schopenhauer's ideas of morality and freedom, right and wrong, the state, and virtue and holiness. The sum-mary judgment Copleston makes is that Schopenhauer's philosophy, despite its radical failure to be in accord with Christianity, is "the most striking statement of the pessimistic *Weltanschauung* in the history of human thought."

Hamlyn, David. *Schopenhauer*. London: Routledge & Kegan Paul, 1980.

David Hamlyn, of Birkbeck College, London, argues that although there is some truth in the claim that Arthur Schopenhauer was not a systematic thinker, a continuous argument runs through *The World as Will and Idea* that constitutes his central philosophical position, and Schopenhauer's other works in one way or another can be seen as filling out that central view.

Hamlyn emphasizes Schopenhauer's doctoral dissertation *The Fourfold Root of the Principle of Sufficient Reason* (written in 1813, revised and enlarged, 1847) as an introduction to Schopenhauer's main work (in line with Schopenhauer's own insistence). Although *The Fourfold Root* says little of Schopenhauer's developed metaphysical view, it provides the first stage of the argument in support of that view.

The principle of sufficient reason is expressed in the words of Christian Wolff: "Nothing is without a reason why it should be rather than not be." According to Hamlyn, Schopenhauer regarded this principle as having a single basic role, and he proceeded to specify this role by reference to its "fourfold root." He does not attempt to prove the principle, for he presumed it to be presupposed in any proof. Hamlyn argues that there is but one root of the single principle; the root, however, may take any one of four forms. Since Schopenhauer regarded the mind as having four and only four kinds of objects, he argued that there must be four and only four kinds of reason or ground.

All knowledge involves a relation between knowing subject and object of knowledge, and all objects of knowledge are "representations." (The term *Vorstellung*, translated as "Idea" in the title of Schopenhauer's masterpiece, covers, Hamlyn claims, perceptions, concepts, images: in short, any object of consciousness, not just intellectual conceptions; hence, Hamlyn prefers the term "representation," as in the translation by E. F. J. Payne, *The World as Will and Representation*).

The four forms of the principle of sufficient reason are (in the order urged by Schopenhauer, although not followed in his exposition) the principle of reason of (1) *being*, (2) *becoming*, (3) *acting*, and (4) *knowing*. The latter, Hamlyn explains, involves representations from (or of) representations; the former three are concerned with immediate representations. The principle of reason of "being" is concerned with time and space; "becoming," with causality; "acting," with the will and law of motivation; and "knowing" with reason and truth.

Hamlyn presents Schopenhauer as suggesting that since the principle of sufficient reason makes reference to a knowing consciousness and its objects and since its objects are "representations" (but not the representations of something-in-itself—and, hence, one might say "presentations"), the principle cannot apply to a world beyond representations, a world-in-itself. Schopenhauer's idealism develops logically from his starting point in the principle of sufficient reason as related to the knowing consciousness, but, Hamlyn points out, Schopenhauer does not make that idealism explicit in *The Fourfold Root*; nor does he argue for it in that work.

After a discussion of the profound influence of Immanuel Kant's work on Schopenhauer's own ideas, Hamlyn proceeds to discuss under the title "The World as Representation" the development of the defense of the central thesis that "The world is my idea (representation)" and hence "my will." The will becomes, for Schopenhauer, the only "thing-in-itself," and his transcendental idealism is a rational development of the basic position that the world *is* will.

(The chapter "The World as Will" provides a careful account of Schopenhauer's conception of the will as the underlying reality.)

Hamlyn discusses also the introduction of the Platonic Ideas into Schopenhauer's philosophy of reality and argues that for Schopenhauer the Ideas are "grades of objectification of the will." Since the Ideas are themselves representations, they do not become another fundamental reality; all that is real and thing-in-itself is will, and the representations are "objects for a knowing consciousness. . . ." Through contemplation of the Ideas, made possible chiefly through the use of the intellect and the artistic faculties, the subject (knowing subject) frees itself from the will and its demands.

Art separates the Ideas from reality, Schopenhauer maintains; thus, art produces a peaceful state of mind because the Ideas free the subject from subjection to the will. Music is to be distinguished from the other arts in that music does not copy Ideas; it is an expression of the will itself.

According to Hamlyn, the notion of the freedom of the will is essential in Schopenhauer's ethics because the moral objective is the will's free denial of itself. The denial of the will entails, of course, the denial of representations and of the world as representation; hence, the resultant nothingness is a positive gain compared to the misery of existence prior to the will's denying itself.

Hamlyn's final appraisal of Schopenhauer and his philosophy is that despite the invalidity of certain lines of thought and despite the austerity and even mysteriousness of Schopenhauer's views, his mind was a "great mind indeed" and his philosophy a "magnificent intellectual construction. . . ."—*I.P.M.*

ADDITIONAL RECOMMENDED READING

Gardiner, Patrick L. *Schopenhauer.* Harmondsworth, England: Penguin Books, 1967. Hamlyn endorses Gardiner's book as one of the few good books in English on Schopenhauer.

Taylor, Richard. "Schopenhauer," in *A Critical History of Western Philosophy.* Edited by D. J. O'Connor. London: Collier-Macmillan, 1964. Both Hamlyn and Gardiner cite Taylor's article as an important contribution.

Tsanoff, R. A. *Schopenhauer's Criticism of Kant's Theory of Experience.* New York: Longmans, Green, 1911. An interesting and scholarly study of Schopenhauer as critic of Kant.

COURSE ON THE POSITIVE PHILOSOPHY

Author: Auguste Comte (1798-1857)
Type of work: Social philosophy
First published: 1830-1842

PRINCIPAL IDEAS ADVANCED

Social dynamics is the science of history; the positive philosophy provides a law of three stages to make historical facts significant.

In the theological state of a society, men invent gods and arrange society accordingly: the priests rule; in the metaphysical stage, intellect deifies itself, authority is challenged, religion becomes sectarian, and individuals abandon their social responsibilities; in the positive stage, the positive sciences provide certainties which make order possible, inspire a moral regeneration, and make social concerns primary for all.

Sociology completes the body of philosophy by tracing out the unity to be found in the various sciences.

The natural sciences, like the societies of men, and like men themselves, have passed through the theological, metaphysical, and positive stages.

The various sciences can be arranged according to their degree of complexity and their dependence on others; beginning with the most general (after mathematics, which is not a natural science), the order is: astronomy, physics, chemistry, biology, physiology, and sociology.

Comte had two distinct aims in writing *Course on the Positive Philosophy.* The first and "special" aim was to put the study of society on a positive foundation, comparable to that at which one by one the natural sciences had arrived. The second and "general" aim was to review the natural sciences, with a view to showing that they are not independent of one another but, as it were, "all branches from the same trunk." As we shall see, the two aims are inseparable.

Comte divided the study of society—sociology or "social physics," as he called it—into two parts, following a distinction which he believed runs through all the sciences: social statics, and social dynamics. The former seems not to have interested him especially. He maintained that in its broader aspects, at least, it was deducible from human physiology, which demands that men live in society, that they form families, and that they obey political authorities. On these grounds, he held that woman is inferior to man and bound to subservience, and that some men and races are constitutionally suited to obey and others to command.

But Comte dealt with these matters only in passing. His interest was not so much in the generic traits which are found in all human societies, as in the laws which govern the transition of a society from one condition to another.

This is what he intended by the term "social dynamics." His work was to be nothing less than a science of history. History, said Comte, had compiled many facts but had been unable to contribute anything of importance to understanding man's condition because, like the data of meteorology, its facts needed a law to become significant. Comte thought that he had discovered that law; he called it the "law of the three stages."

In the first, or *theological stage*, according to this law, man invents gods in order to explain the world to himself, and in so doing he creates the conditions which make possible the specifically human kind of society; for belief in gods gives him some purpose in living beyond the satisfaction of mere bodily wants. At first, the gods are merely tribal fetishes, which do not demand much by way of social organization. But as these are exchanged for astral deities, and eventually for a single god, discipline and order are imposed upon the whole community. Authority characteristically comes to be vested in a priesthood. But a military caste arises, with responsibility for defense, and agricultural labor becomes the foundation of the economy. From the sociological point of view, it is a happy, prosperous condition. A common faith and goal give coherence and strength to the community.

But there is a serpent in the garden. The intellectual turn of mind which made man invent the gods is never content with its creation. Turning critical, it denatures divinity into a set of first principles and eternal essences. Comte called this the *metaphysical stage*. Intellect practically deifies itself, owning allegiance only to truths of reason. Not only theological beliefs, but theological institutions come under criticism. The principle of authority is challenged, and notions of equality and popular sovereignty are offered in its place. As the new attitude permeates the masses, individuals abandon their social responsibilities, and compete with one another to improve their private conditions. Religion becomes sectarian; peasants drift to the cities; military might declines. Sociologically, it is a negative moment, a time of dissolution and decay.

According to Comte, these two stages have appeared again and again in the history of the world, and hitherto there has been no way of saving a society which has passed into the metaphysical stage. But modern Western civilization has the means of breaking out of the old cycle. The negative moment, represented in European history by the Reformation, the Renaissance, and the Enlightenment, has marked the end of a Catholic-dominated culture, and of itself promises nothing but moral and political chaos. Coincident with the rise of libertarian thinking and laissez-faire economics and politics, however, the positive sciences have also made great gains. It is the assured results of these latter which, according to Comte, provide a remedy for metaphysics and make it possible for the mind of man to move forward into a new *positive stage*. Like the theological stage, it will be a time when men will know what to believe; only, this time, there will be no illusion about it—and no chance that the certainties will be overthrown. The new certainties will make possible a reorganization of society, provide a rational system of command, and inspire complete devotion in the hearts of the people. A moral regeneration will make coercive government almost a superfluity. Such regulation of life as the new society requires will rest with a managerial class arising out of industry, while ultimate authority will reside in a new spiritual class, the positive philosophers. Meanwhile, men will have cast away private ambition and personal rivalry, and will have learned to consider all functions as social. They will see the "public utility in the humblest office of cooperation, no less truly than in the loftiest function of government," and will feel "as the soldier feels in the discharge of his humblest duty, the dignity of public service, and the honor of a share in the action of the general economy."

Comte devoted hundreds of pages to the analysis of Western history along the lines indicated. His work is, from one point of view, a speculative undertaking. He considered that he had put history on an indisputably scientific foundation. He wrote: "It certainly appears to me that the whole course of human history affords so decisive a verification of my theory of evolution that no essential law of natural philosophy is more fully demonstrated. From the earliest beginnings of civilization to the present state of the most advanced nations, this theory has explained, consistently and dispassionately, the character of all the great phases of humanity; the participation of each in the perdurable common development, and their precise filiation; so as to introduce perfect unity and rigorous continuity into this vast spectacle which otherwise appears desultory and confused. A law which fulfils such conditions must be regarded as no philosophical pastime, but as the abstract expression of the general reality."

But from another point of view, this Herculean labor was a blueprint for a Brave New World. A youthful disciple of the utopian socialist, Claude Saint-Simon (1760-1825), Comte had as his ultimate purpose in developing the positive philosophy the moral and spiritual regeneration of the West. He believed that by providing an infallible system of truth he was doing the one thing which could bring this regeneration to pass.

With this view of the new science of social dynamics before us, we turn to consider the second aspect of Comte's philosophy, namely, his review of the natural sciences. All the sciences, with the exception of sociology, had already achieved the status of positive knowledge in Comte's time, but their true significance could not be discerned without sociology because, according to Comte, it was a function of the positivist philosopher (himself a sociologist) to trace out the unities and analogies of the sciences. Thus, sociology completes the body of philosophy, not merely as being the last of the sciences, but as "showing that the various sciences are branches from a single trunk; and thereby giving a character of unity to the variety of special studies that are now scattered abroad in a fatal dispersion." Had man been endowed with an angelic intelligence, all the sciences would have sprung into being at the same time, and their hierarchical relation would be evident in an *a priori* fashion. But because man has slowly and painfully arrived at the truth, the only intelligible account of the relationship between the sciences is the empirical one which traces their development. Thus, "all scientific speculations whatever, in as far as they are human labors, must necessarily be subordinated to the true general theory of human evolution," which, being the proper study of sociology, is the warrant for "the legitimate general intervention of true social science in all possible classes of human speculation."

As we have seen, Comte's science of history declared that the social evolution of man is a function of his intellectual evolution and that, broadly speaking, the knowledge of man has passed through three states—theological, metaphysical, and positive. It is not surprising, therefore, that the same cycle governs the development of particular sciences as governs the evolution of knowledge as a whole.

According to Comte, this development is clear on empirical grounds. Every science which has reached the positive state bears the marks of having passed through the others. Astronomy, for example, became truly scientific in Hellenistic times, when observations of the heavens were first coordinated by means of geometrical principles. But myth and astrology are reminders of times when celestial phenomena were explained in terms, first of divine will, and afterwards of impersonal fate. In fact, the more primitive beliefs linger on among less progressive parts of the population; and, according to Comte, they are recapitulated in the development of the mind of each civilized man, who in childhood is a theologian, in youth a metaphysician, and in manhood a natural philosopher.

But Comte held that the empirical account could be supported by reflection, and that it is *a priori* evident (*post factum*) that knowledge must pass through three stages. With Francis Bacon, he held it as a fundamental principle that mere facts are not sufficient to arrive at truth—the mind must form theories; but because intelligent theories cannot be formed without facts, one seems to be confronted with a vicious circle. At least, according to Comte, here is the reason why primitive man did not arrive at scientific truth. Caught, as it were, "between the necessity of observing facts in order to form a theory, and having a theory in order to observe facts, the human mind would have been entangled in a vicious circle but for the natural opening afforded by theological conceptions." Granted that primitive man's speculations owed more to imagination than to experience and reason—what matters is that, by hypothesizing about the gods, he was launched on the intellectual enterprise which could not have been started in any other way. Similarly, according to Comte, the metaphysical stage is necessary before the positive stage can be reached: its abstract and impersonal conceptions prepare the mind for positive knowledge, which is too radically different from theological beliefs for man to accept it immediately.

Comte maintained that different kinds of knowledge have passed through the three stages at different paces. Astronomy became a science before terrestrial physics, physics before chemistry, chemistry before biology, and biology before sociology. According to Comte, it had to be this way. Not only is physics simpler than sociology—it is more general, and hence more fundamental. Here we are introduced to Comte's celebrated hierarchy of the sciences and to the principle upon which it was based. The principle is essentially that of nominalistic logic, according to which the extension of a term is inversely proportional to its intension. Physics has greater extension than biology; that is, more objects of different kinds come under its laws, including both living and nonliving bodies. In Comte's language, physics is more general than biology. Conversely, biology has greater intension than physics; that is, although its laws apply to objects of only one kind, they comprehend more of their aspects. In Comte's language, biology is more complex than physics.

On this principle, Comte arranged the sciences in hierarchical order. Mathematics he placed first, because it is the most general, simple, and independent of all, and serves as the basis of all others. But because of its abstract character, Comte did not regard mathematics as a "natural science." Natural sciences he divided into inorganic and organic. That the latter are more complex than the former is self-evident, inasmuch as organization is a complexity. So, within the two divisions, on the inorganic level, astronomy is less complex than physics, and physics than chemistry; likewise, on the organic level, physiology, which relates to individuals, is less complex than sociology, which relates to aggregates. It may be observed that Comte did not leave a place for psychology in the hierarchy, a notable omission in view of the fact that J. S. Mill, in his *System of Logic* (1843), was to maintain that associationist psychology is as fundamental to all the human sciences as mechanics is to all the physical sciences. Comte argued, however, that because psychology proceeds by the method of introspection and assumes the actuality of the self, mental states, ideas, and the like, it is a relic of the metaphysical stage. Its counterpart in the positive system is cerebral physiology, which had newly come to the fore. In fact, Comte held that it was the discovery of the physiology of the brain which brought biology to perfection and made possible for the first time the new science of sociology.

Comte said of his classification of the sciences that, although it is artificial, it is not arbitrary. It is artificial because it marks out boundaries where none exist in the actual sciences. One of Comte's deepest concerns was to preserve the unity and integrity of man's intellectual pursuit, which he considered threatened to the point of sterility by increasing specialization in his day. He favored the development of a new kind of scientific worker whose task it would be to formulate the general principles of the respective sciences and to connect new discoveries with known truth. By making it possible to keep the whole structure of knowledge in view, these scientific workers would lay a new foundation for education. At the same time they would further research by serving as consultants; for, according to Comte, investigators are often handicapped by their ignorance of what is well known by specialists in other fields.

But while Comte was eager to preserve the unity of knowledge, he maintained that the special sciences are essentially autonomous. Therefore, he insisted that the classification was not arbitrary, and he opposed the view that the sciences can eventually be reduced to one master science and all phenomena explained by a unitary law. "Our intellectual resources," he said, "are too narrow, and the universe too complex, to leave any hope that it will ever be in our power to carry scientific perfection to its last degree of simplicity." The only real unity to science, he said, is that of the positive method, which spurns the idea of asking questions about origins and ends (theological questions) or about essences and causes (metaphysical questions), and settles down to the business of analyzing the circumstances of phenomena and connecting them by the relations of succession and resemblance. It is this method which has led to the division of knowledge into several specialties, so that, in delineating the divisions, positive philosophy was following the requirements of the method itself.

Comte's book derives much of its bulk from the detailed account he gives of all the natural sciences at that time. But he said that it was not his aim to teach the sciences as such: to do so would be endless and would demand more knowledge than one person could hope to muster. In any case, it would miss the point, which was "only to consider each fundamental science in its relation to the whole positive system, and the spirit which characterizes it." He said that his book was a course, not in positive science, but in positive philosophy. In his view, however, positive philosophy was "a whole, solid and entire." From the time of Francis Bacon it had been slowly forming until, in the nineteenth century, only one major gap remained—social physics—which was about to be filled.—*J.F.*

PERTINENT LITERATURE
Spencer, Herbert. "Reasons for Dissenting from the Philosophy of M. Comte," in *Essays, Scientific, Political and Speculative.* Vol. II. New York: D. Appleton and Company, 1891, pp. 118-144.

Auguste Comte's philosophy was made available to the English public in the 1850's by means of Harriet Martineau's abridged translation of the *Cours de philosophie positive* and of George H. Lewes' outline entitled *Comte's Philosophy of the Sciences.* Lewes had said that, although thousands had cultivated the sciences, no one until Comte had conceived the philosophy to which the sciences would give rise, and that on this account Comte deserved the distinction of being the father of positive philosophy. In this connection, Lewes had said that the novelty of Comte's philosophy did not consist in new truths but in the law of the three stages and in the consequent system of classification into which the sciences were placed.

Herbert Spencer's "Reasons for Dissenting from the Philosophy of M. Comte" was an essay in fence-building. In an earlier essay, "The Genesis of Science" (1854), he had found fault with Comte's law of progression; and in a brochure, "The Classification of the Sciences" (1864), he had gone on to develop his own classification. Originally published as an appendix to the latter, "Reasons for Dissenting" (1864) was prompted by an article in a leading French journal in which Spencer had been referred to as one of Comte's followers. Reminding his readers of the continuous line of English scientists and philosophers who, from the time of Francis Bacon and Thomas Hobbes, had dedicated their lives to building up a body of positive truth, Spencer suggested that there was no reason to presume that an English positivist was a disciple of Comte, and that if it was true that Comte's main achievement was the reorganization of knowledge, those who explicitly rejected this organization ought not to be called his followers.

Comte and Spencer were in fact engaged in similar undertakings. Both men maintained that knowledge is limited to appearances and that truth consists in laws describing the uniformities of relation among phenomena. Both assigned to philsophy the task of formulating laws common to all branches of science and of exhibiting the relation of the sciences to one another. Still it is clear that, from the first, Spencer thought along different lines from Comte. Spencer gained a cursory knowledge of Comte's writings when the English translation appeared, but was merely stimulated to work out his own theory of the genesis and classification of the sciences.

In "The Genesis of Science," Spencer raised the fundamental question of how scientific knowledge differs from ordinary knowledge, and he answered that the difference was a matter of degree. All knowledge depends on man's ability to recognize sameness and difference; but whereas ordinary knowledge judges mainly by qualities, scientific knowledge uses measurement. Viewed in this way, the history of science is part of the total fabric of intellectual history; the special sciences progress together, advance in one making possible advance in others. Spencer objected especially to Comte's claim that the simpler sciences must reach a high degree of perfection before more complex sciences can advance. For example, astronomy was said by Comte to be simpler than physics, but historically Sir Isaac Newton's theory of the heavens was dependent on Galileo's experiments with terrestrial bodies. In "The Classification of the Sciences," Spencer grouped the sciences according to subject matter without any pretense to their filiation. Logic and mathematics were called abstract; zoology, psychology, and sociology were called concrete; physics and chemistry, in which natural bodies are treated analytically, were called abstract-concrete.

"Reasons for Dissenting" deals briefly with the matters treated of in the two earlier essays. Against the law of three stages he asserts, "The progress of our conceptions, of each branch of knowledge, is from beginning to end intrinsically alike." The gods of theology and the entities of metaphysics "coalesce in the mind as fast as groups of phenomena are assimilated, or seen to be similarly caused." Historical development within the sciences "*has not* taken place in this . . . or any other serial order. There is no 'true *filiation* of the sciences'. . . . All along there has been a continuous action and reaction between the three great classes—an advance from concrete facts to abstract facts, and then an application of such abstract facts to the analysis of new orders of concrete facts."

Spencer listed other doctrines which, from the English point of view, must seem retrogressive: Comte's rejection of psychology as a science separate from physiology; his refusal to make a place for the theory of organic evolution within biology; and his social and political ideal according to which the functions of government were to be extended, social classes regulated, a hierarchical organization given absolute authority, and individual life subordinated at every turn to the life of society.

While agreeing with Comte's contention that the education of the individual ought to recapitulate the history of the education of mankind, and concurring in his opinion that there should be, besides scientific specialists, a class of generalists whose function would be to coordinate new findings, he could not assent to Comte's claim that the social anarchy and political revolution which characterized the times were the result of intellectual confusion. "Ideas do not govern and overthrow the world," said Spencer; "the world is governed and overthrown by feelings, to which ideas serve only as guides. The social mechanism does not rest finally on opinions; but almost wholly on character."

Mill, John Stuart. *Auguste Comte and Positivism.* London: N. Trübner, 1865.

John Stuart Mill mentions in his *Autobiography* (1863) that he read Auguste Comte's *Cours de philosophie positive* while he was working on his own *System of Logic* (1843), and that thereafter he and Comte corresponded until the latter's social ideas became obsessive. *Auguste Comte and Positivism* was written after Comte's death when, as Mill explains, it had become possible to call attention to Comte's faults without detracting unduly from his merits. The book comprises two articles, reprinted in 1865, from the *Westminster Review.* Part I, "The Cours de philosophie positive," is in the main commendatory. Part II, "Later Speculations of M. Comte," is censorious, containing such expressions as "melancholy decadence" and "intellectual degeneracy." Mill was "appalled at the picture of entire subjugation and slavery, which is recommended to us as the last and highest result of the evolution of humanity."

Mill persuaded himself that Comte's law of the three stages correctly described the evolution of human thought. His chief criticism was that Comte gave too much importance to the metaphysical stage, and that he sometimes used the term "metaphysics" incorrectly to stand for philosophical analysis instead of limiting it to belief in entities that transcend man's experience. As a disciple of Jeremy Bentham, Mill already believed that mankind was entering an era in which all branches of knowledge would soon achieve scientific stature, but he saw it as Comte's achievement to have exhibited the inevitable course by which mankind had come to this stage. "Whoever disbelieves that the philosophy of history can be made of science," he says, "should suspend his judgment until he has read these volumes of M. Comte."

No less gratifying to Mill was Comte's classification of the sciences. That the different branches of knowledge should enter the positive phase in the order of their increasing complexity was inevitable, he said, if only for the reason that the more complex sciences must be able to use laws discovered by the simpler sciences in order to establish their own truths. Mill found this insight helpful when he came to treat of the logic of the moral sciences in his *System of Logic*, where he argues that, just as meteorology and oceanography depend on the physical laws governing mass, heat, fluid, and electricity, so the social sciences, including politics, depend on the psychological laws ("the laws of association") according to which feelings generate one another. In Mill's opinion, Herbert Spencer had misunderstood the purpose of Comte's classification and in his criticisms had failed to observe the distinction between the early empirical and the later scientific stages in the development of a particular science.

Because of his interest in logic, Mill made special note of what Comte had to say about the method proper to the study of society. Observing that human agents, on which history depends, are themselves dependent on history, Comte concluded that one cannot deduce social laws from man's natural constitution but must reach them by generalizing from the phenomena of history, testing these generalizations afterwards against the laws of man's biological (Mill adds, "psychological") nature. This, says Mill, is the reverse of the usual scientific method, for here, instead of turning to experience to verify laws arrived at by deduction, one uses deduction to verify laws arrived at by experience.

Comte was at fault in Mill's eyes for not recognizing the importance of logic. Although he maintained that no hypothesis is legitimate unless factually verifiable, he did not see the need for any canons of proof. Mill attributes this blindness partly to Comte's rejection of the notion of causality, for, says Mill, it is only by postulating universal causation that the canon of induction can be established. But Mill also suspects that Comte did not attach sufficient weight to objective truth as opposed to subjective inclinations, such as the desire for simplicity. He cites as an example Comte's suggestion that chemists treat every unknown as if it were a pair of substances and, when necessary, as a pair of pairs, on the grounds that from "the most philosophical point of view" our picture of the world should satisfy our aesthetic as well as our practical wants.

Comte's refusal to recognize psychology as an independent science Mill could explain only by assuming that Comte had never read English writers in that field. Comte's argument—that intelligence can observe all other things but not itself—Mill regarded as obviously fallacious, refuted even by the distinction that Comte allowed between volitions, feelings, and intelligence. "What we are directly aware of," says Mill, "we can directly observe."

Political differences appear even in Mill's first essay. Comte, reacting against the French Revolution, rejected everything that savored of democracy and liberality as belonging to the metaphysical stage of politics and as having no positive validity as social truth. Mill, following Jeremy Bentham, agreed that the appeal to "natural rights" is metaphysical. Still, he insisted that it was possible to make a case, say, for limited government, on the basis of laws of human nature and our knowledge of history; that is, on positive grounds.

Mill believed, of course, in the natural progress of society; moreover, as opposed to Spencer, he held with Comte that social progress depends on intellectual progress. His criticism of Comte was that, when it came to practical politics, Comte seemed to forget the lessons of history and to deliver himself over to pure fantasy. Alexis de Tocqueville and others had seen in history a steady progress toward democracy and had made this the basis of their political forecasts, but Mill found no such connection in Comte. Hence he raised a doubt as to whether Comte was truly the founder of sociology.—*J.F.*

ADDITIONAL RECOMMENDED READING

Aron, Raymond. "August Comte," in *Main Currents in Sociological Thought*. Vol. I. New York: Basic Books, 1965. The English translation of Aron's Sorbonne lectures. The progress of the human mind seen as holding promise of the unity of mankind.

Comte, August. *August Comte: The Founder of Sociology*. Edited by Kenneth Thompson. John Wiley and Sons, 1975. A book of readings from Comte arranged topically. Chapter One includes selections of philosophical interest.

Hayek, Frederich A. von *The Counter-revolution of Science: Studies on the Abuse of Reason*. Glencoe, Illinois: Free Press, 1952. Chapter Six of Part II summarizes Comte's philosophy and indicates his immediate influence, particularly in England.

Lewes, George H. *Comte's Philosophy of the Sciences: Being an Exposition of the Principles of the* Cours de philosophie positive *of Auguste Comte*.

London: Bell, 1883. A readable and sympathetic introduction to Comte's early thought.

Manuel, Frank. *The Prophets of Paris*. Cambridge, Massachusetts: Harvard University Press, 1962. Five leading thinkers from 1789 to 1848. An objective treatment of the relations between Saint-Simon and Comte.

THE PHILOSOPHY OF HISTORY

Author: Georg Wilhelm Friedrich Hegel (1770-1831)
Type of work: Philosophy of history, metaphysics
First published: 1832

Principal Ideas Advanced
Spirit is freedom and self-consciousness acting to realize its own potentiality.

The real is the rational, and the rational is the real; Idea or Reason is the formative principle of all reality.

The goal of history is the liberation of Spirit from its confinement in Nature in order that Spirit might be reunited with its essence as Idea.

The Spirit could not realize its reunion with Idea were it not for the force of Will, as derived from human passions.

The individual as individual is unimportant; only the historically decisive actor, the hero, makes a significant difference in history; but whether a man be a conventional citizen, a courageous person, a hero, or a victim, he is nothing but the Spirit's instrument.

The embodiment of the Spirit's freedom is the State; the State is the concrete unity of freedom and passion.

History is understood by Hegel as the movement of Spirit toward the attainment of self-consciousness. To comprehend world history as the progress of the consciousness of Spirit it is necessary to arrive at a conceptual grasp of the three constitutive elements which structure historical movement: (1) The Idea of Spirit, (2) the means of actualization, and (3) the State as the final and perfect embodiment of Spirit.

Hegel begins his discussion with a formulation of the abstract characteristics of the Idea of Spirit. The peculiar quality of Spirit is grasped when it is seen in contrast with its opposite—matter. The essence of matter is gravity, which means that it has its center outside itself and thus is dependent upon a central point toward which it tends. The essence of Spirit is freedom, which designates a self-contained existence.

Another characteristic of Spirit is self-consciousness. It is of the essence of Spirit to know itself or be conscious of itself. The self-contained existence of Spirit as freedom is thus self-consciousness. Now in the phenomenon of self-consciousness two modes must be distinguished—the fact *that I know* and *what I know*. There is the self which is conscious, and there is also the self of which the self is conscious. Insofar as in self-consciousness the self is conscious of itself, these two modes are merged into a unity. The self has itself within itself. Self-consciousness is a unity, but it is a unity which expresses a reduplication. I can know myself, I can love myself, and I can hate myself. Spirit as freedom is self-reflexive or self-reduplicative. As it is the nature of

Spirit to know itself, so also it is the nature of Spirit to actualize itself. Spirit forever drives beyond that which it is *potentially* to make itself what it can become *actually*. Spirit yearns for actualization. "The very essence of Spirit is activity; it realizes its potentiality—makes itself its own deed, its own work—and thus it becomes an object to itself; contemplates itself as an objective existence."

Hegel's definition of Spirit must be understood in its context of a rational philosophy which proclaims an identification of reason and reality. In the Hegelian system the laws of logic are at the same time the laws of being. This undergirding principle of Hegel's philosophy was first formulated in his *Phenomenology of Spirit* (1807), and he expressed it thus: the real is the rational and the rational is the real. This principle also governs his interpretation of history. In *The Philosophy of History* he writes: "The only Thought which Philosophy brings with it to the contemplation of History, is the simple conception of *Reason*; that Reason is the Sovereign of the World; that the history of the world, therefore, presents us with a rational process. . . . That this 'Idea' or 'Reason' is the *True*, the *Eternal*, the absolutely *powerful* essence; that it reveals itself in the World, and that in that World nothing else is revealed but this and its honor and glory—is the thesis which, as we have said, has been proved in Philosophy, and is here regarded as demonstrated." Idea or Reason thus constitutes the primary formative principle in Hegel's philosophical system. This Idea expresses itself first in Nature but also in Spirit. The triadic unity of Idea, Nature, and Spirit thus defines the whole of Hegel's system. Expressed in terms of his dialectical logic, Idea is the thesis, Nature the antithesis, and Spirit the synthesis. Nature exhibits the emergence of the Idea in space; Spirit exhibits the actualization of the Idea in time and history. The primary category for Nature is space. The primary category for Spirit is time. Through the workings of Spirit the Idea is wrested from its localization in space and becomes temporized and historicized. Both Nature and Spirit are subject to a development under the impetus of the Idea; but the development in Nature is that of a quiet and subdued unfolding, whereas Spirit expresses a dynamic self-realization in which conflict and alienation are integral movements. "Thus Spirit is at war with itself; it has to overcome itself as its most formidable obstacle. That development which in the sphere of Nature is a peaceful growth, is in that of Spirit, a severe, a mighty conflict with itself. What Spirit really strives for is the realization of its Ideal being; but in doing so, it hides that goal from its own vision, and is proud and well satisfied in this alienation from it." Spirit is alienated from the Idea in its subjugation or bondage to Nature, but in the process of self-realization through which it attains self-consciousness Spirit becomes sovereign over Nature, subordinates Nature to its purposes, and thus drives to a reconciliation of itself with the Idea. It is in the historical consciousness of the Hebrew people, as we shall see later, that Hegel finds the first liberation of Spirit from

Nature. In the Hebrew doctrine of creation Nature is understood as a creature and a servant, and Spirit appears as the creator and the master.

The aim or goal of history is the actualization of Spirit as freedom, wresting itself from its confinement in Nature, and seeking reunion with itself as Idea. This aim or goal defines at the same time God's purpose for the world. Hegel's philosophy of history thus takes on the function of a theodicy—a justification of the ways of God. God's providential activity in the world is the self-realization of Spirit. Hegel converts the truths of philosophical categories and seeks to establish a conceptual justification for the suffering and sacrifices which occur in the course of world history. "Itself is its own object of attainment, and the sole aim of Spirit. This result it is, at which the process of the World's History has been continually aiming; and to which the sacrifices that have ever and anon been laid on the vast altar of the earth, throughout the long lapse of ages, have been offered. This is the only aim that sees itself realized and fulfilled; the only pole of repose amid the ceaseless change of events and conditions, and the sole efficient principle that pervades them. This final aim is God's purpose with the world; but God is the absolutely perfect Being, and can, therefore, will nothing other than himself—his own Will. The Nature of His Will—that is, His Nature itself—is what we here call the Idea of Freedom; translating the language of Religion into that of Thought."

The second constitutive element of the world-historical process is that of the means of actualization. The Idea of Spirit, as the aim or goal of history as such, is merely general and abstract. It resides in thought as a potentiality which has not yet passed over into existence. We must thus introduce a second element—actualization. The source of power which drives Spirit from its potential being into actuality is Will. The author defines Will as "the activity of man in the widest sense." In this definition he seeks to keep the ranges of meaning sufficiently broad so as to include the needs, instincts, inclinations, and passions of men. "We may affirm absolutely," asserts the author, "that *nothing great in the World* has been accomplished without *passion*." Two elements are thus disclosed as essential for an understanding of history. The one is the Idea of Spirit; the other is the complex of human passions. Hegel speaks of the former as the warp and of the latter as the woof of the cloth of universal history. The concrete union of these two provides the third and final element of world history—freedom embodied in the State. The means or material of history is thus the passions and interests of men, used by Spirit for the attainment of its end. Individual men, activated by their inclinations and passions, constitute the power plant for the world-historical process. But these individuals are, in the final analysis, sacrificed for the end or goal of history. History is the slaughter bench at which the happiness and welfare of each individual is sacrificed. The individual constitutes but a moment in the vast general sweep of world history. He remains historically unimportant.

"The particular is for the most part of too trifling value as compared with the general: individuals are sacrificed and abandoned. The Idea pays the penalty of determinate existence and of corruptibility, not from itself, but from the passions of individuals." Spirit uses the passions of men to attain its final self-consciousness. It sets the passions to work for itself. This integration of human passions with the aim of Spirit is accomplished through the "cunning of Reason." The cunning of Reason weaves together all the expressions of passion and makes them contributory to the final goal.

The passions which are put to work by the cunning of Reason arise from the wills of particular individuals, as they play their diversified roles and carry out their variegated functions. These particular individuals are classified by Hegel into four distinct, yet interrelated, historical categories: the citizen, the person, the hero, and the victim.

The *citizen* is subject to what the author calls customary morality. The determinant of action for the citizen is the will of society, the will of a nation-state, or the will of a religious institution. The citizen has not yet apprehended his subjective existence, and consequently has no consciousness of freedom—neither personal nor universal.

The *person* is the individual who can transcend the morality of his particular society and act on the basis of a morality grounded in subjectivity. It is in the person that subjective freedom makes its appearance. The morality of the person is not subordinate. It is determined by a personal consciousness of freedom. The person exhibits an implicit awareness of the Idea as Spirit, and thus drives beyond the static customary morality of the citizen. Hegel finds in Socrates the example *par excellence* of the person who has been liberated from the confining morality of the citizen. "Though Socrates himself continued to perform his duties as a citizen, it was not the actual State and its religion, but the world of Thought that was his true home."

But it is only when we come to the *hero* that we find the "world-historical individual." The hero is the historically decisive actor. Like all other men, he is motivated by private gain and interest, but his actions express at the same time an attunement with the will of the World-Spirit. His own particular will involves at the same time the larger issues of world history. The heroes of history are practical and political men. They are neither philosophers nor artists. They have no theoretical understanding of the Idea which they are unfolding. But they have insight into what is timely and needed, as well as courage to act decisively on the basis of their convictions. They know what their age demands, and they commit themselves to its challenge. Caesar, Alexander the Great, and Napoleon were such men. They responded to the requirements of their times and shaped the history of the world through their decisive actions. After seeing Napoleon ride through the streets of Jena, Hegel retired to his study and wrote: "Today I saw the World-Spirit riding on horseback." Napoleon was an instrument, used by the cunning of Reason, in the actualization of the self-consciousness of freedom. To become heroes or world-historical individuals these men had to sacrifice personal happiness. "If we go on to cast a look at the fate of these World-Historical persons, whose vocation it was to be agents of the World-Spirit—we shall find it to have been no happy one. They attained no calm enjoyment; their whole life was labor and trouble; their whole nature was nought else but their master-passion. When their object is attained they fall off like empty hulls from the kernel. They die early, like Alexander; they are murdered, like Caesar; transported to St. Helena, like Napoleon."

The *victim*, who comprises the fourth category, moves solely in the realm of private desires and inclinations. He has no interest in and offers no contribution to the customary morality of the citizen, nor to the subjective morality of the person, nor to the march of universal freedom exhibited by the hero. He is abandoned to his private situation. His goal is private success and happiness. Hegel has few good words for this type of individual. Obviously, he cannot become historically decisive. In a sense history moves on without him, but in another sense he remains part of the historical pattern insofar as the cunning of Reason must use all the material which passion provides. In the final analysis Spirit makes use of the hero and victim alike. There is a real sense in which both the hero and victim are "victims." The victim is a "victim" of the hero and the age; the hero in turn is a "victim" of the World-Spirit. In all this we see the emergence of the implicatory principle of Hegel's philosophy of history that the individual *as* individual is unimportant.

As Kierkegaard, the chief of all critics of Hegel, has later demonstrated, the existential significance of the individual is sacrificed to the universal and the general. A frank admission of this disregard for individuality is expressed when Hegel writes: "The History of the World might, on principle, entirely ignore the circle within which morality and the so much talked of distinction between the moral and the politic lies—not only in abstaining from judgments, for the principles involved, and the necessary reference of the deeds in question to those principles, are a sufficient judgment of them—but in leaving Individuals quite out of view and unmentioned."

The third constitutive element of world history is the State. The aim or goal of history is Spirit as freedom; the means of actualization are the passions of mankind; the embodiment or fulfillment of this freedom is found in the State. The State, as understood by Hegel, is the concrete unity of universal, objective freedom and particular, subjective passion. Thus the State synthesizes at one and the same time freedom and passion, the universal and the particular, the objective and the subjective. In the State universal freedom becomes concretized and is given substance. The freedom of subjective passion is mere arbitrariness and caprice. The actualized freedom of universal history, on the other hand, is *organized* liberty, or freedom structured by a State.

In the final analysis, the entities which are under consideration in Hegel's philosophy of history are "peoples" or cultural totalities. The State rather than the individual embodies universal freedom. The State does not exist for its subjects—it exists for its own sake. It is its own end. The subjects of a State are means towards its end. It is important not to confuse Hegel's definition of the State with an individual bureaucratic political organization. Such a political organization—British Monarchism, French Constitutionalism, American Democracy—may express the will of a state, but the two are not identical. The State, for Hegel, designates a cultural complex which integrates the art, religion, politics, and technology of a people into a unified self-consciousness. The Third Reich of Hitler, for example, according to the Hegelian philosophy, must be understood as a ghastly distortion of the true meaning of a State. Nazism constituted a pseudostate—a State without cultural content. The State, for Hegel, becomes the foundation for any organization—political or otherwise. The State is responsible for all cultural activities. The implication of this is the subordination of personal morality, personal religion, and political self-determination to a corporate or group substance. This group substance or State, insofar as it provides the foundation for all of man's temporal activities, is understood as an expression of God's purpose for the world. The State is thus defined to be the divine Idea as it exists on earth. There is no room for personal religion and personal morality in Hegel's system. The individual as individual stands outside morality, and outside history itself. Only as a moment in the march of universal freedom, embodied in the State, does the individual become significant. The State or the culture, rather than the individual, is, for Hegel, the bearer of history.

In formulating his philosophy of history Hegel traces the development of the consciousness of freedom as it moves from Eastern to Western civilization. History travels from East to West. Oriental civilization is the childhood of history. Greek civilization marks the period of adolescence. In Roman civilization history develops to manhood. Germanic civilization appears as the fourth phase of world history—old age. The Orientals had acknowledged only *one* man as being free—the despot. And insofar as the freedom of the despot expressed itself in the recklessness of passion, it must be accounted as mere caprice; hence, in Oriental civilization we do not yet find freedom, properly understood. In Greece and Rome, the consciousness of freedom manifested itself in the acknowledgement that *some* men are free. Slavery, with its restriction of freedom, was an accepted institution in both Greece and Rome. It is not until we come to the Germanic nations that we find the acknowledgement that *all* men are free. Germanic civilization, under the influence of Christianity, attained the consciousness of universal freedom.

Among the peoples of China and India, who comprise Oriental civilization, we find only the first glimmerings of a historical consciousness; history as such does not begin until the rise of the Persians. In China and India, the Idea remains bound to Nature. The peculiar determinants of Spirit are lacking. In

China, morality is equated with legislative enactments, individuals are stripped of personality, and the will and the passions of the emperor constitute the highest authority. The emperor as the supreme head of political affairs is also at the same time the chief priest of religion. Religion is thus subordinated to the despotism of a particular bureaucratic organization. Such an organization, according to Hegel, is the very negation of a historical State as a cultural unit. The civilization of India exhibits a similar bondage to Nature. This is expressed particularly in the institution of the caste system. The individual does not choose his particular position for himself. He receives it from Nature. Nature is the governing power. Thus, in Oriental civilization the universal idea emerges in Nature, but it does not drive beyond itself to the self-consciousness of Spirit.

The Persians are the first historical peoples. This historical consciousness is expressed in their use of Light as a symbol for the Good (*Ormuzd*). Light provides the condition for the exercise of choice, and it is precisely choice, action, and deeds which constitute the stuff of history. Historical states are what their deeds are. The Persians understood history as a struggle between Good and Evil, in which the actors were confronted with the inescapability of choice. There is a deficiency, however, in the historical consciousness of the Persians. They failed to grasp the higher unity in which the antithesis of Good and Evil is synthesized. Judaism, which took its rise in the same geographical and cultural milieu, provides a further advance in the progressive development of the consciousness of freedom. In Judaism, Spirit is liberated from Nature and is purified. Both the individual man and Israel as a nation come to a consciousness of themselves as distinct from Nature. Jehovah, as the quintessence of Spirit, is understood as the Lord of Nature. Nature is subordinated to the role of creature. Spirit is acknowledged as the Creator. "The idea of Light has at this stage advanced to that of 'Jehovah'—the *purely One*. This forms the point of separation between the East and the West; Spirit descends into the depths of its own being, and recognizes the abstract fundamental principle as the Spiritual. Nature—which in the East is the primary and fundamental existence—is now depressed to the condition of a mere creature; and Spirit now occupies the first place. God is known as the creator of all men, as He is of all nature, and as absolute causality generally."

Judaism thus marks the transition from East to West. Spirit is acknowledged in its separation from Nature, but neither Spirit nor Nature are yet fully comprehended. In Greek civilization another advance becomes apparent. Greece, as the adolescent period of the historical process, introduces the principle of subjective freedom or individuality. This principle is expressed both in the personal or subjective morality of Socrates (as contrasted with the customary morality of society), and in the rise of Athenian Democracy. As despotism was the peculiar characteristic of the political life of the Orient, so democracy is the peculiar characteristic of the political life of Greece. Spirit becomes introspective and posits itself as particular existence, but it posits itself precisely as the ideal and thus suggests the possible triumph over particularity through a comprehension of universality itself. But the universals of Greek thought are fixed and static essences; hence they are still fettered by the limitations of Nature. They still remain dependent upon external conditions. Therefore, the new direction projected by the consciousness of the Greek Spirit still retains natural elements. A concrete expression of this principle is the continued practice of slavery, which grants freedom to some but not to all. In Rome, in which history attains its manhood, an advance is made from democracy to aristocracy. The institutions of the people are united in the person of the emperor. In the will of the emperor the principle of subjectivity, enunciated in Greek thought, gains unlimited realization. The will of the emperor becomes supreme. But insofar as subjectivity is universalized and objectivized at the expense of the claims of art, religion, and morality, the State which emerges in Roman civilization is still an inferior State, lacking in cultural content.

The State, understood as the concrete embodiment of subjective and objective freedom, comes to its full realization in the German Spirit. The German Spirit, like the Greek, apprehended the principle of subjectivity, but unlike the Greek it became the bearer of the Christian ideal and thus universalized the principle to mean that *all* men are free. The Greek and Roman Spirit still kept some men (the slaves) in chains. The individual interests and passions of men thus find their fulfillment only in the German Spirit. This fulfillment is the unification of the objective Idea of freedom, as the aim of history, with the particular and subjective passions of mankind, in the concrete embodiment of a cultural whole. Subjective freedom, without objective order, is mere caprice—expressed either in the will of a despot or emperor, or in the chaos of anarchy. Thus, subjective freedom cannot be realized until it finds its place within a structured whole—the State. "This is the point which consciousness has attained, and these are the principal phases of that form in which the principle of Freedom has realized itself;—for the History of the World is nothing but the development of the Idea of Freedom. But Objective Freedom—the laws of *real* Freedom—demand the subjugation of the mere contingent Will—for this is in its nature formal. If the Objective is in itself Rational, human insight and conviction must correspond with the Reason which it embodies, and then we have the other essential element—Subjective Freedom—also realized."—*C.O.S.*

PERTINENT LITERATURE

Marcuse, Herbert. *Reason and Revolution: Hegel and the Rise of Social Theory*. London: Oxford University Press, 1941.

No full-length study of Georg Wilhelm Friedrich Hegel's *The Philosophy of History* exists in English. This is due not merely to the fact that the book in question consists of a series of lectures Hegel delivered and, as such, were never authorized for publication by him. The deeper reason is that Hegel's *The Philosophy of History* can scarcely be understood apart from Hegel's system as a whole, and in particular apart from the teleology of his political theory.

Herbert Marcuse's book is a seminal work of political theory as well as a sympathetic treatment of the aims and motives of Hegel's philosophy of history and of the state. Marcuse writes from *within* the Helegian-Marxist tradition and from the perspective of a political philosopher rather than a metaphysician or an epistemologist.

Reason and Revolution was written because the rise of Fascism in Europe called for a reinterpretation of Hegel which would demonstrate that his basic concepts were hostile to Fascist theory and practice. Marcuse's book is in this respect a sort of informed refutation not only of attempts to picture Hegel as a protofascist ideologist but also of later equally misguided attempts to portray him as an enemy of the open society, as was done by Karl Popper, for example. Finally, the book was written not merely to revive an interest in Hegel—which it succeeded in doing—but in the hope of reviving what Marcuse called the power of negative thinking, the essence of the dialectic. In this view, thinking is essentially negation. Marcuse argues that Hegel's most abstract concepts are saturated with experience of a world in which the unreasonable becomes reasonable, in which unfreedom is the condition of freedom and war is the condition of peace. Philosophical-dialectical thinking begins with the refusal to accept this prescribed universe of discourse.

Reason and Revolution consists of two parts. Part I consists of eight chapters which are devoted entirely to Hegel, under the title "The Foundations of Hegel's Philosophy." The first introductory chapter covers the sociopolitical and philosophical setting in which Hegel lived and worked; Chapter II examines Hegel's early theological writings; Chapter III and Chapter IV examine the early attempts at a philosophy of mind, morality, and nature; Chapters V-VII then cover, in turn, Hegel's phenomenology of spirit, his logic, his political philosophy, and his philosophy of history. Part II then consists of two long chapters: "The Foundations of the Dialectical Theory of Society" and a concluding chapter called "The End of Hegelianism." The chapter on the dialectical theory of society covers the negation of philosophy, Søren Kierkegaard, Ludwig Feuerbach, and a brilliant discussion of Karl Marx. The concluding chapter discusses British neoidealism, the revision of the dialectic, and Fascist "Hegelianism," and concludes, appropriately enough, by contrasting National Socialism with Hegelianism.

Marcuse's discussion of Hegel's philosophy of history occupies the book's central chapter (VII) spatially. The emerging *Weltgeist* concretizes the interest of reason and freedom, it is argued, and national history must therefore be understood in terms of universal history. For while Hegel's logical writings had shown the identity of idea and being, the idea unfolds itself "in space" as nature and "in time" as mind. But to exist in time is to exist in the temporal process of history. History, thus, is an exposition of mind in time. The *Logic* demonstrates the structure of reason; *The Philosophy of History* expounds the historical content of reason.

Marcuse's reading of Hegel's philosophy of history as the story of liberty repays close study not only for the power of its exposition but also for its penetrating critical appreciation of Hegel.

Findlay, John N. *Hegel: A Re-examination.* New York: Macmillan Publishing Company, 1958.

John N. Findlay's twelve-chapter study of Georg Wilhelm Friedrich Hegel's philosophy is one of the two most important books on Hegel written in the English language in the past thirty years or so; and it almost certainly joins the ranks of earlier works on Hegel by John M. E. McTaggart, G. R. G. Mure, W. T. Stace, and Jean Hyppolite as classics in the study of Hegel.

The first, introductory chapter not only covers Hegel's life and writings but also attempts to liberate Hegel from the chief misconceptions which have come to dominate an understanding of his philosophy. The misconceptions include treating Hegel as a transcendent metaphysician, or as some sort of subjectivist who thought that our mind or God's made up the universe. Hegel is equally misunderstood if he is treated as a rationalist who deduces the structure and details of experience, or as a political reactionary whose system masks his reactionary intention. What Findlay proposes instead is to relate Hegel's ideas and language to our own time in order to show that he has as much to say to us as to previous generations.

Chapter II treats Hegel's notion of Spirit (*Geist*); Findlay discusses what Hegel says about it, what he means by it, and the historical circumstances which require the notion of Spirit; and, finally, he disposes of standard objections to Hegel's conception. Chapter III treats the dialectical method in detail; Chapters IV and V are devoted to penetrating expositions of Hegel's *Phenomenology of Spirit*; Chapters VI, VII, and VIII are expositions of Hegel's logical writings, *The Science of Logic* and the pertinent sections of the *Encyclopedia of the Philosophical Sciences in Outline*; Chapter IX adumbrates Hegel's philosophy of nature; Chapter X treats Hegel's psychology, under the title "The Philosophy of Subjective Spirit"; Chapter XI compresses Hegel's philosophy of law, state, and history, under the title "The Philosophy of Objective Spirit"; Chapter XII treats his aesthetics, philosophy of religion, and history of philosophy.

The Philosophy of History is discussed in the fifth section of Chapter XI. The point is insisted upon by Findlay that the philosophy of history is a part of the teleological movement of Hegel's system as a whole, of the particular teleology of his political theory. For Hegel here passes from the supreme self-objectification of Spirit—the developed State—to a study of the less developed States that lead up to it. Thus, the philosopher of history is a theodicist, for Hegel, in that he can fathom the deep-set drift which leads to more developed political arrangements and also believes he can articulate the new states of consciousness that events are producing. The philosopher of history follows the Cunning of Reason, in short, but does so with the full consciousness often denied those world-historical figures who labor in its service.

Findlay stresses in his discussion that there is but one single historical line of States, in Hegel's philosophy of history, which represents the unfolding of the State-Idea. Only a single State embodies the State-Idea for its time, the rest serving as satellites or as observers. While Findlay rightly observes that Hegel's philosophy of history is a philosophical reseeing of data, it is not an attempt to write a factual history. Nevertheless, it seems a pity, Findlay thinks, that Hegel was unable to recognize the temporal coexistence of independently significant historical cultures—the Incas and Mayas, for example, in relation to Western European culture. It is also regrettable that Hegel was unable to see that several ordering principles might account for historical data in alternative ways, and that he did not appreciate sufficiently the disruptive and dysteleological features of history.

Taylor, Charles. *Hegel*. Cambridge: Cambridge University Press, 1975.

Charles Taylor's *Hegel* is probably the most comprehensive and thorough study in English. It amounts to almost six hundred large printed pages which are divided into twenty chapters; these, in turn, are organized into six parts.

Part I—"The Claims of Speculative Reason"—consists of three chapters. Chapter I describes the aspirations of the young Romantics of the 1790's, from whom Georg Wilhelm Friedrich Hegel emerged and against whom he defined himself. Chapter II—"Hegel's Itinerary"—sketches Hegel's development; and Chapter III—"Self-positing Spirit"—attempts an outline of his main ideas. Here Hegel is related to earlier figures in the history of philosophy and to the intellectual issues of his time, which are characterized in terms of a pervasive tension between the ideals of individuality and national autonomy on the one hand, and a profoundly felt need to recover unity with nature and within society on the other hand. This pervasive tension between autonomy and unity is taken by Taylor as basic to understanding the Odyssey of self-positing Spirit. Moreover, this tension and longing are not only fundamental to understanding Hegel and his times, but also help to illuminate our own, it is argued.

Part II treats Hegel's *Phenomenology of Spirit* in six chapters; Part III examines his logical writings in five chapters; Part IV treats Hegel's philosophy of history and politics, and the insight he had into modern societies, in three chapters; the three chapters of Part V—"Absolute Spirit"—discusses Hegel's philosophies of art, religion, and the history of philosophy. Part VI, the book's conclusion—"Hegel Today"—argues that Hegel's philosophy is an essential part of the recapitulative conflict of interpretations through which we try to understand ourselves as a civilization.

Chapter XV, "Reason and History," contains a substantial discussion of *The Philosophy of History*. The drama of the sweep of history builds toward Hegel's philosophy of politics, in Taylor's view. The problem is how to reconcile the freedom of the individual who recognizes himself as rationality with a restored *Sittlichkeit*. (*Sittlichkeit*, ethics, is carefully defined by Taylor as the morality which holds all of us in virtue of our being members of a self-subsistent community, to which we owe allegiance as an embodiment of the universal.) History's main drama is then opened by the breakdown of Greek *Sittlichkeit*, the emergence of the individual with universal consciousness. This, in turn, develops in succeeding centuries in individuals and institutions which embody *Sittlichkeit*; and the two—the individual and the institutional—are eventually reconciled in the rational State.

On the wider scale, history can be seen as the succession of communities in which the earlier are imperfect expressions of what is embodied by later ones. Such communities are *Volksgeister*, the spirit of a people. Thus the Idea *qua* history is realized only through the dialectical unfolding of historical civilizations. Despite the looseness of fit between history and logic, Taylor argues that the dialectic of history is to be understood as reflecting the conceptually necessary stages in the self-unfolding of the Idea. And on the widest possible scale, that of the *Weltgeist*, the cunning of Reason is expressed by and expresses itself in the greatness of world-historical individuals, persons whose unconscious motivation—sometimes perceived through a glass darkly—articulates the next stage in the self-unfolding of the Idea.—*B.M.*

ADDITIONAL RECOMMENDED READING

Avineri, Shlomo. *Hegel's Theory of the Modern State*. Cambridge: Cambridge University Press, 1972. One of the most lucid expositions and appraisals of Hegel's theory of the State available in any language.

Bosanquet, Bernard. *The Philosophical Theory of the State*. New York: Macmillan Publishing Company, 1899. A reading of Hegel's philosophy of history by a British idealist which situates the philosophy of history within Hegel's philosophy of right (*Recht*).

Croce, Benedetto. *History as the Story of Liberty*. Translated by Sylvia Sprigge. London: George Allen & Unwin, 1941. An important work by Italy's leading Hegelian.

Kaufmann, Walter. *Hegel: Reinterpretation, Texts, and Commentary*. Garden City, New York: Doubleday, 1965. A general treatment which stresses the

Phenomenology of Spirit and pays less attention to Hegel's idealism or to the dialectic.

Lukács, Georg. *History and Class Consciousness.* Translated by Rodney Livingstone. Cambridge, Massachusetts: MIT Press, 1971. This classic of Marxist thought was repudiated by its author because it treats Marxism as an application of Hegel to history. This is the fountainhead of Western Marxist humanism, against the reigning Soviet orthodoxies.

Marx, Karl. *The German Ideology.* New York: International Publishers, 1933. A standard introduction to Marx's understanding of Hegel and the Hegelians.

MONADOLOGY

Author: Gottfried Wilhelm von Leibniz (1646-1716)
Type of work: Metaphysics
First published: 1840 (written in 1714)

PRINCIPAL IDEAS ADVANCED

Monads are the elements of all things; they are simple substances, created all at once out of nothing; they can neither be altered in quality nor changed internally by any other created thing.

No two monads are perfectly alike; for every individual monad there is some internal difference which accounts for its particular nature.

Perception and apperception are the two chief types of activities by which monads exhibit their natures.

Men are distinguished from the animals by their knowledge of necessary and eternal truths; man reasons according to the principles of contradiction and sufficient reason.

Only through God's mediation is interaction or knowledge of any sort possible; although the monads are isolated, they function and perceive according to God's preestablished harmony.

This is the best of all possible worlds, for God's goodness made him choose it from the infinite number of possible universes.

The *Monadology* is undoubtedly Leibniz's best-known work. Since it is a condensed statement of his main philosophical principles, written late in life, there is good reason for this popularity. On the other hand, its popularity is somewhat strange, since Liebniz himself gave no title to the manuscript and it was published neither by him nor during his lifetime. Written in French, it appeared first in a German translation in 1810. Not until 1840 did the original French version appear, and the title "La Monadologie," given to the work at that time, has remained. Although the *Theodicy* (1710) represents Leibniz's philosophical and theological interests more directly, and his *New Essays* (1765) undoubtedly provoked more immediate interest, the importance of the *Monadology* as a brief metaphysical sketch remains.

The *Monadology* has been called an "encyclopaedia of Leibniz's philosophy," and one of its drawbacks is that in a strict sense the reader needs to know Leibniz's other writings in order to understand its contents properly. Support can be found for considering the *Theodicy* to be a more central work from the fact that Leibniz himself added references in the margin of his manuscript (later named the *Monadology*) referring particularly to passages in the *Theodicy* where the views were more fully expressed. Yet the *Monadology* can be, and usually has been, read alone. As such, it stands in a tradition of brief yet comprehensive metaphysical expositions which have an influence out of all proportion to their length.

Particularly in view of the fact that Leibniz did not himself title the *Monadology*, the work could just as easily be called *On Substance* or *On the Modes of Being*. In subject matter the *Monadology* follows the great tradition of metaphysics in trying to define what the ultimate substance of the world is and in trying to arrange a hierarchy to account for all of the different modes of existence which are possible. The *Monadology* is divided into ninety brief paragraphs, each summarizing some fundamental point. The first paragraph opens with a description of a "Monad," thus introducing Leibniz's most famous doctrine and the single principle in terms of which his entire metaphysics is developed.

Like Spinoza, whom he knew and admired, Leibniz was impressed with mathematical rigor, and he reflects this love of simplicity and brevity in his philosophical writing. The *Monadology* is not an intricately structured work like Spinoza's *Ethics* (1677), but the same love of clarity and of a single first principle is clearly evident in both. Leibniz, who was equally famous as a mathematician, still enjoys the almost unique position of being read by mathematically and logically inclined philosophers as well as by speculative metaphysicians and theologians.

A monad, he tells us, is a simple (indivisible) substance which enters into compounds, and a compound is an aggregation of simple things. Monads are the elements of all things, the atoms of all nature; they are indestructible, since no such simple substance can be destroyed by natural means. Nor can they come into existence artificially within natural limits, since they could not, by their very nature, be formed from anything else. Spinoza's "substance" was so large that it became absolutely infinite and included both God and the world as ordinarily conceived. Leibniz's substances, on the other hand, are the smallest and simplest conceivable entities.

Creation and annihilation are the means of entrance and exit for monads, and here Leibniz's theological dimension is most evident. They are, Leibniz says, created "all at once," which is a condensed reference to the traditional doctrine of creation *ex nihilo*, just as "annihilation" has similarities to traditional eschatological views. Since monads are conceived as having such extra-mundane means of entrance and exit, it is not really surprising that Leibniz asserts that the monads cannot be altered in quality or changed internally by any other created thing. This has overtones of traditional doctrines of predestination, but Leibniz puts it in his dramatic and famous phrase that the monads "have no windows" through which anything could come in or go out. Each is a self-contained, self-developing entity. The means of their coordination will be explained later.

But if monads cannot be altered from without, they would all be identical and indistinguishable were it not for internal differences in quality. The monads derive the qualities they have from internal differences. This is another way of saying that Leibniz denies that there is any general or external principle of individuation. Leibniz then reverses the emphasis from trying to account for a principle of individuation and difference among monads to asserting, in a more radical note, that every monad is absolutely different from every other. No two are perfectly alike; in even the most similar some internal difference of intrinsic quality can be found.

Having covered the basic questions concerning monads as such in eight brief paragraphs, Leibniz then sets forth more general metaphysical principles, built upon the doctrine of the monads as the ultimate simple components of all things. Every created being (and the monad itself is a created thing) is subject to change. All natural changes of the monad come from an internal principle, and the pattern of change which a group of monads characteristically exhibits is its nature. The nature of a thing is its pattern of activity. Perception and apperception (or consciousness) are the two chief types of activity of a monad or of a group of monads, and all activity may be divided under these two headings. The activity which produces change from one perception to another is what Leibniz calls "appetition," and nothing but perceptions and their changes can be found in a simple substance like a monad.

Monads have a kind of self-sufficiency, an internalized and purposeful plan of activity, which is what makes them their own source of their internal activities. Since they have this self-directive action as well as perceptions and desires, they may be called souls, although this title is to be reserved only for those whose perception is distinct and is accompanied by memory.

One perception comes only from another perception, as a motion comes only from another motion. Thus every present state of a monad is a consequence of its preceding state. So understood, any present moment has within it much more of the future than either the past or the present. Leibniz's theory of monads, although in a sense deterministic, is a view which is directed primarily toward the future. Certainly all activity and perception have this orientation. However, men are unique and are to be distinguished from the animals, despite the basic similarity between our component parts and theirs. Such a distinction of man from animal must be based on a distinction of degree; men have knowledge of necessary and eternal truths, but animals do not.

Leibniz began in his theory of monads with a description of a common nature which all things share. Beginning with this separation of men from animals in virtue of man's knowledge of eternal truths, Leibniz concentrates primarily on man and God, and for this reason the common substance we all share receives less emphasis. For man's knowledge of necessary and eternal truths raises him to a knowledge of himself and of God. Reflective self-consciousness has been introduced. Men have a knowledge of necessary truths, and they may think about God's nature—all of which requires a unique type of reasoning.

Man's reasoning is founded on two great principles: the principle of contradiction, which separates the true from the false, and the principle of sufficient reason. The latter tells us that for every fact there is a reason sufficient to account for the fact regardless of whether the reason can be known. Truths in turn are to be divided into two kinds: those of reasoning and those of fact. Truths of reasoning are necessary, and their opposite is impossible; truths of fact are contingent, and their opposite is possible.

Leibniz then offers his arguments for God's existence. The sufficient or final reason for things must be outside the sequence or series of particular contingent things, however infinite the series may be. Thus the final reason for all things must be a necessary substance, and this substance we call God. There needs to be only one God, since this God is sufficient to account for the variety of particulars.

Such a God is absolutely perfect, since perfection as Leibniz defines it is nothing but the presence of positive reality, and God, as an unlimited sequence of possible beings, must contain as much reality as possible. To separate man from God, Leibniz asserts that created beings derive their perfections from God but their imperfections from themselves, since God is infinite but man must be limited. God's infinity seems to be the chief source of his perfection and is the quality which separates him most radically from man, since both are composed of basically similar monads.

Leibniz modifies Anselm's ontological argument for God's existence. Instead of using Anselm's phrase, "necessary existence," Leibniz writes, "He must necessarily exist, if He is possible." This changes Anselm's point and shifts the question of God's existence to one of demonstrating the possibility of a God. Nothing can interfere with the possibility of an infinite God's existence (this part of the reasoning is traditional), but the possibility of a God must first be established (this is new).

One of Leibniz's most famous, and disputed, doctrines is that of the creation of monads. He has asserted that none can be brought into being or destroyed by natural causes, but this leaves open the question of a divine origin. God, it turns out, is the only uncreated monad; all the rest are created or derivative. This process Leibniz calls "fulguration," and it seems to be not a single act but an activity of the Divinity continued from moment to moment. Since no further explanation of this important doctrine of the origin of monads is given, nor any further definition of the key term "fulguration" (except a reference to the *Theodicy*), this theory of Leibniz has been the source of much discussion.

Only through the mediation of God can one monad affect another; and one affects another only in the sense that, in predestinating things from the beginning, God may have considered one monad in determining the activity of another in relation to it. God is said to have a "will" which regulates things according to a principle of the best, but this does not allow him any alternatives in design. Here we discover Leibniz's most famous doctrine, that God has in fact created the best world which it was possible for him to devise.

God does have an infinite number of possible universes to choose from, it is true, but only one of them could become actual through his creative activity. Fitness, or degree of activity in perfection, determines him, so that in that sense his activity in creation is not really free. When all that must be considered and balanced is included, there are no alternatives to the world he did create. His goodness makes him choose it, and his power makes him produce it.

We are not at all cut off in this world. Each living thing is a perpetually living mirror of the universe. It sometimes seems as if we all live in many different worlds, but these are in truth nothing but aspects of a single universe, viewed from the special point of view of each monad. Being joined in this way, we are not really independent. Everybody feels the effect of all that takes place in the universe. Each created monad thus represents the whole universe within itself. All nature shares in this interconnectedness, down to matter itself. There is nothing fallow, nothing sterile, nothing dead in the universe, no chaos, no confusion save in appearance.

God alone is completely without body, although this means merely to be a monad of a special type. The births and deaths of natural bodies are not abrupt transitions (no transition for Leibniz is abrupt). Birth and death are gradual changes. Body and soul both follow their own laws (no soul is without body except God). The body and soul of any entity agree, despite their variant laws, through the "preestablished harmony" of all substances which God has arranged. This is a modern metaphysical version of the traditional theological doctrine of foreordination. Souls act according to the laws of final causes through appetitions, ends, and means. Bodies act according to the laws of efficient causes or motions. Through God's original design, the two realms are in harmony with each other.

Minds are able to enter into a kind of fellowship with God. The totality of all such spirits composes the City of God, and this is the moral world within the natural world. This moral world and natural world are, like body and soul, in perfect harmony. God as architect satisfies in all respects God as lawgiver. The world exceeds all the desires of the wisest men, and it is impossible to make it better than it is. On this high note of optimism, the *Monadology* ends.

One thing which should be noted is that the famous doctrine of the monads occupied only the first part of the unnamed treatise, and in the later sections the traditional theological problems are taken up with less and less mention made of the theory of the monads. The *Monadology* is not the tightly knit and interlocking statement of doctrine it is often thought to be. Within this brief treatise many important theories are merely mentioned; few are argued at all. More independence probably exists between the various theories here than is often recognized, and certainly other of Leibniz's writings need to be studied (primarily the *Theodicy*) before any appraisal at all can be made. What is to be found within the ninety brief paragraphs of the treatise is, without question, a reflection of Leibniz's attempt to meet and to deal with every major philosophical and theological problem.—*F.S.*

PERTINENT LITERATURE

Rescher, Nicholas. *Leibniz: An Introduction to His Philosophy.* Totowa, New Jersey: Rowman and Littlefield, 1979.

Nicholas Rescher's *Leibniz: An Introduction to His Philosophy* is a revision of a study on Gottfried Wilhelm von Leibniz published twelve years earlier. Like its predecessor it is bound to become a standard reference work on Leibniz and thus should not be overlooked by any serious student. In this work, as in the earlier one, Rescher attempts a reconstruction of Leibniz's philosophy. This task is justified on the grounds that Leibniz did not leave us a systematic work. Rather, Leibniz's "system"—if, indeed, he had a single system—is to be found partially in one work, partially in another. What summaries there are, such as *Monadology* (1716), are considerably telescoped, lacking the fuller exposition to be found in a systematic work.

After a brief exposition of the central place occupied in Leibniz's metaphysics by his concept of God, Rescher undertakes his reconstruction of Leibniz's thought. Following Bertrand Russell and Louis Couturat, Rescher takes the view that subject-predicate logic, now transformed into a *metaphysical* thesis, is basic to Leibniz's philosophy. That is, the proposition "A is B" is to be understood in terms of the monad referred to by the subject term, A, and the property, B, asserted by the proposition to belong to A. Put in its most simple form, Leibniz's view is that the proposition "A is B" is true or false depending on whether B is one of the properties to be found among those constituting A's complete individual notion. This is the sense in which Leibniz understood the subject-predicate logic to be a metaphysical thesis.

Rescher then shows how Leibniz constructed three principles on this basis. The first, the Principle of Sufficient Reason (Section 32 in the *Monadology*), holds that in a *true* proposition the predicate is indeed contained in the subject, a fact to be discovered upon analysis, by checking to see if the property named by the predicate is to be found in the complete individual notion of the monad named by the subject. Since monads contain an infinite number of properties for Leibniz, only an infinite analysis of propositions about monads will do. Of course, only God can perform the requisite analysis. The second is the Principle of Identity (what Leibniz in the *Monadology* calls the Principle of Contradiction, 31). This concept applies to cases of finite analysis and holds that every proposition shown to be true on finite analysis is necessarily true.

The third is the Principle of Perfection, which holds that every infinitely analytic true proposition is contingently true. When God is choosing to create a world, he considers all of its monads' complete individual notions via infinite analysis and chooses the world which is characterized by the simplest laws and the greatest variety of being. Rescher takes these twin criteria to complete Leibniz's understanding of the Principle of Perfection (58).

Derivative from these three principles is the principle that the world of monads must be in pre-established harmony (56-62). That is, each monad successively has perceptions of the other monads in its world and they likewise of it. Also, the perceptions of a monad are ordered to unity by appetition (15); none can exist apart from its monad (7). These perceptions, in turn, are the ground of phenomena which are or are not well-founded (*bene fundatum*) in them. Rescher examines the nature of the most important of these phenomena for Leibniz: space and time. Although Leibniz has little to say about space and time in the *Monadology*, Rescher's analysis is nevertheless useful inasmuch as it shows the differences between Leibniz's view and Sir Isaac Newton's, who believed space and time to be real, absolute qualities of things while Leibniz believed them to be concepts abstracted in the mind of the observer.

Rescher also examines Leibniz's views on human knowledge. Leibniz distinguished between truths of fact, which are about the actual work, and truths of reason, which are about all possible worlds and are thus general in character. Rescher also clarifies what might seem an obscure point in the *Monadology*—namely, the relationship between perception and apperception (74 and 30). Perceptions are "based on the mutual perception of all monads"— that is, their representations one of another. In this sense all monads have perceptions. Apperception is the perception by monads of their own basic perceptions. These "reflective acts" (30) distinguish humans as minded spirits from "lower" monads—that is, all other physical creatures and things (82). Reason operates at the level of apperception on the data of basic perceptions.

Rescher concludes with a consideration of Leibniz's metaphysics of God. He highlights Leibniz's crucial revision of the ontological argument and his consequent emphasis on the need for first establishing the possibility of God's existence (8 and 45). The problems posed about the compatability of God's foreknowledge and human freedom are analyzed. Rescher's analysis is helpful in that it delineates the manner in which Leibniz dealt with this problem. It is not the freedom of the individual in isolation that is at stake for Leibniz but that of individuals taken as constituting a world. God would be less than perfect if he chose less than the best possible world. Yet even such a world, Rescher shows, must contain some imperfection because no monad is perfect; only God is.

Rescher's work is valuable to students of Leibniz in two respects. First, he assists the student in grasping the systematic features of Leibniz's thought.

Such a grasp can help to make a work such as the *Monadology* more accessible, since it is not presented to the reader in a systematic fashion. Second, Rescher shows the continuity between Leibniz's metaphysical and moral concerns (87-90), a feature of Leibniz's work underappreciated by other commentators.

Ishiguro, Hidé. *Leibniz's Philosophy of Logic and Language*. London: Gerald Duckworth & Company, 1972.

The title of this book indicates its author's primary concern with Gottfried Wilhelm von Leibniz's philosophy. She begins with a review of the previous scholarship on Leibniz and situates her work within it. Rather than the more ambitious undertaking of Nicholas Rescher, she takes on a few main themes in Leibniz's philosophy. Her study opens with a consideration of Leibniz's Principle of Substitution, *Salve Veritate*. Hidé Ishiguro takes this principle to be one of the most basic to Leibniz's philosophy. This principle holds that "those terms of which one can be substituted for the other without affecting truth are identical." According to Ishiguro, this principle deals with concepts of things and the criterion for their identity. The principle is to be distinguished from related principles—notably, the Identity of Indiscernibles Principle (9).

Ishiguro goes on to consider further the nature of concepts and the role they play in Leibniz's philosophy. Concepts, for Leibniz, are either simple or complex (paralleling the metaphysical remarks at the beginning of the *Monadology*) (1-2). The latter are constituted by the former. The relation between simple concepts and between simple and complex concepts is expressed in Leibniz's Principle of Contradiction (31). The application of this principle is very limited, however, inasmuch as reference to the world must be made in the case of propositions asserting truths of fact. That is, a more complex analysis of propositions about the actual world—about monads and their properties—is necessary.

Monads, Ishiguro asserts, are the only basic existents in Leibniz's metaphysics (1-6), and "universals or facts do not exist over and above individuals." These two claims create a special problem for Leibniz's account of relations. Monads, to use familiar language, mirror the universe; they have relations to all other monads (56). Yet Leibniz also says that relations are ideal things, abstracted in the mind. Some commentators—Rescher and Bertrand Russell, for example—read Leibniz on this point as saying that all relational propositions can be reduced to propositions about the nonrelational properties of monads. Ishiguro takes exception to this view. While Leibniz was interested in developing a clear, formal language that reflected in its structure—subject-predicate logic—the logical and other relations among propositions expressed in it (31-36), he did not thereby mean to eliminate relations altogether from his metaphysics. That is, relational predicates are to be found in the complete individual notion of a monad. Further, more general relational properties can be abstracted from these.

Consider a common Leibnizian example, the proposition "David is the son of Solomon." It is to be analyzed, Ishiguro suggests, in terms of a relational property of David, his being the son of Solomon, and a relational property of Solomon, his being the father of David. The more general properties, son of and paternity, can be abstracted from these two concrete relational properties. These *general* properties Leibniz elsewhere calls ideal things, *entia rationis* (beings of the mind). This ordering of relations Ishiguro calls Leibniz's "Nominalist Thesis." Space and time can be accounted for by this thesis, Ishiguro shows, since they are general relations abstracted from the concrete relations of the side-by-sidedness and succession of individual monads. Hence, they are not to be taken as absolute.

Ishiguro's reading of Leibniz on this central point in his metaphysics is quite different from that offered by Rescher. While both share a common overall strategy in their reading of Leibniz in that they emphasize his logic and epistemology, they differ on the central point of what sort of properties characterize a monad. That is, the two offer quite different accounts of the nature or perceptions, which are the qualities or accidents of monads (7-14). Rescher would have these qualities all be nonrelational in character. Ishiguro, on the other hand, would admit relational properties as well into Leibniz's ontology.

A number of advantages for our understanding of Leibniz's philosophy are gained by Ishiguro's approach. First, those passages in which Leibniz seems to be saying that perceptions are relational in character now make sense (56-57). Second, relational properties are unique to the substances that possess them, since they must make reference to that substance. Hence, as Leibniz puts it, "Accidents cannot be detached from substances and march about outside substances" (7)—that is, be shared by other substances. Nonrelational properties do not make reference to the substances they characterize and thus differ only in number. Third, the doctrine of pre-established harmony is given solid grounding, in that monads are internally related to one another via their perceptions. Thus, it makes sense to assert that those perceptions are coordinated with one another by God—the ground for his doing so is contained within the monads themselves (57). Finally, the unity of the world, the one made up of the many, is secured, since it is anchored in the many, the monads themselves. Thus, Leibniz is successfully able to assert that a world has a great variety of being but only a few simple laws ordering that variety (58).

Another interesting feature of Ishiguro's account is her reference to Leibniz's scholastic forebears. This occurs in her rendition of Leibniz's Nominalist Thesis. Ishiguro indicates Leibniz's awareness of and continuity with philosophical traditions that predate René Descartes and other "modern" philosophers. In doing so, she helps to bring to Leibniz scholarship a historical dimension that it has, for the most part, lacked in the twentieth century.

Martin, Gottfried. *Leibniz: Logic and Metaphysics*. Translated by K. J. Northcott and P. G. Lucas. New York: Barnes and Noble, 1967.

The approach taken by Gottfried Martin to Gottfried Wilhelm von Leibniz's philosophy contrasts with that employed by Nicholas Rescher and Hidé Ishiguro. Martin emphasizes Leibniz's continuity with and preservation of premodern philosophy and the central place occupied in Leibniz's philosophy by metaphysics. It is Leibniz's work in logic, Martin asserts, and not his metaphysics, that makes a decisive break with the past. Since it bears directly on our understanding of the *Monadology*, we will here be concerned with Martin's study of Leibniz's metaphysics.

Martin opens his exposition with an analysis of Leibniz's views on the nature of truth. Truth is objective for Leibniz; that is, it exists in things and not in thought alone (46). Since every true proposition is being constantly thought by God, truth can be understood as divine thought (43). This is so because God conceives of possible worlds and is the ground of the preestablished harmony in each. Hence, objective truth is grounded in and made possible by God's knowledge.

Martin next takes up Leibniz's view of metaphysical good and evil, concepts that play a key role in his talk of best possible worlds. God must be a positive reality and the good of a possible world must consist in its grades or reality, its differing varieties of being. That world characterized by the maximum positive reality is the best possible world (58); and the reality making up any possible world is the multiplicity of monads, the fundamental units of being (1).

The monad comprises perception and appetition (14-15). It is characterized chiefly by unity: it cannot be divided into other free-standing individuals. That is, its parts cannot exist apart from it (3). In addition, monads must differ from one another (8-9). Appetition is the ground of both the monad's unity and its activity, its unfolding of its perceptions (15). That is, monads are *active* unities, unlike the passive matter of René Descartes. Thus, the basic concept in Leibniz's philosophy is individuality—a quite different interpretation from that offered by Rescher and Ishiguro.

All other aspects of Leibniz's metaphysics depend on monads. Qualities, relations, concepts, and universals have their foundation in monads. Thus, for example, secondary qualities such as color are not entities, but are phenomena or appearances of monads. Similarly, and in striking contrast with the thought of Descartes, matter is phenomenal. Hence, monads must be understood as nonmaterial entities, what Leibniz calls souls (74-84). As we have already seen, space and time are phenomenal in character, in opposition to Sir Isaac Newton's views.

Since perceptions are relational in character, the interpretation of the ontological status of relations is one of Martin's central concerns. Martin reads

Leibniz as holding that there are real relations which serve as the basis of our concepts, which are *entia rationis*. Martin maintains that in his account of the ontological status of relations Leibniz relies on older, scholastic views. Individual accidents of relation are real and cannot exist apart from substances. This is the traditional Aristotelian view, as the Scholastic and Late Scholastic philosophers understood it. These real qualities of monads are the basis of general relations such as son of and paternity. They are also the basis of phenomena which are governed by the mechanistic laws of nature. Monads, by contrast, are governed by an internal principle, appetition. Since bodies are phenomenal they are bound by deterministic laws, while monads are not, and, especially in the case of human beings, they are thus characterized by free will (78).

Martin closes with a consideration of Leibniz's metaphysics of God, pointing out that, for Leibniz, philosophy was always synonymous with natural theology. That is, along with monads God occupies a central place in Leibniz's philosophy. Like Rescher, Martin provides a thorough analysis of Leibniz's revision of the ontological proof with its focus on first showing that the concept of God is free of contradiction. God possesses a number of attributes in their perfect form: unity, omniscience, wisdom, goodness, and justice (49).

Martin's work is especially important to Leibniz scholarship because it provides a counterpoint to the school of interpretation begun by Russell and Couturat, that emphasizes Leibniz's logic and epistemology. Martin, by contrast, emphasizes Leibniz's metaphysics and his preoccupation with the nature of individual substances, monads. To be sure, Leibniz's interest in logic and mathematics is relevant, Martin claims, but primarily as it shaped his methods of metaphysical inquiry. That inquiry itself undertakes a traditional task, dating back to Aristotle and Plato: the attempt to understand the nature of being and its determinations. Martin shows in great detail how Leibniz, in his own work, at once extends and is in debt to the Scholastic tradition. Leibniz was certainly a modern philosopher, according to Martin, but he was also one whose philosophy was shaped to a great extent by traditional philosophy. We are in Martin's debt for bringing to light this long-overlooked yet central feature of Leibniz's philosophy.—*L.B.M.*

ADDITIONAL RECOMMENDED READING

Couturat, Louis. *La Logique de Leibniz*. Paris: Felix Alcan, 1901. A pioneering work in Leibniz scholarship in this century, emphasizing the place of logic in Leibniz's philosophy.

Frankfurt, Harry G. *Leibniz: A Collection of Critical Essays*. New York: Doubleday/Anchor, 1972. An examination by a variety of scholars of different aspects of Leibniz's philosophy, it provides an opportunity to study contrasting approaches to understanding Leibniz's logic, epistemology, and metaphysics.

Meyer, Rudolf W. *Leibniz and the Seventeenth-Century Revolution.* Translated by J. P. Stern. Chicago: Henry Regnery Company, 1952. An important study of the broad cultural background against which Leibniz's philosophy should be understood.

Russell, Bertrand. *A Critical Exposition of the Philosophy of Leibniz.* London: George Allen & Unwin, 1937. With that of Couturat, a pioneering work in English on Leibniz. Russell's views should be approached with caution, however, as they are shaped as much by his own philosophical views as by an accurate reading of the Leibnizian texts.

Studia Leibnitiana. An international journal devoted to Leibniz scholarship and the official publication of the International G. W. Leibniz Society, which is based in the Leibniz Archives in Hannover, West Germany.

A SYSTEM OF LOGIC

Author: John Stuart Mill (1806-1873)
Type of work: Logic, philosophy of induction
First published: 1843

PRINCIPAL IDEAS ADVANCED

Terms denote only particulars, and the only particulars we can speak of significantly are those we are acquainted with.

The syllogism is not a form of proof which allows inference to particular statements from general statements, but a form of argument which relates inductive conclusions to present inductive generalizations.

Mathematical propositions are synthetic and empirical (not analytic and verbal), and the only necessity attaching to them is a psychological necessity.

By the methods of agreement, difference, residues, and concomitant variation inductive generalizations are possible.

Inductive inference is based on the principle of the uniformity of nature—which is itself a principle established by inductive argument.

John Stuart Mill is the best known of the English Utilitarians. Educated almost entirely at home—as the heir apparent of the movement—he became fully conversant with the philosophic, social, political, and economic views of James Mill (his father), Jeremy Bentham, David Hartley, and David Ricardo, and through them he received the heritage of Locke, Berkeley, and Hume. While he was not a great original thinker, he assimilated all that was presented to him, analyzed and developed it, made some important changes, and presented it to the world in such a forceful manner that he became the most influential of the Utilitarians. He wrote a number of works ranging from semipopular ethical and social essays to criticisms of the logicians and metaphysicians of his time. He is best known today for *Utilitarianism* (1863), *Essay on Liberty* (1859), and various doctrines presented in his *A System of Logic*, the work that immediately established his reputation among his contemporaries, that had to be reckoned with by any logician during the remainder of the century, and that was still being reprinted in its entirety in the early years of this century.

In Book I, Mill discusses words and propositions with the intention of indicating the limits of meaningful discourse. In defending the traditional doctrine that simple propositions are composed of two names linked by the copula, he makes a number of distinctions, the most important of which are as follows. He distinguishes between *general* names such as "man," which are used to refer to any of an indefinite number of similar things, and *singular* names which are used to denote one specific thing. Singular names may be either *proper* names such as "Peter" or *complex names* such as "the man standing on the step." He also distinguishes between *concrete* terms such as "man" and "white" (that is, "white object") and *abstract* terms such as "humanity" ("manness") and "whiteness." The latter are names of properties. Finally, he distinguishes between *connotative* and *nonconnotative* terms. In the sentence "Peter is white," both terms refer to, designate, or denote Peter, but they do so in different ways. "Peter" functions as an arbitrarily assigned mark used to identify the person, but "white" or "white thing" denotes him by calling attention to or connoting a property he has, the property that is denoted by the abstract term "whiteness." Only proper names and some abstract terms such as "whiteness" are nonconnotative.

If we could not make this last distinction we would be forced to conclude that all propositions are identity statements in which we are asserting only that one thing is denoted by two names. Given the distinction, we can say that we are asserting that whatever is denoted by the subject term has the property connoted by the predicate term. The "is" of predication, which is thus distinguished from the "is" of identity, expresses time through its tenses and expresses denial through the addition of "not," but strictly speaking, it does not assert existence. Hence, we need yet another "is" for this. But since these three uses exhaust the functions of the verb, a simple statement is meaningful only if it asserts an identity, makes a predication, or asserts existence. Of course, we can make statements about causes and about relations, but since causes can be explained as causal relations and since all relations can be regarded as relational properties, these are no more than special cases of predication.

Mill claims that the account given so far is a philosophically neutral one, but he pushes the analysis further in an empirical direction. In the first place, while Mill does not make clear the exact nature of general ideas, his conception falling somewhere between Locke's and Hume's on this matter, he is clear about the denotation of terms: they denote particulars only. Thus, a general name like "man" does not denote a class that is some sort of entity in addition to the individuals that compose it. There are only men, and "man" denotes them. Again, while all men are classified as such because each of them is rational, the abstract term "rational" does not denote a Platonic universal. Rather, it denotes indifferently any of a number of similar properties characterizing different individuals.

The particulars of which we can speak significantly are those we know; these are not the underlying material and spiritual substances of the metaphysician. Mill allows us to speak of causes and relations, but he argues that these can be reduced to predication. He allows us to speak of predicates and of substances, but he insists that all we really know of them are their sensible effects, and therefore that we must restrict ourselves to what is immediately given; namely, to the content of sensation, emotion, and thought. Consequently, to predicate a property of a substance is to say no more than that a phenomenon or set of phenomena denoted by the predicate term accompanies, precedes, follows, or is included in the phenomenon or set of phenomena denoted by the subject term. To assert the existence of anything is to assert the occurrence of some phenomenon, and to assert identity or difference is to compare phenomena.

In Book II, in his discussion of deduction, Mill argues not only that the power of syllogistic reasoning has been greatly overrated, but also that its nature has been misunderstood. He insists that as a method of proof it always begs the question. This is obvious, he says, in the case of the syllogism "All men are mortal, Socrates is a man, therefore Socrates is mortal," for we know that all men are mortal only because we know that Socrates, Caesar, Henry VIII, and others have died. Yet, since we can frame parallel syllogisms in which the person referred to is a living person, the generalization that "All men are mortal" cannot be regarded simply as a summary of facts. Yet, these latter syllogisms are questionable too if they are thought to prove their conclusions, for it is still the case that we have mounted up from the mortality of Socrates, Caesar, and others to the generalization, and have descended from it to the mortality of, say, the United States President. We can think of this sequence as a complex inference in which an inductive inference is followed by a deductive one, but we do not need to, for we might just as well argue directly that because Socrates died, Caesar died, Henry VIII died, and the Duke of Wellington died (among others), so also the said President will die. Since it is superfluous, the syllogism is not the form of the inference, or even of a part of the inference—strictly speaking, the argument is an inductive one. Mill believed this to be true in general: particulars are not inferred from generals, but only from other particulars.

Since Mill did not deny the usefulness of generalizations or of the syllogisms they make possible, he had to reinterpret the function of the major premise. This he did by maintaining in *A System of Logic* that the major premise itself asserts an inference, an inference from particulars to the general, and that it functions as a guide for making inferences, inferences from particulars to particulars. It can function as such a guide because the inference from particulars to a particular is essentially the same as the inference from these particulars to the general statement. Strictly speaking, this guide is superfluous, but it is useful insofar as it reminds us of a valid type of inference, provides supplementary assurance that the present inference is valid, and fosters consistency by leading us to draw inferences in accordance with those we have drawn earlier. The syllogism, then, is not a form of proof in which something is derived from a general premise, but the machinery through which the relevance of earlier inductions is brought to bear upon a present one.

In Book II, Mill also makes his well-known assertions about the nature of mathematics. He recognized that the truth of some propositions follows logically from the meanings of the words contained in them, but that these truths are truths only about words. He agreed with the Kantians of his day in claiming that the propositions of mathematics are synthetic propositions about the world of measurable and countable things, but as an empiricist he could not accept their claim that such propositions express insights into conditions imposed on experience by the knowing mind. They must, then, be experimental truths of a very general and pervasive sort. Strictly speaking, insofar as they refer to magnitudes they are only very close approximations and therefore not literally true—do the measured angles of actual triangles always total 180 degrees?—but the facts agree with them so closely that for all practical and scientific purposes they can be regarded as exceptionless truths. To the objection that they cannot be empirical statements because they are necessarily true, he writes that they are necessarily true only in the sense that it is psychologically impossible to conceive of their falsity. Carrying his position to its conclusion, he insists that even the laws of contradiction and excluded middle are empirical generalizations based upon such facts as that belief and disbelief displace each other, light and darkness exclude each other, and so on. For a number of reasons, this analysis of mathematics and logic has been rejected by almost all serious students of the subject.

In Book III, Mill discusses induction, which is obviously the basic form of reasoning for him. Almost every student of elementary logic is familiar with his four canons: the canon of *agreement* which states that if cases in which a phenomenon occurs have in common only one thing, then that thing is the effect or the cause or part of the cause of the phenomenon; the canon of *difference* which states that if cases in which the phenomenon occurs differ from cases in which it does not in only one respect, that respect, or its absence, is the effect or cause or part of the cause of the phenomenon; the canon of *residues* which states that if we subtract from a phenomenon the effects we know to be due to certain antecedents, then the remainder is the effect of the remaining antecedents; and the canon of *concomitant variations* which states that when one phenomenon varies whenever another does, then either there is a causal relation between the two or they are both related causally to a third thing. Mill regards these methods as ways of both discovering and testing causes. He says that the method of difference is the most important of the four, because it lends itself to experimental applications; of all the purely inductive methods it alone reveals or establishes causes with a high degree of probability. The method of residues requires some deductive steps, the method of concomitant variations is basically but a less useful variation of the method of difference, and the method of agreement is not very effective since we cannot exclude the possibility of plural causes.

Mill believed that inductive inference is based on the principle of the uniformity of nature, the assumption that everything has a cause and that causal laws are invariant. He also believed, and this is more interesting, that this principle itself is established by induction. Having already discovered a good number of empirical laws, such as that fire burns and water drowns, we generalize on the basis of them to attain the principle. We subsequently use the principle when we are making inferences in less obvious situations. To the objection that he begs the question, Mill writes that the principle was not used in the induction that established it or in inductions leading to the laws from which it was induced. While Mill is unclear about the details of his defense, it is clear that to avoid an outright contradiction he would have to modify his earlier assertion that every inductive inference presupposes the principle. Perhaps he would have done this, for he indicates in various ways that he intends to claim only that inductions based on the four methods presuppose the principle. First, these four types of induction are said to comprise "scientific" inference in contrast to induction by simple enumeration, which Mill regards as a much less reliable form of inference. The inductions that precede and establish the principle of the uniformity of nature are "non-scientific" inferences. Again, the four methods are supposed to enable us to detect and test causes, whereas it is not the case that induction by simple enumeration is expected to do so. Consequently, the former is thought to presuppose the principle of universal causation, whereas the latter is not. Furthermore, since the whole point of the principle is that it enables us to recast our inferences in a deductive form, its role is exactly that of the major premise of a syllogism. Consequently, it is not involved as a premise at all. It functions as a guide that is not logically required but which does support the induction insofar as it makes it clear that this induction is similar to ones that are acceptable. Furthermore, Mill writes, once we know that the event does have a cause—and the principle assures us that it does—we have an additional reason for thinking that runs of favorable instances, concomitant variations, and other relationships are more than mere coincidences. In these ways inductions that rise above the "loose and uncertain" status of induction by simple enumeration presuppose the principle.

But if this is what Mill meant, he still leaves us with certain puzzles. For instance, the difference between unreliable inferences of the "All crows are black" type and reliable ones such as "Fire burns" is not at all clear. According to Mill, the difference is that although in the case of fire we have discovered a causal law, in the case of crows we have not. But the introduction of causes raises a number of difficulties. First, there is the difficulty of specifying how we identify a causal relationship, for—as the case of the crows indicates—it cannot be on the basis of the presence of a large number of favorable instances and the absence of any instance to the contrary. Second, the term "cause" must refer to more than Humean conjunctions. Mill asserted that some sort of necessity is presupposed in the assumption that nature will repeat herself, but his reluctance to go beyond Hume prevented him from giving a clear or consistent account. Third, if "All crows are black" is not a reliable scientific inference because, as Mill claimed, the principle of the uniformity of nature is not applicable to it (it is not a causal law), then Mill should have concluded that the generalizations on which the principle rests and the principle itself are similarly unreliable. At least, he should have done so to maintain his own assertion that the question has not been begged because the principle was not involved in the earlier inferences. If the principle is to be reliable and is to be a statement about causality, then the earlier generalizations, such as "Fire burns," must be regarded as reliably confirmed causal laws, but in this case the question has been begged. He equivocated between the positions, but in either case Mill failed to show how the principle can bestow a higher degree of reliability on inferences made in accordance with it. His discussion is confused in part by his failure to distinguish clearly between psychological and logical matters.

Mill himself realized as well as many of his critics that his four methods cannot be applied easily, mechanically, or universally, and that we do, as a matter of fact, hold well-established beliefs that have not and could not have been discovered or tested by the methods alone. Perhaps the most important fact that thwarts the application of the methods is that of the composition of causes. As in the case of the composition of forces in physics, a number of causes can combine to produce one effect and this effect can be such that an inspection of it will not reveal the effect of any one of the component causes. While we cannot apply the methods to such a phenomenon we do have another way of proceeding. For if we know what sorts of causes might, if combined properly, produce this kind of composite effect, and if we know the laws of these causes, we can calculate the net effect of various combinations of these possible component causes until we find one that agrees with the observed complex effect. Thus we have a technique which enables us to explain complicated phenomena in terms of more general laws. If we are successful, there is no reason why we could not apply a similar procedure to these laws to obtain intermediate laws, and to these in turn to obtain yet more basic laws. In this way it is theoretically possible to reduce a whole science to a small set of basic principles from which all the rest can be inferred. This has actually been done for mechanics and astronomy by Newton's laws and for chemistry by Dalton's atomic theory. These intermediate and basic laws are what we call theories.

In discussing the first level explanation of complex phenomena Mill frequently wrote as if we have an exhaustive knowledge of the possible causes and as if the discovery of the correct combinations requires no ingenuity but only the straightforward examination of the possible combinations. The technique of proceeding in this manner is called the "deductive method." But he was well aware that many possible causes and their laws are not known and that in the case of the lower-level ones they can never be discovered by any mechanically applicable procedure. In these cases we have to make assumptions as to what the causal laws might be, just as Newton did when he speculated that the gravitational force varies inversely with the square of the distance and not with the cube. These suppositions, for which we have little or no evidence at the outset, are "hypotheses," and the modified technique is the "hypothetical method." In some of its applications we are looking for basic laws, but in others we are concerned with finding intermediate-level laws that will enable us to infer known empirical laws from accepted principles. The use of this method requires ingenuity, and success is by no means antecedently guaranteed. Since a hypothesis cannot be verified directly, the establishment of its truth depends upon the verification of facts or laws inferred from it. Since two hypotheses might very well be elaborated to explain the same phenomenon, a hypothesis is not really established unless unanticipated consequences that follow from the one hypothesis, but not from the other, are also verified.

Hypotheses and deduction become more and more indispensable as a science develops, for the more inclusive a theory becomes the less likely it is that it can be discovered by a direct examination of the facts. Mill believed that by themselves the four inductive methods will not take us very far, for the first two steps of the required hypothetical method—those of propounding hypotheses and elaborating their consequences—are beyond their scope.

Turning to the social sciences, Mill wrote that experimentation is largely impossible, that the method of agreement is not widely applicable because many phenomena are produced by different causes, and that the method of difference is of little use both because situations are too complex and because many effects are the composite effects of several causes. Consequently, the hypothetical method is even more indispensable in this area. We cannot hope for as high a degree of certainty here because it is usually possible to elaborate different intermediate hypotheses linking basic principles with empirical laws, and there is no convenient way of distinguishing between them. The basic laws are presumably the laws of associational psychology. We encounter additional difficulty when we deal with human beings; man reacts to changes in his environment in such a way that the conditions to which men are subject at one time are not these to which they are subject at another. As a result there is a historical development, even in human nature itself, so that the empirical and intermediate laws are not invariant. Man's changing state of knowledge is the principal factor in this progressive development.

A System of Logic concludes with some remarks that every reader of his *Utilitarianism* should consult. Mill argues that morality is essentially a matter of rules and that consequently moral statements are imperative rather than indicative statements. Since they express precepts and not matters of fact they lie beyond the province of science.—*L.M.*

PERTINENT LITERATURE
Kneale, William and Martha Kneale. *The Development of Logic*. Oxford: Clarendon Press, 1962.

John Stuart Mill's *A System of Logic, Ratiocinative and Inductive, Being a Connected View of the Principles of Evidence and the Methods of Scientific Investigation* was published in London in 1843. In it, William and Martha Kneale tell us, Mill attempted to expound logic in a fashion consistent with the British empiricist tradition. Nevertheless, they add, Mill includes a theory of syllogistic, and hence of formal reasoning, as a subordinate theme in his *A System of Logic*, rather than sharing his fellow empiricists' contempt of formal reasoning.

Further, they add, Mill frees empiricism from nominalism. The nominalism in question is associated with Thomas Hobbes, who, according to the Kneales, held that in every proposition what is signified is the belief of the speaker that the predicate is the name of the same thing as that of which the subject is a name. But, Mill contends, this sort of analysis is sufficient only in the comparatively rare and trivial case in which both the subject term and the predicate term are proper names, and it can have been thought adequate for all cases only on the assumptions that a term is meaningful only if it denotes or names and that a general name differs from a proper name only by virtue of naming more than one individual.

The Kneales report that Mill calls all terms "names" and holds that terms denote what they name (that to which they refer, if they are singular terms, or to which they apply, if they are general terms). General terms, however, connote as well as denote; they connote or imply attributes to the things they apply to. It may be, the Kneales explain, that Mill's view is that connotation is a work that general names perform in addition to their denotational work. In any case, they suggest, it is "connotation" which, in Mill's *A System of Logic*, does duty for "meaning."

The Kneales tell us that, for Mill, definitions are not real; they are not expressions of the essential properties, or natures, of things. Instead, the authors add, Mill's view was that a definition proper tells us only about the use of language. What poses as a real definition will be a definition proper plus assumptions about matters of fact. After Mill's book, real definitions were little spoken of.

The Kneales report that Mill defines "proposition" as "a portion of discourse in which a predicate is affirmed or denied of a subject." This treats all propositions as subject-predicate in form. Similarly, they note, Mill identifies ratiocination with use of syllogism. He holds that every syllogism, viewed as an endeavor to prove a conclusion, begs the question. Thus in "All men are mortal; Socrates is a man; therefore, Socrates is mortal" the conclusion regarding Socrates is already included in the premise regarding all men. Further, the authors of this book indicate, Mill denies that syllogistic reasoning is inference; inference, Mill says, "is from particulars to particulars." A general proposition, in Mill's view, is but a summation of the cases it covers; *All A is B* says *A1 is B* and *A2 is B* and *A3 is B*, and so on through all the *A*'s there are. Thus, Mill says, in "inferring" from *All A is B* that if *This is an A, This is a B*, what one "infers" is already encoded in the general proposition with which one begins.

The Kneales find Mill suggesting sometimes that the syllogism *All men are mortal; Socrates is a man; so Socrates is mortal* is properly viewed as saying *Socrates is a man, so Socrates is mortal*, and at other times holding that it is properly viewed as saying *All other men we have record of have been found mortal, so Socrates, who is a man, is mortal*. On the former account, one derives a singular conclusion from a singular premise, and the argument can be made formally valid by turning it into what Mill calls a syllogism. On the latter account, the conclusion does not follow unless one supposes that the data recorded in the universal proposition justifies one in thinking that a lawlike connection holds between *being mortal* and *being human*.

The authors suggest that the unclarity of Mill's account is caused by his rightly rejecting the view of Thomas Hobbes that logic is merely conventional and the view of certain German Idealists that logic is psychologistic, and holding instead that logic is objective. He could not see how to hold this view—how to account for this objectivity—save by holding that the principles of logic are empirical generalizations. Hobbes (they explain earlier) held that thinking is but the manipulation of signs, and the principles of logic rest only on arbitrary definitions of terms. The German Idealists rested the principles of logic on psychological habits of thought. Mill, they report, rightly rejects both views.

When Mill came to give an account of syllogistic thought, he realized he had to distinguish it from inductive reasoning, and so he suggested the view that the rules of logic are principles governing the use of nonformal principles of inference, these latter being based on inductive grounds. This, the Kneales note, is inconsistent with his view that the principles of logic are generalizations from experience. They believe that while Mill did not explicitly state this view, it is suggested by some of what Mill said.

Frege, Gottlob. *The Foundations of Arithmetic*. Translated by J. L. Austin. Oxford: Basil Blackwell, 1956.

In his *A System of Logic*, John Stuart Mill proposed a certain view about the nature of mathematical propositions. One might think that, say, $2 + 2 = 4$ is obviously a necessary truth—one which could not be false, no matter what. Mill disagrees, holding that $2 + 2 = 4$, and other mathematical claims, are not necessary truths; instead, they are empirical generalizations, based on inductive inference from descriptions of sensory experiences. Gottlob Frege, along with most others, finds this view completely unacceptable, and offers what is surely among the most powerful critiques of it.

For Mill, Frege notes, arithmetical truths are laws of nature, or inductive generalizations over descriptions of sensory experiences. In order to get this result, Frege argues, Mill must interpret the words which are used to express these propositions in a sense they will not bear if they are faithfully to state their mathematical content. For example, Frege notes, to suppose that $1 = 1$ could be false, since a given one pound weight may not be perfectly identical in weight to another, is simply to misconstrue the content of $1 = 1$. Mill, according to Frege, treats the symbol " + " as if it expressed the relation between the parts of a physical body or heap to the whole body or heap. Thus he supposes that, say, $5 + 2 = 7$ tells us that if we pour 5 unit volumes and 2 unit volumes of a liquid into a vat, we will have 7 unit volumes of that liquid in the vat. Whether this is so depends on whether some process or reaction affects the resultant volume, and, about that, $5 + 2 = 7$ has nothing to say. It only says that if you pour 5 units and 2 units, you pour 7 units, with whatever effect. Thus, Frege says, Mill confuses the applications that can be made of mathematical propositions (applications that are often to physical objects and processes and consequently presuppose empirical or observed data) with the pure mathematical propositions themselves, whose truth or falsity does not depend on such data. Addition does not correspond to some physical relationship; we can add, say, great historical events or fictional characters as well as cards in a stack. So, Frege concludes, laws of nature are one thing, and mathematical propositions are another.

Frege then asks: Might mathematical propositions nevertheless be inductively arrived at? Over what will the inductions range? From what will we induce? Presumably, Frege suggests, we will induce from numerical formulae (whose sense will be taken, not from the mathematician's definitions of individual numbers, but from something else). One task will then be to assign some new sense to the formulae. A second task will be to specify the inductive procedure to be followed. The first task is not easy, given that it must be performed in some such way as to prepare the way for the second.

Supposing the first task somehow to have been performed, the inductive procedure cannot assume, but must rather establish, any general propositions which will hold for all numbers. For purposes of constructing the procedure, Frege maintains, we must suppose ourselves ignorant of such propositions, which are after all supposed to be elicited, not presupposed, by the procedure. In ordinary inductive procedures, Frege notes, we often use the proposition that every spatial position, as well as every temporal position, is as good as any other in that it is equally neutral with regard to providing confirmation or disconfirmation of an inductive generalization. Numbers, however, are not in space or time. Further, position in the number series is not a matter of indifference to the properties a number has.

The members of the number series are not related to one another as are the members of a natural species. The numbers, Frege notes, by their nature are arranged "in a fixed, definite, order of precedence"; each has its unique and necessary features. When it is discovered that all the members of the number series share some property, the discovery is made, or else confirmed, not by means of observations, but by offering a proof. These things, Frege says, are not true with regard to the members of natural species. The prospect, then, of using an ordinary inductive procedure to discover general truths regarding numbers is not bright.

Frege suggests the following analogy. Suppose we notice that in a borehole the temperature rises regularly with increase in depth. Suppose, further, we have discovered a considerable variety of rock strata. He suggests that, under these conditions, it would be premature to infer that the regular distribution of temperature will continue, and we cannot infer anything about what sort of strata we will discover if we keep boring. To relate the strata thus far discovered to the deeper strata by means of the concept "whatever you come to by going on boring" will not aid us in making inductive inferences.

Another problem with Mill's approach, Frege notes, is that inductive procedure can establish at most that some proposition which it yields probably is true. But, if we do not confuse such propositions as *2 + 2 = 4* with such propositions as *2 units of one liquid added to 2 units of another liquid will always yield four units of liquid* (rather than an explosion, or some evaporation), we can see that pure mathematical truths are (and are known to be) not merely probably but necessarily true.

Still another problem with Mill's approach, Frege contends, is that it is viciously circular. Inductive procedure, Frege argues, rests on theory of probability. But "how probability theory could possibly be developed without presupposing arithmetical laws is beyond comprehension." Thus the arithmetical laws supposedly arrived at inductively will have been simply presupposed by the inductive procedure all along. One could escape this criticism by regarding induction itself as but a process of habituation—as, say, a process in which persons accustom themselves to having certain expectations. But then the claim can no longer be made that being the product of induction gives some sort of rational sanction to a general proposition.

Thus, Frege concludes, there are strong reasons for refusing to accept Mill's view of the nature of mathematical propositions.—*K.E.Y.*

ADDITIONAL RECOMMENDED READING

Bocheński, I. M. *A History of Formal Logic.* Translated and edited by Ivo Thomas. Notre Dame, Indiana: University of Notre Dame Press, 1961. History of both Western and Indian logic.

Cohen, Morris R. and Ernest Nagel. *An Introduction to Logic and Scientific*

Method. New York: Harcourt Brace and Company, 1934. A discussion of formal and informal logic and scientific method, with many references to Mill.

Copi, I. M. *Introduction to Logic*. New York: Macmillan Publishing Company, 1972. A good introductory statement of Mill's methods.

Pap, Arthur. *Semantics and Necessary Truth*. New Haven, Connecticut: Yale University Press, 1958. A wide-ranging discussion of topics in semantics and logic, with references to Mill.

Prior, A. N. *Formal Logic*. Oxford: Clarendon Press, 1962. Discussion of a wide variety of topics in logic, with references to Mill.

Schneewind, J. B., ed. *Mill: A Collection of Critical Essays*. New York: Anchor Books, 1968. A collection of essays on Mill's thought, including his logic.

EITHER/OR

Author: Søren Kierkegaard (1813-1855)
Type of work: Existential metaphysics
First published: 1843

PRINCIPAL IDEAS ADVANCED

The aesthetical mode of existence is exemplified by both romantic hedonism and abstract intellectualism; both the sensualist and the intellectual fail to commit themselves decisively and thereby to achieve existence and selfhood.

Only through choice is authentic selfhood attained; life is a matter of either/or. The aesthetical way leads to boredom, melancholy, and despair.

In turning toward decision and commitment because of despair, the self passes from the aesthetical stage to the ethical.

In the ethical stage, in virtue of having chosen itself, the self becomes centralized, unified, and authentic.

The third stage of development is the religious; but no stage is sufficient by itself; the ethical stage transfigures the aesthetical, and the religious transfigures the ethical.

Either/Or is a two-volume work in which the author seeks to elucidate the contrasts and interrelationships between the aesthetical and the ethical modes of existence. As with most of the writings of Kierkegaard, *Either/Or* was not published under his own name. The elucidations are penned under various pseudonyms. The first volume contains an analysis and description of the territory of the aesthetical. The literary style is heterogeneous. Use is made of lyrical aphorisms, orations, psychological analyses, drama reviews, and philosophical formulations.

The aestheticist, expressing his views through these various literary forms, is designated as A. The ethical thinker in Volume II, bearing the pseudonym of Judge William, is designated as B. In one of his later works, *Concluding Unscientific Postscript*, Kierkegaard has explained the central theme of *Either/ Or* by informing the reader that A is an existential possibility, superior in dialectics and highly gifted in the uses of wit and poetic style, who nevertheless remains unable to commit himself in decisive action, and thus never exists in the true sense at all. B, on the other hand, represents the ethical man whose whole life is transformed into inwardness, passion, and commitment.

Judge William elucidates the content of the ethical in the form of a letter addressed to A. The communication of ethical truth demands a form or style which is commensurate with it. Ethical truth is existential and concrete, as contrasted with the theoretical and abstract, and consequently requires for its expression a form which has the personal quality of a dialogue or a letter. This constitutes the form of indirect communication. At the outset Judge

William reminds the aestheticist of the biblical story of the Prophet Nathan and David as a supreme example of this form of communication. King David listened attentively to the prophet's parable but remained in a state of theoretical detachment. He intellectualized the parable as an objective story which applied only to the mythical stranger. Not until the Prophet Nathan made the application explicit in his statement, "Thou, O King, art the man," did David apprehend the existential relevance of the parable. The Prophet Nathan used the form of indirect communication. This is also the form used by Judge William.

The aesthetical mode of existence has two primary expressions—romantic hedonism and abstract intellectualism. Mozart's *Don Giovanni* is depicted as the classical representative of the sensual or hedonistic view of life, and Goethe's *Faust* expresses the aesthetical personality of abstract intellectualism. Kierkegaard's archenemy, the Hegelian rationalist, also falls victim to the latter expression. For both the sensualist and the intellectualist inward existence and commitment are accidental and remain a matter of indifference. Neither is able to shoulder his responsibility and commit himself in action. They lack the ethical pathos which characterizes B.

The view of life which characterizes the hedonist is portrayed by the young lover in the "Diary of a Seducer," who carries through his seduction with a diabolical cunning. The young lover is a prototype of Mozart's *Don Giovanni*; he experiments with numerous possibilities but never commits himself to the responsibility of actualizing any particular one in earnestness and seriousness. He experiments with the techniques of seduction but never commits himself in a promise. He experiments with love but never commits himself in marriage. In his aesthetical experimentation the young lover retains the proper abstractness and indifference about him. Every girl is, for him, a *woman in general*. Insofar as the young lover has a guiding principle, it is the hedonistic principle that enjoyment or pleasure constitutes the only end of life. The necessary internal conditions for the attainment of this life of pleasure are physical beauty and health; the necessary external conditions are wealth, glory, and high status. But these conditions provide no ethical pathos for a committed life, and it is precisely a committed life which the young lover seeks to avoid. He lives only in the moment, utilized as an erotic present in which the satisfaction of a desire is maximized. But then the moment passes and a new desire asserts its claim to thrive. His whole life becomes a discontinuous succession of passing from one moment to the next. His personality thus lacks unity and continuity. He has dispersed or lost himself in the present to the neglect of his past and his future. He no longer retains his past in memory, and he retreats from his future which confronts him with the responsibility of decision.

The speculative intellectualist suffers the same loss of selfhood as the romantic hedonist. Whereas the hedonist loses himself in the immediacy of the erotic present, the speculative thinker loses himself in the immediacy of his thought. The speculative thinker seeks to comprehend the whole of reality through the categories of a universal logic. But in such a system the concretely existing subject really does not matter. Just as for the sensualist every girl is a woman in general, so for the intellectualist all reality is dissolved into general categories. Speculative thought sees only the general movement of history, explained through the mediation of logical categories, but forgets the individual who apprehends himself within his particular and concrete history. Thus, both the hedonist and the speculative thinker evade the responsibility of decision. Both flirt with the realm of possibility but neither makes the leap into existence. The hedonist escapes from the future and responsibility for dispersing himself in momentary pleasures. The speculative thinker evades choice by playing the role of a detached observer who speculates about the general movements in world history, but who never participates in his own inner history with pathos and inwardness. Expressing the Socratic irony of which Kierkegaard was a master, his pseudonym is made to say: "To the philosopher world history is concluded, and he mediates. Hence, in our age as the order of the day we have the disgusting sight of young men who are able to mediate Christianity and paganism, are able to play with the titanic forces of history, and are unable to tell a plain man what he has to do in life, and who do not know any better what they themselves have to do." The speculative thinker reduces existence to thought, sacrifices involvement for detached observation, and substitutes a reflective deliberation on universal history for the responsibility of concrete, personal decision. The common denominator of both expressions of aesthetical existence is a retreat from the reality of choice. In both cases the self has not yet found itself. Only through choice is authentic selfhood attained. This demands an awareness that life is a matter of either/or. But the either/or is a matter of indifference for the hedonist and the intellectualist alike. The aestheticist moves in a realm in abstraction from inwardness and existence.

The aesthetical mode or stage of existence leads to boredom and melancholy, and finally to despair. *Either/Or* and the writings of Kierkegaard as a whole contain graphic descriptions of the enveloping character of the moods of boredom, melancholy, and despair. Boredom is depicted as an aesthetical determinant which has plagued man from the very beginning. "The gods were bored, and so they created man. Adam was bored because he was alone, and so Eve was created. Thus boredom entered the world, and increased in proportion to the increase of population. Adam was bored alone; then Adam and Eve were bored together; then Adam and Eve and Cain and Abel were bored *en famille*; then the population of the world increased and the people were bored *en masse*." The aesthetical life of pure pleasure, as well as that of pure thought, leads to an abyss of boredom and tedium. Now it is necessary to distinguish two forms of boredom. In one form boredom is apprehended as an intentional mood which is directed toward a particular object, event, or person. One is bored with a book, a movie, or a boorish conversant. This form of boredom is merely a surface phenomenon which does not yet disclose man's true situation. In the second and more genuine form of boredom one is bored not with an intentionally specified object or person—one is bored with oneself. Man is confronted with a nameless emptiness which threatens life itself with a loss of meaning. This form of boredom brings man to a more intensified awareness of his predicament.

The enigmatic, nameless emptiness which characterizes genuine boredom is also an existential determinant of the melancholy individual. If the melancholy individual is asked what it is that weighs upon him, he is prone to reply, "I know not, I cannot explain it." Melancholy is a "spiritual ailment" or a "hysteria of the spirit" which confronts man with the abyss of emptiness and meaninglessness, and reveals the disquietude and discontinuity of his existence. But for the most part the individual who is subject to the disquieting moods of boredom and melancholy refuses to accept his condition, and seeks to conceal it through various diverting activities.

Like Blaise Pascal, Kierkegaard saw profoundly how man seeks to escape from himself through diversions which provide momentary distraction. The continuing search for diversion is descriptively characterized in the concept of the "rotation method" elucidated in Volume I. Man is bored with life in the country, so he moves to the village; he becomes bored in the village, so he moves to the city; he then becomes bored with his homeland and travels abroad; he becomes bored with life in a foreign land and then entertains the possibility of an endless journeying to alleviate his boredom. So also the melancholy individual engages in a self-defeating and frustrating search for diversion. It is in Nero, says the author, that we find the example *par excellence* of a melancholy nature that had given itself over to an endless search for diverting distractions. Nero sought to divert himself through an immersion into pleasure. He appointed "ministers of pleasure" who were entrusted with the task of finding novel ways to satisfy his desires. Only in the moment of pleasure could Nero find distraction from his melancholy. "Then he grasps after pleasure; all the world's cleverness must devise for him new pleasures, for only in the instant of pleasure does he find repose, and when that is past he gasps with faintness." When the instant of pleasure passes, Nero again plunges into melancholy. Hence a new desire must be created so that another momentary gratification may occur. But there is no end to this sort of thing, and Nero finds himself sucked into an abyss of meaninglessness and emptiness. Finally in his need for pleasure-producing distraction he orders the burning of Rome, but when the last embers die, he again gyrates into an appalling melancholy. This description of Nero's nature, we are reminded by the author, has not been undertaken as an occasion to thank God along with the Pharisee that we are different from Nero. Nero is "flesh of our flesh and bone of our bone," which is to say that in Nero a universal determinant of human existence becomes transparent.

Despair is the most intensive expression of the threat of meaninglessness and emptiness; it constitutes the culmination of the aesthetical mode of existence. The aesthetical life proves itself to be despair. In despair the self experiences a loss of hope because diversion no longer provides its momentary satisfaction. The aestheticist now realizes that he cannot find himself outside of himself—neither in his hedonistic and sensual pursuits nor in the abstractions of his speculative thought. To discover his genuine selfhood he must turn inward. He must turn toward earnestness, passion, decision, commitment, and freedom. Only in this movement will he be able to collect himself out of his dispersed and dissipated existence and become a unified and integrated self. Despair is thus an intensification of subjectivity which constitutes the gateway to authentic or genuine selfhood. In "choosing" despair the self gives birth to itself and passes from the aesthetical stage of indecision to the ethical stage of decisive commitment.

The ethical stage is the stage of decision and resolute commitment. The act of choice is an intensification of the ethical. Even the richest personality, writes the author, must be accounted as nothing before he has chosen himself. On the other hand, the poorest personality is everything for having chosen himself. Choice liberates the self both from the immediacy of pleasure and from the immediacy of reflection or pure thought, and makes possible the discovery of genuine selfhood. Through decision and commitment the self becomes integrated and "centralized." The aestheticist is always "eccentric" in that he seeks the center of his self in the periphery of hedonist or intellectualistic concerns—which means that he has lost his self. The ethical man, by virtue of having shouldered his responsibility in decision, has his center within himself. His life is centralized and unified. The unity of the ethical self is not a unity which is anchored in some residual ego or abiding substratum. The self is not an object which can be abstractly defined as having a permanent nature or a substantial fixity. Unity is achieved, not given. The self achieves or attains its unity and integrity through choice.

Choice thus becomes the central category for the ethical thinker. This is the category which lies closest to the heart and thought of Judge William. Not being a logician, he has no lengthy and impressive list of abstract categories—he has only one concrete denomination: choice. Now choice involves freedom, an either/or, and it is in this that we find the greatest treasure which man can possess. Judge William explains to the reader the central intention of his ethical elucidations when he writes: "For freedom, therefore, I am fighting. . . . I am fighting for the future, for either/or. That is the treasure I desire to bequeath to those whom I love in the world; yea, if my little son were at this instant of an age when he could thoroughly understand me, I would say to him, 'I leave to thee no fortune, no title and dignities, but I know where there lies buried a treasure which suffices to make thee richer than the whole world, and this treasure belongs to thee, and thou shalt not even express thanks to me for it lest thou take hurt to thine own soul by owing everything to another. This treasure is deposited in thine own inner self: there is an either/or which makes a man greater than the angels.'" Judge William's central intention of calling the aestheticist to an awareness of freedom and the importance of choosing is understood as an expression of the Socratic task of attaining self-knowledge. "Know thyself" and "Choose thyself" are conjunctive rather than disjunctive tasks. The knowledge which was the concern of Socrates was an ethical knowledge, and ethical knowledge can be achieved only through choosing. The self becomes transparent to itself only in decisive action.

In the person of Judge William we find the concrete exemplification of the ethical mode of existence. He is a married man who has commited himself in conjugal love. As such he is contrasted with the young lover of the "Diary of a Seducer," who dissipates himself in his various experiments with romantic love. Romantic and conjugal love are thus understood as existential qualities which differentiate the aesthetical and the ethical. Romantic love is experimental and nonhistorical, lacking continuity. Conjugal love expresses an inner history which gives it constancy and stability. The romantic hedonist lives in the present, and this present he experiences in abstraction from existence. The present becomes an instantaneous now, defined as the occasion for enjoyment. The past loses its existential significance and the future is never really faced. The young lover seduces a girl, and after the moment of seduction passes, all is over. The moment then becomes part of an abstracted past which has significance only as an object for melancholy recollection. Romantic love knows no repetition. The romantic hedonist lives his life as though it were a discrete succession of instantaneous nows, each now coming to be and passing away into a past which is bereft of existential importance. Everything is concentrated in the present, which is apprehended as embodying full reality. Conjugal love, on the other hand, strives for repetition. The ideal husband is one who is able to repeat his love every day. The married man thus carries within himself the memory of his past, anticipates his future, and undertakes his daily tasks and decisions in the context of his integrated wholeness. His past, future, and present are unified. It is thus that time and history become of paramount importance for conjugal love. The constancy and continuity of conjugal love are made possible through a unification of the self in its inner history.

In distinguishing between romantic and conjugal love Judge William does not intend an absolute disjunction. He speaks of marriage as the true transfiguration of romantic love. Marriage is its friend, not its enemy. Romantic love is not left behind in the transition to the ethical sphere. It becomes transfigured through the constancy of conjugal love. In the ethical stage ro-

mantic love is historicized and apprehended in terms of its temporal significance. The aesthetical always remains in the ethical, but it remains as a *relative*
and *dependent* mode of existence. "By the absolute choice the ethical is always
posited, but from this it does not follow by any means that the aesthetical is
excluded. In the ethical the personality is concentrated in itself, so the aesthetical is absolutely excluded or is excluded as the absolute, but relatively
it is still left." The romantic hedonist absolutizes the aesthetical as the final
and self-sufficient dimension of existence. The ethical man appropriates the
aesthetical in its relativity and transforms it by the existential determinants
of choice and commitment. At one point in his letter Judge William speaks
of the three stages (aesthetical, ethical, and religious) as "three great allies."
The spheres or stages of existence are not temporally successive levels of
development, excluding each other in a hierarchical ascent. They are modes
of existence, always in some sense present, penetrating the personality in its
process of becoming. They constitute the existential cross section of the self
and coexist interdependently throughout its history. No sphere is sufficient
by itself. The absolutization of one of the three spheres brings about a suf-
focation of the self.

The phenomenon of time, which plays such an important role in ethical
existence, is the focus of a profound analysis of Hegel's teaching on the
alienated or unhappy consciousness. Hegel had already taught that the alienated consciousness is the self that is never present to itself, being absent
from itself either in the past or in the future. The author agrees that Hegel
was right in thus defining the realm of the unhappy consciousness, but argues
that he was wrong in understanding it abstractly rather than existentially.
Hegel "beheld the kingdom from afar off." The author understands himself
to be a native inhabitant of the realm. Consciousness is alienated from itself
when it is severed either from its past or from its future. The alienated
consciousness has lost the memory of its life and has nothing for which to
hope. Thus, it culminates in despair. The unified consciousness has within it
both pastness and futurity. Memory and hope are unified in the center of
personality. The ethical man attains this unified consciousness in the moment
of decisive action. In the act of choice the past is taken up, the future is
acknowledged and faced, and the self is centralized.

The touchstone of the decision through which the self achieves its unity
and integrity is inwardness. An authentic choice is a choice made inwardly
in passion and earnestness. The accent falls on the *way of choosing* rather
than on *what is chosen*. In the ethical sphere man is educated in *how* to
choose. His first concern is not with the choice of the "right," but with the
earnestness and inwardness which determines the movement of choice. This
does not mean that the ethical thinker has no interest in the moral content
of choice. It does mean, however, that the moral content cannot be abstracted
as a *what*—as an objectively determined and legislated moral standard. An

action made solely because of external standards is bereft of moral content. Only that action which proceeds from the depths of inwardness qualifies the self as ethical. Judge William has little interest in a table of virtues which delineates abstract moral requirements. Ethical action is not a matter of following virtues. It is a matter of self-knowledge and self-commitment. Like Nietzsche's strong man, Kierkegaard's ethical man exists "beyond good and evil."

Either/Or concludes with a prayer and a sermon. This is a reminder to the reader that the ethical stage is not the final dimension of existence, but is itself transfigured by a religious state. As the ethical stage transfigures the aesthetical, so the religious transfigures the ethical by introducing the existential determinants of suffering, guilt, sin, and faith. But *Either/Or* does not carry the existential elucidation beyond the ethical. One of the reasons why Kierkegaard wrote his book, *Stages on Life's Way* (which appeared two years after *Either/Or*) was to give proper due to the religious stage.—*C.O.S.*

Pertinent Literature

Solomon, Robert C. "Kierkegaard: Faith and the Subjective Individual," in *From Rationalism to Existentialism: The Existentialists and Their Nineteenth-Century Backgrounds*. New York: Harper & Row Publishers, 1972.

A central goal of Robert C. Solomon in this detailed introduction to existentialism is to defend existentialism from the charge that thinkers of this school are too uncritical and are more literary than philosophical. Solomon is also concerned to respond to a view of some philosophers that the issues and ideas which existentialists discuss are unrelated to those found in traditional philosophy: throughout his book he tries to relate the concerns of existentialists to questions which appear in traditional philosophy. In his discussion of Søren Kierkegaard, Solomon makes many useful comparisons of Kierkegaard to Georg Wilhelm Friedrich Hegel and Immanuel Kant.

An important idea of Kierkegaard, Solomon writes, is his claim that the philosopher's main task should be to develop and present ideas *which people can live by*. The philosopher should not acquire knowledge as an end in itself. The most important issues are those which bear on choice and commitment, he believed. These views led Kierkegaard regularly to attack Hegel's philosophy, Solomon explains. Hegel offered a sophisticated system of "Absolute Knowledge" but no practical wisdom with which one might guide one's life.

The discussion in *Either/Or* centers around a movement between two different "modes of existence" or "stages of life," the aesthetic and the ethical modes. Kierkegaard's idea of different modes of existence and the way in which he orders these modes is similar to Hegel's presentation and ordering of "forms of consciousness" in his *Phenomenology of Spirit*, Solomon explains. For both philosophers the different modes are characterized by different systems of values and different views of oneself and of life. Kierkegaard's aesthetic sphere is similar to the Romantic spirit which Hegel describes in the *Phenomenology of Spirit*. Kierkegaard's depiction of the ethical sphere finds a parallel in Hegel's depiction of an ethical sphere. Both think of ethical life in a Kantian fashion where ethical behavior is conceived of in terms of treating persons as ends in themselves and sacrificing self-interest for moral duty.

The most important difference between Hegel and Kierkegaard in their accounts of the different modes is that for Hegel the movement from one mode to another in the hierarchy results from rational considerations, whereas for Kierkegaard it does not. Kierkegaard's view in *Either/Or* is that although the movement from an aesthetic mode of life to an ethical one is natural or inevitable, one has *no reason* for preferring the latter to the former. To the question "What reason is there for being moral?" Kierkegaard's answer is "None." A choice between fundamentally different life-styles entails a non-rational, arbitrary *leap*.

Solomon sees an important confusion in Kierkegaard's thinking on this subject. An appearance of inconsistency arises in his writings from an ambiguity in the concepts of "reason" which Kierkegaard employs. On the one hand, Kierkegaard claims that we have no reason for choosing the ethical life in preference to the aesthetic (or the religious over the ethical); yet on the other hand, he does say that the movement from one sphere to another is motivated by despair, and he treats the despair created by the aesthetic life as a reason for choosing the ethical life-style. The apparent inconsistency can be resolved, Solomon writes, when we realize that despair does not provide a "reason" in the sense of an objective justification for choosing the one sphere. Despair is a "subjective reason," a consideration which motivates an action without providing objective justification for it, Solomon writes.

In Solomon's view, Kierkegaard's main contribution to existentialism, and his main departure from traditional moral philosophy, lies in this insistence that choices of ultimate values and principles, those which do not gain their importance by being means to the realization of other values and principles, are nonrational and lacking in objective justification.

Gottlieb, Roger S. "A Critique of Kierkegaard's Doctrine of Subjectivity," in *The Philosophical Forum*. IX, no. 4 (Summer, 1978), pp. 475-496.

Søren Kierkegaard's writings have been appreciated for psychological insight and literary quality and not simply for philosophical significance. Indeed, it is sometimes even claimed that Kierkegaard is not a philosopher but a poet, psychologist, or preacher. (It is difficult to locate clearly stated philosophical theses and arguments in his writings.) An unfortunate feature of much that is written about Kierkegaard is that little effort is made to isolate that which is philosophically important in Kierkegaard. Few commentators defend or criticize philosophical views which they see in Kierkegaard: most of them attempt only uncritical exposition or description of his writings.

A valuable feature of Roger S. Gottlieb's article on Kierkegaard is that he does attempt to isolate those ideas that are significant philosophically and to explain and criticize these ideas. One aspect of Kierkegaard's writings which Gottlieb considers philosophically important (especially for ethics and philosophy of religion) is his attack on intellectualism. Kierkegaard objects to theories in ethics or philosophy of history where the actions of men are interpreted as incidental by-products of objective reason, Gottlieb explains. According to Kierkegaard, to view man in this way is to overlook the significance of human freedom and choice. Reason on its own does not produce action. No action occurs until someone chooses to act or to accept some consideration as a reason for acting. A person is free even to reject reason; there is no compulsion to follow reason's recommendations, Kierkegaard writes. Furthermore, there are occasions when reason is unable to provide guidance for action.

In *Either/Or* Kierkegaard stresses that a choice to act morally and the commitment to moral principles is a critical element in being moral. Knowledge of moral principles does not itself guarantee moral action, Gottlieb explains. Being moral requires not merely knowing some principle but choosing to act in accordance with that principle; one can know what is morally right without choosing to do it. Kierkegaard stresses that a choice is present whenever a value is accepted, maintained, or changed, Gottlieb explains.

Although he agrees that Kierkegaard is right to focus on human choice as a mediator between reason and action, Gottlieb criticizes Kierkegaard for being overly antagonistic to reason. In his enthusiasm when attacking deterministic, overintellectualized views of man, Kierkegaard at times treats understanding and choice as independent, mutually exclusive phenomena. Gottlieb responds that choice and reason are compatible and complementary, not mutually exclusive. Although Kierkegaard is right to note that reason does not provide complete, absolute justification for all human action, it does not follow that reason is unable to provide any justification for action. A choice or an act which is not grounded in understanding and reasoning would be blind and absurd, Gottlieb replies.

Gottlieb has further criticism for Kierkegaard's account of ethical life. In *Either/Or* and elsewhere Kierkegaard thinks of acting ethically as acting *for* others rather than acting *with* others, Gottlieb explains. Kierkegaard thinks of the individual as psychologically isolated from other people. He thinks of moral action as arising only through discipline and duty, never through natural inclination. He does not notice that people feel a part of a whole (society), Gottlieb explains, and that often they act morally out of natural inclinations. A genuine concern for the welfare of others is as natural to human beings as is a concern for one's own welfare.

The misrepresentation of ethical life has important consequences in Kierkegaard's thinking, Gottlieb writes. Kierkegaard goes on to claim that ethical life leads to anxiety and guilt and thus is psychologically unsatisfactory. (Only religion can free one from these emotions, Kierkegaard believes.) However, Gottlieb writes, living *with* others and feeling that one is a member of a social group (the possibility of which Kierkegaard overlooks) can provide the desired emotional and moral support.

Dewey, Bradley. "Kierkegaard on Suffering: Promise and Lack of Fulfillment in Life's Stages," in *Humanitas*. IX (1973), pp. 21-46.

In this article Bradley Dewey describes the various modes of life which Søren Kierkegaard portrays and the suffering—the despair, anxiety, and dissatisfaction—which Kierkegaard believes motivates people to put aside one mode of existence in favor of another, "higher" mode. Within his writings Kierkegaard depicts four different modes of life. In *Either/Or* he presents the aesthetic and the ethical. Elsewhere he portrays two kinds of religious life (Religious A and Religious B).

Dewey explains that Kierkegaard intends the fourfold classification to be all-inclusive; that is, he believes that any human action or pursuit will fit into at least one of these four categories. Each life-style is sketched with great refinement and subtlety. The aesthetic life, exemplified in *Either/Or* by Johannes the Seducer (a man dedicated to seducing women), is drawn with sufficient care so that it might represent all people who have immediate pleasure as their goal. The pursuits of wealth, status, comfort, athletic skills, political power, and other ends, Dewey writes, are encompassed within the idea of aesthetic pursuits.

The discussion in *Either/Or* centers around the life-styles of fictional characters. What then is the relationship which Kierkegaard is claiming holds between the characters he has invented and the lives which one lives? Dewey explains that each mode of life has different roles in different people's lives. For some people, the aesthetic mode is dominant. In other people's lives, the ethical or a religious mode dominates; these people have only aesthetic *moments* or *incidents* rather than a life dominated by the aesthetic mode. Most or all people have at least some aesthetic moments and some moments in each of the other modes.

Kierkegaard is not claiming that a person's life at any point is necessarily characterized by only one mode, Dewey explains. Rather, at most times a person's life is a *blend* of some or all of the life-styles. A single act could be motivated by both aesthetic and ethical concerns or by both ethical and religious concerns.

The shift from the aesthetic to the ethical sphere, or from the ethical to a religious sphere, Dewey explains, is motivated by suffering. Johannes the Seducer suffers in his pursuit of the sensuous and erotic. To be successful, the seducer needs to keep a psychological distance between himself and the women he pursues; since he is cut off from genuine companionship, this distance is distressing to him. Connected with his seeking of immediate stimulation is the aesthete's attempt to fight off boredom; the aesthete suffers anxiety as his effort to combat boredom gives rise to a frenzied search for diversions. A distressing satiation-escalation cycle is produced by this pursuit of stimulation, Dewey explains. As the aesthete pursues stimulation he becomes satiated and bored at a given level of stimulus and in consequence needs greater stimulus to satisfy him in the future. Entrapment in this satiation-escalation cycle causes anxiety and despair. Thus, boredom, anxiety, and despair are central features of life in the aesthetic mode.

The ethical life, symbolized in *Either/Or* by marriage and the commitment to another person, produces its own characteristic suffering, Dewey explains. Marriage has disappointments. A person's love for his spouse may fade, and love and kindness then become a burden. The person's sense of security sometimes is jarred by infidelities of his spouse. As a parent one may suffer disappointment from having children who are ungrateful. Failure in an ethical endeavor may bring painful guilt feelings. Thus the comfortable sense of community which an individual seeks from marriage and the ethical life eludes him.—*I.G.*

ADDITIONAL RECOMMENDED READING

Blanshard, Brand. "Kierkegaard on Faith," in *The Personalist*. XLIX, no. 1 (Winter, 1968), pp. 5-23. An excellent philosophical criticism of some central themes in Kierkegaard.

Bolman, Frederick de W. "Kierkegaard in Limbo," in *The Journal of Philosophy*. LXI, no. 25 (December 7, 1944), pp. 711-721. A description of Kierkegaard's insights concerning the interrelationships between beauty, goodness, and self-understanding.

Laird, John. "Either/Or," in *Mind*. LV, no. 218 (April, 1946), pp. 179-181. Laird argues that *Either/Or* has little philosophical merit.

Mackey, Louis. *Kierkegaard: A Kind of Poet*. Philadelphia: University of Pennsylvania Press, 1971. In Chapters 1 and 2 of this exposition of *Either/Or* Mackey maintains that Kierkegaard must be interpreted as a poet as well as a philosopher.

——————. "The Poetry of Inwardness," in *Existential Philosophers: Kierkegaard to Merleau-Ponty*. Edited by George Schrader. New York: McGraw-Hill Book Company, 1967. An interesting discussion of Kierkegaard's writings containing a good account of *Either/Or*.

Swenson, David F. "Kierkegaard's Doctrine of the Three Stages on the Way of Life," in *Something About Kierkegaard*. Minneapolis: Augsburg Publishing House, 1941. An intelligent, illuminating exposition of the aesthetic, ethical, and religious modes of existence in Kierkegaard.

PHILOSOPHICAL FRAGMENTS

Author: Søren Kierkegaard (1813-1855)
Type of work: Existential theology
First published: 1844

PRINCIPAL IDEAS ADVANCED

Men can be separated into three groups, depending on the values they hold: the aesthetes want entertainment, pleasure, and freedom from boredom; ethical men live for the sake of duty, taking on obligations in order to be bound to discharge them; and religious men live in order to obey God.

The Socratic idea of religious truth is that truth in religious matters is not unique, that one learns religious truths by recollection of what one has learned in the realm of Ideas.

The alternative position (the Christian view) is that God in time (Jesus Christ) is the teacher of men, that faith is an organ of knowing, that knowledge comes through the consciousness of sin, and that in a moment of decision a man's life can be changed.

Søren Kierkegaard's *Philosophical Fragments* is the central work in a series of books which are marked by a consistent theme, a most unusual manner of presentation, pervasive irony, and a single-minded effort to present Christianity in a fashion which requires the reader to reach some sort of decision about it. The irony of Kierkegaard is evident even in the title of the book: *Philosophical Fragments.* Very few philosophers would entitle their main work a "fragment," or try to present in less than one hundred pages the core of their position.

In order to read Kierkegaard with some degree of understanding, it is necessary (for most readers, at any rate) to have some knowledge of the general plan of his literary work. One of the essential features of his philosophical position is the doctrine of the "Stages." Kierkegaard believed that men can be separated into three groups, depending on what values they hold as fundamental. He calls these three groups "aesthetes," "ethicists," and "religionists."

The *aesthete* is a person who lives for the interesting; he wants entertainment and variety in his life, and he seeks to avoid boredom as the worst evil that can overtake him. He lives to find immediate satisfactions and he avoids making any long-term commitments. All men have the aesthetic as the basic material of their lives; many remain in the aesthetic stage throughout life. But some men move into another sphere, the ethical.

The *ethicist* lives for the sake of doing his duty; he replaces the interesting versus the boring with the good versus the bad. The kind of man Immanuel Kant had in mind when he urged us to do our duties rather than follow our inclinations is the kind of man Kierkegaard called the ethical man. The ethicist's life is successful if he takes on as many obligations to other men as possible and does his best to discharge these obligations.

Kierkegaard contrasted the ethical man with the aesthete in his first book, *Either/Or* (1843), by posing the question of love and marriage. The aesthete falls in love, lives for a multitude of engagements (but no marriages), wants romance in the Hollywood sense. The ethical man does not fall in love, but rather chooses to love, wants a short engagement so that he may enter the state of being married (and thereby become duty bound to another person for the remainder of his days), and finds his romance in the daily routine rather than in secret, passionate moments.

A great many persons with this kind of ethical concern base the ethical rules which govern their lives in God's will. For such persons, there is no difference between being ethical and being religious. However, Kierkegaard felt that the Christian religion demanded a different orientation from that which characterizes the ethical man. Kierkegaard did not believe that the Christian concept of sin could be explained by saying that to sin is to break an ethical rule. Sin is not violation of rule, but violation of the person of God. Kierkegaard contrasted the ethical man's orientation with the religious man's orientation in his book *Fear and Trembling* (1843), where he considered the problems arising out of Abraham's intended sacrifice of his son, Isaac. As Kierkegaard saw it, Abraham had to choose between the ethical demand to avoid murder and the religious command from God that he sacrifice his son. Kierkegaard raised the question whether it might not be the case that religious commitment sometimes requires a man to suspend his ethical concern. The religious man may at times face the temptation to be good rather than holy.

Such is the doctrine of the stages in Kierkegaard's philosophy. There is one other feature of Kierkegaard's writing that should be pointed out before considering *Philosophical Fragments* in more detail. It is the technique Kierkegaard called "indirect communication." Considerable time might be spent elaborating it, but for the present purpose it will be sufficient to point out that the technique implied that the doctrine of the stages should not be stated directly. The representatives of the various stages should not be described from the point of view of an external observer, but presented "from within," so to speak. To this end, Kierkegaard often adopted pseudonyms in his books. He felt he could best present the aesthetic stage by imagining an aesthete, then writing out what such an aesthetic man would say. *Either/Or*, for example, is an extended correspondence between "a young man" and his older friend, "Judge Wilhelm." Kierkegaard does not directly enter the picture at all, and he offers no judgment between the two views of life presented by the young man and the judge; the reader is left to decide. Kierkegaard was quite successful in this matter, even presenting the imaginary characters with different writing styles. The young man writes beautifully, is poetic, sensitive, and lyrical; the judge writes in a pedestrian style, lecturing as he goes, paying little attention to literary graces.

The pseudonymous author of the *Fragments* is Johannes Climacus—one who is writing about something which is at the climax of the total problem that concerned Kierkegaard throughout his entire literary and philosophical production. Climacus is detached, ironic, and supposedly uncommitted on the immediate problem he is considering; namely, the possibility of giving a different view of religious truth from that presented by Socrates. Socrates is used in the book as a foil, as a man holding a position against which an alternative view can be seen more sharply. Christianity, as Kierkegaard understood it, is the alternative, of course, but, although the reader understands this quite early in the book, the position is not called Christianity until the last paragraph of the book.

The "Socratic" position which Climacus assumes in the book is a rather common interpretation of the Socrates of Plato's dialogues. It may be put briefly as follows: Truth in religious matters does not differ from other kinds of truth. The point of religion is to hold true beliefs about God and to act in accordance with them. Coming to hold true beliefs, in religion as in other areas of human concern, is essentially a matter of recollection, of remembering what a man knew in the realm of the Ideas before birth but forgot when the soul was imprisoned in the body. The teacher, in this case, does not introduce anything new to the learner, but merely serves as midwife, helping the learner to recall what he once knew. After the recollection occurs, the learner adjusts to the true propositions, and the teacher drops out of the knowing relation. The teacher is an occasion, but not a condition, for knowing.

The essential elements in the (Christian) alternative position regarding religious truth are set forth quite openly by Kierkegaard's pseudonym in the "Moral" which he appends to the *Fragments*. The Christian "hypothesis" (as Climacus calls it) differs from the Socratic position, as sketched above, in assuming *faith* as an organ of knowing, in presupposing that there can be in men a *consciousness of sin*, in supposing that there can be a *moment of decision* which changes the course of a man's life, and in assuming a different kind of *teacher* from Socrates—namely, God in time (that is, Jesus Christ). The detachment of Climacus can be seen in the fact that he states these new assumptions so clearly in this "Moral," thus enabling the reader to reject Christianity simply and yet with understanding, if he so desires. Furthermore, Climacus merely states that the hypothesis he has been elaborating differs from Socrates' position in these respects. The question of which hypothesis is true is an entirely different question, he says, and he makes no effort to settle this latter question.

Now if Socrates is right, Climacus argues, the truth is within a man. The teacher merely helps the pupil to realize what he had known all along. In such a case, a man is in the truth rather than in error. In addition, the teacher is not important, since he does not remove the learner from error nor does he introduce him to new truth. Further, the time at which a learner recalls the truth is not important. All in all, the situation is similar to what happened with most, if not all, of us when we learned the basic elements of arithmetic; we can no longer remember who taught them to us or when we were taught. The important thing is that two and two make four, and they always have and always will.

The alternative to this view obviously involves assuming that man is not naturally in the truth but is naturally in error. If this is the case, then the teacher must first give the learner the condition for leaving error and apprehending truth. Then the teacher must provide the truth for the learner to apprehend. The moment at which the learner leaves error and apprehends truth is now quite important and decisive for the learner. And the teacher must be more than an ordinary man, since he is essential to the learner's apprehension of the truth. Indeed, the teacher is so crucial that he is even necessary in order that the learner may recognize that he is in error. Such a teacher, Climacus says, we could appropriately call "Savior."

These elements in Climacus' alternative hypothesis are obviously elements in the traditional Christian account. The fact that one is naturally in error rather than in the truth and also that one does not even recognize such a condition clearly refer to the Christian doctrine of sin, and Climacus does call being in error "sin." The truth that one gains from the teacher is just as obviously the faith that Christians possess. The very unusual teacher who is essential to coming into the truth is, as Climacus calls him, "God in time"; that is, Jesus of Nazareth. And the crucial moment in which a man leaves error for truth is the conversion experience that is the object of so much preaching in the Christian churches. Climacus leaves no doubt that these identifications are appropriate, since he often speaks to the reader about what he has written, citing the original sources of the "hypothesis" he is developing.

In outline, then, the account in the *Fragments* is a very familiar one, differing from the usual Christian account only in the words used to express it and in the reference to the Socratic alternative. There are, however, some implications of Climacus' simple account which are deserving of further treatment. Two matters should be looked into further here: Climacus' account of "the Absolute Paradox," and the question of the "disciple at second hand."

The Absolute Paradox is a discussion of the philosophical significance of the Christian claim that God was incarnate in Jesus of Nazareth. One of the implications of the Socratic view that the truth is somehow within man and needs only to be drawn out by a skillful teacher such as Socrates is that the human mind is adequate for knowing the truth, even religious truth. If, on the contrary, man does not have the truth within himself in some sense, then what a man ought to know or needs to know is beyond man himself—it is the unknown. Or, as Climacus calls it, it is "the other," the absolutely other.

But if it is the absolutely other than man, then man's reason is not competent to know it. Yet man, if he is to achieve the truth, must come to know this absolutely other. To this end, so Christians hold, God—the absolutely other—became incarnate in man; that is to say, the absolutely other became not absolutely other. This requires us to say, then, that the Unknown (God) is both absolutely other and not absolutely other than man. And this statement, clearly, has the form of a self-contradiction.

One of the senses of the word "paradox" is such that a paradox is an apparent contradiction which is seen, on examination, not to be a contradiction. Thus, it is paradoxical to say of a certain member of a group, who is very talkative, that he says less than anyone else in the group. Here, at first glance, it looks as if we are saying that the person both talks a great deal and does not talk a great deal. But the puzzle is resolved quickly when attention is called to the way the words "talk" and "say" are used; namely, although he *talks* a great deal, he *says* very little. Most of his talk is insignificant, it is idle chatter. Such a paradox, then, can be resolved by making some kind of distinction between the apparently incompatible predicates.

In saying that his paradox is "Absolute," however, Climacus seems to be saying that it cannot be resolved. The reason the paradox cannot be resolved lies in the uniqueness of the particular paradox in question. It is essential to Climacus' paradox that the word "absolutely" be included. God both is and is not *absolutely* other than man. If we said of Jones that he is other and not other than Smith, we could go on to specify the similarities and differences between the two men: both are philosophers, but one is interested only in logic, while the other is interested only in ethics. They are alike, yet they differ. But if Jones were said to be *absolutely* other than Smith, then no comparisons could be made at all. When we use the expression "totally different" in ordinary speech, we usually mean to emphasize strongly a difference which is really only partial. We mean that two things differ fundamentally in *some* (but not all) respects. But Climacus is using "absolutely other" in a rather strict way, and this means that even to express the total difference is to go beyond the strict limits of language and understanding. Strictly speaking, we cannot even mention a total difference between two things; the very mention of them indicates at least one respect in which they are not totally different; namely, they are alike in that they can be talked about.

If this is the case, however—that God or the unknown is both totally like and totally unlike man, and yet that we should not even be able to state this—then the paradox Climacus is expressing cannot be resolved. It cannot be resolved because the very language of this paradox, in one sense at least, does not have meaning. The paradox is absolute. Yet we must express ourselves. Or at least Christian men feel that they must express themselves. There is an urge in men, Climacus feels, which drives them to try to express the inexpressible. (Reason, Climacus says, seeks its own downfall.) To come at this point in a somewhat different way, most men can remember trying to express the uniqueness of their beloved in a language which has its power in virtue of expressing the common features, the repeatable elements, the universally instanced qualities of experience. We try to express the unique in terms of the common, and the result is often the paradoxical or the trite. This is why the modern suburbanite's calling his wife "Honey" is at once so full of significance for him, and yet so trite to his neighbors.

If Christianity is true, then its central claim—that God was incarnate in Jesus of Nazareth—leads to a paradox, a paradox which cannot be resolved as paradoxes usually are. But there is also another sense of the word "paradox" which is involved in the discussion in the *Fragments*. Another meaning of the word (its etymological meaning) is "contrary to the received opinion." The Absolute Paradox is paradoxical also in this sense, and this leads to another point Climacus makes in connection with the paradox. Climacus' discussion of the Absolute Paradox is followed by a section in which he claims that man's response to the paradox is to be offended. The religious man, when he has passed through the "moment" and has changed from being in error to being in the truth (to having faith), has his ordinary value commitments upset. Some of Jesus' remarks, at least as they are reported to us in the Christian Scriptures, surely run counter to the prevailing values of everyday life. Common sense— perhaps we have a sample of it in Polonius' advice to his son Laertes in Shakespeare's *Hamlet*: "This above all, to thine own self be true . . ."—surely does not suggest that we turn the other cheek when a man strikes us, nor does it agree that the meek shall inherit the earth. What men usually adopt as a pattern for life is in conflict with the pattern set forth in the Christian Gospels. Men usually want "success" rather than "peace" (in the Christian sense). And so the Christian recommendation, based on its being a revelation from a transcendent God, offends man. Why should one love his neighbor rather than sell to him at a profit? Because God says so. But this recommendation is unreasonable. True enough, but who is to say that God is reasonable? Did not God reveal himself in a most unexpected way? Namely, as the apparently illegitimate son of a poor Nazarene woman, born outside wedlock and in the ancient equivalent of a garage? The Christian account is so contrary to the received opinion of what is of real value that it offends the hearer. Such is Climacus' observation.

Another consequence of the Christian account is that if God revealed himself in Jesus of Nazareth, then it seems he gave special advantages to those men who were contemporary with Jesus and knew Jesus personally, advantages which are denied to the rest of us who are not contemporaries of Jesus. Climacus argues that the immediate followers of Jesus, the "contemporary disciples," enjoyed no advantage over the noncontemporary, the "disciple at second hand." The paradox is the key to Climacus' position here. What the contemporary *saw* was not God, but the man Jesus. It was not apparent or obvious to a normal observer that Jesus is or was more than simply a good man. The divinity which Christians attribute to Jesus was not evident to the senses, but represented an additional characteristic about Jesus which men recognized only in the light of what traditionally has been called the gift of grace from God. Men did not naturally look at Jesus and see his divinity; they beheld only his manhood. Only if God granted grace to the observer, did the observer "see" the divinity of Jesus. Again using the traditional Christian terminology, we can say that even the Apostles could not recognize the divinity of Jesus without having been enlightened by the Holy Spirit. Thus, the contemporary disciple enjoyed no advantage over the disciple at second hand insofar as Jesus' divinity is concerned. The only advantage the contemporary enjoyed concerns Jesus' manhood, his historical existence. Indeed, if there is any advantage, it is the advantage which the disciple at second hand enjoys in having the testimony of several generations that the man Jesus is also God. The reiteration of this claim brings it home as a possibility in a way that the contemporary disciple did not experience.

Such, then, is the position set forth by Kierkegaard, through the pseudonym "Johannes Climacus" in the *Philosophical Fragments*. It is what is at the heart of the (religious) "existentialist" position Kierkegaard gave the name to. The position is elaborated, by the same pseudonym, in a much longer and more involved book, *The Concluding Unscientific Postscript to the Philosophical Fragments* (1846)—which runs to 550 pages as compared with the ninety-three pages of the *Fragments*—but it is the same position nevertheless. It is stated clearly and succinctly in the *Fragments* as a hypothesis; in the *Postscript* an attempt is made to discuss what would happen to a sophisticated person were he to attempt to put into operation in his own life what is discussed merely as a possibility in the *Fragments*. In *The Concluding Unscientific Postscript to the Philosophical Fragments* Climacus concerns himself with the personal question: How do I become a Christian? But the *Postscript* depends upon the *Fragments*, and the *Fragments* is really the central statement of Kierkegaard's position. Rarely does one find such an important question as the philosophical account of Christianity stated with the precision, clarity, and wit which Kierkegaard exhibits in the *Fragments*. Kierkegaard was possessed of a keen intellect, a logical passion, and an ability to give expression to one of the most significant alternatives in Western Civilization in a manner that retains the kernel of Christianity yet makes possible its discussion in the modern milieu. To have done this is a philosophical and literary achievement of the first order.—*R.E.L.*

PERTINENT LITERATURE

Thomas, John Heywood. *Subjectivity and Paradox*. Oxford: Basil Blackwell, 1957.

John Heywood Thomas' *Subjectivity and Paradox* affords a lucid, elegant profile of Søren Kierkegaard's contribution to the philosophy of religion, and is a convincing reply to those scholars who would sharply distinguish between the religious character and the intellectual expression of his thought. The book is also a polemic against those who would contend that religious assertions lack cognitive significance and are reducible merely to statements of inner feeling. Thomas uniquely demonstrates how Kierkegaard by his efforts to communicate to his age about Christian faith and discipleship shows in a concrete way the possibility for meaningful religious discourse. Through a careful examination of two themes—subjectivity and paradox—central to the *Fragments* and to Kierkegaard's work as a whole, Thomas advances a coherent and insightful interpretation of Kierkegaard's view of religious faith and what it means to become a Christian. Documentation is solid and opposing accounts are duly considered.

In an early chapter Thomas supports the view that Kierkegaard's work developed as a powerful criticism of Georg Wilhelm Friedrich Hegel's philosophy of religion. Whereas Hegel's God is totally impersonal, being equated with Absolute Reality or Absolute Spirit, Kierkegaard's God of Christianity is infinitely personal and capable of being appropriated only through an act of intense personal commitment. Hegel acknowledged the Christian doctrine of Incarnation, but for him this meant that God is incarnate in all men and indeed in everything finite, since the world of finitude is nothing other than one moment in the dialectical development of God's nature. For Hegel, Jesus Christ is God incarnate for the simple reason that all men are so; but other than as bearing witness to a metaphysical truth—the unity of God and man—Hegel gave little religious value to the history of Jesus. In dramatic contrast, one of the crucial theses in Kierkegaard's *Fragments* is that for Christianity the Incarnation stands as a unique, momentous, decisive event in history: a necessary condition through which alone it is possible for a person to achieve an intimate relationship with God. Finally, according to Hegel, faith is a form of knowledge; it is spirit knowing spirit, a symbolic type of knowledge which constitutes the first stage on man's road to Ultimate Reality, where the final stage is the appropriation of Absolute Spirit by Reason. It is against precisely this view that Kierkegaard posits his definition of faith as "an objective uncertainty held fast in an appropriation-process of the most passionate inwardness."

The fundamental concern in the *Fragments* is the meaning of Christian faith, although the overt discussion deals with the nature of truth and how far the truth admits of being learned. Thomas acutely perceives that for Kierkegaard the crucial question is not what is truth, but rather what is the individual's proper relation to the truth *qua* Christianity. Kierkegaard brilliantly illustrates that for Christianity truth is not something which can be acquired in the manner of learning information. A truth relationship can never be objective, detached, abstract, or impersonal; rather, from the viewpoint of Christianity truth requires of the person a subjective appropriation, and intense concern—which is nothing other than faith itself. Thomas is therefore able to justify his contention that the principle of subjectivity is rudimentary to unlocking Kierkegaard's concept of faith.

Because for Kierkegaard the very notion of subjectivity implies passion, commitment, and risk, it readily follows that in his view the object of faith by definition must be something uncertain. In an interesting manner Thomas delineates two types of assertions that Kierkegaard makes when describing the object of Christian faith as an objective uncertainty. One type of assertion is that the object of faith is necessarily incapable of being logically demonstrated or objectively known by any sure means. This seems to be what he implies when he speaks of the person's "faith in God." since presumably the existence of God is an objective uncertainty. But in his discussion of the Absolute Paradox he gives every indication of implying that the object of faith is indeed a logical impossibility. Thus in the *Fragments* he proclaims that faith's object is an "offense" to reason; the object of faith is posited not merely as an inherent uncertainty but as an outright absurdity, at least from any objective point of view. Thomas sensibly suggests that Kierkegaard is using this latter description to characterize uniquely the Christian's "faith in Christ," given the fact that to a nonbeliever the Incarnation and the possibility of an eternal being existing in time pose an enigma, a rational incoherence. Interpreting Kierkegaard in this way helps clarify what otherwise might foster perplexities in trying to decipher his discussion of faith, particularly within the context of the *Fragments* and the *Concluding Unscientific Postscript.*

Christian faith means subjectivity for Kierkegaard; but more than that it signifies paradox. Critics have disagreed widely as to what Kierkegaard intended by designating Christianity as a religion of paradox. Thomas gives an account which is at once revealing and provocative by interconnecting paradox, faith, and subjectivity to create a vision of what for Kierkegaard it means to become a Christian. Two uses of the term "paradox" are distinguished. The first points to a paradox proper or, in other words, an apparent contradiction which actually can be resolved upon closer scrutiny. Broadly speaking, the paradoxical nature of faith is manifest by the person's complete and decisive affirmation of faith's object in spite of the fact that the object exists as an objective uncertainty. Uncertainty, then, is an essential condition of faith. Yet in the *Fragments* Kierkegaard makes it quite clear that the subjective appropriation of the truth bears an inner certainty derived from passion although such certainty is very different from that of logic or mathematics, or even science. Viewed in this way, faith appears to involve a paradox by being simultaneously an instance of certainty (inner certitude) and of uncertainty (lack of knowledge). This "paradox" is resolved, obviously, by characterizing faith first by its subjective quality, then by its objective quality.

Kierkegaard employs the notion of paradox more narrowly in a second sense to describe uniquely the faith of Christianity. It is in this sense that he often speaks of Christian faith as faith in the "Absolute Paradox." Here, Thomas argues, Kierkegaard intends a type of paradox which rationally cannot be removed, dissolved, or surmounted. In Christianity Jesus Christ *is* the Absolute Paradox: he is an existing being who at one and the same time is entirely God and entirely man, who is wholly eternal yet wholly temporal. From the point of view of reason the Incarnation is an absurdity, a logical impossibility—yet through faith it acquires the highest degree of certitude for the believer. Kierkegaard is able to conclude that while all faith involves paradox in the broadest sense, Christian faith alone has as its object the Absolute Paradox.

In concluding his discussion of paradox Thomas points out that even though the Absolute Paradox objectively is a blatant contradiction, it is not without meaning for the believer. By virtue of subjectivity, in the "leap" of faith, what before appeared as an absurdity now is grasped with the fullest understanding; what before appeared as an impossibility now is an utmost necessity; and what before appeared as the grossest error ever thought now is appropriated as the highest truth to which a person can attain. In Kierkegaard's thinking, all of this is part of what it means to become a Christian.

Stack, George J. *On Kierkegaard: Philosophical Fragments.* Atlantic Highlands, New Jersey: Humanities Press, 1976.

Contrary to what the title might imply, George J. Stack's book is not a commentary on Søren Kierkegaard's *Fragments*. In a series of six exploratory essays the author sympathetically and imaginatively discusses certain fundamental recurring philosophical themes which he finds interwoven throughout Kierkegaard's works. Emphasis is explicitly given to the philosophical as opposed to the theological dimensions of Kierkegaard's thought. Stack succeeds in his attempt to illuminate the central core of what might be regarded as Kierkegaard's philosophical anthropology. This fresh, revealing study offers a discerning analysis of basic "existential categories" (possibility, necessity, actuality, irony, concern, repetition, and others) which Kierkegaard incorporates in his description of what is man. The book justifies its assumption that Kierkegaard in his pseudonymous works was trying to create a philosophical foundation for prescribing how it is possible for a person to achieve authentic self-realization.

Deserving of serious critical consideration is Stack's suggestive thesis that Kierkegaard's philosophy be interpreted as a response to nihilism. The basic claim is that Kierkegaard's phenomenology of the "stages on life's way" is the product of his constant struggle—both intellectual and personal—with the problem of nihilism. It was Kierkegaard (and not Friedrich Nietzsche) who first recognized the threat of nihilism and existential meaninglessness as an underlying malaise in the world of his time. And it was in Christianity that Kierkegaard saw a genuine possibility for overcoming nihilism, for the passionate resolve and type of ethical-religious commitment necessary to generate and intensify meaningfulness in human existence. Stack advances the same line of thought in a more recent publication, *Kierkegaard's Existential Ethics*, University of Alabama Press, 1977.

Stack's point of departure is *The Concept of Irony*, which he perceives as an initial expression of Kierkegaard's confrontation with nihilism. It is common knowledge that Socrates—dialectician and ironist supreme—represents for Kierkegaard the existential thinker *par excellence*. The key notion in Kierkegaard's interpretation of Socrates is that of irony. In Socrates irony is more than a rhetorical device to show up the ignorance of other people. Rather, it is a mode of being, a perspective which has to be lived through to be fully understood. The ironic standpoint becomes ultimately one of negation, in that it seeks to annul all unexamined assumptions, undermine all certainties, and corrode the secure belief that human reason is the way to Truth. It is in this respect that Kierkegaard views Socratic irony as being essentially nihilistic. The person who has taken up irony into his own existence encounters nihilism head on: a dissolution of all absolutes, a loss of universally accepted values, a psychological sense of the meaninglessness of existence, and a pervasive skepticism about all things. This is not the end of the matter for Kierkegaard, but the beginning.

Kierkegaard realizes that the positive function of irony is to turn the individual back upon himself, to transform the abstract into the personal, and to engender self-consciousness, self-discovery, and the permanent possibility for self-realization. The dominant modality of ironic thought and existence is *possibility*. On the one hand, irony is profoundy nihilistic, seeming to preclude a personal commitment to anything: in the absence of objective certitude and in the midst of infinite negativity and nothingness, what is left for man to embrace? On the other hand, by transposing human existence into the realm of the infinitely possible, irony paves the way for transcending nihilism through a radical affirmation of an objective uncertainty which harbors, nevertheless, meaningfulness in the highest degree. By "nihilating" the actuality of objective truth, the dialectic of irony paradoxically reveals the possibility for subjective truth. The goal of Socrates was not to uncover absolute or metaphysical truths, but to arouse in the person the need for resolution, self-discovery, and a personal truth which can be taken up into one's life to give meaning to one's existence. Irony for Socrates is part of that dialectical process of self-realization. Stack is quick to point out that this is echoed in Kierkegaard's ethics of subjectivity. Thus one sees in Kierkegaard an intimate relationship among irony, possibility, and authentic existence.

As a mode of being, nihilism is not something which can be overcome by thought or reason. What is required is a transformation of the self, a resolute choice of one's own existence or, as Kierkegaard would be most apt to say, a subjective inwardness that holds fast to a truth for which one can live and die. The significance of the negativistic standpoint is that it brings the individual to the brink of despair, hopelessness, and indifference; but in so doing it points the way to meaningfulness and value—that is, subjectivity, commitment, and a passionate striving to become the self one has the potentiality to be.

In the remaining sections of his book Stack discusses Kierkegaard's concept of the aesthetic; then he traces the influence of Aristotle upon Kierkegaard's conception of the ethical; and finally he explicates the concept of existential possibility as the basis for both authentic ethical existence and the "dialectical movements" of religious faith. Still, his most noteworthy contribution is his thesis that Kierkegaard's existential "philosophy of subjectivity" is the result of his confrontation with nihilism and his ensuing quest for meaning.—*R.A.S.*

ADDITIONAL RECOMMENDED READING

Collins, James. *The Mind of Kierkegaard*. Chicago: Henry Regnery Company, 1953. Widely recognized as a superb and reliable commentary on the central themes in Kierkegaard's work, Collins' study remains one of the best available general introductions to Kierkegaard's philosophy. The author establishes a basis for critical evaluation by positioning Kierkegaard's views against the historical, intellectual, and moral background of the Western tradition.

Lowrie, Walter. *Kierkegaard*. New York: Oxford University Press, 1938. A monumental biographical and interpretative work by the translator who has done more than anyone else to make Kierkegaard known to the English reader. This exceedingly thorough, highly detailed study is indispensable as a guide to Kierkegaard's life and thought.

_____ . *A Short Life of Kierkegaard*. Princeton, New Jersey: Princeton University Press, 1942. A compact and lucid portrait of Kierkegaard's psychological and spiritual development which provides penetrating insights into the nature of his writings. In Lowrie's words, this short biography is "not merely an abstract or condensation" of the earlier *Kierkegaard*, but a fresh approach to the events which influenced Kierkegaard's thinking.

Swenson, David F. *Something About Kierkegaard*. Edited by Lillian Marvin Swenson. Minneapolis: Augsburg Publishing House, 1945. As a pioneer Kierkegaard translator and scholar, David Swenson's contribution to the understanding and appreciation of Kierkegaard's significance is immeasurable. The present collection of essays is especially valuable for its explanation of Kierkegaard's existential dialectic and the thought-provoking exposition of Kierkegaard's doctrine of the three stages on the way of life.

Taylor, Mark C. *Kierkegaard's Pseudonymous Authorship: A Study of Time and the Self.* Princeton, New Jersey: Princeton University Press, 1975. A scholarly, carefully wrought treatise which persuasively argues that Kierkegaard's pseudonymous works form a coherent whole. The unifying theme as perceived by Taylor is the temporality of the self as it is revealed in the different stages of existence. Taylor's aim is to show that by entering into the dialogue created by Kierkegaard's pseudonyms it is possible to achieve a meaningful clarification of time and the self, with the ultimate result that the reader will be led to a deeper understanding of himself as an existing individual.

Thompson, Josiah, ed. *Kierkegaard: A Collection of Critical Essays.* Garden City, New York: Doubleday & Company, 1972. This is a well-rounded collection of interpretative papers on Kierkegaard's philosophy of religion, including discussions of such topics as indirect communication, the meaning of subjectivity, the concept of irony, and Kierkegaard's existential ethics.

CONCLUDING UNSCIENTIFIC POSTSCRIPT

Author: Søren Kierkegaard (1813-1855)
Type of work: Existential theology
First published: 1846

PRINCIPAL IDEAS ADVANCED

The subjective thinker is an engaged thinker, one who by his activity commits himself to an understanding of the truth which, by the manner of his existence, he is; he seeks to comprehend himself, not as an abstraction, but as an ethically engaged, existing subject.

Only individuals matter; existence is individual in character.

An existent individual is one in the process of becoming; he moves into an uncertain future.

Since death is imminent every choice has infinite worth, and every moment is a unique occasion for decisive action; each individual achieves his being through decision.

In his development the thinker may pass through the aesthetical stage (in which he experiments but does not commit himself), the ethical stage (in which he acts decisively and commits himself), to the religious stage (in which his sin is acknowledged and he commits himself to God).

Kierkegaard has been called the "Danish Socrates." The *Concluding Unscientific Postscript to the Philosophical Fragments*, which is the central point of his whole authorship, bears out Kierkegaard's legitimate claim to this title. In the *Postscript* Socrates is acknowledged as the illustrious Greek who never lost sight of the fact that a thinker remains an existing individual. The Socratic maieutic method, with its use of ignorance, irony, and dialectics, pervades the whole work. The Athenian gadfly reappears in these pages in a modern counterpart.

The Socratic method is used by Johannes Climacus (Kierkegaard's pseudonym) to elicit from the reader an awareness that truth is subjectivity. The doctrine of "the subjective thinker" stands at the center of this classic, and it provides the pivot point around which all the themes revolve. The subjective thinker is the *engaged* or *involved* thinker whose thought, directed toward a penetration of his inner consciousness, moves in passion and earnestness. He finds in the theoretical detachment of objective reflection a comic neglect of the existing individual who does the reflecting. Objective reflection tends to make the subject accidental and transforms his existence into something indifferent and abstract. The accent for the subjective thinker falls on the *how*; the accent for objective reflection falls on the *what*. Objective truth designates a "what" or an objective content that can be observed in theoretical detachment. Subjective truth is a "how" that must be inwardly appropriated. Truth as subjectivity thus becomes inward appropriation. Truth, subjectively appropriated, is a truth which is *true for me*. It is a truth which I *live*, not merely observe. It is a truth which I *am*, not merely possess. Truth is a mode of action or a manner of existence. The subjective thinker lives the truth; he *exists it*.

One need not proceed far into the pages of the *Postscript* to become aware that Kierkegaard's arch enemy, against whom his Socratic, ironical barbs are directed, is Hegel. Johannes Climacus finds in the systematized, objective and theoretical reflection of Hegel's philosophy a fantastic distortion of truth and an ingenious system of irrelevancy. Climacus never tires of harpooning the System. The Hegelian, in neglecting the crucial distinction between thought and reality, erects a system of thought which comically excludes his own existence. He seeks to comprehend himself as an expression of abstract, universal, and timeless categories; thus he loses himself as a concrete, particular, and temporal existent. "One must therefore be very careful in dealing with a philosopher of the Hegelian school, and, above all, to make certain of the identity of the being with whom one has the honor to discourse. Is he a human being, an existing human being? Is he himself *sub specie aeterni*, even when he sleeps, eats, blows his nose, or whatever else a human being does? Is he himself the pure 'I am I?' . . . Does he in fact exist?" The Hegelian affords an instance of philosophical comedy in which we have thought without a thinker. He erects a marvelous intellectual palace in which he himself does not live. The subject, in Hegel's objective reflection, becomes accidental, and truth as subjectivity is lost.

Descartes shares Hegel's fate of falling under the Kierkegaardian irony and devastating intellectual harpooning. It was Descartes who provided modern philosophy with the *cogito, ergo sum* for its foundation. Now either the "I" which is the subject of the *cogito* refers to a particular existing human being, in which case nothing is proved (If I *am* thinking, what wonder that I *am*!) or else the "I" refers to a universal pure ego. But such an entity has only a conceptual existence, and the *ergo* loses its meaning, the proposition being reduced to a tautology. The attempt by Descartes to prove his existence by the fact that he thinks leads to no real conclusion, for insofar as he thinks he has already abstracted from his own existence. Descartes had already prepared the stage for the later Hegel's identification of abstract thought and reality. Contra Descartes, Climacus is ready to defend the claim that the real subject is not the cognitive subject, but rather the ethically engaged, existing subject. In both Descartes and Hegel he finds that cognition and reason have been viciously abstracted from the concrete particularity of existence.

The subjective thinker emphatically rejects the rationalists' reification of reason, but he in no way denies the validity of thought so long as it is existentially rooted. The subjective thinker is indeed a thinker who makes use of thought in seeking to penetrate the structures of his subjectivity and so to understand himself in his existence. The nobility of the Greek thinker (particularly Socrates) is that he was able to do this. He existed in advance of speculation and the System. The subjective thinker is at the same time a thinker and an existing human being. This is a truth, says Climacus, a statement which, deserving emphasis, cannot too often be repeated, and the neglect of which has brought about much confusion. Kierkegaard was by no means an opponent of thought. He insisted only that thought be placed back into existence, following its vicious abstraction by Hegel. "If thought speaks deprecatingly of the imagination, imagination in its turn speaks deprecatingly of thought; and likewise with feeling. The task is not to exalt the one at the expense of the other, but to give them an equal status, to unify them in simultaneity; the medium in which they are unified is *existence*."

When the subjective thinker thus makes the movement of understanding himself in his existence, he discovers that in the order of reality (as distinct from the order of abstract thought) individuals—and individuals alone—exist. Existence is indelibly individual in character. Kierkegaard's philosophy is a crusade for the reality of the concrete individual. "The individual" (*Enkelte*) was Kierkegaard's central category. It is in this category that he saw bound up any importance that he as a subjective thinker might have. This category was so decisive for his whole literary effort that he asked that it be inscribed on his tombstone (and it was). The human self is not humanity in general. Humanity does not exist; only individual human beings exist. Existential reality resides not in the genus or in the species but in the concrete individual. Universals, like crowds, are abstractions which have neither hands nor feet.

To exist means to be an individual, but to exist also means to be in the process of becoming. "An existing individual is constantly in process of becoming; the actual existing subjective thinker constantly reproduces this existential situation in his thoughts, and translates all his thinking into terms of process." Although Hegel in his *Logic* had much to say about processes in which opposites are combined into higher unities, his doctrine of becoming is ultimately illusory because it does not understand process from the point of view of concrete existence. Logic and pure thought can never capture the existential reality of becoming, for logical entities are *states of being* which are timeless and fixed. In the moment that Hegel wrote his *Logic*, with the intention of encompassing the whole of reality, he forfeited the concrete becoming in which the subjective thinker finds himself disclosed. But this intractable reality of concrete becoming remains as a source of profound embarrassment for the Hegelian—particularly when he is ready to write the last paragraph of his system and finds that existence is not yet finished! Kierkegaardian irony reaches its height when Climacus undertakes to satirize the System. "I shall be as willing as the next man to fall down in worship before the System, if only I can manage to set eyes on it. Hitherto I have had no success; and though I have young legs, I am almost weary from running back and forth between Herod and Pilate. Once or twice I have been on the verge of bending the knee. But at the last moment, when I already had my handkerchief spread on the ground, to avoid soiling my trousers, and I made a trusting appeal to one of the initiated who stood by: 'Tell me now sincerely, is it entirely finished; for if so I will kneel down before it, even at the risk of ruining a pair of trousers (for on account of the heavy traffic to and fro, the road has become quite muddy),'—I always received the same answer: 'No, it is not yet quite finished.' And so there was another postponement—of the System, and of my homage." System and finality are correlative concepts. But existence, which is constantly in the process of becoming, is never finished. Thus, an existential system is impossible. Reality itself is a system— but a system only for God. There can be no system for an existing individual who always stands in the throes of becoming.

As existence involves individuality and becoming, so assuredly does it involve the future. One exists in a process of becoming by facing a future. The subjective thinker is passionately and earnestly interested in the time of immediate experience as it qualifies his existence. Time for the existing subject is not a time in general—an abstract, cosmic time which is spatialized through objectivizing categories. His interest has to do with the time of his inner experience—time as it is concretely lived rather than abstractly known. In the subjective thinker's immediate experience of time, the future has priority. His life is lived primarily out of the future, for in his subjectivity he understands himself as moving into a future. This future generates uncertainty and anxiety. Tomorrow may rob me of all my earthly goods and leave me desolate. The subjective thinker, when he penetrates to the core of his subjectivity, thus finds the uncertainty of life itself. Wherever there is subjectivity, there is uncertainty.

Death is one of the most ethically significant uncertainties of life. Subjective thought discloses death as an imminent possibility. But for the most part man devises means of concealing this imminent possibility. He approaches the fact of death through the eyes of objective reflection and thus conveniently transforms it into something in general. Viewed *objectively*, death is a general and universal occurrence which befalls all forms of life. Viewed subjectively, death is an imminent uncertainty which pertains to my particular existence and which makes a difference for my individual decisions. Death is thus apprehended not as a generalized empirical factuality, but as a task or a deed. "If the task of life is to become subjective, then the thought of death is not, for the individual subject, something in general, but is verily a deed." Death, subjectively understood, becomes a task in that it is defined in terms of its ethical expression. It is experienced and appropriated in an anticipatory conception in such a way that it transforms the whole of man's life. When death is existentially appropriated, then every decision receives a singular importance. If death is imminent every choice has infinite worth, and every moment is a unique occasion for decisive action. Death makes a difference for life.

In the subjective movements of his engaged existence the subjective thinker discloses his existence as qualified by individuality, becoming, time, and death. Already in these movements the pathway is opened for decisive action. The category of decision becomes a centralizing concept for the subjective thinker. In facing a future the existing subject is called to decision. Thus the subjective thinker is at the same time an ethical thinker. He understands his personal existence as a task and a responsibility. He must choose in order to attain his authentic selfhood. His essential humanity is not given. It is achieved through decision. The greatness of man is that he has an *either/or*. This either/or becomes a matter of indifference for the Hegelian. In Hegel's timeless categories there is no place for decisive action or ethical commitment. "Ethics has been crowded out of the System, and as a substitute for it there has been included a something which confuses the historical with the individual, the bewildering and noisy demands of the age with the eternal demand that conscience makes upon the individual. Ethics concentrates upon the individual, and ethically it is the task of every individual to become an entire man; just as it is the ethical presupposition that every man is born in such a condition that he can become one." The objective reflection which is so peculiar to the System transforms everyone into an observer. But existing individuals are actors as well as observers. They make choices which affect the whole of their lives. They are engaged in action which is decisive for themselves as well as for others. The ethically existing subject is thus of utmost importance; but for the Hegelian, who is concerned with the general developments of world history and the meditation of opposites in this world history, the ethical subject remains unacknowledged.

Kierkegaard regarded the existentially decisive act for the ethically engaged subject as not an external action but rather as an internal decision. It is inward passion rather than external consequences which constitutes the criterion of ethical action. The person who does not own a penny can be as charitable as the person who gives away a kingdom. Let us suppose, says Climacus, that the Levite, who found the man that had fallen among thieves between Jericho and Jerusalem, was inwardly concerned to help sufferers in distress. Let us suppose further that when he met the victim he was frightened at the possibility of robbers nearby and hastened on lest he also become a victim. He failed to act, giving no help to the sufferer. But after having left the victim he was overcome by remorse, and hurried back to the scene, but arrived too late. The Samaritan had already helped the victim in his distress. If this were the sequence of events would one not have to say that the Levite acted? Indeed he acted, says Climacus, and in an inwardly decisive sense, even though his action had no external expression.

Much time is devoted in the *Postscript* to a delineation of the "stages" or "existence spheres"—a delineation which Kierkegaard had already undertaken in two of his earlier works, *Either/Or* (1843) and *Stages on Life's Way* (1845). However, for the first time in his writings we have an analysis and description of irony and humor as transitional stages between the aesthetical and the ethical, and the ethical and the religious, respectively. The aesthetical stage is the stage of experimentation. The aestheticist is one who experiments with various possibilities but never commits himself in passionate choice. He experiments with love but never commits himself in marriage. He experiments with thought but never commits himself in action. A constant flight from the responsibility of decision characterizes the aestheticist. Thus he lacks the decisive content of subjectivity—inwardness, earnestness, and passion. It is only in the ethical stage that these decisive determinants appear. The transition to the ethical stage is by way of irony. Climacus speaks of irony as the "boundary zone" between the aesthetical and the ethical. The purpose of irony is to rouse man from his unauthentic aesthetical floundering to an ethical consciousness. Irony elicits the discrepancy between the inward and outward, as this discrepancy is expressed in the life of man. Irony makes man aware of the discrepancy between his inward lack of wisdom and his outward claim of its possession. It makes man aware that his outward profession of virtue betrays an inward lack of it. Irony constitutes the first awareness of the ethical, seeks to bring these suppressed discrepancies to light, and thus drives beyond itself to the next stage.

The ethical stage is the sphere of decisive action and self-commitment. The ethical man has resolutely chosen himself and exists in passion and in inwardness. The personality of the aestheticist is dispersed because of his floundering in possibilities. The personality of the ethical man is unified or centralized because he has been able to commit himself in definite modes of action. But the ground of this unification and the ultimate source of this commitment is not disclosed until the self apprehends itself in the movements of the religious sphere. Although in tension, the ethical and the religious are so close, says Climacus, that they are in constant communication with one another. It is for this reason that the two stages are often hyphenated and designated as the ethico religious sphere. The "boundary zone" between the ethical and the religious is humor. The ethical thinker drives beyond the ethical to the religious through the expression of humor, in which there is a protest against the externalization of ethical norms and standards. The humorist is aware of this externalization, which tends to become identified with the religious, contests it as the proper measure, but still is unable to establish a God relationship in terms of religious passion *stricte sic dictus*. (Kierkegaard's provocative book, *Fear and Trembling*, 1843, incomparably expresses this suspension of an externalized ethics through the movement of faith, exemplified by Abraham in the intended sacrifice of his son Isaac.) Only when the existing subject has apprehended his relationship to God as a relationship qualified by inwardness and passion does he proceed to the religious stage.

The new determinant which is introduced in the religious stage is the determinant of suffering. Suffering is the highest intensification of subjectivity. In it we see the fullest expression of inwardness. The suffering which is acknowledged in this stage, however, must not be confused with the poetic representations of suffering peculiar to the aesthetical stage, nor with the reflection *about* suffering which is always qualitatively different from the fact of suffering, nor with suffering as a simple outward ethical manifestation. Religious suffering is an expression of an inward God-relationship, like that of Job, which remains opaque to the aesthetical and ethical consciousness.

The religious stage is internally differentiated by two levels of existence—religiousness A and religiousness B. Religiousness A is the religion of immanence. Religiousness B is the "paradoxical religiousness," that in which the qualitative distinction between God and man is disclosed, and God's presence in time is revealed in the paradox of Christ. The distinction between A and B also expresses the corresponding distinction between guilt-consciousness and sin-consciousness. Guilt, properly understood, is a determinant of religiousness A; sin is a determinant of religiousness B. Guilt is a disrelationship of the subject with himself. It points to an internal fissure within consciousness which results because of an alienation from his absolute *telos*. It is still a movement within immanence. In religiousness B guilt becomes sin. The disrelationship of the subject with himself is now apprehended as a disrelationship with God. The existing subject can acquire a guilt-consciousness through the purely human movement of dialectics in which he understands himself as alienated from himself in the process of becoming. But sin-consciousness requires a disclosure by God so as to reveal to man that his guilt is at one and the same time an implication of sin. The pagan can have no consciousness of sin. Sin-consciousness emerges only in the subject's awareness of himself as existing in a disrelationship with God. This God is a God who has entered time and history. It is thus that religiousness B finds its supreme expression in Christianity, with its teachings of the "Absolute Paradox" or "Deity in time." As the "paradoxical religiousness," religiousness B affirms a qualitative distinction between God and man. God is wholly and utterly transcendent to the temporal order. Thus, religiousness B breaks with religiousness A. There is no natural kinship between the eternal and the temporal. And so the advent of eternity in time is disclosed as a paradox. Christ is the absolute paradox who reveals God in time, makes man aware of his sin, and calls him to faith and decisive commitment through which sin is overcome.

In his analysis and description of the religious stage as the crown and culmination of the three stages (which must be understood not in terms of temporal sequences of successive development, but rather in terms of copresent qualifications of subjectivity), the author makes his central intention quite apparent. The leading question which concerns Climacus is already put to the reader in the introduction. "The subjective problem concerns the relationship of the individual to Christianity. To put it quite simply: How may I, Johannes Climacus, participate in the happiness promised by Christianity?" It is significant that in the appendix, "For an understanding with the reader," the question is reiterated: "Now I ask how I am to become a Christian." This is indeed Kierkegaard's central question, posed not only in the *Postscript*, but in all of his other writings. Explaining his own perspective as an author, Kierkegaard informs his readers in his book *The Point of View* (1849) that underlying the whole of his literary work is the central concern of how to become a Christian—a task which is extremely difficult in Christendom. —*C.O.S.*

PERTINENT LITERATURE

Johnson, Ralph Henry. *The Concept of Existence in the Concluding Unscientific Postscript*. The Hague, The Netherlands: Martinus Nijhoff, 1972.

Ralph Henry Johnson's interpretation of the *Concluding Unscientific Postscript*, while at times going against the grain of traditional Kierkegaardian scholarship, is intelligible, illuminating, and well-defended. In the main he accomplishes his stated goal, which is to clarify the concept of existence as presented in the *Postscript*.

The title page of the *Postscript* lists the author as "Johannes Climacus," one of Søren Kierkegaard's pseudonyms. Much has been written concerning his use of pseudonyms. Kierkegaard himself discusses the subject in *The Point of View for My Work as an Author*, wherein he cautions readers not to equate the views of his pseudonyms with his own. On this point Johnson takes Kierkegaard quite literally. Whereas most modern critics suppose that in the *Postscript* Kierkegaard actually is speaking for himself, Johnson argues that the separation between Climacus and Kierkegaard should be kept strict and rigid. This becomes the starting point for Johnson's examination of the concept of existence in the *Postscript*—Climacus' concept, he admonishes, but not necessarily Kierkegaard's.

The central, yet often overlooked, theme of the *Postscript*, according to Johnson, is that men have forgotten what it means to *exist*. In this context the term "exist" is not intended in the loose sense of mere presence or being in the world, but rather in a higher, more strict sense that requires elucidation. The significance of the *Postscript*, on Johnson's interpretation, is Climacus' illustration of the "forgetting-claim" through examples from science, philosophy, and religion, with the result being an indirect communication of what individual human existence means in the strictest sense of the term.

Climacus' analysis of human existence is seen by Johnson as a polemic against the type of abstract, systematic, objective thinking exhibited in speculative philosophy and modern science where the individual becomes lost and forgotten. Men need to be reminded, notes Climacus, that to exist as a human being is to exist as an individual. In a chapter which deviates from the content of the *Postscript* but which is interesting nevertheless, Johnson imaginatively considers the differences between science (or the scientific community as an entity) and the individual. His purpose is to show that the more a person gets caught up in scientific thinking, the greater tendency there is to forget that one is a finite and temporal being who must face up to the prospect of death, who is limited in knowledge and understanding (particularly self-understanding), and who exists as more than a cognitive organism. What must not be forgotten is that beyond thinking and knowing, man is fundamentally an emotive and ethical being.

At the heart of Climacus' position is the claim that men have forgotten how to think subjectively. Indeed, in the strictest sense, to exist as a human being is to think subjectively, as opposed to objectively. This is what is meant by the proclamation that truth is subjectivity. Whereas objective thought is externalized, directed away from the thinker's own existence toward something else, subjective thought is characterized by reflective inwardness. In objective thought the relationship between subject and object is one of indifference; but in subjective thought there is an intense, active concern in which the very being of the subject is at stake. The objective thinker is essentially defined by his status as a knowing subject, while the subjective thinker is an ethically existing subject.

In philosophy there is a long history which has it that the kind of thinking that is essential for a truly human existence is abstract thinking; but because not all men are endowed by nature with the ability to think abstractly (or can develop it), it would follow in that view that not all men are capable of achieving a truly human existence. As for Climacus, the kind of thinking that is essential for a truly human existence is subjective thinking, and because all men have the ability to think subjectively, the implication is that every person is, in principle, capable of fully existing as a human being in the strictest sense of the term.

Shmuëli, Adi. *Kierkegaard and Consciousness*. Translated by Naomi Handelman. Princeton, New Jersey: Princeton University Press, 1971.

This intriguing study develops an unconventional but extremely suggestive interpretation of Søren Kierkegaard's thought. Adi Shmuëli views Kierkegaard's philosophy primarily as a theory of human consciousness. The book begins with an examination of the aesthetic, ethical, and religious modes of consciousness, then turns to the problem of alienation, and culminates with a characterization of Christian consciousness as it is actualized through faith, love, and intersubjectivity.

Aesthetic consciousness, which is the lowest level, is defined in terms of immediacy, the here and now. It arises with the momentary awareness of given phenomena, sensations, emotions, volitions, or thoughts. At this stage there is no reflection or self-awareness; the individual is "invisibly present" but "not yet discovered." Thus Kierkegaard depicts the aesthetic life as an unconnected succession of ephemeral experiences, each passing away as quickly as it comes. For the aesthete, the only time is the present, the only truth is the moment, and the only reality is today.

The mark of ethical consciousness is reflection, whence comes self-awareness. Whereas aesthetic consciousness is more a passive apprehension or contemplation, reflective consciousness realizes itself through action. In ethical consciousness there is a positing of ideals and a choosing of a way of life. The future rather than the present takes on the greatest significance for the individual; the ultimate concern shifts from what *is* to what *will be*.

Religious consciousness designates the highest level. In the *Postscript*, Kierkegaard distinguishes between two sorts of "religiousness," what he calls religiousness A and religiousness B. One of the most valuable parts of Shmüeli's study is his penetrating account of this distinction. Religiousness A is basically a deepening and intensification of reflective consciousness, with an additional factor being an awareness of God, the Absolute. Such awareness, however, is neither direct nor transparent. Reflection upon one's own finitude leads the individual to the Infinite; awareness of his temporality brings him to the Eternal; and recognition of his imperfection impels him toward the Perfect. In religiousness A, man's "ethical" choice comes in the form of resignation and surrender to the Absolute.

Religiousness B, on the other hand, which has expression only in genuine Christianity, is constituted by a faith relationship with God. By the miracle of the Incarnation, God—the Absolutely "other"—becomes known to man through Jesus Christ. It is this "absolute relationship with the Absolute" that signifies the consummate form of consciousness for an existing individual.

Shmüeli goes on to explain how for Kierkegaard the actualization of consciousness in the highest form requires a religious "leap" of faith whereby the gap is bridged between the finite and the infinite, the immanent and the transcendent. Until man makes this leap he shall remain forever far from God, hence alienated from the ground of his very being. Disillusionment, melancholy, guilt, and ultimately despair is the tragic finale of alienated consciousness. Only by becoming a Christian is it possible to overcome alienation and achieve total self-realization. Following this line, in the latter sections of his book Shmüeli expands upon Kierkegaard's meaning of Christian consciousness. All in all, the book demonstrates in its own way how Kierkegaard's entire philosophy is directed toward answering the question of what it means to become a Christian.

Solomon, Robert C. "Kierkegaard and 'Subjective Truth,'" in *Philosophy*

Today. XXI, no. 3 (Fall, 1977), pp. 202-215.

What does Søren Kierkegaard mean by his claim that "truth is subjectivity?" When he contrasts "objective truth," which is suprapersonal, necessary, and universal, with "subjective truth," which is intrinsically personal, not necessary, and not universally acceptable, what does he mean by subjective truth? What does he mean when he contends that objective truth is truth for anyone and that subjective truth is truth for an individual? These are the guiding questions in Robert C. Solomon's compact disquisition on Kierkegaard's concept of subjective truth. By combining elements from Hegelian and Kantian philosophy with ideas drawn from contemporary philosophy of language, he offers a fresh approach to what is probably the most fundamental feature of Kierkegaard's thought.

Solomon exposes the fact that even in G. W. F. Hegel the notion of "truth" is understood in more than just an epistemological sense. In science, mathematics, and the like, truth is conceived as a reality or set of facts sought to be known. However, such "cognitive truth" is but one kind of truth. Equally intelligible are the kinds of truth found in morality, religion, art, and music. In morality, truth is right action; in religion, truth is a special relationship with God; in art and music, truth is beauty. Similarly, Kierkegaard's subjective truth must be understood in an extended sense of the term. Kierkegaard is not seeking to reject objective (cognitive) truth totally as it applies in its proper domain, which is science and mathematics. What he does wish to deny is that objective truth is the only kind.

The most provocative section of Solomon's essay is one in which he uses J. L. Austin's celebrated doctrine of "speech acts" as a vehicle for interpreting Kierkegaard. Austin distinguishes between "descriptive" statements (which enable a person to *describe* something) and "performative" statements (which enable a person to *do* something). The statement "Water freezes at thirty-two degrees Fahrenheit" is descriptive. However, a groom uttering the words "I do" during the course of a marriage ceremony is not describing or reporting on a marriage; he is actually engaging in it. In saying those words he is doing something: namely, making a promise, a commitment. Descriptive statements correspond to Kierkegaard's concept of objectivity, while performative statements correspond to subjectivity.

Following through on Solomon's interpretation, it can be said that objective truth is characterized by a "correctness" of description, the final proof being the facts as they exist. Subjective truth, on the other hand, is defined by the sincerity and success of a performative act. A person who says "I promise to repay the loan on Friday" but has no intention of doing so is not "truly" making a promise. Objective truth, quite clearly, is impersonal by nature. The truth that the earth is ninety-three million miles from the sun is not dependent on any particular astronomer, and the truth of Euclidean geometry is not dependent on Euclid's existence. Yet subjective truth is intensely personal by its very definition. In making a promise, it is *my* promise in a way in which no objective truth can ever be mine: it is my commitment, my life, and my decision. Subjective truth depends totally on the particular individual. This approach to Kierkegaard gives new perspective to his doctrine of subjectivity—*R.A.S.*.

ADDITIONAL RECOMMENDED READING

Elrod, John W. *Being and Existence in Kierkegaard's Pseudonymous Works.* Princeton, New Jersey: Princeton University Press, 1975. A thoughtful study which argues that at the heart of Kierkegaard's pseudonymous works is an ontology which serves as a unifying principle for understanding the aesthetic, ethical, and religious modes of existence; focus is upon Kierkegaard's concept of the self and its dialectical development as reflected by the different "stages" of human existence.

Lowrie, Walter *Kierkegaard.* New York: Oxford University Press, 1938. A monumental biographical and interpretative work by the translator who has done more than anyone else to make Kierkegaard known to the English reader. This exceedingly thorough, highly detailed study is indispensable as a guide to Kierkegaard's life and thought.

McCarthy, Vincent A. *The Phenomenology of Moods in Kierkegaard.* The Hague, The Netherlands: Martinus Nijhoff, 1978. An insightful examination of the meaning, function, and interrelationship of four cardinal moods (or states of mind) perceived by Kierkegaard as integral to the emergence of religious subjectivity. The first major study of its kind, this readable, clearly conceived treatise delineates Kierkegaard's idea that spiritual growth is occasioned by personality crises reflected by a sequence of moods—irony, anxiety, melancholy, and despair. A unique contribution toward an understanding of Kierkegaard's philosophical anthropology and religious psychology.

Malantschuk, Gregor. *Kierkegaard's Thought.* Edited and translated by Howard V. Hong and Edna H. Hong. Princeton, New Jersey: Princeton University Press, 1971. A magnificently detailed presentation which examines the dialectical nature of Kierkegaard's writing and the manner in which his individual works coherently fit together as parts of a unified whole. Malantschuk masterfully lays out the basic presuppositions of Kierkegaard's methodology, with a focus upon his progressive shift of emphasis from the objective to the subjective elements which bear on man's existential development. Fully to understand and appreciate this fine piece of scholarship, prior acquaintance with Kierkegaard is essential.

Stack, George J. "The Meaning of 'Subjectivity is Truth,'" in *Midwestern Journal of Philosophy.* (Spring, 1975) pp. 26-40. A scholarly essay which develops the notion of subjectivity in Kierkegaard's thought. The author distinguishes between the subjectivity of authentic ethical existence and the subjectivity of faith, showing how the first is preparatory to the second.

FORCE AND MATTER

Author: Friedrich Karl Christian Ludwig Büchner (1824-1899)
Type of work: Metaphysics, natural philosophy
First published: 1855

Principal Ideas Advanced

There is no force without matter, and no matter without force.
Matter is immortal, and the laws of nature are immutable.
Everything in nature is the result of a natural evolution, not of some creative supernatural force; and there is no evidence of design in nature.
The soul and the brain are inseparably connected.
There are no innate ideas.
There is no strict distinction between organic and inorganic matter, and the soul of man differs only quantitatively from the souls of brutes.

"No force without matter—no matter without force!" This is Büchner's thesis, from which he concludes that there is not and cannot be such a thing as completely inert matter, nor disembodied force. Hence it is impossible for there to have been a creative power that produced the universe out of itself or out of nothing; the universe is eternal. In any case, since a disembodied creative power would exist only when active, it could not have antedated the universe.

The immortality of matter is (presumably) proved by chemistry. "There exists a phrase, repeated *ad nauseam*, of 'mortal body and immortal spirit.' A closer examination causes us with more truth to reverse the sentence." Force is likewise immortal, according to Büchner: "We call the truth simple and self-evident, because it results from a simple consideration of the relation of cause and effect." The eight different forces—gravitation, mechanical force, heat, light, electricity, magnetism, affinity, cohesion—are interconvertible, but their sum is constant.

Matter is very finely divisible, as the microscope shows; Büchner doubts whether there is any limit to divisibility. Space is infinite, and matter is distributed, on the whole, evenly through it; if it were not, the universe would have a center of gravity, and would collapse. (Büchner was unaware of Olbers' proof, 1825, that if the universe were infinite and homogeneous the light at the earth's surface would have an intensity 40,000 times that of sunlight.)

The laws of nature are immutable; there are no miracles. In any case, if there were miracles, their existence would afford an argument *against* the theological conception of God as the Perfect Being: "If the world has been created by God perfect, how can it require any repairs?" One ought not to lament natural necessity, since the conception emancipates man from the degraded state of "a puppet in the hands of unknown powers." Since the natural laws that hold in this part of the universe are in effect everywhere, it is possible, or even probable, that there is life and thought like ours throughout the universe.

The heavens have been formed by the action of gravitational forces on diffuse matter. The whole process is mechanically explicable; "nowhere is there a trace of an arbitrary finger, which has ordered the heavens, or pointed out the paths of comets." The earth is immensely old (more than a billion years); it has evolved from an incandescent state to its present condition gradually, under the influence of forces still operative. To suppose that the whole process is a manifestation of the work of a creative power is "whimsical," for why should such a power have need of "all these roundabouts?"

The fossil record proves an evolution of life also, from simple forms of sea and plant life through gigantic reptiles to mammals and, ultimately, man. (In editions before 1860, Büchner's speculations about the processes of organic evolution are vague and fantastic; after 1860, he writes approvingly of Darwin's work.) Despite the failure of science to exhibit convincing instances of spontaneous generation now, such *must* have occurred at some time in the earth's history when conditions were right; or else the earth was seeded by means of meteorites, some of which have been shown to contain organic compounds. It is probable that the human species is not descended from one original pair, but rather the races arose independently. Evidence for such a theory is provided by the fact that there exist unrelated families of languages. The hierarchy of organic life is continuous. The fossils fill up some of the apparent gaps, and besides, at the present time the black is intermediate between man and ape. (Büchner's views about blacks are all based on citations from "authorities"; it does not seem that he had ever actually seen a black. Thus, his views—absurd today—reflect a prejudice sometimes associated with purely speculative reasoning.)

To impute design to nature, Büchner argued, is to "admire a wonder which the intellect has created itself." "The stag was not endowed with long legs to enable him to run fast, but he runs fast because his legs are long." Diseases, monstrosities, and other imperfections of nature (including the inadequate velocity of light) refute a teleological conception of the universe. "What are the life and the efforts of man, and all humanity, compared with the eternal, inexorable, irresistible, half-accidental, half-necessary march of nature? The momentary play of an ephemeron, hovering over the sea of eternity and infinity."

"The brain is the seat and organ of thought; its size, shape, and structure, are in exact proportion to the magnitude and power of its intellectual functions." Büchner bases his proof on observation of persons who have suffered brain lesions, and on the results of vivisection: "Can we desire any stronger proof as to the necessary connection of the soul and the brain than that afforded by the knife of the anatomist, who cuts off the soul piecemeal?"

Büchner does not explain the nature of the connection of brain and soul; he explicitly refuses to speculate on this matter, contending that having established the *fact* of connection, the "How?" of it can be disregarded. However, he takes to task Vogt, who had said: "To express myself rather coarsely, thought stands in the same relation to the brain, as bile to the liver, or urine to the kidneys." This is wrong because "thought, spirit, soul, are not material, not a substance, but the effect of the conjoined action of many materials endowed with forces or qualities." But of course Vogt was right to stress the *dependence* of thought on the brain.

All of our feelings are in the brain, as we demonstrate by cutting nerves and finding that sensations cease in the parts of the body on the other side of the cut from the brain. "Habit and external appearance have led to the false notion, that we feel in places subjected to external irritation. . . . We falsely attribute the feeling perceived in the brain to the place where the impression is made."

Mediumism and spiritualism are in principle impossible according to Büchner; all mediums and clairvoyants are charlatans.

It is very mistaken and pernicious to despise matter, Büchner wrote— particularly one's body. *Mens sana in corpore sano* should be the ideal of every rational person.

Defenders of body-soul dualism assert that the soul is endowed with certain aesthetic, moral, and metaphysical innate ideas—a false claim, as is shown by the absence of these putative conceptions among deaf-mutes and feral children, and by the facts discovered by anthropologists, who have found the greatest variety of ideas among different peoples, including moral notions the opposites of those entertained in Europe. There is, in any case, no universal standard of morality, whether universally acknowledged or not. "It is well known that the notion of good cannot be defined. The theologians help themselves by saying, that is good which agrees with God's commands. But the commands of God are made by the theologians themselves." Even the conceptions of mathematics originate in sense-perception. Here Büchner's vigorous flogging of the dead horse of innate ideas has led him into absurdity.

In particular, there is no innate idea of God. History shows that the so-called gods of the heathen have nothing to do with the notion of God as a supreme personal being; and many peoples have been discovered who are entirely devoid of religious sentiments. When Moffat, the missionary, explained the tenets of Christianity to "the Bechuanas, one of the most intelligent tribes of the interior of South Africa . . . there only escaped from them exclamations of great surprise, as if these things were too absurd to be listened to by the most stupid." Religion is in fact (as Feuerbach said) human self-idealization.

"Whilst the visible and tangible matter sensually exhibits its indestructibility, the same cannot be asserted of spirit or soul, which is not matter, but merely an ideal product of a particular combination of force-endowed materials." Death is eternal sleep; there is nothing in it to be afraid of. Few people who profess belief in immortality really so believe; and if the soul were immortal, there could be no greater calamity. Büchner praises Buddhism for its denial of God and immortality.

No strict distinction between organic and inorganic is possible; there is no such thing as a vital force. Physiological chemistry does not differ in principle from any other kind; more and more vital processes are being duplicated in the laboratory. "The doctrine of vital power is now a lost affair."

The soul of man differs only quantitatively, not in kind, from the souls of brutes. So-called instinct is only a lower degree of intelligence: "It is not a necessity inborn in themselves and their mental organisation, nor a blind, involuntary impulse, which impels animals to action, but deliberation—the result of comparisons and conclusions." Büchner's evidence for this assertion is anecdotal, as is also his proof that brutes (specifically bees, chamois, baboons, swallows, and storks) have languages. Again, savage races are intermediate with respect to language: "That of the Bushmen is, according to Reichenbach, so poor in words, that it consists mostly of harsh, throat sounds, and clicks, for which we have no representatives in our alphabet, so that they communicate with each other much by signs."

"Free will, to the extent to which man *believes* he possesses it, is a mere chimera. . . . No one . . . who searches beneath the surface can deny that the assumption of a free will must, in theory and practice, be restricted within the narrowest compass." Men's actions are almost entirely determined by their characters, and these in turn are the resultant of external circumstances, particularly climatic. "Deficiency of intellect, poverty, and want of education, are the chief causes of crime. Criminals are rather deserving of pity than of disgust. 'Therefore,' says Forster, 'it were best to judge and to condemn nobody.'" This is not, however, to deny that there is such a thing as crime, nor to object to society's right of self-defense. "What is true is that the partisans of these modern ideas hold different opinions as regards crime, and would banish that cowardly and irreconcilable hatred, which the state and society have hitherto cherished with so much hypocrisy as regards the malefactor."

To the complaint that "modern ideas" if adopted by the populace would lead to moral breakdown and the subversion of society, Büchner replies that "these ideas of God and the world, or moral motives, in so much danger of being wrecked against naturalism, exercise but a very imperceptible influence on the ordinary march of human society." Furthermore, actual European society is egotistical, hypocritical, and rotten: "A society which permits human beings to die of starvation on the steps of houses filled with victuals; a society whose force is directed to oppress the weak by the strong, has no right to

complain that the natural sciences subvert the foundations of its morality."
A more widespread diffusion of the scientific attitude would make possible
a rational reconstruction of society on a humanitarian basis. (Büchner provides no details.) Finally, "truth is above things divine and human; there exist
no reasons strong enough to cause us to abandon it."

"The following pages," Büchner wrote in the Preface to the first edition,
"pretend neither to establish a system nor to be exhaustive. They are merely
scattered, though necessarily connected, thoughts and observations, which,
on account of the difficulty of mastering all the facts of empirical and natural
science, may perhaps meet with some indulgence on the part of the scientific
critic." Such an avowal may serve in some measure to disarm criticism; further,
much ought to be forgiven the author for having produced a book that is (as
its subtitle promises) "intelligibly rendered"—not a common phenomenon in
nineteenth century Germany. Nevertheless, the book has some notable short-
comings.

In the first place, Büchner was a doctor of medicine, which at his time and
place was not at all the same as being a man of science. Thus, despite the
parade of toughmindedness, Büchner was insufficiently skeptical—a fact
which becomes glaringly apparent in his anthropological passages, where the
reports of miscellaneous travelers are set out quite uncritically whenever they
serve his purpose; and in his animal lore, where one point may be supported
by reports of careful research, while the next is "proved" by a recital of a
single anecdote the source of which is not stated.

Nor was Büchner trained as a philosopher. The modern reader may feel
that this was all to the good, in view of the condition of German academic
philosophy in the mid-nineteenth century. However, such giveaway remarks
as "we might as well say, the dog barks, therefore the dog exists" (which,
Büchner naïvely thought, disposed of the Cartesian "I think, therefore I am"
and, in consequence, of all objections to Descartes' position based on the
primacy of consciousness) reveal how inadequately prepared Büchner was to
cope with the two central problems of materialism: consciousness and free
will. One is not surprised to find that the brief passages bearing on these
matters scarcely show awareness of the difficulties.

It might be said in Büchner's defense that despite the reputation of *Force
and Matter* as the bible of what is (in some quarters) disparaged as "old-
fashioned materialism," the author was not committed to any official creed;
and indeed in the Preface to the ninth edition he stated expressly: "Science
or positive philosophy *per se* is neither idealistic nor materialistic, but realistic;
all it aims at is to apprehend facts and their rational connection, without first
adopting some particular system." In the same writing he spoke approvingly
of the positivism of Comte, and averred that "we can know nothing about
the *Why?* all we can ascertain is the *How?* of things, and the laws discovered
in this manner are final solutions." However, if Büchner's philosophy was not

materialism, neither was it really positivism. It was eclectic, in a bad sense; for he availed himself of positivism to excuse his refusal to treat the mind-body problem seriously, while at the same time, as a materialist, he ignored the complexities of theory of knowledge which beset positivism and push it into phenomenalism and idealism. This is not to say that a consistent philosophy embodying Büchner's point of view is impossible; it is to say that Büchner did not even begin to work it out, evidently on account of unawareness of any (even apparent) difficulties in his position. For instance, he was able to say, quite blandly, that we "perceive feeling in the brain" and "falsely attribute it to the place where the impression is made"—and then to drop the subject!

But it is ungrateful, and perhaps irrelevant, to castigate Büchner for lack of philosophical subtlety. *Force and Matter* was designed as a bludgeon, not as a scalpel, and a very effective bludgeon it was. The modern reader is more likely to be bored than shocked by it, a good indication that its battle has been won. As the review of its subject matter has indicated, there is little in it (barring some unfortunate details) that is not today commonplace among literate persons in general. But such was decidedly not the case when it was published. Büchner was, predictably, ejected from his professorial chair; he was denounced throughout Germany; yet his book went through ten editions in fourteen years.

The evaluation by J. F. Collingwood, the editor of the English edition, is still just: "Its subject-matter may not be new to well-informed persons, as it does not aim at original scientific investigation; but the manner of treatment adopted by its accomplished author will be highly appreciated by those who wish for the advancement of mankind through the free exercise of thought." —*W.I.M.*

PERTINENT LITERATURE

Joad, C. E. M. *Guide to Modern Thought*. New York: Frederick A. Stokes Company, 1933.

In the nineteenth century, C. E. M. Joad tells us, the cumulative effect of the scientific discoveries of the preceding three centuries was felt. A view of the universe was developed, based on the mechanics of Galileo and Sir Isaac Newton, in which the physical universe was pictured as a complex and gigantic machine. It was held, Joad continues, that whatever exists and whatever occurs is explicable by reference to the motions of pieces of matter. Further, he suggests, it was held that not only whatever did, but also whatever *could*, exist or occur was explicable in this fashion; for it seemed inconceivable that phenomena should occur other than those ultimately analyzable as movements of matter. Joad adds that, given the experimental and technological successes of the sciences, this materialistic perspective became very influential, and popular thought as a result associated *being real* and *being material*.

The basis for materialism, Joad notes, came from three disciplines: biology, psychology, and physics. At the center of the biological scene, of course, was Charles Darwin. Joad explains that Darwin's discoveries were thought to show that the existence of life and of mind was entirely explicable given only small variations in species, material forces which cause such variations, and laws in accordance with which the movements of matter occur. Thus, Joad adds, life was found to have slowly and continually evolved from nonliving material to its complex form in the human organism. Natural forces, and nothing else, were referred to in describing the process.

Joad notes that very few qualifications of Darwin's account of evolution were required. One qualification concerns the production of new species, which, Joad suggests, are best explained in terms of the sudden appearance of new members of a species which differ substantially from the others; such "mutations" arrive abruptly and constitute a new species which excludes or coexists with its predecessor. Darwin, Joad says, ascribed the variations, including the mutations, to chance, and so does not explain them. The importance of this circumstance, Joad suggests, is the idea that *given the variations*, no force external to or not part of nature need be referred to in explaining the course of evolution and the development of life and mind.

According to Joad, the second discipline that contributed to the rise of mechanistic materialism was psychology, and in particular a certain doctrine concerning mind. As Joad presents it, this doctrine, in effect, has two parts. One part is the claim that mind is very refined matter, or that matter over time has developed an increasingly sophisticated set of capacities which range on up into complex mental or conceptual operations. The other is epiphenomenalism which, as Joad notes, is the view that mental events are always effects, but never causes, of physical events; ". . . mind is a by-product of the functioning of material processes." Given this view of mind, Joad suggests, the doctrine that persons have freedom of choice can only be taken to be an illusion.

The third source of mechanistic materialism, Joad remarks, was physics, which thought of atoms as the basic constituents of matter. These atoms, he tells us, were held to be hard, indestructible, and homogeneous and to interact in accordance with the nonstatistical and deterministically construed laws of mechanics and dynamics.

The net effect of all this, Joad comments, is a view which was expressed in a prophecy in 1874 by John Tyndal, who said that at some future time science would give an account of the "ultimately purely natural and inevitable march of evolution from the atoms of the primaeval nebula to the proceedings of the British Association for the Advancement of Science."

Joad is interested not only in this mechanistic view itself but also in what it entails, or at least is perceived as entailing. Joad argues that it is "readily apparent" that, given mechanistic materialism, life—including human life—

has no particular significance. As he puts it, Copernicus took away the central location and importance of the earth, Darwin removed the primacy of humankind on earth, and materialistic psychology abolished the directive role of the mind in the body.

If (mechanistic) materialism is true, Joad contends, then "matter everywhere determines mind" and "mind nowhere determines matter." Life is caused by, and is analyzable in terms of, nonconscious material processes. This, Joad holds, robs human life and thought of any special significance. Further, a widely accepted consequence of physical theory is the demise of human life on this planet in a frozen future; and, Joad notes, this does nothing to mitigate worries about the significance materialism allows to human life.

In addition to describing mechanistic materialism, Joad expresses reservations concerning it. One reservation concerns radical changes in the concepts of matter (a change foreshadowed by the notions of force and matter and force and energy which Ludwig Büchner, Ernst Haeckel, and others had proffered) and physical law (which, Joad reminds us, has to do with indeterminacy and statistical probability). Another concerns the different sort of view, based on science, presented by such authors as Arthur S. Eddington and J. H. Jeans, who, Joad notes, try to base something like idealism on science. Perhaps the most basic objection is expressed by Joad in describing materialism as "a product of man's mind." (The thesis that if materialism were true, it could not be known to be true or could not without circularity be believed on the ground that it was true has been much discussed, with many attempts to state the view clearly and tellingly and many counter efforts to reply to it critically.)

Chadwick, Owen. *The Secularization of the European Mind in the Nineteenth Century.* New York: Cambridge University Press, 1976.

According to Owen Chadwick, in his 1973-1974 Gifford Lectures, Ludwig Büchner was essentially a popularizer. A doctor of medicine and an active politician, Büchner became, Chadwick reports, a lecturer in medicine at Tübingen. In 1855, he published a book entitled *Kraft und Stoff*, or *Force and Matter*. The publication of the book, Chadwick notes, cost him his lectureship, so that he turned to private medical practice and free-lance writing, and later—in 1881—founded The German League of Freethinkers. By 1904, *Force and Matter* had gone through twenty-one editions in Germany and had been translated into fifteen languages. Further, Chadwick continues, it was reviewed and discussed wherever it was translated.

Chadwick emphasizes that Büchner was neither scientist nor philosopher. Rather, he was an especially successful popularizer of the science of his day. Since *Force and Matter* was published in 1855 and the *Origin of Species* in 1859, Büchner did not, in particular, popularize Charles Darwin's ideas, although in later editions he made use of Darwin's views to support his own perspective.

Büchner's view of the connection between force and matter, Chadwick notes, is that they are identical or interchangeable. From this axiom, Chadwick suggests, Büchner draws certain conclusions. One is that the notion of a spiritual or immaterial force is nonsense. Further, as matter is eternal, there can have been no creation of matter; *creation* is identical with force, and so cannot temporally precede matter.

Other themes in *Force and Matter*, Chadwick tells us, are these. Space must be infinite, as no edge of space can be imagined. (It seems, then, that Büchner found the old argument that you cannot imagine an end to space, since for any space you imagine, you can imagine more space beyond it, to be a persuasive line of reasoning.) Further, pure spirit, or disembodied or unembodied mind, is impossible. Rather, mind depends for its existence and properties upon matter.

Here, perhaps, one gets to the core of Büchner's perspective. Chadwick records that Büchner regards human life, and indeed all life, as an accidental by-product of material phenomena. Thought, too, is a by-product of force or matter; mind is matter thinking. Chadwick specifies the conclusion Büchner draws regarding religion: namely, that nothing miraculous ever occurs, that the universe is nonteleological or has no purpose and heads for no divinely-ordained goal, and that only what Büchner calls "the ignorant layman" can accept the doctrine that a personal Deity is Creator and Providence.

Chadwick then recounts Büchner's conception of the universe as a place in which life arises from nonliving matter; organic life comes from protoplasm in a process which involves no plan; and the human race is headed for destruction in a universe which is running down. Some found this perspective cheerless and depressing, but, as Chadwick indicates, Büchner endeavored to console his readers with a doctrine of a human being as "a proud and free son of Nature"—one who understands and humbly submits to the laws of nature, while endeavoring to forge his or her purposes within the limits these laws set. In this endeavor, Chadwich suggests, Büchner is paradigmatic of the tendency, common in his time, to maintain on the one hand that human beings are merely animals (as opposed to creatures made in the image of God), while, on the other, to maintain that humans are rulers of the world.

Chadwick questions not the popularity but the influence of Büchner's (and similarly wide-selling) popularizing. Very few people, he says, including the readers of *Force and Matter*, have ever believed what the volume propounded. Popular opinion, Chadwick holds, was influenced by the successes, but not therefore by the content, of the sciences. He suggests that *Force and Matter* may have been more a symbol than a textbook—more an attempt to articulate a view of an attitude toward the world which some people wanted to express and could not express for themselves than a summary of shared beliefs.

Chadwick reports that Alex Büchner, Ludwig's brother, thought that the title alone of Ludwig's book was sufficient to guarantee that it would find a publisher; it fit that well into the intellectual climate of its time. The question of Büchner's influence—of how great and how durable it was—Chadwick suggests, is far harder to determine than is its theme. Many inferred that since copies of *Force and Matter* sold in the hundreds of thousands, surely Büchner must have had multitudes of disciples. In fact, Chadwick asserts, Buchner wryly remarks in *Last Words on Materialism* (English translation, 1901), that he looked around for his disciples and found none. In any case, Chadwick remarks that *Force and Matter* reflects, if not the beliefs of its time, at any rate what the people of the time wanted to read and talk about, and this in itself reveals part of the climate of opinion of its day.—*K.E.Y.*

ADDITIONAL RECOMMENDED READING

Copleston, Frederick C. *A History of Philosophy*. Vol. VII. Garden City, New York: Doubleday & Company, 1965. Chapter 18 discusses the materialist movement in which Büchner was involved.

Edwards, Paul, ed. *The Encyclopedia of Philosophy*. Vol. I. New York: Macmillan Publishing Company, 1967. A brief description of Büchner's views plus a short bibliography.

Hocking, William E. *Types of Philosophy*. New York: Charles Scribner's Sons, 1929. Discusses seven types of philosophy, including naturalism, and offers an assessment of each.

Lange, Friedrich A. *The History of Materialism and Criticism of Its Present Importance*. New York: Arno Press, 1974. A multi-volume history, with critique, of materialist views.

Merz, John T. *A History of European Thought in the Nineteenth Century*. London: Blackwood and Sons, 1907-1914. A comprehensive, topically arranged, four-volume intellectual history of nineteenth century Europe.

Perry, Ralph B. *Present Philosophical Tendencies*. New York: George Braziller, 1955. Part II discusses naturalism and, briefly, Büchner.

MICROCOSMUS

Author: Rudolf Hermann Lotze (1817-1881)
Type of work: Metaphysics
First published: 1856-1864

Principal Ideas Advanced

The physicists are right in claiming that the universe is made up of atoms, but the atoms are sentient and they influence one another in a causal fashion predictable according to natural law.

The sentient atoms, or monads, may be considered causally from without, but internally they are the expressions of will.

All nature, which is a mechanism directed by purpose, is the expression of the creative will of God.

Man is unique because of his mind; although, like the other animals, man evolved in the struggle for existence, his history cannot be understood in purely mechanical terms.

Man, who is himself a unity, brings unity to existence by the use of ideas and ideals; wholes in nature are products of mind.

When he selected the title *Mikrokosmus* for his book, Rudolf Hermann Lotze drew upon the ancient tradition, still strong in the eighteenth and nineteenth centuries, which taught that in the little circle of his activities man recapitulates the plan and purpose of the whole world. "As in the great fabric of the universe the creative spirit imposed on itself unchangeable laws by which it moves the world of phaenomena, diffusing the fullness of the Highest Good throughout innumerable forms and events, and distilling it again from them into the bliss of consciousness and enjoyment: so must man, acknowledging the same laws, develop given existence into a knowledge of its value, and the value of his ideals into a series of external forms proceeding from itself." A few years before, the celebrated naturalist Alexander von Humboldt had begun the publication of a panoramic work entitled *Kosmos* (5 volumes, 1845-1862), designed to exhibit in an imaginative synthesis all that was known about the physical world. Lotze's *Microcosmus* sought, in a manner, to redress the balance by focusing attention on man and his achievements. Volume One is an account of the human constitution in its physical, vital, and psychical aspects; Volume Two deals with the physical evolution of man and his mental and social development; Volume Three discusses the meaning of history, not neglecting its metaphysical and theological presuppositions.

For this grandiose undertaking, Lotze was well qualified. To his philosophical labors he brought the prestige of a man of science, reminding us in this respect as in others of the philosopher and mathematician Alfred North Whitehead. The same year that he took his doctor's degree in philosophy he received the degree of doctor of medicine; and his writings on metaphysics and logic were interspersed with works on physiology, pathology, and medical psychology. *Microcosmus* exhibits the results of his labors in these fields.

Lotze's purpose in writing *Microcosmus* was to adjust the differences which divided the educated world of his day into two warring camps, naturalists and humanists, materialists and spiritualists, or what William James was later to call the "tough-minded" and the "tender-minded." Like James, Lotze believed that the truth lies somewhere between the exclusive claims of these parties. He blamed the former for making an idol of truth and renouncing human interests which no man has the right to renounce. But he lamented the irrationalism in which romantic defenders of art, morality, and religion were accustomed to wrap themselves. It was his opinion that the philosophy which takes the realm of value as its starting point is able to frame a consistent and intelligible account of the world by tracing things back to their origin in the purpose of a personal God. And he further argued that the scientific view of the world is not fully intelligible except on this same assumption.

The key to Lotze's proposal for bringing the world view of science into harmony with the world view of aesthetics, morals, and religion is his attitude toward the principle of mechanism. He maintained that the universe is indeed made up of atoms and that these act upon one another in a regular and necessary fashion that can be described in terms of mechanical law. He saw no necessity for limiting or qualifying this causal principle. Some philosophers, in order to preserve freedom and responsibility for man, had set up a dualism of body and soul, arguing that mechanism holds for the former but not for the latter; others had declared for a spiritual monism, maintaining that matter is merely phenomenal and that the chain of causation which appears to determine its movements has no reality in things themselves. Lotze rejected both of these views. He did accept a kind of spiritual monism; the atoms known to physics he held to be actually sentient, like the monads in Leibniz's system. Leibniz, however, had denied that one monad really influences another, explaining their apparent interconnection by his theory of "pre-established harmony." Lotze held that they do influence each other and that their behavior is predictable in terms of law. At the time he wrote, many biologists were contending that mechanistic determinism does not apply to living things. Lotze maintained in his works on physiology that it does, and he did not hesitate to speak of the "mechanism of life."

To that extent Lotze accommodated himself to the views of science. But having admitted that mechanism is universal, he went on to argue that it is everywhere subordinate to purpose. If we consider the atom not from the outside but from within, causality appears in a different aspect. Its essence may be described as feeling, and its activity toward other atoms as excitation and impulse. Nineteenth century materialists were divided into two groups— those who maintained that atoms are qualitatively homogeneous and those who maintained that they are heterogeneous. Lotze took the latter position. He held that each monad or particle has a determinate essence which draws along with it a definite series of possible changes. As it comes into relation with other things it responds in specific ways. Viewed from without, its behavior may be described in terms of law; viewed from within, it is the realization of inclination or will. Like Leibniz, Lotze required a principal monad to complete the picture. Existing things, each ceaselessly acting to realize its own satisfaction, are joined and fitted into harmonious wholes, which in turn go to make up one concordant system, the expression of the creative will of God. It is in the notion of a whole that Lotze found the complement to mechanism which, without subverting causal necessity, subordinates it to an *idea*. The upshot is that mechanism is everywhere operative, but, as is the case with the artifices of men, the laws of nature serve to realize ends.

Lotze's reason for believing that there are unities in the world derives from the peculiarity of mental phenomena. The customary reason given for distinguishing between mind and matter is, according to Lotze, that the one exercises freedom of self-determination which is forbidden to the other. This theory he found inadequate because there is no evidence that conscious choices are determined. Our feeling of freedom could be misleading if it is true that even material particles share with minds the attribute of excitability. The true ground for distinguishing between mind and matter lies in the unity of consciousness, which is totally unlike the kind of unity that we encounter among natural phenomena. On the material plane, two forces, when they combine to produce a third, merge so as to become indistinguishable. But consciousness keeps its objects separate at the same time that it combines them. In this way it gives rise to genuine wholes. Lotze held that it is only in virtue of consciousness (God's or man's) that wholes exist. Moreover, he argued from the fact that minds perceive unity to the unity of minds themselves. It may not appear to us that consciousness is anything but an unconnected plurality; but the very fact that anything which appears does so to *us*, or that the world appears to us as made up of *unities*, is proof incontestable. For only that which is itself a unity can unify manifold phenomena.

Lotze regarded man as occupying a unique status in the world. He is "a phenomenon in space, a connected organism, the head of the animal kingdom," but at the same time he is set off from the rest of creation by "the addition of a wholly new germ of development," namely, the rational *mind*. Writing before the publication of Darwin's *On the Origin of Species* (1859), he laid the groundwork for a mechanistic theory of evolution, including the notions of variation and the selection of existing varieties through the struggle for existence. Nor did he except man from this scheme. But he discerned a deep abyss between the natural history of animals and the intellectual and moral history of the human species. The former can be adequately accounted for in mechanical terms, the latter not by those means at all. *Microcosmus* is the account of man's peculiar development within creation, the story of a creature made in the image of God.

Lotze did not deny that animals have souls, but he did claim that we know too little about animals to speak intelligently on the subject. Their outer lives are all we have to go by. Presumably they experience sensation and desire much as man does, and they cannot be without a kind of intelligence. But, as far as we can tell, they stop short of attaching significance to their experiences and their actions. A dog may find a morsel pleasant to the taste without attaining to a recognition of sweetness; he may bury a bone, but without the thought of providing for tomorrow's need. Man, on the contrary, lives by taking thought, by bringing to bear upon the manifold content of sensation and desire an architectonic structure which transforms the raw product of psychic stimulation into "an organically utilizable thought-atom." Only in view of this creative (or re-creative) function can human phenomena be explained. The bird's song, the beaver's dam, the monkey's capers can all be understood in terms of mechanistic principles. But failure awaits the attempts of materialists (for example, Ludwig Büchner's *Force and Matter*, 1855) to explain the achievements of man by appealing to natural laws. A second principle of explanation must be employed, which takes account of ideas and wholes.

From this latter point of view, Lotze surveyed the whole range of human culture. The structure of language, with its parts of speech and rules of syntax, is the first embodiment of thought, closely following its natural forms. Man's intellectual life, as observable in science and abstract reasoning, further discloses the unique formative activity of the mind as it compares and distinguishes impressions and uncovers relations and connections which it did not originate, lifting out of their spatiotemporal context orders and patterns and beholding their timeless essence. Morality shows similar features, inasmuch as man, unlike the lower creatures, is motivated by ideal principles of duty and obligation and not merely by animal impulse.

In all his specifically human achievements man reveals the presence of mind. Not, indeed, to the exclusion of his body and its laws! Sensation, according to Lotze, is caused by physiological stimulation: the chemical reactions in the brain affect the soul in specific ways, giving rise there to color, taste, and sound impressions. Impressions such as these are the basis for its perceptions. Language originates in spontaneous physiological movements of the respiratory system. Morality is rooted in feelings of pain and pleasure, and when man formulates ideal ends, he is still motivated by antipathy and desire. Lotze claimed that it was proof of the correctness of his theory that it brought together the "theory of an ideal unity in mental life" and the "theory of its mechanical realization." And if his work was directed in the first instance against crude materialism and its attempts to explain civilization in mechanical terms, it was also intended as a corrective of Absolute Idealism, which, he said, "makes the significant Idea float in isolation as a boundlessly shaping power above the low sphere of the ordinary psychic mechanism."

It may be gathered from this quotation that Lotze would not be in sympathy with Hegel's philosophy of history. And this was, indeed, the case. Instead of conceiving history as the logical unfolding of an idea, Lotze viewed it as an interaction between man and his environment. The human mind does not work in a vacuum. In fact, it does not work at all except under the stimulating and guiding influence of various external causes. We may view human activity as an attempt to realize the good, the beautiful, and the just—for these are the ends which man comes to respect; but these goals would never have been sought for themselves, apart from man's bodily and communal needs. And in this connection, such unspiritual factors as climate and rainfall have to be considered, as well as the claims of the ideal.

Lotze saw a development in history. Because of favorable circumstances or because of the possession of peculiar genius or a specially pregnant idea, certain peoples, at least, have developed forms of life which far transcend organic needs; and, in the West, particularly, an overlapping of cultures has permitted later ones to build upon their predecessors' achievements. But Lotze was not greatly impressed with the doctrine of progress as such. In mechanical arts, he granted, it is not difficult to improve upon the achievement of one's predecessors. But he doubted whether there is any progress in art or in the depth and character of mental life from one civilization to another.

Lotze found special difficulty in another feature of the progress-doctrine. It seemed to him irreconcilable with any consistent scheme of values to argue that countless generations of individuals should serve as means to the happiness of those who should come after. On the contrary, he maintained that the life of any generation in any culture has the same intrinsic worth as that of any other. That the whole of history makes up a pattern and has a meaning he was far from denying; but he held that only God knows what it is or can have any satisfaction from it. In fact, Lotze applied the same principle to the cosmos that he applied to history, and one of the reasons which inclined him to view the elemental parts of nature as sentient was his unwillingness to suppose that the vast proportion of the world has no enjoyment of it and exists only for the satisfaction of men.

The arguments by which Lotze arrived at his conception of God as a personal creator are of such a subtle and metaphysical order that it is unprofitable to try to summarize them. Lotze was prepared to prove that the notion of causation presupposes a more fundamental being underlying the interacting particles. His background in chemistry and biology led him to repudiate the notion that atoms are inert extended bodies which interact on one another through external collision; he favored a dynamic conception which explained causation in terms of the internal constitution of things. This led to his discerning patterns or wholes in nature, which, he held, can have no existence apart from a mind which thinks them. The notion that the world is called into being by a purely ideal necessity, as Hegel had suggested, seemed to him inadequate to account for the actuality which things possess and the real causality which they exert on one another. To account for the active quality of existence, he believed it was necessary to hold to an active God, who wills and enjoys, as well as thinks.

When Lotze turned from physical causation to the consideration of value, he found further arguments for a personal creator. He opposed Kant's contention that the highest good is a will determined purely by duty. To make an abstract relation a good seemed to him altogether contrary to experience. In reality, nothing is good except self-satisfaction. A benevolent act is good only if it brings happiness to some other being. And to Lotze, since values are as much a constituent part of the world as existence and law, it was necessary to think of the creator as the one for whom things have preeminent worth. He ventured, with these thoughts before him, to trace the origin of our world to God's eternal love, which, rejoicing in the goodness of his own thoughts, willed that they should have their own existence. Because creation was an act of love, it was not enough that God should enjoy it, but the parts themselves, each in its determinate measure, must know the self-satisfaction of being what they are.

Lotze's philosophy has many loose ends. He reminds himself repeatedly that the finite mind of man, while it can trace the general features of the world, cannot expect to see its ultimate necessity. No philosopher was ever more sophisticated than Lotze—that is to say, less naïve. If he returns to an essentially religious tradition, he does so with due deliberation. It might be true of Kant that his philosophy was an elaborate rationalization of his pietistic faith. This was hardly the case with Lotze, who saw the nihilistic implications in official nineteenth century philosophies and was impelled to take a longer look. He concluded, on the one hand, that our science can never be more than fragmentary, and he warned against exaggerating its findings into systems which impoverish faith without enriching knowledge. On the other hand, he held fast to "the old-fashioned conviction" that there are ways leading to fuller light and that it is man's duty to follow them as far as he can.—*J.F.*

PERTINENT LITERATURE

Passmore, John. *A Hundred Years of Philosophy*. London: Cox and Wyman, 1957.

Rudolf Hermann Lotze wrote *Logic* (1843), *Metaphysic* (1841), and *Microcosmus*. His *System of Philosophy*, which was to be a full account of his views, remained uncompleted at his death, and was posthumously published in 1884. Lotze was born in 1817 and died in 1881; he was trained as a doctor, and his *General Physiology of Bodily Life* (1851) played an important role in the dissemination of materialistic ideas in Germany. Nevertheless, he was not himself a materialist, and his intention in the 1851 volume was to show that mechanism had a mission to fulfill—a mission which requires that mechanism be absolutely universal and that the significance of mechanism be completely subordinate to that of the mission itself.

John Passmore quotes Lotze to the effect that metaphysics is "an inquiry into the universal conditions, which everything that is to be counted as existing or happening at all, must be expected to fulfill." Thus metaphysics, according to this conception, will not tell us what does happen, knowledge of which requires not reflection, but experience.

Talk of universal conditions which everything that exists or occurs must be expected to fulfill suggests that Lotze held a teleological view of the world, and in particular, a view in which physical objects and events serve an overarching purpose of some sort. This is so, Passmore explains, since Lotze held that the laws of mechanism, which describe the order found in physical objects and events, also serve, or provide the condition for, "the realization of Good." Things go as they do in the physical universe because it is best for them to do so. Lotze confessed, Passmore tells us, that he could not prove this teleological view, which combined *realism* (in a sense which involves things happening as they do because they are determined by mechanistic conditions) and *idealism* (in a sense which involves things happening as they do in order to fulfill a plan or realize an ideal). In contrast to Lotze's actual view, which wed realism and idealism (in the senses indicated), many interpreted his view as embracing a bifurcation in sharp distinction between such things as facts and values, or positive (nonevaluative) inquiries and normative (evaluative) inquiries. In any case, Lotze was in the first place a metaphysician who, in impatience at the epistemological preoccupation of various of his contemporaries, wrote in his *Metaphysic* that "the constant whetting of the knife is tedious if it is not proposed to cut anything with it."

Lotze wrote, Passmore says, in logic, aesthetics, ethics, and psychology as well as metaphysics, and was more successful in his specific, more limited, inquiries than in his attempt to paint a coherent conceptual picture of the universe. He was immensely influential in part because he had no specific and detailed system.

Passmore's concentrated discussion of Lotze is brief. What is of at least equal interest to this discussion is Passmore's very frequent further references to Lotze. Passmore informs us that F. H. Bradley offered a characterization of metaphysics whose meaning is identical to that of Lotze; John McTaggart developed his ideas in *Studies in Hegelian Cosmology* (1901) by way of critique of Bradley and Lotze; Bernard Bosanquet's and Bradley's views on logic were indebted to Lotze, as was Edmund Husserl's; James Ward's and G. F. Stout's views on mind and matter were indebted to Lotze; the epistemologies of Andrew Seth and Robert Adamson were influenced by Lotze's views. In sum,

Lotze's writings were widely influential in British philosophy, more so than in his native Germany, as various philosophers picked and chose among his ideas. Thus, while Lotze, strictly speaking, had no disciples, few philosophers, as Passmore puts it, "have been so pillaged."

Kuntz, P. G., ed. "Introduction," in George Santayana's *Lotze's System of Philosophy*. Bloomington: Indiana University Press, 1971.

Rudolf Hermann Lotze, according to P. G. Kuntz, was the most influential German philosopher of his day—namely, the mid-nineteenth century—although he has since fallen into obscurity. His influence, Kuntz notes, was felt in later nineteenth century German thought, and also strongly felt in Great Britain and the United States, where much of philosophy in the nineteenth and twentieth centuries has been dependent on German models.

Like William James, Kuntz reports, Lotze earned an M.D. and moved from physiology through psychology to philosophy. Albrecht Ritschl, the influential liberal German theologian who was himself influential among American liberal theologians, reinterpreted religion as a matter of judgments of value, proceeding on cues provided by Lotze. T. H. Green's activist group in England translated Lotze's *System of Philosophy* into English. In America, Kuntz continues, Lotze's *Outline of the Philosophy of Religion*, with a preface by G. T. Ladd, a Congregational minister and philosophy professor at Yale, was much read. Henry Churchill King taught every B.A. candidate at Oberlin College, using Lotze's *Microcosmus* as a text. Josiah Royce was Lotze's student as well as an admirer. James regarded Lotze as the "deepest philosopher" of his day. In these and other instances, Kuntz documents an impressive variety of German, British, and American thinkers who, in Lotze's classroom or through Lotze's books, came under his influence.

Prior to studying medicine, Lotze had received a classical education, being trained in Greek and Latin. He thus, Kuntz explains, along with other scholars of his time, felt himself to share in an unbroken tradition stretching back to the Greek and Latin authors. Particularly attracted to Lucretius, Lotze could lecture in Latin and came from a humanistic as well as a scientific background.

Kuntz reports that Lotze was both influenced by and critical of his predecessors. He occasionally referred to Plato and Aristotle, usually by way of saying that real things belong to an Aristotelian realm of generation and corruption rather than a Platonic realm of Forms. In the modern period, Kuntz continues, Lotze's interests were in the Continental philosophers, René Descartes, Benedictus de Spinoza, and especially Gottfried Wilhelm von Leibniz, because of Lotze's concern with the question of what the smallest parts of the universe are. In this regard, he was influenced by Leibniz's theory of monads, although, Kuntz informs us, he rejected Leibniz's doctrine of preestablished harmony. On the whole, however, Kuntz suggests, Lotze was critical of his predecessors.

Lotze argued that since philosophers have been developing views for so long, all the possible positions have been developed and abandoned, and the most one can hope for is, not originality, but exactness. The bulk of his historical comments, Kuntz informs us, concern Leibniz, Immanuel Kant, Johann Gottlieb Fichte, and Georg Wilhelm Friedrich Hegel. (Kuntz adds that Lotze simply skips over the medieval philosophers.)

Kuntz informs us that Lotze contends that there is no one starting point in philosophy, nor one philosophical method that applies to all phenomena. He found system-building a pretentious activity. Yet, Kuntz suggests, Lotze is himself "a systematic philosopher seeking to judge among alternative views which comes closest to the truth." Representative of the "pretension" that Lotze rejected, Kuntz tells us, was Fichte's claim that an adequate theory would have to deduce from a single, general principle all the parts of world history. Only a Creator who created the world to serve a specified end, Lotze suggests, could present such a theory.

Kuntz indicates that Lotze also criticizes idealists for (as he sees it) reasoning that, because our representation or experience of the external world is subjective (it would not exist if persons did not), the external world is subjective; for our representation is subjective, whether or not there is a mind-independent and experience-independent world. Nor, Kuntz continues, did Lotze fail to criticize materialists, as he argues that materialism requires some version or other of reductionism—of arguing, for example, that changing color perceptions are caused by light waves of different lengths, and therefore that colors simply are light waves of various lengths.

Kuntz informs us that Lotze was concerned to explain how a unified and orderly world somehow underlies the diverse world presented to our sensory experience—the "problem of the one and the many." In his *Encyclopedia of Philosophy*, Kuntz notes, Lotze gives a brief presentation of his system and uses the metaphor of the world as a melody to try to deal with the relationship between the world and its parts. One thing which, in Lotze's view, makes the metaphor appropriate, Kuntz suggests, is expressed by Lotze's dictum "to be is to be related."

Lotze insisted that philosophy deal with what Kuntz quotes him as calling "those riddles by which our mind is oppressed in life, and about which we are perforce compelled to hold some view or other, in order to be able to really live at all." This, Lotze suggests, will include efforts in science and aesthetics and ethics, but also an endeavor to relate these together in a way relevant to "life's immediate experience." Kuntz quotes Lotze to the effect that philosophy's goal is to establish a view of the world which is "certain, coherent, and of universal validity." Lotze takes it that such a view will include both the conception of a cause which acts according to law and the notion of a cause which acts according to freely adopted ends, allowing each conception its proper scope and relating each to the other.—*K.E.Y.*

ADDITIONAL RECOMMENDED READING

Beck, L. W. *Early German Philosophy*. Cambridge, Massachusetts: Harvard University Press, 1969. A discussion of German philosophy up to Kant, with a final chapter on Kant, by America's leading Kant scholar.

Brightman, E. S. *A Philosophy of Religion*. New York: Prentice-Hall, 1940. An older work with various references to Lotze.

Erdmann, J. E. *A History of Philosophy*. New York: Macmillan Publishing Company, 1890. Good for history of German philosophy, including post-Kantian.

Knudson, A. C. *The Philosophy of Personalism*. New York: The Abingdon Press, 1927. An exposition of the philosophy of personalism—a theistic philosophy—with copious references to Lotze.

Lotze, R. H. *Metaphysics*. Edited by Bernard Bosanquet. Oxford: Clarendon Press, 1897. Deals with ontology, cosmology, and psychology.

Muirhead, J. H., ed. *Contemporary British Philosophy*. London: George Allen & Unwin, 1953. Personal statements by influential British philosophers, with some references to Lotze.

ESSAY ON LIBERTY

Author: John Stuart Mill (1806-1873)
Type of work: Political philosophy
First published: 1859

PRINCIPAL IDEAS ADVANCED

An individual's liberty can rightfully be constrained only in order to prevent his doing harm to others.

Certain areas of human freedom cannot rightfully be denied: the freedom to believe, the freedom of taste, and the freedom to unite (for any purpose not involving harm to others).

Open expressions of opinions should not be repressed, for if the repressed opinion is true, one loses the opportunity of discovering the truth; while if the repressed opinion is false, discussion of its falsity strengthens the opposing truth and makes the grounds of truth evident; furthermore, the truth may be divided between the prevailing opinion and the repressed one, and by allowing expression of both, one makes recognition of the whole truth possible.

Important political thinkers often write like men who are convinced that a bedrock of significant issues underlies the otherwise multitudinous details of human political life. How such men estimate the nature of that bedrock accounts for the important differences of viewpoint among the great political philosophers from Plato to contemporary minds. John Stuart Mill thought long and hard about the theoretical and the practical problems connected with liberal democratic government. Actual service in the British Parliament brought him into intimate contact with applied politics. Beneath the surface of nineteenth century British political experience Mill came upon the one problem he considered central to all men's long-range interests. The clarity with which he stated this problem in the *Essay on Liberty* has earned for him a justified reputation as defender of the basic principles of Liberalism. "The struggle between Liberty and Authority," he wrote in that work, "is the most conspicuous feature in the portions of history with which we are earliest familiar, particularly in that of Greece, Rome, and England." The individual's relation to the organized power of state and popular culture requires that men draw the line between what in principle rightly belongs to each. The liberal task concerns how men are to meet the necessary demands of organized life without destroying the rights of the individual.

Mill mentions two ways in which men gradually subdued sovereign power after long and difficult struggles. First, select groups within a given political domain worked to compel the rulers to grant them special immunities. Second (and historically a later phenomenon), men managed to win constitutionally guaranteed rights through some political body which represented them. These historical tendencies limited the tyrannical aspects of sovereign power without raising questions about the inherited right of the sovereign to rule.

A later European development involved the replacement of inherited rulers by men elected for periodic terms of governing. This was the aim of popular parties in modern European affairs, according to Mill. Men who once wanted to limit governmental powers when such government rested on unrepresentative principles now put less stress on the need of limitation once government received its justification by popular support—say, through elections. "Their power was but the nation's own power, concentrated, and in a form convenient for exercise." Yet Mill criticizes European liberalism for failing to understand that popularly supported governments may also introduce forms of tyranny. There can be what Mill's essay refers to as "the tyranny of the majority." The earlier question went: Who can protect men from the tyranny of an inherited rule? Modern Europeans can ask the question: Who will protect men from the tyranny of custom? The individual citizen's independence is threatened in either instance. He needs protection from arbitrary rulers and also from "the tyranny of the prevailing opinion and feeling." Even a democratic society can coerce its dissenters to conform to ideals and rules of conduct in areas which should belong solely to the individual's decisions.

The chief concern of modern politics, then, is to protect the individual's rights from governmental and social coercion. Mill argues that the practical issue is even narrower—"where to place the limit" which liberal minds agree is needed. Mill understands that organized life would be impossible without some firm rules. Men can never choose to live in a ruleless situation. "All that makes existence valuable to anyone, depends on the enforcement of restraints upon the actions of other people." But *what* rules are to prevail? To this important question the satisfactory answers remain to be realized. Existing rules, which will vary from one culture and historical epoch to another, tend to become coated in the clothing of apparent respect through force of custom; they come to seem self-evident to their communities. Men forget that custom is the deposit of learned ways of acting. Few realize that existing rules require support by the giving of reasons, and that such reasons may be good or bad. Powerful interest groups tend to shape the prevailing morality in class terms. Men also often act servilely toward the rules created by their masters.

Mill credits minority and religious groups, especially Protestant ones, with having altered customs by their once heretical resistance to custom. But creative groups out of step with prevailing modes of action and thought often sought specific changes without challenging in principle the existing rules of conduct. Even heretics sometimes adopted a bigoted posture toward other theological beliefs. As a result many religious minorities could simply plead for "permission to differ." Mill concludes that religious tolerance usually triumphed only where religious indifference also existed side by side with diversified bodies of religious opinion.

A criterion by which rightful interference in a man's personal life can be determined is offered by Mill. Individuals and social groups may so interfere only for reasons of their own self-protection. Society has a coercive right to prevent an individual from *harming* others, but it may not interfere simply for the individual's own physical or moral good. In this latter domain, one may attempt to persuade but not to compel an individual to change his views or his actions. Mill adds a further qualification; namely, the individual must possess mature faculties. Children, insane persons, and members of backward societies are excluded from the use of the criterion. Moreover, the test whether interference is proper can never involve abstract right but only utility—"utility in the largest sense, grounded on the permanent interests of man as a progressive being." Failures to act, as well as overt acts causing harm to others, may be punished by society.

The question is then raised as to how men are to interpret the notion that unharmful acts belong solely to the agent. What are the rights belonging to a man which can never lead to harm to others? There are three broad types of such rights, according to Mill. The types are: one, "the inward domain of consciousnes"; two, "liberty of tastes and pursuits"; three, "freedom to unite, for any purpose not involving harm to others." Mill insists that no society or government may rightfully deny these areas of fundamental human freedom. Men must be permitted and even encouraged to seek their good "in their own way." This means that the repressive tendencies of institutions, including churches and sects, must continually be curbed. Mill points out how even Auguste Comte, the famous French sociologist, encouraged a form of despotism over individuals in society in the name of positivistic rationality. Mill insists that any successful resistance to the individual's coercion by opinion or legislation requires defense of the right to think and to express one's views in the public marketplace.

Mill's famous book addresses several aspects of the problem concerning the relation of authority to the individual: first, the nature of man's freedom of thought and public discussion of controversial ideas; second, the ways in which human individuality is a necessary element in man's well-being; third, the limits of society over the individual. There is then a concluding chapter which shows some practical applications of the liberal principles which Mill has defended.

The first argument against repression of open expression of opinion is that the repressed opinion may be true. Those who silence opinion must act on the dogmatic assumption that their own viewpoint is infallible. But if a given opinion happens to be true, men can never exchange error for its truth so long as discussion is curtailed. On the other hand, if the controversial opinion is false, by silencing discussion of it men prevent more lively truths in existence from gaining by the healthy collision with error. No government or social group should be permitted to claim infallibility for the limited perspective which any given group must inevitably hold toward events. "The power itself is illegitimate," Mill argues, insisting that "the best government has no more title to it than the worst."

Mill lists a number of possible objections to his first argument in defense of free discussion: One should not permit false doctrines to be proclaimed; men should never allow discussion to be pushed to an extreme; persecution of opinion is good in that truth will ultimately win out; and only bad individuals would seek to weaken existing beliefs which are useful. None of these objections proves persuasive to Mill. He answers by asserting: There exists a difference between establishing a truth in the face of repeated challenges which fail to refute it and assuming a truth to prevent its possible refutation; open discussion holds significance only if it applies to extreme cases; many historical instances show that coercive error can interfere with the spread of true opinions; and, finally, the truth of an opinion is a necessary aspect of its utility. Mill reminds men how very learned persons joined with those who persecuted Socrates and Jesus for holding opinions which, later, won many adherents. Such persecution often involves the bigoted use of economic reprisals in many cases, about which Mill says: "Men might as well be imprisoned, as excluded from the means of earning their bread."

Mill's second argument for open discussion concerns the value it holds for keeping established truths and doctrines alive. Such discussion challenges men to know the reasons for their beliefs—a practice which forms the primary basis of genuine education. Without challenge, even accepted religious doctrines become lifeless, as do ethical codes. Discussion of false opinions forces those holding existing truths to know *why* they hold the opinions they do. Mill points out that even in the natural sciences there are instances when alternative hypotheses are possible. Experience indicates that in religious and moral matters one should expect a great range of viewpoints. Organized intolerance of opinions which conflict with the official views kills "the moral courage of the human mind." Mill agrees with the critics who assert that not all men can hope to understand the reasons for their received opinions, but he reminds the critics that their own point involves the assumption that someone is an authority regarding those reasons. Consolidation of opinion requires open discussion. Mill's judgment is that with no enemy at hand, "both teachers and learners go to sleep at their post."

The third argument for free discussion rests on the possibility that competing views may share the truth between them. Even heretical opinions may form a portion of the truth. To the objection that some opinions are more than half-truths, like those associated with Christian morality, Mill replies by stating that this morality never posed originally as a complete system. Christian morality constituted more a reaction against an existing pagan culture than a positive ethical doctrine. Men's notions of obligation to the public stem from Greek and Roman influences rather than from the teachings of the New Testament, which stress obedience, passivity, innocence, and abstinence from evil. Mill's conclusion is that the clash of opinions, some of which turn out to be errors, proves helpful to the discovery of truth.

The question about how freely men may act is more difficult. Mill agrees with those who insist that actions can never be as free as opinions. Actions always involve consequences whose possible harm to others must receive serious consideration. Men need long training in disciplined living in order to achieve the maturity required for a responsible exercise of their judgmental capacities. Yet individuality constitutes an inescapable element in the end of all human action, which is happiness. For this reason men must not permit others to decide all issues for them. The reasons are that others' experience may prove too narrow or perhaps it may involve wrongful interpretations; prove correct and yet unsuited to a given individual's temperament; or become so customary that men's passive acceptance of the experience retards their development of numerous unique human qualities. The man who always acquiesces in others' ways of doing things "has no need of any other faculty than the ape-like one of imitation."

What concerns Mill—a concern prophetic of contemporary difficulties in organized social life—is that society shows a threatening tendency to curb individuality. The pressures of social opinion lead to a deficiency of individual impulses, a narrowing of the range of human preferences, and a decline in spontaneity. At this point Mill, who usually speaks favorably of Protestant resistance to earlier orthodox doctrines, singles out Calvinism for harsh criticism. Modern society evinces dangerous secular expressions of the earlier Calvinist insistence that men perform God's will. The emphasis was on strict obedience. So narrow a theory of human performance inevitably pinches human character. As an ethical teleologist and a Utilitarian, Mill holds that the value of human action must be determined by its tendency to produce human self-realization. Obedience can never be an adequate end of human character.

Mill insists that democratic views tend to produce some conditions which encourage the loss of individuality. There is a tendency "to render mediocrity the ascendent power among mankind." Political democracy often results in mass thinking. To protect human individuality, men must show a great suspicion of averages; for the conditions of spiritual development vary from person to person. In fact, Mill argues that democracy needs an aristocracy of learned and dedicated men who can guide its development along progressive paths. What Mill calls "the progressive principle" is always antagonistic to the coercive stance of customary modes of thinking and acting. Such a principle operates only in contexts which permit diversity of human types and a variety of situations. Mill laments that the latter condition seems on the wane in nineteenth century England. He suggests, also, that the slow disappearance of classes has a causal relation to the growing uniformity in English society. His general conclusion, expressed as a warning, is that the individual increasingly feels the compulsions of social rather than governmental coercion.

To what extent may society influence the individual? Mill asserts that society can restrain men from doing damage to others' interests as well as require men to share the burdens of common defense and of protection of their fellows' rights. Society may rightfully establish rules which create obligations for its members insofar as they form a community of interests. Education aims at developing self-regarding virtues in individuals. Individuals who are persistently rash, obstinate, immoderate in behavior, and filled with self-conceit may even be subject to society's disapprobation. But society must not punish a man by legal means if the individual acts in disapproved ways regarding what he thinks to be his own good. "It makes a vast difference both in our feelings and in our conduct towards him," Mill warns, "whether he displeases us in things in which we think we have a right to control him, or in things in which we know that we have not." Mill rejects the argument that no feature of a man's conduct may fall outside the area of society's jurisdiction. A man has the right to make personal mistakes. Finally, Mill argues that society will tend to interfere in a person's private actions in a wrong manner and for the wrong reasons. Religious, socialistic, and other forms of social censorship prove unable to develop adequate self-restraints. A full-blown social censorship leads, in time, to the very decline of a civilization.

Mill concludes his work by pointing out the circumstances under which a society can with justification interfere in areas of common concern. Trade involves social aspects and can be restrained when it is harmful. Crime must be prevented whenever possible. There are offenses against decency which should be curbed, and solicitation of others to do acts harmful to themselves bears watching. Mill writes: "Fornication, for example, must be tolerated, and so must gambling; but should a person be free to be a pimp, or to keep a gambling-house?" The state may establish restrictions of such activities, according to Mill. Finally, Mill argues that the state should accept the duty of requiring a sound education for each individual.—*W.T.D.*

Pertinent Literature

Wolff, Robert Paul. "Liberty," in *The Poverty of Liberalism*. Boston: Beacon Press, 1968.

The argument with which John Stuart Mill attempts to demonstrate his libertarian principle fails to do what Mill intended it to do, according to Robert Paul Wolff. Mill's argument hinges upon the distinction he draws between the internal sphere of private consciousness and those actions which affect the individual alone, on the one hand, and the individual's interactions with other persons, on the other. In the first, according to Mill, society has no right whatever to interfere, while in the latter, society's guiding rule must be the principle of utility. Indeed, the entire argument of the *Essay on Liberty* is based, according to Wolff, upon the utilitarian principle.

Wolff contends that Mill's defense of the liberty of thought and discussion is based upon a premise that Mill never makes explicit, but which is essential to his argument: that knowledge makes men happy. If, contrary to this assumption, an increase in knowledge would contribute to unhappiness, then, on utilitarian grounds, men ought to refrain from pursuing it. Since Mill does not articulate any evidence in support of this premise, Wolff concludes that the entire argument rests upon an article of faith, one which is at least subject to some doubt in view of the debates among nuclear physicists and geneticists as to the likelihood of further explorations in their fields producing greater misery than happiness among their fellow human beings.

Moreover, a religious believer who is also a utilitarian ought to be opposed to religious liberty, since he would be committed to a belief that adherence to the dogmas of his religion would be more conducive to human happiness than the erroneous beliefs of atheists, agnostics, and members of other cults. Furthermore, it is not clear that even scientific advances depend as much as Mill thought upon absolute freedom of speech and debate. Our schools do not follow Mill's principle, which Wolff suggests would require the establishment of departments of astrology (and, one might add, of creationism and Lamarckian biology) and permission for medical quacks and faddists to practice their arts without official hindrance.

Even in politics, where Wolff concludes that Mill is right, Mill is right for the wrong reasons: It is not truth, but justice, which is served by free and open debate among opposing interest groups.

Wolff concludes by arguing that the weight of empirical evidence is against a strictly utilitarian defense of extreme libertarianism; that welfare-state liberalism is a natural outgrowth of Mill's libertarianism; and that modern American "conservatives" are "merely nineteenth-century Milleans who have refused to admit the facts, and have elevated to the status of absolute and inviolable principles the doctrines which Mill sought to maintain on empirical grounds."

Wolff begins the attack by accusing Mill of failing to distinguish carefully between different types of interests. Mill fails, that is, to observe that the true distinction between the inner and the outer spheres is really a matter of rights or norms, and not of facts. And this causes Mill to blur other important distinctions and to arrive at conclusions which are not supported by the evidence. More importantly, perhaps, Wolff challenges Mill's fundamental assumptions at the root, suggesting, for example, that Mill's personal attachment to the value of individuality misled him into supposing that the absence of all constraint is conducive to its development, whereas it may well be that judicious restraints may be more effective in this regard. In other areas, too, a little meddling may result in considerable reduction of the pain that imprudent persons inflict upon themselves. Even Mill recognized this, as illustrated by his remarks on paternalism vis-à-vis children and savages. Modern welfare-state liberals have rejected Mill's claim that government interference results in greater unhappiness, as evidenced by their adoption of such programs as social security and other forms of regulation; while the conservatives have accepted Mill's factual assessment of the dangers of governmental intrusion into economic and other affairs.

Oddly enough, Mill adopts a paternalistic attitude toward education and culture, which he feels must be imposed upon every child, but tends to be much more liberal (adopting a thoroughly *laissez-faire* position) with regard to material things. Modern liberals, on the other hand, have been loath to impose their aesthetic or doctrinal positions upon the masses, but have not hesitated to regulate drugs, dishwashers, and airfares. Even more paradoxical is Wolff's finding that modern liberals who defend the publication of pornographic materials on the ground that they have "redeeming artistic merits" or "social value" have thereby forsworn the doctrine of absolute freedom of expression, replacing it with appeals to their superior standards of taste—an approach which Mill would have found appalling.

Himmelfarb, Gertrude. *On Liberty and Liberalism: The Case of John Stuart Mill*. New York: Alfred A. Knopf, 1974.

Gertrude Himmelfarb's major thesis is that there is a conflict between the John Stuart Mill of the *Essay on Liberty* and the "other" John Stuart Mill, the bulk of whose work represents a very different trend of liberal thought. Mill's liberalism is suffused with an ambivalence which Himmelfarb maintains has continued to plague liberals to the present day. Her book is divided into three parts: a detailed exposition of the *Essay on Liberty* and an analysis of its contents in the light of Mill's views on the same subjects as expressed in his other writings; an attempt to account for the "extraordinary disparity" between Mill's doctrines in the *Essay on Liberty* and those he expressed in his other writings; and finally, a discussion of the impact Mill's doctrines have had on modern philosophical, social, and legal thinking and the institutions of the Western world.

Much of Himmelfarb's analysis in Part One of her book invokes biographical information and historical settings as well as Mill's own words in order to illuminate the theories he was proposing and the conflicts between his various pronouncements. For example, focusing upon Mill's frequent references to *society*, Himmelfarb notes that this is a radical departure from the views of Mill's father, James Mill, and of James Mill's mentor, Jeremy Bentham, who had regarded "society" as a fiction, insisting that only individuals exist, and that the rulers should be accountable to the people and reflect the interests and the will of the people. It was precisely this notion that Mill inveighed against most fiercely, for in his view, the tyranny of the majority was the greatest evil of all. Society, then, is the chief antagonist in the *Essay on Liberty*, the greatest threat to the individual.

In some of his earlier writings, Mill had contended that there was too much literature and that the public read too much to digest what it read and to exercise its critical faculties over the material upon which it "gorged" itself. He therefore condemned the public for its failure to listen to those who spoke most wisely, preferring instead to listen to those who spoke most frequently. This seems to be quite at variance with Mill's thesis, in the *Essay on Liberty*, that the truth will ultimately prevail if all views are given a free and unimpeded opportunity to be expressed. He even went so far as to recommend the establishment of a "clerisy" supported by the state with the purpose of cultivating and transmitting the national culture, preserving and enlarging the stock of knowledge, and instructing their lesser colleagues, who would serve as residents, guides, guardians, and instructors in their communities. Moreover, Mill had refused to join a writers' society—whose aim was to bring together writers of conflicting opinion—on the ground that he was not interested in assisting anyone in diffusing opinions contrary to his own, but only in promoting those which were "true and just."

At the very time that the *Essay on Liberty* was being published, Mill endorsed the principle that reforms should always be adapted to the framework of the existing constitution. It is "an almost indispensable condition of the stability of free government," he said, to have an "attachment resting on authority and habit to the existing constitution." This appears to be radically at variance with Mill's defense of individualism in Chapter 3 of the *Essay on Liberty*. He argues elsewhere that a "restraining discipline" ought to be the main ingredient of a proper education—and also that when the system of discipline failed on the national level, the disintegration of the state was the inevitable result, with the "natural tendency of mankind to anarchy" reasserting itself. It was therefore necessary, he said, for the state to maintain internal discipline if it was to avoid decline and eventual submission to a despot or to a foreign invader.

Turning to the "applications" Mill makes of his doctrine, Himmelfarb observes that most of these applications seem to be curiously out of touch with the Victorian society in which Mill lived. Indeed, the entire book sounds as though it was aimed at some other society, for, according to Himmelfarb, the Victorians (contrary to prevailing stereotypes) were remarkably liberal in virtually every sense: they engaged openly and sometimes notoriously in extramarital affairs; prostitution was commonplace; they were very free to adopt radical political, religious, and social ideas and to publish them; there were no fetters on scientific inquiry; and people were very free to engage in all kinds of social experimentation. The only norms that were rigidly enforced appear to have been relatively trivial ones which Mill never mentions. Mill himself, in response to some of his critics who made the same points, once claimed that the book was directed at some possible future society which might be more repressive than the one in which he himself was living.

Curiously enough, the one area in which Victorian society was genuinely subject to criticism for its illiberality was almost entirely overlooked by Mill in the book—namely, the equality of women. In other essays, Mill had argued for greater equality of opportunity for women, but in the *Essay on Liberty*, except for a few casual remarks (such as those in connection with polygamy among the Mormons), he has nothing to say about it.

Himmelfarb concludes her book with a look back at the intellectual ancestors of Mill's theory, including John Milton, John Locke, Benedictus de Spinoza, Thomas Jefferson, and Thomas Paine, among others, and at the impact the theory has had upon other thinkers, from Mill's contemporaries to our own time. She distinguishes the kinds of liberty with which he did not choose to deal—political liberty, civil liberties (in the sense of judicial protection of the rights of defendants), and others. Finally, she offers some "paradoxes and anomalies," including a discussion of the controversy over the legalization (or decriminalization) of homosexuality, in which Mill's doctrines played such an important role.—*B.M.L.*

ADDITIONAL RECOMMENDED READING

Berlin, Isaiah. *Four Essays on Liberty*. London: Oxford University Press, 1969. Original essays on some of the issues raised by Mill in the *Essay on Liberty*.

Devlin, Patrick. *The Enforcement of Morals*. London: Oxford University Press, 1968. A recent attack on some of Mill's principal doctrines, in the context of the controversy over the legalization of homosexual relations in Great Britain.

Hart, H. L. A. *Law, Liberty, and Morality*. Stanford, California: Stanford University Press, 1969. A response to Devlin and others, and a defense of Mill's theory, by one of the most distinguished legal philosophers of our time.

Ryan, Alan. *J. S. Mill*. London: Routledge & Kegan Paul, 1974. An excellent summary of Mill's life and works, including a historical and literary analysis of the *Essay on Liberty*.

Schneewind, Jerome B., ed. *Mill: A Collection of Critical Essays*. Garden City, New York: Anchor Books, 1958. A very good collection of recent articles by various authorities on many aspects of Mill's philosophy.

FIRST PRINCIPLES

Author: Herbert Spencer (1820-1903)
Type of work: Philosophy of nature
First published: 1862

PRINCIPAL IDEAS ADVANCED

The business of philosophy is to formulate the laws concerning phenomena common to all the branches of scientific knowledge.

From the principle of the persistence of force can be derived the other principles of natural philosophy, among them the principles of the uniformity of law, the transformation of forces, and the line of least resistance.

The Principle of Evolution and Dissolution is the dynamic and unifying principle of nature; evolution is an integration of matter and a dissipation of motion, during which matter passes from homogeneity to heterogeneity; dissolution occurs when resistance overcomes equilibrium and a system loses its force without adding to its organization.

Society is a kind of superorganism which exemplifies the same principles of differentiation.

Reality is unknowable; we know only appearances.

Spencer intended the *First Principles* to be an introduction to his comprehensive study of the world, entitled *Synthetic Philosophy*. But he made it an independent work, complete in itself, which not merely announced the principles of evolutionary naturalism but illustrated them amply from all fields of knowledge. For good measure, he also raised the issue of science and religion and proposed an amicable solution.

Spencer shared the classical positivist conviction that knowledge consists solely in empirical generalizations or laws. Particular sciences, he held, have the task of formulating the laws which govern special classes of data; but, inasmuch as there are phenomena common to all branches of knowledge, a special science is needed to gather them up into laws. This, he claimed, was the business of philosophy. In his view, that business was now completed. The synthetic philosophy included not only general laws but also one law from which all other laws, both general and specific, could be deduced *a priori*. He therefore offered a new definition of philosophy: it is "completely unified knowledge."

Two highly general principles of natural philosophy were already well-established in Spencer's day; namely, the continuity of motion and the indestructibility of matter. Work in the field of thermodynamics had more recently shown that matter and motion are, in fact, different forms of energy, making it possible to combine these principles into one, which Spencer called the principle of the persistence of force. Here, in his opinion, was a fundamental truth from which all other principles could be deduced. The first principle which Spencer inferred from it was that of the persistence of relations of force, more commonly known as the uniformity of law. The second was that of the transformation of forces; namely, that every loss of motion is attended by an accretion of matter, and vice versa. The third was that motions follow the line of least resistance.

None of these principles, however, sufficed to explain the origin and structure of the ordered world of our experience. What Spencer needed was a unifying principle that applies equally to the burning candle, the quaking earth, and the growing organism. All these events he saw as instances of one vast "transformation." The problem was to find the dynamic principle which governs this metamorphosis as a whole and in all its details. The answer he found in the Principle of Evolution and Dissolution.

Spencer regarded it as his special contribution to philosophy that he was able to show deductively what others (notably the embryologist K. E. von Baer, 1792-1876) had concluded experimentally and on a limited scale; namely, that change is always from a state of homogeneity to a state of heterogeneity. According to Spencer, it is self-evident that homogeneity is a condition of unstable equilibrium. At least this is true of finite masses—though if centers of force were diffused uniformly through infinite space, it might possibly be otherwise; but Spencer held such a state of affairs to be inconceivable. It follows that, because of the inequality of exposure of its different parts, every finite instance of the homogeneous must inevitably lapse into heterogeneity.

Primarily, according to Spencer, evolution was a passing from the less to the more coherent form of energy: for example, the formation of the solar system out of a gaseous nebula. But because the same instability is found in each part of the universe as is found in the whole, the differentiation process will be recapitulated within each new aggregate, giving rise to a secondary evolution: for example, the stratification of the surface of the earth. Primary evolution is a process of integration, the passage from a less to a more coherent form with the dissipation of motion and the concentration of matter. Secondary evolution adds to this a process of differentiation, in the course of which the mass changes from a homogeneous to a heterogeneous state.

But not all heterogeneity is constructive: for example, a tumorous growth. Thus, Spencer had further to qualify his law of change: evolution is change from the indefinite to the definite, from the confused to the ordered. Finally, the same process which has hitherto been stated in terms of matter might equally well be stated in terms of motion: evolution is a concentration of molecular motion with a dissipation of heat.

In sum: "*Evolution is an integration of matter and concomitant dissipation of motion; during which the matter passes from an indefinite, incoherent homogeneity to a definite, coherent heterogeneity; and during which the retained motion undergoes a parallel transformation."*

It was clear to Spencer, however, that evolution cannot go on forever. The redistribution of matter and motion must eventually reach a limit beyond which a simplification takes place: lesser movements are integrated into greater ones, as when the secondary gyrations of a spinning top subside into the main motion. Spencer called this tendency "equilibration." In a harmonious environment, suitably integrated motions continue indefinitely without undergoing noticeable change. Nevertheless, a change is taking place. Resistance, ever so minor, must in time produce its effect upon the system, wearing it down, causing it to dissipate its force without adding to its organization. Even the solar system, which is nearly a perfectly equilibrated system, is losing its energy and must continue to do so until in the distant future it no longer radiates light or heat.

Evolution, therefore, according to Spencer, is only one aspect of the process; it is paralleled by its opposite, dissolution, about which, however, he had little to say because he found it lacking in the interesting features that attend evolution. Still, it is not to be ignored, nor is it a stranger to us. The death of any living organism is "that final equilibration which precedes dissolution, is the bringing to a close of all those conspicuous integrated motions that arose during evolution." And the process of organic decay is dissolution. Particular systems decay while more general systems are still in the state of integration, and Spencer was far from being of the opinion that the evolution of our planetary system has reached its height.

This bare skeleton of Spencer's argument must remain unconvincing without the illustrations which he used to fill it out. To show that the principle of coherence governs even such matters as the evolution of human speech, he pointed out that the primitive Pawnee Indians used a three-syllable word, "ashakish," to designate the animal which the civilized English call by the one-syllable word "dog." The history of the English language offers illustrations of the same tendency toward coherence and integration: witness the passage from the Anglo-Saxon "sunu" through the semi-Saxon "sune" to the English "son"; or, again, from "cuman" to "cumme" to "come." Other examples are taken from politics, industry, art, religion—not to mention the physical sciences. A characteristic one is the following, which shows the change toward heterogeneity in manufactures: "Beginning with a barbarous tribe, almost if not quite homogeneous in the functions of its members, the progress has been, and still is, towards an economic aggregation of the whole human race; growing ever more heterogeneous in respect of the separate functions assumed by separate nations, the separate functions assumed by the local sections of each nation, the separate functions assumed by the many kinds of makers and traders in each town, and the separate functions assumed by the workers united in producing each community."

It was in connection with his argument that homogeneous masses are always unstable that Spencer gave his most explicit account of biological evolution. Given a homogeneous mass of protoplasm, the surface will be subject to different forces from those of the interior, and consequently the two will be modified in different ways. Moreover, one part of the surface is exposed differently from another, so that the ventral features will differ from the dorsal. Again, two virtually identical blobs of protoplasm which chance to arise in different environments—for example, moist and dry—will be modified in different ways. Spencer's theories in these matters had already been published before Darwin's *On the Origin of Species* (1859) appeared, and he saw no reason to change them afterwards. In his view, the real cause of differentiation between species lay in the environmental influences. He thought it probable that modifications in the parent are transmitted through heredity to their offspring. But, in any case, it *must* sometimes happen "that some division of a species, falling into circumstances which give it rather more complex experiences, and demand actions that are more involved, will have certain of its organs further differentiated in proportionately small degrees. . . . Hence, there will from time to time arise an increased heterogeneity both of the Earth's flora and fauna, and of individual races included in them." No doubt Darwin's principle of "natural selection" facilitates the differentiation, he explained in a footnote, but the varieties can be accounted for without it; and without the changes caused by the environment, natural selection would accomplish little.

Spencer's theory of social evolution paralleled his account of biological origins. In his view, society is a kind of superorganism, which exemplifies the same principles of differentiation as those that appear on the inorganic and the organic planes. His was a system of strict determinism which explained social dynamics in terms of universal laws and denied any role to human purpose or endeavor. His guiding principle was the formula that motion follows lines of least resistance. Thus, migrations and wars result from the reaction of societies to climate, geography, and the like. Likewise, internal movements, such as the division of labor and the development of public thoroughfares, arise from the effort to fulfill man's desires in the most economical manner. To the objection that this was only a metaphorical way of viewing social change, Spencer replied that it was not: men are, he said, literally impelled in certain directions, and social processes are in fact physical ones.

Psychology provides further instances. What we think of as mental processes are, from a more fundamental point of view, material ones. Spencer cited as an example the processes of thought engaged in by a botanist who is classifying plants. Each plant examined yields a complex impression; and when two plants yield similar impressions, this "set of molecular modifications" is intensified, "generating an internal idea corresponding to these similar external objects." It is a special case of the general principle called by Spencer "segregation," which states that like units of motion will produce like units of motion in the same or similar aggregates, and unlike will produce unlike.

Such is the tenor of Spencer's system. Philosophy in the traditional sense hardly concerned him. His objective, like that of Descartes, was to put all knowledge on a deductive basis, and his *First Principles*, like Descartes' *Meditations* (1641), merely laid the foundation for the superstructure which was to follow. Unlike Descartes, however, Spencer pleaded ignorance of the underlying nature of things. Following Hume and Kant, he professed that what we know are only appearances, ideas, or impressions in the mind. Reality is unknowable.

Spencer had no intention of wasting his energies on the transcendental problems which concerned Kant and the German speculative philosophers. But he did devote the first hundred pages of his book to "The Unknowable." Here he dealt, very much in the manner of T. H. Huxley, with the limits of human understanding, especially with the claims of revealed religion and of scientific metaphysics. He found it conveniently admitted by Canon H. L. Mansel (1820-1871) of the Church of England that the object of religious devotion cannot be thought. In Mansel's opinion, this belief was due to the relativity of human knowledge, whereas God is, by definition, Absolute. Of course, said Spencer, it is not merely the object of religion that is unknowable. The reality which science describes is also unknowable, if one tries to think of it absolutely. Kant's paralogisms and antinomies make it clear that such concepts as space, time, motion, consciousness, and personality have meaning only in the limited world of experience and tell us nothing about reality.

Nevertheless, said Spencer, the notion of the Absolute is not entirely negative: there is something which defines and limits the knowable; we have a vague, indefinite notion of a being more and other than what we know. Perhaps our closest approach to it is by analogy to the feeling of "power" which we have in our own muscles. The true function of religion is to witness to nature from its mysterious side, as the true function of science is to discover its knowable side. Here as elsewhere Spencer discerned a process of differentiation. The conflict within culture between science and religion is due to "the imperfect separation of their spheres and functions. . . . A permanent peace will be reached when science becomes fully convinced that all its explanations are proximate and relative, while religion becomes fully convinced that the mystery it contemplates is ultimate and absolute."

But, according to Spencer, writing and talking about the problem will not do any good. Cultural changes are not furthered by taking thought concerning them. As presently constituted, men are not ready morally or socially to do without theology: they still need to believe that the Absolute is a person like themselves in order to strengthen their resolve to act rightly. By the time science and religion have differentiated themselves completely, men will presumably have evolved morally to the point that they do good spontaneously.
—J.F.

PERTINENT LITERATURE
Royce, Josiah. *Herbert Spencer: An Estimate and Review*. New York: Fox,
Duffield and Company, 1904.

"Herbert Spencer and his Contribution to the Concept of Evolution" is the
first of two moderately long papers appearing in this volume (the second
concerns Herbert Spencer's theory of education). Spencer's *Autobiography*
had recently appeared. Josiah Royce puts the question: What is the consequence of reconsidering the ideals and methods of Spencer's philosophy in
the light of his autobiography? The paper is in four parts: evolutionary thought
before Spencer's time, the development in Spencer's mind of his view of
evolution, a sketch of Spencer's view in its final form, and some critical
observations.

At the time when Royce was writing, most of those who adhered to
Spencer's system, as well as most of those who opposed it, supposed that
evolution was something new. Royce reviews its history from the Greeks
through the nineteenth century German romantics. Further, he makes the
point that modern thinkers were held back from this way of thinking less by
the dogma of special creation, which, he says, had been discredited among
philosophers from the time of René Descartes and Thomas Hobbes, than by
the dogmas of philosophy itself. It was not supernaturalism but rationalism,
with its one-sided emphasis on universal law and its tendency, favorable to
the development of astronomy and physics, to regard the universe as a permanent order, which delayed the recognition of evolution by philosophers
such as John Stuart Mill and Auguste Comte and by scientists such as George
Lyell and Thomas Henry Huxley.

Spencer's *Autobiography* has an abiding interest for the account it gives of
the author's mental development. Largely self-educated, he read very little,
but was a great "thinker," if only in the sense in which we call a child a great
thinker who sits quietly and puzzles things out. Even so, Spencer was exceptional, if we credit his remark to George Eliot, when she spoke of being
puzzled. "I'm never puzzled," he said; and when she accused him of arrogance
he explained it as a peculiarity of his mind that, left to itself, it seemed to
move automatically from one insight to another. Royce finds this peculiarity
illuminating, and records how Spencer's principles came to him over the years:
a childhood love for tracing causes led to a view of nature that excludes
miracles; love of independence led, in 1843, to a series of letters to *The Non-
Conformist* arguing that government should exercise only police powers; soon
the theory of universal causation took the form of a developmental theory
to account for the origin of living things; then the theory of origins demanded
to be applied to mind as well as to body; finally he found himself in possession
of a coherent theory of nature which not only explained the whole of nature
but also provided a foundation for his individualistic ethics. This line of

development was quite different from that which led Charles Darwin to write *On the Origin of Species*. For about the same reasons that made evolution acceptable to the Presocratics, says Royce, Spencer concluded that natural processes must be responsible for the present variety in nature. Darwin's problem, how to bring the hypothesis of evolutionary origins within the range of scientific inquiry, was no concern of his.

In the third part of his paper Royce attempts to restate Spencer's formula in everyday language. Nature is seen as combining two alternate processes: a primary process in which matter is condensed and solidified into plastic bodies, and a secondary process in which these bodies are liquefied, vaporized, and dissipated. Examples of plastic bodies are our planet and the human brain. As long as a body remains plastic, it contains a great deal of energy, but this is given off as the body further contracts and hardens. The differentiations which come about as a result of such changes bring into play further principles: differentiations are compounded, accenting variety ("multiplication of effects"); new forms unite with like forms ("segregation"), bringing order into confusion—for example, air currents form winds, and floods of water form rivers and tides. In sum, evolution is a change from a state in which there is little firmness and differentiation and orderliness into one in which these are present, the whole process being ultimately describable as a transformation of energy into matter and back.

Royce limits his criticism to one question: How far did Spencer help people to understand evolution? More specifically: Was his attempt to bring the entire world process under one formula sound and enlightening? Royce calls attention to the unresolved duality in Spencer's formula. For example, the law according to which matter condenses while giving off energy, applicable to inorganic evolution, does not explain the development of living things, which absorb energy. Spencer was aware of this, and said that organic evolution is complex, involving both shrinking and swelling, mixing and sorting, variation and order. But this Royce does not find enlightening. The theory becomes so vague that it is equally applicable to dissolution and evolution. What is needed is some way to show how opposing tendencies are brought into the peculiar balance and harmony which makes for development and growth. Royce smiles at Spencer's logical naïveté. "If you found a bag big enough to hold all the facts, that was an unification of science." It was enough for Spencer if he could present an ordered series of illustrations of the principle which he had announced. The requirement that a fruitful hypothesis must serve as an instrument for predicting changes in detail eluded him. Nevertheless, says Royce, his attempt to unify the concepts that make up evolutions is a "permanently inspiring logical idea" likely to bear fruit in the future.

Dewey, John. "The Philosophical Work of Herbert Spencer," in *The Philosophical Review*. XIII, no. 2 (March, 1904), pp. 159-175.

Herbert Spencer's writings, the bible of "advanced thinkers," were coolly received by academic philosophers. For all that, they were an architectural marvel which anyone who was mentally alert had to visit. John Dewey's paper is his attempt to make out this nineteenth century wonder.

It was a wonder that any man could offer subscribers a prospectus for a twelve-volume universal philosophy, as Spencer did in 1860, and devote the remainder of his life to filling in the details. There was something awful and august, Dewey observes, in the way Spencer adhered to his announced program, oblivious to new ideas, new discoveries, and new expansions of life. Other philosophers have produced what, in retrospect, are thought of as systems; Spencer's was a "system in conception, not merely in issue."

A system which can be described in advance is perforce a closed system, and a closed system can emerge only from a self-contained mind. Dewey, who finds it symbolic that Spencer carried ear-plugs so that he could think when in company, describes the seclusion and isolation of Spencer's life: his hit-and-miss schooling, his rejection of the offer of a university scholarship, his refusal to read anything that did not fit in with his ideas. Says Dewey, no intellectual effort has ever been more totally the expression of the makeup of its author. Only Spencer's indifference to the history of thought can explain, for example, how a man devoted to "science" (Dewey supplies the quotation-marks), who thought of himself as "the philosopher of experience," could take it on himself to revive the formal rationalism of the Cartesian school.

Dewey's paper is significant mainly in the manner in which it restores the social and ethical perspective within which Spencer's system was originally conceived. What history was for Karl Marx, evolution was for Spencer, an inevitable progression toward the greatest perfection and happiness of mankind. Characteristically, Spencer was indifferent to history and placed his confidence in laws governing the equilibrium of natural forces. The principles of differentiation and segregation which lead to the development of living organisms and to societies will eventually lead to perfect harmony both within the individual and between individuals and society.

Dewey reminds us that Spencer grew up in a nonconformist home, and points out that the individualism and libertarianism inherited by these remnants of left-wing Puritanism was dogmatic, aggressive, and perfectionalist and differed profoundly from the critical variety of liberalism which formed the mainstream of British political and social thought from John Locke to John Stuart Mill and William Gladstone. It was, says Dewey, more akin to the liberalism of the French Enlightenment, with its faith in human perfectibility and in Nature as working beneficently where not hindered by church or state. In Dewey's opinion, this positive liberalism was what the times required; traditional liberalism having grown thin and remote from practical needs, the only way individualism could be preserved was by coming to terms with new organic concepts of society.

Dewey quotes from Spencer's *Social Statics*, published ten years before the prospect for his *Synthetic Philosophy*. "Man has been, is, and will long continue to be, in process of adaptation, and the belief in human perfectibility merely amounts to the belief that in virtue of these processes, man will eventually become completely suited to his mode of life." Here, says Dewey, although the words "evolution," "environment," and "organism" do not yet come into play, the lineaments of the developed philosophy are all present. The later system is but the projection upon the cosmic screen of the ideals of *laissez-faire* reformism. The social idea was the "far-off event" toward which all moved; biological modes of conception gave it the necessary "scientific coloring"; physical and astronomical speculations provided a causal explanation which make it all look perfectly objective.

This was a far cry from deducing "life, mind, and society" from one universal postulate concerning force, but it was an achievement fully deserving the honor bestowed on it in popular imagination. The fact that Spencer's and Charles Darwin's works appeared at the same time was a great piece of luck for both men, says Dewey: what Spencer lacked in the way of scientific credibility Darwin supplied, and what Darwin lacked in the way of moral complacency Spencer supplied. "Each blended into and fused with the other in the minds of readers and students."

The immediate popularity of Spencer's system betrays its inevitable weakness: people accepted it because it measured up to the intellectual level of the time, not because it asked them to believe anything new. For the same reason the whole system could be laid out in advance: all that Spencer really did was to supply headings under which to dispose of material already at hand. But, in Dewey's opinion, this "wholesale disposal" of material did have the beneficial effect of clearing the ground for new, unthought-of speculation.

Dewey's own radicalism appears in the final paragraph of his paper, where he asks whether what Spencer taught was really evolution. While he spoke of evolution and environment, underneath the new language remained the old rationalist concept of Nature as fixed and eternal. But if there be evolution, says Dewey, nothing can be thought of as fixed: origins, laws, and goals must be defined in terms of process, not vice versa. Spencer offered a world that moved within a fixed frame. Dewey dares to contemplate a world in which reality evolves its own frame.—*J.F.*

ADDITIONAL RECOMMENDED READING

Bowne, Borden P. *Kant and Spencer; a Critical Exposition.* Boston: Houghton Mifflin Company, 1912. Part II, "The Philosophy of Spencer," is a detailed criticism of *First Principles* under the headings agnosticism, doctrine of science, and law of evolution.

Hudson, William Henry. *An Introduction to the Philosophy of Herbert Spencer.* London: Chapman and Hall, 1897. Popular lectures on Spencer's philosophy by an Englishman teaching in an American college. Strongly pro-Spencer.

Kennedy, James G. *Herbert Spencer*. Boston: Twayne, 1978. A general introduction to Spencer's life and work.

Medawar, P. B. "Onwards from Spencer," in *Encounter*. XXI (September, 1963), pp. 35-43. The 1963 Herbert Spencer Lecture by the 1960 Nobel Prize winner in medicine considers the misunderstandings which have led to the belief that living organisms circumvent the Second Law of Thermodynamics.

Randall, John Herman, Jr. "Romantic Faith in Mechanistic Evolution," in *Philosophy After Darwin*. New York: Columbia University Press, 1977. Treats of Spencer with Comte and Marx as accepting evolution as an up-to-date Providence for the salvation of mankind.

Rogers, A. K. "Naturalism and Evolution," in *English and American Philosophy Since 1800*. New York: Macmillan Publishing Company, 1922. A critical evaluation of Spencer's epistemology, ethics, and religious philosophy, as well as of his evolutionary theory.

UTILITARIANISM

Author: John Stuart Mill (1806-1873)
Type of work: Ethics
First published: 1863

PRINCIPAL IDEAS ADVANCED
Those acts are right and good which produce the greatest happiness for the greatest number of persons.

An act derives its moral worth not from its form but from its utility.

Although it is the intrinsic worth of pleasure which gives value to acts conducive to pleasure, some pleasures are better than others in quality.

The proof of the value of pleasure is that it is desired, and the proof of the claim that some pleasures are better than others is that experienced, rational men prefer some pleasures to others.

Justice is the appropriate name for certain social utilities by which the general good is realized.

The central aim of John Stuart Mill's *Utilitarianism* is to defend the view that those acts are right and good which produce the greatest happiness of the greatest number. This ethical position did not originate with Mill. An influential predecessor, Jeremy Bentham, earlier championed pleasure and pain as the sole criteria for judging what is good and bad. The utility yardstick measures good by asking: Does an act increase pleasure, and does it decrease pain? Bentham's crude "Push-pin is as good as poetry" interpretation of the yardstick led to numerous criticisms. Therefore, Mill states the principle of utility in its most defensible form both to counter some specific criticisms of it and to make clear what are the sanctions of the principle. He also offers a proof of the principle. The work concludes with a discussion of the relation of utility to justice.

The ethics of Utilitarianism influenced a large number of public men and helped to shape important reform legislation in nineteenth century British political life.

Utilitarianism opens with the author's lament that little progress has occurred through centuries of ethical analysis. Ethical philosophers seeking to define the nature of "good" have left a number of incompatible views to their intellectual posterity. Mill admits that history of scientific thought also contains confusion about the first principles of the special sciences. Yet this is more to be expected in the sciences than in moral philosophy. Legislation and morals involve practical rather than theoretical arts. Since such arts always aim at ends of action rather than thought, they require agreement about a standard by which the worth of those ends can be evaluated. There is greater need of fixing the foundation of morals than of stating the theoretical principles underlying bodies of scientific knowledge. The sciences result from accumulation of many particular truths, but in moral philosophy "A test of right and wrong must be the means, one would think, of ascertaining what is right or wrong, and not a consequence of having already ascertained it."

Ethical intuitionists insist that men possess a natural faculty which discerns moral principles. Against them, Mill argues that appeal to a "moral sense" cannot solve the problem of an ultimate ethical standard for judging acts. No intuitionist claim about knowledge of moral principles can provide a basis for decisions regarding cases. Intuitionist and inductive moral theorists usually disagree about the "evidence and source" grounding moral principles. Clearly, then, the main problem facing moral philosophers is that of justifying our judgments in the light of a defensible principle.

Mill asserts that even those philosophers must invoke the greatest happiness principle who wish to reject it. For example, the German philosopher Immanuel Kant claimed that the basis of moral obligation involves a categorical imperative: "So act that the rule on which thou actest would admit of being adopted as a law of all rational beings." Mill insists that numerous, even contradictory, notions of duties can follow from this imperative. Kant's noble effort thus leads to decisions which can be shown to be immoral only because the consequences of some universally adopted acts would be unwanted by most men.

The fact that men tacitly employ the utility yardstick is not the same as a proof of its validity. Mill offers to present such a proof. He makes clear that no absolutely binding proof, "in the ordinary and popular meaning of the term," is possible. To give a philosophical proof means to advance reasons directed at man's rational capacities. Philosophical proofs are their own kinds of proofs. It is in this sense of proof that Mill promises to make good after he has first more fully characterized the Utilitarian doctrine.

Mill must first perform an important polemical function in replying to critics who find problems with the Utilitarian doctrine. The polemic is to serve the persuasive goal of winning over critics to a proper understanding of Utilitarianism, whose basic view of life is "that pleasure and freedom from pain are the only things desirable as ends." A corollary to this claim is that all things desirable are so either for the pleasure they can directly produce or for ways in which they serve as means to other pleasures or preventions of pain. Aware that some thinkers view his idea as a base moral conception, Mill states a number of outstanding objections to it. He argues that the objections represent either misunderstandings of the Utilitarian doctrine or, if they contain some truth, views which are not incompatible with it.

Mill rejects the argument that Utilitarianism chooses to picture human nature at the lowest animal level. Clearly, animals are incapable of experiencing many pleasures available and important to men. Every "Epicurean theory of life" also admits that intellectual pleasures are more valuable than those of simple sensation. "It is quite compatible with the principle of utility to recognize the fact that some kinds of pleasure are more desirable and more valuable than others." Pleasures must be judged in terms of quality as well as quantity. Mill suggests a way in which the value of two possible pleasures may be determined. Only that man can decide who, out of wide experience, knows both pleasures and can thus state a comparative judgment. Apparently Mill believed this test is adequate. He assumed that the man of experience actually knows the worth of competing pleasures in a manner which is not simply psychological but objective. Rational beings should choose pleasures of higher quality. Not all men are equally competent to render decisive judgments. In a striking sentence Mill writes: "It is better to be a human being dissatisfied than a pig satisfied."

A summary statement of important criticisms of the Utilitarian doctrine, along with brief descriptions of Mill's replies, is here in order. First, the Utilitarian "greatest happiness" principle is said to be too exalted in expecting human beings to adopt a disinterested moral posture. Mill's reply is that in serving the interests of one's fellow creatures the motive may be either self-interest or duty. The resulting act rather than the motive must be judged, though the motive of duty can influence us to honor also the character of the doer. Men can promote the general interests of society without always fixing "their minds upon so wide a generality as the world, or society at large." Second, to the charge that Utilitarianism will make men cold and unsympathizing, Mill answers that men should show interest in things other than those concerned with standards of right and wrong. Yet it is necessary to emphasize the need of making judgments of right and wrong and to supply moral standards for human behavior. Third, Mill calls simply false the view that Utilitarianism is a godless doctrine. Religiously inclined men can use the Utilitarian standard to determine what in detail the will of God means for human action. Fourth, some critics complain that Utilitarianism will end in expediency. Mill's rebuttal is that the utility principle does not justify acts which result only in the pleasure of the lone individual. The social standard must always operate. Fifth, Mill argues that Utilitarianism can account even for the actions of martyrs and heroes. Heroism and martyrdom involve individual sacrifices whose ultimate aim is the increase in the happiness of others or of society as a whole. Other criticisms—that Utilitarianism overlooks lack of time for men to decide the results of given actions and that Utilitarians may use the doctrine to exempt themselves from moral rules—are shown to apply equally to other ethical doctrines.

Mill goes on to admit that other questions about a moral standard can be raised. For what reasons should any person adopt the standard? What motivates one to apply it? Such questions about the sanctions of a moral standard Mill treats as if they are meaningful. There are two possible kinds of sanction for Utilitarianism—an external and an internal one. Desire of favor and also fear of displeasure from one's fellows, or from a sovereign God, constitute the Utilitarian principle's external sanctions. Given feelings of affection for other men or awe for a God, men may act also out of unselfish motives which can "attach themselves to the Utilitarian morality, as completely and powerfully as to any other."

Conscience makes up the internal sanction of the principle. Mill defines conscience as "a pain, more or less intense, attendant on violation of duty." This sanction is really a feeling in the mind such that any violation of it results in discomfort. Even the man who thinks moral obligation has roots in a transcendental sphere acts only conscientiously insofar as he harbors religious feelings about duty. There must be a subjective feeling of obligation. But is this feeling of duty acquired or innate? If innate, the problem concerns the objects of the feeling. Intuitionists admit that principles rather than the details of morality get intuited. Mill argues that the Utilitarian emphasis on regard for the pleasures and pains of others might well be an intuitively known principle. Some regard for interests of others is seen as obligatory even by intuitionists who insist on yet other obligatory principles. Mill thought that any sanction provided by a transcendental view of the origin of obligation is available to the Utilitarian doctrine.

Nevertheless, Mill's view was that men's notions of obligation are actually acquired. Though not a part of man's nature, the moral faculty is an outgrowth of it. This faculty can arise spontaneously in some circumstances as well as benefit from proper environmental cultivation. The social feelings of mankind provide a basis of natural sentiment which supports the Utilitarian doctrine. "Society between equals can only exist on the understanding that the interests of all are to be regarded equally." Proper education and social arrangements can encourage the moral feelings toward virtuous activity. By education men can learn to value objects disinterestedly which, in the beginning, they sought only for the sake of pleasure. Mill claims that virtue is one good of this kind.

In *Utilitarianism* Mill raises the peculiar question as to whether the utility principle can be proved. It is difficult to understand what kind of question Mill thought he was asking here. The setting for this question appears to involve something like the following: When someone asks if the principle has any sanctions, it is as if he were to ask: "Why should I seek the good even if the utility principle is sound?" But when someone asks for a proof of the principle, it is as if he were to inquire: "How can I know *that* the utility principle is true?" Strangely, this question comes up only after Mill has already refuted a whole range of criticisms of the Utilitarian doctrine as well as shown the sanctions which support it.

Mill argues that "the sole evidence it is possible to produce that anything is desirable, is that people do actually desire it." One difficulty with this assertion concerns the word "sole." Even if it is true that nothing can be desirable which is not desired by someone, would it follow necessarily that one's desire of an object is sufficient evidence of its desirability? If not, what besides desire would account for an object's desirability? Contextually, it would appear that Mill might have to agree that though everything desirable must be desired, not everything desired need be desirable. This would follow from his earlier claim that some pleasures are qualitatively better than others. A human being who desired to live like a pig would seek to evade realizing the highest kind of happiness available to him. To this argument Mill might have wanted to reply that, in fact, no man really does want to live like a pig. Yet the most controversial aspect of Mill's proof occurs when he insists that "each man's happiness is a good to that person, and the general happiness, therefore, a good to the aggregate of all persons." Some philosophers call this statement an example of an elementary logical fallacy—attribution of a property applicable to the parts of a collection to the collection itself. The Utilitarian stress on men's obligation to seek the happiness of the greatest number raises a question about the relation of individual pleasures to social ones. A man may desire to drive at high speeds as an individual, yet not have grounds for making desirable the changing of the speed rules. What Mill wants to underline is that in conflicts between social and individual interests, the individual interests must often give way.

Ultimately a conception of human nature must serve as justification of Mill's use of the utility principle. The proof runs to the effect that men are, after all, naturally like that. If they do not seek happiness directly, they seek other ends as a means to it. To a skeptic convinced that the principle cannot be proved by an appeal to human nature, Mill might have said: "Obviously, you misunderstand what you really desire." In this case the utility principle is proved in that it conforms to what men are like. On this basis, however, it seems peculiar to want to argue that men *ought* to use the principle in making moral judgments. To say that men ought to act in a given way is to imply that they may not.

The concluding chapter of *Utilitarianism* discusses the relation of justice to utility. The idea of justice tends to impede the victory of the Utilitarian doctrine, according to Mill. Men's sentiment of justice seems to suggest existence of a natural, objective norm which is totally divorced from expediency and hedonistic consequences. Mill's task was to indicate how the Utilitarian doctrine could accommodate this sentiment and nevertheless remain the sole acceptable standard for judging right and wrong.

One must examine objects in the concrete if he wants to discover whatever common features they may contain. This is true of the idea of justice. Several fundamental beliefs are associated in popular opinion with notions like "just" and "unjust." Justice involves respect for the legal and moral rights of other people. It implies the wrongfulness of taking away another's moral rights by illegal or even legal means. There can be bad laws. The notion of desert is also important. This notion entails belief that wrongdoing deserves punishment and the doing of right, reciprocation in good acts. Justice cannot mean doing good in return for evil, according to Mill. Nevertheless men may waive justice when they are wronged. Furthermore, men ought not to break promises which are willingly and knowingly made. This is so even in the case of implied promises. Justice precludes breach of faith. Finally, justice implies impartiality and equality in the treatment of men and claims. This means that men ought to be "influenced by the considerations which it is supposed ought to influence the particular case in hand." Mill concludes that several general features rather than one are common to these opinions about justice. Turning to the etymology of the word, he asserts that the primitive meaning of justice is "conformity to law." The Greeks and Romans, recognizing the possibility of bad laws, came to view injustice as the breaking of those laws which ought to be obeyed. The idea of justice in personal conduct also involves the belief that a man ought to be forced to do just acts.

To say that justice accepts the idea of the desirability of compelling someone to do his duty tells men what justice is about. Yet it does not mark off the peculiar nature of justice from other branches of morality. According to Mill, justice involves the notion of perfect obligation. Duties of perfect obligation imply the existence of a correlative right in a person or persons. "Justice implies something which it is not only right to do, and wrong not to do, but which some individual person can claim from me as his moral right." This view of justice admits a distinction between moral obligation and the domains of beneficence and generosity. In men the sentiment of justice becomes "moralized," spread over a social group or community. Justice then involves the feeling that one ought to punish those who harm members of that community. Men's need of security plays a role here. The idea of right does also. Justice involves a belief that there are rights which morally society must defend. Thus justice is compatible with the utility principle, for "when moralized by the social feeling, it only acts in directions conformable to the general good."

The idea of justice requires belief in a rule of conduct applicable to all men, plus a sentiment which sanctions the rule. This sentiment, which insists that transgressors be punished, is compatible with the utility principle if the idea of justice is taken to refer to special classes of moral rules. These are the rules without which the realization of the general good would be impossible. An important example of such rules would be those forbidding one person to harm another. Such rules presuppose the Utilitarian doctrine that one person's happiness must be considered as important as another's. Mill's conclusion is that "Justice remains the appropriate name for certain social utilities which are vastly more important, and therefore more absolute and imperative, than any others are as a class."

Utilitarianism is a book of significance for thinkers concerned about the problem of moral fairness in a social setting. Mill attempted to show that men's notions of obligation can be made compatible with the utility principle. What animates the work is Mill's clear conviction that even the more exalted moral claims of intuitionists and Kantian moralists make sense only if the Utilitarian doctrine is the true one. Only with justice and binding rules of obligation can man achieve the greatest happiness of the greatest number. —*W.T.D.*

PERTINENT LITERATURE

Albee, Ernest. *A History of English Utilitarianism*. London: Sonnenschein, 1902.

Just as Ernest Albee's book *A History of English Utilitarianism* offers a survey of its general subject matter, so Chapters X-XII present a survey of the more specific topic of John Stuart Mill's version of Utilitarianism. In doing so they give their reader considerable information concerning the relationships between Mill's theories and those of other writers within the Utilitarian tradition, as well as a view of the development of Mill's own thinking on ethical issues. Finally, in these chapters Albee offers a systematic explanation and a detailed critical analysis of Mill's central tenets in moral philosophy.

Chapter X is devoted to Mill's early essays on ethical topics, which consist mainly of commentaries on the views of contemporary writers such as Jeremy Bentham, Samuel Taylor Coleridge, and William Whewell. Albee makes a point of emphasizing that in these essays Mill is not only beginning to formulate the positions that he will develop fully later but that, in the process, he is also commencing the task of transforming Utilitarianism from a relatively narrow and rigid conception of morality into one that is broader and more humane. Of particular interest is the discussion of Mill's essay *Bentham* (1838), for Albee makes it clear that even at such an early date Mill, far from being a slavish disciple of his mentor, was acutely aware of major weaknesses in the Benthamite position.

In Chapter XI Albee turns to more mature expressions of Mill's ethics that appear in several writings, beginning with an examination of his views on the controversy between determinism and free will, and the conclusions he draws from them regarding the possibility of developing a science of human nature. It was Mill's conviction that such a science is possible, Albee emphasizes, that was to determine the direction that his subsequent reasoning in ethics would take. It also, Albee adds, explains the ultimate failure of Mill's enterprise; for since ethics cannot be reduced to the natural sciences, it cannot be dealt with through a methodology patterned on theirs.

According to Albee, Mill had come to recognize the impossibility of basing his ethics simply on an analysis of human nature by the time he completed his essay *Utilitarianism*. As far as the details of the theory presented in that essay are concerned, Albee attaches considerable importance to Mill's departure from Bentham, embodied in his claim that pleasures differ from one another qualitatively as well as quantitatively. In Albee's opinion, such a view, besides being inconsistent with Mill's stated hedonism, is historically significant because it represents a break from the narrower Utilitarianism of the past to a wider form of the theory yet to be successfully articulated. Albee continues his account with detailed remarks on the various issues raised in *Utilitarianism*, taking special note of Mill's emphasis on sympathy as a motivating force for moral action, a view that also set him apart from earlier Utilitarians, with their conception of universal psychological egoism. Albee does not devote much space to Mill's argument in support of hedonism that appears in Chapter IV of *Utilitarianism*, offering little criticism of it—a lacuna in his account that was filled shortly afterwards by G. E. Moore. His substantive discussion of Mill's ethics ends with some remarks on Mill's attempt to incorporate the duty of justice within the framework of his hedonistic ethics, as this appears in the final chapter of *Utilitarianism*. Albee sums up Mill's special contribution to our philosophical tradition with the comment: "Seldom, indeed, has a personality accounted for more in the whole history of Ethics."

Moore, G. E. *Principia Ethica*. New York: Cambridge University Press, 1903.

The classic critique of John Stuart Mill's ethics appears in Chapter III of G. E. Moore's *Principia Ethica*. Until recently the criticisms Moore levels there against Mill's case for hedonism in *Utilitarianism* have been considered by most moral philosophers to be so decisive as neither to require further supplementation nor to countenance successful defense of the views they attack.

Moore's main objection to hedonism, which he states at the beginning of the chapter, is that the arguments by which it is generally supported commit the naturalistic fallacy; they mistakenly identify the concept of "good" with that of "pleasure" and by doing so consequently fail "to distinguish clearly that unique and indefinable quality which we mean by good." Pursuing his case in detail, Moore concentrates his attention on Chapter IV of *Utilitarianism*, which contains Mill's celebrated "proof" of the principle of utility. After having noted that Mill assumes, for the purpose of his argument, that the term "desirable" is equivalent to "good," he points out that Mill then reduces the notion of what is desirable to that of what is in fact desired. In doing so he commits the naturalistic fallacy, being led into this error through drawing a false analogy between the meaning of "desirable" on the one hand and that of "audible" and "visible" on the other. The falsity of the analogy, of course, lies in the fact that the first concept is normative and the second two are descriptive; it is this confusion on Mill's part that motivates Moore's description of his error as an example of the naturalistic fallacy.

Turning to the second step in Mill's argument, the attempt to establish that pleasure is the only thing that we desire, hence (by his first argument) the only thing good, Moore begins by pointing out that Mill actually denies his own thesis through his admission that we do in fact desire things other than pleasure. To repair this flaw in his argument he goes on to contend that, ultimately, we do desire nothing but pleasure because, in desiring these other things, we are desiring them as a part of our pleasure. Moore examines Mill's reasoning on this issue at length, laying bare a number of confusions in it, including particularly Mill's mistaken view that pleasure is the object of our desires, rather than the view, for which support can be given, that it is a cause of our desires, and the even more egregious error that leads him to affirm that money (that is, physical coins), when desired for its own sake, must be identical with feelings in our consciousness. Against such fallacious argumentation, Moore considers the best antidote to lie in an epigram taken from Joseph Butler, which he reproduces on the title page of *Principia Ethica*: "Everything is what it is, and not another thing."

On the positive side, Moore argues that the question of whether hedonism is true or false, even though it cannot be resolved by the type of argument that Mill employed in *Utilitarianism*, is susceptible to rational adjudication. Ultimately, he contends, the issue must be settled by an appeal to intuition or direct insight into values. We are capable of such insight, and our capacities can be heightened by deliberate effort and buttressed by argument. At their best, Moore concludes, they reject Mill's hedonistic thesis that pleasure is the only good thing good as an end.

Ryan, Alan. *J. S. Mill*. London: Routledge & Kegan Paul, 1974.

Alan Ryan's approach to the ethics of John Stuart Mill is representative of a relatively recent trend toward viewing Mill's contribution to Utilitarianism with greater sympathy than had critics under the influence of G. E. Moore. Ryan does not refrain from criticism, but he also tries to evaluate individual arguments in terms of the total context of Mill's thought, with the result that their deficiencies do not appear so glaring as they had to Moore. His general perspective is that, despite the numerous logical errors he committed in defending his position, Mill made a major contribution to one of the most important theories in the history of ethics.

Ryan begins his discussion of *Utilitarianism* by pointing out that it is necessary to an understanding of Mill's line of argument to appreciate the general intellectual setting in which it was written and the kind of audience to whom it was addressed. To gain acceptance for his Utilitarian view Mill believed it necessary to resolve three problems, all of them associated with a perceived antagonism between a secular ethics such as Utilitarianism and the traditional

Christian creed, which had become embodied in the intuitionistic moral pronouncements of eighteenth century English divines. (1) The appeal to consequences as a guide to moral action lacks the clarity and immediate authority of an appeal to rules of conduct already laid down. (2) Such an appeal also runs the danger of undermining the individual's sense of duty, and hence of encouraging immorality. (3) The Utilitarian goal of the maximization of pleasure was considered by many to be morally obnoxious, as witness Thomas Carlyle's description of Utilitarianism as a "pig philosophy." If, in reading *Utilitarianism*, one imaginatively puts himself into the historical situation in which it was written, Ryan contends, he will recognize that Mill's case was largely shaped by his attempts to find answers to these objections to his theory.

Ryan views Mill's ethics as forming a central component of a wider interest, which he calls "the Art of Life." Mill is not clear about what is included within this broader domain, but indicates that, in addition to morality, it comprises prudence and aesthetics. In all of these realms the standard by which our actions should be guided, according to Mill, is that of the maximization of good (pleasurable) consequences.

On the vexed question of Mill's "proof" of the principle of utility, Ryan accepts the verdict of critics that the argument in Chapter IV of *Utilitarianism* is rent with errors, but suggests that some plausibility can be given to Mill's effort if we turn to other passages in which he states his case in a different form. Specifically, if we remember that in his *Logic* Mill had offered an inductive argument in support of induction, we can view him in *Utilitarianism* as doing the same for the principle of utility, defending the appeal to consequences as the ultimate justification of moral action on the grounds that people tacitly do accept such an appeal already. The difficulty with this form of inductive argument, however, lies in its inability to draw a vital distinction— between the grounds on which we actually make moral judgments and the grounds on which we ought to make them.

Ryan concludes his chapter with a review of Mill's Utilitarian explanation of justice. Of it he writes: "Mill's account of justice is one of the most interesting parts of his moral theory; it is also better argued than most. . . ." He nevertheless does not agree with Mill's interpretation but rather finds it deficient in two related respects. First, he agrees with most critics in finding unacceptable Mill's attempt to explain the concept of "desert" (for example, in justifying rewards and punishments) in terms of the good consequences that a just procedure will produce and an unjust procedure prevent. Second, he argues that Mill's Utilitarianism cannot explain either the rules we have for what we discern to be cases of just ways of acting or our obligation to follow these rules in practice.—*O.A.J.*

ADDITIONAL RECOMMENDED READING
Anschutz, R. P. *The Philosophy of J. S. Mill*. Oxford: Clarendon Press, 1953.

A survey of Mill's philosophy, beginning with a chapter on his ethics.

Britton, Karl. *John Stuart Mill*. London: Penguin Books, 1953. A short account of Mill's philosophy with a chapter devoted to his ethics.

McCloskey, H. J. *John Stuart Mill: A Critical Study*. London: Macmillan and Company, 1971. A critical account of Mill's thought, including his ethics.

Plamenatz, J. P. *The English Utilitarians*. Oxford: Basil Blackwell, 1949. A brief history of the main Utilitarian writers with a chapter devoted to Mill.

Schneewind, J. B., ed. *Mill: A Collection of Critical Essays*. Garden City, New York: Anchor Books, 1968. Nineteen essays on Mill by contemporary scholars, concentrating primarily on his ethics.

Stephen, Leslie. *The English Utilitarians*. London: Duckworth and Company, 1900. A classic survey of the English Utilitarians in their social and historical settings; most of Volume III is devoted to Mill.

THE PHILOSOPHY OF THE UNCONSCIOUS

Author: Eduard von Hartmann (1842-1906)
Type of work: Metaphysics
First published: 1869

PRINCIPAL IDEAS ADVANCED

An unconscious will is the ground and true cause of everything that comes to be.

Morality, history, and the mind of genius all show the unconscious will at work.

The universe is composed of atoms, but the atoms are atoms of force, not matter.

Although the unconscious will never errs, in evolving consciousness, which is its opposite, it shows itself to be irrational in its creative process.

The philosopher, who prizes consciousness and rationality, is the enemy of the will; by being conscious he triumphs over will.

Man reaches "old age," or philosophical maturity, only after passing through the "childhood" stage (in which happiness is sought), the stage of "youth" (in which one counts on the rewards in heaven), and the stage of "manhood" (in which man labors to build a paradise on earth).

Hartmann completed this most celebrated book, of some thirty which came from his hand, before he was twenty-five years of age. More than a thousand pages long (in the English translation), it revived the agnostic spirit of German speculative philosophy to combine it with the findings of empirical science. (It bears the subtitle, "Speculative Results According to the Inductive Method of Physical Science.") Its protest against the mechanistic view of nature and against the liberal and optimistic view of man found a large and appreciative audience. Its appeal to nature ministered to the sentimentality of dying romanticism, and its teleological outlook strengthened religious orthodoxy in its struggle against Darwinism. But it has the more enduring claim of being one of the wellsprings of modern irrationalism as expressed in the literature of psychoanalysis and in the political theories of right-wing socialism.

At the center of Hartmann's thought is the notion of an unconscious will which is the ground and only true cause of everything that comes to be. He has drawn freely from Fichte, Schelling, Hegel, and Schopenhauer, as well as from Herbart and Fechner. But, broadly speaking, what he has done is to combine the Hegelian notion of the unconscious self-unfolding of the Idea with Schopenhauer's notion of a blind, striving will. In his opinion, Schopenhauer did not do justice to the fact that every act of willing presupposes a purpose. The future state must be contained in the present existing state, and since it cannot be there actually, it must be there ideally, as representation.

On the other hand, Hegel did not bring out clearly what is involved in the conception of Absolute Idea which has not yet been externalized in nature or become conscious in mind. If the ideal realm is not thought of as residing in God, considered as conscious and therefore as Spirit (which, for Hegel it was not, since Spirit is the fulfillment of the System), then it remains that it is unconscious and present only as will.

Hartmann's choice of the term "will" to designate his first principle is based on the analogy of conscious activity. Volition is "the form of causality of the ideal with respect to the real." When a man wills, he imagines a future event which he is in a position to bring about, but only through intermediate causes. The infallible mark of will is that it gives rise to preconceived action. But, argues Hartmann, we have only to open our eyes to see that preconceived action is going on all around us, and that conscious willing is only a special case of a universal phenomenon. The only straightforward and intelligible name for this universal cause is "will."

As *The Philosophy of the Unconscious* is divided, the first two parts, which are entitled "The Unconscious in Bodily Life" and "The Unconscious in Mind," are devoted to illustrating the author's thesis that everything in nature and history is the working out of an unconscious purpose. The third part, called "Metaphysic of the Unconscious," traces the evolution of the cosmos out of the unconscious and explores the moral consequences of this knowledge.

Writing only ten years after the appearance of Darwin's *On the Origin of Species*, Hartmann found the theory of natural selection a good target. Not that he repudiated altogether the mechanistic type of explanation—nature does operate to a great extent according to mechanical principles—but these pertain only to means and pay no regard to ends. Hartmann elaborates a proof against the chances of our world's having emerged mechanically by using the well-worn method of mathematical probabilities. For example, the physiology of that day enumerated thirteen conditions necessary for the existence and maintenance of normal vision. All are there at birth, although the occasion for their exercise has never arisen. The material conditions of the blastoderm offer not the slightest probability that any one of the conditions (say, the optic nerve) should develop. Clearly something is missing in a purely mechanical explanation.

From the argument based on abstract probability, Hartmann turns to the ever-startling evidences of teleological behavior in nature. There is, for example, a wisdom of the body not confined to the cortex—the beating of the heart, the rhythm of the stomach-muscles, the minute adjustments commonly referred to as "reflexes." Add to these a catalogue of the curious instincts of spiders and bees, the reparative powers in the limbs of a crab, and the whole science of embryology. Everywhere we meet immanent purpose, or will. Hartmann does not limit himself to such commonplace examples; perhaps much of the excitement which the work held for the nineteenth century reading public lay in the thoroughness of his compilation, which must have cost him many hours with books on nature.

No less comprehensive than his treatment of the inner teleology of nature is his account of the works of the unconscious in the character and conduct of man. For many readers today, Hartmann's chief significance doubtless lies in the manner in which he anticipated depth psychology when he pointed out the obliquely purposive quality of many of our seemingly unintentional acts. But Hartmann's interest in these facts extends merely to the support they lend to his thesis of universal teleology, and he does not linger over them. In fact, he is less concerned with the bizarre behavior which occupies the medical psychologists than with the social and cultural achievements of the race. Thus, speech is originally as unpremeditated as the cry of a bird; but it contains the rudiments of logic and philosophy—a point of his system which he allows was ably developed before him by Schelling. And there is more than an echo of the romantic philosophers in his account of artistic production, where he distinguishes between genius and talent and exalts the products of inspiration (Plato's "divine frenzy") over so-called art which is the product of rules and conscious design. He places taste on the level of instinct, together with morality. His teaching is that moral principles are innate, and that when a people emerges from barbarism to a civilized estimate of moral principles, there is then a coming to consciousness of judgments which were subconsciously present all the time. Not merely the fruits of civilization, but the historical process itself is the working out of a secret plan. History makes sense, and the great upheavals and movements which mark its course give expression to unconscious Ideas. Like Hegel, Hartmann holds that these are sometimes disclosed to masses of men, as when a new conception takes possession of an entire people without anyone consciously discovering it; but perhaps more often they are revealed through the mind of a single genius, more conscious than his fellows, who serves as a prophet for the coming of the will.

Writing as he did against the background of post-Kantian speculation, Hartmann was especially concerned with the question of the status to be given to the individual in relation to the absolute. The unconscious, in his system, is unity, and for Hartmann, as for his predecessors, the world of appearance is an unfolding of infinite potentialities hidden there. In the last analysis, therefore, everything that comes to pass owes its existence to this Primal Being. But Hartmann tried to overcome the complaints which had arisen since Hegel's time against Idealism on the grounds that it did not do justice to the reality either of nature or of the personality of the individual. Instead of conceiving the world as a purely ideal representation, he thought of it as built up of atoms, very much in accordance with the chemistry and biology of his day. The distinctive thing in his account, which made it possible for him to reconcile scientific realism with his doctrine of the will, was that he conceived of the atoms purely as forces. He distinguished between body-atoms and ether-atoms, representing respectively the forces of attraction and of repulsion; and by the behavior of these, he accounted for the laws of matter. This part of his system he called "dynamic atomism," and he claimed that by atoms of force he could account for anything which more conservative scientists could explain in terms of atoms of matter. At bottom, of course, each of his atoms was thought of as an expression of the unconscious and as fulfilling a unique purpose in the world plan.

From this beginning, Hartmann went on to explain the rise of living crea-tures, from the simplest organisms to man. A striking feature of his system (which inevitably reminds us of Leibniz's) is the way in which he argues that psychic activity is present in the lowest organisms and that sensibility is present in plants as well as in animals. The natural world, therefore, is as real as anything else. The Neoplatonic prejudice against materiality has no hold here. Higher forms of being have exactly the same kind of reality as lower. For although the world is an ascending evolution in which the potentialities of the unconscious are ever more completely actualized, the higher products are always conditioned by the lower. Even consciousness, which is the goal and end product of the whole development, is bound to physiological conditions. It is found only in higher vertebrates and is absolutely dependent upon the healthy working of a brain and nervous system.

In this way, Hartmann "saves" appearance, preserving for the world of nature the reality demanded by the physical scientists, for the world of eco-nomics the reality demanded by political agitators, and for human ambitions and aspirations the reality demanded by moralists and philosophers of reli-gion. They are, in the final analysis, only appearances, because they are really expressions of the sovereign purpose of the unconscious will. They have the only kind of existence that is conceivable to partial and particular things separated from the world ground. They are what Hartmann calls "objectively real phenomena."

Thus, he comes to the border of a still more difficult problem: Why is there something instead of nothing? If the unconscious is the ground of being, why did it extend itself to become something which it was not? Is there a second world principle independent of the unconscious which seduces it out of the eternal night? Is creativity a "fall"? Space has sometimes been thought to function in this way, as the void disturbed the eternal calm of Plotinus' One. But for Hartmann, following Kant, space is itself posited by the unconscious as the theater for its tragic representation. And in any case, a dualistic ex-planation offends our deepest philosophical instincts. The only possible ex-planation is that the dynamism which causes the unconscious to unfold itself lies within the original unity itself. This would be the case if, as Hartmann held, the unconditioned is neither the pure Idea of Hegel nor the pure will of Schopenhauer, but will and Idea inextricably combined, an irrational impulse ever stirring itself to accomplish rational ends. According to Hartmann, the unconscious is, from one point of view, perfectly rational. When it comes to realizing its ends, it is infallible. It never hesitates, it never errs, but in virtue of an absolute clairvoyance, it achieves with minimal effort the goal which it has set before it. In this sense, ours is the best possible world, and the eighteenth century was correct in its praises of the wisdom of divine providence. But the other side of the question is whether no world at all would not have been better than this one, whether a fully rational being would have permitted any world to be. The answer is not to be given in terms of our egoistic satisfaction, but from the point of view of reason itself. And the fact that the direction of evolution is toward the production of consciousness, which is the contradictory of its original, makes it clear that creation is irrational and yet, in terms of its own conditions, it should not be. It is self-defeating, hence absolutely bad. Pure, blind chance would not have been evil in any profound sense. But an absolute in which the rational and the irrational are inseparably and eternally one is criminal. It is "willful" in the derogatory sense of that word.

Hartmann's pessimism differed from the *Weltschmerz* of the romantics in that it was theoretically based and not merely an expression of frustrated hedonism. This base accounts for the apparent ambiguities in his attitudes toward evolution and progress. Creation and history are a madman's tale which must be condemned *in toto*. They are also to be condemned for the point of view of the individual ego, which tries to maintain its own private worth and satisfaction. But the tendency of evolution is to produce ever higher consciousness. And insofar as an individual is so fortunate as to be endowed with superior understanding, he can affirm that evolution is progress and that the end result is good. He does so by depending on the inherently contradictory unconscious. For the unconscious tends to destroy itself, and the true philosopher, insofar as he lives on the plane of consciousness, is its nemesis. Knowing this, he affirms rationality and intelligibility wherever these manifest themselves in evolution and history. He can even affirm pain, because that is an ingredient in consciousness and a condition for the emergence of free intelligence.

Consciousness, according to Hartmann, is the emancipation of idea from will, just as unconsciousness is the inseparable unity of idea and will. It extricates the rational elements of being from their native soil, the realizing will, and in this way disarms the cunning of the absolute or diverts it into channels where it can do no harm. Hartmann is, in this respect, on the side of enlightenment and intelligence; he has no patience with those who would make voluntarism an excuse for resigning themselves to the movements of the unconscious. According to Hartmann, man cannot with impunity neglect the use of his higher endowments, for when the unconscious evolves a complicated machine to do a certain work, it makes no provision for that work to be done in other ways. Thus, when man received intelligence, he was deprived of instinct. The unconscious does nothing in vain, and a human being who refuses to think is simply discarded like so much rubbish. Man has to reason, to plan, and to decide. The other side of the issue, however, is that intellect can never cut itself free from the unconscious; and this is particularly true when production and creativity are involved. Reason can impose limits on nature's caprice, preserve and heighten those effects which are harmonious, and weed out those that disturb. By analysis it can anticipate the unfolding of Idea, and speed up the progress of cosmic development. But it must never lose touch with concrete reality or suppose that it can revise the conditions of human existence. In this respect, Hartmann set himself against what he calls the "mock enlightenment" of the eighteenth century and against the rationalist mentality in his own time.

Mankind as a whole, Hartmann believed, is a long way from being able to make any proper use of consciousness. The history of civilization is the record of elaborately cultivated illusions. Such consciousness as man has achieved scarcely has done more than make him aware of the evils of existence and compound them with folly and vice, from which he has fled into worlds of fancy and hope. Several stages are discernible. Ancient man, in the "childhood" stage of the race, supposed that happiness is attained in the present life. He worked, sacrificed, endured disappointment and defeat, believing that wealth, fame, and friendship have the power to bring satisfaction. Disenchanted with the more obvious goals, he tried religion and vice, or turned to art and invention—always persuaded that somewhere the world must offer fulfillment to those who know how to court its favor. But at last experience convinced him of the contrary and led to the conclusion, "All is Vanity."

Hartmann calls the second stage "youth." It is represented in history by the Christian idea which, condemning the present life, promised treasure in heaven where mortal ills cannot prevail. The fancied nearness of the other world taught men to sacrifice present benefits for future gain; but it did little or nothing to weaken the individual's pride and self-will. And when, with further understanding, man found it impossible any longer to keep up the illusion, he turned his hope again to this life.

The post-Christian mind, however, maintains its own illusion. This stage Hartmann labels "manhood." It signifies the stage in which man plans and labors for future generations, persuading himself that he can build a cooperative paradise on earth. Such was the prevailing attitude in Western society when Hartmann was writing his book. It too, according to Hartmann, is an illusion, a life-lie. There is no historical basis for believing that science or education or democratic government contributes anything to social harmony or to private happiness; and thoughtful consideration of the factors which limit human existence shows that under no conceivable circumstances can real pleasure counterbalance real pain. Fortunately, however, in "old age," or philosophical maturity, man finds that when he has cast off illusion, the pain and disappointment of life are not intolerable. He discovers that ego is not ultimately real and that its desires and ambitions are merely part of the primal urge. And in the very act of understanding them, he cuts their nerve and dissipates their forces, while freeing himself for rational and aesthetic satisfactions. Few men, according to Hartmann, have reached this level. And when the race as a whole achieves it, history and civilization will come to some sort of rest. The reader who desires to know how it may work out is advised to read Bernard Shaw's *Back to Methuselah.—J.F.*

PERTINENT LITERATURE
Sully, James. *Pessimism: A History and a Criticism.* London: Henry S. King and Company, 1877.

The distinction between mind and consciousness, familiar since Gottfried Wilhelm von Leibniz, was first clearly formulatd by Eduard von Hartmann, who supported it with a mass of evidence. His psychology was an all-out attack on older consciousness psychologies which undertook to erect a science of mind on introspective evidence. *Pessimism* is a counterattack by the last important representative of the school of Jeremy Bentham, John Stuart Mill, and Alexander Bain. While dealing with pessimism in its full extent, James Sully gives special attention to Hartmann, along with Arthur Schopenhauer, because of the elaborate metaphysical and scientific claims which they brought to the support of pessimism.

Sully gives full and objective accounts of the philosophies of both Schopenhauer and Hartmann before undertaking his criticism. Chapter Five, devoted to Hartmann, is a very detailed exposition of *The Philosophy of the Unconcious*, especially of the parts dealing with psychology and with metaphysics. As explained by Sully, Hartmann's task was to show how the unconscious attains to real existence in matter, and how matter evolves through organic forms until it reaches consciousness in man. Sully stresses the complexity of the activity of the unconscious in developed organisms, pointing out that, besides being embodied in atoms, in organs, in the nervous system, and in psychic processes, the unconscious presides over the local manifestations and every now and then "interferes with their action," directing the life history of the individual in concert with nature as a whole. "The main part of the development," Sully explains, "both of plants and animals, is due to the direct action of the organizing Unconscious."

When he turns from exposition to criticism, Sully makes clear the reservations with which a disciple of Bentham and Mill must approach any German metaphysician. For Sully, no principle can explain the world, because explanation is something confined to thought, and thought is part of the world to be explained. Passing various ontological hypotheses in review, he concludes that each of them is the projection of some element or function of man's mind. Ontology, he says, has exhausted psychology, objectifying one after another of its elements and using it to explain the world.

Pressing this objection, Sully argues at length against the notion that will is the active force in nature. It is staggering, he says to be told that will, which is known to us only by introspection and is therefore a component of conscious mind, is also present in inanimate nature. Adding that consciousness has been differently defined, he nevertheless argues that feelings, desires, and thought processes, which we sometimes call unconscious because they lie outside the cone of attention, must yet be conscious because they can be attended to by persons trained in introspection. Hence, he concludes that it is contradictory to try to think of an unconscious mind. The same conclusion follows when mind is approached objectively as an aggregate of mental states extended in time and developing with the growth of the cerebral structure from simple and homogeneous to multiform and heterogeneous. Once again, if we are to avoid contradiction, we must not infer the presence of mental events where there is no "serial mental life."

If it be objected that what Hartmann has done is to give the names "intelligence" and "will" to the mysterious forces which are evidently at work in nature, including our own bodies, Sully's reply is that modern science does not admit the existence of force any more than it admits the existence of matter. Both these notions, he says, are nowadays known to be nothing more than useful fictions: science knows nothing of any "dynamic reality" that could be construed as "will in nature." Nor is will in man "something one and substantial, a single permanent substratum in the individual mind." As a science of phenomena and their laws, psychology knows several processes which, as having a tendency to eventuate in bodily motions, are called will; but, although conceptually distinct from other processes called feeling and intelligence, they are not found in isolation from these.

Hartmann's argument for pessimism is partly *a priori*, based on his metaphysics of will, and partly *a posteriori*, based on his calculus of the pain and pleasure observable in different human activities. Sully tries to show that both lines of argument rest on a confusion of will and desire. The *a priori* argument says merely that because it is the nature of will never to be satisfied, creatures of will can never find fulfillment. But it is desire and not volition which brings pain when unsatisfied. Desire, according to Sully, is a mental state in which a pleasurable idea fails to call forth an appropriate volition because of some external hindrance. What distinguishes will from feelings and desires is that will results in action. Willing is neither painful nor pleasant, although its natural tendency is to lessen pain and to increase pleasure.

Hartmann's *a posteriori* argument is more complicated, due, among other things, to the problems of forgetfulness and illusion and to the need to recognize and balance indirect and direct pleasures and pains. Sully maintains, however, that Hartmann has prejudiced the argument by maintaining that pleasure and pain are homogeneous, differing only in quantity, being merely degrees of satisfaction and nonsatisfaction of will. Viewed in this light, dissatisfaction (for example, hunger), which normally makes itself known in consciousness, easily outweighs satisfaction, which normally passes unnoticed.

Hall, G. Stanley. *Founders of Modern Psychology.* New York: D. Appleton and Company, 1912.

G. Stanley Hall, who spent six years in Germany as a student between 1870 and 1882, tries in this book to transmit to a new generation some appreciation for the German speculative tradition which had been neglected since the introduction of experimental methods into psychology. The six chapters are an amplification of lectures, each dealing with a major figure. The account of Eduard von Hartmann, whom the author had visited on Sunday afternoons in his suburban Berlin home, is a sympathetic introduction to the man and his work.

Hartmann, who turned to writing when an incurable illness compelled him to abandon a military career, remained outside the academic world, living in retirement with a wife as sensitive and cultivated as himself. When a professorship was offered him, he refused, partly for health reasons and partly in order to preserve his independence. Nevertheless, in Hall's opinion, his books establish him as the most comprehensive writer since Georg Wilhelm Friedrich Hegel, as well as the most consistent and intelligible. Hall sees him as reviving and keeping alive what was best in the German philosophical tradition, and he suggests that if a new idealism ever appears, it will be "along the lines of Hartmann's Unconscious."

On his advocacy of the unconscious, says Hall, rests Hartmann's claim to a place in history. In demonstrating the "eccentric, prenumbral, peripheral, marginal nature of consciousness," he carried through the true Copernican revolution. From the time of René Descartes, philosophy had sought to make consciousness its point of departure, with the result that the phenomenal world either stood between man and the real world or was affirmed to be the only world there is. Hartmann explained consciousness as an adventitious product of the unconscious. Sensations are "nodes of collision" that arise when will is checked. These "reaction-feelings' are synthesized, and as life ascends from lower to higher forms, sensations are intellectualized.

According to Hall, the fact that consciousness is derivative does not, in Hartmann's view, imply that knowledge is illusory. On the contrary, only by recognizing the origins of our ideas are we in a position to resolve the basic problem of epistemology. Holding, against Immanuel Kant, that causality is an ontological category, Hartmann maintained that we can attain to knowledge of reality beyond and independent of consciousness by means of inference. Philosophy, like science, progresses only by observation and induction. The only knowledge which man can have in his present stage of development is hypothetical, and the only certainty he can attain to is practical. But Hartmann hopefully predicted that the time will come when man will intuit things as they are.

Hall reminds us that, like Arthur Schopenhauer, Hartmann was devoted to the arts. Beauty, he held, although phenomenal, brings us closer than does knowledge to the *Ding-an-Sich* (thing-in-itself), and a work of art is truer than metaphysics. Aesthetic feeling is a special way of experiencing the world, more universal and less egoistic than pragmatic perception. The unconscious works spontaneously in the artist, revealing the higher purpose in nature and in man, thereby bringing evolution to a new level of perfection. Art in man's present condition is largely idealization; it anticipates the day when consciousness will attain to complete harmony with the unconscious.

Hall passes somewhat briefly over Hartmann's writings on religous subjects, pointing out that, although an opponent of Christianity, Hartmann was not opposed to religion and put his faith in what he called the "religion of the future," which would be a synthesis of teachings from all the great religions. Zarathustra, prophet of Light in its eternal struggle against Darkness, seemed to be the exemplification of the struggle between Intelligence and Will.

Of special interest to Hall is Hartmann's *Phenomenology of Moral Consciousness*, a major work which he thinks worthy of a place alongside *The Philosophy of the Unconscious*. In the Hegelian manner, but without Hegel's dialectic, Hartmann brought under review all the classical ethical systems, pointing out the limitations of each and concluding with his own version of Absolute Morality. Part One reviews "pseudo-moral systems," including hedonism, eudaemonism, and Christianity. These are predominantly false because they perpetuate egoism. Part Two, "True Ethical Consciousness," considers those systems which subordinate the individual's will to a higher purpose; although each contains some truth, none is adequate. For example, utilitarianism, while properly subordinating the individual to the group, is inimical to culture because it knows no higher good than the satisfaction of individual desires. Absolute Morality, as Hartmann envisages it, is based on the twofold truth of the identity of each individual with every other and the identity of man with God. Here morality joins hands with religion. Man's highest duty is the service of God, who, in Hartmann's opinion, does not stand in need of love but does stand in need of pity. Man's chief end is, in Hartmann's words, "to ameliorate the negative eudaemonism of the Absolute"—that is, to help free the Absolute from the blind need to create.

Hall tries to keep Hartmann's pessimism in perspective, pointing out that even in the 1870's when he defended pessimism with ardor in private conversation, he would also remark that if one wanted to see contented faces, he must go among pessimists. This suggests to Hall that what Hartmann meant to emphasize was not the relative prepotency of pain over pleasure but the therapeutic power of intellect. Only when we know ourselves objectively do we overcome pain and attain peace and rest.—*J.F.*

ADDITIONAL RECOMMENDED READING

Butler, Samuel. *Unconscious Memory*. London: A. C. Fifield, 1910. As part of his campaign to vindicate the independence of his theory of evolution, the author of *Erewhon* translated and commented on Hartmann's chapter on instinct.

Caldwell, W. "The Epistemology of Ed. Von Hartmann," in *Mind*. II, no. 6 (April, 1893), pp 187-207. A criticism of "transcendental realism" as set forth in Hartmann's writings on the theory of knowledge.

——————— . "Von Hartmann's Moral and Social Philosophy," in *The Philosophical Review*. VIII, nos. 4, 5 (July, September, 1899), pp. 465-483, 589-603. A study of the *Phenomenology of the Moral Consciousness*.

Höffding, Harald. *A History of Modern Philosophy*. Translated by B. E. Meyer. Vol. II. New York: Macmillan Publishing Company, 1915, pp. 532-540. Hartmann is considered, along with Lotze and Fechner, in the chapter entitled "Idealistic Construction on a Realistic Basis."

Loemker, L. E. "Hartmann, Eduard von," in *Encyclopedia of Philosophy*. Edited by Paul Edwards. Vol. III. New York: Macmillan Publishing Company, 1967, pp. 419-421. Topical treatment of Hartmann's doctrine.

Siwek, Paul, S. J. *The Philosophy of Evil*. New York: Ronald Press, 1951. Chapter 10, "Pessimism," is mainly concerned with Hartmann's philosophy.

Tsanoff, R. A. "Hartmann's Philosophy of the Unconscious," in *The Nature of Evil*. New York: Macmillan Publishing Company, 1931, pp. 308-341. Best popular introduction in English to the above work.

A GRAMMAR OF ASSENT

Author: John Henry Cardinal Newman (1801-1890)
Type of work: Metaphysics, epistemology
First published: 1870

PRINCIPAL IDEAS ADVANCED

There is no qualitative break between our knowledge of God and other kinds of knowledge.

Since God is the most concrete and determinate of beings, knowledge of him must be real apprehension—intelligent acceptance through personal, concrete experience.

Assent does not depend on inference, and inference is not always of the formal sort described by logicians.

The right to assent to religious truths comes from personal involvement in the concrete situations in which God manifests himself.

Cardinal Newman may not be thought of by many as a philosopher, possibly because he is a sort of philosophical outsider without specific ancestry or descent: and histories of philosophy, victims of their own schemes of classification, find it difficult to include such individualists. In our own day, however, when men have grown dissatisfied with established traditions and have taken to reviewing the history of thought with a view to discovering where we may have gone astray, Newman's writings have excited a new interest. And this is the case, not primarily among Roman Catholics, whose scholastic revival is quite foreign to Newman's way of thinking, but chiefly among realists and empiricists, who are drawn to him because of his appreciation of the whole person, and his recognition that man's thought processes are complex and cannot be understood apart from the rest of man. Scholars have suggested that he anticipated Bergson in his interpretation of the roles of intuition and intellect, that what he calls a "Grammar" of assent and certitude is a very model of phenomenological analysis, and that his emphasis upon the distinct kind of reality belonging to man and to God (in virtue of personality, concreteness, individuality, and vitality) discloses existentialist insights. Whatever the truth of these claims, they serve to dispel the notion that Newman was primarily an antiquarian. Perhaps as much as any Victorian Englishman, he found himself abreast the stream of post-modern thought.

A Grammar of Assent is concerned with the problem of knowledge, which, like his predecessors of the British school, Newman approaches by analyzing the activity of mind in perception and reasoning. The central problem is that of "assent," and it corresponds to the problem of "belief" in Hume and in Reid. Newman considers it in two relations which give the divisions of his book: assent and apprehension; assent and inference.

The term *apprehension* is standard in the literature of empirical thought, and there is nothing exceptional in the way Newman defines it: "Apprehension is an intelligent acceptance of the idea or of the fact which a proposition enunciates." We can "assert" a matter without apprehending it, that is, without grasping the significance of what we are saying.

On the other hand, Newman argues that we can apprehend a meaning without "understanding" it in any concrete, experiential sense. Here we sense the special quality of Newman's thinking, which is powerfully inclined toward the concrete and sensible and away from the abstract and intellectual. There are, in general, two ways of apprehending a truth: we may grasp it in a merely "notional" sense, or we may grasp it as a "reality." The former is the work of the intellect. It involves naming, comparing, distinguishing, and classifying. It reduces real things to notions or concepts, to symbols and linguistic signs. The latter way is the work of sensation, imagination, and memory. Only through these do we have experience of the concrete, singular thing. And the more experience we have, the more real our apprehension. For example, a French economist may write about facts well known to himself with a view to being understood by others who are furnished with comparable facts. A bright schoolboy could translate his work into English with but the faintest understanding of what the treatise really maintained; yet his apprehension of all the terms would be correct enough to enable an informed Englishman to understand the French author.

We may now see the relation of apprehension to *assent*. Assent is "belief," but belief as fully specified to fit Newman's observations. He defines it: "the absolute acceptance of a proposition without any condition."

Assent is, thus, a sort of internal assertion. We may assert without apprehending; but if we apprehend what we assert, the assertion is an assent. How much must we apprehend? Merely the predicate term. For example, a child asks, "What is lucern?" If his mother answers, "Lucern is food for cattle," the child apprehends the predicate. He assents to it, even though he has never seen lucern, and he can henceforth go further, even to assenting to propositions where "lucern" is the predicate; for example, "That field is sown with lucern." If, however, his mother were to reply, "Lucern is medicago sativa of the class of diadelphia," he can then assert this; but since he does not apprehend, he cannot assent to it. There is, indeed, an indirect way in which he can assent to this proposition also—if it be given a new predicate such as "That lucern is medicago sativa is true," he can assent to it, which he does because he believes his mother. This latter would be, incidentally, a notional apprehension: and, as we shall see, notional apprehensions lead to assertion only in a conditional or inferential manner; that is, on the basis of some previous assent.

As between real and notional assents, Newman holds that the former are generally stronger because of the vividness with which they strike the imagination. Imagination plays an important role in Newman's thought, not as creating assent (after the manner of Hume) but as intensifying it, giving it body and substance and making it easier for us to hold onto it. This is a "natural and rightful effect of the acts of imagination," and it is important for educators to bear this in mind. Notional assents may become real—for example, a passage of poetry or Scripture, once held only in a notional way, may as a result of some private experience come to "mean more" to us than it did before; it becomes concrete.

We have not yet considered the reasons or grounds of assent. This is the burden of the second part of the work, where Newman comes to treat of the relation between assent and *inference*. In his view, traditional philosophy has taken too theoretical a view of the grounds of assent by consulting an idea of how the mind ought to act instead of interrogating human nature as an existing thing. One would think, from reading Plato or Locke, that there is really no such thing as assent apart from inference, and that our degree of confidence in the truth of a proposition is proportional to the strength of the reasons that can be brought for and against it. Newman shows that there are instances in which correct inference fails to produce assent, and others in which we assent without any inference at all.

There is such a thing as *simple* assent which does not rest on argument. It is "adhesion without reserve or doubt to the truth of a proposition." Ordinarily it follows automatically from real apprehension: from what I see, what I remember, what I have on good authority. But it is possible to pass from simple assent to *complex* assent, based on inference. For example, I may believe the proposition "Great Britain is an island," without any thought of the reasons on which this belief is established. This is simple assent. But if called upon to do so, I could call up the reasons, and do this without any suspension of the belief while I was thinking of them. When it is done, however, the assent is in a manner altered. I now assent deliberately, hypothetically, conditionally. In fact, it will be observed, I am now asserting a new proposition, namely "That Great Britain is an island is true." This act of the mind is reflexive. Newman distinguishes it from the other by calling it "certitude." It is more than assent as "following on investigation and proof, accompanied by a specific sense of intellectual satisfaction and repose, and [in] that it is irreversible."

Certitude, according to Newman, is essential to the whole pursuit of knowledge. Without it, truth would still be truth; but knowledge of truth would ever be beyond us and unattainable. Philosophers, with their preconceptions of how the mind should work, have contradicted the plain facts of experience. We do know many things for certain; and, as a general rule, certitude does not fail us. The fact that sometimes we are mistaken does not destroy other certitudes any more than the fact that clocks are sometimes wrong destroys our confidence in clocks. "No instances of mistaken certitude are sufficient to constitute a proof that certitude itself is a perversion." Newman seriously considers the case against this position, showing that we often have a conviction of certainty and are proved wrong. But in at least some instances where this seems to be the case, we have been careless about the distinction between propositions which we hold for certain and those of which we are strongly persuaded but not certain. If we bother to keep these apart, Newman thinks, it is rare that a certainty has to be given up. We are made for truth, can attain it, and having attained it can keep it, recognize it, and preserve the recognition. Though errant, the mind is capable of discipline, of progress, of approaching by practice to perfection.

Newman's analysis of inference may be said to put logic in its place. Reasoning, he maintains, is as spontaneous to man as are perception and memory. "By means of sense we gain knowledge directly; by means of reasoning we gain it indirectly." But there is too strong a tendency in Western intellectual history to restrict inference to the *formal* process. The Aristotelian syllogism is merely an attempt to analyze a natural process of the mind and "invent a method to serve as a common measure between man and man." It succeeds so far as words can capture the subtleties of thought; but its inability ever to do this completely should make us cautious about taking the syllogism for a norm.

Here is the place to speak of the role of intelligence in Newman's philosophy. Its world of abstractions and symbols makes possible the whole realm of human science—mathematical, physical, biological. But it has serious limits, and is far from being the whole of mind. The great vice of the Enlightenment, the Age of Reason, was to suppose that all truth is of this conceptual order, and that in ordering and judging among its notions we are dealing with reality. "Science in all its departments has too much simplicity and exactness from the nature of the case to be the measure of fact. In its very perfection lies its incompetency to settle particulars and details." The human mind includes more than can be described by the syllogism or by the most refined mathematical calculus. Consider any actual problem—for example, one in literary criticism. "How short and easy a way to a true conclusion is the logic of good sense; how little syllogisms have to do with the formation of opinion; how little depends upon the inferential proofs, and how much upon those preexisting beliefs and views, in which men either already agree with each other or hopelessly differ, before they begin to dispute, and which are hidden deep in our nature, or, it may be, in our personal peculiarities."

Besides considering formal inference, Newman analyzes what he calls *informal* inference. It is carried out in the concrete, is largely implicit, and is chiefly an accumulation of probabilities. There is, in addition, what he calls *natural* inference, which is the immediate perception of relations without proof, granted to spirits of high genius. Examples: Napoleon's disposal of troops in battle, or Newton's rule for discovering imaginary roots of equations.

To designate the normative processes of inference, Newman uses the term "illative sense," which he justifies by setting it alongside the parallel faculties by which we judge duty and taste. He remarks its similarity to the *phronesis* (judgment) by which Aristotle said that we have our perception of the "mean." He points to the taste of a Phidias or a Raphael, which is more subtle and versatile than any treatise on art could ever grasp. Corresponding to these special senses is the "illative sense," which deals with truth. It is the same for all kinds of subject matter, although one individual may by endowment or training be skilled in applying it in one area and not in another; and because it proceeds always in the same way, its processes may be described by logic and extended in mathematical calculus. But in no case is there any test of the truth beyond the trustworthiness of the illative sense just as there is no other test of beauty or morality beyond their special senses.

Man's business, Newman says, is not to justify this illative sense, but to use it. We are in a world of facts: it would be out of place to demand the credentials of earth, air, fire, and water. So of our own mental capacities: "Our being, with its faculties, mind and body, is a fact not admitting of question, all things being of necessity referred to it." This commonsense remark could have been made by Reid; but note that Reid and his followers never actually made it. They took their stand within the circle of consciousness and had the problem of breaking out and establishing the not-self. Newman took his stand on the world as a whole; he regarded man's existence as something that was certainly known. From his point of view, he had more in common with the Greeks than with his own age, dominated as it was by subjectivism. "My first disobedience," he says, in a pointed criticism of the spirit of modern philosophy, "is to be impatient at what I am and to indulge an ambitious aspiration after what I cannot be, to cherish a distrust of my powers, and to desire to change laws which are identical with myself."

A larger proportion of the *Grammar* is given over to the discussion of religion than this review has indicated. But the application of Newman's general principles to religion can be quickly shown. For Newman, there is no qualitative break between our knowledge of God and other kinds of knowledge. Man requires no special faculty by which God comes to be known to him, no special feeling of dependence, or sense of the numenous. We know reality at any level in the degree that we have concrete, personal, living experience of it. We know our old clothes, our customary surroundings, our familiar acquaintances in a peculiarly solid and satisfactory way. Our knowledge of our friends illustrates this very clearly. The first meeting leaves us with scarcely more than a silhouette. It is as we renew the impression in a variety of ways that it begins to take on depth and fullness. The roles of sensation and imagination are more important in this getting acquainted than our abstractive powers which, in a sense, are the enemy of true knowledge— there is a kind of routine familiarity that is compatible with profound ignorance. Now, God being the most concrete and determinate of all beings, our knowledge of him must be just as particular.

For Newman, religion consists in real apprehension, and theology in merely notional. The true religion commands *assent* because God has manifested himself in tangible and imaginable forms—through the lives of holy men, the liturgy and hymns, and the sacraments. Its *certitude*, when that is called for, is founded on the witness of conscience, and upon the evidences of history and anthropology. Like the Thomists, Newman argues from natural revelation to special: but instead of appealing, as they do, to philosophical proofs (natural theology), he argues from sacrifice and prayer among primitive peoples (natural religion). "Revelation begins where Natural Religion fails. The Religion of Nature is a mere inchoation, and needs a complement—it can have but one complement, and that very complement is Christianity."

In Newman we are dealing with an authentic person: his whole life bears the stamp of autonomy and self-determination. What is impressive in his account of religious truth is that in listening to his presentation of it, we are not listening to a mere philosopher who is trying to fit religious phenomena into a satisfactory world view, but to a religious genius who is at the same time a profound and disciplined thinker. *A Grammar of Assent* is not an attempt to prove religion, or even to expound a doctrine. It is an attempt to render intelligible the actuality of a life (Newman's own) founded on the knowledge of God. In this province, he says that "egotism is true modesty. In religious inquiry each of us can speak only for himself, for himself he has a right to speak."—*J.F.*

Pertinent Literature
D'Arcy, M. C., S. J. *The Nature of Belief.* London: Sheed & Ward, 1931.

Writing for the so-called "lost generation" after World War I, a generation which seemed not to believe anything, the author sets aside the traditional apologetic of the Church which treats reason as a prelude to faith, and, borrowing from the Gestalt psychology of his day, argues that belief in Christianity is a global impression that comes all at once. There are patterns in nature and in history; moreover, each of us carries within us patterns or complexes which determine our apprehension of the world. When a nonbeliever embraces Christianity, he does so as a result of changes in the way he perceives the evidence. Faith, says M. C. D'Arcy, is interpretation.

What gives the book its enduring interest is D'Arcy's attempt to relate his conclusions to the line of argument developed in *A Grammar of Assent*, which he commends as a "masterpiece which no one can safely neglect," adding, "It is always a pleasure to find one's own thought already adumbrated or forestalled in the pages of a great writer." In a very readable summary of John Henry Newman's book, he singles out three points for emphasis: that our assent is usually independent of formal reasoning; that certainty attaches to real apprehension but fades when apprehension becomes purely notional; and that conviction comes not through reason but through the illative sense. This summary is followed by two chapters of criticism, one examining the thesis that assent attaches to real apprehension and is independent of inference, the other attempting to improve on Cardinal Newman's account of the illative sense.

Much of D'Arcy's criticism reflects the standpoint of Neo-Thomism, which became the official philosophy of the Catholic Church after Newman had written *A Grammar of Assent*, and is less a criticism of Newman than of the empiricist and commonsense tradition of British philosophy within the framework of which Newman developed his position. Two faults D'Arcy attributes to this philosophical tradition: first, the nominalist interpretation of notions. The low estimation in which Newman held notional apprehension, as against real apprehension, D'Arcy traces to the belief that only individual things, apprehended through the senses and laid hold of by means of the imagination, are real, whereas, according to D'Arcy, notions apprehended directly by the intellect are as real as the individual properties apprehended through the senses and are prior to these in the order of knowledge. Then there is the fault residing in the faculty psychology which referred different kinds of judgment to different senses. Newman was justified, says D'Arcy, in rebelling against the Lockean distinction between demonstrative and probable knowledge and in maintaining that certitude attaches more readily to informal than to formal inference. Nevertheless, had it not been for the skimpy philosophical tradition within which he worked, he would have recognized that "the power of knowing the real world" is not a separate faculty but belongs to the intellect as the Thomists understand it. It is difficult, says D'Arcy, to fit an illative sense into an acceptable philosophical system, "whereas there is a heap of evidence to be drawn from modern psychology, from observation of the methods employed in the sciences, in historical investigation, in the fine arts, and from everyday experience, which fits in with what I have called interpretation, and this fact of interpretation is in turn easily fitted into a sound philosophical theory."

The Lockean term "probabilities," used by Newman in his account of informal inference, is unacceptable to D'Arcy, but replacing it with the term "evidences," he acknowledges that certitude is produced by an accumulation of independent evidences too numerous to mention and too subtle to be converted into syllogisms. He explains this fact by what he calls "the unity of indirect reference." Why do I believe that England is an island? I may give particular reasons, but the real reason lies in "an infinite number of other certainties or facts, all of which would have to be wrong" if this statement were to be denied.

By "interpretation" D'Arcy means the process of thought by means of which the mind discerns unity in a group of phenomena, as when one perceives letters as forming a word and words as forming sentences. The process is not an inference; yet it can, and in most cases does, lead to certitude. Applied to religious faith, interpretation means reading the evidence of Christ's history, character, and teaching, and fitting it into what one already knows about God and man. There is, to begin with, a secular interpretation of history; for we have no difficulty in discerning "the purposes of man written across the surfaces of the earth in every age." In religious faith, "we are swung into a divine order and exchange our human pattern for the divine."

A Grammar of Assent grew out of Newman's correspondence with William Froude, a lifelong friend who as a result of his scientific and engineering studies had drifted from Christianity into scientific naturalism. Newman had, therefore, the task of explaining how it is that assent may fail or that assent may be withheld in the presence of cogent evidence. In this connection he spoke of "prepared positions," or what D'Arcy, following modern psychology, calls complexes and patterns. Our mind, D'Arcy notes, is active in perception. In normal learning, patterns reinforce and enrich one another, but affective and desirous elements frequently produce distortions. Thus, even as the natural enlargement of knowledge through experience is sufficient to account for the relatively high achievements of natural religion, so also the darkening of the mind by the partial elements of the personality explains the need for supernatural assistance if we are to see the world as God sees it, and to partake of the "unspeakably love and union" which is the message of the Gospel.

Price, H. H. *Belief*. New York: Humanities Press, 1969.

Theologians often puzzle themselves over the difference between knowledge and belief, belief and opinion, belief *in* and belief *that*, belief as an act and belief as a state. Moreover, such distinctions are also puzzles for epistemologists, as H. H. Price demonstrates in his 1960 Gifford Lectures. The lectures throughout are addressed to such problems, and the views of traditional philosophers (notably René Descartes, John Locke, David Hume, and John Henry Newman) are introduced only in connection with those problems on which their writings shed light.

The distinction which leads Price to refer to Newman's *A Grammar of Assent* is that between "two uses of the word belief, or a difference of opinion as to what the correct usage is." For the most part we allow that belief admits of degrees, ranging from conviction at one end of the scale to doubt at the other, with opinion in between. There are, however, occasions in which belief admits of no degrees, as when we say that a person believes in God or believes that all men are equal. In this latter sense, to use Price's example, we can admit that Archibald has opinions on many matters but that he does not believe anything. Price develops this distinction by considering Locke's claim that degrees of assent are or ought to be proportional to the strength of evidence, and Newman's counterclaim that assent is a substantive act that does not admit of degrees.

From the outset Price sides with Locke, but the virtuosity of Newman's analysis makes it worthy of attention. Two main questions emerge: first, what Newman understood by inference when he accused Locke of failing to distinguish between inference and assent; second, why he held that conditionality is a character of inference but not of assent.

As to the first question, Price points out that, although Newman used "inference" to include both inferences ("because p therefore q") and entailments ("if p then q"), he was aware of the difference and understood that assenting to an entailment is different from assenting to a premise or a conclusion. With this distinction in mind he could go on to distinguish between assenting to the proposition "There are reasons for believing q" and believing q. And, says Price, "if this is what Newman means when he insists upon the difference between inference and assent, he is clearly right and is drawing our attention to an important distinction."

As to the second question, why inferences have to be conditional, Price suggests that Newman may have overlooked the distinction between inferring and thinking about inferences—what we have learned to call first-order and second-order statements. When one thinks about an inference, he cannot avoid noticing that the conclusion can be drawn only on condition of our acceptance of the premises. But when he actually draws an inference this conditionality need not appear at all, as we see in Newman's own words: "We reason when we hold this by virtue of that." "'*Holding* this by virtue of that,'" says Price, "is something more than just noticing that this would follow provided that were true."

Having in this way blunted Newman's arguments against Locke, Price introduces the personal element. The dispute, he thinks, was largely verbal. While denying that there are degrees of assent, Newman agreed with Locke that our attitude toward propositions (inclination or disinclination to assent) admits of degrees. The difference between the two men was that Locke looked on the bright side when he thought about probabilities, and Newman took a gloomy view and saw only uncertainty and doubt.

The question whether belief admits of degrees was part of Price's original program of lectures. But in preparing the series for publication, the author introduced additional material, including a chapter on Newman's distinction between notional and real assent, which Price calls "interesting and important," and which he considers Newman's most original contribution to the epistemology of belief.

Price's discussion is partly designed to show that, although it does make a difference whether we assent to a proposition in a real or in a notional way, the distinction is a matter of degree and not of kind. Even when we assent to a vividly imagined object, what we assent to is not the picture that is before the mind but the proposition "There is a state of affairs which these images accurately represent"; and this proposition is purely notional. The distinction between notional and real is further blurred, says Price, when we consider that for certain theoretically trained minds notional propositions come to exercise the same psychic power which Newman rightly attributed to real propositions, as in the case of a mathematician's passion to understand complex numbers.

For the rest, Price is chiefly concerned with the role of "imaging" and "imagining" in Newman's discussion of real assent. Newman's account of his own exceptionally vivid visual imagination leads Price to refer to Francis Galton's survey of individual differences in this respect and to note that Newman failed to take into consideration persons whose imagination is almost entirely verbal. Price also raises the question whether Newman did not confuse two senses of the word "image": for example, having an image of a train and having an image of the British Railways. Admittedly, mental pictures stimulate motive powers; but among such images Newman lists honor, gain, Divine Goodness, and eternal life, which are ordinarily thought to be concepts. In exploring what Newman means, Price concludes that "imagine" often has the sense of imagining *that* and imagining *as*. For example, a person may imagine himself *as* refusing to betray a friend and may imagine *that* he is being interrogated by the police, without having any images of persons, although he may use verbal imagery. It is in this extended sense of imagining that Price understands Newman when he speaks of having an image *of* God and of giving real assent to the proposition *that* God exists. Newman stressed in this connection the voice of conscience as bringing us directly into the presence of our Lord and Master. But this, says Price, is necessarily imaging *as* or imagining *that.—J.F.*

ADDITIONAL RECOMMENDED READING

Collins, James Daniel. *Philosophical Readings in Cardinal Newman*. Chicago: Henry Regnery Company, 1961. Selections with explanatory articles. Best introduction to Newman's philosophy.

Dessain, C. S. *John Henry Newman*. Stanford, California: Stanford University Press, 1971. Brief life of Newman with emphasis on his intellectual development.

Pailin, David A. *The Way to Faith: An Examination of Newman's 'Grammar of Assent' as a Response to the Search for Certainty in Faith*. London: Epworth Press, 1969. A commentary.

Sillem, Edward A., ed. "General Introduction to the Study of Newman's Philosophy," in John Henry Newman's *The Philosophical Notebook*. Vol.

I. Louvain, Belgium: Nauwelaerts Publishing House, 1969. Representative of contemporary Newmanism in the Catholic Church.

THE METHODS OF ETHICS

Author: Henry Sidgwick (1838-1900)
Type of work: Ethics
First published: 1874

PRINCIPAL IDEAS ADVANCED

Modern man uses three different methods of ethics, three ways of resolving moral problems: egoism, intuitionism, and utilitarianism.

Egoistic hedonism, the theory that one ought to seek his own pleasure, is one of the natural methods of ethics; its primary disadvantage is the difficulty of measuring and evaluating pleasures.

The ethics of right and duty employs an a priori *method, utilizing intuition, or direct cognition, as a way of discovering duties; but it is difficult to find moral principles that do not need qualification and that do not admit exceptions.*

Certain moral principles are manifestly true: the principle of impartiality, the principle of prudence, and the principle of benevolence.

Utilitarianism is true to the principles of impartiality and benevolence; but it is difficult to reconcile egoism and utilitarianism.

Henry Sidgwick held that ethics has to do with the reasons which men use in deciding between two courses of action and that the study of ethics is the attempt to bring these reasons together in a coherent system. Modern Western man uses three different "methods" of ethics; that is, three different ways of answering the question, "Why should I do such and such?" He may reason with a view to self-interest; he may ask what his duty is; he may try to estimate the effect of the action in question on the general well-being. Sidgwick held that the ordinary man does not find it necessary to choose between these methods: on some occasions he uses one, and on other occasions another.

Professed moralists, however, have condemned this slackness and have insisted that all ethical reasoning should proceed from one principle and employ one method. Some have maintained that ethics is the reasoned pursuit of happiness, whether one's own or that of all mankind. Others have denied this and maintained that man's reason knows immediately what acts are right and what are wrong. In Sidgwick's view, neither of these approaches could be carried through consistently without unduly constraining the moral intention of ordinary men. He accepted the ideal of unity and consistency which governs all theoretical inquiry; but he was wary of Procrustean solutions, and thought it better to leave certain questions unresolved than to do violence to important aspects of moral experience. Thus, instead of championing only one method, he sought to find a higher unity in which the distinctive contribution of each of "the methods of ethics" is preserved.

A work with such a thesis might have turned out to be a tiresome piece of eclecticism. Actually, it is a masterpiece in philosophical analysis, a pioneer work which set the style for philosophy at Cambridge University for at least two generations afterwards. Sidgwick aimed at synthesis, but his conclusions were modest and imperfect. The strength of his work lies in the sympathetic treatment which he accorded each method, the care he expended in defining and testing claims, and the hopeful and tentative manner in which he developed rival positions.

Sidgwick broke with the practice, which had prevailed in English philosophy before his time, of treating moral philosophy as an adjunct of metaphysics, or of divinity, or of psychology. Whether moral law has its foundation in the will of God or in the evolution of society, whether the will of man is an efficient cause, whether man is naturally selfish or social are questions which do not enter into ethical inquiry. Ethics is a search for "valid ultimate reasons for acting or abstaining." Problems concerning God, Nature, and Self belong not to ethics but to general philosophy. "The introduction of these notions into Ethics is liable to bring with it a fundamental confusion between 'what is' and 'what ought to be,' destructive of all clearness in ethical reasoning."

Limiting his field, therefore, to what would today be called "the phenomenology of morals," (see Husserl, *Ideas*), Sidgwick brought under review three methods of ethical reasoning and their corresponding principles. He called them, for brevity, egoism, intuitionism, and utilitarianism. British ethical opinion, when his book first appeared, could fairly well be summed up in these three positions. The neo-Hegelian position, represented by T. H. Green and F. H. Bradley, had not yet challenged the "national philosophy." When it did, beginning with the publication in 1875 of Green's *Introduction to Hume's Treatise*, the picture was no longer so simple. In subsequent editions (the sixth appeared posthumously in 1901), Sidgwick undertook to refute the new philosophy. But historians question whether he could have conceived and written the kind of book he did if idealism had taken root in England a decade earlier.

The first method discussed by Sidgwick is egoistical hedonism. We have mentioned Sidgwick's concern to separate ethical questions from psychological ones. But historically, ethical hedonism has always been closely connected with psychological hedonism and has been thought to draw support from it. For example, Jeremy Bentham maintained that "the constantly proper end of action on the part of any individual" is his own happiness. This is an ethical proposition. But Bentham also said that "on the occasion of every act he exercises, every human being is inevitably led to pursue that line of conduct which, according to his view of the case, taken by him at the moment, will be in the highest degree contributory to his own greatest happiness." This is a psychological proposition. Sidgwick said that, if the psychological statement be construed strictly, the ethical statement is meaningless: there is no point in maintaining that one "ought" to pursue the line of conduct which will bring him the greatest happiness if he is incapable of following any other line. But even if the psychological law is taken in a weak and approximative sense, "there is no necessary connection between the psychological proposition that pleasure or absence of pain to myself is always the actual ultimate end of my action, and the ethical proposition that my own greatest happiness or pleasure is for me the *right* ultimate end."

Ethical hedonism does, however, deserve consideration as a method of ethics apart from the alleged psychological law. When a man makes "cool self-love" the ordering principle of his life, he is, according to Sidgwick, using one of the "natural methods" by which men judge between right conduct and wrong. And the philosophical egoist who defines the good in terms of pleasure is doing no more than stating this view in clear and meaningful terms.

One problem, for example, that is implicit in the popular conception of estimating satisfactions—say, the relative value of poker and poetry—is to find a common coin by which they can be measured. Pleasure, conceived of as "the kind of feeling that we seek to retain in consciousness," serves as that coin. To give the theory further applicability, pain may be regarded as commensurable with pleasure, along a scale on either side of a "hedonistic zero."

Sidgwick submitted these notions to searching criticism, the most damaging of which, in his estimation, was that methodical and trustworthy evaluation of the pleasures involved in two different courses of action is impractical. He did confess, however, that "in spite of all the difficulties that I have urged, I continue to make comparisons between pleasures and pains with practical reliance on their results." But he concluded that for the systematic direction of conduct other principles were highly desirable. He thought that this would be recognized by the man who is concerned only with his own happiness.

Common morality, however, although it allows a place for reasonable self-love, does not admit that a man has the right to live for himself alone. This brings us to the second "method" of ethics, which Sidgwick called intuitionism. From this point of view, right conduct has very little to do with desires and selfish enjoyment. What matters to it is duty and virtue.

Sidgwick held that the notions of "right" and "ought," which are fundamental to the intuitionist point of view are "too elementary to admit of any formal definition." They cannot be derived from the idea of the good, if this is understood to consist in happiness. If, on the other hand, it is understood to consist in excellence, this is merely another way of referring to what ought to be. The judgment that a certain course of action is right presents itself as a direct cognition. It may be accompanied by feelings, such as sympathy or benevolence, but it is itself a dictate of reason. Unlike egoistic hedonism, which reasons *a posteriori* in its effort to estimate future good, the ethics of right and duty employs an *a priori* method, reasoning from self-evident truth. Sidgwick called it, therefore, the method of intuition.

Sidgwick maintained, however, that it is one thing to recognize the *prima facie* claims of moral insight—that they are simple and categorical—and something else to grant that their claims are veridical. The point he wished to make is that man would not have the notions of morally right and wrong (as distinct from instrumentally right and wrong and logically right and wrong) except for some kind of direct moral insight.

The systematic moralist soon discovers that not all moral intuitions are trustworthy. There are, said Sidgwick, three levels on which the claims of obligation present themselves to man's conscience. First, there is the kind of judgment ordinarily referred to as the voice of conscience, which functions after the analogy of sense perception and testifies to the rightness or wrongness of single acts or motives. But the slightest experience with men is enough to convince us that conscience, in the sense of an intuitive perception, is not infallible. Virtuous men differ in their judgment of a course of action. In their effort to persuade one another, they appeal from the particular instance to general rules which seem to be self-evident. This is the second level of intuitive moral reasoning. It comprises rules such as these: that we govern our passions, obey laws, honor parents, keep promises, and the like.

To the unreflective mind, these rules seem unexceptionable. But a serious attempt to give them precise meaning and application discloses at once their ambiguity. For example, it is said to be intuitively certain that "the promiser is bound to perform what both he and the promisee understood to be undertaken." But on examination, all sorts of qualifications come into view, which are just as obviously reasonable as the original principle. The promisee may annul the promise if he is alive; and there are circumstances in which it seems that promises should be annulled if the promisee is dead or otherwise inaccessible. Again, a promise may conflict with another obligation. Or, a promise may have been made in consequence of fraud or concealment. Sidgwick explored these and other possibilities in detail, and concluded "that a clear consensus can only be claimed for the principle that a promise, express or tacit, is binding, if a number of conditions are fulfilled," and that "if any of these conditions fails, the consensus seems to become evanescent, and the common moral perceptions of thoughtful persons fall into obscurity and disagreement."

Recognizing the weakness of common moral axioms, philosophers, ancient and modern, have sought to raise the principle of intuition to the level of an axiomatic science by formulating abstract principles of morality so clearly that they cannot conceivably be doubted or denied. For example, "we ought to give every man his own," and "it is right that the lower parts of our nature should be governed by the higher." These alleged axioms are self-evident, but only because they are tautologies. Sidgwick called them "sham axioms." They are worth even less than popular moral rules.

It might seem, from this analysis, that the entire attempt to base ethical reasoning upon intuition was a mistake and should be abandoned. Such, however, was not Sidgwick's contention. "It would be disheartening," he said, "to have to regard as altogether illusory the strong instinct of common sense that points to the existence of such principles, and the deliberate convictions of the long line of moralists who have enunciated them." And if the "variety of human natures and circumstances" is so vast that rules are not helpful in determining particular duties, there are, nevertheless, "certain absolute practical principles, the truth of which, when they are explicitly stated, is manifest."

The first such principle is that of justice or impartiality. It states that "if a kind of conduct that is right for me is not right for someone else, it must be on the ground of some difference between the two cases other than the fact that I and he are different persons." Sidgwick saw this as an application of the principle of the similarity of individuals that go to make up a logical whole or genus.

The second principle is that of prudence. It states "that Hereafter *as such* is to be regarded neither less nor more than Now." In other words, a man ought to have a care for the good of his life as a whole, and not sacrifice a distant good for a nearer one. Sidgwick said that this was an application of the principle of the similarity of the parts of a mathematical or quantitative whole.

The third principle is that of benevolence, and follows from the other two. If we combine the principle of justice (equal respect for the right of every man) with the principle of the good on the whole, we arrive at "the notion of Universal Good by comparison and integration of the goods of all individual human—or sentient—existences." "I obtain the self-evident principle that the good of any one individual is of no more importance, from the point of view of the universe, than the good of any other. . . . And it is evident to me that as a rational being I am bound to aim at good generally."

In Sidgwick's opinion, these formal principles of intuition are an indispensable part of systematic ethics, providing the rational necessity on which the whole structure is based. Egoistic hedonism would have no kind of rational foundation apart from the axiom of prudence here expressed. Nor would universal hedonism, or utilitarianism, without the other two axioms, those of justice and benevolence.

But the axioms of intuition do not offer practical guidance by themselves. They must be given content and direction in terms of the good—not merely in terms of the formal concept of the good as "excellence," but in terms of the material concept of the good as "happiness," that is, "desirable consciousness." We have seen the validity of this concept in connection with egoism. All that remains is to accept it as the ultimate criterion or standard which ought to govern our actions toward our fellowmen.

Sidgwick's discussion of utilitarianism, the third of his three "methods," is brief. It need not be extensive because its main principles have already been stated—that the good is pleasure was shown under egoism and that the right action has regard to the happiness of the whole was shown under intuitionism. As we have seen, Sidgwick does not try to base our duty to mankind at large on "feelings of benevolence," or "natural sympathy." It rests on a moral cognition, as Jeremy Bentham, because of his affinities with the Age of Reason, saw better than John Stuart Mill. Sidgwick declared that utilitarianism requires a man to sacrifice not only his private happiness but also that of persons whose interests natural sympathy makes far dearer to him than his own well-being. Its demands are sterner and more rigid than traditional notions of duty and virtue. And the Utilitarian who follows his principles will find the whole of organized society rising up against him "to deter him from what he conceives to be his duty."

The fact that he found the rationale of utilitarianism implicit in the axioms of intuitionism was, for Sidgwick, a great step toward bringing the diverse methods of ethics into a higher synthesis. That egoism finds its rule of prudence among them was also encouraging. But one fundamental breach remained to be healed. How to reconcile egoism with utilitarian duty?

Theologians have resolved the problem by the doctrine of immortality and eternal rewards. But Sidgwick refused that solution in the interests of preserving the autonomy of ethics. He did not deny the desirability of such an arrangement but he saw no rational evidence for it. "It only expresses the vital need that our Practical Reason feels of proving or postulating this connection of virtue and self-interest, if it is to be made consistent with itself. For," he says, "the negation of this connexion must force us to admit an ultimate and fundamental contradiction in our apparent intuitions of what is Reasonable in conduct."

That would be tantamount to admitting that rational ethics is an illusion. It would not mean abandoning morality, "but it would seem to be necessary to abandon the idea of rationalizing it completely." And this, in turn, would have the practical consequence that in a conflict between duty and self-interest, the conflict would be decided by "the preponderance of one or other of two groups of non-rational impulses."

Sidgwick's conclusion has about it the inconclusiveness of many a Socratic dialogue. He suggested that we may be faced with the alternative of accepting moral propositions "on no other grounds than that we have a strong disposition to accept them," or of "opening the door to universal scepticism."

—*J.F.*

PERTINENT LITERATURE

Broad, C. D. "Sidgwick," in *Five Types of Ethical Theory*. Paterson, New Jersey: Littlefield, Adams & Company, 1959.

C. D. Broad's pioneering critical study of Henry Sidgwick's *The Methods of Ethics* originally appeared in 1930, and it is still the most detailed and thoroughgoing critical work on *The Methods of Ethics,* and among the fairest and most lucid. Broad's overall opinion of the work is extremely high; he ranks it as the best treatise on ethics ever written. Nevertheless, he disagrees with Sidgwick on a number of important points of substance and method and assesses his arguments as inconclusive or even fallacious in some cases.

Broad arranges his critique into seven major topics, three of which will be touched upon here: Sidgwick's classification of the methods of ethics, discussion of the three methods, and examination of the relations among the methods.

Broad says that Sidgwick's method of classification of the various methods of ethics uses both epistemic and ontological distinctions and results in cross-divisions. Broad prefers a distinction of methods into deontological and teleological, and he classifies Sidgwick as primarily a teleologist who accepts certain highly abstract deontological principles about the proper distribution of happiness.

Broad agrees in the main with Sidgwick's critique of the morality of common sense. Sidgwick lays down several requirements for genuine moral axioms: they must be clear and determinate, the principles must continue to seem self-evident no matter how closely they are examined and in the face of whatever difficulties confront them, and they must be mutually consistent. Sidgwick finds that the dogmatic intuitionistic principles of commonsense morality do not fulfill the requirements. It is for that reason that Sidgwick turns to the alternative of a teleological view supplemented with a very few deontological principles about distribution. Broad suggests a different alternative. He argues that the dogmatic intuitionist makes two fundamental mistakes: he simply identifies rightness with fittingness of an action to the situation in which it occurs and fails to notice that utility is also a relevant consideration; he also takes it for granted that the fittingness of an action to its situation is a simple function of its relation to only a very short train of events, what Broad calls the initial situation or the phase that immediately succeeds the action. But remote consequences are also relevant to its fittingness as well as to its utility. These mistakes can be rectified by a view which holds that the rightness or wrongness of an action is a function of both its fittingness and its utility. Deontological principles will cease to be absolute and instead concern the tendencies of certain kinds of acts to be right or wrong. Estimates of rightness and wrongness in particular cases will become very complex and uncertain. No doubt this alternative is not so simple as Sidgwick's utilitarianism, but it may be closer to the truth.

Broad devotes a great deal of thoughtful discussion to Sidgwick's universal hedonistic view of intrinsic goodness. Sidgwick holds that the one and only intrinsically good thing is the experience of pleasure, and that nothing is relevant to the intrinsic value of an experience but its hedonic quality—its pleasantness or painfulness. With Jeremy Bentham he also holds that nothing is relevant to the goodness or badness of an experience as a means except its fecundity, by which he means its tendency to produce pain or pleasure in the future. Broad thinks that this cannot be true and that Sidgwick and others who try to show that it is true commit a fallacy. His telling counterexample is the case of malice. Suppose someone takes pleasure in thinking of the undeserved suffering of another. Is malice not an intrinsically bad state of mind precisely because it is pleasant and the more pleasant the more intrinsically bad? On the other hand, the sorrowful contemplation of the undeserved suffering of another is not intrinsically bad. Therefore, Broad concludes, we must be prepared to accept the possibility that there is no single simple feature of an experience necessary and sufficient to make it intrinsically good or bad; the goodness or badness will depend on the constituents of the experience and how they are related. Attempts to prove that pleasantness is sufficient for intrinsic goodness seem to follow this line of reasoning: For any particular nonhedonic quality, an experience can be intrinsically good if it is pleasant but lacks that quality. Therefore it could be intrinsically good if it lacked all such nonhedonic qualities. That is fallacious, Broad thinks, in the same way that it would be fallacious to argue that since something can be round without having any particular area, it could be round without having any area at all. Broad thinks that Sidgwick is guilty of this fallacy and that the doctrine of hedonism is almost certainly false.

Broad distinguishes three forms of hedonism: egoistic, altruistic, and universalistic. He notes that common sense regards egoism as "grossly immoral" and altruism as Quixotic. It is not sure about the universal form. While Sidgwick thinks the principles of egoistic hedonism and universalistic hedonism are both self-evident, he confesses that they are clearly contradictory, and he can find no way of refuting egoism. Broad thinks that egoism, far from being self-evident, is plainly false, and that universalistic hedonism is not obviously true. For example, he thinks that although the total net happiness in a group could be increased by increasing the size of the group but diminishing the average happiness of its members, to do so would be plainly immoral. Broad also thinks that fecundity is not the only relevant consideration in deciding how to distribute happiness. For example, he thinks that a very unequal distribution is *ipso facto* somewhat objectionable even though it might finally be justified on utilitarian grounds. Thus Broad believes that Sidgwick's theory cannot be the whole truth about ethics.

Darwall, Stephen L. "Pleasure as Ultimate Good in Sidgwick's Ethics," in *The Monist*. LVIII, no. 3 (July, 1974), pp. 475-489.

Henry Sidgwick regards himself as an intuitionist, or at least a utilitarian on an intuitionist basis, thus dissociating himself from empiricism. Despite that, argues Stephen L. Darwall, Sidgwick's utilitarian view is largely analogous to an empiricist epistemology and arises from his account of pleasure and its role as the ultimate good. Darwall believes that Sidgwick's view is mistaken and that to understand it as the analogue of epistemological empiricism enables one to see why it is mistaken.

Briefly, Sidgwick defines pleasure as a feeling a sentient being, at the time of feeling it, apprehends to be desirable, when considered merely *as* a feeling, irrespective of its objective conditions or consequences. It is not a particular kind of feeling; what makes various experiences or feelings pleasures is their relation to desire. Darwall says that this account of pleasure has the merit of being able to explain how pleasure can be a reason for action as well as solving some of the difficulties inherent in psychological hedonism. The account seems true in many instances, but seems implausible in many others, among them some of the most important for moral philosophy.

For example, one takes pleasure in the thought that the war is over or that one has helped a friend or done a good job. Darwall says that on Sidgwick's account, in all these cases if I am to get pleasure from these thoughts, I apprehend my having these thoughts as desirable *however they might happen to have come about.* This he thinks is clearly untrue; if I am to get pleasure I must believe the thoughts to be correct or justified. What I take pleasure in, what I apprehend as desirable, is not a feeling or thought at all, but rather some objective condition, some state of affairs.

Sidgwick holds that pleasure is the ultimate good and that (roughly) rightness consists in promoting it, so that his view about rightness is essentially teleological. One line of support he gives for that view is that the mere existence of human organisms is not in itself desirable, but is desirable only because it is accompanied by consciousness. He concludes that therefore this consciousness is what must be regarded as the ultimate good. Darwall sees this argument as a *non sequitur*, as had James Seth before him. It does not follow from the fact that I cannot take pleasure in some state of the world unless I am aware of it, that what I apprehend as ultimately desirable is my awareness of it. Darwall suggests that Sidgwick's acceptance of this fallacious argument, together with his claim that pleasure is the ultimate good, constitutes an empiricism comparable to epistemological empiricism—this notwithstanding the fact that Sidgwick himself remarks that experience cannot tell us that anyone ought to seek pleasure. Pleasure plays the role of the "given" and the foundation of morality just as sense data play the role of the "given" and the foundation of knowledge. Naturally then, according to Darwall, Sidgwick's view falls prey to some of the same problems which beset empiricism. Egoistic hedonism becomes the same vexing problem for Sidgwick that solipsism became for the empiricists. It is one's own pleasure which is presented in experience as desirable. How, then, can one come to know, or can one know at all, that the aggregate pleasure of all persons is good?

Sidgwick concedes that the egoist may decline to agree that there is any such thing as the universal good, and he admits that if the egoist does so decline, he knows of no way to prove him mistaken. Sidgwick ultimately acknowledges the possibility of a fundamental and irredeemable contradiction in our intuitions about what is reasonable in conduct.

The lessons to be learned from Sidgwick's errors are similar to those Immanuel Kant taught about early empiricism. Moral philosophy ought to begin not with the question of what presents itself to us as in itself desirable, but with the question of what constitutes *practical* experience which we can reason about. Darwall says that if there are principles which govern practical experience, these principles are surely relevant to a theory of the right, and they cannot be found in the direction in which Sidgwick is looking for them. That is because their ground is that they are constitutive principles of practical experience of rational agents and not that they are apprehended as desirable. Sidgwick's teleological approach, then, must actually reverse the proper order of inquiry. As Darwall puts it, "A theory of the right is prior to a theory of value."

Raphael, D. D. "Sidgwick on Intuitionism," in *The Monist.* LVIII, no. 3 (July, 1974), pp. 405-419.

D. D. Raphael discusses Henry Sidgwick's account of intuitionism and its role in relation to the particular sort of utilitarianism that Sidgwick himself embraces. Sidgwick attempts a kind of reconciliation between intuitionism and utilitarianism, calling himself a utilitarian on an intuitionist basis. He distinguishes three kinds of intuitionism: perceptual, dogmatic, and philosophical. Perceptual intuitionism is the view that in each particular case we apprehend what is right without employing general rules to reason to conclusions. Dogmatic intuitionism holds that there are several general, independent, and self-evident moral principles and that we refer to these principles in making judgments about particular cases. Sidgwick thinks that this is the method used by enlightened common sense, but that it is defective in several important respects. The principles do not form a coherent system; indeed, they often conflict with one another, and the method gives no guidance about how the conflicts should be settled. The principles are often indeterminate in their application to particular cases; and upon close scrutiny, the principles raise skeptical doubts about their supposed self-evidence.

Philosophical intuitionism finally attempts to refine dogmatic intuitionism by providing a set of principles which are undoubtedly self-evident, coherent, clear, and determinate, that will enable us to resolve conflicts and show us the relationships of the rules of morality to one another. Sidgwick's own version of philosophical intuitionism attempts to remedy the defects of dogmatic intuitionism by combining principles of justice, prudence, and rational benevolence. Justice as a principle separate from utility is purely formal; it amounts to impartiality—treating like cases alike. Substantive justice, Sidgwick believes, is grounded entirely on utility. Departures from equality of treatment can be justified, according to Sidgwick, only on some reasonable ground. Raphael points out that such a ground can only be utilitarian, for any other ground would require additional self-evident principles beyond those Sidgwick is willing to admit. Further, says Raphael, as a utilitarian Sidgwick must hold that when such reasonable grounds exist, discrimination is not only permissible but also morally required, and consequently equity as an independent moral principle becomes trivial. Sidgwick's principle of impartiality seems on the surface to require impartiality in cases in which common sense also requires it, but if utility is the one and only reasonable ground for discrimination, there can be cases in which the agent's own personal satisfaction in acting partially toward one of several parties, say, because he likes him, can tip an otherwise equal balance of utility and justify or, indeed, require discrimination.

Even if we ignore such cases, Raphael believes Sidgwick's principles to be still relatively trivial, for they require equal treatment only when the consequences of alternatives appear to be equal with regard to happiness. That is because a difference in utility, in Sidgwick's view, is always a sufficient reason for preferring one course of action to another. Raphael thinks that, on the contrary, equity and utility can give rise to opposed claims, requiring a striking of a balance between them.

This consideration leads Raphael to his last and most significant comment on Sidgwick's argument for utilitarianism as a way of rationalizing the morality of common sense. Sidgwick, when describing the principles of commonsense morality, does not include the principle of utility among them, and can therefore introduce the principle as a higher order, one which is able to act as moral arbiter when commonsense principles conflict. Sidgwick does not take into account the real possibility of conflict between the principle of utility itself and other moral principles. Sidgwick seems to make the assumption that the principle of utility plays no role at the lower level of commonsense morality, an assumption Raphael regards as absurd. It is true that practical moral conflicts are sometimes settled by appeal to the principle of utility, but this is an appeal to one principle already belonging to the morality of common sense, not a new, higher level principle. Sidgwick likewise overlooks the fact that sometimes conflicts are also settled by appeal to other principles, such as justice or conscientiousness. Thus, according to Raphael, Sidgwick's attempt to rationalize dogmatic intuitionism by appeal to utility as a higher order principle at once self-evident, providing the main foundation for morality, and capable of resolving conflicts, falls to the ground.—*G.D.R.*

ADDITIONAL RECOMMENDED READING

Havard, William C. *Henry Sidgwick and Later Utilitarian Political Philosophy*. Gainesville: University of Florida Press, 1959. Mainly historical rather than critical. Defines Sidgwick's place in the British utilitarian and Liberal tradition. On Sidgwick's differences with Bentham and Mill and his reconciliation of utilitarianism with intuitionism, see especially Chapter 4, "Reconstruction of the Utilitarian Ethic."

The Monist. LVIII, no. 3 (July, 1974). Entire issue devoted to Sidgwick. Contains several excellent historical and critical articles by J. B. Schneewind, W. K. Frankena, M. Singer, and P. Singer, among others, in addition to those reviewed above.

Schneewind, J. B. "First Principles and Common Sense Morality in Sidgwick's Ethics," in *Archiv fur Geschichte der Philosophie*. XLV, Heft 2 (1963), pp. 137-156. Gives an account of the methodology Sidgwick uses to support utilitarianism.

_____ . *Sidgwick's Ethics and Victorian Moral Philosophy*. Oxford: Clarendon Press, 1977. Gives the historical context for the problems Sidgwick was addressing. Contains the longest and possibly the best expository interpretation of *The Methods of Ethics* itself, as well as a brief account of Sidgwick's later disagreements with T. H. Green, F. H. Bradley, and Herbert Spencer.

ETHICAL STUDIES

Author: Francis Herbert Bradley (1846-1924)
Type of work: Ethics
First published: 1876

PRINCIPAL IDEAS ADVANCED

To be morally responsible a person must be intelligent, capable of making moral distinctions, uncoerced, and actively involved in a situation in which not all of his behavior is predictable in advance.

To ask, "Why should I be moral?" is to ask a senseless question, for it presupposes the instrumentality of moral action.

The sense in which morality as an end in itself is an end for man is that through moral action man realizes himself.

Self-realization is a creative process whereby a self, which is a unity, aims at the higher unity made possible through social cooperation with others.

In *Ethical Studies*, F. H. Bradley did not attempt to delineate a complete system of moral philosophy; rather, this book contains a discussion of problems in ethics which seemed to Bradley to be of particular importance. He believed that the function of ethics "is not to make the world moral, but to reduce to theory the morality current in the world." Consequently, the discussion begins with a consideration of the facts of ordinary morality.

What does the average person mean when he says that someone is morally responsible? Moral responsibility means that a person must answer for some or all of the things that he has done, that he must answer to some moral authority, and that it is right that he should so answer if called upon. He must be the same person when he committed the deed as when he is called upon to answer for it; he must have a certain amount of intelligence; he must be capable of making moral distinctions.

A person is not responsible for every act. For example, he may be forced to do something that is contrary to his desire. He might even know what he is doing in the sense that an insane man knows and still is not responsible. But if a person wills an act, even though he is persuaded to will it, the persuasion alone does not relieve him of moral responsibility.

An ethical act must be in some sense freely done. What meaning can we attach to freedom? It is sometimes said that freedom means liberty to do what a person wills to do and liberty to choose what he wills to do. However, to be free to choose does not mean that the choice is not motivated. A choice without motives is no choice at all; one must choose something on some grounds. But if every act of a person could be predicted in advance, we would be unlikely to say that he was free at all. The truth is that some prediction is compatible with freedom, while some is not. We must know how a moral person will act under certain circumstances, but it does not follow that we can know how he will act under all circumstances. The first sort of prediction is founded on knowledge of character; the second sort, the prediction of all his acts, annihilates him as an individual, denies him a character and a self. The character of a man is not made, but makes itself out of the man's disposition and environment. Thus the ordinary person does not believe that mind can be explained in terms of purely physical laws.

The unsophisticated person believes that there is a necessary connection between punishment and guilt. Punishment is the penalty that someone pays because he owes it. He merits the punishment because he has done wrong, and the wrong exists in the self or in the will of the doer. Punishment is thus an end in itself. Its purpose is not to correct the criminal nor is it to protect society. It is the denial of wrong by the assertion of right.

If I am responsible, if I am free, if I have a theory of punishment, I might still ask the question, "Why should I be moral?" Before this question can be answered, its meaning must be made clear. Bradley points out that this is a strange question. Usually when one asks, "Why should I do it?" one is asking for information concerning the value of the act. But it seems odd to ask, "What is morality good for?" The answer seems to be that morality is good for its own sake. If this is not the answer, then we seem to imply by the question that only means are good and that there is some end beyond morality. But where every good is a good *for*, everything is good because everything can be a means to something else. However, no one would ask, "Why should I be moral?" and then accept the answer, "You cannot be otherwise."

What, then, can the question mean? It may mean, "What should I get by being moral?" This question rests again on the assumption that there is an end in itself that is not morality. But Bradley believes that he has shown that morality cannot be concerned merely with means. He concludes that a genuine ethical theory must be concerned with ends. Therefore, the "*Why?*" in "Why should I be moral?" asks nothing, has no meaning.

There is one other possible interpretation of the question. One might ask, "What does it mean to say that morality as an end in itself is the end for man?" The term which comes closest to expressing the end for man is self-realization. What can this term mean? To understand its meaning clearly, Bradley thinks that we must understand the meanings of "*self*," "*real*," "*realize*," and "*end*." These terms can be understood only within a system of related meanings and such a system would be in the area of metaphysics, with which this book by Bradley is not concerned.

What we can show is that when we act morally, we do try to realize ourselves. We act to secure some end or object that we desire, and "all we can desire is, in a word, self." A desired object is a thought of an object as desired by the individual. What we aim at is the object as desired; that is, at the self in the object. But do we aim at a series of states of the self, discontinuous and fragmented? No, we aim at the sum of these states, a sum to which this particular state contributes. "The question in morals," Bradley says, "is to find the true whole."

If we ask ourselves what it is we most wish for, we shall answer with some general term such as "happiness," "security," "position." This is the whole toward which we intend our acts to aim. Every choice that we make is a choice relative to the self which stands above the particularity of the choice. This self is a unity in a diversity. It is not merely unity, which is static, nor yet merely diversity, which is chaotic; but it is both realized in one infinite whole. Bradley affirms, "'Realize yourself as an infinite whole,' means, 'Realize yourself as the self-conscious member of an infinite whole, by realizing that whole in yourself.'"

But why aim at self-realization when one can aim at some specific thing such as happiness? A concern with happiness is central in the utilitarian theory of ethics. Bradley wishes to dispose of this theory. He answers his question by saying that happiness is not a specific thing. It is what everyone wants but wants in a thousand different ways. Most agree that happiness is not the search for pleasure. Pleasure, when achieved, is found as an accompaniment of some other goal. But suppose that pleasure for pleasure's sake were a workable goal. Would it be a moral goal? To say that my aim is to feel pleased as much as possible and as long as possible seems to be contrary to every notion of morality that a person could have unless he accepted the theory. A goal must present itself as a concrete whole which we can realize by our acts. But pleasure is never realized in this way. It is a momentary internal state of an organism, various and perishing. When the pleasure is gone, we are no longer satisfied. But the goal of the theory is to achieve a sum of these momentary pleasures. Such a goal is impossible, Bradley believes. No organism ever reaches the end of possible pleasures until it is dead. Further, past pleasures are not pleasures but only ideas of pleasures, and they cannot be added to real pleasures.

The hedonist tells us that we should not aim at pleasure but at some reasonable course of action that will bring pleasure. What guarantee is there that any such course will result in pleasure? In whose pleasure will it result? What is pleasure to one may be pain to another. The injunction to act so as to achieve one's own personal pleasure is neither a general rule nor a moral mandate. Also, Bradley says that "to aim at pleasure is not to get it, and yet the getting of it is a moral duty." The seeking of personal pleasure gives no practicable end to life.

Most moralists have believed that judgments must be made as to the goodness of means as well as of ends. They believe that a good end does not justify evil means. Bradley believes that the hedonist cannot, on his own theory, be concerned with the ethics of means. If the end increases happiness, any means is justified as a means. Is prostitution an evil? The question for the utilitarian is, "Does it increase the general happiness?" There is no way in which an answer to this question could be found; and even if one were found, it could hardly be relevant to the moral problem.

What does it mean to say that pleasure is a moral end? John Stuart Mill wrote in *Utilitarianism* (1863), "Each person's happiness is a good to that person, and the general happiness, therefore, a good to the aggregate of all persons." Bradley replies that the conclusion does not follow. A person desires his own happiness on psychological grounds, and he desires the happiness of others either as a means to his own happiness or on some non-utilitarian moral ground such as unselfish duty toward others. Because my own happiness is desired and the happiness of others is desirable, it does not follow that the combination of both is desired and desirable. Bradley concludes this phase of his argument by remarking that Mill's argument "is not a good theoretical deduction, but it is the generation of the Utilitarian monster, and of that we must say that its heart is in the right place, but the brain is wanting."

The argument stemming from the question, "Why should I be moral?" has shown that the moral good as an end in itself must be sought for its own sake. One theory which stresses this view is the duty for duty's sake ethics of Immanuel Kant. Briefly, Bradley's criticism of Kant's ethical theory is that the theory is too abstract to be used as a guide for practical action. To do a duty is to do a specific act; but the reason for doing it, duty's sake, gives no specific object for the act. Duty's sake is an abstract concept. One can give this concept meaning, but one cannot deduce any concrete meaning from it.

The moral end for Bradley is self-realization, not the isolated self as with the utilitarians, not the abstract self acting for the sake of duty as with the Kantians, but a self having a relation to other selves in a community. Only individuals are real, but they become real through relations with other individuals in families, states, and nations. These communities are the means through which the individual can realize his real self. He has a place in a system of selves which requires that he act in certain ways in relation to the whole and to the other selves which are parts. The obligation that he has in relation to this system is summed up by Bradley as follows: "In short, man is a social being; he is real only because he is social, and can realize himself only because it is as social that he realizes himself." It is true that a person can choose his station within certain limits, but everyone has a station and duties pertaining to it. Certain circumstances and a certain position require certain acts. The theory establishes a relation between the subjective person and the objective world which is the society in which he lives. When a person wills to act morally, he wills to fill an objective place in the concrete world. When he succeeds, that is, realizes himself morally, something which ought to be in the world is in it. Then the person is what he ought to be, and he is content and satisfied.

The next problem is to determine how a person can know what particular act is right or wrong. This is an important question, but for Bradley it is not the function of philosophy to answer it. Philosophy does not deal with particulars. This is the area of common sense, science, and other fields of practical action. Philosophy tries "to understand what is."

Within Bradley's self-realization theory of ethics, we can still raise the question as to whether morality and self-realization are the same thing. A person may realize himself through his work, but we would not be inclined to say that he was moral just because he was a good scientist or a good artist. On the other hand, we would not be inclined to call a person moral if, although he failed to transgress any moral rules, he had done nothing at all. The moral man seems to be one who tries to do well in everything that he attempts. The moral demand is that one do his best both in work and in play. Of course, there are courses of action which are not moral choices. One may go to another city by train, car, or bus and the choice need not be a moral one (although it could be), even though the act of going is morally desirable.

If a moral act is a good act, and if a moral act is one which realizes the self, we may say, according to Bradley, that morality is coextensive with the realization of the ideal self. What is the ideal self? It is both a social and a nonsocial idea. As a social ideal it is realized in society, in one's station and its duties. But one also has duties to oneself, duties beyond the station. A good man is a man who strives for good whether he achieves it or not. Not all goods will be realized; much that is striven for will not be attained. One's good in one's station is a good made visible in the world; the good beyond the good of the ideal self.

Morality is self-realization insofar as this may be taken as an expression of the will for good. It is a devotion to what seems best as against what we happen to like. Its achievement is the compatibility of reason and passion, of demand and accomplishment. It is the state in which all individual acts are subsumed under one collective end. The nature of this end is the subject of metaphysics.

In contrast, the bad self is one that has no coherence. It acts on no principle; it acts toward no coherent end. It turns away from its social dimension, contradicting and opposing the good self. Acts that accord with the good self give us pleasure because they accord with our real being and that of the world, but the bad self is self-contradictory; it has no center to which its acts are related. It is driven by lust from one course of action to another, from one supposed end to some different one. The bad self is not self-conscious. If it were, it would become the good self by selecting some unifying ideal for self-realization. Nor can the bad self be desired for its own sake. An evil act may be desired but not insofar as it is evil. If morality is self-realization, then to desire evil would be to hate the self.

Reflection on morality leads us beyond it. On the one hand, it demands that we explain the self as a metaphysical entity. On the other, it leads us into a philosophy of religion to answer the question of the connection between religion and morality. One fact is clear—that the person who is religious and does not act morally is an impostor. Religion requires some act, and that act is a moral one. But morality is not religion. Mere morality is an ideal; religion is belief in a real object.

An ideal, something only in our imagination, cannot be the object of religion. Faith is the recognition of one's true self in an object. It includes the belief that the course of the world converges on some purpose and that the real human self and the divine self are one. Justified by faith, the ideal self, through religion, finds its objective realization in God.—*J. Co.*

PERTINENT LITERATURE

Vander Veer, Garrett L. *Bradley's Metaphysics and the Self.* New Haven, Connecticut: Yale University Press, 1970.

In his Introduction to *Bradley's Metaphysics and the Self* Garrett L. Vander Veer of Vassar College quite frankly acknowledges that his study of Francis Herbert Bradley was undertaken by one interested in developing a metaphysical system, a kind of Absolute Idealism. This is worth noting for two reasons: in the first place, metaphysics is unpopular among the majority of twentieth century philosophers (even when, unwittingly, they practice it); in fact, analytic philosophers, those who regard the study of language as central to philosophy, are generally inclined to contend not only that metaphysics is uninteresting as an archaic remnant of theology but also (and even worse) that it is not even meaningful. Insofar as metaphysical problems exist, such analytical philosophers contend, the problems arise from misconceptions about or misuses of language. And, second, the question arises whether to trust an explicator sympathetic to the line of thought under examination; can a metaphysician be trusted to find the weaknesses in work similar to his own?

But Vander Veer is a clear writer and a clear thinker (the two skills tend to go together), and the fact that he is sympathetic to Bradley's approach means that he has given to Bradley's work the kind of initial readiness to comprehend that makes it possible for him to grasp Bradley's meaning and to appreciate his objective, that of presenting a clear and persuasive defense of the view that reality is unified, coherent, and accessible to thought, even though any thought, as necessarily partial, must present "appearance" and not reality itself.

Vander Veer's treatment is especially significant in that its author is aware of the content and theme of contemporary analytic philosophy, and he comes to grips in a clear and forceful way with analytic challenges to metaphysics and to Absolute Idealism in particular.

In his discussion of Bradley's theory of judgment, of reality as exhibiting coherency and value, and of the self (in the seven chapters of Part II), Vander

Veer deals with matters central to Bradley's ethics. The emphasis in Bradley's ethics, Vander Veer claims, is upon personal identity; and he quotes Bradley's comment that "Without personal identity responsibility is sheer nonsense." Conceding that Bradley's conception of personal identity as not absolute involves the logical consequence that responsibility, as a function of personal identity, cannot be absolute either, Vander Veer calls attention to the tendency in moral judgment to recognize degrees of responsibility, and he argues that Bradley's theory supports this customary tendency in judgment.

Since Bradley's ethics is a form of "self-realization" theory in that he argues that the objective of right action is the realization of the ideal self, Bradley's conception of the self is particularly critical. Vander Veer points out that although the self may appear to be an exemplar of the "real" since each person is convinced that he is unique, existent, and real, it would be an error to presume that from the recognition of the self's existence one can move uncritically to an assumption of the self's reality. Although Bradley rejects the conception of the self as transexperiential in that it is only in experience that we find assurance of the self, he also criticizes those idealists who argue that the self is an "ultimate concept" providing an embodiment of the kind of unity constitutive of reality. The experience of the self is incomplete, and hence the self is not known as an organic whole. "To find the real," Vander Veer writes in explication of Bradley's position, "we must look beyond the unity present in a self to a unity that . . . implies the extinction of the subject-object relation so essential to selfhood."

The key to understanding the self or the world, according to Vander Veer's view of Bradley's position, is the "proper" experience of the world. The world, including the self, is not a substance beyond experience and presumed by it, nor is it as common sense, influenced by conventional interpretations of experience, supposes it to be. One grasps reality—including the reality of the self—through felt experience that reveals the misleading thrusts of interpretations conditioned by feeling, as in perception and thinking.

In fact, the self as conceived in various ways has all the appearance of appearance, not reality. In a chapter titled "Bradley's Conclusions About the Self," Vander Veer explains that Bradley found it impossible to discover any single, consistent meaning of the term "self." Vander Veer quotes Bradley as concluding that "Anything the meaning of which is inconsistent and unintelligible is appearance and not reality." This conclusion is in line with Bradley's insistence that relational thinking must fail to grasp the whole reality it posits as its object; explanations fail because, writes Vander Veer, "the things to be explained retain some independence from the context that supplies the reason for their relatedness."

Vander Veer's effort is to show that Bradley's view of the self as only an aspect of a "felt totality" that is a finite center, what we might uncritically be inclined to call a "person," is compatible with his claim that moral responsibility requires personal identity. If there were no felt whole as a reality subject to interpretation, there would be no possibility of personal identity. Thus, even though personal identity is a matter of degree, there remains the possibility of will as, in Bradley's words, "the self-realization of an idea with which the self is identified." The moral objective appears to be, then, the realization of the whole through and in the strivings of the self.

Wollheim, Richard. *F. H. Bradley*. Harmondsworth, England: Penguin Books, 1969.

Richard Wollheim's careful and intensive critical examination of Francis Herbert Bradley's philosophy emphasizes Bradley's critical method, his practice of examining conventional and traditional ideas, whether those of common sense or philosophy, finding them unsatisfactory, and then struggling to find what went wrong and what could be done about it. The book is, then, both a study of Bradley's method and of his conclusions; in fact, the thesis of the book appears to be that unless one appreciates Bradley's negativism (in his rejection of inadequate ideas) and the progress of his thought, one cannot grasp his distinctive philosophical position.

Hence, after examining Bradley's logic and his rejection of the phenomenological approach to the resolution of philosophical problems, Wollheim elaborates Bradley's case against pluralism, his ideas on thought and truth, and his account of appearance and reality. Bradley's metaphysics, Wollheim argues, has the content one might expect from the workings of his logic. The central doctrine in Bradley's philosophy, according to Wollheim, is that reality is one, that every effort to conceive of the world as made up of independent things fails, and that every intellectual effort to understand reality by abstracting relationships also fails. Wollheim calls attention to four levels of experience that Bradley distinguished: the level of feeling, of immediate experience; the level of relational thinking; the level of thinking "in which all relations are internal," and the level of thought that may be described as "supra-relational" in that it no longer proceeds relationally. It is only when thought reaches the supra-relational level that the misconceptions and partial conceptions that stem from the relational interpretations of experience are avoided. In escaping the conceptual, relational, and hence partial way of grasping experience and in allowing experience to be of the whole, the one reality, one finally recognizes that although appearances are unreal, they survive as aspects of the Absolute to be grasped, if at all, only in an organic context. (Wollheim concedes the difficulty of understanding Bradley's contention that phenomena, as appearances, are unreal and false outside the Absolute but real and true inside it; metaphor is of some help in attempting to communicate the conception of the fourth level of thinking and of the Absolute it reveals, but the basic idea of "transcendence" is "on all levels incomprehensible.")

In ethics as in metaphysics, Wollheim contends, Bradley proceeded from the rejection of ordinary views to the development of a philosophy that hopefully would avoid the inconsistencies inevitably generated by conventional methods of analysis. Wollheim regards Bradley's *Ethical Studies* as the most Hegelian of his writings, primarily because of Bradley's dialectical method, an elaborate process of criticism, rejection, modification, further rejection, synthesis, and final resolution.

Bradley's position in ethics is summed up in the proposition that the ultimate end for man is self-realization. Wollheim notes that Bradley did not attempt to prove this proposition because to make clear the meanings of such terms as "self" and "realization" would involve the development of a system of metaphysics, a task Bradley did not choose to take up at the time of writing the *Ethical Studies*.

Bradley did, however, examine, analyze, and reject both hedonism (utilitarianism)—the view that the end of action is the maximization of happiness or pleasure—and Kantianism—the view that right action consists in doing what is one's duty for the sake of doing so. Hedonism is unacceptable both because of the hedonistic paradox—namely, that if you pursue pleasure, you will not get it, while if you want pleasure, you have to seek something else—and because hedonism substitutes the pursuit of pleasure for moral motivation; one is morally motivated only insofar as one seeks virtue, not its rewards.

Kantian ethics is also rejected, Wollheim reports, because it presumes that if the good will (the will to act in conformity with the moral law) is formal (in that the moral law provides the form of right action) it concerns itself exclusively with the formal. But moral choice involves the particular and the determinate; it cannot be exclusively formal.

Bradley's doctrine of "My Station and Its Duties" attempts to salvage from hedonism and Kantianism their positive contributions—the ideas that morality is related to the world of individuals and their likes and dislikes, and the idea that morality requires the good will. Bradley maintains that the self is to be realized only as the self of the social organism to which it belongs.

After defending the view at length, Wollheim writes, Bradley found serious objections to it. The conception requires the conformity of the individual self to the ideal self, but the social context fails to provide any such ideal self as a reality. Bradley finally attempts to escape the dilemma by contending that religion satisfies the demands of morality in that the religious object is the ideal self, a higher will that ought to be. Morality is intelligible and not contradictory only when it is transcended in religion. Finally, although one cannot find a theoretical consistency in religion any more than in science or morality, to demand such consistency in religion is unreasonable. Although both God and religion involve inconsistencies, God is real to a higher degree than anything else we might consider; to correct the conception of God is beyond the powers of anyone who approaches the problem in a systematic or conceptual way.

Wollheim's book concludes with a defense of Bradley's monistic vision and its relation to the demands of the psyche to see life steadily and to see it whole while enhancing the grasp of reality by maintaining faith in the ideal.— *I.P.M.*

ADDITIONAL RECOMMENDED READING

Blanshard, Brand. *The Nature of Thought*. London: George Allen & Unwin, 1939. A fellow idealist offers criticism of Bradley's position while developing his own.

Bradley, Francis Herbert. *Appearance and Reality*. Oxford: Clarendon Press, 1955. An understanding of Bradley's ethical theory requires a grasp of his metaphysical view of reality as a monistic absolute.

Moore, George Edward. *Some Main Problems of Philosophy*. London: George Allen & Unwin, 1953. (See also Moore's *Principia Ethica*, London: Cambridge University Press, 1903.) Moore's criticism of metaphysical ethics and his discussion of the uses of the terms "real" and "unreal" apply directly to Bradley's ethics.

Warnock, Mary. *Ethics Since 1900*. London: Oxford University Press, 1960. Warnock's book begins with an account of Bradley's ethics.

Wilson, John Cook. *Statement and Inference*. Oxford: Clarendon Press, 1926. Many regard this work as containing the best criticism of Bradley's account of relations.

PROLEGOMENA TO ETHICS

Author: Thomas Hill Green (1836-1882)
Type of work: Ethics, metaphysics
First published: 1883

PRINCIPAL IDEAS ADVANCED

Nature is dependent upon a self-distinguishing consciousness that is prior to finite minds.

Human consciousness stands between nature and the divine consciousness; man is free because he has understanding and the capacity to will.

The Utilitarians are mistaken in claiming that pleasure is the greatest good; man's good is whatever satisfies man when, as a moral being, he is motivated by the ideal of realizing his capacities, the divine in him.

Virtue, rather than pleasure, is the moral good.

What Green called "the national philosophy" of Britain was represented in the nineteenth century of J. S. Mill, T. H. Huxley, and Herbert Spencer. It was rooted in materialism and sensationism and found its political and ethical expression in altruistic hedonism. In the universities, to be sure, a more classical, theologically grounded tradition remained; and such British men of letters as S. T. Coleridge and Thomas Carlyle had, through their writings, familiarized the literate public with the flavor of German Transcendentalism. But "the national philosophy" was effectively challenged for the first time by a group of academic philosophers, chiefly at Oxford, who fell under the spell of Kant and Hegel. It has been said that they invented the "Hegel-myth" in order to counteract the "Darwin-myth" which Huxley was so successfully propagating at the time, which may indicate that important elements in the British religious and moral heritage were not adequately represented in "the national philosophy."

Such, at any rate, is the contention of Green in his *Prolegomena to Ethics*, originally given as lectures at Oxford. The work falls naturally into two parts, of which the first is concerned with the metaphysical foundations of moral and the second with moral principles and their application. But both parts are developed in antithesis to traditional British philosophy; they point out in turn the failings of naturalism as metaphysics and of Utilitarianism as ethical theory. Under the impetus of Darwinism, according to Green, empiricism had come near to explaining morality out of existence. Newly enlightened, the moralist could no longer mock the misery of the poor or flatter the complacency of the prosperous by speaking of obedience to law, because it had been demonstrated to him that laws were not the sort of things that could be disobeyed, and that it was laws that had brought the poor their misery and the others their prosperity. The charm of this discovery was that it removed much that had previously seemed mysteriously beyond human comprehension; but when its implications had had an opportunity to sink in, a reconsideration had to come. Nothing, Green maintained, could be more contrary to the ideals of enlightened reason.

Green begins his reconsideration by raising the question "whether a being that was merely the result of natural forces could form a theory of those forces explaining himself." If not, if science presupposes a principle which is not one of the facts which it explains, then we shall have learned that, at least in respect of knowing, man is not merely a child of nature but is possessed of a principle that is higher than nature. Green argues that because the data of the natural sciences are all given within consciousness, the latter is the prerequisite for our knowledge of nature and cannot conceivably be the byproduct of material forces, as Huxley was maintaining. Not merely are the data known through consciousness—they are constituted by it. Motion, for example, "has no meaning except such as is derived from a synthesis of the different positions successively held by one and the same body." We cannot think of it without engaging mental processes which give continuity and form to a manifold of sense impressions.

But, as the argument develops, man's knowledge of nature is only an instance of the wider principle that consciousness is prerequisite to the existence of nature itself. By nature we mean "a system of unalterable relations." Now, any relation involves the familiar problem of unity in diversity. But the source of unity and connection cannot be inside nature, for nature is a process of change, and that which gives the world its permanent character cannot itself be subject to change. Intelligence, however, readily accomplishes that which in nature is inconceivable. A multiplicity of feelings and sense impressions is ordered and unified at every moment of our experience. This is the way the world becomes one for each individual. But, since nature is obviously not dependent on particular human intellects for its existence, there must be a unifying factor prior to our finite minds. It must be the common source of the relations which constitute nature and our conception of it; and, "because the function which it must fulfil . . . is one which, on however limited a scale, we ourselves exercise in the acquisition of experience, and exercise by means of such a consciousness," we are justifed in concluding that it, too, is "a self-distinguishing consciousness."

For Green, human consciousness stands between the divine consciousness and nature. Man exists in time: his bodily changes are causally related to everything else in nature. And his kinship with the latter is not limited to his body: his sensations are connected with changes in the brain, which in turn are influenced by light and motion. From this side, the mind may well be thought of as "a stream of consciousness." That, however, is only half the truth, for if consciousness were merely a stream it would never arise to self-awareness. Only because man is able to take a stand outside the stream, to find a point unmoved by change, does he know anything. In this aspect, his thought transcends nature and is related to the eternal consciousness. According to Green, the relation is peculiarly intimate: the divine consciousness "reproduces itself" in man, using feeling and sensation to objectify itself there. The reproduction takes place piecemeal and by degrees because its vehicle is part of nature, because it takes up into itself the "constant succession of phenomena in the sentient life." But though our knowledge is partial, it is nevertheless identical in essence with the eternal consciousness which it reproduces.

Herein lies the secret of man's freedom. He alone of all natural creatures is a self, able to stand apart from the world and, by virtue of the fragment of divinity which is in him, subdue nature and have dominion over it. In addition to understanding he has the capacity to will, and the world appears to him not merely for what it is but also for what it should be.

Just as analysis of knowledge made it necessary to distinguish a *punctum stans* over the flux of sensation by means of which sensations were integrated into facts of nature, so the analysis of volition presupposes, as standing over our feelings, appetites, and desires, a conscious moment in virtue of which these impulses are converted into motives. Wants are natural: man shares them with other animals. But, properly speaking, a want becomes a desire only when it is present to consciousness as an object; that is to say, as an ideal end. There is no desire apart from intellect. But knowing a want involves comparing it with others, preliminary to deciding whether it is to be satisfied. The choice between desires is determined by volition; that is, by the character of the individual. Green opposed the contention of empirical psychology that man's actions are determined by the strongest desire. Desires only condition our choices, which are determined by the self. And a man's self, as Green has maintained, is only partially contained in nature.

On the strength of these metaphysical considerations, Green was prepared to challenge the naturalistic theory of morals and to develop an idealistic one. Both parties—the naturalists and the idealists—were agreed that insofar as man acts morally he seeks self-satisfaction. They were also agreed that intellect plays an important role in determining which acts are good and which are bad. The difference between them lay, as we might anticipate, in whether man's satisfaction is to be found on a purely natural level, or whether it involves an ideal that transcends nature. It should be noted that in practice Green was closer to his opponents than their theories might suggest. Both were progressive and humanitarian in outlook, condemning heartless ambition and lazy indulgence. Both were active and optimistic in politics, sharing the vision of peace and brotherhood among men. The problem was to provide the correct theoretical account of what morality consists in. And each side believed that theory matters and that wrong thinking is likely to lead to evil conduct.

In its simplest form, the question was: Is a maximum of pleasure what man always desires? Green maintained that it is not—that the object chosen is always the satisfaction of some specific desire and never pleasure on its own account. The thought of the pleasure which accompanies the realization of the object may increase our eagerness for the object; but desire defeats itself if pleasure becomes the chief object of our striving. There is, moreover, a logical contradiction in maintaining that the *summum bonum* is the greatest sum of pleasures. Pleasures are instantaneous, and the sum of pleasures is not a pleasure but an intellectual abstraction, according to Green. To say that we seek the sum of pleasures is to abandon hedonism and to admit that man finds his satisfaction on an ideal plane. Green pointed to J. S. Mill's *Utilitarianism* (1863) as an example of the inconsistencies into which hedonism leads. Mill had amended the doctrine of earlier Utilitarians in conceding that pleasures vary in quality, and he tacitly admitted that what properly motivates man is a sense of his own dignity. Nature does not provide us with any such ideal: we are thrown back, as in the case of knowledge, upon the notion of a divine consciousness present to man's mind and working there for its own fulfillment.

For Green, therefore, the moral good must be distinguished from good in general as "that which satisfies the desire of a moral agent, or that in which a moral agent can find the satisfaction of himself which he necessarily seeks." The practical definition of that good admittedly presents some difficulties. Man is bent on realizing to the full extent his moral capacities; but he cannot know those capacities until he has realized them. Nevertheless, in the moral struggle for the better life in which men through the centuries have been engaged, the direction is evident. It has become clear, on the one hand, that the life of intemperance and self-indulgence is no way to realize the good; nor, on the other, is the life of ruthless self-seeking. We have no difficulty, therefore, in marking out certain general lines of moral advance. The good is *personal* and it is *social*.

Although the divine plan is for all humanity, it can be realized only when individual men freely submit to the direction of the eternal consciousness as it is manifest in their lives. In different historical settings, the ideal appears to change; but the formal element in every moral situation is the same. The good for man is never anything but loyalty to the ideal. Suspended as he is between nature and divinity, man is ever compelled to choose whether he will identify himself with his physical appetites or with that which stands to him as a divine command. His realization of selfhood demands that he choose the latter. In Kant's language, he must follow duty for duty's sake.

But it is not possible to respect the demands of reason in one's own person without respecting them in all others. On this Kantian axiom, Green developed his account of the common good, once again finding himself in opposition to "the national philosophy," which, although it had recognized the principle of benevolence or altruism, had never been happy in its attempts to show why a man should sacrifice his own happiness for that of others if he were not inclined to do so. The fact is, according to Green, the "better reason" which presents itself as a law to the individual also presents itself as a law to every man and for the same reason, "as prescribing means to the fulfillment of an idea of absolute good, common to him with them."

Virtue, then, instead of pleasure is the good which man ought always and everywhere to pursue; and, according to Green, the course of moral progress is best traced in terms of the extent to which men were interested in the cultivation of virtue rather than in material prosperity. Reviewing the history of Western morality from the Greeks to the present, he maintained that while Plato and Aristotle adequately understood the personal aspect of moral goodness, they were deficient in their appreciation of its scope—a defect supplied by Christianity. If modern morals are superior to those of the Greeks, it is in the greater renunciation which they impose upon the individual—a self-denial which, however, is not mistaken for a good in itself, but as a means to assisting "in the struggle upward of the many."

The final portion of the book concerns the question of the value of moral theory in helping persons know their duty. In Green's opinion, theory is important because the moral ideal is to make men aware of their true natures, which requires that they reflect on their conduct and on the adequacy of accepted standards. As between the "greatest happiness" theory and that which finds man's good in "self-realization," the former appears to provide the clearer criteria; and Green credited the leaders of the Utilitarian movement with important moral and political gains. But, inasmuch as the hedonistic theory gave no adequate account of duty, it seemed to Green to pose a threat to moral initiative and, indeed, dangerously to weaken the individual's ability to resist evil. Green's own theory, as he acknowledged, offers no technique for making moral choices—the philosopher's judgments, like those of other men, being largely an intuitive application of the ideal. But it has the advantage of keeping uppermost the claims of the ideal, and in cases of moral conflict it may help the individual choose "the higher but more painful good."—*J.F.*

Pertinent Literature
Sidgwick, Henry. *Lectures on the Ethics of T. H. Green, Mr. Herbert Spencer, and J. Martineau.* New York: Macmillan Publishing Company, 1902.

In his *The Methods of Ethics*, Henry Sidgwick took the ground that ethics is an autonomous philosophical discipline, independent of theology, metaphysics, and psychology. The appearance shortly thereafter of Herbert Spencer's *Data of Ethics* and of Thomas Hill Green's *Prolegomena to Ethics* drew quick response, first in articles published in *Mind*, then in the course of

Cambridge University lectures which make up the present volume. Since Sidgwick's time the autonomy of ethics has been generally accepted, but his *Lectures* have permanent interest as a classical example of philosophical analysis.

Without undertaking to challenge the cogency of Green's metaphysical arguments, Sidgwick maintains that even if they are valid they do not have the relevance to ethics that their author assumes. Green's proofs for the existence of an eternal, self-distinguishing consciousness are based on man's cognitive faculty. The divinity, as Green has presented him, is merely an eternal intelligence to which endless succession is known as present. For all that he has shown to the contrary, the succession may be a purposeless round of change: nowhere does Green explain how we are to get from this synthesizing and objectivizing consciousness to the ideal of holiness and to the infinitely and perfectly good will which his moral theory requires.

Turning to Green's ethical psychology, Sidgwick argues that, in spite of his strenuous advocacy of freedom, Green cannot avoid explaining human choices in causal terms. The self-determining consciousness, which is supposed to raise the self above the stream of natural events, does nothing toward explaining why one person chooses good and another evil. It is the particular elements in each person's makeup that determine his choices; and, by Green's own admission, these elements are the result of one's social environment and past life.

Furthermore, Sidgwick maintains, Green's account of the moral act precludes the possibility of a person's willfully doing wrong. Green tries, by setting aside the traditional view according to which the will weighs desires and resolves one against the other, to bring desire, understanding, and will together into a single act of self-objectification. According to Sidgwick, however, experience upholds the old view. It is quite possible, he insists, to entertain desires which one knows are incompatible with one's own good and then to act on them. In his opinion, Green remains too much under the influence of the ancient Greeks in excluding the "willful choice of wrong known to be wrong" which Christian moral consciousness recognizes as sin.

Sidgwick's criticism of Green's ethical ideal turns on the ambiguities inherent in his account of the true good as the idea which each person has of his own greatest self-satisfaction on the whole.

There is first a question whether the good aimed at is objective or subjective. Green fails to distinguish between "good as *attained* or *realized* and good *as sought*." In his system, the wrongdoer is one who thinks he can find satisfaction where there is none—for example, the voluptuary. Looked at in this way, the good is objective and consists in an end to be realized. In this view, whenever a person chooses, he makes a prediction about the results of his action. But in other passages Green treats goodness as subjective; for example, in his account of a person who finds satisfaction in a life of suffering deliberately chosen to fulfill what he conceives to be his mission. In this case, when an agent chooses, he is not predicting anything but is adopting an end, and his good lies not in the attainment but in the choice.

The confusion is compounded, Sidgwick argues, when Green goes on to speak of the true good as an abiding satisfaction of an abiding self. The difficulties here turn on the notion of the self, which is thought of sometimes as "a function of the social organism, which is being made a vehicle of the eternal consciousness" and sometimes as "that eternal consciousness itself, making the animal organism its vehicle, and subject to certain limitations in so doing." Swinging between these two views of the self, Green's answer to the question, What will afford an abiding satisfaction to an abiding self?, takes first one form then another. In a broad sense, man's true good includes the realization of various natural capacities; in a narrow sense, it is limited to the realization of the moral capacities. Taken in either sense, Sidgwick finds that important questions remain unanswered. If the true good includes the realization of our sensitive, emotional, and intellectual capacities, then Green ought to provide a criterion for deciding which capacities are to be realized; for some capabilities are realized in every action. As an example, one of the deepest impulses that prompt men to vice is the desire for richness of experience. On the other hand, if the good is restricted to moral fulfillment, it becomes empty and devoid of practical guidance. "Suppose us all willing the good, what should we all will?" Sidgwick is aware that in practice such a question cannot arise; but his argument is with Green's claim to have made morality philosophically comprehensible.

In large part, Green's *Prolegomena to Ethics* is an attack on Utilitarianism; and we might expect Sidgwick, whose own teachings are included in the attack, to come to the defense of that system in his *Lectures*. This he finds it unnecessary to do. He does, however, take up Green's claim to have overcome one of the chief difficulties of altruistic hedonism: the possibility that A's greatest happiness may be incompatible with B's. Certainly, says Sidgwick, it would be an achievement if Green could support the claim that his system "does not admit of the distinction between good for self and for others." He belies this claim, however, as Sidgwick shows, in his own discussion of justice and self-sacrifice; for example, when he represents the conscientious man asking whether in seeking his own well-being he may not be doing so at the cost of impeding the well-being of some other person. Sidgwick admits that the pagan Greek could say that the good of each was the good of all; but he could do this because he was not concerned, as Green is, with the self-satisfaction of each person.

Richter, Melvin. *The Politics of Conscience: T. H. Green and His Age.* Cambridge, Massachusetts: Harvard University Press, 1964.

Thomas Hill Green's reputation today rests mainly on his contribution to English political thought; but, as Melvin Richter shows in this full-length portrait, Green's contribution to the idea of positive liberalism is not intelligible apart from his account of man's nature and of the true good, given in the *Prolegomena to Ethics*. For example, the common good, much spoken of in his *Lectures on Political Obligation*, simply means the true good, explained at length in the *Prolegomena to Ethics*; and freedom, treated as a political objective, means the power to fulfill one's higher capabilities, not some unconscionable right to do whatever one pleases.

Richter's book is a comprehensive study of the forces that helped to mold Green's thought and to prepare its enthusiastic reception by the rising generation. Among these forces were his evangelical background, his active interest in radical politics, and his role in university reform. It is in the latter connection that we see Green turning to the philosophies of Immanuel Kant and G. W. F. Hegel to fill what he perceived as a void in the way philosophy was then being taught. With science challenging theology, which hitherto had provided answers to questions of meaning and conduct, students demanded a fuller training in philosophy than English universities were accustomed to provide. This, says Richter, accounts for two paradoxical elements in Green's thought: a determination to follow reason wherever it leads, and a confidence that reason will provide answers to questions hitherto regarded as religious.

Richter's account is useful to the philosophical reader as showing the close affinity between Green's method and that of Kant. Like Kant, he approached his problems by asking how knowledge, morality, and society are possible, and concluded that they are possible only on the basis of certain presuppositions. Three such presuppositions, according to Richter, dominate Green's thought: (1) the theory of internal relations, according to which no element of experience is knowable apart from its relations to other elements; (2) the theory that all knowledge implies an organizing consciousness which combines the elements into a whole; and (3) the theory of teleology, according to which all experience fits into a scheme of progress. Throughout, Green's method is opposite to that employed by the empirical sciences: instead of trying to prove that there is a good at which all men aim, he maintains that unless such a good is presupposed the moral enterprise becomes unintelligible.

That Green defined the true good in terms of moral perfection rather than in terms of happiness is also owing to Kant, who had proclaimed that the only thing that is good in itself without qualification is the good will. Here Green found not only philosophical expression of the Puritan concept of conscience, but also the ascetic and activist ideal that motivated many secular reformers. According to Richter, however, Green was troubled by Hegel's criticism of Kant's subjective individualism and tried to mend the defect of his pure deontologism by embracing a teleological view of history.

Kant, of course, had made the point that in recognizing one's own life as an end in itself, a person perceives that the same must be true of the lives of all men. Still, the ideal of fellow-service remains formal and abstract until it is fleshed out in an established system of communal ties, with reciprocal rights and obligations. It is in such a community that personality emerges and character is formed. Thus, in a sociological sense, individuals are secondary to societies, which define the limits of self-realization and determine that, so far as individual choice of good is concerned, "each has primarily to fulfill the duties of his station." In a metaphysical perspective, however, the individual person is prior to society. Consciousness, by means of which all relations are determined, is the property of individuals, as is the idea of the good— that "parent of institutions and usages" through which human life has been bettered. In short, institutions are not the product of animal instinct and chance association, but are the vehicle of reason, even as history is the revelation of God's purpose.

Libertarians have attacked these Hegelian features of Green's philosophy as a threat to individual rights. When set alongside the actual influence that Green exercised, however, these criticisms seem doctrinaire; for, as Richter shows, Green's thought did not rob men of personal freedom but instead made possible urgently needed economic and social reforms which had been blocked by traditional individualism.

Does Green's Idealist method, with its *a priori* approach to personal and social behavior, offer an objective means of determining value, or does it merely indicate individual preference? While admitting Green's good faith, Richter agrees with Sidgwick and G. E. Moore that Green's actual analysis is anything but convincing. The fault, as Richter sees it, follows inevitably from Green's determination to provide his students with a philosophy of life. As the leader of a moral crusade, he needed an *a priori* method which would free men from the necessity of constantly examining their presuppositions. Moreover, to knit together a following from diverse backgrounds, he found it expedient to disregard clarity where it divided men: for example, Green seems never to have declared for or against the belief in personal immortality—a doctrine certainly relevant to what he had to say about the abiding satisfaction of the abiding self.

As Richter notes, Green's Oxford followers were divided. F. H. Bradley, for example, denied that metaphysics is relevant to ethics; and Bernard Bosanquet joined Bradley in arguing that personality has no reality. From Cambridge, the younger men (Bertrand Russell and Moore) were to create a climate hostile to the whole Idealist movement. Whether they did so by force of logic or by inventing a pathos of their own, Richter refuses to say.—*J. F.*

ADDITIONAL RECOMMENDED READING

Caird, Edward. "Professor Green's Last Work," in *Mind*. VIII, no. 32 (October, 1883), pp. 544-561. An appreciative summary of the *Prolegomena to Ethics* by a leading representative of Green's school.

Lamont, William D. *Introduction to Green's Moral Philosophy*. London: George Allen & Unwin, 1934. A sympathetic reworking of Green's ideas.

Milne, A. J. M. "T. H. Green's Theory of Morality," in *The Social Philosophy of English Idealism*. London: George Allen & Unwin, 1962. Useful for comparing Green with Bradley, Bosanquet, and Josiah Royce.

Taylor, A. E. *The Problem of Conduct*. London: Macmillan and Company, 1901. Chapter II, "Some Arguments in Favor of a Metaphysical Ethic Considered," is a sharp criticism of Green.

THUS SPAKE ZARATHUSTRA

Author: Friedrich Wilhelm Nietzsche (1844-1900)
Type of work: Ethics
First published: Parts I and II, 1833; III, 1884; IV, 1885

PRINCIPAL IDEAS ADVANCED

Life is the will to power, and he who would truly live must overcome the beliefs and conventions of common men; he must become an overman (or "superman").

Those who teach the Christian virtues of pity and meekness seek to corrupt man, to destroy his will to power, and to make him submit to those who prosper from the conventional way.

Men who do not have the courage to live seek to escape by sleeping, by prizing the soul more than the body, and by seeking peace instead of war.

The overman is virtuous when he frees himself from the belief in God and from the hope of an afterlife; he is nauseated by the rabble, and his joy comes from surpassing those who live by false hopes and beliefs.

Worship of any sort is a return to childhood; if men must worship, let them worship donkeys if that suits them.

It is difficult to decide whether Nietzsche is greater as a literary figure or as a philospher. He was a literary master of the German language. He influenced such writers as Bernard Shaw, H. L. Mencken, Theodore Dreiser, Robinson Jeffers, Frank Norris, and Jack London. He is neither a systematic philosopher in the sense of Hegel, nor a meticulous critical philosopher in the sense of Ernst Mach, the philosopher of science. Nietzsche belongs rather to the traditon of philosophers who wished to tell men how to live. His injunction is for one to become an individual, and to follow one's own desires—if necessary, through the destruction of others.

Nietzsche is often inconsistent, sometimes contradictory; but he is almost always provocative. His criticisms of nineteenth century institutions remind the reader of those of his contemporaries, Søren Kierkegaard and Fyodor Dostoevski, and like theirs often seem to apply to our own century. His positive doctrine is rejected by most people and is accepted not, as Nietzsche had hoped, by potential leaders but by those hopelessly defeated by modern civilization.

There are three principal themes in *Thus Spake Zarathustra*: the will to power, the consequent revaluation of values, and the doctrine of eternal recurrence. Life is essentially a will to power, the feeling that one is in command of oneself and of the future. In controlling the future, one finds that the values which most people accept are inadequate and that one must adopt a new, in many cases opposite, set of values. But neither power nor the new set of values is desirable for its consequences. If one were to use power to accomplish some final end, one would no longer need it; if one were to realize the new values, one would no longer need them. For Nietzsche there are no final ends. Power and the revaluation of values are good in themselves; and, consequently, there is no millennium, nothing but an eternal recurrence of people, things, and problems.

These three themes are developed carefully in *Thus Spake Zarathustra*. This exposition will follow Nietzsche's manner of development which is both self-conscious and purposive.

The main theme in Part I is that the individual stands alone with his fate in his own hands. He can expect no help from others either in this life or in some imagined future life. He must "make himself" to use the phrase of the modern existentialists. As Part I opens we find that Zarathustra has spent ten years on a mountain in meditation. His companions have been his eagle, a symbol of pride, and his serpent, a symbol of wisdom. He has just decided to go into the world of men to teach some of the wisdom that he has acquired during his period of meditation.

On the way down the mountain, he meets a saint who tells him that the way to help men is to stay away from them and to save them through prayer. Here Nietzsche announces one of his important ideas, that the individual can expect no supernatural help because God is dead.

Zarathustra reaches a town where, finding a crowd engaged in watching a tightrope walker perform his act, he says to them, "*I teach you the overman. Man is something that shall be overcome.*" He explains that man has evolved from apes but that he is still apelike. Man is poisoned by those who teach that salvation is found not in this world but in the next, and by those who teach the Christian ethics of virtue, justice, and pity. But the people in the crowd are not ready for Zarathustra's message. They think that he is announcing the tightrope walker's act. He reflects that they cannot be taught since they are not ready to take the first step toward learning by recognizing that their present beliefs are false. What Zarathustra must find is those "who do not know how to live except by going under, for they are those who cross over."

The tightrope walker falls and is killed. Zarathustra and the corpse are left alone in the marketplace. Zarathustra then realizes that one of his great problems will be to communicate his message to people too indifferent or too stupid to understand him. But his purpose remains firm, "I will teach men the meaning of their existence—the overman, the lightning out of the dark cloud of man." Since he cannot teach the multitude, he decides that he will have to select a few disciples who will follow him "because they want to follow themselves. . . ."

Throughout the rest of Part I, Nietzsche expresses a series of more or less disconnected criticisms of the men of his time. Most people are sleepers because sleep robs them of thought, makes them like inanimate objects, and imitates death. Man uses sleep as a means of escape, just as God created the world as a diversion, as an escape from himself.

Another sort of escape is found by accepting the injunction to renounce the body and love the soul. But the soul is only a part of the body; and one must love the whole more than one loves any part. Love of the soul to the exclusion of the body is a kind of renunciation of life. Another is the belief that life is full of suffering. So it is, but the overman will see to it that his is not one of the sufferers. War brings out many of the best qualities in men, Nietzsche argues. "You should love peace as a means to new wars—and the short peace more than the long. . . . You say it is the good cause that hallows even war? I say unto you: it is the good war that hallows any cause."

The state, another escape from reality, is one of the greatest enemies of individualism. It tells the citizen what to do, how to live; it replaces his personality with its own.

Another renunciation of life is dedication to the ideal of chastity. To deny the lust of the flesh is often to affirm the lust of the spirit. Why deny lust? Nietzsche asks. Women are only half human at best, more like cats or cows. What is great is the passion of love between men and women, for all creation is the result of passion. The solution to all of women's problems is child-bearing; and this is the only interest women ever have in men. A man needs two things, danger and play. His interest in woman is that she is "the most dangerous plaything." She is "the recreation of the warrior. . . ." Her hope should be that she will bear the overman. Men are merely evil, but women are bad. That is why they are dangerous. Men can overcome them only by subjugating them completely. An old crone agrees with Zarathustra and adds her advice, "You are going to women? Do not forget the whip!"

How should one die? Only when one has perfected his life; but if one cannot live a perfect life, then it is best to die in battle. Death must come because one wants it.

Part I ends with the injunction that through Zarathustra's teaching one should not become merely a disciple and imitator of the prophet, but should learn through him to understand oneself. The section ends on a note that has become familiar: "'*Dead are all gods: now we want the overman to live*'—on that great noon, let this be our last will."

In Part II Nietzsche develops the notion of the will to power. The first part is largely negative, but the second part provides the positive doctrine. It begins with the idea that the conjecture of God is meaningless because it defies the imagination. However, the conjecture of the overman is within the scope of the human mind if one first eliminates error. One cause of error is pity; but the overman is willing to sacrifice himself, and so he is willing to sacrifice others. Priests cause error. They have taken death as their God's triumph; they need to be redeemed from their Redeemer. They are virtuous because they expect a reward in the afterlife, but there is no reward. For the overman, to be virtuous is to be true to oneself and to follow where the self leads. The mass of people want power and pleasure too, but they want the wrong kinds. The overman must seek the higher powers and pleasures. He must be nauseated by the rabble that is around him.

This category of nausea is also found in works by Dostoevski and Jean-Paul Sartre, In *Notes from the Underground*, the sickness is caused by the loathsomeness of life; in Sartre's *Nausea*, it is caused by the meaninglessness of existence. For Nietzsche, the malaise comes from seeing the rabble as one would see a field of dead, decaying animals, from seeing their "stinking fires and soiled dreams. . . ."

Nietzsche's statement of his positive doctrine is often interrupted by fell criticisms. The contrast between the desires of the masses and those of the overman reminds him of the belief that all men are equal. But if men were born equal, there could be no overman. Those who have preached equality have told the people what they wanted to hear rather than the truth. The truth can be discovered only by the free spirit that wills, desires, and loves. Such a free spirit finds that not all things can be understood, and that some must be felt. The will to truth is just one aspect of the will to power. Such a will carries the free spirit beyond truth and falsity and beyond good and evil as well. The slave thinks that he can conquer his master by his servility; he has the will to power, but in its lowest form. The forerunner of the overman has the will to be master, the will to command, the will to conquer. Since he is incapable of positive action, the slave can do neither good nor evil. The master with his capacity for evil has a capability for good. If the good requires positive action, so does the beautiful. Zarathustra asks, "Where is beauty?" and answers, "Where I must will with all my will; where I want to love and perish that an image may not remain a mere image."

If one cannot find truth among those who tell the people what they want to hear, still less can one find it among the scholars, who have removed themselves from the possibility of action and who "knit the socks of the spirit." Neither can one turn to the poets. They know so little they have to lie to fill the pages they write. They are the great mythmakers; they created God. Zarathustra's mission is to lead men away from myths toward an assertion of the will. Men who accept the myths are like actors who play the parts assigned to them but who can never be themselves. The man who exercises the will to power can do so only by being himself.

The Third Part of *Thus Spake Zarathustra* introduces the theme of eternal recurrence, but it is almost obscured by other themes. The main question is: What does one experience when one travels? Zarathustra decides that no matter where one travels one can experience only oneself. But if this is the case, then the individual is beyond good and evil, both of which require some absolute standard or criterion of judgment. There is none. Man lives in a world, not of purpose, knowledge, law, and design, but of accident, innocence, chance, and prankishness. "In everything, one thing is impossible; rationality." Of course one may use a little wisdom, but only as a joke.

But what of people who cannot accept this doctrine because they are weak in body and in mind? They cannot be expected to accept the truth; they talk but cannot think. They ask only for contentment and refuse to face life. They expect teachers of contentment, flatterers who will tell them they are right. They want those who will condemn as sins the acts that they never commit, and who will praise their small sins as virtues. But Nietzsche continues. "'Yes, I *am* Zarathustra the godless!' These teachers of resignation! Whatever is small and sick and scabby, they crawl to like lice, and only my nausea prevents me from squashing them."

Although much that Nietzsche says is negative and critical, he constantly warns the reader that criticism should be given only out of love and in preparation for a positive doctrine to follow. Condemnation for its own sake is evidence only of an interest in filth and dirt.

If God is dead, how did he die? Here Nietzsche cannot resist a criticism of the musician Wagner, with whom he had been closely associated and with whom he had finally quarreled. Wagner had written an opera, *Götterdämmerung* (*The Twilight of the Gods*). It is a highly dramatic story of the destruction of the Norse gods. Nietzsche says that the gods did not die in the way that Wagner describes. On the contrary, they laughed themselves to death when one of their number announced that there was only one god. This jealous god had lost his godhead by saying the most godless word; and the other gods died laughing.

What are often considered evils turn out on close examination by Nietzsche to be goods. Sex, which is cursed by "all hair-shirted despisers of the body," is a virtue for the free and innocent. Lust to rule, which destroys civilizations, is a fit activity for the overman. Selfishness, a vice only of masters as seen by their slaves, is a necessary virtue of great bodies and great souls. The first commandment is to love yourself; the great law is "*do not spare your neighbor! Man is something that must be overcome.*"

Nietzsche turns at last to the doctrine of eternal recurrence. The theory that history repeats itself in identical cycles is familiar to us through Plato, who derived it from the writings of Egyptian and Babylonian astronomers. It requires a concept of time that has not been congenial to Western thought ever since it was attacked by Saint Augustine. For us, time seems to move in a straight line that has no turnings. Nietzsche, knowing that his doctrine would not be well received, stated it first of all as coming from Zarathustra's animals: "Everything goes, everything comes back; eternally rolls the wheel of being." Whatever is happening now will happen again and has happened before. The great things of the world recur, but so do the small. The recurrence of the small things, of the men farthest removed from the overman, seems at first impossible for Zarathustra to accept. That the return is exactly the same—not that the best returns, not that the part returns, not that all except the worst returns, but that *all*, best and worst, returns—is difficult for him to acknowledge. But at last he is willing to abandon the doctrine of progress for the truth of eternal recurrence.

The Fourth Part of *Thus Spake Zarathustra*, not intended by Nietzsche to be the last, is concerned with the consequences of accepting some portion of Zarathustra's teachings without accepting the whole. One must take all or none. Much of this part consists of parodies of Christian views—for example, that one must become like a little bovine to enter the kingdom of heaven.

Zarathustra, who is still concerned with the overman, wonders what he will be like. As he goes from place to place in the world, he sees that man is fit only to be despised unless he is the prelude to the overman. Man is not to be preserved; he is to be overcome. Man must be brave even though there is no God; man must be strong because he is evil; and he must hate his neighbor as a consequence of the will to power.

But once more, this doctrine is too strong for the people who listen to Zarathustra. Although God is dead, it is necessary for them to make a god of their own; and this time they choose a donkey. The animal fulfills all of the requirements for a god. He is a servant of men. He does not speak and therefore is never wrong. The world, created as stupidly as possible, is in his own image. Everyone is able to believe in the donkey's long ears. Zarathustra, after upbraiding the people for worshiping a donkey, is told by them that it is better to worship some god, even a donkey, than no god at all. At least here is something that the worshiper can see, touch, hear, and even smell and taste if he wants to. God seems more credible in this form. The first atheist was the man who said that God is spirit.

Zarathustra replies to this plea for the donkey by pointing out that worship of any sort is a return to childhood. The overman has no wish to enter the kingdom of heaven; he wants the earth. However, if the people need to worship, let them worship donkeys if such a belief helps them.

No man except Zarathustra has seen the earth as it is. But the overman will come, and he will see it. He will command the earth and it will obey. With this vision in mind, Zarathustra turns again to the world to search for and bring into perfection the overman.—*J.Co.*

Pertinent Literature

Kaufmann, Walter. *Nietzsche: Philosopher, Psychologist, Antichrist.* Princeton, New Jersey: Princeton University Press, 1950, 1974.

Any discussion of Friedrich Wilhelm Nietzsche's reception in English-speaking countries must acknowledge Walter Kaufmann's pioneering book. It remains the most widely read work on Nietzsche by English-speaking persons to this day. When Kaufmann's book first appeared in 1950 Nietzsche was in eclipse in Europe and censured in the United States as a protofascist ideologist. He was seldom taken seriously philosophically, at any rate. This book changed all that; and, coupled with eleven elegant translations that he produced, Kaufmann's contributions remain a bench mark for Nietzsche scholarship.

Kaufmann's work situates Nietzsche in the mainstream of Western thought, argues that he was a great philosopher, and relates his thought to Socrates and Plato, Martin Luther and Jean Jacques Rousseau, Immanuel Kant and Georg Wilhelm Friedrich Hegel, Johann Wolfgang von Goethe, and Heinrich Heine. In doing this Kaufmann emancipates Nietzsche from Charles Darwin, Arthur Schopenhauer, and Adolf Hitler alike, by reference to whom he had previously and typically been understood.

The book is divided into four parts, preceded by a "prologue" and succeeded by an "epilogue." The Prologue, "The Nietzsche Legend," undermines the various distortions of Nietzsche which had then gained widespread currency. Part I, "Background," treats three preliminary matters: Nietzsche's life as the background of his thought, Nietzsche's method, and the death of God and the Revaluation. Part II, "The Development of Nietzsche's Thought," examines his views on art and history, *Existenz* versus the State, Darwin, and Rousseau, and introduces Nietzsche's initial discovery of the will to power. Part III, "Nietzsche's Philosophy of Power," then examines the will to power in several contexts: in relation to morality and sublimation; sublimation, *Geist*, and Eros; power versus pleasure: the master race; overman and eternal recurrence. Part IV, "Synopsis," treats Nietzsche's repudiation of Christ and his attitude toward Socrates. The "Epilogue" treats Nietzsche's heritage.

Thus Spake Zarathustra is discussed throughout, but crucially in the last chapter of Part II and all of Part III. These chapters constitute the philosophical core of the book; for Kaufmann argues that the will to power is *the* core of Nietzsche's philosophy, and Zarathustra is its teacher. Hence *Thus Spake Zarathustra* is a central (perhaps *the* central) Nietzschean *opus*.

Zarathustra was chosen as the great protagonist, Kaufmann suggests, because of Nietzsche's own dualistic tendencies, which he sought to overcome through the doctrines of will to power and eternal recurrence. For the will to power is developed by Nietzsche not only as a psychological concept of sublimation but as nothing less than a generic definition of morality, all morality. Common to all moral codes—that of the Greeks, the Persians, the Jews, and the Germans—is the generic element, will to power *as* self-overcoming. Nietzsche proposed to explain all human behavior in terms of will to power, according to Kaufmann.

The process of self-overcoming which the will to power expresses is *sublimation*, and Kaufmann spends considerable time elucidating the manifold ways in which the concept of sublimation is forged by Nietzsche, anticipating, for example, Sigmund Freud's later development of sublimated sexuality. Nietzsche suggests over and over in *Thus Spake Zarathustra* and elsewhere that the sexual impulse could be channeled into creative spiritual activity, instead of being fulfilled directly. Olympic contests, the rivalry of tragedians, and the Socratic-Platonic dialectic could be construed usefully as sublimated strivings to overwhelm one's adversaries, for example.

Nietzsche is a dialectical monist, according to Kaufmann, and the philosophy of power which Nietzsche has Zarathustra articulate culminates in the dual vision of the overman (*Übermensch*) and the eternal recurrence.

According to Kaufmann, Nietzsche's overman is not some new species or higher type; rather, it is the person who, like Goethe, has overcome his animal nature, has sublimated his impulses, has organized the chaos of his passions, and has given "style to his life." In its quintessential expression, being an overman is to be an artistic Socrates or, to vary the metaphor, Christ's soul in Caesar's body.

The doctrine of eternal recurrence is referred to by Kaufmann as "the Dionysian faith." The overman, the person who has transmuted his life into a beautiful totality, would also want to affirm all that is, has been, or will be, in affirming his own being. Those who achieve self-perfection want an eternal recurrence out of the fullness of their own being, out of their delight in the moment. Thus, Kaufmann argues, eternal recurrence was for Nietzsche less an idea than an experience: the experience of a life supremely rich in suffering, pain, agony, and their overcoming.

But it was not only an experience. Kaufmann argues that the doctrine of eternal recurrence was a "meeting place" of science and philosophy. He maintains that Nietzsche thought that the doctrine of eternal recurrence was implied by modern science. If science assumes a finite amount of energy in a finite space and an infinite time, it might follow that only a finite number of configurations of the power quanta is possible. Thus, argues Kaufmann, Nietzsche regarded the doctrine of eternal recurrence—despite the experiential thrust stressed in *Thus Spake Zarathustra*—as "the most scientific of all possible hypotheses." And, of course, Zarathustra was its prophet and its teacher.

Alderman, Harold. *Nietzsche's Gift.* Athens: Ohio University Press, 1977.

Harold Alderman's *Nietzsche's Gift* is an extremely difficult book to describe, primarily because it is a work which insists that philosophy is a kind of theater of self-enactment rather than a statable series of issues about questions which are decidable in principle. The chief reason for including it here, then, is that it is the *only* book-length treatment of Friedrich Wilhelm Nietzsche's *Thus Spake Zarathustra* available in the English language. It moves within the orbit of the phenomenological tradition and is most indebted to Martin Heidegger. Its principal "adversaries" are commentators like Arthur C. Danto on the one hand—persons who try to see the argument beneath the surface prose and try to relate this to perennial questions in the history of philosophy—and Walter Kaufmann on the other hand. Kaufmann's book would be characterized by Alderman as a "historical-comparative" study, one which he wishes to contrast with his "philosophical" study. Books about Nietzsche, Alderman asserts, are not books *of* philosophy, a deficiency he seeks to remedy in treating Nietzsche as the foremost "philosopher of philosophy."

Alderman's investigation of *Thus Spake Zarathustra* emerges against the background of three questions: What do we do in trying to deal theoretically with the diffuse problems and perplexities we encounter in one another and the world? What are the conditions and limitations of our theoretical explications of our *praxis*? What does it mean to be serious about thinking?

In seeking to answer such questions, Alderman argues that *Thus Spake Zarathustra* is itself an exhibition of the structures of philosophical experience. As a result, the narrative content of *Thus Spake Zarathustra* becomes an essential feature of its meaning, and the voiced character of an idea is central to understanding the sense in which a thinker becomes both free and responsible in acknowledging the playful character of his philosophizing.

The book consists of eight chapters. The first chapter, "Nietzsche's Masks," is concerned primarily to differentiate Alderman's reading from other readings. It is suggested that *Thus Spake Zarathustra* is Nietzsche's *magnum opus*, that it is the touchstone for any interpretation of Nietzsche's work. It also argues suggestively how Nietzsche's dictum—whatever is profound loves masks—applies self-referentially in that Nietzsche's aphoristic style, along with the use of allegories and metaphors, constitutes his masking device.

The second chapter, "The Camel, the Lion, and the Child," takes Zarathustra's opening speech—"On the Three Metamorphoses"—as its hermeneutic guide in order to illustrate the cyclical structure of experience, which must necessarily be reenacted in the process of self-encounter. According to Alderman, the three metamorphoses state the structure of "the theatre of philosophy." The section of *Thus Spake Zarathustra* to which this speech belongs, Part I, culminates with the speech "On Voluntary Death." Here, Alderman argues, we are confronted on the literal level with human finitude and on the metaphorical level with the temporary character of all self-conceptions and ideas. Alderman suggests that Nietzsche's injunction—"Die at the right time!"—indicates that a genuine human life is not to be measured by the length of its duration; but it also suggests for him that within the boundaries of a finite existence no permanent meaning may be assumed. This latter point may be generalized to identify Alderman's approach. He argues throughout that it is Nietzsche's view that all meanings are finite which are invoked to cope with human finitude. There are no final, univocal interpretations of life and world available, as long as the need to interpret life remains.

Chapter III, "Silence and Laughter," advances Alderman's historicist theme further. It is argued that to understand Nietzsche's doctrines we must understand why they are spoken, understand that in *Thus Spake Zarathustra* a philosophical revolution occurs through the rediscovery and exploration of the range and limits of human speech.

Chapter IV, "The Thinker at Play: Value and Will," explores the relationship between value and will to power within the existential-phenomenological matrix. In the course of that discussion Alderman offers an interesting list of the identifying characteristics of the "slave" and "master" moralities—a list which is of course meant to be neither exhaustive nor logically necessary:

Slave/Master

1. resentful/expresses anger directly
2. reactionary (negative)/creative (positive)
3. other-directed/self-directive
4. other-worldly/this-worldly
5. self-deceptive/self-aware
6. humble (meek)/proud (*not* vain)
7. altruistic/egoistic
8. prudent/experimental
9. democratic (self-indulgent)/aristocratic (value hierarchy)
10. confessional/discrete (masked)
11. morality of principles/morality of persons
12. weak-willed/strong-willed
13. Good (weakness) vs. Evil (strength)/Good (strength) vs. Bad (weakness)

The remaining four chapters cover "The Drama of Eternal Recurrence," "The Comedy of Affirmation," "Philosophy as Drama: Nietzsche as Philosopher," and an epilogue, "Who is Nietzsche's Zarathustra?" The doctrine of eternal recurrence is discussed in detail and it is argued not only that the cosmological version is untenable but also that Nietzsche never intended to teach a cosmological doctrine.

Chapter VI is a detailed discussion of Part IV of *Thus Spake Zarathustra*. It is argued that Nietzsche's serious and comedic recapitulation of his major themes indicates the personal conditions under which affirmation of any doctrine may be appropriately made. Chapter VII briefly relates Alderman's construction of *Thus Spake Zarathustra* to four other works Nietzsche published: *The Birth of Tragedy*, *Beyond Good and Evil*, *The Gay Science*, and *Toward a Genealogy of Morals*. The epilogue, Chapter VIII, is Alderman's attempt to differentiate his interpretation from that of Martin Heidegger.
—B.M.

ADDITIONAL RECOMMENDED READING

Danto, Arthur C. *Nietzsche as Philosopher*. New York: Macmillan Publishing Company, 1965. An attempt to relate Nietzsche's thought to the analytic tradition and to isolate the specifically philosophical features of his work.

Heidegger, Martin. *Nietzsche*. 2 vols. Pfullingen: Neske, 1961. One of the world's most influential interpretations of Nietzsche by one of its major twentieth century philosophers. Now being translated into English, in four volumes, for Harper & Row.

Jaspers, Karl. *Nietzsche: An Introduction to the Understanding of His Philosophical Activity*. Tucson: University of Arizona Press, 1965. This translation of Jasper's seminal work on Nietzsche provides the other influential interpretation of Nietzsche by a famous existential philosopher.

Magnus, Bernd. *Nietzsche's Existential Imperative*. Bloomington: Indiana University Press, 1978. An interpretation of Nietzsche which focuses on his doctrine of eternal recurrence and takes *Thus Spake Zarathustra* as its principal source.

Morgan, George A. *What Nietzsche Means*. Cambridge, Massachusetts: Harvard University Press, 1941. Less philosophical than the others mentioned so far, but a clear and sympathetic attempt to understand Nietzsche.

THE ANALYSIS OF THE SENSATIONS

Author: Ernst Mach (1838-1916)
Type of work: Philosophy of mind, epistemology
First published: 1886

PRINCIPAL IDEAS ADVANCED

The special sciences are systems of symbols by means of which man orders the facts immediately given in experience; the world is the sum of all phenomena.

Since physical objects, bodies, and sensations are all phenomenal in character, it is possible that sensations are connected with physical events.

Our perception of dimensional space represents the experience of countless generations; the conceptions of our bodies as moving and of the environment as fixed are fixed in racial memory.

The common sense, realistic view of the world is a product of nature developed in the course of evolution.

The concepts of science are useful fictions, names for complexes of phenomena.

The ostensible purpose of Mach's *Contributions to the Analysis of the Sensations* was to report certain experiments which he had made on the relationship between sensations and neural physiology. But the permanent interest of the book is due less to the experiments themselves than to the radically empirical standpoint which the author adopted in the exposition of his findings. Setting aside the traditional mind-body problem as "metaphysical," he proposed that psychology and physiology alike be restricted to describing facts and their connections. These two sciences, he argued, do not treat of different kinds of facts but of the same kind of facts in different relations. More generally, he maintained that all facts are of the same kind, namely, what is immediately given in experience, and that the special sciences are systems of symbols by means of which man orders the facts to suit his several interests.

Mach did not claim to be a professional philosopher. As a worker in the field of science, he was compelled to raise philosophical questions in order to overcome difficulties which confronted him when he tried to move from one scientific discipline to another. "I only seek to adopt in physics a point of view that need not be changed the moment our glance is carried over into the domain of another science; for, ultimately, all must form one whole." Is the world an electromagnetic field, or is it a swarm of molecules which in turn are composed of indestructible atoms? Too much intellectual energy, said Mach, was being diverted from real problems in an effort to resolve pseudoproblems such as these.

The gulf that separated physics from psychology was one of these pseudoproblems. In order to help bridge it in an intelligible manner, Mach had adopted Leibniz's theory of monads. But he soon concluded that he was giving too prominent a place to the "artificial scaffolding" as distinguished from "the facts which really deserve to be known." He therefore discarded "this cumbrous artifice" and turned to a simpler view—one which had intrigued him almost from childhood; namely, the view that the world consists solely of sense-impressions.

Educated in the German tradition, Mach approached empiricism through the philosophy of Kant rather than through the English or French sensationalists. He was only fifteen when he read Kant's *Prolegomena to Any Future Metaphysics* (1783). Of it, he said, "The book made at this time a powerful and ineffaceable impression upon me, the like of which I never afterward experienced in any of my philosophical reading." However, some two or three years thereafter he detected Kant's blunder in introducing the "thing in itself." "On a bright summer day under the open heaven, the world with my ego suddenly appeared to me as *one* coherent mass of sensations, only more strongly coherent in the ego. Although the actual working out of this thought did not occur until a later period, yet this moment was decisive for my whole view." The reason it did not work itself out at once lay, he said, in his scientific training. "With the valuable parts of physical theories we necessarily absorb a good dose of false metaphysics." Only as he alternated his scientific studies with readings in the history of science, and his physical investigations with psychological research, did he see his way clear to break with tradition and reconstruct his scientific views along the bold lines suggested by his youthful vision.

In this view, the world is the sum of all phenomena, that is, of all sounds, colors, smells, and so on, that ever did or will exist, together with the connections which tie them into parcels and link them into chains and meshes. Initially, Mach spoke of them as "sensations," in a manner that resembled Hume (without his being acquainted at the time with Hume's writings); but he later determined to call them by a neutral term, "elements." He did this because it was essential to his theory that the same elements which are called sensations when joined together to make up what we know as consciousness are called physical properties when they are joined together to make up what we know as the world, or that singular border-territory between consciousness and the world which we call "our body."

Mach adopted the following kind of schematism, which he used throughout the book to illustrate his meaning. Let *ABC* represent elements in nature; let *KLM* represent elements in "our body"; and let *abc* represent elements in our mind. *ABC*, *KLM*, and *abc* are all phenomenal in character. But *ABC* might stand for the sensible qualities of an apple; *KLM* for the observable properties of my digestive system; and *abc* for my sensations of red, juicy, sweet. For even though the elements are interchangeable, my vital interest compels me to distinguish the apple from my digestive system, and both of them from my feelings or sensations.

Here is the first merit which Mach claimed for his philosophy. Whereas common sense regards the complexes of elements as forming more or less permanent entities ("bodies" and "souls"), and metaphysics goes further and invents eternal substances ("matter" and "mind"), Mach reverted to pure experience and acknowledged the existence only of what is immediately given. By abolishing metaphysics, he claimed to have rid mankind of numerous "supposititious" problems, and by illuminating common sense, he prepared the way for the unification of the sciences.

The application to problems of physiological psychology lay immediately to hand. On Mach's assumptions, it is not necessary to show how matter can influence mind and vice versa. The ego or soul has only that existence which belongs to individual elements of consciousness and their connections; and the same is true of nerves and muscles. Moreover, since the elements we have designated *abc* are no different essentially from those we have designated *KLM*, and since the connection which joins *a* to *b* is no different in kind from that which joins *K* to *L*, there is no reason why combinations of the sort *KLa*, and *AKa* may not exist. In other words, sensations may be connected with physical events quite as plausibly as with other sensations.

The experiments in psychophysics which Mach's book was designed to give to the public were an attempt to show that such sensations as those by which a person judges distances in space of intervals of time are functions of his nervous and muscular activities. One of his simpler experiments consisted of attaching putty to his eyeballs and noting his sensations as he tried to use his eyes in gauging distances. "The will to perform movements of the eyes, or the innervation to act, is itself the space-sensation," he concluded. Time-sensation, he conjectured, is probably "connected with the organic *consumption* necessarily associated with consciousness. . . . The fatiguing of the organ of consciousness goes on continually. . . . The sensations connected with greater expenditure of attention appear to us to happen *later*."

A question which has long interested philosophical empiricists is whether we have a sensation of distance. The eighteenth century followers of Locke were of the opinion that we do not—that judgments of this sort are the product of experience and have to be learned by practice, possibly requiring two different senses, vision and touch. Mach's analysis might have led him to similar conclusions if it had not been for the theory of evolution, which dominated his thought. Mach agreed that our perception of dimensional space is learned—but he held that it represents the experience of countless generations of men, not to speak of their subhuman ancestors. In other words, it is firmly established in the racial memory and is to be explained in terms of its biological value. A simple experiment was used to prove his point. When a person's body is in motion on a turntable or on a moving train, his eyes do not sweep the environment in a continuous motion, but move in jerks from one fixed point to another. This is true even of small children, proving that it is not the result of individual learning but of racial evolution. The conception of our bodies as moving and of the environment as fixed has impressed itself upon the memory of mankind because of its utility. "We understand why it is that, in our numerous turnings and ramblings in the streets and in buildings, and in our passive turnings in a wagon or in the cabin of a ship—yes, even in the dark—we do not lose our sense of direction. . . ."

Like Kant, therefore, Mach held that man brings to his experience the forms of intuition of space and time, although, unlike Kant, Mach explained these as the product of human evolution. In the same way he explained other basic notions and beliefs with which the ordinary mind is endowed. Man brings with him a ready capacity, which he easily perfects by practice, of seeing, not unrelated colors and forms, but solid objects. Likewise, he has a strong disposition to interpret certain sequences as necessarily (we say, "causally") related. In short, the whole common sense or "naïvely realistic" view of the world "has arisen in the process of immeasurable time without the conscious assistance of man. It is a product of nature, and is preserved and sustained by nature."

Mach attributed the highest importance to this natural inheritance in which we all share. Nothing which man's conscious art and reflection have added to it by way of philosophy and science can begin to compare with it. Nor can we ever leave it behind, but, having made our flights into higher mathematics and speculative physics, we must return "to the universal point of view held by all men in common." And if these commonsense beliefs are "true" only in the sense that they have biological value and are "formed for special, practical purposes and with wholly provisional and limited ends in view," exactly the same is true of our sophisticated theories.

We come now to the second merit which Mach claimed for his philosophy. While showing that the concepts of science (electricity, atoms, forces, laws, and so forth) are fictions, it also was able to show why fictions are necessary. They are labor-saving devices by which the mind brings under surveillance and control vast numbers of facts which otherwise would be unmanageable. If we had the kind of omniscience which would make it possible to grasp in detail the phenomena which go to make up an earthquake, for example, we would not require a scientific account of it. But because we would lose ourselves in the literal description, we observe complexes of phenomena and give them names—such as "fault" and "volcano." To mistake these concepts for entities and causes would be to lapse into the ways of metaphysics. But if we recognize them for what they are, "indirect descriptions" and "intellectual abridgements," we can use them just the same and not prejudice the advance of knowledge or prevent other scientists from developing alternative symbols to describe the same phenomena.

Mach recognized the contribution which felicitous images have made to the advancement of science. For example, the Scottish chemist Joseph Black supposed heat to be a fluid substance which passes from one body to another. This was a useful concept. On the other hand, this image prevented Black's successors from using their eyes, and they overlooked an important group of phenomena where heat is produced by friction. Hence, Mach warned investigators not to be led astray by their representations.

A theory, according to Mach, is always a "representation." It "puts in the place of a fact something *different*, something more simple, which is qualified to represent the fact in some *certain* aspect, but for the very reason that it is different does *not* represent it in other aspects." Scientific concepts, theories, and laws, because they are representations, exist in the mind only. For this reason, Mach's studies in psychology were finally determinative of his attitude toward all the other sciences. Either for practical ends or for theoretical ("removing intellectual discomfort"), the mind evolves new ideas which will represent old ones in a more satisfactory fashion. To quote Mach's schematic language again, "Science arises where in any manner the elements *ABC* . . . or the elements *KLM* . . . are reproduced or representatively mimicked by the elements *abc* . . . or the latter by one another. For example, physics (in its broadest signification) arises through representatively reproducing by *abc* . . . the elements *ABC* in their relations to one another, the physiology or psychology of the *senses*, through reproducing in like manner the relations of *ABC* . . . *to KLM*. . . ; physiology, through reproducing the relations of *KLM* . . . to one another and to *ABC*. . . ; while the reproducing of the *abc* . . . themselves by other *abc* leads to the psychological sciences proper."

In speaking of concepts as representations, Mach did not, however, intend to imply that they outline or copy phenomena in any literal sense. In language which is similar to that employed by pragmatists, Mach emphasized the "operational" role of scientific terms. "In using a word denoting a concept," he said, "there is nothing involved in the word but a simple *impulse* to perform some familiar *sensory operation*, as the *result* of which a definite sensuous element (the mark of the concept) is obtained." Elsewhere (*Popular Scientific Lectures*, 1894), he used the striking analogy of musical notation: "The concept is to the physicist," he said, "what a musical note is to a piano-player."

Mach had an important part in popularizing the positivist view of knowledge. But his views were in various degrees paralleled by the writings of other scientists and mathematicians of his day, such as Karl Pearson and Henri Poincafe. As Professor of the History and Theory of Inductive Science at the University of Vienna, he particularly influenced the men who came to be known as the Vienna Circle of Logical Positivists.—*J.F.*

PERTINENT LITERATURE

Mises, Richard von. *Positivism: A Study in Human Understanding.* Cambridge, Massachusetts: Harvard University Press, 1951.

Richard von Mises states at the beginning that although this book is by a positivist (a former member of the Vienna Circle), it is not a book about positivism. Nevertheless, writing with the general reader in view, Mises gives a valuable account of the positivist movement, devoting one chapter to Ernst Mach's doctrine of sensational elements, and other chapters to the connection between Mach's doctrine and that of his successors.

There was a generation gap between Mach and the logical positivists. The generation for which Mach wrote *The Analysis of the Sensations* was concerned with such topics as realism versus idealism, materialism versus spiritualism, and naturalism versus agnosticism. It is against this background and in the context of discussions concerning psycho-physical parallelism and interactionism that Mach's doctrine of elements is properly understood. The generation that carried on the positivist tradition after 1920 was mainly occupied with problems posed for a sensationalist theory of knowledge by new developments in the physical sciences. It is well known, for example, that Mach argued against both Albert Einstein's theory of relativity and Max Planck's theory of the atom. Broadly speaking, logical positivism, while keeping the door barred against metaphysical notions such as mind and energy, opened it far enough to admit such abstract constructions as were necessary for theoretical developments in the sciences. This end was achieved by appealing not to experience directly but to experience once removed—that is, to language; and by translating the original claim that only what is sensed is real to the claim that only statements expressing facts which can be tested by experience are meaningful (the exception being statements which say nothing about reality but are true or false by virtue of syntactical rules).

Mises leans as far as possible in the direction of giving Mach credit for the developed positivist doctrine. According to Mises, the goal of logical positivism is to construct a system of "mutually connectible statements" embracing everything open to experience. The building blocks of this system must be "simple sentences, the meanings of which are self-evident." Mach, it is true, spoke of simple facts rather than of simple sentences; but, according to Mises, *The Analysis of the Sensations* was completely successful in its aim of reducing experiences to irreducible elements. Moreover, when Mach made the sensations do double duty, he solved the problem of connectibility. If we are observing changes in color of a piece of iron which is being heated, we are studying physics; if we are concerned with retinal changes or skin sensations in the observer, we are studying physiology. Meanwhile, because we are immediately aware of the connection between the two groups of phenomena, we are in a position to view the sciences of physics and physiology as divisions within a unified science.

Although Mach did not make use of the logical distinction between material and formal modes of expression employed by Rudolf Carnap, Mises argues that the doctrines which he formulated as material (factual) statements ("the world consists for us of a complex of sensations") can be easily translated into linguistic sentences ("our statements about the world are reducible to statements about sensations"). Mises illustrates his point by developing Mach's answer to certain questions concerning the identity of bodies undergoing change: for example, whether water is the same in its liquid, vaporous, and solid forms. Mach, who included space and time among the sensations, argued that when some elements of a complex undergo change while other elements remain the same, it is merely a question as to the limits of language whether one speaks of it as the same or not the same. In any case, he found no need to look for some mysterious thing-in-itself behind the appearances.

Mach deals in the same way with questions concerning the self. Just as we speak for practical purposes of a material object being the same from day to day in spite of changes in its appearance, so we speak of our egos as if they were well-defined and enduring wholes, whereas, as David Hume recognized, what we call the self is merely a sequence of sensation-elements (a pain, a memory, the blue of the sky, the tone of a piano). Translated into formal language, what Mach meant to say is: All sentences that state anything about the ego are reducible to sentences in which only sensations and their appropriate connections are mentioned. According to Mises, Mach had no wish to disturb customary ways of talking about persons and everyday objects, but only to "demarcate the boundaries" within which these locutions are useful and beyond which they give rise to pseudo-problems, such as: How is it possible for sensations to be caused by the motions of atoms? Does the self survive the death of the body?

In the formal language of logical positivism, Mach's elements were replaced by simple statements known as protocol sentences. It seemed legitimate to imagine all relevant experiences as if they were recorded in verbal form for purposes of further study. The theory became excessively complicated, however, because what might seem to be the simplest statements in a laboratory protocol were far from being epistemologically simple. A measurement in ohms, for example, which is a protocol sentence in physics, is not an original protocol, since it does not describe immediately observed facts. The original protocol must take the form of short expressions such as "here pointer at five." Even words such as "pointer" and "five" denote complex experiences which require many protocols. The epistemologist, however, is not interested in carrying out the analysis in detail so long as it is possible in principle.

Blackmore, John T. *Ernst Mach: His Work, Life, and Influence.* Berkeley: University of California Press, 1972.

Ernst Mach liked to say that he was a scientist and not a philosopher. Partly this was a maneuver to avoid confrontation with professional philosophers, notably with fellow-Viennese Franz Brentano (1883-1917), but partly also, says John T. Blackmore, it was a ruse by which Mach won disciples to his philosophy under the impression that what he was teaching was not philosophy but science. Writing as a historian of science, Blackmore makes no effort to conceal his antipathy to much that Mach stood for. He leaves no room for doubt, however, as to the high level of Mach's genius, his intellectual integrity, and the heroism with which he pursued his work under severe personal affliction. Although this book should be read in its entirety, persons interested in philosophy will want to reread chapters devoted to Mach's philosophical development, his philosophy of science, and his world influence among philosophers.

In tracing Mach's philosophical development, Blackmore mentions the influence on Mach's thought of George Berkeley and Immanuel Kant, and he quotes Mach as saying that in his youth he shared for a while Berkeley's belief in a perceiver distinct from what is perceived but that, influenced by Johann Friedrich Herbart and Georg Christoph Lichtenberg, he arrived in the 1860's at a position similar to that of David Hume, whose writings he had not yet read. Blackmore finds the year 1860 symbolic of the direction which Mach chose to take. It was the year in which Charles Darwin's *On the Origin of Species* became known in Germany, and it was the year in which Gustav Fechner's *Elements of Psychology* was published: to the former Mach owed his theory of "economy"—namely, that knowledge is subservient to biological needs; to the latter, his view that psychology and physics deal with the same elements. There was that same year, however, a third major scientific event, one that left Mach untouched. The event was a conference of German chemists called to help solve the problem of valences, which eventuated in general acceptance of Amedeo Avogadro's law giving the atomic weight of elements, an event which not only lent support to the atomic theory in chemistry but also caused physicists to take a new interest in atomic theory. Blackmore finds it significant that, at a time when for most of the scientific community "elements" were chemical entities, for Mach, following Fechner, "elements" were sensations.

Blackmore characterizes Mach's philosophical position as a particular kind of phenomenalism. Not only was he an epistemological phenomenalist in holding that we can know only sensations, and an ontological phenomenalist in holding that only sensations exist; he was also a referential phenomenalist, in holding that one can refer meaningfully only to sensations. In this last respect, however, Mach was not always consistent; and Blackmore traces some of the confusions that surround Mach's thought to the fact that on occasion he used a commonsense approach to reference. For example, Mach is on record as both accepting and rejecting atomic theory: in terms of his referential phenomenalism, he accepted atoms as ideal constructions useful to the scientist in dealing with phenomena at a certain level—but that Mach was capable of understanding and employing a nonphenomenalist theory of reference appears from his occasional assertions that he did not believe that atoms are real. Apparently he was not persuaded to the contrary (as some have believed) by scintillations from alpha particles visible on a zinc sulfide screen; for, in the 1912 revision of *The Analysis of the Sensations*, he wrote: "If ordinary 'matter' must be regarded merely as a highly natural, unconsciously constructed mental symbol for a relatively stable complex of sensational elements, much more must this be the case with the highly hypothetical atoms and molecules of physics and chemistry."

Throughout his book, Blackmore contrasts Mach's phenomenalist viewpoint with what he calls the commonsense or representationalist viewpoint shared by Galileo and Sir Isaac Newton, and by most practical scientists to this day. Unlike naïve realism, which identifies the physical world with sensory objects, commonsense realism assumes the causal theory of perception according to which conscious experience provides evidence from which we infer the characteristics of physical objects that lie outside conscious experience. The difference between presentationalism and representationalism is sometimes described by positivists as being no more than a matter of linguistic conventions; but, according to Blackmore, it actually has to do with one's understanding of reference—whether, as presentationalists assume, reference is a relation between sensible objects, or, as representationalists assume, it is an intentional act.

Mach's presentationalist epistemology was to exercise extensive influence on twentieth century academic philosophy. Denying that any meaning can be attached to material forces outside actual or possible experience, Machians took the same tack as Berkeley and appropriated object-language for their own use. The dispute early in the century between neo- and critical-realists was a confrontation between presentationalists and representationalists, with the former adopting a functional and the latter a causal account of the relation between objects and sensations. At mid-century, influenced by the linguistic ideas of Ludwig Wittgenstein and Rudolf Carnap, some members of the movement tried to shift from phenomenalism to realism, but got no further than to adopt an object-language. "No aspect of modern philosophical usage," says Blackmore, "is more misleading and regrettable than identifying the word 'realism' with views based on a presentationalist or idealist (in eighteenth century terms) epistemology." In Blackmore's opinion, the person chiefly responsible was Mach.—*J. F.*

ADDITIONAL RECOMMENDED READING

Alexander, Peter. "Ernst Mach," in *A Critical History of Western Philosophy*. Edited by D. J. O'Connor. London: Collier-Macmillan, 1964, pp. 403-409. Good general introduction to Mach's philosophy.

Bradley, J. *Mach's Philosophy of Science*. London: Athlone Press of the University of London, 1971. Problems of physics viewed in the light of Mach's theory of elements.

Čapek, Milič. "Ernst Mach's Biological Theory of Knowledge," in *Boston Studies in the Philosophy of Science*. Edited by R. S. Cohen and M. W. Wartowsky. Vol. V. Dordrecht, The Netherlands: D. Reidel Publishing Company, 1969, pp. 400-420. Shows how Mach's acceptance of the evolutionary origin of man's cognitive functions differentiates his epistemology from that of pre-Darwinian empiricists.

Frank, Philipp G. "Einstein, Mach, and Logical Positivism," in *Albert Einstein, Philosopher-Scientist* (The Library of Living Philosophers). Edited by Paul A. Schilpp. Evanston, Illinois: Open Court, 1949, pp. 269-287. Logical positivism viewed as a movement away from elemental and observational terms toward abstract terms and symbols required in modern physics.

Popper, Karl R. "Three Views Concerning Human Knowledge," in *Conjectures and Refutations: The Growth of Scientific Knowledge*. New York: Harper & Row Publishers, 1965, pp. 97-119. Mach's instrumentalist view of knowledge fails to account for scientific progress because it makes impossible the falsification of a theory by crucial experiments.

BEYOND GOOD AND EVIL

Author: Friedrich Wilhelm Nietzsche (1844-1900)
Type of work: Ethics
First published: 1886

PRINCIPAL IDEAS ADVANCED

Ideas which preserve life and add to a man's power are more important than ideas sanctioned by logicians and seekers after the absolute.

The metaphysical interest in the freedom of the will should give way to an interest in the strength of the will.

Men must turn conventional values upside down in order to live creatively; the established values of society were invented by the weak to enable them to triumph over the strong.

Scientific minds are weak when they fail to pass judgment; whoever denies the will denies the power of life.

Progress in life is possible only if there are men of action who have the courage to trust will and instinct; new values arise which go beyond conventional good and evil when the will to power asserts itself.

Friedrich Nietzsche holds a commanding historical significance in modern thought in spite of a continuing controversy about his stature as a philosophical mind. Many scholars refuse to judge Nietzsche's brilliant writings as serious philosophical contributions. They prefer to view him as a poet, or as a critic of culture and religion, or even as a superb master of the German language. Yet some contemporary scholars insist on Nietzsche's importance as a genuine philosophical figure—a lonely, disturbed thinker who anticipated contemporary criticism of the classical ideal of a rigorously deductive model of philosophical knowledge and of the accompanying belief in the possibility of a completed metaphysics. Nietzsche felt keenly the impact of Darwinian evolutionary views which so stirred many nineteenth century thinkers in a number of intellectual fields. As a philosopher, he must be included in that group of thinkers for whom the philosopher's primary function is to lay bare the unexamined assumptions and buried cultural influences lurking behind supposedly disinterested moral and metaphysical constructions.

Symptomatically, *Beyond Good and Evil* begins with a chapter entitled "About Philosophers' Prejudices." Written during Nietzsche's intellectual maturity, hard on the heels of a lengthy literary development yet prior to the tragic illness which ended his career and made him a mental case, this book reflects the many important central tendencies of his thought. Its contents illustrate the surprisingly wide range of Nietzsche's intellectual interests—the origin and nature of moral valuations, the history and psychology of religion, the psychology of human motivation, and the relation of man and historical processes. Nietzsche often uses aphorisms (as he does in the fourth section of *Beyond Good and Evil*) which, though unsystematic from a logical point of view, manage to express a tolerably consistent philosophical viewpoint.

Nietzsche's writings contain numerous passages which suggest similar positions worked out in greater psychotherapeutic detail by Sigmund Freud. Frequently he shows greater interest in the question, "What are the motives of philosophizing?" than in "What do philosophers say?" When he turns to an analysis of moral judgments, Nietzsche worries about what may hide submerged in such valuations—much as a student of icebergs wants to discover what exists beneath the surface. Perhaps the valuations produced by moralists always represent a perspective on things in the sense that there may exist no final metaphysical standpoint from which to render such valuations. In a similar manner, the philosophical quest after truth may peculiarly express what Nietzsche terms the "will to power" rather than a disinterested description of things. Even assuming that genuine truth can be obtained in principle, Nietzsche points out that the value of an idea has greater significance than the truth of the idea. The value perspectives by which individuals live may be necessary and yet not objective. "Un-truth" may carry greater value than "truth" in many situations. Such perspectives must be judged in terms of the degree to which they are life-furthering. "Even behind logic and its apparent sovereignty of development stand value judgments," Nietzsche suggests early in *Beyond Good and Evil*; "or, to speak more plainly, physiological demands for preserving a certain type of life." On this supposition, a psychologist would ask of any belief whether it is conducive to sound health (a therapeutic matter) rather than whether it is true. "True" and "health-producing" become synonymous in Nietzsche's treatment of ideas.

Nietzsche criticizes a philosopher like Immanuel Kant for having assumed existence of an unknowable "thing-in-itself" behind the phenomenal universe available to science. Similarly, he shows scorn for Hegel, who sought to find in the antithetical aspects of existence (passions, ideas, moral valuations) the expressions of a more fundamental rational reality. The tendency toward dualism, by which the "I" as subject stands independent of that which is perceived (as well as logically distinct as "subject" over against "object"), receives criticism as a possible grammatical prejudice erected into a false and misleading metaphysical argument. Rather than philosophizing in "the grand manner," Nietzsche encourages piecemeal treatment of a host of specific, clearly stated problems. Physiology may hold the key to solution of a number of old and baffling questions, including moral ones.

A philosophical investigator must forego easy solutions happening to fit his prejudices—just as physiologists must cease thinking that the basic drive behind organic life is that toward self-preservation. The will to power may prove more fundamental than desire of self-preservation. The will to power expresses an expansive, assimilating, positive, value-creating tendency in existence, nonhuman as well as human. There may also be no immediate certainties like the philosopher's "I think" or "Schopenhauer's superstition, 'I will.'" The older superstition that thinking activity results from a human will requires sophisticated and subtle analysis, for "A thought comes when 'it' and not when 'I' will." Indeed, even to say, "*It* is thought," instead of "I think," may cause another set of misleading metaphysical puzzles to arise. Nietzsche also argues that the metaphysical question about freedom of the will results from misuses of terms like "cause" and "effect," which are simply concepts. These concepts are fictions useful for the facilitation of common understanding but not as explanations. Men must stop creating myths about an objective reality based on pure concepts useful for other ends. There is neither "free" nor "non-free" will, according to Nietzsche, but simply "strong will and weak will."

Psychological investigations done previous to Nietzsche's day are found suspect because of the subtle ways in which their conclusions reflect human prejudices and fears. This theme sounds constantly throughout Nietzsche's writings. Nietzsche wanted a new kind of psychologist able to resist the unconscious forces in himself influencing him to accept conclusions dictated by his "heart." The evidence is what must count in such investigations. He asks his readers to imagine an investigator in physiology-psychology who possesses the courage to believe that greed, hatred, envy, and such passions are "the passions upon which life is conditioned, as things which must be present in the total household of life." So, too, the new philosophical breed will approach the study of the origins of morals with a ruthless honesty.

In a later book, *Toward a Geneology of Morals* (1887), Nietzsche in practice attempted the kind of historical-genetic investigation his *Beyond Good and Evil* recommends in principle. In the former book it is suggested that the concepts "good" and "bad," as well as "good" and "evil," arose out of a spiteful transvaluation of classical values by the meek and the lowly. "Bad" is the valuation placed on acts previously termed "good" in an aristocratic, healthy culture. Jewish and Christian priests, expressing their hatred of life, described as "evil" those biological functions fundamental to creation and healthful strength.

The central suggestion in *Beyónd Good and Evil* is that another transvaluation of human values must now follow from the evolutionary notion of the will to power—that the cultural standpoint of Western Europe so influenced by Christian valuations must undergo a deep change certain to usher in gigantic, even sometimes cataclysmic, alterations in the table of values. Man is seen as a being who must "get beyond" existing valuations in order to live creatively and even dangerously. A culture whose established values are foundering, in which the faith in metaphysical absolutes wobbles unsteadily on aging legs, throws up the question whether the belief in the possibility of an objectively justifiable morality is not an illusion. Never does Nietzsche say that men can live without making valuations. Nor does he argue that moral valuations are unqualifiedly relative—one as good as another. His point is psychological and critical. Nietzsche believed that man's nature, a product of evolution, demands the constant creation of new valuations even in the face of the absence of absolute standards. This aspect of his thought brings to mind contemporary existentialist thought which, however differently expressed by numerous existentialist writers, responds to the anguish of the human situation by making value judgments possible even though absolutes are lacking.

Nietzsche warns that the new philosopher must guard against some of the characteristics of the "intellectuals." This is a theme expressed early in his literary life (in *The Use and Abuse of History*, 1874, for example), when Nietzsche cautioned against bringing up a German generation so preoccupied with history that the *value* of those things whose history is studied could receive neither affirmation nor denial. Intellectualistic pursuit of objective knowledge tends to weaken the critical and evaluative capacities needed by men as a basis for living. Nietzsche never ridicules the scientific quest after objective knowledge as such. What he warns against is the production of scientific minds unable to make judgments about better and worse. Objective knowledge functions valuably only as a means to some other end or ends, like those which actualize human potentiality in all its possible varieties. Scientific knowledge fails to show men what things they should say "Yes" and "No" to from a valuational standpoint. Judgment is a function of the will— something which the scientific man can never determine.

For long centuries men decided on the value of actions by reference to their consequences. Nietzsche calls this the *pre-moral* period. Since he elsewhere caricatures English utilitarian thought, one must assume that Nietzsche thinks little of a value standard based on the tendency of acts to produce pleasure rather than pain. A second period, lasting for the past ten thousand years (according to Nietzsche who made no anthropological survey of such an enormous space of historical time), is marked by a predominant tendency to judge the value or worthlessness of an act by its origins. "The origin of an action was interpreted to rest, in a very definite sense, on an *intent*." Such an intentional yardstick for judging actions reflected an aristocratic stance. In his own time, Nietzsche believed neither the intent nor the consequences of an act would play the crucial role. This would be the *amoral* period. In a famous passage, Nietzsche characterizes the nature of the philosophers who would conduct new amoral analyses of human valuations: "A new species of philosopher is coming up over the horizon. I risk baptizing them with a name that is not devoid of peril. As I read them (as they allow themselves to be read—for it is characteristic of their type that they wish to remain riddles in some sense), these philosophers of the future have a right (perhaps also a wrong!) to be called: *Experimenters*. This name itself is only an experiment, and, if you will, a temptation." These thinkers will view pain and suffering as the necessary preconditions of any new valuations. They will also issue commands rather than simply describe or explain.

Nietzsche's treatment of what he calls "the peculiar nature of religion" bears a crucial relation to his prophesied transvaluation of existing values. According to Nietzsche, a student of religious phenomena should develop that kind of malicious subtlety which the moral investigator needs in all times and places if he is to succeed in his work. Although he despised the moral values taught by traditional Christianity, Nietzsche nonetheless admired the psychological self-discipline of the Christian saints. Religious phenomena fascinated him. The faith demanded of early Christians, a rarely attained reality, provides an example possessing peculiarly tough and lasting appeal. Nietzsche writes that contemporary men lack the corresponding toughness to appreciate the paradoxical statement of faith: God dies on a cross. Early Christian faith demanded qualities found in a modern Pascal, according to Nietzsche. In Pascal this faith "looks in a horrible way like a continuous suicide of the reason, a tough, long-lived, worm-like reason which cannot be killed at one time and with one blow." Nietzsche believed that such a faith would require careful study if the new experimenters were to learn how to succeed in their own transvaluation of Christian values. Especially intriguing are the three restrictions associated with what Nietzsche calls "the religious neurosis"— solitude, fasting, and sexual abstinence. For a student to understand the earlier historical transvaluation which occurred he must answer the question: "How is the saint possible?" Genuinely to understand how from the "bad" man one gets, suddenly, a saint requires one to compare Christianity's valuations to the lavish gratitude characteristic of earlier Greek religion before fear made Christianity a possibility.

Nietzsche argues that the study of moral and religious phenomena can never be the work of a day or a brief season. Modern thinkers can hope only to assemble the necessary evidence, slowly and painstakingly. Their first concern is the statement of a morphology of morality rather than the former ambitious attempt to give a philosophical justification of the derivation of a morality. Only "the collection of the material, the conceptual formalization and arrangement of an enormous field of delicate value-feelings and value-differences which are living, growing, generating others, and perishing" is possible at the present time along with some observations about recurrent features of these value growths. Investigators must know where to look for the proper evidence. For this task, the scientific man lacks the capacities needed for directing the investigations. The scientific man functions best as an instrument—an enormously valuable one. Yet the instrument "belongs in the hands of one who has greater power"—one who commands what uses the instrument shall be put to. Most philosophers also fail to qualify for this kind of moral analysis. The reason is that they have reduced philosophizing to theory of knowledge, which produces a value skepticism when what is required is action—value-commanding and value-judging.

The whole problem of understanding moral valuations is reminiscent of the older Faith versus Reason controversy in theology. Does "instinct" (the tendency to act creatively without always knowing how to give reasons for one's actions) hold a more important place in the subject matter of moral analysis than reasoning (the capacity to give reasons for one's valuations)? This problem emerges early in the character of Socrates—a philosopher whom Nietzsche admires for his magnificent irony and dialectical skills even though Nietzsche denounces "Socratism," the dogma that beliefs are valuable only insofar as they are capable of logical justification. Nietzsche considers Socrates a much greater figure than Plato. Socrates knew how to laugh at himself, realizing that his superior powers failed to discover the means by which to justify many beliefs he held important. Plato was more naïve than Socrates. Plato left a moral prejudice which Nietzsche simply rejects: the view that instinct and reason ultimately seek the same end—"God" or "*the* Good." Plato, in thus dissolving all that Nietzsche finds fascinating in the Faith-Reason controversy, made possible a later Christian institutionalization of herd-morality.

Fundamentally, Nietzsche distrusted individuals who venerate reason and deny the value of instinct. He insists that men of action illustrate the gap that exists between those who merely know (intellectually) and those who act. Any existing morality needs a horizon provided by men of action who say: "It shall be thus!" This command source of any morality must itself go unjustified and unquestioned. Any existing morality is in this sense always "problematic." By this Nietzsche probably meant that after reasons for the existing valuations have been given, there must remain, at last, a self-justifying command for which no further reasons are possible. Indeed, all morality containing progressive aspects stems from an aristocratic type of commanding. Every command requires a commander, some individual who supplies the necessary value horizon which others must simply accept. There can be no objectively grounded perspective of all perspectives. Life as an expanding process requires the cutting off of deliberative procedures at some point.

Nietzsche was willing to accept some of the painful consequences of this view of the command origin of all moral valuations. One consequence is that any existing morality requires sacrifice of numerous individuals and of many nuances of feeling and human tendency. Morality requires the application of command in such a way that not all legitimately natural instincts can find total expression at any one time. It also rests on exploitation as a necessary element in the creation of values. Some instincts must give way to others—and the commanding ones ought to be domineering and aristocratic. There must occur "the forcing of one's own forms upon something else."

Nietzsche's analysis of morality led him to dislike equalitarian democracy and herd-utilitarianism ("the greatest happiness of the greatest number"). An order of rank must exist. Between commander and commanded must arise a social distance based upon the former's greater value. The new philosopher seeking to transform valuations must stand "against his own time"—finding a value standpoint "beyond" the accepted valuations of his own era. To do so requires hardness and patient waiting. Philosophical success is thus partly a result of circumstances beyond any individual philosopher's control. *What his creative response shall be is a function of what the situation is in which he finds himself.* In this sense the philosopher must always be a lonely man, "beyond" the good and evil of conventional morality. This loneliness will produce anguish.

In *Thus Spake Zarathustra* (1883-1885), Nietzsche describes the anguish which results from the discovery that no God is found beyond good and evil. Nor is there a higher, more ultimate Platonic harmony. The new philosopher must learn to embrace existence for its own sake. Nietzsche attempts to express the nature of this love of existence through a doctrine of "eternal recurrence," which seems sometimes to function even mystically in his thought. The philosopher of existence must say "Yea" to reality while knowing that "God is dead." Any new values which arise in the evolutionary process do so as expressions of man's self-commanding capacity. Error and pain inevitably and necessarily are aspects of existence. "That everything recurs, is the very nearest approach of a world of Becoming to a world of Being: the height of contemplation," he wrote in the second volume of *The Will to Power* (a work published by Nietzsche's sister, 1901-1904, from remaining notes). The new philosopher of "beyondness" needs this doctrine of eternal recurrence, since he must command new values in an existence which expresses the will to power rather than a rational scheme of things.

In Nietzsche's style one finds a brilliance to match his intellectual daring— a wealth of suggestion, irony, maliciousness, a fine balancing of value antitheses, and playful criticism coupled with the most serious intention. The understanding of Nietzsche's works requires that one attempt to read them sympathetically, returning to them again and again. If he is to be judged severely for his unsystematic methods and for the disordered expression of his complex anxieties, his age and culture must also be so judged. Nietzsche was (as he says all men are) a philosopher who worked from an inner necessity to achieve self-understanding. Of philosophers he wrote: "But fundamentally, 'way down below' in us, there is something unteachable, a bedrock of intellectual destiny, of predestined decision, of answers to predestined selected questions."—*W.T.D.*

Pertinent Literature

Kaufmann, Walter. *Nietzsche: Philosopher, Psychologist, Antichrist.* Princeton, New Jersey: Princeton University Press, 1950.

Walter Kaufmann's *Nietzsche: Philosopher, Psychologist, Antichrist* is the most thorough study in English of Friedrich Wilhelm Nietzsche's work. It brings Nietzsche's philosophy into focus while also tracing his development and actively criticizing other major interpretations of his thought.

In Part III, "The Philosophy of the Will to Power," Kaufmann makes his most extensive use of *Beyond Good and Evil*. There he is concerned, perhaps overzealously, to show that Nietzsche was not an irrationalist. Although Nietzsche repudiates the traditional dualism of reason and impulse and explains all human behavior in terms of the will to power, it nevertheless remains true that he regarded reason as the highest manifestation of the will to power, for reason gives man power not only over nature but also over himself. Those who stand at the top of the power scale, according to Nietzsche, neither act on impulse nor extirpate their passions, but, in a manner reminiscent of Aristotelian man, act rationally by instinct, through an "attained unconsciousness" or "second nature." Nietzsche, who never prescribes moral norms but finds human conduct reflected universally in nature, often equates the will to power that nature displays with the "instinct of freedom" or with Eros. For him all life is a striving to transcend and perfect itself. Accordingly, "Nothing that is alive is sufficient unto itself," but everything strives to overcome itself as it denies itself gratification for more life and more power. Human life is a dialectic of commanding and obeying. Although most men, contenting themselves with the strength of the herd in their bid for power, obey other men's laws, genuine creativity generates its own standards. Thus, Kaufmann maintains, "One of the most significant connotations of the phrase 'beyond good and evil' is that all established codes must forever be transcended by men who are creative."

Kaufmann gives scant attention to Nietzsche's master and slave moralities. He emphasizes that Nietzsche in no way identifies with the master despite his polemic against weakness. Every man would in fact be a mere animal were it not for the ambiguous marvel of bad conscience which imposes itself on an intransigent, suffering material, burning a "No" into the soul. For Nietzsche what is called "higher culture" rests on the channeling and spiritualizing of cruelty. Here Kaufmann finds grounds for saying that Nietzsche's very evaluation of suffering and cruelty springs out of his respect for rationality.

The offspring of man's self-inflicted travail is the "overman" or superman, humanity in its highest form. This overman may possibly be willed and bred in the future, but until now it has appeared only as a fortunate accident of history in the human being who has inherited the supra-abundant power of passion and reason stored up from the experience of generations. Such a one, glimpsed in Caesar and perhaps Goethe, in performing "his unique deed of self-integration, self-creation, and self-mastery," overcomes the highest resistance from his epoch and from the ordinary humanity in himself. Just as he redeems his every impulse in the wholeness and sublimity of his own nature, so he believes that likewise every particular may have meaning in the vast macrocosm of nature as a whole. He therefore joyously affirms the fatality allotted him in embracing what is at once the most nihilistic and "*most scientific of all possible hypotheses*," the eternal return of the same. Simultaneously the overman realizes his full power as the "single one." And this is the only goal that history can have. Kaufmann sees both the overman and the eternal recurrence as denying, equally, indefinite progress and the eternal beyond. Both express the repudiation of any depreciation of the moment, the finite, and the individual. Hence Kaufmann sees Nietzsche's dual vision, whose foci might seem antithetical in character, as one of complete rational consistency.

Danto, Arthur C. *Nietzsche as Philosopher*. New York: Macmillan Publishing Company, 1967.

Arthur C. Danto's *Nietzsche as Philosopher* is the first book to attempt an analytical assessment of Friedrich Wilhelm Nietzsche's philosophy. Much of it is an indictment of Nietzsche for his inconsistency, vagueness, erroneous assumptions, and rhetorical excesses. Throughout Nietzsche's books, Danto writes, there is the sense of "an irresponsible shifting of ground and an infuriating skeptical juggling in which the juggler is part of what he manages to keep aloft through some miraculous feat of light-handedness."

Although Nietzsche claims that morality belongs to a stage of ignorance in which the concept of reality is lacking, his own *perspectivism*, "the doctrine that there are no facts but only interpretations," makes it impossible, Danto says, for Nietzsche himself to distinguish the real from the imaginary. In his teaching about the *Übermensch* (overman) Nietzsche leaves singularly unspecific the goal for life that he proclaims. His contrasting of this ideal with the contemporary herd crassly revives the ancient idea that some men (now the bulk of mankind) are natural slaves. However, Danto insists, the notion that simply because the common man is not exceptional, he is sick, weak, or impotent is "as nakedly a fallacious inference as could be drawn." Again, Nietzsche's assertion that the strong simply are their acts of strength, when coupled with his denial that the subject is the agent of action, appears to offer a mere triviality of logic as the foundation of a metaphysics of morals. Danto finds Nietzsche's anti-Darwinism to be based on little more than a pun, and his counterdoctrine, that the weak prevail over the strong, to be manifestly illogical. Furthermore, he considers that Nietzsche, in exhorting the strong to passionate action, is guilty of assuming that the gratuitous causing of suffering is justified by the mere fact of metabolism and that any antisocial impulses can suffice to provide new moral horizons.

For all this, Danto maintains that most of Nietzsche's irrationality lies not in his thought but in his misuses of language. Although Nietzsche wrote "what seem to be bald apologies for and exhortations to lust, cruelty, violence, hatred, and brutality of every sort," in his approach to morality, through the juxtaposing of reason to passion, he scarcely deviated from a tradition that goes back at least as far as Socrates. Repeatedly he resorted to excessive language in order to drive home his points. Danto believes that out of self-indulgence and self-dramatization he often overestimated the difficulties of his own thinking. On the other hand, his utterances do sometimes verge on the mystical, offering us enigmatic paradoxes, for he was actually groping toward a breakthrough in thought.

Danto states that *Beyond Good and Evil* represents Nietzsche's most mature philosophy. He takes as his task the reconstructing of a Nietzschean system that he finds embedded in its aphorisms. That system's central concept is total nihilism, the recognition that "every taking-for-true (*Fuer-wahr-halten*) is necessarily false; because there is no true world at all." Accepting this insight need not lead to a will to nothingness. Rather it should lead to an embracing of fate, to a Dionysian affirmation of the world just as it is. Precisely this yes-saying to the world as sheer chaos and meaninglessness opens the way to creativity, for it includes the view that the world is an infinity of "power quanta" whose essential characteristic is "the will to overpower and to resist being overpowered." Danto takes no real cognizance of Nietzsche's notion of self-overcoming as intrinsic to the will to power or of Nietzsche's portrayal of the will to power as a single force coursing through all phenomena. He speaks only of isolated centers of will, each seeking to organize the world solely from its own perspective and each locked in perpetual combat with the rest. The key to creativity is knowing that the only source of form, meaning, and value lies in this contest. In ably propounding this interpretation, Danto continually introduces a metaphysical framework largely alien to Nietzsche's thinking. Paradoxically enough, this structuring allows a host of Nietzschean pronouncements that fit readily into Danto's schema simultaneously to qualify Nietzsche as a progenitor of some branch or other of contemporary analytical philosophy.

Camus, Albert. "Nietzsche and Nihilism," in *The Rebel.* Translated by Anthony Bower. New York: Vintage Books, 1956.

Albert Camus, in the section of *The Rebel* entitled "Nietzsche and Nihilism," portrays the Friedrich Wilhelm Nietzsche of the period of *Beyond Good and Evil* as the philosopher in whom "nihilism becomes conscious." Nietzsche was the first complete nihilist of Europe because he refused to evade the outlook common to all men of his time, which was not the simple belief in nothing but, rather, the inability to believe in what exists. Determined to live as a rebel and to destroy everything that kept nihilism from view, Nietzsche made it his mission to bring men to awareness of their lack of faith in God, while simultaneously he attacked the ideals of traditional morality for undermining faith in the world.

But the active nihilist who casts out God and the enslavement to moral idols finds, in anguish, that to be without law also is to lack freedom. Rather than live under the servitude of moral anarchy in a world of pure chance, he chooses complete subordination to fate. An eager embracing of total necessity becomes his definition of freedom. His rebellion thus culminates in the asceticism that transforms Karamazov's "If nothing is true, everything is permitted" into "If nothing is true, nothing is permitted."

To be sure, under this deification of fate, the individual is annihilated, submerged in the destiny of a species, lost in the vast ordering of the cosmos as a whole. Yet through this same acquiescence the individual becomes divine, since he participates in the divinity of the world. In saying yes to the world, he re-creates the world and himself. He becomes the great artist-creator.

In this "magnificent consent" Camus sees something analagous to the Pascalian wager. It involves a heroic game of mental subterfuge. The lucidity that began by rebelling against illusions ends by finding evasions of its own. Writing during the aftermath of the Nazi atrocities, Camus notes that this man who claimed to be the last antipolitical German, in accepting evil as a possible aspect of the good "dreamed of tyrants who were artists." He remained blind to the fact that "tyranny comes more naturally than art to mediocre men." The same Nietzsche who, with his mind only, said yes even to murder, had also to admit that, in fact, he could not bear even to break his word. But the moment Nietzsche said yes to the world as it is, he opened the way to others who could bear to lie and kill and who would actually gain strength from such acts. Originally Nietzsche's rebellion had been a protest against a lie. His affirmative, "forgetful of the original negative, disavows rebellion at the same time that it disavows the ethic that refuses to accept the world as it is."

Nietzsche's responsibility extends still further. As the solitary man of lucidity, he seemed to assent to the world quite uncomplicatedly just as it was. But accepting the world included accepting history, and accepting history included accepting the will to power as the sole legitimate motivation for human action. "Nietzscheanism," Camus contends, "would be nothing without world domination." Nietzsche, as the prophet of nihilism, knowing its internal logic, foresaw its ascendency and sought to transform the sordid apocalypse that threatened into a renaissance by redirecting it toward a superior type of humanity. Ironically, he could not prevent the "free-thinkers" whom he detested from taking hold of the will to power for themselves and, through the very logic of nihilism and the doctrines of social emancipation, ushering in their own superhumanity. Thus there are those today, Camus writes, who have corrected Nietzsche with Karl Marx and who choose to give assent solely to history instead of to the whole of creation. Camus believes that such an alliance could happen only because Nietzsche, like Marx, had replaced the Beyond with the Later-On. Once this great rebel had emancipated himself from God's prison, his immediate concern was to construct yet another, the prison of history and reason. Sanctioning tyranny, he ended by camouflaging and consecrating the very nihilism that he claimed to have overcome.—*C. W. L.*

ADDITIONAL RECOMMENDED READING

Heidegger, Martin. *Nietzsche.* Translated by David Farrell Krell. Vol. I. New York: Harper & Row Publishers, 1979. Volumes II, III, and IV are forthcoming. In this monumental work, Heidegger is often doing what he calls "thinking the unthought in a thinker's thought." He nevertheless provides numerous insights into Nietzsche.

—————— . "Nietzsche's Word: 'God is Dead,'" in *The Question Concerning Technology and Other Essays.* Translated by William Lovitt. New York: Harper & Row Publishers, 1977. Heidegger explicates Nietzsche's philosophy in the light of Nietzsche's avowed intention to overturn traditional metaphysics through his revaluing of all values. In so doing he goes on to show from his own point of view that Nietzsche actually still stands squarely in that tradition and indeed embodies its culmination.

Hollingdale, R. J. *Nietzsche.* London: Routledge & Kegan Paul, 1973. Quoting extensively from *Beyond Good and Evil*, Hollingdale considers it and *Toward a Genealogy of Morals* to be probably Nietzsche's best books.

Jaspers, Karl. *Nietzsche: An Introduction to the Understanding of His Philosophical Activity.* Translated by Charles F. Wallraff and Frederick J. Schmitz. Chicago: Henry Regnery Company, 1969. In Jaspers' book we are to realize in dialogue with Nietzsche that genuine freedom and authenticity are found only in creativity; Jaspers makes extensive use of *Beyond Good and Evil.*

Löwith, Karl. *From Hegel to Nietzsche: The Revolution in Nineteenth Century Thought.* Translated by David E. Green. New York: Holt, Rinehart and Winston, 1964. A brief but penetrating analysis dealing with nihilism, the herd, work, education, and the Superman in Nietzsche.

Magnus, Bernd. *Nietzsche's Existential Imperative.* Bloomington: Indiana University Press, 1978. Magnus sees the doctrine of the Eternal Return as the central theme in Nietzsche's thought.

Morgan, George A. *What Nietzsche Means.* Cambridge, Massachusetts: Harvard University Press, 1941. Morgan provides one of the most cogent and richly documented analyses of Nietzsche's thought available anywhere.

Solomon, Robert C., ed. *Nietzsche: A Collection of Critical Essays.* Garden City, New York: Anchor Books, 1973. A superb collection of essays on Nietzsche written from a wide range of perspectives.

Stern, J. P. *A Study of Nietzsche.* New York: Cambridge University Press,

1979. Stern singles out *Beyond Good and Evil* for special attention, providing in Chapter V an invaluable sketch of all nine parts.

MARX: SELECTED WORKS

Author: Karl Marx (1818-1883)
Type of work: Philosophical anthropology, philosophy of social science, social and political philosophy, philosophy of history
First published: Various times

PRINCIPAL IDEAS ADVANCED

The postulation of transcendent divine beings is a function of incomplete and distorted self-identification among men.

Incomplete human self-identification is a function of nonegalitarian and incompletely developed modes of production.

The state is the ideologically legitimated power of ruling classes over laboring classes; its disappearance under genuine egalitarian and advanced productive and social conditions is thus necessary by definition.

Socially mediated production on the basis of foresight and skill distinguishes human from animal production; blockages in the development and expression of these basic capacities, reaching a peak in capitalism, are entitled "alienation."

Human history can be represented and explained as a sequence of changes in the modes of human production, upon which are raised corresponding sociopolitical structures and modes of thought.

The capitalist mode of production and its corresponding social and ideological forms will predictably give way to a socialist order which expresses human capabilities and thus overcomes alienation.

A number of circumstances have until recently led to an underestimation of the philosophical dimensions and interest of Karl Marx's work. First, the general disrepute of "speculative" as opposed to "empirical" thought in the later nineteenth century led Friedrich Engels and his collaborators to stress the hardheaded empiricism, scientism, and even positivism of Marx's work when they undertook to turn it into the ideology of a mass movement during the 1880's. Marx himself was probably involved in this effort. In any case, its success was ensured by consolidation of power in Russia by a group of Marxists schooled exclusively in this view. Second, the manuscripts of Marx which could shed a different light on the origins and foundations of Marx's thinking were not published until this century. This fact is obviously not unconnected with the first. Here Marx's complicity derives from his habit of keeping his philosophical way of thinking out of view in the works he prepared or authorized for publication, largely in order to preclude any intimation of idealism, which he felt would undermine the urgency of his message to the working class. The publication in the last fifty years of four groups of Marx's manuscripts, however, has thrown much new light on his deeper philosophical roots, commitments, and habits, and has given rise to a scholarly enterprise in which the expertise of philosophers has been particularly prominent and effective. These "manuscript clusters" are (1) Marx's *Critique of Hegel's Philosophy of Right* (written 1843, published 1927), together with the "Introduction" to it which Marx did publish shortly after completing the larger manuscript; (2) the famous *Economic and Philosophic Manuscripts of 1844* (published in 1932) together with some related papers, especially the essay "On the Jewish Question," which appeared in 1844, and the "Notes on James Mill," which did not; (3) the complete text of *The German Ideology* (written 1846, published in full 1932), which Marx wrote with Engels, along with the short but important "Theses on Feuerbach," which Engels found and published in 1886; and (4) the *Grundrisse* or "Rough Draft of Capital," a rich but unwieldly group of notebooks (written in 1857, published ineffectively in 1939 and effectively in 1953, and translated in full by 1973). It is on these works that the following sketch is based.

Like his Young Hegelian companions, Marx as a graduate student began to suspect that Georg Wilhelm Friedrich Hegel's philosophy leads to the unwarranted positing of transcendent entities—notably, Absolute Spirit. The point is not that Hegel takes this line; it is that he is unable, whatever his intentions, to escape it. By 1843 Marx had become especially intrigued by Ludwig Feuerbach's *causal* explanation of the positing of transcendent objects. For Feuerbach they are projections, roughly, of an "ideal self" displaced into another world because of factual restrictions placed on self-recognition and self-validation in this world. These restrictions come about generally from the domination of nature over man, but more particularly they arise whenever some men systematically dominate others. Given such an artificial division within the species "man" (as if differences between classes or races or other social groupings were like, or took the place of, differences between whole species) individual human beings are prevented from seeing in themselves what is characteristic of all men and seeing in all men what is characteristic of themselves. Full recognition and expression of one's "species being," then, is blocked. (An assumption of this argument is that rational persons basically experience themselves and other beings in terms of categories like natural kinds.) This blockage is expressed by the ascription of ideal human characteristics to divine beings. For Feuerbach, the degree of progress in history, then, is marked by stages in which men take back into self-characterizations predicates that had been projected onto fantastic beings. This process culminates in the refusal to countenance, however bloodlessly and undescriptively, any divinity at all. In such ideal circumstances, there will, by definition, be no religion. Further, the only entities which will be ontologically certified are those which have their roots exclusively in sensory experience and which can be referred back to sensory particulars as their subjects. Hegel's philosophy, since it fails to pass this ontological test, is not nearly as far beyond religious thinking as its author hopes. Meanwhile, however, Feuerbach's own theory remains deeply ambiguous about the relation it posits between empiricism and the demand that our experience is categorized in essentialistic terms such as "species being." The basic problem is that one may talk about kinds in ontological terms (roughly essentialism) without thoroughgoing empiricism, and vice versa. Feuerbach seems never to have faced this tension squarely, or even to have recognized it fully. The ambiguity is passed on to Marx. Feuerbach's theory does, however, propose a test for its own verification. It will be verified if there comes to exist a social reality which is jointly characterized by (a) a throughgoing empiricism, (b) the disappearance of religion, and (c) sufficiently democratic political institutions to express social equality—that is, by hypothesis, seen as underlying the joint existence of the first (a) and (b), and so providing an arena for complete mutual recognition among human beings.

What is crucial is that Marx deeply accepted this complex hypothesis. Some of his first works are an attempt to *further* Feuerbach's analysis by showing why *merely formal democracy* is not sufficient to bring about (a) and (b). Marx became convinced, on the basis of contemporary sociological information, especially about America and France, that formal democracy not only can coexist with religion, but can bring about an intensification and interiorization of religious belief. These apparent countercases to Feuerbach's theory never led Marx to suspect the general thesis itself, but did propel him to find some additional factor (d) which is alleged to be preventing the joint coexistence of (a), (b), and the "real or true democracy" needed for (c). Under the increasing influence of socialist literature, Marx came to find this additional factor in *pure private property*.

Thus, already in his crucial interpretation (in 1843) of Hegel's political philosophy, Marx shows that Hegel's countenancing of transcendent objects and his contempt for empiricism—indeed his whole "upside down" ontology and epistemology, which makes particular space-time substances dependent on abstract universals rather than the opposite—is of a piece with his justification of antidemocratic politics and private property. The one supports the other. Within the political theory itself, moreover, where Hegel promises a solidarity between rulers and ruled, Marx finds marked "alienation" and "division." Deceptive idealist rhetoric to the contrary, there is no common mind in the state portrayed by Hegel—only the domination of some by others, and naked self-interest by all. This estrangement at the political level, Marx concludes, is integrally connected to the justification of private property that Hegel built into his state-construct. It is at this point that Marx commits himself to the thesis that political community (in a Rousseauean sense) is possible if and only if private property is dismantled. Although he speaks of this as a *fulfillment* of democracy (as had the extreme left wing of the popular party during the great French Revolution, to whose views Marx's here hark back), it is unclear whether Marx at this time is speaking of a fulfillment of democracy in a democratic *state*; or had already come to believe what he later clearly proclaimed—that such a "democracy" requires the disappearance and delegitimation of the state itself. The state, in this latter view, comes *by definition* to refer to an institution functioning to restrict property to a particular class or set of classes. Its disappearance, therefore, in genuinely equal social conditions is analytically guaranteed.

However one analyzes Marx's views on "true democracy," it is certainly the case that by the time of his essay "On the Jewish Question" Marx held, in opposition to his former mentor Bruno Bauer, that formal democracy as a political institution exists *merely* to preserve bourgeois property rights. As these lead to human separation, competition, and the privatization of experience, they result in the religious-displacement illusions postulated by Feuerbach and in a political life which is something apart from, and dominating, the activities of the individual.

In the *Economic and Philosophic Manuscripts of 1844* Marx deepened this analysis by showing *why* private property in its developed bourgeois form (where entitlement to property rests on no qualification beyond formal personhood) leads to this sociopolitical and religious alienation. He first situates this kind of private property in its larger context: that production and distribution system we call *laissez-faire* capitalism. He does this by way of an analysis of the writings of the political economists. He then more generally lays down what he thinks has since the beginning distinguished the human species from other animal species: a productive capability which is characterized by (1) the intervention of intelligence and foresight into the productive process; and (2) a thoroughgoing social organization of production. (Marx couples these two characteristics in such a way that without the one, the other will not continually change and develop.) These conjoint capacities express themselves in the creation of a "humanized nature" in which men *cooperate* to transform the found materials of their environment into objects which are media for self-expression and which thus permit mutual human recognition in a public sphere. In creativity conceived along artistic lines, then, Marx locates the *sine qua non* of the full mutual recognition that, in different ways, Hegel and Feuerbach were concerned to make possible. Marx's insistence on "social *praxis*" centers on this view of "transformative activity" as the locus of human expression, development, and recognition. This is man's "species being." Indeed, in a productive system that appears *most* distinctively human, self-expression and mutual recognition provide the motive for production, and the securing of more basic needs appears as a concomitant and by-product of the achievement of these recognition-needs. Conversely, where human production is centered on the preservation of "mere existence," human life appears less distinguishable from that of other species, and human production approximates the narrowness of animal production.

Marx goes on to show that this latter pole is most closely approached in capitalism. Because of the complete dominance of pure private property under capitalism, the worker is alienated (1) from the product of his work, since he does not own it, and it cannot therefore express him, (2) from the process of his work, since he sells his own labor capacity which is his most basic human ("inalienable") attribute, and (3) from other men, since although capitalist production is *de facto* enormously cooperative and thus socialized, (1) and (2) prevent it from being experienced as the work of consciously cooperating human beings and as a product of their joint activity. Indeed, on the contrary, the economic system appears as something to which men subject themselves as to a fact of nature. It therefore becomes a fetish to them. Socialism, Marx concludes, *by removing private property*, allows the basic defining dispositions of human beings to operate freely. This is a program whose time has come, because the skills, tools, and productive capacity of capitalism itself provide the necessary conditions for this fulfillment of human aspiration. Marx found such a call in contemporary communist propaganda literature, which, although frequently written by intellectuals, he took to be a genuine and spontaneous expression of the experience and intelligence of the working class itself. He was also delighted to find in this literature a concomitant rejection of religion and of formal democracy, and thus a confirmation not only of Feuerbach's thesis, but also of his own interpretation of it. Marx's enormous and lasting confidence in the working class—which has presented great problems for twentieth century Marxists—derives, one is tempted to conclude, from his astonishment that the working class had independently arrived at Feuerbach's and his own insights.

Marx's strategy of situating types of property relations within larger and more comprehensive types of productive relations, first used in 1844, when combined with the judgment that man's productive activity is the most central aspect of his experience, suggests a larger project still: redoing Hegel's and Feuerbach's accounts of the historical development of humankind toward full self and mutual recognition on the basis of these presuppositions. Against Hegel, it will be stressed by Marx that successive types of consciousness do not unfold out of their own conceptual resources, but rather on the basis of changes in man's socially mediated interchange with the environment. Marx believed that Hegel had at one point grasped this, in a left-handed way, in the *Phenomenology of Spirit*, when he spoke of the slave's sense of self-identification as superior to the master's, because the former's transformative interaction with nature gives him a solidly achieved sense of self, while the latter is subject to the shifting tides of honor and opinion in an elitist world cut off from its productive roots. But these ideas were soon buried, and Hegel constructs his history as the history of consciousness moving on its own steam toward "theoretical" self-appropriation. (See *1844 Manuscripts*, "On Hegel's Dialectic.") Against Feuerbach, it will be stressed that the progressive taking back of alienated human properties from postulated divinities cannot be displayed as moving toward a passive, sensationalistic empiricism of the English sort, with its concomitant pleasure ethic, political indifference, and historical blindness. For Marx, men recognize their own essence (*"Wesen"*) in and by their productive activity, and therefore progressively in proportion as they make nature a home that expresses themselves ("humanized nature"). This Marx calls "active or practical materialism," as opposed to Feuerbach's "speculative" materialism. (See Marx's "Theses on Feuerbach," 1886.)

The first attempt to carry out this historical project occurs in *The German Ideology* (1846), on which Marx collaborated with Engels. What stands out in this account is a conscious attempt both to suppress the essentialistic language which had hitherto characterized Marx's thinking and to insist upon the empiricist credentials of the authors. What is to be traced is a *factual* history of the human race, in which changing forms of production determine corresponding sociopolitical patterns and legitimating ideologies. Essentialistic language would automatically imply, it is asserted, that the determination works the other way around, as in Hegel, and (it is now insisted) in the Young Hegelians as well. Nevertheless, looked at more closely, what we actually find here is a history with a high degree of quasilogical and dialectical patterning, and a suspicion arises that the forecast of the coming socialist order with which the work culminates is derived as much from his dialectical machinery as from the empiricistic data base on which we are merely *told* that it rests. It is plausible to think, then, that some essentialism, and indeed some Hegelian dialectic of consciousness, lurks inside these empiricist trappings. The resolution of this tension between contingent empirical fact and necessary quasilogical unfolding in accounting for human history constitutes the most difficult and vital problem in the analysis of Marx's mature philosophical commitments. Two other problems are associated with it. (1) How is either empiricism or quasilogicism consistent with Marx's claim that human agents freely make their own history? and (2) How is Marx capable of exempting his own analyses from the sociopolitical and economic determinism on which, in his view, it would appear *all* intellectual products rest?

Orthodox Marxism had long committed itself and Marx to a rather deterministic theory of the kind worked out by Engels in *Anti-Düring* and *The Dialectics of Nature*, and had thus allowed Marx's insistence on free human activity to escape from view. The problem of self-referencing was also bypassed by simply asserting that Marxism is a "science" which grounds its judgments in the way that natural science does. The publication of the early manuscripts may well have scandalized proponents of these views, but it was always possible to take the tack of calling these manuscripts juvenilia. For several decades the central issue in Marx scholarship, then, centered on where precisely to draw the line between the young Marx and his mature scientific-deterministic successor, who presented in *Das Kapital* the laws by which capitalism inevitably gives way to socialism. The publication of the *Grundrisse*, however, demonstrated that the habits of mind frequently associated with the younger Marx were still operating in Marx's thinking while he was writing *Das Kapital*, if somewhat behind the scenes. Those who still wished to speak of two Marxes were then driven to think of them as two alternating sides of a single Marx which vied with each other until the end. More challenging approaches, however, have tried to demonstrate that the new understanding of *Das Kapital* that the study of the *Grundrisse* makes possible shows a coherence of the later view with the earlier one at the expense of Marx's alleged scientism. The main point is to challenge the quasideterministic interpretation of *Das Kapital* itself. The correct disposition of these issues, however, is still far from accomplished.—*D. J.D.*

PERTINENT LITERATURE

Avineri, Shlomo. *The Social and Political Thought of Karl Marx*. Cambridge: Cambridge University Press, 1968.

Shlomo Avineri's study is based largely on a detailed reading of Karl Marx's *Critique of Hegel's Philosophy of Right* (1843). It is the first major study to investigate the bearing of this early manuscript on Marx's subsequent thought. It is an important part of Avineri's thesis to show that Marx later remained faithful to what he had already worked out in this *Critique*.

Avineri's interpretation of the *Critique* is built on the premise that Marx means what he says in terming his an internal critique of Georg Wilhelm Friedrich Hegel's political philosophy. It accepts Hegel's own premise—that reality *qua* reality is penetrated with reason—and demonstrates that the sociopolitical vision of the modern state that Hegel articulates and recommends in the *Philosophy of Right* is still irrational when judged by standards that Hegel himself should accept. The demonstration of this irrationality is accomplished by Marx's use of Ludwig Feuerbach's "transformative method." In this interpretive device, Hegel's habit of ascribing existential import to concepts apart from their instantiations, and of treating the latter as deductions from, or at best exemplifications of, the concepts, is replaced by treating what Hegel regards as "predicates" as "subjects." Thus, the concept of the monarch is nothing other than an abstraction from real, earthly monarchs, and less attractive on that account. This technique is taken over by Marx and used to strip Hegel's *Philosophy of Right* of an appearance of rationality that it does not yet deserve, since rational social life is not yet realized.

The chief dimension of irrationality is the gap between the real "material" life of civil society and the separation from it of political "form." This dialectic between state and civil society, which is central to Marx's argument, yields a theory of historical development that, according to Avineri, throws much light on Marx's later materialist theory of history. In classical Greco-Roman society, no civil society emerges in contradistinction to the political life of the citizen. That is where his real identity is. In the Middle Ages, there is also no split between civil and political life: political life expresses itself entirely in terms of the work roles of civil society, rather than the reverse (guilds, corporations, and the like). Modern society, however, is basically characterizable as a mutual separation of state and civil society, the state becoming alien to the concrete life of the social individual, while the economic life of civil society becomes itself more and more abstract, one-sided, and non-self-expressive as pure private property and capitalism emerge. Marx goes on to speak of their reunion both as "true democracy" and as "communism" (*"Gemeinwesen"*).

Thus Avineri believes that the issue of whether Marx at this time was a left-wing democrat or a communist is empty. Common productive life, on the basis of the anthropology soon to be worked out in detail in the *1844 Manuscripts, fulfills* political life while trancending it as a separate kind of life, while the communizing of productive and economical life makes it humanly expressive in a way that classical political theory, including Hegel's, must either promise without delivering, or ignore with peril to its own claim to rationality.

In turning to how a rational society *is* to be realized, Avineri interestingly points out how Marx assigns to the proletariat the role of "universal class" that Hegel had reserved in the *Philosophy of Right* for the bureaucracy. The connection is in the role assigned to both to bring about rationalization of the sociopolitical structure, and in the claim that Hegel makes for the bureaucrats and Marx for the proletarians that they have in mind the interest of the whole society (hence "universal"). What is different, of course, is that in Hegel's case the method for rationalizing is administrative domination, while in Marx's case it is revolutionary liberation. According to Marx, Hegel's bureaucrats are really corrupted by and embedded in the egoism of a society based on private property. Marx's proletarians do not fall back into this because they have nothing to protect; they also can acquire positive cooperative and fulfilling values in the transformative activity of work itself.

Avineri believes that Marx remains faithful in his later works to the theory worked out in 1843-1844, although terminology, accent, and matters of details do shift. One interesting argument that Avineri proposes about the later Marx is designed to undercut the idea that Marx moved, in *Das Kapital*, to a kind of deterministic scientism. Avineri argues that *Das Kapital* is a model of a free-market society already approximated by the England of the 1850's. The *projection* toward socialism proceeds by noting ways in which the free-market model tries, by many devices, to rectify its own instability and inherent mutability. These interventions, however, bring about by their very nature an integration of collective political decisionmaking and the economic infrastructure. Thus socialism grows up within the world of capitalism itself.

It would be small exaggeration to conclude that, for Avineri, Marx came not to reject Hegel but to fulfill him—to mark out what a truly rationalized society would be like, where rationality is conceived of as an organic unity between social matter and political form.

Ollman, Bertell. *Alienation: Marx's Conception of Man in Capitalist Society*. Cambridge: Cambridge University Press, 1971, 1976.

In combating the common interpretation of Karl Marx's historical materialism, which holds that the sociopolitical and ideological superstructure are causally determined and explained by the economic base, Bertell Ollman takes a daring tack: this *cannot* be the case for Marx because this model of causal explanation assumes an ontology in which one (sort of) thing has effects on another that is fully discriminable from it. Marx, Ollman argues, consistently subscribed to an ontology of "internal relations" in which any one "thing" is simply the totality of its relations. No entity, that is, has defining properties which are statable in nonrelational terms. Causal analysis of the type referred to, then, is to be replaced by accounts of inherently changeable and constantly changing configurations of "elements" that are themselves relations. Ontologies of this sort were most fully articulated by British Hegelians at the turn of the century. Ollman holds that, like them, Marx read such a doctrine out of Georg Wilhelm Friedrich Hegel, as when, for example, he refers to the sun and plants in the *1844 Manuscripts* as mutually "objects" to each other. An object (*Gegenstand*) is for Marx that to which an entity is related in order to be what it is, and without reference to which it would have no identity conditions sufficient to posit it as existing at all.

Such a view has advantages in enabling us to separate Marx's "essentialism" from the usual sense of a preestablished entelechy which limits the development and operation of any kind of being in precise directions. It thus preserves, within a broader sense of "essentialism," Marx's insistence that man's "nature" is constantly changing as the range of the "objects" with which man deals, and to which he relates himself, is increased. It also helps make sense of Marx's reiterated insistence that the individual person is not something constituted prior to or apart from his social relations, but comes to be an individual precisely in and through those relations. What speaks against the thesis are, first, the possibility that a doctrine of internal relations is not formulatable in a way that does not depend on an idealism which Marx trenchantly rejects, at least in his maturity. Second, any such doctrine takes upon itself the perhaps unfulfillable task of preserving a sense for "individuation" which squares with our experience. To the first of these objections, Ollman replies by taking seriously Friedrich Engels' attempt to work out a "materialist dialectic," and Marx's approval of that chore. (Thus Ollman makes a more positive assessment of Engels' work than is customary among nonorthodox Marxists.) As to the second problem, Ollman believes that although "individuation" is indeed always relative to a point of view on the ontologically constituted whole, such points of view can do justice to the way we break up our experience for purposes of understanding it and dealing with it. Putting these two points together, Ollman arrives at an account in which a "materialist" doctrine of internal relations is seen as truly reflecting and reporting how the whole of experience coheres with and can be best explained from *the perspective of human productive activity*. On the basis of this general theory, Ollman offers an interpretation of the key Marxian concept of "alienation," as it is worked out in the *1844 Manuscripts* and as it is presumed to underlie Marx's thinking thereafter. Alienation, roughly, is a condition in which human productive activity in interaction with "objects" is narrowed, contracted, and reduced below what human needs, wants, and capacities are, *at any given time*, capable of. In such a condition, and especially under capitalism, experience becomes "abstract" or "one-sided." Thus, in Ollman's reading, Marx's frequent attacks on "abstraction" refer to a separating off of aspects from a concrete whole, as notably the separation of the "commodity" in capitalism from the reference of social production to social life. Such separated elements cannot adequately explain matters presumed to be separated from them, or in turn be explained by other "abstractions." Thus the conventional model of historical materialism frequently assumed to be Marx's is for Ollman contrary to his view.

Rader, Melvin. *Marx's Interpretation of History*. New York: Oxford University Press, 1979.

In addressing himself to the conflict between traditional interpretations of Karl Marx and more recent readings which stress Marx's roots in Georg Wilhelm Friedrich Hegel, Melvin Rader suggests that we might distinguish between several "models" of historical process which Marx uses heuristically and alternately. Thus Rader separates the traditional "base-superstructure" model from a more Hegelian "organic totality" model. The former may take either a fundamentalist or a more sophisticated form. In its fundamentalist version, the base-superstructure model severely separates out the various strata of social reality and ascribes to the lowest stratum, the stratum of "forces of production," all casual and explanatory roles. The more sophisticated version, preferred by Friedrich Engels, may be called "dialectical" at least in the rather weak sense that it permits of causal interaction among the strata, while nevertheless insisting on the ultimate weight of the base "in the long run." The strength of the base-superstructure model generally is that it maintains the characteristically Marxian stress on the role of modes and forces of production in historical process. Its weakness is its tendency to reductionism, and, in the case of the fundamentalist version, to epiphenomenalism. Moreover, the rules for separating out and then relating the various strata have proved to be very difficult to formulate and to use with sufficient precision.

The "organic totality" model does away with these problems at a stroke; but it does so only by getting into the turgid area of "internal relations." Nevertheless, this model is, for Rader, more faithful on the whole to Marx's work both early and late. Rader takes pains, then, to clarify Marx's views about internal relations.

First, he argues that neither in the early nor the mature writings does Marx's theory of internal relations—relations such as constitutively obtain among parts of organisms and in social relations—extend as far as a universal ontology committed to the view that anything and everything is logically incomplete except by its relation to everything else. Rader casts doubt on Bertell Ollman's ascription of such a view to Marx. (See above review of Ollman's *Alienation*.) Marx's invocation of internal relatedness focuses on the world of human activity and its situation within the wider sphere of organic activity; and even in these restricted contexts Marx is quite open about the degree of interpenetration that needs to be postulated for explanation in particular cases. Degrees of internal relatedness are a matter for empirical investigation rather than *a priori* legislation.

Second, Rader is concerned to point out that there is less inherent tension between Marx's two models than one might assume. In Marx's early period, the dominant use of the organic totality model is nevertheless accompanied by insistencies that employ, or at the very least foreshadow, the base-superstructure model. For example, in his very early critique of Hegel's political theory Marx traces defects in Hegel's state-construct to underlying economic and property relations. Conversely, in *Das Kapital* Rader finds much use of organic conceptualization. Indeed, it is only that model which can provide the normative foundations for Marx's attack on capitalist societies and his approbation of socialist ones. Without being buffered by the expressive humanism available in that model, the exclusive use of base-superstructure talk to explain historical process might be taken as involving an "economic determinism" in which the stages of history unfold by alleged immutable laws of social development into a socialist order whose desirability is, in this account, both beside the point and ungrounded in relevant sorts of arguments. Rader holds that Marx never envisioned the matter in this deterministic light.

Indeed, Rader is concerned to point out that there are areas of real compatibility between the organic totality and the base-superstructure models. There can be hierarchical dependence between the parts of organisms without undermining their internal relatedness. Some organs and functions are more basic to the preservation and functioning of a living whole than others, and thus play greater causal-explanatory roles. So too in societies, the "forces of production" are basic to social functioning. Where this works eufunctionally we see a harmony among the various aspects of social life, and between individual and society, that can best be represented in terms of the descriptions available in the organic totality model. Where it is dysfunctional we see the social organism separate into "abstract" relations which can best be described and explained in terms of the base-superstructure model. The separability of the elements featured in this model describes and explains dysfunctional relations within a presumed, but defective, organic totality. It thus plays a significant role in explanations of periods of social revolution. —*D.J.D.*

ADDITIONAL RECOMMENDED READING

Cohen, G. A. *Karl Marx's Theory of History: A Defense.* Princeton, New Jersey: Princeton University Press, 1978. Well-argued functionalist interpretation of the traditional base-superstructure model.

Gould, Carol. *Marx's Social Ontology: Individuality and Community in Marx's Theory of Social Reality.* Cambridge, Massachusetts: MIT Press, 1978. Seeks insight into Marx's use of internal relations in his connection with Aristotle.

Lichtheim, George. *Marxism: An Historical and Critical Study.* New York: Frederick A. Praeger, 1961. A view of subsequent streams of Marxist thought built up on a sound reading of Marx himself.

McLellan, David. *Karl Marx: His Life and Thought.* New York: Harper & Row Publishers, 1974. Reliable and nontendentious biography.

——————. *The Young Hegelians and Karl Marx.* New York: Frederick A. Praeger, 1969. Traces influence on the early Marx of such figures as Bruno Bauer, Moses Hess, Arnold Ruge and Feuerbach, as well as Hegel.

Schmidt, Alfred. *The Concept of Nature in Marx.* London: New Left Books, 1973. Refutation of dialectical materialist interpretation of Marx's ontology and epistemology.

TIME AND FREE WILL

Author: Henri Bergson (1859-1941)
Type of work: Metaphysics
First published: 1889

PRINCIPAL IDEAS ADVANCED

It is inappropriate to limit thought to spatial concepts; time, in particular, should not be conceived of as extension.

It is misleading to conceive of dynamic matters by the use of static concepts.

In giving accounts of aesthetic feelings or sensations, philosophers often attempt to describe qualitative changes in a quantitative fashion.

Space is the material with which mind builds up the conception of number, but the sensations by means of which we form the idea of space are themselves unextended and qualitative, not quantitative.

Time is duration, and duration may very well be nothing but a succession of qualitative changes permeating each other.

A self of pure duration is not subject to the distinctions which are imposed upon the self considered symbolically; the self is free when its acts spring from the whole personality.

Bergson stands as one of the great names in late nineteeth and early twentieth century philosophy, and the question of the freedom of the will is one of philosophy's classical problems. However, it is interesting to note that Bergson's little book is one of the few which treat this problem directly. Plato, Aristotle, and Augustine give classical analyses of time, but these come about in the course of the development of larger works. The problems which surround freedom of the will are numerous, but few have attacked the problem directly. In fact, it is probably safe to say that the focus upon freedom of the will as a central issue is a development of modern philosophy. Theology developed this as a major part of the question of God's foreordination. Classical philosophy dealt with freedom only incidentally. Modern philosphy singled it out as a major issue, and Bergson wrote one of the few direct and systematic treatments of the issue.

The approach in this work is through psychology and particularly through an analysis of psychic states. Not only had philosophy not yet been separated in Bergson's time from psychology as a discipline, but the interest in psychology had really only begun to grow within philosophy. The empirical psychology, and the interest in sense perception so typical of British empiricism, combined with continental phenomenology to bring psychology to the foreground in philosophy, and this is Bergson's approach. As a Frenchman, the introspective analysis of Descartes has left its mark, although Bergson is noted as the great opponent of the strict Cartesian rationalism. The author is adept at detecting approaches which are inadequate to their subject matter, and so here he starts out by noting the inappropriateness of always thinking in spatial concepts. His problem (free will) is common to both metaphysics and psychology, and he begins by trying to point out a confusion of duration with extension, which has complicated the treatment of the problem of free will.

The first of the three chapters discusses the intensity of psychic states. In considering intensity in relation to extension, Bergson finds that intensity contains the image of something virtually extended. As is so often the case with Bergson, he breaks down barriers and finds in two apparently different phenomena elements of similarity and aspects of community. Again, Bergson considers the reflective consciousness as a way of looking at things and finds that it is repelled by the wholly dynamic way of perceiving. Such static-dynamic oppositions are Bergsons' prime target, and he makes the case for dynamic views without surrendering more traditional approaches.

As an example of gradual transition which results in change in kind, Bergson cites aesthetic feelings as a striking example of the progressive intrusion of new elements, which in reality are merely altered emotions and not an increase in magnitude as they appear to be. In an aesthetic feeling we sympathize with the feeling that is expressed. Art aims at impressing feelings on us rather than at expressing them. The feeling of the beautiful is no specific feeling, but every feeling experienced by us assumes an aesthetic character, if it has been suggested and not caused.

Bergson continues with his analysis of sensations, emotions, and muscular effort after finishing his discussion of feeling. The magnitude of a representative sensation, he concludes, depends upon our transferring the cause into the effect. The intensity of the affective element depends, on the other hand, on the more or less important reactions which prolong the external stimulations and find their way into the sensation itself. We promote the changes of quality into variations of magnitude.

Bergson opposes some postulates of what he calls a psychophysical interpretation, on the grounds that they cannot be verified unless the postulates are first granted. He resists the reduction of all psychological phenomena to physical states, and he insists that there is no point of contact between the unextended and the extended, between quality and quantity. There is no radical opposition; both arise as resultant variations in degree and are not disparate in nature.

Conscious states should not be considered in isolation from one another. Their proper context is in concrete multiplicity, for they unfold themselves in pure duration. Then you have to go on to inquire what the multiplicity of our inner states becomes, what form duration assumes when the space in which it unfolds is eliminated. The usual radical opposition has been broken down by Bergson, and now the problem becomes one of giving an adequate account of duration as the source.

In the second long chapter Bergson studies duration and begins by breaking down the concept of number into a synthesis of the one and the many. The idea of number implies the simple intention of a multiplicity of parts or units, which are absolutely alike. Every clear idea of number implies a visual image in space. For counting material objects means thinking of these objects as being together, thereby leaving them in space. Space is, accordingly, the material with which mind builds up number, the medium in which the mind places objects.

Ultimately, Bergson finds two kinds of multiplicity: that of material objects, to which the conception of number may be applied; and the multiplicity of states of consciousness. The latter cannot be thought of as numerical without the help of some symbolic represention, and in this a necessary element is space. But now we ask, has duration anything to do with space? It could be that space comes in as a later addition. The sensations by means of which we form the notion of space are themselves unextended and simply qualitative—this is the most likely hypothesis.

In actuality, space is what enables us to distinguish a number of identical and simultaneous sensations from one another. It is a principle of differentiation but not a qualitative one. Consequently, it is a reality with no quality. The mind perceives under the form of extensive homogeneity what is given it as qualitative homogeneity. There are two kinds of reality, one heterogeneous (that of sensible qualities), the other homogeneous (space). Because the latter is clearly conceived by the human intellect, we are able to use clearcut distinctions, to count, to abstract, and also to speak. However, we still regard time as an unbounded medium, different from space but, like it, homogeneous. We can thus conceive of succession without distinction, and think of it as a mutual penetration, as interconnection and organization of elements. Each one represents the whole and cannot be distinguished or isolated from it except by abstract thought.

Pure duration might well be nothing but a succession of qualitative changes which melt into and permeate one another without precise outline. Yet it is extraordinarily difficult to think of duration in its purity. The real concrete self is made of such pure duration; its symbolic substitute has all of the artificial distinctions, and thus contradictions, implied in the problems of freedom, causality, and personality. An inner life, it is true, with well-distinguished moments and with clearly characterized states will answer better the requirements of social life. But a self of pure duration overcomes problems of freedom and causation by not being subject to their distinctions.

Dynamism is what Bergson prefers, and this starts from the idea of voluntary activity, given by consciousness. (Mechanism takes the opposite path.) The self experiences a first feeling and, according to the dynamic theory, has already changed to a slight extent when the second feeling takes its place. In this way a dynamic series of states is formed which permeates and strengthens the feeling states which are its members. Freedom depends on such a series. We are free, Bergson says, when our acts spring from our whole personality. Our acts express our personality. They have that indefinable resemblance to it which one sometimes finds to exist between an artist and his work. The believer in free will assumes that the same series of antecedents could issue in several different acts, all equally possible.

For Bergson freedom must be sought in a certain shade or quality of the action itself and not in the relation of this act to what it is not or to what it might have been. There are two ways of assimilating antecedent events, the one dynamic and the other static. Yet we still cannot analyze the outcome of a free action, for we cannot know the value of the antecedents without knowing the final act, which is the very thing that is not yet known. The question is whether the definite regularity of antecedent to consequent is found in the domain of consciousness, too. That is the whole problem of free will.

Of course, if we stand by experience, then we would say that we feel ourselves free, that we perceive force (rightly or wrongly) as a free spontaneity. The relation of inner causality is purely dynamic and has no analogy with the relation of two external phenomena which actually condition each other. Freedom is the relation of the concrete self to the acts which it performs, "This relation is indefinable, just because we are free." Every demand for an explanation of freedom comes back to the question: Can time be adequately represented by space? If you are dealing with time flow, then the answer is yes. Freedom is therefore a fact, among the facts which we observe; there is none which is clearer.

Bergson thus used his famous doctrine of conscious time as flowing from a primitive apprehension of undivided duration. By his doctrine he attempted to release causal action from the grip of mechanical regulation and to place the source for free acts in a consciousness ultimately free from space and its rigid divisions. In *Time and Free Will* Bergson thus argues for an undivided duration behind conscious states and normal distinctions and thereby leaves an area for spontaneity and free decision in psychic states if not in physical matter.—*F.S.*

Pertinent Literature

Höffding, Harald. *Modern Philosophers and Lectures on Bergson.* Translated by Alfred C. Mason. London: Macmillan and Company, 1915.

In 1913, Harald Höffding delivered a series of lectures at the University of Copenhagen on Henri Bergson's philosophy. These lectures, along with his 1902 lectures on Wilhelm Wundt, Freidrich Wilhelm Nietzsche, William James, and others, were published under the title *Modern Philosophers and*

Lectures on Bergson. In his lectures on Henri Louis Bergson, Harald Höffding outlines Bergson's thought, comments on it in relation to other philosophies, and takes issue with many of Bergson's conclusions. There are six lectures: "The Problem of Philosophy," "Intuition," "Psychology and Physiology," "The Philosophy of Evolution," "The Psychology of Will and Laughter," and "Metaphysics."

The first lecture contains biographical information about Bergson and identifies some of the major characteristics of his philosophy. Höffding regards Bergson as a philosopher in the tradition of Michel Eyquem de Montaigne, Blaise Pascal, Jean Jacques Rousseau, and Maine de Biran. For each of these thinkers, the human being is not fundamentally a rational being; the intellect is only a part of the human being, and, in the end, not the most important part.

The second lecture, "Intuition," considers Bergson's thought in *Données immediates de la conscience* (published in English as *Time and Free Will*). Höffding summarizes Bergson's objections to the mechanical psychologies of David Hume, James Mill, John Stuart Mill, and Herbert Spencer and offers an analysis of Bergson's own theory of the two selves. According to Bergson, the surface self views reality from the outside and is characterized by intelligence, while the inner self, the true self, is characterized by intuition. Höffding points out the relative merits of this theory of the two selves, but finally rejects it on the grounds that it leaves each individual as if he or she were a separate individual unable to communicate with the other. Höffding is not satisfied with what he takes to be a fundamental dualism in Bergson's philosophy of the self.

The third lecture, "Psychology and Physiology," follows Bergson's thought through *Matter and Memory*. Höffding believes that Bergson's position in *Matter and Memory* is a continuation of his position in *Time and Free Will*. In *Matter and Memory* the dualism between the two selves is presented as a distinction between perception and memory. Again Höffding objects, maintaining that Bergson's division between perception and memory is little more than a new version of the traditional dualism between material things and thinking things and that it is plagued with the same unsolvable problems.

Höffding's lectures "The Philosophy of Evolution" and "The Psychology of Will and Laughter" analyze Bergson's thought as expounded in *Creative Evolution* and *Laughter*. His concluding lecture, "Metaphysics," gives a final assessment of Bergson's thought. These lectures are weaker than the first three, but are nevertheless worth reading.

Höffding has delved deeply into Bergson's thought. Although he disagrees with many of Bergson's conclusions, he is appreciative of Bergson's work.

Russell, Bertrand. *The Philosophy of Bergson.* London: Macmillan and Company, 1914.

Bertrand Russell is one of Henri Louis Bergson's harshest critics. It is his judgment that Bergson's critique of intellect and his belief in freedom are unfounded and dangerous. In *The Philosophy of Bergson* Russell states his basic disagreement with Bergson. The book also contains a brief response to Russell's analysis of Bergson's philosophy by H. Wildon Carr—a man who finds Bergson's thought convincing—and Russell's rejoinder to Carr. (Russell's critical appraisal of Bergson's philosophy can also be found in his book *A History of Western Philosophy*, New York: Simon and Schuster, 1945.)

According to Russell, there are two characteristic features of Bergson's thought: first, his critique of intellect and his endorsement of intuition and, second, his belief in an undetermined freedom of the will. Apart from these two doctrines, Russell believes that Bergson's philosophy amounts to nothing. Russell contends that Bergson's valuation of intuition over intellect stems from his understanding of space and that his belief in an externally undetermined and hence "free" self has its roots in his analysis of time. If Russell can show that Bergson misunderstands both space and time, he can undermine Bergson's philosophy.

Before turning his attention to Bergson's doctrines of space and time, however, Russell makes it clear that Bergson's philosophy is dangerous. If Bergson is correct, if intuition is more accurate than intellect, and if there is real freedom, the world moves forward without rhyme or reason. Indeed, Russell begins his critique of Bergson by pointing out that Bergson's philosophy was used by Georges Sorel to legitimate a revolutionary labor movement which had no definite goal.

Russell maintains that Bergson's understanding of space is flawed. According to Russell, Bergson's notion that the intellect can deal only with spatialized concepts—concepts which are extended images—is simply not true. Bergson, in Russell's estimation, wrongly identifies an abstract concept with some particular manifestation and therefore mistakenly assumes that the concept has the same properties as the thing which is concrete.

Russell is also convinced that Bergson's analysis of time is based on a confusion. He maintains that Bergson's concept of duration—time as known in the act of memory—confuses past and present. For Bergson the reason that there is freedom is that nothing exists independently of the present; the past is always being determined in the present. Because memory consists of the effect of past facts on present experience, however, Russell argues that the distinction between past *as past* and past *as present* is blurred in Bergson's thought. In the end, Russell contends, Bergson denies time altogether.

H. Wildon Carr argues that Russell's criticisms of Bergson are not well founded, that Russell misunderstands Bergson and contradicts himself. According to Carr, Bergson is not guilty of confusing abstractions with concrete instances of those abstractions; furthermore, Bergson does not confuse the object known with the knowing of it, which is to say that he does not confuse the past as past with the past as present. Russell, however, is not persuaded by Carr's arguments.

Russell's treatment of Bergson is instructive even though it is not sympathetic. Russell is certainly correct in pointing out that intuition and freedom are central to Bergson's philosophy, and he is right in maintaining that space and time are crucial to Bergson's notion of intuition and belief in freedom. Russell's criticism of Bergson's philosophy deserves thoughtful consideration.

Levi, Albert William. *Philosophy and the Modern World*. Bloomington: Indiana University Press, 1959.

Philosophy and the Modern World is divided into two parts: *The Problems* and *The Prophets*. In Part I, Albert William Levi discusses what he considers to be the major problems facing the twentieth century—namely, personal, social, and intellectual fragmentation—and the philosophical roots of these problems. In Part II, he summarizes and analyzes the thought of those he considers to be contemporary "prophets"—Henri Louis Bergson, Sigmund Freud, John Dewey, Alfred North Whitehead, and others—who have tried to explain the problems confronting the twentieth century and to point the way to a promised land where these problems do not exist. Levi's book is an excellent introduction to these persons who have shaped the contemporary world with their thought.

Levi's presentation and analysis of Bergson's work is particularly outstanding. Levi began his philosophical career as a Bergsonian, and his understanding and his appreciation for Bergson's thought is evident. In addition to tracing the overall development of Bergson's thought, Levi is able to show how Bergson's individual works are related to one another. Bergson's discovery in *Time and Free Will* of the underlying self, for example, leads him to the further exploration of the self in *Matter and Memory* and then, in *Creative Evolution*, into a general theory of nature.

Another strong point of this essay, especially in its exposition of *Time and Free Will*, is that it employs various literary works as a means of illustrating Bergson's philosophy. For example, Levi's use of extended passages from Marcel Proust's *Remembrance of Things Past* sheds much light on Bergson's thought. Levi contends that Proust understood reality in exactly the same way as Bergson. A careful reading of Proust's great work of fiction, in Levi's estimation, provides one with the same insight that can be obtained from reading *Time and Free Will* and *Matter and Memory*.

Still another strength of this very solid essay is that it locates Bergson's thought in relation to preceding and succeeding philosophies. Levi considers some of the similarities and dissimilarities which exist between René Descartes' philosophy and that of Bergson. He also comments on how Bergson's important distinction between "time by the clock" and "time lived" preceded similar distinctions made by Bertrand Russell, Arthur S. Eddington, Alfred North Whitehead, and the Existentialists. (Levi considers the distinction between two types of time to be one of the focal issues of contemporary philosophy.) He also provides a helpful comparison between Bergson's thought and Immanuel Kant's thought. Levi agrees with A. D. Lindsay, Jacques Maritain, and others who understand Bergson's philosophy as a kind of "inverted Kantianism." Kant's concern is how to account for our knowledge of the natural world, whereas Bergson's concern is how to account for our knowledge of the inner self. In these discussions of the differences and commonalities between Bergson and other thinkers, Levi is able to highlight Bergson's originality and at the same time show his relation to the dominant thinkers in the Western tradition.

Levi's book is a very sound work and deserves to be read with care. His treatment of Bergson's thought will be of great assistance to anyone who desires to understand Bergson's major contributions to philosophy.—*M.F.*

ADDITIONAL RECOMMENDED READING

Carr, H. Wildon. *The Philosophy of Change; a Study of the Fundamental Principle of the Philosophy of Bergson*. London: Macmillan and Company, 1914. *The Philosophy of Change* is a sympathetic and careful study of Bergson's major philosophical doctrines.

Chevalier, Jacques. *Henri Bergson*. Translated by Lilian A. Clare. New York: Macmillan Publishing Company, 1928. In this book Chevalier discusses Bergson's intellectual environment, his life, and his major works (*Time and Free Will*, *Matter and Memory*, and *Creative Evolution*); he also discusses Bergson's concept of God.

Gunter, Pete A. *Henri Bergson: A Bibliography*. Bowling Green, Ohio: Philosophy Documentation Center, Bowling Green University Press, 1974. This work contains an introduction which includes a biographical sketch, a list of works by Bergson, and a complete list of works published about Bergson; it is an invaluable research tool.

Hanna, Thomas, ed. *The Bergsonian Heritage*. New York: Columbia University Press, 1962. *The Bergsonian Heritage* is a collection of three essays and seven short papers dealing with the importance of Bergson's thought. The essays are "What Bergson Means to Us Today" by Edouard Morot-Sir; "Bergson Among the Theologians" by Jaroslav Pelikan; and "Bergson and Literature" by Enid Starkie.

Lindsay, Alexander D. *The Philosophy of Bergson*. London: J. M. Dent & Sons, 1911. Lindsay's thesis is that Bergson's thought is best understood in comparison to Kant's. Like Kant, Bergson was interested in resolving the antinomies found in uncritical thought by reassessing the limits of philosophy and by establishing a new method.

Pilkington, A. E. *Bergson and His Influence: A Reassessment*. Cambridge:

Cambridge University Press, 1976. Pilkington provides a brief overview of Bergson's thought before engaging in his study of Bergson's influence. Pilkington's work focuses on Bergson's influence on Charles Péguy, Paul Valéry, Marcel Proust, and Julien Benda.

APPEARANCE AND REALITY

Author: Francis Herbert Bradley (1846-1924)
Type of work: Metaphysics
First published: 1893

PRINCIPAL IDEAS ADVANCED

The distinction between primary (sensed) qualities of physical objects and secondary (structural) qualities is based on appearance; in reality there is no such distinction.

Upon analysis it turns out that space, time, objects, and selves are appearances, not realities; the concepts do not stand up because alleged differences vanish when it is discovered that definitions are circular, empty, or inconsistent.

The logical character of reality is that it does not contradict itself; the metaphysical character of reality is that it is one; and the epistemological character of reality is that it is experience.

Reality, or the Absolute, must be because appearances are the appearances of reality.

In judgment, an idea is predicated of a real subject; a judgment is true insofar as it predicates harmonious content, removing inconsistency—but since predicates are ideal, every truth is but a partial truth, every error but a partial error.

F. H. Bradley wrote with the confidence of a leader in the main stream of British philosophy between the 1870's and the 1920's. His speculation, strongly influenced by Hegel, was highly metaphysical; and his intention was to arrive at ultimate truths about the universe as a whole. His general method was to show that the world regarded as made up of discrete objects is self-contradictory and, therefore, a world of appearances. The real is one, a world in which there are no separate objects and in which all differences disappear. Curiously enough, Bradley's conclusions about reality have not been of primary interest to contemporary philosophers. It is, rather, his critical method that they have found important, his destruction of the world of appearance.

In his Preface to *Appearance and Reality*, Bradley describes metaphysics as "the finding of bad reasons for what we believe on instinct, but to find these reasons is no less an instinct." He warns the reader that many of the ideas he presents must certainly be wrong; but since he is unable to discover how they are wrong, others will have to be critical of his conclusions.

If metaphysics is so liable to error, why should Bradley bother to study it, much less write over six hundred pages about it? He reminds us that we have all had experiences of something beyond the material world and that we need metaphysics to understand these experiences, at least insofar as they admit of being understood. Metaphysical speculation on its constructive as well as on its critical side protects us from the extremes of cross materialism and dogmatic orthodoxy. We learn from the study of metaphysics that either of these solutions is too simple, that both are peremptory. "There is no sin, however prone to it the philosopher may be," Bradley says, "which philosophy can justify so little as spiritual pride."

Appearance and Reality is divided into two parts. In the first part, "Appearance," Bradley deals with some of the recurring problems of philosophy, such as quality, relation, space, time, causation, and self. His general intention was to show that these problems have been formulated in such a way that no determinate solution can be found for them, that the world viewed from their perspective is contradictory and, therefore, appearance.

The first problem with which Bradley deals is the division of the properties of objects into primary and secondary qualities. Those who maintain this division mean by primary qualities those spatial aspects of things that we perceive or feel. All other qualities are secondary. Primary qualities, these advocates hold, are constant, permanent, self-dependent, and real. Secondary qualities, such as color, heat, cold, taste, and odor are relative to the perceiver.

In one of his arguments against this view, Bradley grants that secondary qualities are mere appearances because he wishes to show that the same thing is true of primary qualities. If an object has secondary qualities, even though they are relative to the perceiver, they must have some ground in the object. A thing can be relative only if the terms of the relation are real. For example, in the sentence, "The table is to the left of the chair," the relation, "to the left of" can hold only if there are a table and a chair. Consequently, to show that a quality is relative is to show that it is grounded in an object. The ground or terms of the relation must be real for the relation to hold. Consequently, secondary cannot mean unreal, as some proponents of the theory seem to argue that it does. Again, primary qualities must also be perceived and would be relative for the same reason given for secondary qualities. The division of the properties of objects into primary or secondary qualities turns out on close examination to be mistaken. This division, which has seemed real to many philosophers, is merely an appearance.

The structure of Bradley's argument, which often recurs in this section of the book, might be stated as follows: Some opponent maintains that x is different in kind from y, but both x and y are seen to depend on a. The opponent takes a as the defining property of x; therefore he is inconsistent in not taking it as the defining property of y. Thus x and y are not different in kind. The opponent defined them from different points of view and concluded that they were different in kind from his difference in definition. The alleged difference is merely one of appearance.

Metaphysicians are often quoted as saying that space is unreal. One of Bradley's arguments that space is unreal or an appearance involves the question of whether space has an end. If one thinks of a small portion of space, one thinks of it as bounded. The space between the table and the chair is bounded by the table and the chair. But space itself cannot be bounded. What would be outside it? However, precise boundaries determine space. This difficulty arises from regarding space first of all as a relation with the table and chair as its terms and then regarding it as a quality which is unlimited. Space cannot be a relation because any space can be divided into smaller spaces. But to divide space is to have a relation with another relation as its terms. "Space," says Bradley, "is essentially a relation of what vanishes into relations, which seek in vain for their terms. It is lengths of lengths of— nothing that we can find."

But what of space as a quality? If it is a quality, it must have limits because it is a quality in contrast to some other quality. But there is no such other. If there were, space would be a relation. According to Bradley, the philosophers who have thought of space as real have wanted to think of it both as infinite and ideal and as limited and experienced. Neither of these views by itself is enough, but one can be maintained only at the expense of the other.

A similar argument applies to time. Suppose that time is composed of units; then it has no duration. Suppose it has duration; then it has no units and no before or after. As he had said of space, Bradley avers, "Time . . . must be made and yet cannot be made of pieces."

The world seems to be made up of things or objects. But what is a thing? A minimum qualification for being a thing is to be located somewhere and probably at some time. But we cannot make clear the notions of spatial or temporal location. Not only must a thing be located but also it must have qualities; yet here again is a notion to which we cannot give any determinate meaning. In Bradley's analysis the world of this and that has disappeared.

But if the external world is appearance, what of the self? Surely here is a constant point of reference. However, the word "self" has many meanings. If the self is defined in terms of what is not self, that is, the external world, then this external world must have some meaning. If the self is understood by self-examination, then it is at once subject and object—an impossibility.

Now that objects and selves have become appearances, Bradley has only the world of things-in-themselves to deal with. But if things-in-themselves are absolutely unknown, then their existence itself is unknown; and to the extent that things-in-themselves are known, they are not things-in-themselves.

Here we come to the end of Bradley's section on appearance. What conclusion are we to draw from this part of *Appearance and Reality*? Whatever we have examined has turned out to be appearance, to be inconsistent with itself. But we have not proved that these inconsistent entities have no connection with the real. Reality completely divorced from appearance would have no meaning. We must look for some way in which appearance and reality can be joined, and it is to this problem that the second part of the book, "Reality," is devoted.

Bradley maintains that there are three fundamental properties of reality, one logical, one epistemological, and one metaphysical. The logical character of reality is that it does not contradict itself. This immediately differentiates reality from appearance. The metaphysical property is that reality is one, another characteristic to be contrasted with appearance. The epistemological property is that reality is experience. This is Bradley's way of putting the central doctrine of philosophical Idealism that the real is the rational. For him, to be rational is to be in some mind. A rational, nonmental world could at best be merely potentially rational. But to be in some mind is to be experience. These three principles, as Bradley develops them, are seen to be constitutive of all reality and, as such, are metaphysical principles.

Reality, taken as the totality of all that exists, Bradley calls the Absolute. There must be such a reality because something can be an appearance only if it is the appearance of something. The problem now is to show how such things as appearance, evil, finite objects, error, time, and space are related to and are compatible with this Absolute.

Before the question of the Absolute can be settled, we must have a definition of truth. What is a real object? Bradley says that every real thing has at least two properties, existence and characteristics. We have to be able to say that the entity *is* and *what* it is. But to be able to say something is to have ideas, and through judgment an idea is predicated of a real subject. Existence, then, is contained in the subject, and the predicate contains an ideal character which it relates to the real subject. We are now ready for Bradley's definition of truth: "Truth is the object of thinking, and the aim of truth is to qualify existence ideally." Furthermore, "Truth is the predication of such content as, when predicated, is harmonious, and removes inconsistency and with it unrest." But a truth is never wholly adequate. The predicate is only ideal, not real. Therefore, every truth is a partial truth and is capable of being expanded and extended indefinitely towards more truth.

If one can account for truth, one must also account for error. The Absolute exists and what is not a part of the Absolute does not exist. Error seems to be an exception. It cannot exist as part of the Absolute because it is in contradiction with it and is hence, error. It cannot be nonexistent because people really do make errors. It is as naïve to think that there is no error as it is to think that there is no evil in the world. On the other hand, there is a sense in which error is a partial truth. The subject and predicate refer to real things and the relation asserted between them does exist. But this partiality is also the source of error. It is a partiality which must be supplemented to become truth. Its error is in its one-sidedness; but in spite of that, it expresses one side or aspect of the Absolute.

If solipsism were true, it would be a forceful argument against the Absolute. The argument in favor of solipsism may be stated as follows: Whatever I am conscious of is an experience. But every experience is my private experience. Therefore, all I can know are various states of my own mind. Bradley's answer to this view is through definitions of the term "experience." There are two meanings that the term may have. One is that experience is a succession of bare mental states, unrelated to one another. This meaning of experience is not enough for the solipsist because he must be able to talk about a self or mind which is the agent or subject of the experiences. Thus the experiences on which solipsism is based must be more than bare mental states. They are experiences that go beyond the moment of feeling. But the solipsist may say that experience in going beyond the present moment stops short at the self. Even for him this self must have a past and a future, which are constructed by inference from the present self. But in the same way that he infers the existence of other states of his own self, he could infer other selves. The truth in solipsism is that one can know the universe only through one's own experiences and sensations. Its falsity is that it wishes to stop the expansion of experience at an arbitrary point. For Bradley, the expansion of experience, once begun, cannot stop short of the Absolute.

Are things more or less real and statements more or less true? Bradley says, "The Absolute considered as such, has of course no degrees; for it is perfect, and there can be no more or less in perfection." But if the Absolute is perfectly real and statements of it perfectly true, then true statements of anything other than the Absolute must be less true and refer to something less real. It seems odd to say that one thing is less real than another. One would be inclined to think that a thing is either real or not: this chair is real; ghosts never are. But it is easy to see Bradley's difficulty. Either every statement must be of the Absolute or some must be less true than others. The same consideration must be applied to existence. Properly speaking only the Absolute exists, and you, I, and the gatepost exist only partially.

No propositions are adequate to the Absolute; and Bradley must say, "There will be no truth which is entirely true, just as there will be no error which is totally false. With all alike, if taken strictly, it will be a question of amount, and will be a matter of more or less." But even this doctrine must have a proviso: "Our thoughts certainly, for some purposes, may be taken as wholly false, or again as quite accurate; but truth and error, measured by the Absolute, must each be subject always to degree."

Bradley discussed morality in his *Ethical Studies* (1876). In *Appearance and Reality*, he treats goodness as a metaphysical category. One might ask the question, "Is the Absolute good?" The answer is that good is an incomplete category, simply one aspect of perfection. Beauty, truth, and so on are good, but they are something else besides. Good is limited in its scope; but, limited, it cannot be a property of the Absolute. "Goodness, as such, is but appearance which is transcended in the Absolute."

Surely, then, the Absolute must be God. But the God of religion must be an object to man. The God of religion must be available. But if he has these properties, then he is appearance. The logic of development in Bradley's metaphysics cannot be suspended even for God. If God is another name for the Absolute, then he is unavailable to man. But if he is not the Absolute then he is subordinate to it. The God of religion must remain in the world of appearances.

Thus religion would have little to recommend it if it were knowledge. The essential factor in religion is not knowledge. It is, Bradley says, "the attempt to express the complete reality of goodness through every aspect of our being."

Most of the doctrines that we have attributed to Bradley have been negative. Many of the things in which we most firmly believe have turned out to be appearances, half-truths at best. But only the Absolute is true. What can we say about it? We can only approach a description of the Absolute because no statements are infinite as statements of this sort would have to be. The Absolute is perfection. Insofar as a statement approaches perfection, insofar as the system approaches completeness, our statements become more nearly true. A statement will be more nearly complete to the extent that its opposite is inconceivable. A statement is inconceivable when its truth would falsify a system of truths. Thus a true statement is one related to other truths within a system, and the more comprehensive the system, the more nearly true the statement.

Truth about the Absolute is only one part of the Absolute itself. Truth refers to statements that are abstract, but the Absolute itself is reality and concrete. Philosophy, the concern of which is truth, can only hope to be partial at best. Bradley says, "Truth, when made adequate to Reality, would be so supplemented as to have become something else—something other than truth, and something for us unattainable." But there are degrees of truth; and insofar as their limits are determined, truths are genuine.

In an early chapter of *Appearance and Reality*, Bradley tells us that "what is *possible*, and what a general principle compels us to say *must be*, that certainly *is*." There is some sense in which this statement is the key to what Bradley does in *Appearance and Reality*. His sharp, critical mind led him to reject much of what common sense would admit. The few principles that remain he accepted reluctantly because they seemed to him impervious to attack. What could he construct with the material that he had left? Logical necessity led him into a world in which none of us can feel at home, a world which transcends the scope of philosophy and even of language.—*J. Co.*

PERTINENT LITERATURE
Wollheim, Richard. *F. H. Bradley*. Baltimore: Penguin Books, 1959.

This study, although selective, offers a critical appreciation of F. H. Bradley's entire philosophy—logic, epistemology, metaphysics, ethics, and theology. It concentrates on topics and themes germane to contemporary philosophic concerns. While citations of *Appearance and Reality* surface throughout Richard Wollheim's book, Chapter Five is expressly a commentary on this masterpiece.

According to Wollheim, Bradley's principal doctrine is Monism—that the system of reality is one, and, however many different things may be found in the world, there is one vast thing, the World, which contains everything else. Bradley's argument in behalf of Monism is twofold: (1) that pluralism is untenable—in other words, the existence of many realities is impossible, and (2) that there can be but one Substance.

On the impossibility of many realities, Bradley's argument is primarily negative. It operates in the first part of *Appearance and Reality*, where Bradley demolished *seriatim* the categories of common sense and traditional philosophy—quality, relation, space, time, motion and change, causation, thing, even the self. The key target of Bradley's negative dialectic is relation, for as Wollheim shows not only in Chapter Five but also in other parts of his book, relation is fundamental to discursive thought and is implicated in all the other traditional categories. Bradley's gravamen against relations rests on his classification of them into two kinds: (1) external and (2) internal. As external, relations lie outside their terms, and so cannot relate them without intervening relations *ad infinitum*. As internal, a relation falls inside one of the terms and so fails to link this term with any other. Hence, the category of relation is self-contradictory, so that realities cannot be related to one another, as pluralism affirms. Since, moreover, discursive thought involves relations, it too proves inadequate to penetrate reality, which, to be self-consistent, must be suprarelational. All self-contradictory entities and relations are for Bradley appearances. Bradley's ultimate thrust on relations and all other appearances is that as contents they find their ground in a self-consistent whole that includes them. In this sense Bradley favored the theory of the internality of relations. As Wollheim contends, this doctrine lends support to Bradley's monistic metaphysics of Substance.

In using the term "Substance" to designate Bradley's Monism, Wollheim correctly points out that the philosopher himself never used the term in this way; Bradley's preferred term is the Absolute. However, Wollheim believes that the category of substance, as employed, for example, by Benedictus de Spinoza, soundly represents Bradley's metaphysical intentions. Thus Wollheim construes Bradley's "Reality" to be one substance that underlies and embraces all particular things, which are termed "appearances." Nevertheless, it does not follow that these appearances are illusions to be disregarded in any final account of reality. Rather, appearances exist; they are appearances of Reality; they are parts of the whole, attributes of the one Substance. It follows that to the extent that discursive thought centers on particular things, appearances, without regard for the whole, it falls short of adequate and valid cognition.

Wollheim's immediate philosophical heritage is the realistic, analytic tradition that stems from G. E. Moore and Bertrand Russell. From the perspective of this tradition, he explores and critically evaluates Bradley's arguments. Yet he does not ignore or lightly dismiss these arguments; he provides instead a judicious accounting of the philosopher's dialectical hits and misses. Noteworthy is his scrutiny of Bradley's equation of the Absolute, Reality, Substance with idealistic content—"experience" being Bradley's preferred term. He finds that Bradley's arguments for idealism are derived from George Berkeley and consequently share the strengths and weaknesses of the Berkeleyan philosophy. At the same time he insists on the singularity of Bradley's philosophical position.

Wollheim distinguishes two major groups of metaphysicians. One group is made up of those who contend that our beliefs are mistaken, and who consequently propose to direct our understanding to discover or construct new, valid beliefs to replace the inherited, bankrupt ones. The other group consists of those metaphysicians who maintain that our beliefs are correct but are misunderstood, and who undertake, therefore, to amend our understanding so that our beliefs may be properly understood. According to Wollheim, Bradley belongs to neither group. It is not our beliefs but our vision that Bradley seeks to correct, so that we "see the whole world—knowledge, and knowledge of knowledge, and the object of knowledge—in a new light."

Church, Ralph Withington. *Bradley's Dialectic*. Ithaca, New York: Cornell University Press, 1942.

This difficult but rewarding volume is an intensive study of F. H. Bradley's masterpiece. It is packed with quotations, interwoven with elucidations and commentary. Primarily, Ralph Withington Church intends to explicate the essential nature of Bradley's dialectic. Secondarily, he subjects Bradley's dialectic to criticism.

Church demonstrates that Bradley's dialectic, while derivative from G. W. F. Hegel, contains novel features. Bradley rejected the Law of Identity, expressed as "A is A," on the grounds that it is an inane tautology. The only kind of identity that he acknowledged is dialectical identity in difference. He also revised the Law of Non-Contradiction, repudiating the logic of contradictories and installing the dialectic of contraries. Clarification is required to grasp Church's very dense, abstruse argument. Contradiction is illustrated in the following formula where "S" stands for a subject and "P" for a predicate: "All S is P" is contradicted by "Some S is not P." Contrariety may be expressed by "All S is P" and "No S is P." Or, simply put, contradiction is represented by "S" and "not-S"; contrariety by "S" and "non-S". Thus Bradley admitted a middle term between any two coopponents and consequently also rejected the Law of Excluded Middle. By means of his dialectic of contrariety, according to Church, Bradley attacked all traditional categories, conventional things, qualities, and relations. He argued that they are discrepant intrinsically and also discrepant with one another, and concluded that they are not realities but appearances.

Church retraces Bradley's dialectic as it dissolves relation, quality, space, time, and thing into appearances. He takes Bradley's dialectical dissolution of relation into unreality as paradigmatic for the treatment of appearances. He further examines Bradley's conception of the real as the self-consistent, his coherence theory of truth and reality, and his climactic thesis that reality is the Absolute interpreted idealistically as Experience.

Bradley sought to save appearances by considering them to be appearances of the Absolute. As fundamental and pervasive appearances, qualities and relations are moments of experience. Relations are moments wherein immediacy recedes and mediation (or undifferentiation) dominates; conversely, qualities are moments wherein immediacy dominates and mediation recedes. Hence Appearance, as the summary totality of appearances, may be viewed as a process of becoming or development, with all qualities and relations moving toward a comprehensive embrace, a systematic network of moments of immediacy related by their differences.

How, then, are the many relational, mediated, discrepant appearances united with the sole, suprarelational, unmediated reality as Absolute? It is tempting to reply to this question by suggesting that the Absolute is simply the systematic totality of appearances. According to Church, however, Bradley rejected this solution. Instead of finding the Absolute by means of intellect and then intelligibly relating it to appearances, Bradley confessed that his own intellect fell short in this regard, and he concluded that the Absolute is a whole not merely of but beyond thought, a suprarelational Experience. Thus Church admits that it is difficult to see how, for Bradley, the Absolute may in any sense be related to its appearances.

Church devotes Chapter VIII of his study to an examination of some basic difficulties in Bradley's dialectic. He observes that Bradley's metaphysics is ultimately monistic and that the validity of the monism depends upon the theory of relations and the dialectic of quality and relation. Difference relates; identity differentiates. Every quality, by virtue of its internal relatedness within the whole, is unique. Although Bradley denied that the uniqueness of a quality is numerical only, Church suggests that the dialectic does not foreclose number as the sole criterion of uniqueness, and this, in turn, jeopardizes the doctrine of the Absolute as the concrete universal that is the sole Individual. Furthermore, Church criticizes Bradley for lacking criteria for the coherence theory of truth and of reality, with its corollary theory of degrees. He denies that Bradley's appeal to self-consistency as the criterion of reality fulfilled in the conception of the Absolute will serve, for the relation of the Absolute to appearances remains essentially the unanswered question at issue.

Saxena, Sushil Kumar. *Studies in the Metaphysics of Bradley*. New York: Humanities Press, 1967.

This sympathetic but penetrating work focuses on F. H. Bradley's metaphysics. Sushil Kumar Saxena presents studies of Bradley's conception of metaphysics, his definitions of reality and appearance, his position on immediate experience, his theory of relational form, his account of the relation of thought and reality, and his doctrine of the Absolute. He takes pains to examine thoroughly and to respond in detail to the main objections and criticisms that have been raised against Bradley by such distinguished philosophers and commentators as G. E. Moore, Bertrand Russell, A. C. Ewing, James Ward, Ralph Withington Church, C. A. Campbell, Morris Lazerowitz, and Richard Wollheim. He also endeavors to illuminate the relevance of Bradley's thought to contemporary metaphysics.

Bradley's commitment to metaphysics sprang from his quest for a system that transcends all particular regions of thought and experience treated by the special sciences, as well as by the institutions of art, morality, and religion. This system, moreover, promises an inclusive unity that is self-consistent, unlike the subordinate regions, each of which is permeated with contradiction. In metaphysics Bradley sought to go beyond ordinary experience, common sense, and the traditional categories of thought, for these are self-contradictory and fragmentary; he strove for ultimate reality, which is consistent and inclusive.

Bradley's program, therefore, seems to be totally at odds with the plain sense of human beings who esteem ordinary things, processes, and events as realities. It seems to dismiss this commonsense world as illusory. Saxena meticulously canvasses Bradley's various usages of the terms "appearance" and "reality" to refute the claim that the philosopher reduced the commonsense world to illusion. On the contrary, Bradley distinguished "existence" from "reality." While things, processes, and events in this world as we ordinarily experience and understand them are not real, since they are proven to be self-contradictory, nevertheless they exist. Hence they are not illusions, although they are appearances. By means of dialectic they are shown to be unreal, although existent. This is tantamount to driving thought to find their ground in some higher, inclusive, self-consistent reality that appears through and in them. Thus appearances exist, serving as the subject matter on which thought operates dialectically in its quest for reality. Bradley's name for reality as self-consistent and all-inclusive is, of course, the Absolute.

Saxena probes the relation of experience and thought to the Absolute and also the relation of the Absolute to its appearances. Immediate experience fuses its contents without relations; it portends the sort of form the Absolute would have. At the same time immediate experience is always particular and partial; it invites the reflection of thought and the function of understanding.

Thus immediate experience becomes the material of thought, and thought proceeds by means of relations. Relation, as Saxena and other commentators contend, is the central category in Bradley's negative dialectic. When it is shown to be self-contradictory and therefore appearance, all experience and thought fall with it. Saxena traces Bradley's dialectic in this regard, but he does not succumb to the line of criticism which maintains that, since thought is inherently relational, it must commit suicide in order to attain suprarelational reality. Rather, he attempts to show that thought is logically stimulated by the appearances to seek the reality beyond them. Thought's indication of a transcendent Absolute that embraces it and all other appearances is not suicidal death, but consummation.

How is the Absolute related to its appearances? This question is posed, in the first place, in terms of the self-contradictory category of relation and also from the standpoint of finite appearances. Since we never can, in our finitude, reach the standpoint of the Absolute except as an idea, we can never precisely explain how the Absolute contains its appearances, or why it appears at all. But given the appearances, we can, Saxena argues in the footsteps of Bradley, understand that they are appearances and that their existence demands that they be grounded in a consistent, inclusive reality. Although for Bradley Experience and not vacuous Being is the term appropriate to the nature of the Absolute, Saxena detects in Bradley's argument for the Absolute a stand of metaphysical thought akin to Martin Heidegger's quest for Being.—*A.J.R.*

ADDITIONAL RECOMMENDED READING

Campbell, C. A. *Scepticism and Construction*. London: George Allen & Unwin, 1931. A critique by a major British philosopher who calls into question Bradley's conception of the Absolute.

Cunningham, G. Watts. *The Idealistic Argument in Recent British and American Philosophy*. New York and London: The Century Company, 1933. An expository and critical account of Bradley's philosophy and its place in recent Anglo-American idealism.

Eliot, T. S. *Knowledge and Experience in the Philosophy of F. H. Bradley*. New York: Farrar, Straus and Company, 1965. The officially approved doctoral dissertation by the famous Anglo-American poet, who was never awarded the degree because he did not return to Harvard for its oral defense.

Muirhead, John H. *The Platonic Tradition in Anglo-Saxon Philosophy*. London: George Allen & Unwin, 1931, pp. 257-273. One of five chapters on Bradley's philosophy, devoted to a critical but appreciative interpretation of *Appearance and Reality* as an epoch-making articulation of Hegelian Idealism.

Reck, Andrew J. *Speculative Philosophy*. Albuquerque: University of New

Mexico Press, 1972, pp. 170-175. A brief sketch of Bradley's system as a variant of idealism.

Vander Veer, Garrett L. *Bradley's Metaphysics and the Self*. New Haven, Connecticut: Yale University Press, 1970. A constructive study that brings Bradley's metaphysics into contact with contemporary discussion.

COLLECTED ESSAYS

Author: Thomas Henry Huxley (1825-1895)
Type of work: Epistemology, ethics, philosophy of science
First published: 1893-1894 (in nine volumes)

PRINCIPAL IDEAS ADVANCED

Not only has science had practical benefits, but also it has brought about a revolution in man's conception of man and of his place in the universe.

Education is learning the rules of the game of life; the educated man possesses skills, a trained intellect, and knowledge of facts; but he is no ascetic.

There is but one kind of knowledge, and that is to be found in the verifiable conclusions of the natural sciences.

Although all life has a protoplasmic basis, it is an error to conclude that materialism is superior to spiritualism; the fact is that both theories involve empty and unverifiable conceptions.

It is wrong for a man to say that he is certain of the truth of a proposition unless he can produce evidence, and it is wrong to demand belief from others when evidence is not available to substantiate the belief.

Nature is nonmoral; to make progress man cannot count on evolutionary processes; he must use his best energies and his intelligence.

Huxley was a surgeon by profession, whose original investigations into natural history led to his election in 1850 to the Royal Society and to his appointment in 1854 to a lectureship at the School of Mines. But after the publication of Charles Darwin's epoch-making work in 1859, Huxley renounced whatever ambition to scientific fame he might have cherished in order to devote himself to the task of promoting a general increase in scientific knowledge, "to the popularization of science; to the development and organization of scientific education; to the endless series of battles and skirmishes over evolution; and to untiring opposition to that ecclesiastical spirit, that clericalism, which . . . is the deadly enemy of science." The papers which make up the *Collected Essays* were written over a period of thirty years and were brought together by their author near the close of his life.

Undoubtedly Huxley's fundamental motivation was humanitarian. He believed that man ought to take an active part in improving his own condition, and it was plain to him that the increase of natural knowledge was the only effective means. But he rejected the view that science is merely "a sort of comfort-grinding machine." In an early essay entitled "On the Advisableness of Improving Natural Knowledge," he maintained that science "has not only conferred practical benefits on men, but, in so doing, has effected a revolution in their conceptions of the universe and of themselves, and has profoundly altered their modes of thinking and their views of right and wrong." The vision of the infinite magnitude of space and of the endless modifications of life, with every atom determined in a fixed order by an unchanging causation, satisfied Huxley's "spiritual cravings"; and the stern demands imposed upon man's intellect by the increasing hazards of the human condition seemed to him "the foundations of new morality." With it all, there was a note of sadness, but, according to Huxley, such is the essence of all religion—"this consciousness of the limitation of man, this sense of an open secret which he cannot penetrate."

It was clear to Huxley that science had opened the door to a new era in human history. He saw, moreover, some of the perils which technological advancement holds for nations which are not sufficiently matured in spirit to assume the responsibilities which material progress brings in its train. In his view, compulsory primary education was an imminent necessity. It was needed in order to prove trained leadership in proportion to the increased demands of the new age. But it was also needed in order to save society from the danger of revolution by a miserable and ignorant proletariat.

When the Education Act of 1870 was being debated, Huxley wrote an essay entitled "Administrative Nihilism," in which he argued against laissez faire individualists who were opposed to involving the state in education. He quoted John Locke (*Of Civil Government*), who had said, "The end of Government is the Good of Mankind," and he went on to maintain that the general welfare demands new kinds of legislation to meet changing times. "I take it," he said, "that the good of mankind means the attainment, by every man, of all the happiness which he can enjoy without diminishing the happiness of his fellows." He admitted that it is unnecessary and undesirable for the state to undertake directly to increase either the material prosperity of its people or their personal happiness. But he thought that, just as there are indirect ways in which legislation aids industry and commerce, so there are indirect ways in which it can aid the improvement of morals and the advancement of art and science, among the most patent of which is the education of the young.

Huxley was not merely concerned to make education more widely accessible. It seemed to him that in the age of science important revisions had to be made in what is taught. In this connection, he undertook to redefine "A Liberal Education." Life, he said, is like a game in which every man's happiness depends upon knowing the rules. "Education is learning the rules of this mighty game. In other words, education is the instruction of the intellect in the laws of Nature . . . and the fashioning of the affections and of the will into an earnest and loving desire to move in harmony with those laws." He explained that when he spoke of the laws of Nature, he included those which govern the behavior of men, so that he was not to be understood as favoring the physical sciences to the exclusion of the social. Moreover, as a man of great breadth and depth of "culture," in Matthew Arnold's sense of the word, he insisted on the importance of literature and history, and sanctioned what is called the "education of taste." He saw the educated man as one possessing bodily skills, a trained intellect, a mind well supplied with facts—"one who, no stunted ascetic, is full of life and fire, but whose passions are trained to come to heel by a vigorous will, the servant of a tender conscience; who has learned to love all beauty, whether of Nature or of art, to hate all vileness, and to respect others as himself." Such, he said, was the goal of a "liberal education."

To the view, prevalent in literary and academic circles, that a liberal education is synonymous with instruction in humane letters, Huxley opposed two propositions. The first was that knowledge of Greek and Roman antiquity does not have as much direct value, either in terms of its subject matter or in terms of the mental discipline which it demands, as a comparable training in the physical sciences. The second was that, supposing one must choose between an exclusively scientific education and an exclusively literary education, the former is at least as effectual as the latter "for the purpose of attaining real culture." In fact, Huxley saw no need of making education so exclusive. The omission of the classical languages, said he, is not incompatible with the mastery of the mother tongue and the reading of the Bible, Shakespeare, and Milton, whom he thought not inferior to Homer and Vergil. Huxley rejected the distinction between pure and applied science, maintaining that the latter is "nothing but the application of pure science to particular classes of problems." He did not envisage the new scientific colleges, which were then coming into existence, as narrow trade schools. "Industry," he said, "is a means and not an end." And he saw it as one of the main functions of education to enlarge men's minds, so as to ennoble their aspirations and enhance their capacities for higher goods, notably the pleasures of the mind. But, he argued, in the age of Newton and Darwin the mind which is not trained to think scientifically is more impoverished than one which is ignorant of Greek.

Classical education, however, had not formed the mind of the larger British public. And in Huxley's view, the most serious obstacle to intellectual and social advance came not from traditional education but from popular religion. The issue, for all practical purposes, was the conflict between naturalism and supernaturalism. In an article called "The Progress of Science," Huxley maintained that there is only one kind of knowledge—the kind shared by the physical sciences, namely, physics, chemistry, and biology. These all have the same objective, "the discovery of the rational order which pervades the universe," and the same method, that "of observation and experiment for the determination of the facts of Nature; of inductive and deductive reasoning for the discovery of their mutual relations and connections." Futhermore, they rest on the same three assumptions which, strictly speaking, are indemonstrable, but which have vindicated themselves in terms of the results they make possible. These are the existence of an "extended, impenetrable, mobile substance" termed matter; "the universality of the law of causation"; and the eternal validity of the "laws of Nature." Natural sciences, said Huxley, deserve the name of knowledge because their findings are verifiable. And he pleaded with his age to lay aside the consideration of any hypotheses which are unverifiable.

Although Huxley spoke the language of materialism, he preserved a sophisticated attitude toward this language, which he saw as being merely symbolical, "the aid by which Nature can be interpreted in terms apprehensible by our intellects." In an essay entitled "On the Physical Basis of Life," he said that, judging from the direction biology was taking, he saw no alternative to concluding that all life has a protoplasmic basis. At the same time, he protested that he himself was not a materialist. He believed that materialism is a grave error because it involves an unverifiable, empty conception of matter. "What do we know," he asks, "about this terrible 'matter', except as a name for an unknown and hypothetical cause of states of our own consciousness? . . . And what is the dire necessity and 'iron' law under which men groan? Truly, most gratuitously invented bugbears." The argument for using "materialistic terminology" is that this way of thinking of the world has made possible the discovery of truths of Nature, "whereas the alternative, or spiritualistic, terminology is utterly barren, and leads to nothing but obscurity and confusion of ideas."

Huxley's position was essentially the same as that which Herbert Spencer had outlined under the heading of "The Unknowable," in his *First Principles*. By suspending judgment about ultimate being, Huxley avoided systematic materialism, with its implicit threat to moral responsibility. At the same time, he was delivered from the necessity of admitting spiritual entities into the naturalistic account of the world. If our minds are not capable of knowing ultimate being, he argued, we are no more justified in calling it spirit than in calling it matter. Let it remain out of bounds for human inquiry, particularly in view of the fact that the kind of knowledge which science gives us is ample for our needs.

These views Huxley shared with many nineteenth century positivists. His characteristic contribution was to grace them with a name—agnosticism. In a piece by that name, he gave an amusing account of the origin of the word. When he was accustomed to attend meetings of a certain Metaphysical Society, where everyone else was an-*ist* of one kind or another, he felt like the proverbial fox which had lost its tail. "So I took thought, and invented what I conceived to be the appropriate title of 'agnostic.' It came into my head as suggestively antithetic to the 'gnostic' of Church history, who professed to know so much about the very things of which I was ignorant; and I took the earliest opportunity of parading it at our Society, to show that I, too, had a tail like the other foxes." In a later article, "Agnosticism and Christianity," he went on to explain precisely what the term stands for. An agnostic, he said, is not simply an unbeliever, much less one who from indifference or sloth has not troubled to inform himself about higher matters. His is the ethical or intellectual principle "that it is wrong for a man to say that he is certain of the objective truth of any proposition unless he can produce evidence which logically justifies that certainty." Huxley was more cautious, in this respect, than Spencer and many of the positivists, inasmuch as he did not wish to lay it down as a dogma that no knowledge of ultimate reality is possible. However, he confessed that knowledge of ultimate reality was beyond him, much though he regretted it, and he was tolerably certain that it was beyond everyone else. Huxley was especially vexed with ecclesiastics who maintained that it is wrong not to believe certain dogmas, no matter what evidence science brings against them, and he saw it as compounding the "abomination" when they further declared that their doctrines must be taught, even if they are not true, on the grounds that they are necessary for morality. "Surely the attempt to cast out Beelzebub by the aid of Beelzebub is a hopeful procedure as compared to that of preserving morality by the aid of immorality. . . . The course of the past has impressed us with the firm conviction that no good ever comes of falsehood."

In the popular mind, the great issue between science and religion in Huxley's day centered about evolution. Huxley was unambiguously on the side of the latter. He had rejected pre-Darwinian theories of evolution as being purely speculative, but when Darwin brought forward the theory of natural selection, Huxley embraced it as providing for the first time a hypothesis which made evolution scientifically verifiable. Still, he was never completely convinced that Darwin's hypothesis was correct. In 1892, he wrote, "That the doctrine of natural selection presupposes evolution is quite true; but it is not true that evolution necessarily implies natural selection." What stood out in his mind at that time was not any particular explanation as to the origin of species, but a great body of facts all tending to the same conclusion: embryology attested that the evolution of individual plants and animals is taking place every day; and paleontology attested that species arose in just those morphological relations in which they would have arisen supposing that evolution had taken place. To these facts, he said, "all future philosophical and theological speculations will have to accommodate themselves."

With the example of such men as Herbert Spencer and Ernst Haeckel before him, Huxley repudiated anything that could be called a "philosophy of evolution." Attempts to construct such a philosophy might be admirable but, in his opinion, they were premature. In particular he opposed attempts to give an evolutionary account of ethics, as Spencer and others were doing.

Nature, Huxley insisted, is nonmoral. When we study it with our minds, we find cause for admiration; but when we view it in terms of our moral sympathies, we can only shudder. The Mother-goddess of middle Eastern cults, in whom were combined the attributes both of generation and of destruction, seemed to him a fairly accurate representation of nature. This conception preserved a healthy balance between the optimism which supposes that the world exists to make man happy, and the pessimism which concludes that it makes happiness impossible.

According to Huxley, man, in becoming civilized, has ventured on an undertaking for which he alone is responsible and for which he can expect no help or sympathy. Everywhere in nature, the struggle for existence goes on, unrelieved by generosity or scruple; and originally the human species, like every other, must have been engaged in "a Hobbesian war of each against all." But civilization, or what we call society, is man's attempt to escape from that condition by setting limits to the struggle. In return for exercising self-restraint and cooperating with his fellows, man not merely satisfies his biological needs more adequatley than he could do in a savage state; entirely new dimensions are opened to him. But, in Huxley's view, of these the cosmos knows nothing. He rejected the argument that moral propensities are the result of evolutionary processes, pointing out that immoral propensities are no less so. And to the supposition that the struggle for survival, if permitted to continue, will automatically bring men to ethical perfection, he replied that the kind of fitness which enables an organism to survive bears no relation to the human ideal.

If men want to preserve civilization, Huxley argued, they must devote to it their best energies and intelligence. Distinguishing evolution from progress, he deplored the mental confusion of persons who made the principle of survival of the fittest an argument for competition within society. In his view, man's survival demands more cooperation and more planning; and he declared his faith that "intelligence and will, guided by sound principles of investigation, and organized in common effort, may modify the conditions of existence. . . . And much may be done to change the nature of man himself." One of the problems which he said demanded attention was that of overpopulation. Nature overpopulates itself, and this is one of the causes of the struggle for survival. If man is to eliminate war and famine, he must take in hand the problem of stabilizing the population.

In the end, Huxley admitted, the cosmic process must defeat the human enterprise. Like Spencer, he held that evolution is counterbalanced by dissolution. Civilizations rise and fall. So do planetary systems. To this grander prospect Huxley responded in Stoic fashion. "We should cast aside the notion that escape from pain and sorrow is the proper object of life." It is time, he said, to put away youthful confidence, but without plunging, like so many nineteenth century men of letters, into "the no less youthful discouragement of nonage." As mature men, strong in will, we must cherish the good that falls our way, and bear the evil "with stout hearts set on diminishing it."
—J.F.

PERTINENT LITERATURE

Shafer, Robert. "Huxley," in *Christianity and Naturalism*. New Haven, Connecticut: Yale University Press, 1926, pp. 121-155.

Since World War II, philosophical naturalism has attracted little attention. This was not the case in 1926. Robert Shafer, who views naturalism as a protest not so much against supernaturalism as such as against "the supernatural conceived as arbitrary, incoherent, and chaotic," finds it as old as philosophy and predicts that in some form it will persist as long as men construct philosophical systems. It has supported material progress and has freed men's minds from irrational fears and imaginary dangers. On the other hand, its implicit claim that human intelligence can comprehend the universe runs counter to many enduring facts of life which are recognized and given sound meaning in historic Christianity, although, according to Shafer, one need not be a Christian to be fully alive to the inner substance of its message.

Shafer sees Thomas Henry Huxley as a controversial writer, excelling as a lecturer and essayist, but lacking in depth and above all in consistency. One who reads the *Collected Essays* looking for guidance is confronted with several Huxleys, says Shafer, two of which stand out.

First, there is Huxley the apostle of truth, the teacher of men, as his first biographer called him. Huxley's training in science seemed to him, as it did to others, a royal road, just opened to travel, which would lead to the only correct interpretation of life. His problems arose from the fact that, professing to follow truth with an unprejudiced mind, he was in reality pledging himself to the special view which the world presents to our external senses. Moreover, in spite of his professed empiricism, Huxley unconsciously embraced such rationalistic assumptions as that the universe is one and the same throughout and that there is no ultimate difference between organic and inorganic matter and between matter and consciousness. Although he liked to say that the foundation of morality is to have done with lying, he suffered from a serious inability to understand himself. Consequences followed from his scientific world view that he himself could not avow. Shafer cites from an essay in which Huxley says that men are conscious automata, free only in the sense that without interrupting the chain of natural causation we are sometimes "able to do as we like." In the same essay he compares consciousness to the whistle of a locomotive, indicative of change but not itself a causal factor. This all had the ring of scientific truth. In other essays, however, Huxley discussed human conduct in terms which presuppose the power of will and intelligence to modify behavior, silently admitting the falsity of his claim that a single causal order reigns throughout the universe.

Huxley's much-publicized break with evolutionary ethics was a more or less open repudiation of his monistic philosophy. At the same time, it shows him relaxing the rules of empirical science and appealing to inner guidance. Humanitarian sympathy, moral purity, patience, nobility—these for Huxley were part of an ideal which every man ought to reverence and want to realize. Huxley, when asked why, appealed to moral intuition; the truth, he said, was self-evident.

The other Huxley that claims Shafer's attention is the shrewd debater. This was Huxley the skeptic, or, as he came to call himself, the agnostic. Although not trained in philosophy, Huxley had studied René Descartes' *Discourse on Method*; and when it suited him, he would say that the only certainty a person ever has is "that at any given moment the feeling which he has exists." He was also familiar with David Hume's *A Treatise of Human Nature* and, in order to fend off the charge of having a closed mind, he would make the astonishing claim that, for all we can know, anything is possible at any time. When discussing human immortality, he said that he had no *a priori* reasons for not believing that the soul survives the death of the body: the fact that we have not been able to float on clouds in the past is no reason for believing that we shall not be able to do so in the future. Such knowledge as we command depends on evidence which the mind can comprehend and test. If this is true of the small difficulties which the experimenter succeeds in resolving in his laboratory, one can hardly expect the great mysteries of life and death to be opened to him on easier terms. Shafer finds the argument less than candid, coming from a man who has already made up his mind that what we call consciousness is dependent on the activity of the brain.

Huxley put on much the same act in dealing with the supernatural element in the gospels. A person has no more right to believe that the world is haunted by demons than to believe that the south pole swarms with sea serpents. The scientist, he says, is always open to conviction; but he may decline to waste his time investigating old wives' tales and forecastle yarns. This comes off somewhat better, in Shafer's opinion. Still, for a distinguished paleontologist to say that he is open to conviction on the subject of sea serpents, and for an avowed enemy of superstition to say that he suspends judgment in respect to evil spirits strikes Shafer as disingenuous because it obscures the distinction between not believing something and disbelieving it. Honest skepticism, says Shafer, would have served Huxley well; but he never learned that his own views needed sifting as well as those of his opponents. For him, skepticism was merely a weapon that he used in shielding his sacred verities.

Shafer does not belittle Huxley's courage or the nobility of his purpose in single-handedly attacking widespread superstition and prejudice. Huxley's achievement in overthrowing the biblical view of creation and establishing evolutionism in its place accords him permanent recognition. It was when he attempted a theory of knowledge and a philosophy of culture in naturalistic terms that he ran into trouble.

Paradis, James G. *T. H. Huxley: Man's Place in Nature*. Lincoln: University of Nebraska Press, 1978.

"Man's Place in Nature" was the title of Thomas Henry Huxley's first book. However, James G. Paradis uses the phrase to designate not the book but the problem, which was to hold a central place in Huxley's lectures and essays for thirty years after the book appeared. Huxley was by no means alone in his concern with the significance of the sciences for our understanding of human nature: Thomas Carlyle, before Charles Darwin's breakthrough, and Matthew Arnold and Thomas Hardy after the event, dealt with the same problem. Huxley was unique among major writers of the time mainly because he insisted that the scientist rather than the poet or novelist or literary critic was the person best prepared to deal with the question.

Paradis notes that the scientist, as a pure, disinterested seeker after truth, was Huxley's invention, and that he strove religiously to realize the ideal in his own person. Huxley was also a scientist in the specialized sense: his contributions in the fields of botany and zoology were recognized by men such as Darwin. But the scientist who came forward as a public lecturer and essayist was a generalist, his ancestry going back to Francis Bacon, whose famous classification of the sciences made a point of bringing natural history and human history under one head. For several years Huxley compiled notes for what was to have been a systematic work that would comprehend both man's biological development and the history of human culture. But the project fell by the wayside. According to Paradis, Huxley was not a systematic thinker, able to bring widely different aspects of experience together in a harmonious synthesis, but rather a visionary in whose imagination the world appeared as an orderly whole. Paradis' book traces the development of Huxley's thought, showing the transition it underwent from youthful romanticism, through physical determinism, to *fin-de-siècle* disillusionment.

Huxley's equivalent to Alfred Tennyson's "Flower in the crannied wall" was the cell under a microscope: by extrapolation one might know, within the limits of our understanding, ". . . what God and man is." Paradis finds the key to this idealization of nature in Huxley's 1860 lecture, "A Lobster," where, after reporting on recent studies in embryology which showed that organisms as different as man and fish appear identical in their early stages, he went on to declare that "unity of plan everywhere lies hidden under the mask of diversity of structure." The lobster machine is integral to an order which in its harmony and perfection man's mind can only dimly apprehend.

With this vision before him, Huxley called upon his audience to discard their anthropocentric prejudices, to tear down the artificial wall of civilization, and to recognize that the natural is the ideal, that the cosmic order is more just than the human, that health and happiness can come only through conformity to nature's laws. Man's place in nature is miniscule: it was absurd to suppose that our species is in any sense privileged. Paradis calls this aspect of Huxley's thought "scientific Calvinism."

Problems arose when the vision was subjected to analysis. First, there were questions of methodology. As Huxley recognized, his ideal nature was a fusion of two concepts: the empirically founded order studied by science, and the transcendent order demanded by reason. Huxley insisted that the unities described by the zoologist are not simply man's way of looking at things but are "the expression of deep-seated natural facts." Nevertheless, says Paradis, he was aware of having posited a perfection in nature that could only be called an act of faith. The agnostic principle, as Paradis views it, was largely an attempt to reconcile the experiential and speculative parts of Huxley's philosophy.

Second, there were metaphysical questions. In the scientific vision there was no place for Mind, and almost no place for minds. This changed. Huxley went so far as to admit that the phenomena which the scientist investigates are in the last analysis known only as acts of consciousness; on the other hand, he maintained that what is given to us in consciousness is practically knowable only by the formulae of physics. Moreover, in a paper written shortly before his death, he introduced teleology into his vision and made a place for Cosmic Mind, objectively present in physical nature and conscious of itself in the human mind. In another paper, comparing the universe to a kaleidoscope, he spoke with enthusiasm of the beatitude with which a pure intelligence might be filled on contemplating the mathematical symmetry which governs physical change.

Third, there were ethical questions. In his figure of the kaleidoscope, Huxley was careful to specify that his ideal observer must be free from the experience of pain, whether sensible or moral. Man, of course, is not free from these experiences; and, more and more, especially in the final years of his life, Huxley faced up to the fact that intellectual abstractions distorted his account of man's place in nature. For practical purposes at least, the scientist must leave his observer's station to lend a hand in repairing the walls of civilization and in doing so must view the world through the visor of a man. In a section entitled "Revolt Against Nature," Paradis shows how completely Huxley left behind the Baconian hope of fitting civil history into natural history. That consciousness makes a difference was all too clear; volition is a fact that must be taken into account. The structuring impulses of man, all of a type, are found in no other animals. In effect, the human enterprise is antagonistic to nature, this appearing even in the human psyche, where the ethical sense is at war with animal impulses. How this could be, Huxley left veiled in mystery. If the antagonism of a part of nature to the whole poses logical difficulties, "I feel sorry for logic," Huxley says, "because, as we have seen, the fact is so."—*J.F.*

ADDITIONAL RECOMMENDED READING

Ashforth, Albert. *Thomas Henry Huxley*. New York, Twayne, 1969. Introduction to Huxley's life and evaluation of his achievement as a man of letters.

Ayres, Clarence E. *Huxley*. New York: Norton, 1932. Huxley as the creator of Darwinism, no less than its defender.

Bibby, Cyril. *T. H. Huxley: A Scientist, Humanist, and Educator*. New York: Horizon Press, 1960. Standard biography presenting Huxley mainly as an educational statesman.

Irvine, William. *Apes, Angels, and Victorians: The Story of Darwin, Huxley, and Evolution*. New York: McGraw-Hill Book Company, 1955. A popular narrative account.

Peterson, Houston. *Huxley: Prophet of Science*. New York: Longmans, Green & Company, 1932. A sympathetic picture of Huxley and his scientific and philosophical achievements.

THE SENSE OF BEAUTY

Author: George Santayana (1863-1952)
Type of work: Aesthetics
First published: 1896

PRINCIPAL IDEAS ADVANCED

Our preferences are ultimately nonrational; things are good because they are preferred.

Beauty is pleasure objectified; when a spectator regards his pleasure as a quality of the object he sees, he calls the object "beautiful."

Form pleases when in perception the excitation of the retinal field produces a semblance of motion while the mind synthesizes the elements perceived.

The aesthetic component "expression" is the result of the emotional associations excited by contemplation of the aesthetic object.

George Santayana is one of the few philosophers whose writings have a beauty of style which can be appreciated independently of their philosophical worth. Literary ability should not be taken as a substitute for clarity in presenting ideas; but at his best Santayana had the fortune of combining both well. In this early work not only does he present a provocative account of aesthetics in what may be called a "naturalistic" vein, but in addition he gives an insight into the development of his later metaphysics and ontology.

The Sense of Beauty is divided into four parts. In the opening part Santayana discusses the nature of beauty. He points out that the term "aesthetics" originally meant "perception" and that it was associated, by use, with a particular object of perception and its study, that which we call "the beautiful." This can be put in a different but related manner if we speak of a perceptual quality which we are to analyze; namely, "beauty." Here one should remind himself of words which make use of the "perception" meaning of "aesthetics"; for example, we use the term "kinaesthesis" to refer to a certain sense which our muscles have, and we speak of "anaesthesis" as the loss of our sensations.

To return to the sort of perceptive activity with which this analysis is to be concerned, it should be pointed out that we are not examining the world of facts considered independently of any observer. Such a world is neutral as far as value is concerned, for it is not good (or evil) for any one. Herein we see a basis for Santayana's naturalism. The existence of worth or value depends upon the presence of somebody's consciousness; nature has purpose or growth only in that one values what nature exhibits. Nature is not itself aware of the changes. Since the consciousness that observes must also appreciate if it is to hold patterns of value, there is a nonrational as well as rational basis for our judgment of the world as one in which phenomena are loved or hated. Santayana lays bare his indebtedness to Spinoza and Hume when he proclaims that our preferences regarding the events of the world are ultimately non-rational. Things are good because we prefer them; they are not preferred because they are good.

One should point out, however, that Santayana's view that values must be separated from facts rests upon a distinction which is false in fact. It is not meaningless to contend that we are creatures who have desires because objects in the world provoke our interests; in this sense, it is as much true that we desire things because they are good as that they are good because we desire them. Either philosophical view, the one that says that values are independent of consciousness and intrinsic to the world (the so-called "absolutist position"), or that which claims values wholly dependent upon and relative to the attitudes of subjects, is incomplete and only part of the story.

Santayana goes on to discuss the difference between moral and aesthetic values. The analogy that he draws is between work and play, between duty and amusement. Morality prepares us for the serious aspects of life: death, disease, passion, and, only against the background of these, the possibility of salvation. To seek pleasure, to enjoy experience—these are but futile pursuits, trivial and potentially dangerous against the stark reality of existence. Actions are looked upon in terms of the consequences they will have in preparing us for our stern lives. There is no time to give oneself to the pleasure of an experience enjoyed for its own sake, which aims at nothing else. This attitude toward the world is akin to the biblical attitude toward work; one must labor by the sweat of his brow because of man's first disobedience, which brought death and disease into the world. As the pressures upon a society lessen and it becomes more secure in its struggle with its environment, the seriousness of life lifts and individuals are more likely to take on a holiday air; play and freedom go together and with them the love of immediate pleasures for their own sake, free from fear and independent of consequences. In the distinction between duty and pleasure, work and play, constraint and freedom is to be found the difference between moral and aesthetic values.

In defining beauty, Santayana points out that as a pleasure it has certain peculiar characteristics which allow us to distinguish it from other pleasures. Most pleasures that we get from perceiving (in the wide sense of the term) can be distinguished from the object perceived. We usually go through certain actions before the pleasure is felt. In eating, drinking, inhaling, the activity is entered upon and thereby pleasure follows. There are certain pleasures that seem to occur in the process of perception itself; when this happens to us we then intuit the pleasure as a quality of the thing perceived. Santayana holds that the very mechanism or structure of the mind by which we perceive various qualities as one homogeneous object also objectifies this type of pleasure, as it were, so that it, too, is felt as an integral part of the object. This is the kind of pleasure that is considered to be intrinsic, enjoyable in itself, and, of course, of positive value in the sense that it belongs to the play, holiday, free class rather than to the moral one. For Santayana, beauty is *positive, intrinsic, objectified pleasure* or *pleasure regarded as the quality of a thing*.

Although some hold that in nature we can find such aesthetically pleasant objects, generally speaking it is to man and his creations that we look for objects in which we can take some contemplative pleasure. Santayana has a problem, however, in considering beauty as he does; for if we identify those objects as works of art, we then have the problem of tragedy and of painful works of art. We shall later see how he meets this challenge.

In "The Materials of Beauty," Santayana discusses the substance of beauty—sound, color, and fragrance—as well as other topics concerned with the appeal of our lower senses in relation to the total aesthetic experience. There are those who have argued that the experiences which we must have by *direct* contact with an object (because of the structure of certain parts of our sensorium) cannot be of the beautiful. The bouquet and taste of wine, the touch of brocade, of marble, or sandalwood, are pleasant yet do not seem to be beautiful. Santayana claims, however, that all contribute to the ultimate experience of beauty in that they teach us to appreciate the pleasant, to delight in things sensuous. Those who find the height of aesthetic experience in objects appealing to the eye and ear through their formal structure must recognize that form and meaning can be presented only in something sensible. To divorce content from a work of art is to present something utterly barren.

In the third part of his work, Santayana analyzes form as a main aspect of beauty. In the previous section we noted that certain elements presented to the senses charm or please in themselves. We need look no further than the coolness of a summer breeze to explain the pleasure we feel in its company. But there is a pleasure we encounter which, although immediate and intrinsic, is yet puzzling and perhaps mysterious when we come upon it. There are presented to us objects which have elements none of which is particularly pleasing yet which, because of their arrangement, combination, or pattern, are pleasing. The *form* of the object is the aesthetician's name for it, and he insists that to reduce it to its elements destroys its distinctive, pleasing effect, although without those elements there could not be form.

Santayana turns to the psychology of perception to explain, hypothetically, the pleasure which one derives from form in its various manifestations, as well as to indicate why some forms are either boring or incomplete as visual wholes. (He concentrates on visual form and specifically omits auditory form as too technical to analyze in this work, although he indicates that in principle it should be the same.) Briefly, he claims that the visual image is gathered as a series of sensitive points about the center of the retina. These points or spots each have their peculiar quality of sensation and are associated with the muscular tension and relaxation that occurs with the turning of one's eyes. As the associations are formed they establish a field which is such that when certain elements (or perhaps a single element) are presented to the eye the entire field is excited. The excitation produces a semblance of motion; there is a radiation about the points that tends to re-create the associated image, so that the point leads the mind to the possible field. Various geometrical figures affect the eyes in ways that lead to a graceful and rhythmic completion by the mind (depending to a certain degree, if not entirely, on the figure given) which is pleasing. The muscular movement is not itself smooth, but rather a series of jerks; the visual effect, however, is one of movement full and graceful, combining actual and possible (or perhaps imaginary) rays.

The form presented does not automatically produce a pleasing effect. Because of their gross or tiny size some forms fail to excite the eye and its muscles significantly.

Symmetry is a good example of aesthetic form, where it is an aid to unification, where it helps us to organize, discriminate, and distinguish—in other words, to bring a semblance of harmonic order to a confused or chaotic jumble—the effect is pleasing. Form then may be looked upon as the perception of unity in variety, whereby a conscious and attentive effort, we are able to bring comprehension to what might otherwise not be understood. In this sense, it is an activity of mind as well as of perception. The elements may stimulate and excite, but it is the mind that synthesizes, that has an insight into the order of the elements.

Santayana goes on to discuss various aspects of form which illustrate both its aesthetic value and its dangerous (from an aesthetic point of view) possibilities. There is unity in variety, as noted, but also there is multiplicity in uniformity. The starry skies present to us a picture of an infinite number of similar bodies. The field that is the sky is peppered by a multiplicity of objects that is overwhelming, yet they do not blend into one, for each retains (or at least enough do) its individuality. In its presentation to us the heavens' beauty is increased by the very material composing it—the blackness of the heavens glittering with the light of the stars—so that form and substance are blended in perfect union.

It should be noted that multiplicity as an aesthetic component may lead to boredom and disinterest if not properly presented. The attention span of the individual and his ability to synthesize may be brief when the same elements are given repeatedly. Just as sheer variety becomes another name for confusion, so mulitiplicity is synonymous with dullness when presented for its own sake.

Aestheticians have long pondered the question, "Are all things beautiful?" Santayana addresses himself to this question, and it is not difficult, cued as we are by what has been presented of his system so far, to guess what his reply would be. Since the world independent of consciousness and will would be valueless, and since what is good (or beautiful) depends upon our desires, nothing in principle can be ruled out as a possible object of beauty. One makes a mistake, however, if one concludes from this possibility that everything is equally beautiful. As Santayana states: "All things are not equally beautiful because the subjective bias that discriminates between them is the cause of their being beautiful at all. The principle of personal preference is the same as that of human taste; real and objective beauty, in contrast to a vagary of individuals, means only an affinity to a more prevalent and lasting susceptiblity, a response to a more general and fundamental demand. And the keener discrimination, by which the distance between beautiful and ugly things is increased, far from being a loss of aesthetic insight, is a development of that faculty by the exercise of which beauty comes into the world."

The most important aspect of form, and the one which best expresses Santayana's view, is that in a neutral universe there are elements which are susceptible to the imaginative activity of our mind. By means of such activity the world is constructed by reference to ideals into unities from elements which are diverse in themselves. In this activity lies the basis for the life of reason and contemplation and for the discovery of the world of phenomena which we know and the beauty which it has. Although a naturalist in his outlook on value, Santayana comes close to a variety of Kantian idealism in his consideration of the imaginative, synthesizing character of mind by which the world of objects and the beauty therein is constructed.

In the final section of *The Sense of Beauty* the aesthetic component called "expression" is discussed. In the presence of beautiful objects the mind is affected by and contributes to both the material and the formal aspects of the aesthetic object. There is an additional feature, however, which, given the object and the mind's activity, must be mentioned. There is present, both with the immediate perception of the object and after it is no longer perceived, an emotional overtone which colors the sensation and our memory of it. This aura is the result of associations which we have made and which affect our memory as well as our immediate perceptions; this quality we call "the expression of the object."

Form and substance constitute aesthetic value in the first term, whereas expression is value in the second term. The latter value is found in the associations, the moral values, the history, the accouterments—all of which may go with the presentation of a work of art. These, accompanying the work itself, are raised to the level of beauty, when in themselves they present a joy and sweetness which transcends the utilitarian or functional character that they ordinarily have.

The difficult question which was raised earlier as to the place of tragedy as an aesthetic object in a theory which emphasizes that pleasure is beauty when seen as the quality of a thing can now be answered. It is by expression that tragedy is beautiful. The events of *Hamlet* or *Oedipus* can be imagined as reported in a newspaper; in this context they would hardly constitute that which we would call "beautiful." Moral and pathetic, perhaps, if written well, but the utility of the journalistic presentation would doubtless preclude any feeling of pleasure. The horror, the pain, the sadness of life would come through; the world of moral value, of duty, of work, and, rather than that of beauty, of play, and of joy would be given to us. But these events can, when placed in the context of the theater or treated under the brush of the painter or pen of the composer, take on a positive value and thus move, as it were, to a new plane. The moral, negative in itself, may then take on the character of a first term value and become positive.

In this way we turn the evil in life into a good; we see in the tragic lesson something to be learned, something which makes us better for it, something which points toward a possible and, we hope, realizable perfection. And in the transference of the negative value into something good we prepare the way for the events to be a source of pleasure. The tragic elements are there, but through their expressiveness they have been made by mind into a thing of beauty. It is in this way that Santayana analyzes the object of beauty into its material, formal, and expressive aspects and prepares the way for an analysis of the life of reason through which man raises the world which is given, a world of no value, into one in which, ultimately, good is supreme. —*T.W.*

PERTINENT LITERATURE

Arnett, Willard E. *Santayana and the Sense of Beauty*. Bloomington: Indiana University Press, 1955.

Willard E. Arnett is concerned with aesthetic quality and with George Santayana's theory of art and of aesthetics, not only in *The Sense of Beauty* but in the other works as well. He stresses that Santayana's philosophy is fundamentally a moral philosophy, centered on a life of reason aiming at happiness and creativity. Nevertheless, he insists that Santayana refrained from separating moral from aesthetic values, that he classified beauty as a moral good, describing harmony, which is both a goal and an instrument of reason, as an aesthetic principle which is also moral. In the course of this book, Arnett dilates on Santayana's style, which was leisurely and imaginative, as befitting the expression of detached aesthetic enjoyment or contemplation as the desirable end for human moral endeavor. He even treats Santayana's realms of being from the aesthetic point of view, for which they are ontological landscape to be envisaged and appreciated. Although the intent of Arnett's interpretation is to maintain that Santayana subordinates art and aesthetics to morality, its import is to establish an aesthetic construction of ethical value.

Following Santayana, Arnett distinguishes art from aesthetics. Art is the means reason employs to alter the environment to produce objects of utilitarian or aesthetic value, objects of utility constituting industrial (or servile) arts, and objects of aesthetic value, the fine arts. Aesthetic value is linked to all objects, whether natural or artificial (or man-made), insofar as they are capable of producing the sort of pleasure involved in beauty.

Arnett observes that *The Sense of Beauty* opens with a psychological account of sensibility, and that Santayana sought to explain in mechanistic terms the advent of aesthetic value in consciousness, to locate aesthetic value within human life as a whole, and to establish the nature of aesthetic judgment and criticism. He tries to clarify Santayana's famous formula that beauty is "pleasure objectified." He comments that, strictly speaking, it is not a definition, but rather a statement of the relativist theory of aesthetic value. Accordingly, Santayana attributed the advent of beauty to a certain sort of pleasure produced in an observer by an object, such that the image of the object, which it also produces, is suffused with the feeling of pleasure. Hence the beauty, reduced to the pleasure, comes to be predicated of the object. Since in fact the beauty is not an objective property of the object, aesthetic judgment is necessarily relative to the human subject who enjoys the pleasure and makes the judgment.

Arnett examines the three sources or conditions and types of beauty presented by Santayana in *The Sense of Beauty*: matter, form, and expression. Although Santayana admitted that the unpleasant materials of pain, suffering, and evil could be incorporated in such art as tragedy if they were subordinated to forms that give pleasure and, moreover, constituted objects of aesthetic expression that embraced the individual within society and universal humanity, he was hostile to much contemporary art because of its incapacity to produce beauty in the sense of pleasure.

Arnett concedes that the early Santayana elevated the fine arts over the servile (or industrial) arts, partly as a consequence of the critical conservatism he espoused, with its affinity for classical forms. As Santayana matured, Arnett surmises, the philosopher, while constant in his devotion to the fine arts as consummatory values, developed an appreciation for the value of the servile (or industrial) arts. Here Arnett draws upon Santayana's *Reason in Art* from *The Life of Reason*.

Ashmore, Jerome. *Santayana, Art, and Aesthetics*. Cleveland: The Press of Western Reserve University, 1966.

Jerome Ashmore's central thesis in this slender volume is that George Santayana did not esteem fine art as primary in his aesthetics and philosophy of art. On the contrary, Santayana's aesthetics is more intimately connected with psychology, with the ontology of essence, and with morality, than with fine art. More expository than critical, Ashmore sketches the historical development of Santayana's aesthetics, providing notes replete with quotations from the philosopher, organized by chapters, and relegated to the back of the book. He modestly acknowledges that what he offers is a commentary on, instead of an original interpretation of, Santayana's work.

In the first, introductory chapter, Ashmore establishes the boundaries of his study. Despite Santayana's disclaimer, he shows that the philosopher had, in fact, formulated an aesthetics and a philosophy of art, although lodged firmly within a moral philosophy with its emphases on the rational life, happiness, and freedom. In consonance with the refusal to separate art and aesthetics from morality, Santayana did not contend, according to Ashmore, that the fine arts alone offer unique and independent aesthetic experiences. He further relates that for Santayana aesthetic experience and the production of art presuppose three basic principles: (1) the subjective self, (2) harmony, and (3) the moral goal of happiness by means of reason.

Chapter II, "The Aesthetic Experience," consists of a commentary on *The Sense of Beauty*. As Ashmore reports, Santayana's theory of aesthetic experience rests on (1) an associationist functional psychology, (2) a mechanistic theory of causation, which prevails throughout the physical universe in which experience (mind or consciousness) emerges, and (3) a hedonistic theory that equates value with pleasure and defines pleasure as the satisfaction of impulse or desire. Beauty—the value intrinsic to aesthetic experience—is defined as objectified pleasure. In other words, an object arouses a noncognitive element in a subjective self, so that the self responds with a feeling of pleasure that it then projects upon the object. Aesthetic pleasure, moreover, differs from other sorts of pleasure in that the subject does not locate it within its organism or its parts, but rather in the object. The materials of beauty therefore are easily divorced from the experiencing subject and transferable to objects, such as the aesthetic experiences excited by color and sound rather than taste and odor. When the subject perceives a combination of sensible materials, this, too, may induce a pleasure that is objectified. Hence, form as beauty arises. It depends upon a synthesis of imagination guided by a norm. In addition to matter and form, there is a third source of beauty: expression. It requires an object of sensuous beauty as well as a train of associations which the subject contributes. In any event, beauty in all its types is really not a property of objective things, and aesthetic judgment and criticism are inescapably relative.

In Chapter VI Ashmore discusses the revised position that Santayana assumed in his later review article, "The Mutability of Aesthetic Categories," in *The Philosophical Review*, XXXIV (May, 1925), pp. 281-291. Following his discovery of essence, Santayana held that the contents of all experience, including the pleasure felt in aesthetic experience, are not subjective but objective, requiring therefore no special act of objectification. The pleasure felt, moreover, does not constitute the beauty; it is, however, a precondition for the apparition of beauty. Hence Santayana's mature doctrine of beauty, according to Ashmore, is that beauty is a visionary essence, an indefinable quality intuited in a special emotion. Although this concept marks a major departure from *The Sense of Beauty*, Ashmore nevertheless lauds the early work as a significant contribution to aesthetics as a branch of empirical psychology.

Singer, Irving. *Santayana's Aesthetics: A Critical Introduction*. Cambridge, Massachusetts: Harvard University Press, 1957.

In this dense, tightly argued book, Irving Singer seeks to clarify George Santayana's aesthetics and to propose original solutions to problems he uncovers in these fields. To his purpose he brings to bear not only Santayana's ontology and epistemology, but also the views of John Dewey and C. I. Lewis. He attributes Santayana's difficulties to his adherence to the philosophical tradition that radically separates the pure, intuited given from belief or interpretation, essence from existence. While he finds fault with Dewey and Lewis as well as with Santayana for subscribing to this tradition, he finds in the views of the pragmatists suggestions for the new philosophy which he espouses, a philosophy which denies that knowledge or experience requires foundations in a pure given of uninterpreted data or nonexistent essences.

Singer scrutinizes Santayana's famous definition of beauty as objectified pleasure and concludes that it is not a definition. He acknowledges that Santayana's choice of language has misled his readers in this regard. But he insists that Santayana's theme was not beauty but, as the title of his book declares, the *sense* of beauty—that is, the definition of the sense of beauty, the nature of the sense of beauty, the conditions of the sense of beauty. Even in *The Sense of Beauty* Singer discovers the doctrine of essence, manifest in its Platonic "Introduction" where Santayana states that value judgments invoke absolute, intrinsic, ultimate standards (ideals) by which they measure actual objects, events, persons. Thus Singer declares that Santayana was consistent with his early intentions when he identified beauty as an essence, a complex essence which combines pleasure and an image, both themselves essences. Santayana and others erred, however, in regarding this essence to be indefinable. On the contrary, according to Singer, it is definable in the explication of its component essences, and also in the explanation that it is the capacity of an object to enter into aesthetic experience.

For an object to enter into aesthetic experience it must meet certain requirements. These requirements are represented as the conditions for the sense of beauty or the elements in our consciousness which contribute to beauty. They are matter, form, and expression, and Singer examines each in turn. He infers that Santayana's preference for form—and in particular for classical forms—is tied to his latent doctrine of essence. For Santayana favored the kind of aesthetic form that is a harmonious unification of diverse components, a singular complex essence accessible to the spectator's intuition and conformable to an idealized type. Expression, which relates two terms, an aesthetic expressive object and an expressed chain of association contributed by the subject, invites Singer's discussion in that it has misled some critics, but not Santayana, to separate radically the two terms, one the given and the other the interpretation. Nevertheless, he criticizes Santayana for having confused three distinct things: (1) the definition of beauty, (2) the components of an art object, and (3) the effects produced in aesthetic experience by an object.

Singer also examines Santayana's position *vis à vis* the fine arts. He repudiates Santayana's distinction between the fine arts and the servile (industrial) arts, since any productive activity, whether it consists of the manufacture of useful things or the creation of objects of so-called fine art such as paintings or statues, and any object produced by such activity, may possess or lack the capacity to enter into aesthetic experience. He consequently finds Santayana's alleged preference for fine art indefensible.—*A.J.R.*

ADDITIONAL RECOMMENDED READING

Ames, Van Meter. *Proust and Santayana: The Aesthetic Way of Life.* Chicago: Willett, Clark and Company, 1937. A felicitous study of Marcel Proust and Santayana along lines suggested by the philosopher's interpretation of the French novelist as a spectator of essences remembered, with insightful remarks on the differences in regard to pleasure and evil between *The Sense of Beauty* and *Le Temps Retrouvé.*

Boas, George. "Santayana and the Arts," in *The Philosophy of George Santayana* (The Library of Living Philosophers). Edited by Paul A. Schilpp. La Salle, Illinois: Open Court, 1940, pp. 241-263. A compact essay which contains an incisive discussion of the definition of beauty as objectified pleasure.

Kirkwood, M. M. "The Young Philosopher," in *Santayana: Saint of the Imagination.* Toronto: University of Toronto Press, 1961. Santayana's biography as a young philosopher interwoven with an exposition of *The Sense of Beauty* to emphasize the role of imagination in the philosopher's life, work, and theory of art.

Pepper, Stephen. "Mechanistic Criticism," in *The Basis of Criticism in the Arts.* Cambridge, Massachusetts: Harvard University Press, 1945. Analysis of Santayana's aesthetics as the basis for criticism on mechanistic (psychological) foundations with a hedonistic conception of aesthetic value as pleasure.

Ransom, John Crowe. "Art and Mr. Santayana," in *The Virginia Quarterly Review.* XIII, no. 3 (Summer, 1937), pp. 420-436. A sweeping critique of Santayana's aesthetics and philosophy of art by a leading American poet and literary critic.

Reck, Andrew J. "The Authority of Morality over Aesthetics in Santayana's

Philosophy," in *The Southern Journal of Philosophy*. X (1972), pp. 149-158. An interpretation of Santayana as a moralist and not an aesthete.